Lecture Notes in Computer Science 8998

Commenced Publication in 1973
Founding and Former Series Editors:
Gerhard Goos, Juris Hartmanis, and Jan van I ......n

Editorial Board

David Hutchison
  Lancaster University, UK
Takeo Kanade
  Carnegie Mellon University, Pittsburgh, PA, USA
Josef Kittler
  University of Surrey, Guildford, UK
Jon M. Kleinberg
  Cornell University, Ithaca, NY, USA
Friedemann Mattern
  ETH Zurich, Switzerland
John C. Mitchell
  Stanford University, CA, USA
Moni Naor
  Weizmann Institute of Science, Rehovot, Israel
C. Pandu Rangan
  Indian Institute of Technology, Madras, India
Bernhard Steffen
  TU Dortmund University, Germany
Demetri Terzopoulos
  University of California, Los Angeles, CA, USA
Doug Tygar
  University of California, Berkeley, CA, USA
Gerhard Weikum
  Max Planck Institute for Informatics, Saarbruecken, Germany

Martin Wirsing   Matthias Hölzl
Nora Koch   Philip Mayer (Eds.)

Software Engineering for Collective Autonomic Systems

The ASCENS Approach

 Springer

Volume Editors

Martin Wirsing
Matthias Hölzl
Nora Koch
Philip Mayer
Ludwig-Maximilians-Universität
Institut für Informatik
Oettingenstraße 67, 80538 München, Germany
E-mail: {wirsing, hoelzl, kochn, mayer}@pst.ifi.lmu.de

ISSN 0302-9743   e-ISSN 1611-3349
ISBN 978-3-319-16309-3   e-ISBN 978-3-319-16310-9
DOI 10.1007/978-3-319-16310-9
Springer Cham Heidelberg New York Dordrecht London

Library of Congress Control Number: 2015932507

LNCS Sublibrary: SL 2 – Programming and Software Engineering

© Springer International Publishing Switzerland 2015
This work is subject to copyright. All rights are reserved by the Publisher, whether the whole or part of
the material is concerned, specifically the rights of translation, reprinting, reuse of illustrations, recitation,
broadcasting, reproduction on microfilms or in any other physical way, and transmission or information
storage and retrieval, electronic adaptation, computer software, or by similar or dissimilar methodology
now known or hereafter developed. Exempted from this legal reservation are brief excerpts in connection
with reviews or scholarly analysis or material supplied specifically for the purpose of being entered and
executed on a computer system, for exclusive use by the purchaser of the work. Duplication of this publication
or parts thereof is permitted only under the provisions of the Copyright Law of the Publisher's location,
in ist current version, and permission for use must always be obtained from Springer. Permissions for use
may be obtained through RightsLink at the Copyright Clearance Center. Violations are liable to prosecution
under the respective Copyright Law.
The use of general descriptive names, registered names, trademarks, service marks, etc. in this publication
does not imply, even in the absence of a specific statement, that such names are exempt from the relevant
protective laws and regulations and therefore free for general use.
While the advice and information in this book are believed to be true and accurate at the date of publication,
neither the authors nor the editors nor the publisher can accept any legal responsibility for any errors or
omissions that may be made. The publisher makes no warranty, express or implied, with respect to the
material contained herein.

Typesetting: Camera-ready by author, data conversion by Scientific Publishing Services, Chennai, India

Printed on acid-free paper

Springer is part of Springer Science+Business Media (www.springer.com)

Preface

A collective autonomic system consists of collaborating autonomic entities that are able to adapt at runtime, adjusting to the state of the environment and incorporating new knowledge into their behavior. These highly dynamic systems are also known as ensembles. To ensure the correct behavior of ensembles it is necessary to support their development through appropriate methods and tools that can guarantee an autonomic system lives up to its intended purpose; this includes respecting important constraints of the environment.

This book addresses the engineering of such systems by presenting the methods, tools, and theories developed within the ASCENS project. ASCENS[1] was an integrated project funded in the period 2010–2015 by the 7th Framework Programme (FP7) of the European Commission as part of the Future Emerging Technologies Proactive Initiative (FET Proactive). The ASCENS Consortium consisted of 14 partners of seven countries and one third party, from which nine are universities, three research organizations, and three companies (two SMEs). The project was coordinated by the Ludwig-Maximilians-Universität München. ASCENS participated in the coordination actions AWARENESS[2] and FOCAS[3].

The ASCENS approach is both formal and pragmatic. Formal means that it provides a range of foundational theories and methods that support requirements engineering, modeling, programming, formal reasoning, validation and verification, monitoring and dynamic adaptation of autonomic systems. As a guide for performing these tasks, ASCENS has defined a process model for systems development called the Ensemble Development Life Cycle (EDLC). The EDLC takes both the design and runtime of an autonomic system into account, and includes mechanisms for enabling design changes based on the system's and environmental awareness obtained during runtime.

The pragmatic nature of the ASCENS approach manifests itself in three case studies: autonomic robot swarms performing rescue operations, autonomic cloud computing platforms transforming numerous small computers into a supercomputing environment, and autonomic e-mobility support that addresses decision making in transportation systems.

This book is divided into four parts corresponding to the research areas of the project and their concrete applications: (I) language and verification for self-awareness and self-expression, (II) modeling and theory of self-aware and adaptive systems, (III) engineering techniques for collective autonomic systems, and, last but not least, (IV) challenges and feedback provided by the case studies of the project in the areas of swarm robotics, cloud computing, and e-mobility.

---

[1] http://www.ascens-ist.eu/

[2] http://www.aware-project.eu/

[3] http://focas.eu/

Many people contributed to the success of the ASCENS project. We extend our sincere thanks to all of them. We are particularly grateful to the EC project officers Wide Hogenhout, Dagmar Floeck, and Dalibor Grgec. We thank the reviewers Richard Anthony, Jim Davies, Paola Inverardi, Fernando Orejas, Ralf Reussner, and Carles Sierra for their always constructive criticism and helpful suggestions. We are also grateful to Springer for the assistance in producing this book. Our sincere thanks go to all authors for the high quality of their scientific contributions and to the reviewers of the book chapters for their careful reading and suggestions for improvements. Finally, we thank all ASCENS members for the excellent work, their inexhaustible effort and never-ending enthusiasm for achieving the goals of the project and even going further in their research activities.

February 2015

Martin Wirsing
Matthias Hölzl
Nora Koch
Philip Mayer

Project Partners

Ludwig-Maximilians-Universität München, Germany
Università di Pisa, Italy
Università di Firenze, Italy
Fraunhofer Gesellschaft, Germany
Université Joseph Fourier Grenoble 1, VERIMAG Laboratory, France
Università di Modena e Reggio Emilia, Italy
Université Libre de Bruxelles, Belgium
Ecole Polytechnique Fédérale de Lausanne, Switzerland
Volkswagen AG, Germany
Zimory, Germany
University of Limerick, Ireland
IMT Lucca, Italy
Mobsya, Switzerland
Charles University, Czech Republic
Istituto di Scienza e Tecnologie della Informazione "A. Faedo", Italy

Table of Contents

Part III: Engineering Techniques for Collective Autonomic Systems

Part IV: Case Studies: Challenges and Feedback

Part I:
Language and Verification for Collective Autonomic Systems

The first chapters of this book explore foundations for reliable and trustworthy ensembles: languages and verification techniques for individual components, for systems consisting of many individual components, and for the networks and connectors with which components communicate.

The first chapter introduces the SCEL language, a formal language for modeling and programming systems consisting of interacting autonomic components. Each SCEL component contains processes operating on a knowledge repository and is equipped with an interface consisting of attributes that describe the features of the component. Components can dynamically form ensembles based on predicates over interface attributes. Behaviors and interactions in SCEL can be controlled by policies. FACPL is a language for expressing hierarchically-structured, high-level policies. jRESP is a framework that allows Java programs to use the linguistic constructs of SCEL.

The second chapter focuses on foundational aspects of the infrastructure for adaptive systems: networks and reconfigurable connectors. The authors define the Network-Conscious Pi-calculus (NCPi), an extension of the pi-calculus in which network nodes and links are explicitly represented. NCPi can serve as framework for modeling and and verifying systems with programmable network infrastructure, such as peer-to-peer networks. The NCPi calculus is applied to various modeling and verification tasks, e.g., for the PASTRY protocol. The second part of the chapter introduces BIP, the main language for verifying components and ensembles of ASCENS. It also establishes a correspondance between BIP and Petri nets and presents two extensions, reconfigurable and dynamic BIP.

Verification of system properties is an important goal of the ASCENS project, and the third chapter presents various techniques and tools that were developed as part of ASCENS. The techniques comprise qualitative methods that verify Boolean properties, as well as quantitative methods that evaluate a system's performance according to a metric. It is well known that many verification techniques suffer from state explosion: the time or memory to verify a system grows rapidly in the size of its state space. To address this, the chapter stresses the use of compositional verification techniques, in which properties of a system are established based on independent verification of properties of its subsystems. Security aspects are verified using a framework for information-flow analysis that is particularly well suited to checking non-interference and therefore the preservation of information confidentiality.

M. Wirsing et al. (eds.): Collective Autonomic Systems, LNCS 8998, p. 1, 2015.
© Springer International Publishing Switzerland 2015

CHAPTER I.1

The SCEL Language:
Design, Implementation, Verification*

Rocco De Nicola[1], Diego Latella[2], Alberto Lluch Lafuente[1,3], Michele Loreti[4],
Andrea Margheri[4], Mieke Massink[2], Andrea Morichetta[1], Rosario Pugliese[4],
Francesco Tiezzi[1], and Andrea Vandin[1,5]

[1] IMT Institute for Advanced Studies Lucca, Italy
[2] Istituto di Scienza e Tecnologie dell'Informazione 'A. Faedo', CNR, Italy
[3] DTU Compute, The Technical University of Denmark, Denmark
[4] Università degli Studi di Firenze, Italy
[5] University of Southampton, UK

Abstract. SCEL (Service Component Ensemble Language) is a new
language specifically designed to rigorously model and program autonomic components and their interaction, while supporting formal reasoning on their behaviors. SCEL brings together various programming
abstractions that allow one to directly represent aggregations, behaviors
and knowledge according to specific policies. It also naturally supports
programming interaction, self-awareness, context-awareness, and adaptation. The solid semantic grounds of the language is exploited for developing logics, tools and methodologies for formal reasoning on system
behavior to establish qualitative and quantitative properties of both the
individual components and the overall systems.

Keywords: Autonomic computing, Programming languages, Adaptation policies, Formal methods, Verification

1 Introduction

Nowadays much attention is devoted to software-intensive cyber-physical systems. These are systems possibly made of a massive numbers of components,
featuring complex intercommunications and interactions both with humans and
other systems and operating in open and unpredictable environments. It is therefore necessary that such systems dynamically adapt to new requirements, technologies and contextual conditions. Such classes of systems include the so-called
ensembles [44]. Sometimes ensembles are explicitly created by design, while some
other other times they are assembled from systems that are independently controlled and managed, while their interaction "mood" may be cooperative or

* This research was supported by the European project IP 257414 (ASCENS) and by
the Italian PRIN 2010LHT4KM CINA.

M. Wirsing et al. (eds.): Collective Autonomic Systems, LNCS 8998, pp. 3–71, 2015.
© Springer International Publishing Switzerland 2015

competitive; then one has to deal with systems coalitions, also called *systems of systems*. Due to their inherent complexity, today's engineering methods and tools do not scale well to ensembles and new engineering techniques are needed to address the challenges of developing, integrating, and deploying them [53]. The design of such systems, their implementation and the verification that they meet the expectations of their users pose big challenges to language designers and software engineers. It is of paramount importance to devise appropriate abstractions and linguistic primitives to deal with the large dimension of systems, to guarantee adaptation to (possibly unpredicted) changes of the working environment, to take into account evolving requirements, and to control the emergent behaviors resulting from complex interactions.

It is thus important to look for methodologies and linguistic constructs that can be used to build ensembles while combining traditional software engineering approaches, techniques from autonomic, adaptive, knowledge-based and self-aware systems, and formal methods, in order to guarantee compositionality, expressiveness and verifiability. It has to be said that most of the basic properties of the class of systems we have outlined above are already guaranteed by current service-oriented architectures; the novelties come from the need of self-awareness and context-awareness. Indeed, self-management is a key challenge of modern distributed IT infrastructures spanning almost to all levels of computing. Self-managing systems are designed to continuously monitor their behaviors in order to select the optimal meaningful operations to match the current status of affairs. After [30], the term *autonomic computing* has been used to identify the self-managing features of computing systems. A variety of inter-disciplinary proposals has been launched to deal with autonomic computing. We refer to [47] for a detailed survey.

In this chapter, we propose facing the challenge of engineering autonomic systems by taking as starting point the notions of *autonomic components* (ACs) and *autonomic-component ensembles* (ACEs) and defining programming abstractions to model their evolutions and their interactions. Building on these notions, we define SCEL (Software Component Ensemble Language). This is a kernel language that takes a holistic approach to model and program autonomic computing systems. SCEL aims at providing programmers with an appropriate set of linguistic abstractions for programming the behavior of ACs and the formation of ACEs, and for controlling the interaction among different ACs.

SCEL permits governing the complexity of such systems by providing flexible abstractions, by enabling transparent monitoring of the involved entities and by supporting the implementation of self-* mechanisms such as self-adaptation. The key concepts of the language are those of *Behaviors*, *Knowledge*, *Aggregations* and *Policies* that have proved fruitful in modelling autonomic systems from different application domains such as, e.g., collective robotic systems, cloud-computing, and cooperative e-vehicles.

One of the distinguishing features of SCEL is the use of flexible, *group-oriented*, communication primitives that allows one to implicitly select the set of components (the ensemble) to communicate with, by evaluating a given predicate

$\mathcal{P}$ used as the target. When a communication action has predicate $\mathcal{P}$ as a target, it will involve all components that satisfy $\mathcal{P}$. For example, if a system contains elements that export attributes such as *serviceProvided* and *QoS* and one would like to program a component willing to interact with the ensemble of all the components that provide a service s and offer a QoS above q, (s)he can use the predicate *serviceProvided* $= s \wedge QoS > q$ to select the component's partners.

We would like to add that SCEL is, somehow, minimal; its syntax fully specifies only constructs for modeling Behaviors and Aggregations and is parametric with respect to Knowledge and Policies. This choice permits integrating different approaches to policies specifications or to knowledge handling within our language and to easily superimpose ACEs on top of heterogeneous ACs. Indeed, we see SCEL as a *kernel* language based on which different full-blown languages can be designed. Afterwards, we will present a simple, yet expressive, SCEL's dialect that is equipped with a specific language for defining access control policies and that relies on knowledge repositories implemented as distributed *tuple spaces*. The small set of basic constructs and their *solid semantic grounds* permits us to develop logics, tools and methodologies for formal reasoning on systems behavior in order to establish qualitative and quantitative properties of both the individual components and the ensembles.

In this chapter, we will present most of the work that has been done within the ASCENS project on the SCEL language. We shall introduce the main linguistic abstractions for components specification and interaction together with different alternatives for modeling knowledge and for the operations for knowledge handling (we refer to Chapter II.3 [54] for more sophisticated forms of knowledge and to Chapter II.4 [27] for other knowledge-based reasoning techniques). We shall also discuss different possibilities for describing interaction and authorization policies. We shall describe a Java runtime environment, to be used for developing autonomic and adaptive systems according to the SCEL paradigm and thus for the deployment of SCEL specifications (we refer to Chapter III.5 [1] for other software tools for supporting the development of this class of systems). Finally, we shall introduce tools and methodologies for the verification of qualitative and quantitative properties of SCEL programs (we refer to Chapter I.3 [17] for other verification techniques and tools).

The main features of SCEL will be presented in a step-by-step fashion by using, in most of the following sections, a running example from the swarm robotics domain described below (we refer to Chapter IV.2 [42] for a comprehensive presentation of the swarm robotics case study). A complete account of the specification of this scenario is given in Section 5.2.

A Swarm Robotics Scenario. We consider a scenario where a swarm of robots spreads throughout a given area where some kind of disaster has happened. The goal of the robots is to locate and rescue possible victims. As common in swarm robotics, all robots playing the same role execute the same code. According to the separation of concerns principle fostered by SCEL, this code consists of two parts: *(i)* a process, defining the functional behaviour; and *(ii)* a collection of policies, regulating the interactions among robots and with their environment and generating the (adaptation) actions necessary to react to specific (internal or environmental) conditions. This combination permits a convenient design and enacts a collaborative swarm behaviour aiming at achieving the goal of rescuing the victims.

A robot initially plays the *explorer* role in order to look in the environment for the victims' positions. When a robot finds a victim, it changes to the *rescuer* role starting the victim rescuing and indicating the victim's position to the other robots. As soon as another robot receives the victim's position, it changes to the *helpRescuer* role going to help other rescuers. During the exploration, in case of critical battery level, a robot changes to the *lowBattery* role to activate the battery charging. Notably, the role changes according to the sensors and data values, e.g. when the robot is close to a victim that needs help.

Outline of the Chapter. The rest of this chapter is structured as follows. Section 2 introduces the key principles underlying the design of SCEL together with the syntax and the operational semantics of the language. Section 3 presents two different knowledge handling mechanisms, i.e. *tuple spaces* and *constraint stores*, and illustrates how components can exploit external *reasoners* for taking decisions. Section 4 introduces a language for defining access control, resource usage and adaptation policies. Section 5 presents a full instantiation of SCEL: it uses tuple spaces as knowledge handling mechanism and the language presented in Section 4 as policy language. Section 6 describes a Java runtime environment that provides an API for using SCEL's linguistic constructs in Java programs. Section 7 deals with the issue of enriching SCEL with information about action duration, by providing a stochastic semantics for the language. Section 8 deals with verification of qualitative and quantitative properties of SCEL specifications via the analysis tools provided by the runtime environment illustrated in Section 6, the MAUDE framework [16], and the SPIN model checker [28]. Section 9 concludes by also touching upon directions for future work.

This chapter collects a large body of work around SCEL developed along many different research directions. The reader interested in further details on the presented ideas and their relationship with the relevant literature is thus referred to our published papers cited in this contribution.

2   The Parametric Language SCEL

In this section we first introduce the key principles underlying the design of the SCEL language. Then, we formally present its syntax and operational semantics.

2.1   Design Principles

Autonomic Components (ACs) and Autonomic-Component Ensembles (ACEs) are our means to structure systems into well-understood, independent and distributed building blocks that may interact and adapt.

ACs are entities with dedicated knowledge units and resources; awareness is guaranteed by providing them with information about their state and behavior via their knowledge repositories. These repositories can be also used to store and retrieve information about ACs working environment, and thus can be exploited to adapt their behavior to the perceived changes. Each AC is equipped with an *interface*, consisting of a collection of *attributes*, describing component's features such as identity, functionalities, spatial coordinates, group memberships, trust level, response time, etc.

Attributes are used by the ACs to dynamically organize themselves into ACEs. Indeed, one of the main novelties of our approach is the way groups of partners are selected for interaction and thus how ensembles are formed. Individual ACs can single out communication partners by using their identities, but partners can also be selected by taking advantage of the attributes exposed in the interfaces. Predicates over such attributes are used to specify the targets of communication actions, thus permitting a sort of *attribute-based* communication. In this way, the formation rule of ACEs is endogenous to ACs: members of an ensemble are connected by the interdependency relations defined through predicates. An ACE is therefore not a rigid fixed network but rather a highly flexible structure where ACs' linkages are dynamically established.

We have identified some linguistic abstractions for uniformly programming the evolution and the interactions of ACs and the architecture of ACEs. These abstractions permit describing autonomic systems in terms of Behaviors, Knowledge and Aggregations, according to specific Policies.

- *Behaviors* describe how computations may progress and are modeled as processes executing actions, in the style of process calculi.
- *Knowledge* repositories provide the high-level primitives to manage pieces of information coming from different sources. Each knowledge repository is equipped with operations for *adding*, *retrieving*, and *withdrawing* knowledge items.
- *Aggregations* describe how different entities are brought together to form ACs and to construct the software architecture of ACEs. Composition and interaction are implemented by exploiting the attributes exposed in ACs' interfaces.
- *Policies* control and adapt the actions of the different ACs for guaranteeing accomplishment of specific tasks or satisfaction of specific properties.

By accessing and manipulating their own knowledge repository or the repositories of other ACs, components acquire information about their status (*self-awareness*) and their environment (*context-awareness*) and can perform *self-adaptation*, initiate *self-healing* actions to deal with system malfunctions, or install *self-optimizing* behaviors. All these *self-** properties, as well as *self-configuration*, can be naturally expressed by exploiting SCEL's higher-order features, namely the capability to store/retrieve (the code of) processes in/from the knowledge repositories and to dynamically trigger execution of new processes. Moreover, by implementing appropriate security policies, e.g. limiting information flow or external actions, components can set up *self-protection* mechanisms against different threats, such as unauthorised access or denial-of-service attacks.

Our aim is to provide a common semantic framework for describing meaning and interplay of the abstractions above, while minimizing overlaps and incompatibilities. In the subsection below we introduce the constructs of SCEL, while their precise semantics will be presented in the next one.

2.2 Syntax

We present here the syntax of SCEL. We would like to stress that we have taken a minimal approach and SCEL syntax specifies only constructs for modeling Behaviors and Aggregations and is parametric with respect to Knowledge and Policies.

Concretely, an AC in SCEL is rendered as the term $\mathcal{I}[\mathcal{K}, \Pi, P]$. This is graphically illustrated in Figure 1 and consists of:

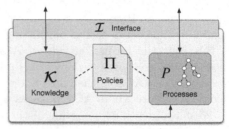

Fig. 1. SCEL component

- An *interface* $\mathcal{I}$ publishing and making available information about the component itself in the form of *attributes*, i.e. names acting as references to information stored in the component's knowledge repository. Among them, attribute *id* is mandatory and is bound to the name of the component. Component names are not required to be unique; this allows us to easily model replicated service components.

- A *knowledge repository* $\mathcal{K}$ managing both *application data* and *awareness data*, together with the specific handling mechanism. Application data are used for enabling the progress of ACs' computations, while awareness data provide information about the environment in which the ACs are running (e.g. monitored data from sensors) or about the status of an AC (e.g. its current location). The knowledge repository of a component stores also the information associated to its interface, which therefore can be dynamically manipulated by means of the operations provided by the knowledge repositories' handling mechanisms.

- A set of *policies* Π regulating the interaction between the different parts of a single component and the interaction between components. Interaction policies and Service Level Agreement policies provide two standard examples of policy abstractions. Other examples are security policies, such as access control and reputation.

- A *process* P, together with a set of process definitions that can be dynamically activated. Some of the (sub)processes in P execute local computations, while others may coordinate interaction with the knowledge repository or perform adaptation and reconfiguration. *Interaction* is obtained by allowing ACs to access knowledge in the repositories of other ACs.

SCEL syntax is reported in Table 1. Its basic category is the one defining PROCESSES that are used to build up COMPONENTS that in turn are used to define

Table 1. SCEL syntax (KNOWLEDGE $\mathcal{K}$, POLICIES Π, TEMPLATES T, and ITEMS t are parameters of the language)

SYSTEMS: $S ::= C \mid S_1 \parallel S_2 \mid (\nu n)S$

COMPONENTS: $C ::= \mathcal{I}[\mathcal{K}, \Pi, P]$

PROCESSES: $P ::= \mathbf{nil} \mid a.P \mid P_1 + P_2 \mid P_1 \mid P_2 \mid X \mid A(\bar{p})$

ACTIONS: $a ::= \mathbf{get}(T)@c \mid \mathbf{qry}(T)@c \mid \mathbf{put}(t)@c \mid \mathbf{fresh}(n) \mid \mathbf{new}(\mathcal{I}, \mathcal{K}, \Pi, P)$

TARGETS: $c ::= n \mid x \mid \mathsf{self} \mid \mathcal{P} \mid p$

SYSTEMS. PROCESSES specify the flow of the ACTIONS that can be performed. ACTIONS can have a TARGET to determine the other components that are involved in that action. As stated in the Introduction, SCEL is parametric with respect to some syntactic categories, namely KNOWLEDGE, POLICIES, TEMPLATES and ITEMS (with the last two determining the part of KNOWLEDGE to be retrieved/removed or added, respectively).

Systems and Components. SYSTEMS aggregate COMPONENTS through the *composition* operator _ $\parallel$ _. It is also possible to restrict the scope of a name, say n, by using the *name restriction* operator (νn) . In a system of the form $S_1 \parallel (\nu n)S_2$, the effect of the operator is to make name n invisible from within S_1. Essentially, this operator plays a role similar to that of a *begin . . . end* block in sequential programming and limits visibility of specific names. Additionally, restricted names can be exchanged in communications thus enabling the receiving components to use those "private" names.

Running example (step 1/7) The robotics scenario can be expressed in SCEL as a system S defined as follows

$$S \triangleq \text{ROBOT}_1 \parallel \ldots \parallel \text{ROBOT}_n$$

Each robot is rendered as a SCEL component ROBOT$_i$, which has the form $\mathcal{I}_{R_i}[\mathcal{K}_{R_i}, \Pi_R, P_R]$. These components concurrently execute and interact. Each interface $\mathcal{I}_{R_i}$ specifies the attribute *role*, which can assume values *explorer*, *rescuer*, etc. according to the current role played by the robot.   □

Processes. PROCESSES are the active computational units. Each process is built up from the *inert* process **nil** via *action prefixing* ($a.P$), *nondeterministic choice* ($P_1 + P_2$), *controlled composition* ($P_1 \mid P_2$), *process variable* (X), and *parameterized process invocation* ($A(\bar{p})$). The construct $P_1 \mid P_2$ abstracts the various forms of parallel composition commonly used in process calculi. Process variables support *higher-order* communication, namely the capability to exchange (the code of) a process and possibly execute it. This is realized by first adding an item containing the process to a knowledge repository and then retrieving/withdrawing this item while binding the process to a process variable. We assume that A ranges over a set of parameterized *process identifiers* that are used in recursive process definitions. We also assume that each process identifier A has a *single* definition of the form $A(\bar{f}) \triangleq P$. Lists of actual and formal parameters are denoted by $\bar{p}$ and $\bar{f}$, respectively.

Running example (step 2/7) The process P_R running on a robot has the form $(a_1. P_1 + a_2. P_2) \mid P_3$ meaning that it is a parallel composition of two sub-processes, where the one on the left-hand side of the controlled composition can either execute the action a_1 and thereafter continue as P_1, or execute the action a_2 and thereafter continue as P_2.   □

Actions and Targets. Processes can perform five different kinds of ACTIONS. Actions $\mathbf{get}(T)@c$, $\mathbf{qry}(T)@c$ and $\mathbf{put}(t)@c$ are used to manage shared knowledge repositories by withdrawing/retrieving/adding information items from/to the knowledge repository identified by c. These actions exploit templates T as patterns to select knowledge items t in the repositories. They heavily rely on the used knowledge repository and are implemented by invoking the handling operations it provides. Action $\mathbf{fresh}(n)$ introduces a scope restriction for the name n so that this name is guaranteed to be *fresh*, i.e. different from any other name previously used. Action $\mathbf{new}(\mathcal{I}, \mathcal{K}, \Pi, P)$ creates a new component $\mathcal{I}[\mathcal{K}, \Pi, P]$.

Action $\mathbf{get}$ may cause the process executing it to wait for the expected element if it is not (yet) available in the knowledge repository. Action $\mathbf{qry}$, exactly like $\mathbf{get}$, may suspend the process executing it if the knowledge repository does not (yet) contain or cannot 'produce' the expected element. The two actions differ for the fact that $\mathbf{get}$ removes the found item from the knowledge repository while $\mathbf{qry}$ leaves the target repository unchanged. Actions $\mathbf{put}$, $\mathbf{fresh}$ and $\mathbf{new}$ are instead immediately executed (provided that their execution is allowed by the policies in force).

Different entities may be used as the target c of an action. Component names are denoted by $n, n', \ldots$, while variables for names are denoted by $x, x', \ldots$. The distinguished variable self can be used by processes to refer to the name of the component hosting them. The possible targets could, however, be also singled out via predicates expressed as boolean-valued expressions obtained by logically combining the evaluation of relations between attributes and expressions. Thus targets could also be an explicit *predicate* $\mathcal{P}$ or the name p of a predicate that is exposed as an attribute of a component interface whose value may dynamically change. We adopt the following conventions about attribute names within predicates. If an attribute name occurs in a predicate without specifying (via prefix notation) the corresponding interface, it is assumed that this name refers to an attribute within the interface of the *object* component (i.e., a component that is a target of the communication action). Instead, if an attribute name occurring in a predicate is prefixed by the keyword this, then it is assumed that this name refers to an attribute within the interface of the *subject* component (i.e., the component hosting the process that performs the communication action). Thus, for example, the predicate this.*status* = *"sending"* $\wedge$ *status* = *"receiving"* is satisfied when the status of the subject component is *sending* and that of the object is *receiving*.

In actions using a predicate $\mathcal{P}$ to indicate the target (directly or via p), the predicate acts as a 'guard' specifying *all* components that may be affected by the execution of the action, i.e. a component must satisfy $\mathcal{P}$ to be the target of the action. Thus, actions $\mathbf{put}(t)@n$ and $\mathbf{put}(t)@\mathcal{P}$ give rise to two different primitive forms of communication: the former is a *point-to-point* communication, while the latter is a sort of *group-oriented* communication. The set of components satisfying a given predicate $\mathcal{P}$ used as the target of a communication action are considered as the *ensemble* with which the process performing the action intends to interact. Indeed, in spite of the stress we put on ensembles, SCEL does not have any specific syntactic category or operator for forming ACEs. For example, the names of the components that can be members of an ensemble can be fixed via the predicate $id \in \{n, m, o\}$. When an action has this predicate as target, it will act on all components named n, m or o, if any. Instead, to dynamically characterize the members of an ensemble according to the role they are currently playing in the system, by assuming that attribute *role* belongs to the interface of any component willing to be part of the ensemble, one can write *role*="*rescuer*" $\lor$ *role*="*helpRescuer*" to refer to the ensemble of components playing either the role *rescuer* or *helpRescuer*.

It is worth noticing that the group-oriented variant of action **put** is used to insert a knowledge item in the repositories of all components belonging to the ensemble identified by the target predicate. Differently, group-oriented actions **get** and **qry** withdraw and retrieve, respectively, an item from *one* of the components satisfying the target predicate, non-deterministically selected.

Running example (step 3/7) By specifying actions a_1 and a_2 as a **qry** and a **get** action, respectively, the process P_R becomes

$$(\mathbf{qry}(\text{``}victimPerceived\text{''}, \mathsf{true})@\mathsf{self}.\, P_1$$
$$+\, \mathbf{get}(\text{``}victim\text{''}, ?x, ?y, ?c)@(role=\text{``}rescuer\text{''} \lor role=\text{``}helpRescuer\text{''}).\, P_2) \mid P_3$$

The sub-process on the left-hand side of the controlled composition allows the robot to recognise the presence of a victim, by means of the **qry** action, or to help other robots to rescue a victim, by means of the **get** action. In the latter case, the action binds the victim's coordinates to variables x and y, and the number of other robots needed for rescuing the victim to variable c.   □

2.3 Operational Semantics

The operational semantics of SCEL is defined in two steps. First, the semantics of processes specifies *commitments*, i.e. the actions that processes can initially perform and the continuation process obtained after each such action; issues like process allocation, available data, regulating policies are ignored at this level. Then, by taking process commitments and system configuration into account, the semantics of systems provides a full description of systems behavior.

Table 2. Semantics of processes

$$a.P \downarrow_a P \qquad\qquad P \downarrow_\circ P$$

$$\frac{P \downarrow_\alpha P'}{P + Q \downarrow_\alpha P'} \qquad\qquad \frac{Q \downarrow_\alpha Q'}{P + Q \downarrow_\alpha Q'} \qquad\qquad \frac{P\{\bar{p}/\bar{f}\} \downarrow_\alpha P'}{A(\bar{p}) \downarrow_\alpha P'} \ \ A(\bar{f}) \triangleq P$$

$$\frac{P \downarrow_\alpha P' \quad Q \downarrow_\beta Q'}{P \mid Q \downarrow_{\alpha[\beta]} P' \mid Q'} \ \mathrm{bv}(\alpha) \cap \mathrm{bv}(\beta) = \emptyset \qquad\qquad \frac{P' \downarrow_\alpha P''}{P \downarrow_\alpha P''} \ P \equiv_\alpha P'$$

Semantics of Processes. Process commitments are generated by the following production rule

$$\alpha, \beta \quad ::= \quad a \mid \circ \mid \alpha[\beta]$$

meaning that a commitment is either an action a as defined in Table 1, or the symbol $\circ$, denoting *inaction*, or the composition $\alpha[\beta]$ of the two commitments α and β. We write $P \downarrow_\alpha Q$ to mean that "P can commit to perform α and become Q after doing so".

The relation $\downarrow$ defining the semantics of processes is the least relation induced by the inference rules in Table 2.

The first rule says that a process of the form $a.P$ is committed to do a and then to continue as process P. The second rule allows any process to stay idle. The third and fourth rules state that $P + Q$ non-deterministically behaves as P or Q. The fifth rule says that a process invocation $A(\bar{p})$ behaves as the invoked process P , where the formal parameters $\bar{f}$ have been replaced by the actual parameters $\bar{p}$. The sixth rule, defining the semantics of $P \mid Q$, states that a commitment $\alpha[\beta]$ is exhibited when P commits to α and Q commits to β. However, P and Q are not forced to actually commit to a meaningful action. Indeed, thanks to the second rule, which allows any process to commit to $\circ$, α and/or β may always be $\circ$. The semantics of $P \mid Q$ at the level of processes is indeed very permissive and generates all possible compositions of the commitments of P and Q. This semantics is then specialized at the level of systems by means of interaction predicates that take also policies into account. Notice that, in general, commutative. Condition $\mathrm{bv}(\alpha) \cap \mathrm{bv}(\beta) = \emptyset$ ensures that the variables used by the two processes P and Q are different, to avoid improper variable captures. In fact, $\mathrm{bv}(\alpha)$ denotes the sets of *bound* variables occurring in α, with **get** and **qry** being the only binding constructs for variables. Similarly, the action **fresh** is a binding construct for names. The last rule states that *alpha-equivalent* ($\equiv_\alpha$) processes, i.e. processes differing only for bound variables and names, can guarantee the same commitments.

Running example (step 4/7) The process P_R running on the robots, apart for the trivial case $P_R \downarrow_{\circ[\circ]} P_R$ and the commitments of P_3 (not specified here), produces the following meaningful commitments

$$PR \downarrow_{\textbf{qry}(\text{``}victimPerceived\text{''},\textsf{true})@\textsf{self}[\circ]} (P_1 \mid P_3)$$

$$PR \downarrow_{\textbf{get}(\text{``}victim\text{''},?x,?y,?c)@(role=\text{``}rescuer\text{''}\lor role=\text{``}helpRescuer\text{''})[\circ]} (P_2 \mid P_3)$$

□

Semantics of systems. The operational semantics of systems is defined in two steps. First, the possible behaviors of systems without occurrences of the name restriction operator are defined. This is done in the SOS style [43] by relying on the notion of Labeled Transition System (LTS). Then, by exploiting this LTS, the semantics of generic systems is provided by means of a (unlabelled) Transition System (TS) only accounting for systems' computation steps. This approach allows us to avoid the notational intricacies arising when dealing with name mobility in computations (e.g. when opening and closing the scopes of name restrictions).

The labeled transition relation of the LTS defining the semantics of systems without restricted names is induced by the inference rules in Tables 4, 5 and 6. We write $S \xrightarrow{\lambda} S'$ to mean that "S can perform a transition labeled λ and become S' in doing so". Transition labels are generated by the following production rule

$$\lambda ::= \tau \mid \mathcal{I} : \textbf{fresh}(n) \mid \mathcal{I} : \textbf{new}(\mathcal{J}, \mathcal{K}, \Pi, P)$$
$$\mid \mathcal{I} : t \triangleleft \gamma \mid \mathcal{I} : t \blacktriangleleft \gamma \mid \mathcal{I} : t \triangleright \gamma \mid \mathcal{I} : t \bar{\triangleleft} \mathcal{J} \mid \mathcal{I} : t \bar{\blacktriangleleft} \mathcal{J} \mid \mathcal{I} : t \bar{\triangleright} \mathcal{J}$$

where γ is either the name n of a component or a predicate P indicating a set of components, and $\mathcal{I}$ and $\mathcal{J}$ range over interfaces[6]. The meaning of labels is as follows: τ denotes an internal computation step; $\mathcal{I} : \textbf{fresh}(n)$ denotes the willingness of component $\mathcal{I}$ to restrict visibility of name n; $\mathcal{I} : \textbf{new}(\mathcal{J}, \mathcal{K}, \Pi, P)$ denotes the willingness of component $\mathcal{I}$ to create the new component $\mathcal{J}[\mathcal{K}, \Pi, P]$; $\mathcal{I} : t \triangleleft \gamma$ (resp. $\mathcal{I} : t \blacktriangleleft \gamma$) denotes the intention of component $\mathcal{I}$ to withdraw (resp. retrieve) item t from the repositories at γ; $\mathcal{I} : t \triangleright \gamma$ denotes the intention of component $\mathcal{I}$ to add item t to the repositories at γ; $\mathcal{I} : t \bar{\triangleleft} \mathcal{J}$ (resp. $\mathcal{I} : t \bar{\blacktriangleleft} \mathcal{J}$) denotes that component $\mathcal{I}$ is allowed to withdraw (resp. retrieve) item t from the repository of component $\mathcal{J}$; $\mathcal{I} : t \bar{\triangleright} \mathcal{J}$ denotes that component $\mathcal{I}$ is allowed to add item t to the repository of component $\mathcal{J}$. Moreover, in the rules, we use $\mathcal{I}.\pi$ to denote the policy in force at the component $\mathcal{I}$, $\mathcal{I}[\Pi/\mathcal{I}.\pi]$ to denote the update of the policy of the component $\mathcal{I}$ with the policy Π, $\bullet$ to denote a placeholder for the policy of a component and $S[\Pi/\bullet]$ to denote the replacement of the placeholder $\bullet$ with a policy Π in a system S.

The labeled transition is parameterised with respect to the following two predicates:

---

[6] The names of the attributes of a component are pointers to the real values contained in the knowledge repository associated to the component. This amounts to saying that in terms of the form $\mathcal{I}[\mathcal{K}, \Pi, P]$, $\mathcal{I}$ only includes the names of the attributes, as their corresponding values can be retrieved from $\mathcal{K}$. However, when $\mathcal{I}$ is used in isolation (e.g., within a label), we assume that it also includes the attributes' values; we then use, for example, $\mathcal{I}.id$ to denote the value associated to the attribute id in the corresponding repository.

– The *interaction predicate*, $\Pi, \mathcal{I} : \alpha \succ \lambda, \sigma, \Pi'$, means that under policy Π and interface $\mathcal{I}$, process commitment α yields system label λ, substitution σ (i.e., a partial function from variables to values) and, possibly new, policy Π'. Intuitively, λ identifies the effect of α at the level of components, while σ associates values to the variables occurring in α and is used to capture the changes induced by communication. The generated system label λ must be one among τ, $\mathcal{I} : \mathbf{fresh}(n)$, $\mathcal{I} : \mathbf{new}(\mathcal{J}, \mathcal{K}, \Pi, P)$, $\mathcal{I} : t \triangleleft \gamma$, $\mathcal{I} : t \blacktriangleleft \gamma$ and $\mathcal{I} : t \triangleright \gamma$. Π' is the policy in force after the transition; in principle it may differ from the one in force before the transition. This predicate is used to determine the effect of the simultaneous execution of actions by processes concurrently running within a component that, e.g., exhibit commitments of the form $\alpha[\beta]$.

– The *authorization predicate*, $\Pi \vdash \lambda, \Pi'$, means that under policy Π, the action generating the system label λ (which can be thought of as an *authorization request*) is allowed and the policy Π' is produced. Labels λ taken as argument by the authorization predicate are system labels of the form $\mathcal{I} : \mathbf{fresh}(n)$, $\mathcal{I} : \mathbf{new}(\mathcal{J}, \mathcal{K}, \Pi, P)$, $\mathcal{I} : t \bar{\triangleleft} \mathcal{J}$, $\mathcal{I} : t \bar{\blacktriangleleft} \mathcal{J}$, or $\mathcal{I} : t \bar{\triangleright} \mathcal{J}$. This predicate is used to determine the actions allowed by specific policies, and the (possibly new) policy to be enforced. The authorization to perform an action is checked when a computation step can potentially take place, i.e. when it becomes known which is the component target of the action.

Many different interaction predicates can be defined to capture well-known process computation and interaction patterns such as interleaving, monitoring, asynchronous communication, synchronous communication, full synchrony, broadcasting, etc. In fact, depending on the considered class of systems, one can prefer a communication model with respect to the others.

A specific interaction predicate is given in Table 3; it is obtained by interpreting controlled composition as the *interleaved* parallel composition of the two involved processes. Notably, this simple predicate does never modify the policy currently in force. Notice also that process commitments corresponding to inaction ($\circ$, $\circ[\circ]$, etc.) are disallowed. In the table, function $[\![\cdot]\!]_{\mathcal{I}}$ denotes the evaluation of terms with respect to interface $\mathcal{I}$ with attributes occurring therein being replaced by the corresponding value in $\mathcal{I}$. Moreover, $match(T, t)$ denotes a partial function performing matching between a template T and an item t; when they do match, the function returns a substitution σ for the variables in T (we use $\{\}$ to denote the empty substitution), and is otherwise undefined. We have a rule for each different kind of process action; for example, the third rule states that, once the target γ of the action and an item t matching the template T' through a substitution σ have been determined (by also exploiting the interface $\mathcal{I}$ for evaluating c and T), an action **qry** at the level of processes corresponds to a proper transition label at the level of systems semantics. The last two rules ensure that in case of controlled composition of multiple processes only one process at a time can perform an action (the other stays still).

Like the interaction predicate, many different reasonable authorization predicates can be defined, possibly resorting to specific policy languages. One of such

Table 3. The interleaving interaction predicate

$$\Pi, \mathcal{I} : \mathbf{fresh}(n) \succ \mathcal{I} : \mathbf{fresh}(n), \{\}, \Pi \qquad \frac{[\![\, T \,]\!]_{\mathcal{I}} = T' \quad [\![\, c \,]\!]_{\mathcal{I}} = \gamma \quad match(T', t) = \sigma}{\Pi, \mathcal{I} : \mathbf{get}(T)@c \succ \mathcal{I} : t \lhd \gamma, \sigma, \Pi}$$

$$\frac{[\![\, T \,]\!]_{\mathcal{I}} = T' \quad [\![\, c \,]\!]_{\mathcal{I}} = \gamma \quad match(T', t) = \sigma}{\Pi, \mathcal{I} : \mathbf{qry}(T)@c \succ \mathcal{I} : t \blacktriangleleft \gamma, \sigma, \Pi} \qquad \frac{[\![\, t \,]\!]_{\mathcal{I}} = t' \quad [\![\, c \,]\!]_{\mathcal{I}} = \gamma}{\Pi, \mathcal{I} : \mathbf{put}(t)@c \succ \mathcal{I} : t' \rhd \gamma, \{\}, \Pi}$$

$$\Pi, \mathcal{I} : \mathbf{new}(\mathcal{J}, \mathcal{K}, \Pi, P) \succ \mathcal{I} : \mathbf{new}(\mathcal{J}, \mathcal{K}, \Pi, [\![\, P \,]\!]_{\mathcal{I}}), \{\}, \Pi$$

$$\frac{\Pi, \mathcal{I} : \alpha \succ \lambda, \sigma, \Pi}{\Pi, \mathcal{I} : \alpha[\circ] \succ \lambda, \sigma, \Pi} \qquad \frac{\Pi, \mathcal{I} : \alpha \succ \lambda, \sigma, \Pi}{\Pi, \mathcal{I} : \circ[\alpha] \succ \lambda, \sigma, \Pi}$$

---

languages inspired by, but simpler than, the OASIS standard for policy-based access control XACML [39], will be presented in Section 4. There, we will stress also how the actual semantics of this policy language is intertwined and integrated with SCEL semantics.

The labeled transition relation also relies on the following three operations that each knowledge repository's handling mechanism must provide:

- $\mathcal{K} \ominus t = \mathcal{K}'$: the *withdrawal* of item t from the repository $\mathcal{K}$ returns $\mathcal{K}'$;
- $\mathcal{K} \vdash t$: the *retrieval* of item t from the repository $\mathcal{K}$ is possible;
- $\mathcal{K} \oplus t = \mathcal{K}'$: the *addition* of item t to the repository $\mathcal{K}$ returns $\mathcal{K}'$.

We now briefly comment the rules in Table 4. Rule *(pr-sys)* transforms process commitments into system labels by exploiting the interaction predicate. As a consequence, a substitution σ is applied to the continuation P' of the process that committed to α. When α contains a $\mathbf{get}(T)$ or a $\mathbf{qry}(T)$, σ replaces in P' the variables occurring in T with the corresponding values. The application of the rule also replaces, in the generated label, self with the corresponding name. When α is a **fresh**, it is checked if the name is not already used in the creating component, except for the process part that will likely use n as, e.g., an information to be added to some knowledge repository (notation n(E) is used here to denote the sets of names occurring in a syntactic term E); this condition can be always made true by exploiting alpha-equivalence among processes. Moreover, as a consequence of the evaluation of the interaction predicate, the policy in force at the component performing the action may change; this update is registered in the produced system label by applying $[\Pi'/\mathcal{I}.\pi]$ to the label λ generated by the interaction predicate. Notably, the component generated by this transition contains a placeholder • in place of the policy; it will be replaced by a (possibly new) policy during the rest of the derivation (see, e.g., the use of $[\Pi'/\bullet]$ in rule *(freshn)*).

The possibility of executing actions **fresh** and **new** is decided by using the information within a single component. However, since these actions affect the

Table 4. Systems' labeled transition relation (1/3): base rules

$$\frac{P \downarrow_\alpha P' \quad \alpha = \mathcal{I} : \mathbf{fresh}(n) \Rightarrow n \notin \mathrm{n}(\mathcal{I}[\mathcal{K}, \Pi, \mathbf{nil}]) \quad \Pi, \mathcal{I} : \alpha \succ \lambda, \sigma, \Pi'}{\mathcal{I}[\mathcal{K}, \Pi, P] \xrightarrow{\lambda[\Pi'/\mathcal{I}.\pi]} \mathcal{I}[\mathcal{K}, \bullet, P'\sigma]} \; (pr\text{-}sys)$$

$$\frac{C \xrightarrow{\mathcal{I}:\mathbf{fresh}(n)} C' \quad \mathcal{I}.\pi \vdash \mathcal{I} : \mathbf{fresh}(n), \Pi'}{C \xrightarrow{\tau} (\nu n) \, C'[\Pi'/\bullet]} \; (freshn)$$

$$\frac{C \xrightarrow{\mathcal{I}:\mathbf{new}(\mathcal{J}, \mathcal{K}, \Pi, P)} C' \quad \mathcal{I}.\pi \vdash \mathcal{I} : \mathbf{new}(\mathcal{J}, \mathcal{K}, \Pi, P), \Pi'}{C \xrightarrow{\tau} C'[\Pi'/\bullet] \parallel \mathcal{J}[\mathcal{K}, \Pi, P]} \; (newc)$$

$$\frac{\Pi \vdash \mathcal{I} : t \triangleleft \mathcal{J}, \Pi' \quad \mathcal{K} \ominus t = \mathcal{K}'}{\mathcal{J}[\mathcal{K}, \Pi, P] \xrightarrow{\mathcal{I}:t \triangleleft \mathcal{J}[\Pi'/\mathcal{J}.\pi]} \mathcal{J}[\mathcal{K}', \Pi', P]} \; (accget)$$

$$\frac{\Pi \vdash \mathcal{I} : t \, \tilde{\triangleleft} \, \mathcal{J}, \Pi' \quad \mathcal{K} \vdash t}{\mathcal{J}[\mathcal{K}, \Pi, P] \xrightarrow{\mathcal{I}:t \tilde{\triangleleft} \mathcal{J}[\Pi'/\mathcal{J}.\pi]} \mathcal{J}[\mathcal{K}, \Pi', P]} \; (accqry)$$

$$\frac{\Pi \vdash \mathcal{I} : t \triangleright \mathcal{J}, \Pi' \quad \mathcal{K} \oplus t = \mathcal{K}'}{\mathcal{J}[\mathcal{K}, \Pi, P] \xrightarrow{\mathcal{I}:t \triangleright \mathcal{J}[\Pi'/\mathcal{J}.\pi]} \mathcal{J}[\mathcal{K}', \Pi', P]} \; (accput)$$

$$\frac{S_1 \xrightarrow{\lambda} S_1' \quad \lambda \notin \{\mathcal{I} : t \triangleright \mathcal{P}, \mathcal{I} : t \triangleright \mathcal{J}\}}{S_1 \parallel S_2 \xrightarrow{\lambda} S_1' \parallel S_2} \; (async)$$

system, as they either create a name restriction or a new component, their execution by a process is indicated by a specific system label $\mathcal{I} : \mathbf{fresh}(n)$ or $\mathcal{I} : \mathbf{new}(\mathcal{J}, \mathcal{K}, \Pi, P)$ (generated by rule *(pr-sys)*) carrying enough information for the authorization request to perform the action to be checked according to the local policy and for the modification of the system to take place (rules *(freshn)* and *(newc)*). Notably, the authorization predicate is evaluated under the policy produced by the interaction predicate (rule *(pr-sys)*); thus, the component performing the action will enforce the (possibly new) policy so generated. Notably, rule *(freshn)* relies on the condition checked in rule *(pr-sys)*, about the freshness of the new name n in the creating component, in order to put in place its scope.

The successful execution of the remaining three actions requires, at system level, appropriate synchronization. For this reason, we have a pair of complementary labels corresponding to each action. Rules *(accget)*, *(accqry)* and *(accput)* are used to generate the labels denoting the willingness of components to accept the execution of an action. More specifically, rule *(accget)* generates the label $\mathcal{I} : t \triangleleft \mathcal{J}$ indicating the willingness of component $\mathcal{J}$ to provide the item t to component $\mathcal{I}$. Notably, the label is generated only if such willingness is authorized by the policy in force at the component $\mathcal{J}$ (by means of the authorization predicate

Table 5. Systems' labeled transition relation (2/3): point-to-point communication rules

$$\frac{C \xrightarrow{\mathcal{I}:t \triangleleft n} C' \quad n = \mathcal{I}.id \quad C'[\mathcal{I}.\pi/\bullet] \xrightarrow{\mathcal{I}:t \triangleleft \mathcal{I}} C''}{C \xrightarrow{\tau} C''} \; (lget)$$

$$\frac{S_1 \xrightarrow{\mathcal{I}:t \triangleleft n} S_1' \quad S_2 \xrightarrow{\mathcal{I}:t \triangleleft \mathcal{J}} S_2' \quad \mathcal{J}.id = n \quad \mathcal{I}.\pi \vdash \mathcal{I} : t \triangleleft \mathcal{J}, \Pi'}{S_1 \parallel S_2 \xrightarrow{\tau} S_1'[\Pi'/\bullet] \parallel S_2'} \; (ptpget)$$

$$\frac{C \xrightarrow{\mathcal{I}:t \blacktriangleleft n} C' \quad n = \mathcal{I}.id \quad C'[\mathcal{I}.\pi/\bullet] \xrightarrow{\mathcal{I}:t \blacktriangleleft \mathcal{I}} C''}{C \xrightarrow{\tau} C''} \; (lqry)$$

$$\frac{S_1 \xrightarrow{\mathcal{I}:t \blacktriangleleft n} S_1' \quad S_2 \xrightarrow{\mathcal{I}:t \blacktriangleleft \mathcal{J}} S_2' \quad \mathcal{J}.id = n \quad \mathcal{I}.\pi \vdash \mathcal{I} : t \blacktriangleleft \mathcal{J}, \Pi'}{S_1 \parallel S_2 \xrightarrow{\tau} S_1'[\Pi'/\bullet] \parallel S_2'} \; (ptpqry)$$

$$\frac{C \xrightarrow{\mathcal{I}:t \triangleright n} C' \quad n = \mathcal{I}.id \quad C'[\mathcal{I}.\pi/\bullet] \xrightarrow{\mathcal{I}:t \triangleright \mathcal{I}} C''}{C \xrightarrow{\tau} C''} \; (lput)$$

$$\frac{S_1 \xrightarrow{\mathcal{I}:t \triangleright n} S_1' \quad S_2 \xrightarrow{\mathcal{I}:t \triangleright \mathcal{J}} S_2' \quad \mathcal{J}.id = n \quad \mathcal{I}.\pi \vdash \mathcal{I} : t \triangleright \mathcal{J}, \Pi'}{S_1 \parallel S_2 \xrightarrow{\tau} S_1'[\Pi'/\bullet] \parallel S_2'} \; (ptpput)$$

$\Pi \vdash \mathcal{I} : t \triangleleft \mathcal{J}, \Pi'$) and if withdrawing item t from the repository of $\mathcal{J}$ is possible $(\mathcal{K} \ominus t = \mathcal{K}')$. An effect of this transition is also the update of policy Π in Π' (both in the resulting component and in the produced label). Rules *(accqry)* and *(accput)* are similar to *(accget)*, the only difference being that they invoke the retrieval $(\mathcal{K} \vdash t)$ and the addition $(\mathcal{K} \oplus t = \mathcal{K}')$ operations of the repository's handling mechanism, respectively, rather than the withdrawal one. Finally, rule *(async)* states that all actions different from a **put** for group-oriented communication and an authorization for a **put** can be performed by involving only some of the system's components. Therefore, if there is a system component able to perform the authorization for a **put**, there is no way to infer that such component in parallel with any other one (hence the system as a whole) can perform the action. This ensures that when a system component is going to execute a **put** for group-oriented communication all potential receivers are taken into account.

The rules in Table 5 model the variants of the three communication actions implementing point-to-point interaction, while the rules for group-oriented communication are shown in Table 6.

In case of point-to-point interaction, action **get** can withdraw an item either from the local repository *(lget)* or from a specific repository with a point to point access *(ptpget)*. In any case, this transition corresponds to an internal computation step. The transition labelled by $\mathcal{I} : t \triangleleft \mathcal{I}$ in the premise of *(lget)* can only be produced by rule *(accget)*; it ensures that the component $\mathcal{I}$ authorizes

Table 6. Systems' labeled transition relation (3/3): group communication rules

$$\frac{S_1 \xrightarrow{\mathcal{I}:t \triangleleft \mathcal{P}} S_1' \quad S_2 \xrightarrow{\mathcal{I}:t \bar{\triangleleft} \mathcal{J}} S_2' \quad \mathcal{J} \models \mathcal{P} \quad \mathcal{I}.\pi \vdash \mathcal{I}:t \bar{\triangleleft} \mathcal{J}, \Pi'}{S_1 \parallel S_2 \xrightarrow{\tau} S_1'[\Pi'/\bullet] \parallel S_2'} \quad (grget)$$

$$\frac{S_1 \xrightarrow{\mathcal{I}:t \blacktriangleleft \mathcal{P}} S_1' \quad S_2 \xrightarrow{\mathcal{I}:t \bar{\blacktriangleleft} \mathcal{J}} S_2' \quad \mathcal{J} \models \mathcal{P} \quad \mathcal{I}.\pi \vdash \mathcal{I}:t \bar{\blacktriangleleft} \mathcal{J}, \Pi'}{S_1 \parallel S_2 \xrightarrow{\tau} S_1'[\Pi'/\bullet] \parallel S_2'} \quad (grqry)$$

$$\frac{S_1 \xrightarrow{\mathcal{I}:t \triangleright \mathcal{P}} S_1' \quad S_2 \xrightarrow{\mathcal{I}:t \bar{\triangleright} \mathcal{J}} S_2' \quad \mathcal{J} \models \mathcal{P} \quad \mathcal{I}.\pi \vdash \mathcal{I}:t \bar{\triangleright} \mathcal{J}, \Pi'}{S_1 \parallel S_2 \xrightarrow{\mathcal{I}[\Pi'/\mathcal{I}.\pi]:t \triangleright \mathcal{P}} S_1' \parallel S_2'} \quad (grput)$$

$$\frac{S \xrightarrow{\mathcal{I}:t \triangleright \mathcal{P}} S' \quad (\mathcal{J} \not\models \mathcal{P} \ \vee \ \Pi \not\vdash \mathcal{I}:t \bar{\triangleright} \mathcal{J}, \Pi' \ \vee \ \mathcal{I}.\pi \not\vdash \mathcal{I}:t \bar{\triangleright} \mathcal{J}, \Pi')}{S \parallel \mathcal{J}[\mathcal{K}, \Pi, P] \xrightarrow{\mathcal{I}:t \triangleright \mathcal{P}} S' \parallel \mathcal{J}[\mathcal{K}, \Pi, P]} \quad (engrput)$$

the local access to item t and that the component's knowledge and policy are updated accordingly. When the target of the action denotes a specific remote repository *(ptpget)*, the action is only allowed if n is the name of the component $\mathcal{J}$ simultaneously willing to provide the wanted item and if the request to perform the action at $\mathcal{J}$ is authorized by the local policy (identified by notation $\mathcal{I}.\pi$). Of course, if there are multiple components with the same name, one of them is non-deterministically chosen as the target of the action. Action **qry** behaves similarly to **get**, the only difference being that, if the action succeeds, after the computation step all repositories remain unchanged. Its semantics is modeled by rules *(lqry)* and *(ptpqry)*. Finally, action **put** adds item t to a repository. Its behavior is modeled by rules *(lput)* and *(ptpput)*, that are similar to those of actions **get** and **qry**, with the major difference being that, if the action succeeds, after the computation step an item is added to the target repository.

Let us now comment the rules for group-oriented communication that are shown in Table 6. When the target of action **get** denotes a set of repositories satisfying a given predicate *(grget)*, the action is only allowed if one of these repositories, say that of component $\mathcal{J}$, is willing to provide the wanted item and if the request to perform the action at $\mathcal{J}$ is authorized by the policy in force at the component performing the action. Relation $\mathcal{J} \models \mathcal{P}$ states that the attributes of $\mathcal{J}$ satisfy predicate $\mathcal{P}$; the definition of such relation depends on the kind of the used predicates. In any case, if the action succeeds, this transition corresponds to an internal computation step (denoted by τ) that changes the repository of component $\mathcal{J}$. Rule *(grqry)* is similar, but in the case of action **qry** the item is not removed from the repository. Differently from the two previous actions that only capture the interaction with one target component arbitrarily chosen among those satisfying the predicate $\mathcal{P}$ and willing to provide the wanted item, **put**(t)@$\mathcal{P}$ can interact with all components satisfying $\mathcal{P}$ and willing to accept the item t. In fact, rule *(grput)* permits the execution of a **put** for group-oriented communication when there is a parallel component, say $\mathcal{J}$, satisfying the target of the action and whose policy authorizes this remote access. Of course, the action must be authorized to use $\mathcal{J}$ as a target also by the policy in force at the component performing the action (which is updated after each evaluation of the authorization predicate). Notably, the resulting action is still a **put** for group-oriented communication, thus further authorization actions performed by other parallel components satisfying the target of the action can be simultaneously executed.

The capability of a component to perform a **put** for group-oriented communication is not affected by those system components not satisfying predicate $\mathcal{P}$, i.e. not belonging to the ensemble, or not authorising the action according to the policy in force at the sending component or at the target ones (rule *(engrput)*). Therefore, when there is a system component able to perform a **put** for group-oriented communication, by repeatedly applying rules *(grput)* and *(engrput)* it is possible to infer that the whole system can perform such an action (which in fact means that a component produces an item which is added to the repository of all the ensemble components that simultaneously are willing to receive the item).

Running example (step 5/7) Let us suppose that $\mathcal{I}_{R_2}.role=$ "*rescuer*" and $\mathcal{I}_{R_3}.role=$ "*helpRescuer*", while $\mathcal{I}_{R_i}.role=$ "*explorer*" for $4 \leq i \leq n$. Suppose also that $\mathcal{K}_{R_3}$ contains an item indicating that the victim has position $(3,5)$ and that 3 additional robots are needed for rescuing it.

Now, by exploiting the operational rule *(accget)*, the third component can generate the following labelled transition

$$\mathcal{I}_{R_3}[\mathcal{K}_{R_3}, \Pi_R, P_R] \xrightarrow{\mathcal{I}_{R_1}:\langle\text{"victim"},3,5,3\rangle \triangleleft \mathcal{I}_{R_3}} \mathcal{I}_{R_3}[\mathcal{K}_{R_3} \ominus \langle\text{"victim"},3,5,3\rangle, \Pi_R, P_R]$$

Recall that $\mathcal{K}_{R_3} \ominus \langle\text{"victim"},3,5,3\rangle$ means that the information about the victim is withdrawn from the knowledge repository $\mathcal{K}_{R_3}$.

Instead, by exploiting the operational rule *(pr-sys)*, the first component can generate the following labelled transition

$$\mathcal{I}_{R_1}[\mathcal{K}_{R_1}, \Pi_R, P_R] \xrightarrow{\lambda} \mathcal{I}_{R_1}[\mathcal{K}_{R_1}, \bullet, (P_2\{3/x, 5/y, 3/c\} \mid P_3)]$$

where λ is

$$\mathcal{I}_{R_1}[\Pi'_R/\Pi_R] : \langle\text{"victim"},3,5,3\rangle \triangleleft (role=\text{"rescuer"} \vee role=\text{"helpRescuer"}).$$

Hence, by exploiting the operational rule *(grget)* and assuming $\Pi'_R \vdash \lambda, \Pi''_R$, the overall system can perform the transition

$$S \xrightarrow{\tau} \mathcal{I}_{R_1}[\mathcal{K}_{R_1}, \Pi''_R, (P_2\{3/x, 5/y, 3/c\} \mid P_3)] \parallel \text{ROBOT}_2$$
$$\parallel \mathcal{I}_{R_3}[\mathcal{K}_{R_3} \ominus \langle\text{"victim"},3,5,3\rangle, \Pi_R, P_R] \parallel \text{ROBOT}_4 \parallel \ldots \parallel \text{ROBOT}_n \triangleq S'$$

$\square$

Table 7. Systems' transition relation

$$\frac{S \xrightarrow{\ \tau\ } S'}{(\nu\bar{n})S \succ\!\!\longrightarrow (\nu\bar{n})S'} \ (tau) \qquad\qquad \frac{S \xrightarrow{\ \mathcal{I}:t\rhd\mathcal{P}\ } S'}{(\nu\bar{n})S \succ\!\!\longrightarrow (\nu\bar{n})S'[\mathcal{I}.\pi/\bullet]} \ (put)$$

$$\frac{(\nu\bar{n}, n'')(S_1 \parallel S_2\{n''/n'\}) \succ\!\!\longrightarrow S' \qquad n'' \ fresh}{(\nu\bar{n})(S_1 \parallel (\nu n')S_2) \succ\!\!\longrightarrow S'} \ (top)$$

$$\frac{(\nu\bar{n})(S_2 \parallel S_1) \succ\!\!\longrightarrow S'}{(\nu\bar{n})(S_1 \parallel S_2) \succ\!\!\longrightarrow S'} \ (comm) \qquad\qquad \frac{(\nu\bar{n})((S_1 \parallel S_2) \parallel S_3) \succ\!\!\longrightarrow S'}{(\nu\bar{n})(S_1 \parallel (S_2 \parallel S_3)) \succ\!\!\longrightarrow S'} \ (assoc)$$

The unlabeled transition relation ($\succ\!\!\longrightarrow$) of the TS providing the semantics of generic systems is defined on top of the labeled one by the inference rules in Table 7. As a matter of notation, $\bar{n}$ denotes a (possibly empty) sequence of names and $\bar{n}, n'$ is the sequence obtained by composing $\bar{n}$ and n'. $(\nu\bar{n})S$ abbreviates $(\nu n_1)((\nu n_2)(\cdots(\nu n_m)S\cdots))$, if $\bar{n} = n_1, n_2, \cdots, n_m$ with $m > 0$, and S, otherwise. $S\{n'/n\}$ denotes the system obtained by replacing any free occurrence in S of n with n'. When considering a system S, a name is deemed *fresh* if it is different from any name occurring in S.

Rule *(tau)* of Table 7 accounts for the computation steps of a system where all (possible) name restrictions are at top level. Rule *(put)* states that, besides those labeled by τ, computation steps may additionally be labeled by $\mathcal{I} : t \rhd \mathcal{P}$, corresponding to group-oriented communication triggered by an action **put**(t)@$\mathcal{P}$ performed by component $\mathcal{I}$, and thus transforms them into transitions of the form $\succ\!\!\longrightarrow$. This rule also takes care of updating the policy in force at the sending component with the policy produced by the last evaluation of the authorization predicate in the inference of transition $S \xrightarrow{\ \mathcal{I}:t\rhd\mathcal{P}\ } S'$. Rule *(top)* permits to manipulate the syntax of a system, by moving all name restrictions at top level, thus putting it into a form to which one of the first two rules can be possibly applied. This manipulation may require the renaming of a restricted name with a freshly chosen one, thus ensuring that the name moved at top level is different both from the restricted names already moved at top level (to avoid name clashes) and from the names occurring free in the other (sub)systems in parallel (to avoid improper name captures). Rules *(comm)* and *(assoc)* state that systems' composition is a commutative and associative operator. Notably, by exploiting these two rules, we can manipulate systems and avoid adding analogous rules to those defining the labeled transition relation.

Running example (step 6/7) The robotics system can thus evolve by performing the reduction $S \succ\!\!\longrightarrow S'$.   □

3 Knowledge Management

As we have seen in the previous section, the SCEL language definition abstracts from a few ingredients of the language. In this section, we show two different knowledge mechanisms that can be used to instantiate the knowledge parameter. We start presenting the simplest, yet effective, instantiation of knowledge repositories based on multiple distributed *tuple spaces* à la KLAIM [20]. Then, we consider *constraints*, which are suitable to represent partial knowledge, to deal with multi-criteria optimization, to express preferences, fuzziness, and uncertainty. Finally, we show how knowledge can be exploited by external *reasoners* for taking decisions according to (a partial perception of) the context.

3.1 Tuple Spaces

Table 8 shows how to instantiate knowledge repositories, items and templates to deal with tuple spaces. Knowledge ITEMS are *tuples*, i.e. sequences of values, while TEMPLATES are sequences of values and variables. KNOWLEDGE repositories are then *tuple spaces*, i.e. (possibly empty) multisets of stored tuples $\langle t \rangle$. We use $\emptyset$ to denote an empty 'place' and the operator $\_ \parallel \_$ to aggregate items in multisets. Values within tuples can either be targets c, or processes P or, more generally, can result from the evaluation of some given expression e. We assume that expressions may contain attribute names, *boolean*, *integer*, *float* and *string* values and variables, together with the corresponding standard operators. To pick a tuple out from a tuple space by means of a given template, the *pattern-matching* mechanism is used: a tuple matches a template if they have the same number of elements and corresponding elements have matching values or variables; variables match any value of the same type ($?\,x$ and $?\,X$ are used to bind variables to values and processes, respectively), and two values match only if they are identical. If more tuples match a given template, one of them is arbitrarily chosen.

This form of knowledge representation has been already used in the running examples shown in the previous section. For instance, the template ("victim", $?x, ?y, ?c$) is used as argument of a **get** action to withdraw a 4-element tuple from the repository of one of the robots that knows the victim position. The first element of such a tuple must be the string "victim"; the other three values will be bound to variables x, y, and c, respectively.

The three operations provided by the knowledge repository's handling mechanism, namely *withdrawal* ($\mathcal{K} \ominus t$), *retrieval* ($\mathcal{K} \vdash t$) and *addition* ($\mathcal{K} \oplus t$) of an item t from/to repository $\mathcal{K}$, are inductively defined by the inference rules shown in Table 9. Notably, when a matching tuple is withdrawn from $\mathcal{K}$, it is replaced by the empty place $\emptyset$.

3.2 Constraints

In this section, we report some basic definitions concerning the concept of (soft) constraints. Among the many available formalizations, hereafter we refer to the one based on *c-semirings* [7,45], which generalizes many of the others.

Table 8. Tuple space syntax (e is an EXPRESSION)

KNOWLEDGE:	ITEMS:	TEMPLATES:
$\mathcal{K} ::= \emptyset \mid \langle t \rangle \mid \mathcal{K}_1 \parallel \mathcal{K}_2$	$t ::= e \mid c \mid P \mid t_1, t_2$	$T ::= e \mid c \mid ?x \mid ?X \mid T_1, T_2$

Table 9. Tuple space operations ($\ominus, \vdash, \oplus$)

$\langle t \rangle \ominus t = \emptyset$	$\dfrac{\mathcal{K}_1 \ominus t = \mathcal{K}'}{(\mathcal{K}_1 \parallel \mathcal{K}_2) \ominus t = \mathcal{K}' \parallel \mathcal{K}_2}$	$\dfrac{\mathcal{K}_2 \ominus t = \mathcal{K}'}{(\mathcal{K}_1 \parallel \mathcal{K}_2) \ominus t = \mathcal{K}_1 \parallel \mathcal{K}'}$
$\langle t \rangle \vdash t$	$\dfrac{\mathcal{K}_1 \vdash t}{(\mathcal{K}_1 \parallel \mathcal{K}_2) \vdash t}$ $\dfrac{\mathcal{K}_2 \vdash t}{(\mathcal{K}_1 \parallel \mathcal{K}_2) \vdash t}$	$\mathcal{K} \oplus t = \mathcal{K} \parallel \langle t \rangle$

Intuitively, a constraint is a relation that gives information on the possible values that the variables of a specified set may assume. We adopt a functional formulation. Hence, given a set V of variables and a domain D of values that the variables may assume, assignments and constraints are defined as follows.

Definition 1 (Assignments). *An* assignment η *of values to variables is a function* $\eta : V \to D$.

Definition 2 (Constraints). *A* constraint χ *is a function* $\chi : (V \to D) \to \{\mathsf{true}, \mathsf{false}\}$.

A constraint is then represented as a function that, given an assignment η, returns a truth value indicating if the constraint is satisfied by η. An assignment that satisfies a constraint is called a *solution*.

When SCEL's knowledge repositories are instantiated as multiple distributed constraint stores, D could be taken as the set of SCEL *basic values* (e.g., integers and strings). Variables in V, that we call *constraint variables* to take them apart from those of SCEL processes, could be written as pairs of names of the form $n@n'$ (e.g., $batteryLevel@robot_i$), where n is the variable name and n' the name of the component that *owns* the variable. Different components may own variables with the same name; such variables are distinct and may thus store different values.

We denote an assignment as a collection of pairs of the form $n@n' \mapsto v$, where $n@n'$ and v range over variables and values, respectively. Such pairs explicitly specify the associations for only the variables relevant for the considered constraint; these variables form the so-called *support* [8] of the constraint, which is assumed to be finite. For example, given the constraints $batteryLevel@robot_i \geq 20\%$ and $lifetime@robot_i = batteryLevel@robot_i \cdot 3000$, the assignment $\{batteryLevel@robot_i \mapsto 25\%, lifetime@robot_i \mapsto 1000\}$ satisfies the first constraint (i.e., returns true) but does not satisfy the second one (i.e., returns false).

The constraints introduced above are called *crisp* in the literature, because they can only be either satisfied or violated. A more general notion is represented by the *soft constraints*. These constraints, given an assignment, return an element of an arbitrary constraint semiring (*c-semiring* [7]). C-semirings are partially ordered sets of 'preference' values equipped with two suitable operations for comparison $(+)$ and combination $(\times)$ of (tuples of) values and constraints.

Definition 3 (C-semiring). *A c-semiring is an algebraic structure $\langle S, +, \times, 0, 1 \rangle$ such that: S is a set and $0, 1 \in S$; $+$ is a binary operation on S that is commutative, associative, idempotent, 0 is its unit element and 1 is its absorbing element; $\times$ is a binary operation on S that is commutative, associative, distributes over $+$, 1 is its unit element and 0 is its absorbing element. Operation $+$ induces a partial order $\leq$ on S defined by $a \leq b$ iff $a + b = b$, which means that a is more constrained than b or, equivalently, that b is better than a. The minimal element is thus 0 and the maximal 1.*

Definition 4 (Soft constraints). *Let $\langle S, +, \times, 0, 1 \rangle$ be a c-semiring. A soft constraint χ is a function $\chi : (V \rightarrow D) \rightarrow S$.*

In particular, crisp constraints can be understood as soft constraints on the c-semiring $\langle \{\text{true}, \text{false}\}, \vee, \wedge, \text{false}, \text{true} \rangle$.

By lifting the c-semiring operators to constraints, we get the operators

$$(\chi_1 + \chi_2)(\eta) = \chi_1(\eta) + \chi_2(\eta) \qquad (\chi_1 \times \chi_2)(\eta) = \chi_1(\eta) \times \chi_2(\eta)$$

(their n ary extensions are straightforward). We can formally define the notions of consistency and entailment. The *consistency* condition $\chi \neq 0$ stands for

$$\exists \eta : \chi(\eta) \neq 0$$

i.e. a constraint is consistent if it has at least a solution; the *entailment* condition $\chi_1 \leq \chi_2$ stands for

$$\forall \eta, \; \chi_1(\eta) \leq \chi_2(\eta)$$

When constraints are used as the argument of actions **put**, **qry** and **get**, these actions play the role of actions **tell**, **ask** and **retract**, respectively, commonly used in the CCP paradigm [48] to add a constraint to a store, to check entailment of a constraint by a store and to remove a constraint from a store. These constraints may only involve constraint variables whose owner is the component target of the action. This ensures that all the constraints stored in the same repository only involve variables owned by the same component, which is the owner of the repository. Thus, for example, it will never happen that the $robot_2$'s repository stores a constraint like $batteryLevel@robot_1 < 100\%$.

The three operations provided by the knowledge repository's handling mechanism, namely *withdrawal* $(\mathcal{K} \ominus \chi)$, *retrieval* $(\mathcal{K} \vdash \chi)$ and *addition* $(\mathcal{K} \oplus \chi)$ of a constraint χ from/to repository $\mathcal{K}$, are inductively defined by the inference rules

Table 10. Constraint store operations $(\ominus, \vdash, \oplus)$

$$\mathcal{K} \ominus \chi = \begin{cases} \mathcal{K}' & \text{if } \mathcal{K} \equiv \mathcal{K}' \parallel \chi \\ \mathcal{K} & \text{otherwise} \end{cases}$$

$$\mathcal{K} \vdash \chi \qquad\qquad \text{if } \mathcal{K} \equiv (\chi_1 \parallel \ldots \parallel \chi_m) \text{ and } (\chi_1 \times \ldots \times \chi_m) \leq \chi$$

$$\mathcal{K} \oplus \chi = \mathcal{K} \parallel \chi \quad \text{if } \mathcal{K} \equiv (\chi_1 \parallel \ldots \parallel \chi_m) \text{ and } (\chi_1 \times \ldots \times \chi_m \times \chi) \neq 0$$

---

shown in Table 10. We use $\mathcal{K}_1 \equiv \mathcal{K}_2$ to denote that $\mathcal{K}_1$ and $\mathcal{K}_2$ are equal up to commutation of items. In the definition of $\mathcal{K} \vdash \chi$ and $\mathcal{K} \oplus \chi$, if the constraint store is empty (i.e. $m = 0$), then it suffices to verify that χ is a tautology (i.e., it is a constant function returning the c-semiring value 1 for any assignment) and that χ has at least a solution (i.e., it differs from the c-semiring value 0), respectively.

As an example of use in our robotics scenario of the constraint-based interaction, $robot_1$ could perform the action $\mathbf{qry}(lifetime@robot_2 > 1000)@robot_2$ to check if the lifetime of $robot_2$ is at least 1000 seconds (which could be, e.g., the minimum time to transport the victim to a safe area). Assuming that the $robot_2$'s repository stores the constraints $batteryLevel@robot_2 = 50\%$ and $lifetime@robot_2 = batteryLevel@robot_2 \cdot 3000$, the entailment of constraint $lifetime@robot_2 > 1000$ is satisfied and, hence, the execution of the robot behaviour can proceed with the continuation process of the $\mathbf{qry}$ action.

3.3   External Reasoners

As discussed, SCEL is sufficiently powerful for dealing with coordination and interaction issues. However, it does not provide explicit machineries for specifying components that take decisions about the action to perform based on their context. Obviously, the language could be extended in order to encompass such possibilities, and one could have specific reasoning phases, or dedicated SCEL components, triggered by the perception of changes in the context.

The general perspective. In our view, it is however preferable to have separate reasoning components specified in another language, that SCEL programs can invoke at need. Having two different languages for computation and coordination, and for *reasoning*, does guarantee *separation of concerns*, a fundamental property to obtain reliable and maintainable specifications. Also, it may be beneficial to have a methodology for integrating different reasoners designed and optimised for specific purposes.

What we envisage is having SCEL programs that whenever have to take decisions have the possibility of invoking an external reasoner by providing it information about the relevant knowledge they have access to, and receiving in exchange informed suggestions about how to proceed. In a scenario like the robot rescue one, reasoners could for example be exploited by robots to "improve" their random walk phase, e.g. trying to minimise collisions in an environment densely populated by robots moving in an unexpected way. Intuitively, the current robot's perception of the surrounding environment should be provided to a reasoner, which would return the "best" movement direction according to the probability of colliding with other robots and, possibly, to other criteria.

As a matter of fact, in [5] we provided a general methodology to enrich SCEL components with reasoning capabilities by resorting to explicit *reasoner integrators*, we instantiated the methodology for MISSCEL[7], a SCEL interpreter, and we discussed the integration of MISSCEL with the PIRLO reasoner [4]. This permits to specify *reasoning service component ensembles*, and also paves the way towards the exploitation of tools and techniques for analysing their behaviour, allowing thus to *reason on* reasoning service component ensembles. An example is the collision avoidance scenario considered in [5], which has been analysed exploiting MULTIVESTA [51], a recently proposed statistical model checker. More details about the scenario and its analysis are provided in Section 8.2.

In the following we present our approach to enrich SCEL components with external reasoning capabilities, in particular focusing on a SCEL instance where repositories are implemented as multisets of tuples (as in Section 3.1), while we refer to [5] for details about its instantiation for MISSCEL.

The methodology. We aim at enriching SCEL components with an external reasoner to be *invoked* when necessary (e.g. by a robot before performing a movement). Ideally, this should be done by minimally extending SCEL. In Figure 1 we depicted the constituents of a SCEL component: interfaces, policies, processes and repositories. Interfaces will not be involved in the extension, as they only expose the local knowledge to other components. Moreover, we currently restrict ourselves to not explicitly consider policies in the extension. Since, in the considered dialect, processes store and retrieve tuples in repositories, the interaction between a process and its local repository is a natural choice where to plug-in a reasoner: we can use special data (*reasoning request tuples*) whose addition to the local knowledge (i.e. via a **put** at **self**) triggers the reasoner. For example, assuming we have a reasoner offering the capability of computing the best direction where to move so as to minimize the probability of collisions, a robot may invoke the reasoner before performing a movement by resorting to an action like **put**(*"reasoningRequest"*, *"computeDirection"*, *perceivedEnv*)@self, where *perceivedEnv* is the current perception that the robot has of the surrounding environment (e.g. the number and position of robots within a certain range). Reasoning results can then be stored in the knowledge as *reasoning result tuples*, allowing local processes to access them as any other data (e.g. via a **get** from **self**). For example, the direction *"dir"* generated by the reasoner can be accessed by resorting to an action like **get**(*"reasoningResult"*, *dir*)@self.

Figure 2 depicts such an *enriched* SCEL *component*, together with a generic external reasoner R. With respect to Figure 1, now local communications are filtered by *RI*, a *reasoner integrator*. As depicted by the grey arrow between *RI*

---

[7] http://sysma.lab.imtlucca.it/tools/misscel/

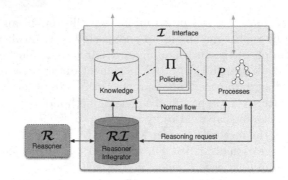

Fig. 2. Enriched SCEL component

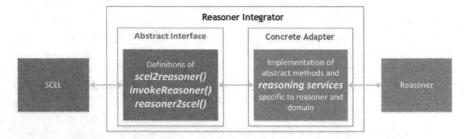

Fig. 3. An architectural perspective of the reasoner integrator

and R, in case of reasoning requests RI invokes R, which evaluates the request and returns back the result of the reasoning phase. RI then stores the obtained result in the knowledge, allowing the local processes to access it via common **get** or **qry**. In case of normal data the flow goes instead directly to the knowledge. Note that only local **put** of reasoning request tuples trigger a reasoner.

Actually, RI has the further fundamental role of translating data among the internal representations used by SCEL and by the reasoner, acting hence as an adapter between them. For example, the reasoner may use a different representation for the space (and thus for the positions of the other robots) with respect to SCEL. To sum up, RI performs three tasks: it translates the parameters of the reasoning requests from SCEL's representation to the reasoner's one (*scel2reasoner*), it invokes the reasoner (*invokeReasoner*), and finally it translates back the results (*reasoner2scel*). Clearly, each reasoner requires its own implementation of the three operations. Hence, as depicted in Figure 3, we separate the RI component into an *Abstract Reasoning Interface* and a *Concrete Adapter*. The former is given just once and contains the definition of the three operations, while the latter is reasoner- and domain-specific, and provides the actual implementation of the three operations. In [5] we discussed the instantiation for MISSCEL of the Abstract Reasoning Interface, together with an example of a concrete adapter for the reasoner PIRLO in the context of the mentioned collision avoidance robotic scenario.

Note that the presented methodology is not restricted to a particular reasoner. Moreover, many reasoners could be used at the same time, each performing particular reasoning tasks for which they are best suited. To this end, particular *reasoning services* (like e.g. the *computeDirection* one) can be requested by a SCEL process according to the task at hand.

Finally, it may be worth to remark that, as mentioned, we did not investigate yet the role of policies in extending SCEL's components with reasoning capabilities. However, they already play an important role in our methodology, as they can manipulate the flow of data among processes and local repositories, and thus can intercept, modify or generate reasoning requests and results. Moreover, we can easily foresee a scenario in which complicated policies, possibly involving reasoning tasks, resort to a reasoner as well, following the proposed methodology. For example, in case of a group **get** like, e.g. the second action of the process presented in the *step 3/7* of our running example, which is used to help other robots for rescuing a victim, it may be useful to allow policies to use reasoners in order to select the *best* tuple among the many matching ones present in a distributed repository (e.g. different help requests) according to some specific criteria (e.g. the one regarding the nearest robot, or the most urgent one).

4 A Policy Language

The SCEL programming constructs presented in Section 2 define the computational behaviour of components in a procedural style. According to the SCEL design principles, the interaction and adaptation logics are defined separately by means of behavioural policies. These policies have to be intuitive and easy-to-maintain, therefore the use of a declarative paradigm for their specification is advocated. Recently, *policy languages* (see e.g. [18,31,29]) are receiving much attention in different research fields, varying, e.g., from access control to network management. In fact, policies can regulate multiple system's aspects and, by using a declarative approach, can be easily integrated with other programming languages.

Here, we present a simplified version[8] of FACPL (Formal Access Control Policy Language) [36], a simple, yet expressive, language for defining access control, resource usage and adaptation policies, which is inspired by the XACML [39] standard for access control. We refer the interested reader to [35] for a presentation of the full version of FACPL, which contains additional aspects that are not exploited in the integration with SCEL. Syntax and semantics of policy abstractions are presented in Section 4.1 and Section 4.2, respectively.

4.1 Policies and Their Syntax

Policies are sets of rules that specify strategies, requirements, constraints, guidelines, etc. about the behaviour of a controlled system. The syntax is presented

---

[8] In the rest of the paper, unless when explicitly mentioned, we use the acronym FACPL for referring to this simplified version.

Table 11. Policy constructs

POLICIES:	π ::=	$\langle \alpha$ target $:\tau^?$ rules $:r^+$ obl $:o^* \rangle$
	$\mid$	$\{\alpha$ target $:\tau^?$ policies $:\pi^+$ obl $:o^* \}$
COMBINING ALGORITHMS:	α ::=	deny-overrides $\mid$ permit-overrides
	$\mid$	deny-unless-permit $\mid$ permit-unless-deny
	$\mid$	first-applicable $\mid$ only-one-applicable
RULES:	r ::=	$(d$ target $:\tau^?$ condition $:be^?$ obl $:o^*)$
DECISIONS:	d ::=	permit $\mid$ deny
TARGETS:	τ ::=	$f(pv,sn) \mid \tau \wedge \tau \mid \tau \vee \tau$
MATCHING FUNCTIONS:	f ::=	equal $\mid$ not-equal $\mid$ greater-than
	$\mid$	less-than $\mid$ greater-than-or-equal
	$\mid$	less-than-or-equal $\mid$ ...
OBLIGATIONS:	o ::=	$[d\ s]$
OBLIGATION ACTIONS:	s ::=	$\epsilon \mid a.s$

in Table 11. As a matter of notation, symbol ? stands for optional elements, $*$ for (possibly empty) sequences, and $+$ for non-empty sequences. For the sake of readability, whenever an element is missing, we also omit the possibly related keyword; thus, e.g., rule $(d$ target $:\tau$ condition $:$ obl $:$ $)$ will be written as $(d$ target $:\tau)$.

A POLICY is either an *atomic policy* $\langle ... \rangle$ or a *policy set* $\{...\}$. An atomic policy (resp. policy set) is made of a target, a non-empty sequence of rules (resp. policies) combined through one of the combining algorithms, and a sequence of obligations.

A TARGET indicates the authorisation requests to which a policy/rule applies. It is either an atomic target or a pair of simpler targets combined using the standard logic operators $\wedge$ and $\vee$. An *atomic target* $f(pv,sn)$ is a triple denoting the application of a matching function f to *policy values*[9] pv from the policy and to policy values from the evaluation context identified by *attribute (structured) names*[10] sn. In fact, an attribute name refers to a specific attribute of the request or of the environment, which is available via the evaluation context. In this way, an authorisation decision can be based on some characteristics of the request, e.g. subjects' or objects' identity, or of the environment, e.g. CPU load. For

---

[9] The set of policy values depends on the system where the policies are enforced. In case of SCEL systems, this set contains action identifiers (i.e., **get**, **qry**, **put**, **fresh** and **new**), items and templates, and all the other knowledge values that can be used within the evaluation.

[10] A structured name has the form *name/name*, where the first name stands for a category name and the second one for an attribute name.

example, the target greater-than(90%,*subject/CPUload*) matches whenever 90% is greater then the CPU load of the subject component. Similarly, the structured name *action/action-id* refers to the identifier of the action to be performed (such as **get**, **qry**, **put**, etc.) and, thus, the target equal(**get**, *action/action-id*) matches whenever such action is the withdrawing one.

Rules are the basic elements for request evaluation. A RULE defines the tests that must be successfully passed by attributes for returning a positive or negative DECISION — i.e. permit or deny — to the enclosing policy. This decision is returned only if the target is 'applicable', i.e. the request matches the target; otherwise the evaluation of the rule returns not-applicable. In fact, as shown in Section 4.2, the semantics of the policies is defined over a three-valued decision δ that, in addition to permit and deny, can also assume the value not-applicable. Rule applicability can be further refined by the CONDITION expression *be*, which permits more complex calculations than those in target expressions. *be* is a boolean expression which acts on policy values and structured names. Notably, these expressions, as well as the matching functions, can be extended in order to properly deal with specific data types.

A COMBINING ALGORITHM computes the authorisation decision corresponding to a given request by combining a set of rules/policies' evaluation results. The language provides the following algorithms:

- deny-overrides: if any rule/policy in the considered list evaluates to deny, then the result of the combination is deny. In other words, deny takes precedence, regardless of the result of evaluating any of the other rules/policies in the list. Instead, if at least a rule/policy evaluates to permit and all others evaluate to not-applicable or permit, then the result of the combination is permit. If all policies are found to be not applicable to the decision request, then the policy set evaluates to not-applicable.
- permit-overrides: this algorithm is the dual of the previous one, i.e. this time permit takes precedence over the other results.
- deny-unless-permit: this algorithm is similar to permit-overrides, because it is intended for those cases where a permit decision takes precedence over deny decisions; differently from permit-overrides, this algorithm never returns not-applicable, i.e. it is converted to deny.
- permit-unless-deny: this algorithm is the dual of the previous one, i.e. deny takes precedence over permit decisions and not-applicable is never returned.
- first-applicable: rules/policies are evaluated in the order of appearance in the considered list of rules/policies and the combined result is the same as the result of evaluating the first rule/policy in the list that is applicable to the decision request, if such result is either permit or deny. If all rules/policies evaluate to not-applicable, then the overall result is not-applicable.
- only-one-applicable: if one and only one rule/policy in the considered list is applicable by virtue of its target, the result of the combining algorithm is the result of evaluating the single applicable rule/policy. Otherwise, the result is not-applicable.

An OBLIGATION is a sequence (ϵ denotes the empty one) of actions that should be performed in conjunction with the enforcement of an authorisation decision. It is returned when the authorisation decision for the enclosing element, i.e. rule, policy or policy set, is the same as the one attached to the obligation. An OBLIGATION ACTION is a generic action that can be used for enforcing additional behaviours in the controlled system and whose arguments may also contain expressions and structured names that are fulfilled during request evaluation. Like policy values, the set of obligation actions depends on the system where the policies are enforced. For example, w.r.t. a given request, the obligation

$$[\,\mathsf{deny}\ \mathbf{put}(\text{``}goTo\text{''}, env/station.x, env/station.y)@\mathsf{self}\,]$$

returned when the authorisation decision for the enclosing element is deny, could be fullfilled as follows

$$\mathbf{put}(\text{``}goTo\text{''}, 5.45, 3.67)@\mathsf{self}$$

and could be used to set the robot movement's direction with respect to the coordinates of the closest (charging) station. Notably, the coordinates are retrieved at evaluation-time through the context, as indeed obligation actions can use context-dependent arguments.

4.2   Semantics of the Policy Language

Before presenting the semantics, we introduce the key notion of *authorisation requests*. They are functions, ranged over by ρ, mapping structured names to policy values and are written as collections of pairs of the form (sn, pv). As an example, consider the following request:

$$\begin{aligned}
\rho = \{ &(subject/subject\text{-}id, \text{``}cmp\text{''}), (subject/attr, 4), \ldots \\
&(action/action\text{-}id, \text{``}act\text{''}), \ldots \\
&(object/resource\text{-}id, \text{``}res\text{''}), (object/attr, 3), \ldots \}
\end{aligned}$$

Here, the subject identified by the string "*cmp*" requires the authorisation to execute the action "*act*" on the object identified by string "*res*". Notably, authorisation requests contain all attributes needed to evaluate them, forming the so-called evaluation context, including environmental properties.

The language semantics permits, given a policy π and a request ρ, to obtain a decision $\delta \in \{\mathsf{permit}, \mathsf{deny}, \mathsf{not\text{-}applicable}\}$ and a (possibly empty) sequence s of (fulfilled) obligation actions. This is expressed by the judgement $\pi, \rho \vdash \delta, s$. When we only consider permit and deny as resulting decisions, we use d instead of δ. The semantics is defined by the inference rules for the evaluation of policy elements, reported in Table 12, and of policy combining algorithms, reported in Table 13. In the next two subsections we comment the rules of the two tables, respectively.

Semantics of Policies' Elements. The inference rules of Table 12 are grouped according to the type of element they refer to. Thus, from top to bottom, we have the inference rules concerning policies, rules, targets and obligations. To

Table 12. Semantics of policies' elements

POLICIES

$$\frac{\tau,\rho \vdash \text{applicable} \qquad \alpha(r^+),\rho \vdash d,s \qquad o^*,\rho,d \vdash s'}{\langle\alpha \ \text{target}:\tau \ \text{rules}:r^+ \ \text{obl}:o^*\rangle,\rho \vdash d,s.s'}$$

$$\frac{\alpha(r^+),\rho \vdash d,s \qquad o^*,\rho,d \vdash s'}{\langle\alpha \ \text{rules}:r^+ \ \text{obl}:o^*\rangle,\rho \vdash d,s.s'} \qquad \frac{\alpha(r^+),\rho \vdash \text{not-applicable},\epsilon}{\langle\alpha \ \text{rules}:r^+ \ \text{obl}:o^*\rangle,\rho \vdash \text{not-applicable},\epsilon}$$

$$\frac{\tau,\rho \vdash \text{not-applicable} \quad \vee \quad (\tau,\rho \vdash \text{applicable} \ \wedge \ \alpha(r^+),\rho \vdash \text{not-applicable},\epsilon)}{\langle\alpha \ \text{target}:\tau \ \text{rules}:r^+ \ \text{obl}:o^*\rangle,\rho \vdash \text{not-applicable},\epsilon}$$

RULES

$$\frac{\tau,\rho \vdash \text{applicable} \quad [\![be]\!]_\rho = \text{true} \quad o^*,\rho,d \vdash s}{(d \ \text{target}:\tau \ \text{condition}:be \ \text{obl}:o^*),\rho \vdash d,s} \qquad \frac{\tau,\rho \vdash \text{applicable} \quad o^*,\rho,d \vdash s}{(d \ \text{target}:\tau \ \text{obl}:o^*),\rho \vdash d,s}$$

$$\frac{[\![be]\!]_\rho = \text{true} \quad o^*,\rho,d \vdash s}{(d \ \text{condition}:be \ \text{obl}:o^*),\rho \vdash d,s} \qquad \frac{o^*,\rho,d \vdash s}{(d \ \text{obl}:o^*),\rho \vdash d,s}$$

$$\frac{\tau,\rho \vdash \text{not-applicable}}{(d \ \text{target}:\tau \ \text{condition}:be^? \ \text{obl}:o^*),\rho \vdash \text{not-applicable},\epsilon}$$

$$\frac{[\![be]\!]_\rho = \text{false}}{(d \ \text{condition}:be \ \text{obl}:o^*),\rho \vdash \text{not-applicable},\epsilon}$$

$$\frac{\tau,\rho \vdash \text{applicable} \quad [\![be]\!]_\rho = \text{false}}{(d \ \text{target}:\tau \ \text{condition}:be \ \text{obl}:o^*),\rho \vdash \text{not-applicable},\epsilon}$$

TARGETS

$$\frac{\tau_1,\rho \vdash \text{applicable} \quad \vee \quad \tau_2,\rho \vdash \text{applicable}}{(\tau_1 \vee \tau_2),\rho \vdash \text{applicable}} \qquad \frac{\tau_1,\rho \vdash \text{applicable} \quad \tau_2,\rho \vdash \text{applicable}}{(\tau_1 \wedge \tau_2),\rho \vdash \text{applicable}}$$

$$\frac{\tau_1,\rho \vdash \text{not-applicable} \quad \tau_2,\rho \vdash \text{not-applicable}}{(\tau_1 \vee \tau_2),\rho \vdash \text{not-applicable}} \qquad \frac{\tau_1,\rho \vdash \text{not-applicable} \quad \vee \quad \tau_2,\rho \vdash \text{not-applicable}}{(\tau_1 \wedge \tau_2),\rho \vdash \text{not-applicable}}$$

$$\frac{f([\![pv]\!]_\rho,\rho(sn)) \vdash \text{true}}{f(pv,sn),\rho \vdash \text{applicable}} \qquad \frac{sn \notin dom(\rho) \quad \vee \quad f([\![pv]\!]_\rho,\rho(sn)) \vdash \text{false}}{f(pv,sn),\rho \vdash \text{not-applicable}}$$

$$\frac{pv > pv'}{\text{greater-than}(pv,pv) \vdash \text{true}} \qquad \frac{pv \not> pv'}{\text{greater-than}(pv,pv') \vdash \text{false}}$$

$$\cdots$$

OBLIGATIONS

$$\frac{}{\epsilon,\rho,d \vdash \epsilon} \qquad \frac{d' = d \quad [\![s]\!]_\rho = s' \quad o^*,\rho,d \vdash s''}{[d' \ s]o^*,\rho,d \vdash s'.s''} \qquad \frac{d' \neq d \quad o^*,\rho,d \vdash s'}{[d' \ s]o^*,\rho,d \vdash s'}$$

---

save space, we do not show the inference rules of policy sets, as they are similar to those of atomic policies, and of some matching functions.

Some inference rules use the evaluation function $[\![\cdot]\!]_\rho$ that first replaces each attribute occurring in its argument expression with the corresponding value retrieved from the request ρ and then makes possible (boolean, integer, float, string, etc.) calculations. For example, given the request shown before, the arithmetic expression $subject/attr + object/attr$ is evaluated as follows

$$[\![\, subject/attr + object/attr \,]\!]_\rho = \rho(subject/attr) + \rho(object/attr) = 3 + 4 = 7$$

In case of occurrence of run-time errors, e.g. a function is not defined for arguments of a certain type, the expression evaluation halts and the policy evaluation does not complete.

The judgement $\pi, \rho \vdash \delta, s$ defines the semantics of policies and is inferred via the inference rules for targets, obligations and rules, combined together using the inference rules for the combining algorithms. Specifically, when a policy π is applied to a request ρ, first it is checked if the policy's target matches the request. If this is the case the evaluation proceeds by applying the policy's combining algorithm to the (sequence of) enclosed rules, thus obtaining a policy decision d and a sequence of obligation actions s. The decision d is then used to fulfill the sequence of policy's obligations thus obtaining a sequence s' of obligation actions that, in the resulting authorisation statement, is appended to s. If the target is empty then it matches any request. Finally, if the target does not match the request or the decision obtained by the combining algorithm is not-applicable, the policy does not apply and the decision not-applicable is returned together with an empty sequence of obligations. A policy set is evaluated like a policy, the only difference is that the combining algorithm is applied to a sequence of policies and/or policy sets, rather than rules.

When a rule r is applied to a request ρ, first it is checked if the rule's target matches the request. Additionally, in this case, a condition expression, if present, is evaluated. If its evaluation returns true, the rule applies, otherwise the decision not-applicable is returned. If the condition expression is absent, then it is considered true. When the rule's target matches the request and the condition expression returns true, the rule's effect, i.e. permit or deny, is returned, together with the sequence of obligation actions resulting from fulfilling the sequence of rule's obligations.

A target τ matches a request ρ, i.e. its evaluation returns applicable, if the combination of its atomic targets matches ρ. A composed target of the form $(\tau_1 \vee \tau_2)$ matches ρ, if one between τ_1 and τ_2 matches the request, while in case of target $(\tau_1 \wedge \tau_2)$, both τ_1 and τ_2 must match the request. An atomic target of the form $f(pv,sn)$ matches a request ρ if the matching function f, applied to (the evaluation of) the policy value pv and the value identified by the structured name sn in the request, i.e. $\rho(sn)$, returns true. Before applying the matching function, the policy value must be evaluated, since it may be a template containing expressions. This is not necessary for the structured name; indeed, although it may be an item, it will not contain expressions since it has been retrieved from the request. Instead, the evaluation of an atomic target returns not-applicable either if the structured name does not identify any value in the request, i.e. it does not belong to the request's domain ($sn \notin dom(\rho)$), or if the matching function returns false. The rules for matching functions are straightforward. For example, greater-than(pv,pv') returns true only when pv is greater than pv'.

The last three rules account for fulfilment of a sequence of policy's obligations when the decision for the enclosing element is d, i.e. permit or deny. If the sequence is empty, then an empty sequence of obligation actions is returned. Otherwise, the obligations in the sequence are fulfilled sequentially and the resulting sequences of obligation actions are linked together preserving the same order. The fulfilment of an obligation with attached effect equal to the decision d of the enclosing element consists in evaluating all argument expressions by using function $[\![\cdot]\!]_\rho$. Instead, if the attached effect differs from d, the last rule permits to continue the fulfilment while ignoring the current obligation.

Semantics of Policy Combining Algorithms. The rules of Table 13 rewrite formally the combining algorithms descriptions presented in Section 4.1. For each algorithm, we have separate, but quite similar, rules that deal with the case that the algorithm is applied to a sequence of rules or of policies. Therefore, to save space, we only report and comment the first type of rules and, for dual algorithms (e.g. permit-overrides and deny-overrides), we avoid to report both set of rules.

In the inference rules, given a non-empty sequence r^+ of rules, notation $\exists\, r, \rho \vdash \delta, s$ ($\nexists\, r, \rho \vdash \delta, s$, resp.) means that there is (not, resp.) a rule in the sequence satisfying the judgement. The variants with universal quantifier or where the index of rules is explicitly considered have a similar meaning.

The rules for the algorithm permit-overrides (resp. deny-overrides) are straightforward: if there is a rule in the sequence to which the algorithm is applied returning decision permit (resp. deny) then the algorithm returns permit; instead, if all rules in the sequence are not-applicable, then the algorithm returns not-applicable; otherwise, i.e. no rule returns permit and there is at least one rule returning deny (resp. permit), then the algorithm returns deny.

The rules for the algorithm deny-unless-permit (resp. permit-unless-deny) are similar to those for permit-overrides (resp. deny-overrides) but in this case the decision not-applicable is never returned. Thus, the algorithm returns permit (resp. deny) if there is a rule in the sequence returning it; otherwise, it returns deny (resp. permit).

In the previous inference rules, the sequence of obligation actions returned by an algorithm together with a decision d is any of those returned by one of the rules, in the sequence to which the algorithm is applied, returning the same decision d (if there is no such rule, then it is the empty sequence). However, no assumption is made about the evaluation order of the rules in the sequence. Thus, when more rules return permit or deny, the returned sequence of obligation actions is somehow nondeterministically chosen. Namely, id the execution halts at the first permit or deny result, the resulting obligation sequence s is composed by only the actions returned together with such a result.

Table 13. Semantics of policy combining algorithms

PERMIT-OVERRIDES

$$\frac{\exists\, r, \rho \vdash \mathsf{permit}, s}{\mathsf{permit\text{-}overrides}(r^+), \rho \vdash \mathsf{permit}, s} \qquad \frac{\nexists\, r', \rho \vdash \mathsf{permit}, s' \quad \exists\, r, \rho \vdash \mathsf{deny}, s}{\mathsf{permit\text{-}overrides}(r^+), \rho \vdash \mathsf{deny}, s}$$

$$\frac{\forall\, r, \rho \vdash \mathsf{not\text{-}applicable}, \epsilon}{\mathsf{permit\text{-}overrides}(r^+), \rho \vdash \mathsf{not\text{-}applicable}, \epsilon}$$

DENY-UNLESS-PERMIT

$$\frac{\exists\, r, \rho \vdash \mathsf{permit}, s}{\mathsf{deny\text{-}unless\text{-}permit}(r^+), \rho \vdash \mathsf{permit}, s} \qquad \frac{\nexists\, r', \rho \vdash \mathsf{permit}, s' \quad \exists\, r, \rho \vdash \mathsf{deny}, s}{\mathsf{deny\text{-}unless\text{-}permit}(r^+), \rho \vdash \mathsf{deny}, s}$$

$$\frac{\forall\, r, \rho \vdash \mathsf{not\text{-}applicable}, \epsilon}{\mathsf{deny\text{-}unless\text{-}permit}(r^+), \rho \vdash \mathsf{deny}, \epsilon}$$

FIRST-APPLICABLE $i \in \{1, 2, \ldots, |r|\}$

$$\frac{r_i, \rho \vdash d, s \qquad \forall\, 1 \le j < i : r_j, \rho \vdash \mathsf{not\text{-}applicable}, \epsilon}{\mathsf{first\text{-}applicable}(r^+), \rho \vdash d, s}$$

$$\frac{\forall\, i : r_i, \rho \vdash \mathsf{not\text{-}applicable}, \epsilon}{\mathsf{first\text{-}applicable}(r^+), \rho \vdash \mathsf{not\text{-}applicable}, \epsilon}$$

ONLY-ONE-APPLICABLE $i \in \{1, 2, \ldots, |r|\}$

$$\frac{r_i, \rho \vdash d, s \qquad \forall\, j \ne i : r_j, \rho \vdash \mathsf{not\text{-}applicable}, \epsilon}{\mathsf{only\text{-}one\text{-}applicable}(r^+), \rho \vdash d, s}$$

$$\frac{\exists\, i, j : \quad i \ne j \ \wedge\ r_i, \rho \vdash d_i, s_i \ \wedge\ r_j, \rho \vdash d_j, s_j}{\mathsf{only\text{-}one\text{-}applicable}(r^+), \rho \vdash \mathsf{not\text{-}applicable}, \epsilon}$$

Differently from the previous cases, the inference rules for the algorithm first-applicable ensure that the rules to which the algorithm is applied are evaluated sequentially. The decision returned is then the first one differing from not-applicable, if any, or not-applicable, otherwise.

Finally, the rules for the algorithm only-one-applicable check if only one of the rules to which the algorithm is applied returns a decision differing from not-applicable: if this is the case, then such decision is returned (together with the associated sequence of obligation actions), otherwise not-applicable is returned.

To sum up, policies, and their evaluation, are hierarchically structured as trees: the evaluation of leaf nodes, i.e. rules, return a 'starting' decision, permit, deny or not-applicable, while the intermediate nodes, i.e. policies, combine the decisions and obligations returned by the evaluation of their child nodes through the chosen combining algorithm. Policy evaluation terminates when the root is reached producing a decision and a sequence of obligations. This sequence

Table 14. pattern-match function

$match(T,t) = \sigma$	$\nexists\sigma : match(T,t) = \sigma$
pattern-match$(T,t) \vdash$ true	pattern-match$(T,t) \vdash$ false

consists of fulfilled actions that will enforce the consequences resulting from the authorisation process.

5   A Full-Fledged SCEL Instance

In this section, we present a full instantiation of the SCEL language, called PSCEL (Policed SCEL). PSCEL uses as knowledge the tuple spaces presented in Section 3.1 and as policy language the version of FACPL presented in Section 4.1. Therefore, each PSCEL component has its own tuple repository and a collection of policies controlling the behaviour of such a component and consequently the interactions with others.

Section 5 introduces the formal integration of FACPL with SCEL by outlining the integration steps which must be followed in order to obtain fully-interoperable abstractions. Then, Section 5.2 shows PSCEL at work on the considered swarm robotics scenario.

5.1   PSCEL: Policed SCEL

We present the syntax refinement, followed by the formal integration in the SCEL operational semantics.

Syntax. FACPL policies are specialised by instantiating the obligation actions as the set of SCEL actions reported in Table 1, and by defining the matching function pattern-match, which aims at comparing knowledge values with policy ones. In particular, this function defines, by using the pattern-matching mechanism presented in Section 3.1, the matching of a template with a knowledge item. The formal rules for the new comparison function are reported in Table 14.

To explicitly represent the fact that the policies in force at any given component can dynamically change while the component evolves, we use a sort of automata somehow reminiscent of *security automata* [49]. Thus, a POLICY AUTOMATON Π is a pair $\langle A, \pi \rangle$, where

- A is an automaton of the form $\langle Policies, Targets, \mathcal{T} \rangle$ where the set of states *Policies* contains all the policies that can be in force at different times, the set of labels *Targets* contains the security relevant events (expressed as the TARGETS in Table 11) that can trigger policy modification and the set of transitions $\mathcal{T} \subseteq (Policies \times Targets \times Policies)$ represents policy replacement.
- $\pi \in Policies$ is the current state of A.

Dynamically changing policies is a powerful mechanism that permits controlling, in a natural and clear way, the evolution of adaptive systems having a very high degree of dynamism, which in principle would be quite difficult to manage. In Section 5.2 a full application of such an automaton is provided.

Semantics. PSCEL specialises the SCEL operational semantics by connecting the evaluation of the authorization predicate with the inference rules of Tables 12 and 13. More specifically, the authorization predicate in PSCEL also considers the outcome of policy evaluation; this is an authorization decision δ and a sequence of actions s. The authorization predicate takes the form $\Pi \vdash_s^\delta \lambda, \Pi'$ meaning that the action generating the label λ is evaluated with respect to the policy automaton Π to a decision δ (i.e., permit, deny or not-applicable), along with a (possibly empty) sequence s of actions to perform, and a (possibly adapted) policy automaton Π' to enforce. To calculate an authorization decision, we need first to generate a request ρ from label λ and then to evaluate it with respect to the current policy state π of Π.

The authorization request is produced on demand when an action that needs to be authorised is going to be performed. The production is done by function $\lambda 2\rho(\cdot)$ that maps (a subset of) the SCEL labels to requests and is defined as follows:

$$\lambda 2\rho(\mathcal{I} : \mathbf{fresh}(n)) = \{(subject/attr, val) \mid (attr, val) \in \mathcal{I}\}$$
$$\cup \{(action/action\text{-}id, \mathbf{fresh})\}$$
$$\cup \{(object/attr, val) \mid (attr, val) \in \mathcal{I}\}$$

$$\lambda 2\rho(\mathcal{I} : \mathbf{new}(\mathcal{J}, \mathcal{K}, \Pi, P)) = \{(subject/attr, val) \mid (attr, val) \in \mathcal{I}\}$$
$$\cup \{(action/action\text{-}id, \mathbf{new})\}$$
$$\cup \{(object/attr, val) \mid (attr, val) \in \mathcal{J}\}$$

$$\lambda 2\rho(\mathcal{I} : t \triangleright \mathcal{J}) = \{(subject/attr, val) \mid (attr, val) \in \mathcal{I}\}$$
$$\cup \{(action/item, t), (action/action\text{-}id, \mathbf{put})\}$$
$$\cup \{(object/attr, val) \mid (attr, val) \in \mathcal{J}\}$$

$$\lambda 2\rho(\mathcal{I} : t \triangleleft \mathcal{J}) = \{(subject/attr, val) \mid (attr, val) \in \mathcal{I}\}$$
$$\cup \{(action/item, t), (action/action\text{-}id, \mathbf{get})\}$$
$$\cup \{(object/attr, val) \mid (attr, val) \in \mathcal{J}\}$$

$$\lambda 2\rho(\mathcal{I} : t \blacktriangleleft \mathcal{J}) = \{(subject/attr, val) \mid (attr, val) \in \mathcal{I}\}$$
$$\cup \{(action/item, t), (action/action\text{-}id, \mathbf{qry})\}$$
$$\cup \{(object/attr, val) \mid (attr, val) \in \mathcal{J}\}$$

Each value for subject and object, retrieved from $\mathcal{I}$ and $\mathcal{J}$, respectively, is bound to an attribute identifier, e.g. the identifier of the subject component is bound to $subject/subject\text{-}id$. Notably, the *item* attribute identifies the exchanged item in a communication action, thus it is undefined in the case of **fresh** and **new**.

Finally, if we let $\Pi \triangleq \langle A, \pi \rangle$, $\Pi'' \triangleq \langle A, \pi' \rangle$ and $\rho \triangleq \lambda 2\rho(\lambda)$, the authorization predicate can be formally defined in terms of the semantics of policies by the following rule:

$$\pi, \rho \vdash \delta, s \quad \Pi' = \begin{cases} \Pi'' & \textit{if } \langle \pi, \tau, \pi' \rangle \in A \ \wedge \ \tau, \rho \vdash \text{applicable} \\ \Pi & \textit{otherwise} \end{cases}$$

$$\overline{\Pi \vdash_s^\delta \lambda, \Pi'}$$

Intuitively, an action λ is allowed if the corresponding request ρ satisfies $\pi, \rho \vdash$ permit, s; moreover, if for some target $\tau \in Targets$, such that $\tau, \rho \vdash$ applicable, the automaton A has a transition $\langle \pi, \tau, \pi' \rangle$, then the state of A after the request evaluation becomes π'. On the other hand, if we get $\pi, \rho \vdash$ deny, s, then the action is disallowed but, as a consequence of evaluation of the authorization predicate, and similarly to the previous case, the policy in force within the component can change. Notably, the current policy in Π does not change unless there is a target τ matching the request ρ and producing a transition in the policy automaton. Of course, if the automaton has a single state or an empty set of transitions, the policy in force at a component never changes.

The refinement of the authorization predicate forces a slight modification of the SCEL operational semantics, for appropriately dealing with the authorization decisions permit and deny, and the discharge of obligation actions. For the sake of simplicity, the PSCEL operational semantics does not take into account the decision not-applicable. This means that the rules do not explicitly deal with situations where none of the policies is applicable to a given request, or the combining algorithms do not convert not-applicable into permit or deny. These situations are handled as runtime errors that induce the executing process to get stuck. They could be easily avoided by using an appropriate combining algorithm, as e.g. permit-unless-deny, at top level of each state of the policy automaton Π.

PSCEL operational rules are similar to those presented in Section 2.3, therefore in Table 15 we only report some significant ones[11]. As a matter of notation, $\mathcal{I}.p$ indicates the process part of component $\mathcal{I}$ and, when $s = \epsilon$, $s.P$ stands for P. Notably, all labels taken as argument by the authorization predicate, i.e. $\mathcal{I} : \mathbf{fresh}(n)$, $\mathcal{I} : \mathbf{new}(\mathcal{J}, \mathcal{K}, \Pi, P)$, $\mathcal{I} : t \triangleleft \mathcal{J}$, $\mathcal{I} : t \blacktriangleleft \mathcal{J}$ and $\mathcal{I} : t \triangleright \mathcal{J}$, have a counterpart corresponding to decision deny which is obtained by application of functional notation $\oslash(\cdot)$ to the label. Thus, label $\oslash(\mathcal{I} : t \triangleleft \mathcal{J})$ indicates that action $\mathbf{get}$ is denied. Some comments on the rules in Table 15 follow.

The interaction predicate, used in rule *(pr-sys)*, is instantiated by the interleaving interaction predicate of Table 3. Moreover, the rule here is tailored for taking into account the discharge of the obligation actions generated by the inference. To this aim, the component obtained after the transition contains the placeholder $*$ in place of the process part; it will be replaced by the continuation of process P, possibly prefixed by a sequence of obligations, during the rest of the derivation (see, e.g., the use of $[s.(\mathcal{I}.p)/*]$ in the rule *(ptpget-p-p)*). Notably, this mechanism permits to apply the substitution σ also to the obligation actions, so that the variables possibly contained get instantiated.

---

[11] We refer the interested reader to the technical report [37] for a complete account of the operational rules.

Table 15. PSCEL (excerpt of) operational semantics (p stands for permit in $\vdash_s^p$, while d stands for deny in $\vdash_s^d$)

$$\frac{P \downarrow_\alpha P' \quad \alpha = \mathcal{I}: \mathbf{fresh}(n) \Rightarrow n \notin \mathrm{n}(\mathcal{I}[\mathcal{K}, \Pi, \mathbf{nil}]) \quad \Pi, \mathcal{I}: \alpha \succ \lambda, \sigma, \Pi'}{\mathcal{I}[\mathcal{K}, \Pi, P] \xrightarrow{\lambda[\Pi'/\mathcal{I}.\pi, P'/\mathcal{I}.p]} \mathcal{I}[\mathcal{K}, \bullet, *\sigma]} \quad (pr\text{-}sys)$$

$$\frac{\Pi \vdash_s^p \mathcal{I}: t \vartriangleleft \mathcal{J}, \Pi' \quad \mathcal{K} \ominus t = \mathcal{K}'}{\mathcal{J}[\mathcal{K}, \Pi, P] \xrightarrow{\mathcal{I}: t \vartriangleleft \mathcal{J}[\Pi'/\mathcal{J}.\pi, s.P/\mathcal{J}.p]} \mathcal{J}[\mathcal{K}', \Pi', s.P]} \quad (accget\text{-}p)$$

$$\frac{\Pi \vdash_s^d \mathcal{I}: t \vartriangleleft \mathcal{J}, \Pi'}{\mathcal{J}[\mathcal{K}, \Pi, P] \xrightarrow{\oslash(\mathcal{I}: t \vartriangleleft \mathcal{J}[\Pi'/\mathcal{J}.\pi, s.P/\mathcal{J}.p])} \mathcal{J}[\mathcal{K}, \Pi', s.P]} \quad (accget\text{-}d)$$

$$\frac{C \xrightarrow{\mathcal{I}: t \vartriangleleft n} C' \quad n = \mathcal{I}.id \quad C'[\mathcal{I}.\pi/\bullet, \mathcal{I}.p/*] \xrightarrow{\mathcal{I}: t \vartriangleleft \mathcal{I}} C''}{C \xrightarrow{\tau} C''} \quad (lget\text{-}p)$$

$$\frac{C \xrightarrow{\mathcal{I}: t \vartriangleleft n} C' \quad n = \mathcal{I}.id \quad C \xrightarrow{\oslash(\mathcal{I}: t \vartriangleleft \mathcal{I})} C''}{C \xrightarrow{\tau} C''} \quad (lget\text{-}d)$$

$$\frac{S_1 \xrightarrow{\mathcal{I}: t \vartriangleleft n} S_1' \quad S_2 \xrightarrow{\mathcal{I}: t \vartriangleleft \mathcal{J}} S_2' \quad \mathcal{J}.id = n \quad \mathcal{I}.\pi \vdash_s^p \mathcal{I}: t \vartriangleleft \mathcal{J}, \Pi'}{S_1 \parallel S_2 \xrightarrow{\tau} S_1'[\Pi'/\bullet, s.(\mathcal{I}.p)/*] \parallel S_2'} \quad (ptpget\text{-}p\text{-}p)$$

$$\frac{S_1 \xrightarrow{\mathcal{I}: t \vartriangleleft n} S_1' \quad S_2 \xrightarrow{\oslash(\mathcal{I}: t \vartriangleleft \mathcal{J})} S_2' \quad \mathcal{J}.id = n \quad \mathcal{I}.\pi \vdash_s^p \mathcal{I}: t \vartriangleleft \mathcal{J}, \Pi'}{S_1 \parallel S_2 \xrightarrow{\tau} S_1 \parallel S_2'} \quad (ptpget\text{-}p\text{-}d)$$

$$\frac{S_1 \xrightarrow{\mathcal{I}: t \vartriangleleft n} S_1' \quad S_2 \xrightarrow{\mathcal{I}: t \vartriangleleft \mathcal{J}} S_2' \quad \mathcal{J}.id = n \quad \mathcal{I}.\pi \vdash_s^d \mathcal{I}: t \vartriangleleft \mathcal{J}, \Pi'}{S_1 \parallel S_2 \xrightarrow{\tau} S_1[\Pi'/\bullet, s.(\mathcal{I}.p)/*] \parallel S_2} \quad (ptpget\text{-}d\text{-}p)$$

$$\frac{S_1 \xrightarrow{\mathcal{I}: t \vartriangleleft n} S_1' \quad S_2 \xrightarrow{\oslash(\mathcal{I}: t \vartriangleleft \mathcal{J})} S_2' \quad \mathcal{J}.id = n \quad \mathcal{I}.\pi \vdash_s^d \mathcal{I}: t \vartriangleleft \mathcal{J}, \Pi'}{S_1 \parallel S_2 \xrightarrow{\tau} S_1[\Pi'/\bullet, s.(\mathcal{I}.p)/*] \parallel S_2} \quad (ptpget\text{-}d\text{-}d)$$

The rules denoting the willingness of components to accept the execution of an action operating on their local repository are now split in two rules: one rule, e.g. *(accget-p)*, corresponding to the fact that the action is authorised, and one rule, e.g. *(accget-d)*, corresponding to the the fact the action is denied. In the former rule, the label of the transition is updated with the new policy (as in the SCEL corresponding rule) and with the the obligation actions s that have to be performed before the continuation process. In the latter rule, the transition label is updated similarly, although the action on the repository, i.e. the withdrawing of item t, is not performed.

When considering the transitions that a single component can perform, the main difference is that we have one rule, e.g. *(lget-p)*, for the case the action is allowed by the authorization predicate, and one rule, e.g. *(lget-d)*, for the case it is denied. Notably, in this latter case, even though the action is not performed (indeed the last premise of *(lget-d)* starts from C and not from C'), the new policies and the obligation actions produced by evaluation of the authorisation predicate are installed (indeed, in the conclusion of the rule, C evolves to C''); they in fact may adapt the system to allow a subsequent successful execution of the action or to enable an alternative execution path.

Similarly, in case of synchronisation between two components, for each different type of action we have four cases to consider, corresponding to the pairs consisting of the values permit and deny. For example, the action **get** can withdraw an item from a specific repository with a point to point access according to the rule *(ptpget-p-p)* of Table 15. The label $\mathcal{I} : t \triangleleft \mathcal{J}$, generated by rule *(accget-p)*, denotes the willingness of component $\mathcal{J}$ to provide the item t to component $\mathcal{I}$. The label is generated only if such willingness is authorised by the authorization predicate in force at component $\mathcal{J}$ and if withdrawing an item t from the repository of $\mathcal{J}$ is possible $(\mathcal{K} \ominus t = \mathcal{K}')$. The target component $\mathcal{J}$ is modified by removing t from the repository and by installing the policy and the sequence of obligation actions produced by the evaluation of the authorization predicate. Thus, when the target of the action denotes a specific remote repository *(ptpget-p-p)*, the action is only allowed if n is the name of the component $\mathcal{J}$ simultaneously willing to provide the wanted item, and if the request to perform the action at $\mathcal{J}$ is authorised by the policy at the source component $\mathcal{I}$ (identified by notation $\mathcal{I}.\pi$). The authorization to perform the action could be denied by the local policy (rule *(ptpget-d-p)* for remote ones) or by the policy of the target component (rules *(accget-d)* and *(ptpget-p-d)*) or by both policies (rule *(ptpget-d-d)*). Note that the policy and the sequence of obligation actions produced by evaluation of the authorisation predicate are always installed on the source component, except when the action is authorised by the local policy but not by the policy of the target component, i.e. as in the case of rule *(ptpget-p-d)*. In the target component, the installation occurs only when the action has been authorised by the source component.

The rules for group-oriented communication rely on the same basic ideas described above (i.e., there are four rules for each kind of action). Thus, due to space limitations, they are not reported here.

5.2   PSCEL at Work

We show here the effectiveness of the PSCEL approach by providing a complete model of the robot swarm scenario used as a running example in the previous sections and informally presented in Section 1. Notably, this model exploits the fact that a process, which represents the behaviour of a robot, can read tuples produced by sensors, e.g. the tuple $\langle$ *"collision"*, true $\rangle$ indicating that an imminent collision with a wall of the arena has been detected, and can add tuples that trigger the activation of actuators, e.g. the tuple $\langle$ *"goTo"*, 4.34, 3.25 $\rangle$ forcing the

robot to reach a specific position. Therefore, as these tuples are produced (resp.,
consumed) by sensors (resp., actuators), no additional data/assumptions on the
initial state are needed. It is also worth noticing that sensors and actuators are
not explicitly modelled in PSCEL, as they are robot's internal devices while
the PSCEL model represents the programmable behaviour of the robot, i.e. its
running code. We clarify the practical role of sensors and actuators in Section 6.

The scenario is modelled as a set of components ($\mathrm{ROBOT}_1 \parallel \ldots \parallel \mathrm{ROBOT}_n$)
where each ROBOT_i has the form $\mathcal{I}_{R_i}[\mathcal{K}_{R_i}, \Pi_R, P_R]$. The behaviour of a single
robot corresponds to the following PSCEL process

$$
\begin{aligned}
P_R \triangleq (\ &\mathbf{qry}(\text{``}victimPerceived\text{''}, \mathsf{true})@\mathsf{self}. \\
&\mathbf{put}(\text{``}victim\text{''}, x, y, 3)@\mathsf{self}.\ \mathbf{put}(\text{``}rescue\text{''})@\mathsf{self} \\
&+ \mathbf{get}(\text{``}victim\text{''}, ?x_v, ?y_v, ?count)@(role=\text{``}rescuer\text{''} \vee role=\text{``}helpRescuer\text{''}). \\
&HelpingRescuer\ ) \\
&|\ RandomWalk\ |\ IsMoving
\end{aligned}
$$

A robot follows a random walk to explore the disaster area. To this aim, the
process *RandomWalk* randomly selects a direction that is followed until either
a wall is hit or a *stop* signal is sent to the wheels actuator. The robot recognises
the presence of a victim by means of the **qry** action, while it helps other robots
to rescue a victim by means of the **get** action and according to the *HelpingRescuer* process definition. When a victim is found, information about his position
(retrieved by the attributes x and y of the robot's interface) and the number of
other robots needed for rescuing him (3 robots in our case, but a solution with
a varying number can be easily accommodated) is locally published. Then, the
tuple ⟨*"rescue"*⟩ is locally inserted to start the rescuing procedure.

The *RandomWalk* process calculates the random direction followed by the
robot to explore the arena. The robot starts moving as soon as the first direction is calculated. When the proximity sensor signals a possible collision, by
means of the tuple ⟨*"collision"*, true⟩, a new random direction is calculated. This
behaviour corresponds to the following PSCEL process

$$
\begin{aligned}
RandomWalk \triangleq\ &\mathbf{put}(\text{``}direction\text{''}, 2\pi\mathrm{rand}())@\mathsf{self}. \\
&\mathbf{qry}(\text{``}collision\text{''}, \mathsf{true})@\mathsf{self}.RandomWalk
\end{aligned}
$$

The process defines only the direction of the motion and not the will of moving.

The *HelpingRescuer* process is defined as follows

$$
\begin{aligned}
HelpingRescuer \triangleq\ &\mathbf{if}\ (count > 1)\ \mathbf{then}\ \{\ \mathbf{put}(\text{``}victim\text{''}, x_v, y_v, count\text{-}1)@\mathsf{self}\ \}. \\
&\mathbf{put}(\text{``}goTo\text{''}, x_v, y_v)@\mathsf{self}. \\
&\mathbf{qry}(\text{``}position\text{''}, x_v, y_v)@\mathsf{self}.\ \mathbf{put}(\text{``}rescue\text{''})@\mathsf{self}
\end{aligned}
$$

This process is triggered by a *victim* tuple retrieved from the rescuers ensemble
(see P_R). The tuple indicates that additional robots (whose number is stored
in *count*) are needed at position (x_v, y_v) to rescue a victim. If more than one

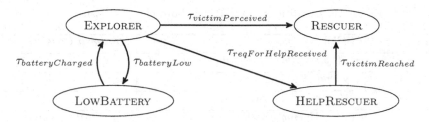

Fig. 4. Swarm robotics scenario: policy automaton

robot is needed, a new *victim* tuple is published (with decremented counter). Then, the robot, which becomes a helper of the rescuer, goes towards the victim position. Once it reaches him (i.e., its current position coincides with the victim's one), it becomes a rescuer and starts the rescuing procedure. It is worth noting that, if more victims are in the scenario, different groups of rescuers will be spontaneously organised to rescue them. To avoid that more than one group is formed for the same victim, we assume that the sensor used to perceive the victims is configured so that a victim that is already receiving assistance by some rescuers is not detected as a victim by further robots. This assumption is also feasible in a real scenario, where a light-based message communication among robots can be used [40]. Thus, once a robot has reached the victim, by using a specific light color, it signals not to "discover" the victim next to it (see Chapter IV.2 [42]).

Notably, the effectiveness of this approach relies on the assumption that robots cannot fail. In fact, when a robot that knows the victim's position fails, it cannot be ensured that such position is correctly communicated. Specific handling can be used in such a case, e.g. by enabling the perception of a victim if the robots already taking care of the victim are not active.

Finally, in order to check the level of the battery during the exploration, and possibly halting the robot when the battery is low, we need to capture the movement status. This information is represented by the tuple $\langle$ *"isMoving"* $\rangle$, which is produced by the wheels sensor, and monitored by the following process

$$IsMoving \triangleq \mathbf{qry}(\text{``isMoving''})@\mathsf{self}.IsMoving$$

The reading of this datum is exploited by a rule of the authorisation policy.

Each robot dynamically adapts its role, as well as the enforced policies, according to external conditions and stimuli. Thus, each role corresponds to a different enforced policy. The transitions triggering the policy changes are defined by the policy automaton shown in Figure 4.

Before presenting the policies of some of the automaton states, we briefly outline the conditions of the policy automaton transitions, whose details are reported in Table 16. These transitions, which mimic the role changing previously described, define the conditions on the action the process wants to execute,

Table 16. Conditions of the Policy Automaton Transitions

Condition	PSCEL action	Additional Constraint
$\tau_{victimPerceived}$	**qry**(*"victimPerceived"*, true)@self	-
$\tau_{victimReached}$	**qry**(*"position"*,_,_)@self	-
$\tau_{reqForHelpReceived}$	**get**(*"victim"*,_,_,_)@(role=*"rescuer"* ∨...)	-
$\tau_{batteryLow}$	**qry**(*"isMoving"*)@self	$subject/batteryLevel < 20\%$
$\tau_{batteryCharged}$	**qry**(*"charged"*)@self	-

and (if needed) some additional constraints on environmental values. For instance, the EXPLORER state evolves to the RESCUER one when the condition $\tau_{victimPerceived}$ holds, that is as soon as the perception of a victim has to be authorised (i.e., the action **qry**(*"victimPerceived"*, true)@self can complete). To move from EXPLORER to LOWBATTERY, it is required that the robot is moving (i.e., the action **qry**(*"isMoving"*)@self can complete), and the battery level is less then 20%. All the other conditions are defined in the same way.

In the EXPLORER state, to stop the robot as soon as a victim is perceived and to diagnose a critical level of the battery, we define the following policy

```
⟨ permit-unless-deny
    rules : (permit  target : equal(qry,action/action-id)
                            ∧ pattern-match((“victimPerceived”, true),action/item))
                obl : [ permit  put(“stop”)@self] )
            (deny  target : equal(qry,action/action-id)
                            ∧ pattern-match((“isMoving”),action/item)
                            ∧ greater-than(20%,subject/batteryLevel)
                obl : [ deny  put(“goTo”, env/station.x, env/station.y)@self] )⟩
```

The first positive rule has the only purpose of returning the obligation action **put**(*"stop"*)@self when the corresponding **qry** is executed. This obligation instructs the wheels actuator to stop the movement. The negative rule checks the battery level of the robot, and when the level is critical (i.e., lower then or equal to 20%), the obligation **put**(*"goTo"*, $env/station.x, env/station.y$)@self is returned in order to change the robot direction. Notably, the position of the charging station is provided by the evaluation context during the obligation fulfilment.

The policy enforced in the HELPRESCUER state is defined similarly: it controls the robot movement towards the previously received victim's position. In particular, the policy halts the robot as soon as the victim's position is reached and forbids unexpected direction changes during the movement.

In the case of LowBattery state, we define instead the following policy

⟨ permit-unless-deny
   rules : (permit target : equal(**qry**,*action/action-id*)
                            ∧ pattern-match((*"position"*, _, _),*action/item*))
                  obl : [permit **put**(*"stop"*)@self.**put**(*"charge"*)@self.
                         qry(*"charged"*)@self])
    (deny target : equal(**qry**,*action/action-id*)
                    ∧ (pattern-match((*"victim"*, _, _),*action/item*)
                        ∨ pattern-match((*"victimPerceived"*, true),*action/item*)))
    (deny target : equal(**put**,*action/action-id*)
                ∧ pattern-match((*"direction"*, _),*action/item*)))⟩

When the position of the charging station is reached, the first rule halts the movement and returns the actions needed for enacting the charging behaviour. In particular, the battery charging process is started by the **put**(*"charge"*)@self action, while the **qry**(*"charged"*)@self blocks the robot until the end of the charging process. Note that the transition condition $\tau_{batteryCharged}$ holds when the latter action requests for authorisation, and therefore in the continuation the robot will play the Explorer state.

Finally, the policy enforced in the Rescuer state is as follows

⟨ permit-unless-deny
    rules : (permit target : equal(**put**,*action/action-id*)
                     ∧ pattern-match((*"rescue"*),*action/item*))
                     ∧ less-than(40%,*subject/batteryLevel*)
               obl : [permit **put**(*"camera"*, *"on"*)@self])⟩

This policy does not forbid any actions, it is only used for turning on the robot's camera if there is enough battery; other functionalities could be activated as well.

As shown in this section, the design of a PSCEL specification involves processes, policies, and obligations. In order to decide which design approach, e.g. defining a process action or an obligation, is more appropriate, we can follow the *separation of concerns* principle. According to it, we decouple the functional aspects of the components behaviour from the adaptation ones. Thus, the application logic generating the computational behaviour of components is defined in a procedural style, in the form of processes, while the adaptation logic is defined in a declarative style, in the form of policies enclosing obligations. Processes and policies have indeed different features:

– a process contains the actions that *should* be executed. Thus, when an action is not authorised, the process is blocked until a positive authorisation for such action is received;
– a policy decides whether to authorise a process action and can force processes to perform additional actions which can depend on contextual information or on the authorisation of remote actions.

Of course, a process could decide by itself whether to execute an action or not, without resorting to a policy. However, this would lead to a specification where application and adaptation logics are mixed up, which is more difficult to develop and maintain. Moreover, it would require, at least, some additional efforts to introduce: (i) conditional choices for checking contextual information; (ii) actions monitoring the knowledge items for, e.g., discovering when a remote **get** is performed. These additional tasks significantly affect the burden of specifying a process. Indeed, the use of policies and obligations is advocated not only to decide the authorisation of process actions but also to define actions that are not executed all the times. Furthermore, by means of the policy automaton, policies can dynamically change to react to external conditions, while processes cannot. On the other hand, policy evaluation is triggered by a process action, therefore additional demon processes, such as the *isMoving* process, could be needed.

6   A Runtime Environment for SCEL

In this section we present jRESP[12], a Java runtimeenvironment providing a framework for developing autonomic and adaptive systems according to the SCEL paradigm. Specifically, jRESP provides an API that permits using in Java programs the SCEL's linguistic constructs for controlling the computation and interaction of autonomic components, and for defining the architecture of systems and ensembles.

The implementation of jRESP fully relies on the SCEL's formal semantics. The close correspondence between the two languages enhances confidence on the behaviour of the jRESP implementation of SCEL programs, once the latter have been analysed via formal methods, which is possible given there is a formal operational semantics.

The SCEL language, as explained in Section 2, is parametric with respect to some aspects, e.g. knowledge representation and policy language, that may be tailored to better fit different application domains. For this reason, also jRESP is designed to accommodate alternative instantiations of the above mentioned features. Indeed, thanks to the large use of design patterns, the integration of new features in jRESP is greatly simplified.

SCEL's operational semantics abstracts from a specific communication infrastructure. A SCEL *program* typically consists of a set of (possibly heterogeneous) components, each of which is equipped with its own knowledge repository. These components concur and cooperate in a highly dynamic environment to achieve a set of *goals*. In this kind of systems the underlying communication infrastructure can change dynamically as the result of local component interactions. To cope with this dynamicity, the jRESP communication infrastructure has been designed to avoid *centralized control*. Moreover, to facilitate interoperability with other tools and programming frameworks, jRESP relies on JSON[13]. This is an open data interchange technology that permits simplifying the inter-

---

[12] jRESP (Java Run-time Environment for SCEL Programs) website: http://jresp.sourceforge.net/.

[13] JSON (JavaScript Object Notation) website: http://www.json.org/.

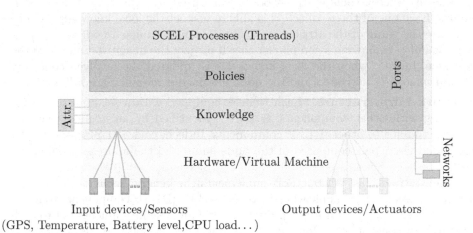

Fig. 5. Node architecture

actions between heterogeneous network components and provides the basis on which SCEL programs can cooperate with external services or devices.

The overall environment and the programming constructs are presented in Section 6.1, while the integration of FACPL is detailed in Section 6.2. Finally, Section 6.3 reports the jRESP implementation of the robot swarm scenario.

6.1 Programming Constructs

Components. SCEL components are implemented via the class Node. The architecture of a node is shown in Figure 5. Nodes are executed over virtual machines or physical devices providing access to input/output devices and network connections. A node aggregates a knowledge repository, a set of running processes, and a set of policies. Structural and behavioral information about a node are collected into an *interface* via *attribute collectors*. Nodes interact via *ports* supporting both *point-to-point* and *group-oriented* communications (whose implementation is described in the *Network Infrastructure* paragraph below).

Knowledge. The interface Knowledge identifies a generic knowledge repository and indicates the high-level primitives to manage pieces of relevant information coming from different sources. This interface contains the methods for withdrawing/retrieving/adding a piece of knowledge from/to a repository. Currently, a single implementation of the Knowledge interface is available in jRESP, which relies on the notion of tuple space presented in Section 3.1.

External data can be collected into a knowledge repository via *sensors*. Each sensor can be associated to a logical or physical device providing data that can be retrieved by processes and that can be the subject of adaptation. Similarly, *actuators* can be used to send data to an external device or service attached to a node. This approach allows SCEL processes to control exogenous devices that identify logical/physical actuators.

The interface associated to a node is computed by exploiting *attribute collectors*. Each one of these collectors is able to inspect the local knowledge and to compute the value of the attributes. This mechanism equips a node with *reflective capabilities* allowing a component to self-project the image of its state on the interface. Indeed, when the local knowledge is updated the involved collectors are *automatically* activated and the node interface is modified accordingly[14].

Network Infrastructure. Each Node is equipped with a set of ports for interacting with other components. A port is identified by an *address* that can be used to refer to other jRESP components. Indeed, each jRESP node can be addressed via a pair composed of the node name and the address of one of its ports.

The abstract class AbstractPort implements the generic behaviour of a port. It implements the communication protocol used by jRESP components to interact with each other. Class AbstractPort also provides the instruments to dispatch messages to components. However, in AbstractPort the methods used for sending messages via a specific communication network/media are abstract. Also the method used to retrieve the address associated to a port is abstract in AbstractPort. The concrete classes defining specific kinds of ports extend AbstractPort to provide concrete implementations of the above outlined abstract methods, so as to use different underlying network infrastructures (e.g., Internet, Ad-hoc networks, ...).

Currently, four kinds of port are available: InetPort, P2PPort, ServerPort and VirtualPort. The first one implements point-to-point and group-oriented interactions via TCP and UDP, respectively. In particular, InetPort implements group-oriented interactions in terms of a UDP broadcast. Unfortunately, this approach does not scale when the size of involved components increases. To provide a more efficient and reliable support to group-oriented interactions, jRESP provides the class P2PPort. This class realises interactions in terms of the *P2P* and *multicast* protocols provided by Scribe[15] [14] and FreePastry[16] [46]. A more centralized implementation is provided by ServerPort. All messages sent along this kind of port pass through a centralized server that dispatches all the received messages to each of the managed ports. Finally, VirtualPort implements a port where interactions are performed via a buffer stored in memory. A VitualPort is used to *simulate* nodes in a single application without relying on a specific network infrastructure.

Behaviors. SCEL processes are implemented as threads via the abstract class Agent, which provides the methods implementing the SCEL actions. In fact, they can be used for generating fresh names, for instantiating new components and for withdrawing/retrieving/adding information items from/to shared knowledge repositories. The latter methods extend the ones provided by Knowledge with another parameter identifying either the (possibly remote) node where the

---

[14] This mechanism is implemented via the *Observer/Observable* pattern.

[15] Scribe is a generic, scalable and efficient system for group communication and notification.

[16] FreePastry is a substrate for peer-to-peer applications.

target repository is located or the group of nodes whose repositories have to be accessed. As previously mentioned, group-oriented interactions are supported by the communication protocols defined in the node ports and by attribute collectors.

Policies. In jRESP, like in SCEL, policies can be used to authorise local actions and to regulate the interactions among components. When a method of an instance of class Agent is invoked, its execution is delegated to the policy in force at the node where the agent is running. The policy can authorise or not the execution of the action (e.g., according to some contextual information) and, possibly, adapt the agent behaviour by returning additional actions to be executed. The interface IPolicy permits to easily integrate different kinds of policies in jRESP Nodes. When a Node is instantiated, if no policy is provided, a default policy is used, which allows any operation to be executed.

6.2 Policing Constructs

The interface IPolicy is currently implemented by two different classes: Default-PermitPolicy and PolicyAutomaton. The former is the default policy of each node; it allows any action by directly delegating its execution to the corresponding node. The latter policy implements a generic POLICY AUTOMATON Π (like the one presented in Section 5) which triggers policy changes according to the execution of agent actions. In particular, a PolicyAutomaton consists of a set of IPolicyAutomatonStates, each of which identifies the possible policies enforced in the node, and of a reference to the current state, which is used to *authorise* agent actions with respect to the current policies.

When a PolicyAutomaton receives a request for the execution of a given action, first of all an AutorisationRequest representing the action (like the request ρ introduced in Section 5) is created. This request identifies the action an agent wants to perform, thus it provides the action name, its argument, its target and the list of attributes currently published in the node interface. The created AuthorizationRequest is then evaluated with respect to the current policy state via the (abstract) method evaluate(AutorisationRequest r) defined in the class IPolicyAutomatonState. The request evaluation can trigger an update of the current state of the PolicyAutomaton. Indeed, for each state, a sequence of *transitions* is stored in the automaton. The transitions are instances of the class PolicyAutomaton-Transition which provides two methods: apply(AutorisationRequest r): boolean and nextState(): IPolicyAutomatonState. A transition is *enabled* if the first method returns true, while the next state is then obtained by invoking nextState() on the enabled transition. If no transitions are enabled, the current state is not changed.

Therefore, the full PSCEL implementation can be now achieved by defining the class FacplPolicyState, which extends IPolicyAutomatonState and wraps the Java-translated FACPL policies[17]. The overwritten method evaluate(AutorisationRequest r) delegates the authorisation to the referred FACPL

---

[17] These translated policies can be automatically obtained by using the FACPL Eclipse IDE available from the FACPL website (http://www.ascens-ist.eu/facpl).

policies, which return an instance of the class AuthorisationResponse containing a *decision*, i.e. permit or deny, and a set of *obligations*. The latter ones are rendered as a sequence of Actions that must be performed just after the completion of the requested action. Hence, if the decision is permit, the corresponding agent can continue as soon as all the obligations are executed. Instead, if the decision is deny, the requested action cannot be performed and the obligations possibly returned must be executed. After their completion, the action previously forbidden can be further evaluated.

6.3   Exploitation

We report here the code[18] of the jRESP implementation of the specification, presented in Section 5.2, of the robot swarm scenario.

In the previous sections we saw that jRESP, like SCEL, is parametric with respect to the knowledge representation and the policy language. The default implementations of these components provided with jRESP, i.e. the knowledge represented via *tuple space* and policies regulated according to the classes described in Section 6.2, allow a programmer to execute PSCEL specifications. The Java classes reported in this section permit appreciating how close the SCEL (resp. PSCEL) processes are to their implementation in jRESP.

For the considered scenario, in jRESP we have a Node for each robot operating in the arena[19]. Each node is equipped with the appropriate sensors and actuators that provide the machinery for interacting with the robots circuits/components. Sensors include the ones used to detect a *victim*, to check the *battery level*, to detect possible *collisions*, to access the robot position and to verify if a robot is *moving*. Actuators are used to set *robot direction*, to *stop* the movement and to start the *battery recharging activity*.

The current state of a robot is modelled via a tuple of the form ("role" , r), where r can be *explorer, rescuer, help rescuer* or *low battery*. This values correspond to the states of the policy automaton considered in Figure 4. The tuple identifying the robot state is stored in the local tuple space of each node and, together with the values read from the sensors, is used to infer the *node interface*. In the interface of each node, besides the role and the *id* of the corresponding robot, the current position is also published. The latter is identified by the attributes x and y.

Running at a node there are four agents: Explorer, HelpingRescuer, RandomWalk and isMoving. Agents Explorer and HelpingRescuer represent respectively the two branches of the non-deterministic choice[20] in process P_R defined

---

[18] The complete source code for the scenario, together with a simulation environment, can be downloaded from http://jresp.sourceforge.net/.

[19] These nodes could be executed directly on physical robots assuming that these are able to execute java code

[20] Non-deterministic choice is rendered in jRESP in terms of concurrent execution of agents (which are implemented as Java threads) regulated by checks on the current status of the robot (corresponding to the state of the policy automaton).

in Section 5.2. Since there is almost a one-to-one correspondence between the class implementing an agent and its definition in PSCEL, here we only present the code of agent Explorer that is reported below. The interested reader can refer to the jRESP web site for a detailed description of the other classes.

```
1   public class Explorer extends Agent {
2     public Explorer() {
3       super("Explorer");
4     }
5     protected void doRun() throws Exception {
6       query(
7         new Template(
8           new ActualTemplateField("VICTIM_PERCEIVED"),
9           new ActualTemplateField(true)
10        ),
11        Self.SELF
12      );
13      // Pass to RESCUER state
14      put(new Tuple("role", Scenario.RESCUER), Self.SELF);
15      double x = getAttributeValue( "x" , Double.class );
16      double y = getAttributeValue( "y" , Double.class );
17      put(
18        new Tuple(
19          "victim",
20          x,
21          y,
22          3
23        ),
24        Self.SELF
25      );
26    }
27  }
```

When an instance of class Agent is executed, the method doRun() is invoked. This method defines the agent behaviour. In the case of Explorer, it consists of the sequence of steps needed to detect a victim and to broadcast its position to the other robots. The method query(), used to retrieve data from a knowledge repository, is defined in the base class Agent and implements the SCEL's action qry[21]. The method takes as parameters an instance of class Template and a target, and returns a matching tuple. In the code above, the target is the local component (referred by Self.SELF) while the retrieved tuple is one consisting of two fields: the first field is the constant "VICTIM_PERCEIVED" while the second field is the boolean value true. This tuple is not retrieved from the local knowledge but from the *victim sensor* when the robot is able to perceive the victim. After that, the agent retrieves the actual robot position via the attributes x and y stored in the node interface. To perform this operation method getAttributeValue is used. This method takes as parameter the name of the attribute to evaluate and its expected types and returns the collected value; null is obtained when the requested attribute is not published in the interface or when its value has not the requested type. Finally, method put is invoked to publish in the local knowledge repository the tuple witnessing that a victim has been perceived at position (x,y) and 3 robots are needed to rescue it.

The policies in force at each node are managed by an instance of the class PolicyAutomaton that implements the automaton reported in Figure 4. This au-

---

[21] Class Agent also provides methods put() and get() that implement actions **put** and **get**, respectively.

tomaton is instantiated as a list of FacplPolicyState, each of which contains the reference to a particular FACPL policy, and a list of transitions. For the sake of simplicity, the, straightforward, Java translation of the transition's conditions defined in Table 16 is not reported. In the following code, we show, instead, the Java implementation of the policy in page 43 that defines the automaton state RESCUER.

```
1   public class Policy_Rescuer extends Policy {
2
3      public Policy_Rescuer() {
4        addCombiningAlg(PermitUnlessDeny.class);
5        addRule(new RuleCameraOn());
6      }
7
8      class RuleCameraOn extends Rule{
9
10        RuleCameraOn(){
11          addEffect(RuleEffect.PERMIT);
12
13          addTarget(new TargetTreeRepresentation(TargetConnector.AND,
14                 new TargetTreeRepresentation(new TargetExpression(
15                       Equal.class, ActionID.PUT,
16                       new StructName("action", "action-id"))),
17                 new TargetTreeRepresentation(new TargetExpression(
18                       PatternMatch.class, new Template(
19                             new ActualTemplateField("rescue"),
20                             new FormalTemplateField(Double.class),
21                             new FormalTemplateField(Double.class)),
22                       new StructName("action", "item"))),
23                 new TargetTreeRepresentation(new TargetExpression(
24                       LessThan.class, 40,
25                       new StructName("object", "battery_level")))
26          ));
27
28          // The PUT for adapting the process
29          addObligation(new ScelObligationExpression(RuleEffect.PERMIT,
30                 ActionID.PUT, new Tuple("cameraOn"), Self.SELF));
31        }
32      }
33   }
```

The policy is formed by the combining algorithm permit-unless-deny, which is passed as class reference, and the rule *CameraOn*. This rule is implemented as an inner class containing an authorization effect, which is RuleEffect.PERMIT, a target and an obligation. The target contains checks on: (i) the action's identifier (i.e., ActionID.PUT); (ii) the action's template (i.e., a tuple starting with the string "rescue" and followed by two formal double values; (iii) the battery level (i.e., more than 40). Finally, the instance of the class ScelObligationExpression defines the **put** action that triggers the activation of the robot's camera.

7   Quantitative Variants of SCEL

In this section we address the issue of enriching SCEL with information about action duration, by providing a stochastic semantics for the language. There exist various frameworks that support the systematic development of stochastic languages [22]. However, the main challenge in developing a stochastic semantics for SCEL is in making appropriate modeling choices, both taking into account the specific application needs and allowing to manage model complexity and size. Our contribution in this work is the proposal of four variants of STOCS, a Markovian extension of a significant fragment of SCEL, that can be used to support quantitative analysis of adaptive systems composed of ensembles of cooperating components [32]. In this chapter, we focus on only one of the four variants, the so called *Network oriented* one (NET-OR, for short). The reader interested in the full spectrum of STOCS semantics and their complete formal definition is referred to [32] and to the technical report [33]. In summary, STOCS is essentially a *modeling language* which inherits the purpose and focus of SCEL. STOCS extends SCEL by modeling the time of state-permanence as a *random variable* (r.v.) with negative exponential distribution and by replacing non-determinism by a probability distribution over outgoing transitions, thus adopting an operational semantics based on *continuous time Markov chains* (CTMC) [21]. Finally, an important aspect in a modelling language concerns the need of devising an appropriate syntax to express the environment model. In STOCS, like in SCEL, the only point of contact with the environment is the knowledge base, which contains both internal information and externally-sensed events.

7.1 StocS: Stochastic SCEL

The syntax of STOCS is essentially a subset of that of SCEL. In the presentation that follows, we deliberately omit to incorporate certain advanced features of SCEL, such as the presence and role of policies; we focus mainly on action durations and their stochastic modelling. Furthermore for the sake of simplicity, we consider only **put**, **get**, and **qry** actions and in $\mathbf{get}(T)@c$, $\mathbf{qry}(T)@c$ and $\mathbf{put}(t)@c$ we restrict targets c to the distinguished variable self and to component *predicates* p. In order to be able to obtain a CTMC from a STOCS model specification, all sources of non-determinism must be given a probabilistic interpretation. This is true also for knowledge repositories, where patterns may match different values. We push the probabilistic view a bit further, assuming that *all* repository operations have probabilistic behaviour, thus providing more flexibility to modellers (e.g. the possibility to model faulty/error outcomes and related probabilities). Letting $\mathbb{K}, \mathbb{I}$ and $\mathbb{T}$ denote the classes of all possible *knowledge states*, *knowledge items* and *knowledge templates* respectively, we require that the operator $\oplus : \mathbb{K} \times \mathbb{I} \to \mathsf{Dist}(\mathbb{K})$ for adding an item to a repository returns a *probabilistic distribution* over repositories as a result. Similarly, the withdraw operator $\ominus : \mathbb{K} \times \mathbb{T} \hookrightarrow \mathsf{Dist}(\mathbb{K} \times \mathbb{I})$ and the infer operator $\vdash : \mathbb{K} \times \mathbb{T} \hookrightarrow \mathsf{Dist}(\mathbb{I})$ are assumed to return a *probability distribution* over repositories paired with items, and over items, respectively. Functions $\ominus$ and $\vdash$ are partial: if no matching item is found the result is undefined. No further assumptions are required on knowledge repositories and, in fact, STOCS is parametric w.r.t. to knowledge repository, like SCEL. Finally, it is assumed that an assignment of appropriate r.v. parameters is given which characterises the transmission and processing durations of the several phases of STOCS action execution, as sketched below.

The semantics of SCEL does not consider any time related aspect of computation. More specifically, the execution of an action of the form $\mathbf{act}(T)@p \,.\, P$

(for **put/get/qry** actions) is described by a *single* transition of the underlying SCEL LTS semantics. In the system state reached by such a transition it is guaranteed that the process which executed the action is in its local state P and that the knowledge repositories of all components involved in the action execution have been modified accordingly. In particular, SCEL abstracts from details concerning: (a) when the execution of the action starts; (b) when the possible destination components are required to satisfy p; and (c) when the process executing the action resumes execution (i.e. becomes P); and their consequent time relationship. If we want to extend SCEL with an explicit notion of (stochastic) time, we need to take into account the time-related issues mentioned above. These issues can be addressed at different levels of abstraction, reflecting a different choice of details that are to be considered in modelling pobabilistic/timed aspects of SCEL actions.

Point (a) above does not require particular comments.

Point (b) requires to define *when* a component satisfies p with respect to a process executing an action, when time and possibly space are taken into consideration. We assume that source components are not aware of which are the components satisfying predicate p. Therefore, we define the notion of *observation* of the component by the process, the result of which allows to establish whether the component satisfies the predicate or not. In the context of distributed systems this is very often realised by means of a message sent by the process to the component. According to this view, the check whether a component satisfies predicate p is performed *when the message reaches* the component. This means that a STOCS action may require broadcast communication to be executed, even if its effect involves a few (and possibly no) components. In distributed systems, different components may have different response times depending on different network conditions and one can model explicitly the message delivery, taking into account the time required to reach the component.

Finally, point (c) raises the issue of when source component execution is to be resumed. In particular, it is necessary to identify how the source component is made aware that its role in the communication has been completed. Get/query actions are blocking and they terminate when the source receives a knowledge item from any component. A reasonable choice is that further responses received are ignored. We assume appropriate mechanisms that ensure no confusion arises between distinct actions and corresponding messages. Put actions are non-blocking, so it is sufficient that the source component is aware that the observation procedure of all components has started. Our choice is to make the source side set-up the transmission of one request of predicate evaluation for each component and then resume the execution of the source process immediately. The evaluation of the predicate against each component and the corresponding (possible) knowledge repository modification will take place at the target side(s).

In a *network-oriented* view of the system, the execution of the various phases sketched above is explicitly modelled in detail by the operational semantics, which entails that actions are *non-atomic*. Indeed, they are executed through several intermediate phases, or activities, each of which requires appropriate time duration modeling, as we illustrate by means of the following simple example. Let us consider three components, as illustrated in Fig. 6: $C_1 = \mathcal{I}_1 [\mathcal{K}_1, P_1]$, $C_2 = \mathcal{I}_2 [\mathcal{K}_2, P_2]$, and $C_3 = \mathcal{I}_3 [\mathcal{K}_3, P_3]$ and let us assume process P_1 is defined as **put**$(v)@p . Q$. Note that different components may be in different locations. The interaction we illustrate starts with process P_1 executing the first phase of **put**$(v)@p$, i.e. creating two[22] copies of the special "envelope" message $\overline{\{v@p\}}$, one for component C_2 and one for component C_3, and sending these messages; they play the role of *observers*: each of them travels in the system and reaches the component it is associated with. The special message creation and message-component association phase has a duration, denoted in grey in the figure, which is determined by rate λ: this value is computed as a (given) function of several factors, among which (the size of) v. After message creation, P_1 can proceed without waiting for their arrival at the destination components— since **put** actions are non-blocking—behaving like Q (the light-grey stripe in the figure illustrates the resumed execution of C_1). Each special message has to reach its destination component (in the figure this is illustrated by two dashed arrows), which checks whether its own interface satisfies p, and if so, it delivers v in its own knowledge repository. Observer delivery to C_2 (C_3 respectively) is performed with rate μ_2 (μ_3, respectively), which may depend on v and other parameters like the distance between C_1 where P_1 resides and the target component C_2 (C_3 respectively). Therefore, a *distinct* rate μ_j is associated to each target. In practice, one can be interested in modelling also the event of failed delivery of the observers. This is interesting both for producing more realistic models (with unreliable network communication), and for allowing the application of advanced analysis techniques based on fluid approximation [10], such as fluid model-checking [9]. Therefore, we add an error probability to the observers delivery, which we denoted p_{err} (or simply err, in Fig. 7). This more detailed semantics of the **put**$(v)@p$ action is described below in more detail. The execution of **get/qry** actions is a little bit more complicated because the executor must remain *blocked* as long as a value matching the required pattern is sent back from *one* of the potential target components. This is realised by exploiting the *race condition* which arises from multiple competing potential target components and sophisticated use of interleaving semantics; the interested reader is referred to [33] for details.

7.2   Semantics of a StocS Fragment

In this section we present the fragment of the formal semantics definition for the **put** action in the *Network oriented* variant of STOCS.

   We recall that the interface $\mathcal{I}$ of a component makes information about the component available in the form of attributes, i.e. names acting as references to

---

[22] For the sake of notational simplicity, here we assume that predicate p in process actions implicitly refers only to the *other* components, excluding the one where the process is in execution.

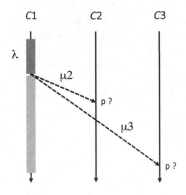

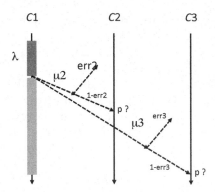

Fig. 6. Dynamics of the **put** action

Fig. 7. Actual model of **put**

information stored in the component's knowledge repository. It is convenient to make this dependency of the interface on the current knowledge $\mathcal{K}$ explicit. We do this by using the notation $\mathcal{I}(\mathcal{K})$ for the *evaluation* of the interface $\mathcal{I}$ in the knowledge state $\mathcal{K}$. The set of possible interface evaluations is denoted by $\mathbb{E}$. Interface evaluations are used within the so-called *rate function* $\mathcal{R} : \mathbb{E} \times Act \times \mathbb{E} \to \mathbb{R}_{\geq 0}$, which defines the rates of actions depending on the interface evaluation of the *source* of the action, the action itself (where Act denotes the set of possible actions), and the interface evaluation of the *destination*. For this purpose, interface evaluations will be embedded within the transition labels to exchange information about source/destination components in a synchronisation action. We will conventionally use σ (δ, respectively) for the interface evaluation of a source (destination, respectively) component. The rate function is not fixed but instead is a parameter of the language. Considering interface evaluations in the rate functions, together with the executed action, allows us to take into account, in the computation of actions rates, various aspects depending on the component state such as the position/distance, as well as other time-dependent parameters. We also assume to have a *loss probability function* $f_{\mathsf{err}} : \mathbb{E} \times Act \times \mathbb{E} \to [0,1]$ computing the probability of an error in message delivery.

As briefly sketched in Section 7.1, in the NET-OR semantics of STOCS, several phases, or activities, are identified during the execution of an action. It is convenient to distinguish between output activities (those issued by a component) and input activities (those accepted by a component). To simplify the synchronisation of input and output activities , we assume input activities are "passive" and *probabilistic*, i.e. described by (discrete) probability distributions, and output activities have durations which are *stochastic*, therefore the composition of output and related input activities yields stochastic durations with parameters (i.e. rates) computed directly through multiplication.

The operational semantics rules of STOCS are given in the FuTSs style [22] and, in particular, using its Rate Transition Systems (RTS) instantiation [21]. In RTSs a transition is a triple of the form $(P, \alpha, \mathscr{P})$, where the first and second components are the source state and the transition label, as usual, and the third component, $\mathscr{P}$, is the *continuation function* that associates a real non-negative value with each state P'. A non-zero value represents the rate of the exponential distribution characterising the time needed for the execution of the action represented by α, necessary to reach P' from P via the transition. Whenever $\mathscr{P} P' = 0$, this means that P' is not reachable from P via α[23]. RTS continuation functions are equipped with a rich set of operations that help to define these functions over sets of processes, components, and systems, as we will see.

Let $\mathbf{FTF}(S, \mathbb{R}_{\geq 0})$ denote the class of total functions from set S to $\mathbb{R}_{\geq 0}$ with finite support[24]. Given countable, non-empty sets S (of states) and A (of transition labels), an A-*labelled* RTS is a tuple $(S, A, \mathbb{R}_{\geq 0}, \rightarrowtail)$ where $\rightarrowtail \subseteq S \times A \times \mathbf{FTF}(S, \mathbb{R}_{\geq 0})$ is the A-labelled *transition relation*.

As for the standard SOS definition, also FuTS-based semantics are fully characterised by the smallest relation induced by a set of axioms and deduction rules [22]. The operational semantics of STOCS is the FuTS induced by the rules for systems, which in turn are defined using those for processes and components. In Table 17 (18, 19, respectively) we show only the rules for **put** actions performed by processes (components and systems, respectively). It is worth noting that the rules in the tables use a structure for the transition labels which is simpler than that of the labels used in Section 2, due to the fact that we consider only a fragment of the language. Furthermore, for the sake of readability and given that our labels are simpler, we prefer to use explicit action names (e.g. **put**) instead of symbols (e.g. $\triangleright$). Finally, we typically use annotated transition labels $\overline{\alpha}$ for output activities α, while input activities are used as labels without annotations; labels for activities α which are not intended for synchronisation, i.e. *internal* activities, are denoted by $\overleftrightarrow{\alpha}$.

Rule *(env)* models the delivery of the envelope message, with delivery-time rate μ. The notation $[\mathbf{nil} \mapsto \mu]$ states that the only process which can be reached by $\{t@p\}_\mu$ via activity $\overline{\{t@p\}}$ is **nil** and the relevant rate is μ. This is a special case of the general notation $[d_1 \mapsto \gamma_1, \ldots, d_m \mapsto \gamma_m]$ for the function which associates γ_i with d_i and 0 with the other elements; $[]$ denotes the 0 constant function in $\mathbf{FTF}(X, \mathbb{R}_{\geq 0})$ and is used in Rule *(env$_B$)*, which in fact states that $\overline{\{t@p\}}$ is the only activity $\{t@p\}_\mu$ can perform. A process of the form $\mathbf{put}(t)@c\,.\,P$ lounches the execution of an output activity $\overline{\mathbf{put}(t)@c}$, as postulated by Rule *(put)*. Note that the process transition is *parameterized* with respect to the evaluation σ of the interface of the specific component which the process will be running within, in the specific knowledge repository (state), as we will see when discussing Rule *(c-puto)*. Similarly, the rate λ for the execution time of the local activity of the **put** action is given by the (global) *rate function* $\mathcal{R}$ which takes σ as parameter, besides (a description of) the action itself. Note that λ does not depend on any specific destination.

---

[23] We use Currying for continuation function application.

[24] A function $\mathscr{F}$ has *finite support* if and only if there exists finite $\{s_1, \ldots, s_m\} \subseteq S$, the *support* of $\mathscr{F}$, such that $\mathscr{F} s_i \neq 0$ for $i = 1 \ldots m$ and $\mathscr{F} s = 0$ otherwise.

Table 17. Operational semantics of **put** actions (processes, NET-OR)

$$\frac{}{\{t@p\}_\mu \xrightarrow{\overline{\{t@p\}}} [\mathbf{nil} \mapsto \mu]} \; (env) \qquad \frac{\alpha \neq \overline{\{t@p\}}}{\{t@p\}_\mu \xrightarrow{\alpha} []} \; (env_B)$$

$$\frac{\lambda = \mathcal{R}(\sigma, \mathbf{put}(t)@c, \_)}{\mathbf{put}(t)@c \,.\, P \xrightarrow{\overline{\mathbf{put}(t)@c}}_\sigma [P \mapsto \lambda]} \; (put) \qquad \frac{\alpha \neq \overline{\mathbf{put}(t)@c}}{\mathbf{put}(t)@c.P \xrightarrow{\alpha} []} \; (put_B)$$

Table 18. Operational semantics of **put** actions (components, NET-OR)

$$\frac{\sigma = \mathcal{I}(\mathcal{K}) \quad P \xrightarrow{\overline{\mathbf{put}(t)@\mathsf{self}}}_\sigma \mathscr{P} \quad \mathcal{K} \oplus t = \pi}{\mathcal{I}[\mathcal{K},\, P] \xrightarrow{\overleftrightarrow{\sigma:\mathbf{put}(t)@\mathsf{self}}} \mathcal{I}[\pi, \mathscr{P}]} \; (c\text{-}putl)$$

$$\frac{\sigma = \mathcal{I}(\mathcal{K}) \quad P \xrightarrow{\overline{\mathbf{put}(t)@p}}_\sigma \mathscr{P}}{\mathcal{I}[\mathcal{K},\, P] \xrightarrow{\sigma\,:\,\mathbf{put}(t)@p} \mathcal{I}[(\mathcal{X} \mathcal{K}), \mathscr{P}]} \; (c\text{-}puto)$$

$$\frac{\delta = \mathcal{I}(\mathcal{K}) \quad \mu = \mathcal{R}(\sigma, \{t@p\}, \delta) \quad p_{\mathsf{err}} = f_{\mathsf{err}}(\sigma, \{t@p\}, \delta)}{\mathcal{I}[\mathcal{K},\, P] \xrightarrow{\sigma\,:\,\mathbf{put}(t)@p} [\mathcal{I}[\mathcal{K},\, P] \mapsto p_{\mathsf{err}},\; \mathcal{I}[\mathcal{K}, P|\{t@p\}_\mu] \mapsto (1 - p_{\mathsf{err}})]} \; (c\text{-}puti)$$

$$\frac{P \xrightarrow{\overline{\{t@p\}}} \mathscr{P} \quad \mathcal{I}(\mathcal{K}) \models p \quad \mathcal{K} \oplus t = \pi}{\mathcal{I}[\mathcal{K},\, P] \xrightarrow{\overline{\{t@p\}}} \mathcal{I}[\pi, \mathscr{P}]} \; (c\text{-}enva) \qquad \frac{P \xrightarrow{\overline{\{t@p\}}} \mathscr{P} \quad \mathcal{I}(\mathcal{K}) \not\models p}{\mathcal{I}[\mathcal{K},\, P] \xrightarrow{\overline{\{t@p\}}} \mathcal{I}[(\mathcal{X}\mathcal{K}), \mathscr{P}]} \; (c\text{-}envr)$$

Rule *(c-putl)* makes **put** actions *internal*, when they are targeted to self. The rule uses the notation $\mathcal{I}[\pi, \mathscr{P}]$; for interface $\mathcal{I}$ and continuation functions $\mathscr{F}_1$ and $\mathscr{F}_2$, function $\mathcal{I}[\mathscr{F}_1, \mathscr{F}_2]$ returns $(\mathscr{F}_1\, \mathcal{K}) \cdot (\mathscr{F}_2\, P)$ when applied to component $\mathcal{I}[\mathcal{K},\, P]$, and 0 otherwise. Rule *(c-puto)* lifts the (start of the) execution of a non-local **put** at the source component level; the (Curried) characteristic function $\mathcal{X}$, with $\mathcal{X}\,\mathcal{K} = [\mathcal{K} \mapsto 1]$, is used in the obvious way. The *output* label $\sigma\,:\,\mathbf{put}(t)@p$ is used for launching a broadcast; note, in the transition label, the indication of the source σ which is the evaluated interface of the component at hand and which is required to be the same as the parameter of the process transition used in the premiss. As established by Rule *(c-puti)*, every (potentially target) component can perform an activity with the dual *input* label $\sigma\,:\,\mathbf{put}(t)@p$. The result is the instantiation of the envelope process $\{t@p\}_\mu$ in the component. In this way, a specific instance of the envelope is associated with the specific component. The transmission of the envelope will be modelled by the execution of $\{t@p\}_\mu$, with transmission time characterized by rate μ (see Rule *(env)* again). Note that rate μ

Table 19. Operational semantics of **put** actions (systems, NET-OR)

$$\dfrac{S_1 \xrightarrow{\overline{\sigma\,:\,\mathbf{put}(t)@p}} \mathscr{S}_1^o \quad S_1 \xrightarrow{\sigma\,:\,\mathbf{put}(t)@p} \mathscr{S}_1^i \quad S_2 \xrightarrow{\overline{\sigma\,:\,\mathbf{put}(t)@p}} \mathscr{S}_2^o \quad S_2 \xrightarrow{\sigma\,:\,\mathbf{put}(t)@p} \mathscr{S}_2^i}{S_1 \parallel S_2 \xrightarrow{\overline{\sigma\,:\,\mathbf{put}(t)@p}} \mathscr{S}_1^o \parallel \mathscr{S}_2^i + \mathscr{S}_1^i \parallel \mathscr{S}_2^o} \quad (s\text{-}po)$$

$$\dfrac{S_1 \xrightarrow{\sigma\,:\,\mathbf{put}(t)@p} \mathscr{S}_1 \quad S_2 \xrightarrow{\sigma\,:\,\mathbf{put}(t)@p} \mathscr{S}_2}{S_1 \parallel S_2 \xrightarrow{\sigma\,:\,\mathbf{put}(t)@p} \mathscr{S}_1 \parallel \mathscr{S}_2} \quad (s\text{-}pi)$$

$$\dfrac{S_1 \xrightarrow{\overleftarrow{\sigma\,:\,\mathbf{put}(t)@\mathsf{self}}} \mathscr{S}_1 \quad S_2 \xrightarrow{\overleftarrow{\sigma\,:\,\mathbf{put}(t)@\mathsf{self}}} \mathscr{S}_2}{S_1 \parallel S_2 \xrightarrow{\overleftarrow{\sigma\,:\,\mathbf{put}(t)@\mathsf{self}}} \mathscr{S}_1 \parallel (\mathcal{X}\,S_2) + (\mathcal{X}\,S_1) \parallel \mathscr{S}_2} \quad (s\text{-}spl)$$

may depend both on the source (σ) and on the specific destination components (δ); furthermore, the successful transmission of the envelope is subject to the absence of errors (with probability $1 - p_{\mathsf{err}}$). Rules *(c-enva)* and *(c-envr)* ensure that the repository is updated if the interface evaluation satisfies the predicate. Finally, Rules *(s-po)* and *(s-pi)* together realise the broadcast communication a component uses for sending the envelope to all the other components, while *(s-spl)* takes care of local, consequently internal, **put** actions. For continuation functions $\mathscr{F}_1$ and $\mathscr{F}_2$, function $\mathscr{F}_1 \parallel \mathscr{F}_2$ returns $(\mathscr{F}_1\,S_1) \cdot (\mathscr{F}_2\,S_2)$ when applied to a system $S_1 \parallel S_2$ and 0 otherwise, whereas function $\mathscr{F}_1 + \mathscr{F}_2$ is the point-wise extension of +, i.e. $(\mathscr{F}_1 + \mathscr{F}_2)S = (\mathscr{F}_1\,S) + (\mathscr{F}_2\,S)$.

8   Verification

In this section we present the verification approaches developed so far for guaranteeing properties of systems modelled in SCEL. Currently, rather than developing new ad-hoc verification tools for SCEL, we have exploited existent tools. In particular, for verifying *qualitative* properties we use the well-established model checker Spin, while for verifying *quantitative* ones we use a statistical model-checking approach relying on either the simulation environment provided by jRESP or the MAUDE-based interpreter of SCEL specifications MISSCEL.

8.1   Simulation and Analysis via jRESP

To support analysis of autonomic systems specified in SCEL, the jRESP provides a set of classes that permits simulating jRESP programs. These classes enable the execution of *virtual components* over a simulation environment that can control component interactions and collect relevant simulation data. In fact, although in principle jRESP code could be directly executed in real robots (provided that a Java Virtual Machine is running on them and that jRESP's sensors

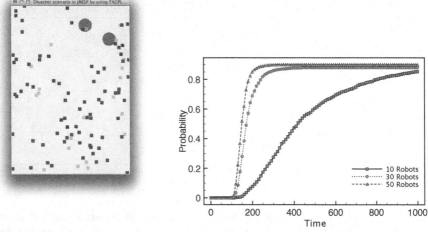

Fig. 8. Simulation and analysis of the robot swarm scenario in jRESP

and actuators invoke the API of the corresponding robots' devices), this may not be always feasible. Therefore, jRESP also provides simulation facilities.

The simulation environment integrated in jRESP is based on a *discrete event simulator* and on a specialised variant of class Node, named SimulationNode, that allows the execution of SCEL programs in the simulated environment.

jRESP agents can be also directly executed on a SimulationNode (which shares the same interface of class Node). In this case, agents are rendered as specific simulation processes instead that Java threads. The discrete event simulator is responsible for scheduling the execution of SCEL actions. Actions execution time is computed by an instance of class DelayFactory. This class, following the same approach considered in Section 7, computes the execution time of a SCEL action by considering the type of action performed, its arguments and the interfaces of the involved components. Notice that, STOCS semantics can be easily obtained when DelayFactory computes the action execution time via the appropriate sampling of exponential distributed random variables.

To set-up the simulation environment in jRESP one has also to define a class that provides the machinery to manage the physical data of the scenario. This data includes, e.g., robots positions, direction and speed. Sensors and actuators *installed* in a SimulationNode are used to collect data from the scenario and to update the state of the simulation. This mechanism, for instance, can be used to *stop* the movement of a robot or to regulate its direction. In our case, we consider the class ScenarioArena that, in addition to the above mentioned data, also provides the methods for updating robots position and computing collisions. These methods are periodically executed by the jRESP simulation environment. For the sake of simplicity, in the simulation, only collisions with the borders of the arena are considered, while collisions among robots are ignored.

By relying on the jRESP simulation environment, a prototype framework for *statistical model-checking* has been also developed. A randomised algorithm is used to verify whether the implementation of a system satisfies a specific property with a certain degree of confidence. Indeed, the statistical model-checker is parameterized with respect to a given *tolerance* ε and *error probability* p. The algorithm guarantees that the difference between the computed value and the exact one is greater than ε with a probability that is less than p.

The model-checker included in jRESP can be used to verify *reachability properties*. These permit evaluating the probability to reach, within a given deadline, a configuration where a given predicate on collected data is satisfied. In the considered scenario, this analysis technique is used to study how the number of robots affects the probability to reach the victim within a given deadline.

In Figure 8, we report a screenshot of the simulation simulation (left-hand side) and the results of the analysis (right-hand side) of the robot swarm scenario. In the screenshot, red semi-circles represent the locations of the victims, while squares represent robots, whose color is used to show their current state. Robots in the *explorer* state are *blue*, *rescuers* are *green*, *help rescuers* are *light blue* while the ones with *low battery* are *yellow*. The analysis results are represented as a chart showing the probability of rescuing the victims within a given time according to different numbers of robots (i.e., 10, 30 and 50). In the performed analyses we consider two victims each of which needs a swarm of three robots to be rescued. Notably, the victims can be rescued only after 100 time steps and, beyond a certain threshold, increasing the number of robots is not worthwhile (in fact, the difference in terms of rescuing time between 50 and 30 robots is marginal with respect to the cost of deploying a double number of robots).

8.2   Maude-Based Verification

SCEL comes equipped with solid semantics foundations laying the basis for formal reasoning. This is exploited in MISSCEL (MAUDE Interpreter and Simulator for SCEL) which is an implementation of SCEL's operational semantics in the MAUDE framework [16]. MISSCEL currently focuses on a SCEL dialect where repositories are implemented as multisets of tuples (as in Section 3.1), while the processes of a SCEL component evolve in a pure interleaving fashion (i.e. the interaction predicate is the interleaving one defined in Table 3). Access control policies are supported, even if no policy language has been integrated yet: by default, every request is currently authorized.

Why Maude? MISSCEL exploits the rich MAUDE toolset to perform:

- automatic state-space generation;
- qualitative analysis via MAUDE's invariant and LTL model checkers;
- debugging via probabilistic simulations and animations generation;
- statistical model checking via the recently proposed MULTIVESTA [51], a distributed statistical analyser extending VESTA and PVESTA [3,52].

A further advantage of MISSCEL is that SCEL specifications can now be intertwined with raw MAUDE code, exploiting its expressiveness. This allows us to obtain sophisticated specifications in which SCEL is used to model behaviours, aggregations, and knowledge manipulation aspects, leaving scenario-specific details like, e.g. robots movements or computation of distances to MAUDE.

Reasoning in MISSCEL. In Section 3.3 we discussed about the enrichment of SCEL components with reasoning capabilities via external reasoners. As a matter of fact in [5] we have showed how to enrich MISSCEL components (and thus SCEL components) with reasoning capabilities exploiting the reasoner PIRLO [4], implemented in Maude as well, and we analyzed a collision-avoidance robotic scenario. Collision avoidance is a key feature of the robot navigation. For example, in our robot disaster scenario, collision avoidance can be used to minimise collisions during the random walk phase, which is characterised by a high density of robots arbitrarily moving in unpredictable ways. Collision avoidance is also an archetypal example of how external reasoners can be applied to the scenario considered in this paper.

Using MISSCEL we can specify and evaluate two different random walks strategies: a normal one and an informed one. We considered two kinds of robots distinguished by the strategy they apply: *normal robots*, and *informed robots*. Normal robots choose randomly (with a uniform distribution) among five actions: to perform random walk in one of the four cardinal directions, or to stay idle. Informed robots monitor their surrounding environment by relying on proximity sensors, and exploit this information to choose actions aiming at reducing the number of collisions. The amount of environment perceived by an informed robot depends on its perception range. The positions up, right, down and left are reachable with a single move, while the diagonal ones are reachable with two moves. However, the perception of the diagonal positions is also useful for the computation of the next action, as a robot located there (e.g. one perceived in down-left) could move towards the same position chosen by the informed robot (e.g. up, if the informed robot moves left).

Statistical Analysis with MULTIVESTA. In [5] we exploited MISSCEL and the recently proposed statistical model checker MULTIVESTA to perform a statistical quantitative analysis of the robotic collision avoidance scenario.

MultiVeStA is a Java-based distributed statistical model checker which allows its users to enrich existing discrete event simulators with automated and statistical analysis capabilities. The analysis algorithms of MultiVeStA do not depend on the underlying simulation engine: MultiVeStA only makes the assumption that multiple discrete event simulations can be performed on the input model. The tool has been used to reason about public transportation systems [26], volunteer clouds [50], crowd-steering [41] and robotic collision avoidance [5] scenarios. Note however that MISSCEL is an executable operational semantics for SCEL, and as such, given a SCEL specification representing a system's state (i.e. a set of SCEL components), MISSCEL executes it by applying a rule of SCEL's semantics to (part of) the state. According to such semantics, a system evolves

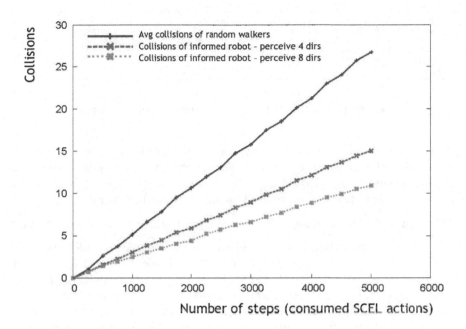

Fig. 9. Collisions of normal and informed robots at varying of number of steps.

non-deterministically by executing the process of one of its components, and in particular by consuming one of its actions. As usual (especially in the MAUDE context, e.g. [6,11,2,25]), in order to perform statistical analysis it is necessary to obtain probabilistic behaviours out of non-deterministic ones by resolving non-determinism in probabilistic choices. For this reason, we defined a Java wrapper for MISSCEL together with a set of external schedulers which permit to obtain probabilistic simulations of SCEL specifications, which can then be exploited by MULTIVESTA to perform statistical model checking.

In our analysis in [5], we considered two scenarios with ten normal robots and an informed one, varying the size of the perception range of the informed robot. In the first scenario the informed robot perceives only the four surrounding positions (up, right, down, left). In the second scenario the informed robot has a wider perception range, allowing to perceive also the positions in the four diagonal directions (up-right, down-right, down-left, up-left). For both scenarios we first studied the expected value of the average number of collisions of the normal robots when varying of number of execution steps. Not surprisingly, we obtained very similar measures for both the scenarios, and hence we use only one plot in Figure 9 ("Avg collisions of random walkers"). More interesting is the case of informed robots. As depicted by the plots "Collisions of informed robot - perceive 4 dirs" and "Collisions of informed robot - perceive 8 dirs", informed robots do significantly less collisions than the normal ones, and wider perception ranges allow to further decrease the number of collisions.

```
1   SC(I(tId('SCId), tId('role), tId('x), tId('y), ...,
2     K(< tId('SCId) ; av(id('robot-1)) >, < tId('role) ; av("rescuer") >,
3       < av("pos") av(41) av(3)>, < tId('x) ; av(41)>, < tId('y) ; av(3)>  ...,
4     Pi(INTERLEAVING-PROCESSES_AUTHORIZE-ALL),
5     P(pDef('ProcessName))
6   )
```

Listing 1. A MISSCEL component representing a robot

Implementation details. Listing 1 provides an excerpt of a possible MISSCEL representation of a robot. As discussed, each robot of our scenario is modelled as a SCEL component. In MISSCEL, a SCEL component is defined as a MAUDE term with sort `ServiceComponent` built with the following operation

`op SC : Interface Knowledge Policies Processes -> ServiceComponent`

As an implementation choice, in MISSCEL tuples may have an identifier (e.g. `< tId('role) ; av("rescuer") >` is a tuple with identifier `role`), but it is not mandatory (e.g. `< av("pos") av(41.0) av(3.0) >` has no identifier). Note that, for implementation reasons, actual values (e.g. strings and integers) are enclosed in the constructor `av`. Note moreover that `'role` is a MAUDE term with sort quoted identifier (similar to strings) built by prefixing alphanumeric words with the operator "`'`". However, only tuples with identifiers can be exposed by the interface, as identifiers are used as pointers to the actual values of the tuples stored in the knowledge. Then, as depicted in line 1 of Listing 1, an interface is just a set of tuple identifiers enclosed in the MAUDE operation `I`, while, as depicted in lines 2-3, the knowledge is a multiset of tuples enclosed in the operation `K`. For example, the sketched robot has id `id('robot-1)`, role `rescuer` and position $(41,3)$. Line 4 specifies that the default policy is enforced.

Line 5 specifies that the behaviour of the robot is provided in the process definition `'ProcessName`. To provide an example of process definition, the MISSCEL representation of the process P_r of Section 5.2 is provided in Listing 2. Note the almost one-to-one correspondence between the process specification and its MISSCEL representation. SCEL variables with type value are built with the MAUDE operations `?x` (when act as binders, e.g. in a `get` or `qry` as in line 5) or `x` (when instantiated, e.g. as in line 7), having as parameter the name of the variable (we also have the corresponding process variables `?X` and `X`). Listing 2 also provides an hint on how MISSCEL deals with process definitions and their invocations. As depicted in lines 1-10, the body of a process is provided in the form of a MAUDE equation. MAUDE equations are *executed* by the MAUDE engine to rewrite occurrences of terms (in this case `invoke(pDef('Pr))`) matching the left-hand side (LHS) of the equation (i.e. before the `=`) in the term specified in the right-hand side (RHS) of the equation (i.e. after the `=`), in this case the body of the process. Intuitively, once all the preceding actions have been executed, a process definition (e.g. `pDef('Pr)`) is *invoked*. That is, it is encapsulated in the operation

`op invoke : ProcessDefinition -> Process`

```
1   eq invoke(pDef('Pr)) = (
2       (qry(< av("victimPerceived") av(true) >)@self.
3         put(< av("victim") x y av(3) >)@ self.
4         put(< av("rescue") >)@ self +
5       get(< av("victim") ?x('x) ?x('y) ?x('count) >)@ Prescuers .
6         pDef('HelpingRescuer)
7         put(< av("victim") x('x) x('y) 3 >)@ self.
8         put(< av("rescue") >)@ self
9       ) | pDef('RandomWalk) | pDef('IsMoving)
10  ) .
11
12  op Prescuers : -> Predicate .
13  eq Prescuers
14  = remote. tId('role) = av("rescuer") OR
15    remote. tId('role) = av("helpRescuer") .
16  op PrescuersWithDist : FormalOrActualValue FormalOrActualValue -> Predicate .
17  vars xvic yvic : ActualValue .
18  eq PrescuersWithDist(xvic,yvic)
19  = (remote. tId('role) = av("rescuer") OR
20    remote. tId('role) = av("helpRescuer")) AND
21    dist(xvic,yvic, remote. tId('x), remote. tId('y)) <= 10 .
```

Listing 2. The MISSCEL representation of process P_r of Section 5.2

(e.g. invoke(pDef('Pr))), which can then be matched with the LHS of the corresponding equation, causing the replacement of the process definition with its body.

Predicates are defined as MAUDE operations with sort **Predicate**. As depicted in line 5 of Listing 2, we exploited the predicate **Prescuers**, specified in lines 12-15. In line 12 we define the MAUDE operation **Prescuers** with sort **Predicate** having no parameters. Then, in lines 13-15 we provide the body of the predicate in the form of a MAUDE equation, similarly to what done for process definitions. Note that in predicates we follow the convention of prefixing tuple identifiers referring to the target of the communication with the keyword **remote** (while we use **this** for local ones).

Interestingly, predicates can also be defined with parameters. An example is **PrescuersWithDist** of lines 16-21, having as parameter the position of the victim, so to send the message only to rescuers *near* to the victim. In line 16 we define the MAUDE operation **PrescuersWithDist** with sort **Predicate** having as parameters two **FormalOrActualValue** (i.e. either SCEL variables or actual values). Then, similarly to **Prescuers**, in lines 18-21 we provide the body of the predicate in the form of a MAUDE equation. Given that at line 17 we specify the MAUDE variables (i.e. place-holders for any term with the same sort) xvic and yvic with sort **ActualValue**, we have that only instantiated occurrences of the predicate (i.e. where all the SCEL variables have been replaced by actual values) match with the LHS of the equation.

Line 21 of listing 2 provides an interesting example demonstrating the usefulness of mixing SCEL and MAUDE specifications: dist is a MAUDE operation which computes the distance between two points (e.g. the positions of two robots), which could for example correspond to the Euclidean distance. Noteworthy, in case we would consider *distances* with different assumptions, e.g.

```
1   op commit : Process -> Commitment .
2   rl commit(P) => commitment(inaction,P) .
3   rl commit(a . P) => commitment(a,P) .
4   crl commit(P + Q) => commitment(a, P1) if commit(P) => commitment(a, P1) .
```

Listing 3. The first four rules of SCEL process semantics implemented in MISSCEL

congested areas, it would be sufficient to change the MAUDE operations leaving unchanged the SCEL specification.

Coming to semantics-related aspects, we have seen in Section 2.3 that the operational semantics of SCEL is defined in two steps. The same happens in MISSCEL. For the sake of presentation, we now exemplify the correspondence of SCEL semantics and its implementation in MISSCEL for the semantics of processes only.

Let us consider the first four rules of the SCEL process semantics reported in Table 2. Listing 3 depicts (omitting unnecessary details) how we implemented these rules in MISSCEL, where P, Q and P1 are MAUDE variables with sort Process (i.e. place-holders for any term with the specified sort), while a is an Action variable. The correspondence is straightforward. Note that we need only one rule for the + operator, as we defined it with the comm axiom, meaning that it has the commutative property, i.e. when applying a rule to P + Q, MAUDE will try to match the rule also with Q + P.

8.3   Spin-Based Verification

We present here a verification approach for SCEL specifications based on the Spin model checker [28]. Specifically, we provide a translation of SCEL specifications into Promela, the input language of Spin, and show how to exploit it to verify some properties of interest of the swarm robotics scenario with Spin.

From SCEL to Promela. For the sake of presentation, we consider a simple instance of SCEL with no policies, standard interleaving interaction (as in Table 3), and knowledge repositories based on multiple distributed tuple spaces (as in Section 3.1). Moreover, we do not consider other sophisticated features of SCEL such as higher-order communication and dynamic creation of new names and components.

We present below the key points of the translation from SCEL to Promela by resorting to the robotics scenario[25]. The translation is defined by a family of functions $[\![\cdot]\!]$, whose formal definitions are given in [23].

---

[25] The complete specification of the scenario can be retrieved from http://rap.dsi.unifi.it/scel/docs/SpinSpecificationSwarmRoboticsScenario.pml.

```
1   /* Constants declaration */
2   #define NROBOTS 10        /* Number of robots*/
3   #define CAPACITY 10       /* Maximum size of knowledge repositories */
4   ...
5
6   /* The type of the interface as a struct of attributes */
7   mtype={rescuer, helpRescuer, explorer}
8   typedef interface{
9           int id;
10          mtype role;
11  }
12
13  /* A component-indexed array of interfaces */
14  interface I[NROBOTS];
15
16  /* Component-indexed array of knowledge repositories */
17  mtype={victim, direction}
18  chan K[NROBOTS]=[CAPACITY] of {mtype, int, int, int};
19
20  /* Components specification */
21  active [NROBOTS] proctype Robot(){
22          /* Attribute initialization */
23          int id=_pid;
24          I[id].id=id;
25          I[id].role=explorer;
26
27          /* Component's process specification */
28          ...
29  }
```

Listing 4. Promela specification of the swarm robotics scenario

Specifications. The Promela specification resulting from the translation (of a simplified variant) of the SCEL specification of the swarm robotics scenario is shown in Listing 4. It contains the declaration of the necessary data structures for representing interfaces, knowledge, components and processes. Data structures representing interfaces and knowledge repositories are declared with a global scope; in this way, attributes and knowledge items can be directly accessed by Promela processes.

Interfaces. The translation declares a structured type interface (lines 8–11) as a collection of variables, one for each attribute. In our scenario, all robots expose two attributes: id, ranging over integer values, and role, ranging over names in {rescuer, helpRescuer, explorer}. All interfaces are then recorded in the array I (line 14), whose size is given by the number of robots, defined by the constant NROBOTS (line 2).

Repositories. All knowledge repositories are grouped together in the array K (line 18). Each repository is implemented as a channel of tuples, whose length is given by the maximum length of items used in the specification. In fact, to simplify message management in Promela, all tuples have the same length and are composed only of a value in {victim, direction} followed by integer values. To fulfil this assumption, messages representing shorter items are completed by using dummy values. The dimension of repositories is set by means of the constant CAPACITY (line 3).

Components. The translation of a component $\mathcal{I}_i[\mathcal{K}_i, \Pi_i, P_i]$ corresponds to a declaration of a Promela process, via the proctype construct (line 21), that initializes the data structure modelling the component attributes with values in $\mathcal{I}_i$ (lines 23-25). In our example, the data structure modelling the knowledge repository, i.e. channel K[i], is not initialized because $\mathcal{K}_i$ is initially empty. Notably, component translations are automatically instantiated in the initial system state (by means of the keyword active).

Processes and actions. The composition of SCEL processes can be naturally translated into Promela process declarations and their composition. For example, multiple run statements can be used for the parallel execution of processes. Then, each SCEL action is translated in a small piece of Promela code that basically performs output or input operations on channels K[i]. For example, the group-oriented action get("victim", $?x, ?y, ?count$)@($role$="rescuer" ∨ $role$="helpRescuer"), used by a robot to receive a request for help by other robots, is rendered in Promela as a non-deterministic choice among a set of input operations on each K[i]. In particular, for each robot component i, there is a choice branch

$$::\text{atomic}\{(\text{g\_i} \rightarrow \text{K[i]??victim,x,y,count}\}$$

where the guard g_i is as follows:

$$(\text{I[i].role==rescuer} \;||\; \text{I[i].role==helpRescuer}) \;\&\&\; \text{K[i]??[victim,\_,\_,\_]}$$

This guard ensures the transition to fire only if the target predicate holds for component i (i.e., the component plays either role rescuer or helpRescuer) and i has a matching victim tuple in its repository. If that is the case, the tuple is indeed removed using the (consuming) input operation K[i]??victim,x,y,count. It is worth noticing that the atomic block is used to guarantee atomic execution of the operations.

Spin Verification. We illustrate in this section some examples of how Spin can be used to check and verify properties of SCEL specifications, by resorting to the translation of the SCEL specification of our swarm robotics scenario.

Checking Deadlock Absence. A first property one would like to check is absence of deadlocks. Below, we report the result of invoking Spin for checking deadlock absence in our scenario with 10 robots:

```
State-vector 2188 byte, depth reached 415289, errors: 0
   415290 states, stored
```

The result is positive (no errors) and Spin explores more than 400.000 states.

Checking liveness. Another typical use of Spin that is very convenient for our purposes is to look for interesting executions, that is, we characterise them by means of an LTL formula. For example, in our scenario, we can specify a formula

```
[](I[i].role==helpRescuer ->
   <>(positionX[i]==VICTIMX && positionY[2]==VICTIMY))
```

which states that whenever the robot i becomes a HELPRESCUER, it eventually reaches the victim. Spin provides a positive answer, since in our simplified scenario robots' batteries never discharge. We have also defined a variant of the scenario where each robot component has a battery level value that decreases after each movement. In this case, the formula is not satisfied and Spin returns a counterexample showing an execution of the system in which the robot becomes a HELPRESCUER but then stops moving because the battery is completely discharged.

9   Concluding Remarks

We have presented the kernel language SCEL and its Java implementation together with alternative linguistic primitives and with automatic tools to support verification of qualitative and quantitative properties of its programs. To assess to which extent SCEL meets our expectations, we have used it to tackle a number of case studies from robotics [15,24,13,34], service provision domains [19,23], cloud-computing [36,38] and e-Mobility domains [12]. Moreover, to verify the impact of SCEL on autonomic programming we have shown how it can be used to model a key aspect such as self-expression [13] and how it can flexibly model different adaptation patterns [15].

Our holistic approach to programming autonomic computing systems permits to govern systems complexity by providing flexible abstractions for modeling behaviors, knowledge and policies and for exploiting external reasoners whenever informed decisions need to be taken. We are now working on two different, almost opposite, directions.

On the one hand, we are developing a high-level programming language that, by enriching SCEL with standard constructs (e.g., control flow constructs such as while or if-then-else), simplifies the programming task. This would enable us to implement an integrated environment for supporting the development of autonomic systems at different levels of abstraction: from a high-level perspective, based on SCEL, to a more concrete one, based on jRESP. (Semi-)Automatic analysis tools, based on the SCEL's formal semantics, will be integrated in this toolchain. On the other hand, we are distilling from SCEL a minimal calculus where communication partners are selected according to predicates on attributes exposed by the different processes. Our aim is to understand the full impact on distributed programming of this novel paradigm that has proved very fruitful in modeling the interaction of large numbers of autonomic systems. For the new calculus we plan to develop behavioral relations, axiomatizations and logics that will help to devise new tools for supporting specification and verification of SCEL programs.

Other interesting topics that deserve further investigation are those connected to policies, reasoners and adaptation. We are currently working on defining different interaction policies to study the possibility of modeling different forms of synchronization and communication, and for example to guarantee local synchronous interaction and global asynchronous interaction between components. Moreover, we are studying the connections between knowledge handlers, reasoners and components goals described by means of appropriate knowledge representation languages. In this case the aim is the development of methodologies that enable components to take decisions, possibly after consulting external reasoners, about possible alternative behaviors by choosing among the best possibilities while being aware of the consequences.

Acknowledgements. We would like to thank all friends of the ASCENS project, without their contributions and stimuli, SCEL would not have been conceived.

References

1. Abeywickrama, D.B., Combaz, J., Horký, V., Keznikl, J., Kofroň, J., Lafuente, A.L., Loreti, M., Margheri, A., Mayer, P., Monreale, V., Montanari, U., Pinciroli, C., Tůma, P., Vandin, A., Vassev, E.: Tools for Ensemble Design and Runtime. In: Wirsing, M., Hölzl, M., Koch, N., Mayer, P. (eds.) Software Engineering for Collective Autonomic Systems. LNCS, vol. 8998, pp. 429–448. Springer, Heidelberg (2015)
2. Agha, G.A., Meseguer, J., Sen, K.: PMaude: Rewrite-based specification language for probabilistic object systems. In: Cerone, A., Wiklicky, H. (eds.) QAPL 2005. ENTCS, vol. 153(2), pp. 213–239. Elsevier (2006)
3. AlTurki, M., Meseguer, J.: pVeStA: A parallel statistical model checking and quantitative analysis tool. In: Corradini, A., Klin, B., Cîrstea, C. (eds.) CALCO 2011. LNCS, vol. 6859, pp. 386–392. Springer, Heidelberg (2011)
4. Belzner, L.: Action programming in rewriting logic (technical communication). Theory and Practice of Logic Programming, Online Supplement (2013)
5. Belzner, L., De Nicola, R., Vandin, A., Wirsing, M.: Reasoning (on) service component ensembles in rewriting logic. In: Iida, S., Meseguer, J., Ogata, K. (eds.) Specification, Algebra, and Software. LNCS, vol. 8373, pp. 188–211. Springer, Heidelberg (2014)
6. Bentea, L., Ölveczky, P.C.: A probabilistic strategy language for probabilistic rewrite theories and its application to cloud computing. In: Martí-Oliet, N., Palomino, M. (eds.) WADT 2012. LNCS, vol. 7841, pp. 77–94. Springer, Heidelberg (2013)
7. Bistarelli, S., Montanari, U., Rossi, F.: Semiring-based constraint satisfaction and optimization. J. ACM 44(2), 201–236 (1997)
8. Bistarelli, S., Montanari, U., Rossi, F.: Soft concurrent constraint programming. ACM Trans. Comput. Log. 7(3), 563–589 (2006)

9. Bortolussi, L., Hillston, J.: Fluid model checking. In: Koutny, M., Ulidowski, I. (eds.) CONCUR 2012. LNCS, vol. 7454, pp. 333–347. Springer, Heidelberg (2012)
10. Bortolussi, L., Hillston, J., Latella, D., Massink, M.: Continuous approximation of collective system behaviour: A tutorial. Perform. Eval. 70(5), 317–349 (2013)
11. Bruni, R., Corradini, A., Gadducci, F., Lluch Lafuente, A., Vandin, A.: Modelling and analyzing adaptive self-assembly strategies with Maude. In: Durán, F. (ed.) WRLA 2012. LNCS, vol. 7571, pp. 118–138. Springer, Heidelberg (2012)
12. Bures, T., De Nicola, R., Gerostathopoulos, I., Hoch, N., Kit, M., Koch, N., Monreale, G.V., Montanari, U., Pugliese, R., Serbedzija, N., Wirsing, M., Zambonelli, F.: A Life Cycle for the Development of Autonomic Systems: The e-mobility showcase. In: Proc. of SASOW, pp. 71–76. IEEE, Los Alamitos (2013)
13. Cabri, G., Capodieci, N., Cesari, L., De Nicola, R., Pugliese, R., Tiezzi, F., Zambonelli, F.: Self-expression and dynamic attribute-based ensembles in SCEL. In: Margaria, T., Steffen, B. (eds.) ISoLA 2014, Part I. LNCS, vol. 8802, pp. 147–163. Springer, Heidelberg (2014)
14. Castro, M., Druschel, P., Kermarrec, A.-M., Rowstron, A.: Scalable Application-Level Anycast for Highly Dynamic Groups. In: Stiller, B., Carle, G., Karsten, M., Reichl, P. (eds.) NGC 2003 and ICQT 2003. LNCS, vol. 2816, pp. 47–57. Springer, Heidelberg (2003)
15. Cesari, L., De Nicola, R., Pugliese, R., Puviani, M., Tiezzi, F., Zambonelli, F.: Formalising adaptation patterns for autonomic ensembles. In: Fiadeiro, J.L., Liu, Z., Xue, J. (eds.) FACS 2013. LNCS, vol. 8348, pp. 100–118. Springer, Heidelberg (2014)
16. Clavel, M., Durán, F., Eker, S., Lincoln, P., Martí-Oliet, N., Meseguer, J., Talcott, C.: All About Maude - A High-Performance Logical Framework. LNCS, vol. 4350. Springer, Heidelberg (2007)
17. Combaz, J., Bensalem, S., Tiezzi, F., Margheri, A., Pugliese, R., Kofron, J.: Correctness of Service Components and Service Component Ensembles. In: Wirsing, M., Hölzl, M., Koch, N., Mayer, P. (eds.) Software Engineering for Collective Autonomic Systems. LNCS, vol. 8998, pp. 107–159. Springer, Heidelberg (2015)
18. Damianou, N., Dulay, N., Lupu, E.C., Sloman, M.: The Ponder Policy Specification Language. In: Sloman, M., Lobo, J., Lupu, E.C. (eds.) POLICY 2001. LNCS, vol. 1995, pp. 18–38. Springer, Heidelberg (2001)
19. De Nicola, R., Ferrari, G.-L., Loreti, M., Pugliese, R.: A Language-Based Approach to Autonomic Computing. In: Beckert, B., Damiani, F., de Boer, F.S., Bonsangue, M.M. (eds.) FMCO 2011. LNCS, vol. 7542, pp. 25–48. Springer, Heidelberg (2013), http://www.ascens-ist.eu/scel
20. De Nicola, R., Ferrari, G., Pugliese, R.: Klaim: A Kernel Language for Agents Interaction and Mobility. IEEE Trans. Software Eng. 24(5), 315–330 (1998)
21. De Nicola, R., Latella, D., Loreti, M., Massink, M.: Rate-based transition systems for stochastic process calculi. In: Albers, S., Marchetti-Spaccamela, A., Matias, Y., Nikoletseas, S., Thomas, W. (eds.) ICALP 2009, Part II. LNCS, vol. 5556, pp. 435–446. Springer, Heidelberg (2009)
22. De Nicola, R., Latella, D., Loreti, M., Massink, M.: A uniform definition of stochastic process calculi. ACM Comput. Surv. 46(1), 1–5 (2013)
23. De Nicola, R., Lluch Lafuente, A., Loreti, M., Morichetta, A., Pugliese, R., Senni, V., Tiezzi, F.: Programming and verifying component ensembles. In: Bensalem, S., Lakhneck, Y., Legay, A. (eds.) From Programs to Systems. LNCS, vol. 8415, pp. 69–83. Springer, Heidelberg (2014)
24. De Nicola, R., Loreti, M., Pugliese, R., Tiezzi, F.: A Formal Approach to Autonomic Systems Programming: The SCEL Language. TAAS 9(2), 7 (2014)

25. Eckhardt, J., Mühlbauer, T., AlTurki, M., Meseguer, J., Wirsing, M.: Stable availability under denial of service attacks through formal patterns. In: de Lara, J., Zisman, A. (eds.) Fundamental Approaches to Software Engineering. LNCS, vol. 7212, pp. 78–93. Springer, Heidelberg (2012)
26. Gilmore, S., Tribastone, M., Vandin, A.: An analysis pathway for the quantitative evaluation of public transport systems. In: Albert, E., Sekerinski, E. (eds.) IFM 2014. LNCS, vol. 8739, pp. 71–86. Springer, Heidelberg (2014)
27. Hölzl, M., Gabor, T.: Reasoning and Learning for Awareness and Adaptation. In: Wirsing, M., Hölzl, M., Koch, N., Mayer, P. (eds.) Software Engineering for Collective Autonomic Systems. LNCS, vol. 8998, pp. 249–290. Springer, Heidelberg (2015)
28. Holzmann, G.J.: The model checker SPIN. IEEE Trans. Softw. Eng. 23(5), 279–295 (1997)
29. IBM: Autonomic Computing Policy Language – ACPL, http://www.ibm.com/developerworks/tivoli/tutorials/ac-spl/
30. IBM: An architectural blueprint for autonomic computing. Tech. rep., IBM, Third edition (June 2005)
31. Khakpour, N., Jalili, S., Talcott, C.L., Sirjani, M., Mousavi, M.R.: Formal modeling of evolving self-adaptive systems. Sci. Comput. Program. 78(1), 3–26 (2012)
32. Latella, D., Loreti, M., Massink, M., Senni, V.: Stochastically timed predicate-based communication primitives for autonomic computing. In: Bertrand, N., Bortolussi, L. (eds.) Proceedings of the Twelfth Workshop on Quantitative Aspects of Programming Languages (QAPL 2014). Electronic Proceedings in Theoretical Computer Science (EPTCS), pp. 1–16 (2014), doi:10.4204/EPTCS.154.1
33. Latella, D., Loreti, M., Massink, M., Senni, V.: On StocS: a Stochastic extension of SCEL. Tech. Rep. 11, ASCENS Project (February 2014), http://www.ascens-ist.eu/
34. Loreti, M., Margheri, A., Pugliese, R., Tiezzi, F.: On programming and policing autonomic computing systems. In: Margaria, T., Steffen, B. (eds.) ISoLA 2014, Part I. LNCS, vol. 8802, pp. 164–183. Springer, Heidelberg (2014)
35. Margheri, A., Masi, M., Pugliese, R., Tiezzi, F.: A Formal Software Engineering Approach to Policy-based Access Control. Tech. rep., DiSIA, Univ. Firenze (2013), available at http://www.ascens-ist.eu/scel
36. Margheri, A., Pugliese, R., Tiezzi, F.: Linguistic Abstractions for Programming and Policing Autonomic Computing Systems. In: UIC/ATC, pp. 404–409. IEEE, Los Alamitos (2013)
37. Margheri, A., Pugliese, R., Tiezzi, F.: Linguistic abstractions for programming and policing autonomic computing systems. Tech. rep., Univ. Firenze (2013), http://www.ascens-ist.eu/scel
38. Mayer, P., Klarl, A., Hennicker, R., Puviani, M., Tiezzi, F., Pugliese, R., Keznikl, J., Bure, T.: The autonomic cloud: A vision of voluntary, peer-2-peer cloud computing. In: Proc. of SASOW, pp. 89–94. IEEE, Los Alamitos (2013)
39. OASIS XACML TC: eXtensible Access Control Markup Language (XACML) version 3.0 (January 2013), http://docs.oasis-open.org/xacml/3.0/xacml-3.0-core-spec-os-en.pdf
40. O'Grady, R., Groß, R., Christensen, A.L., Dorigo, M.: Self-assembly strategies in a group of autonomous mobile robots. Auton. Robots 28(4), 439–455 (2010), doi:10.1007/s10514-010-9177-0
41. Pianini, D., Sebastio, S., Vandin, A.: Distributed statistical analysis of complex systems modeled through a chemical metaphor. In: HPCS (MOSPAS workshop), pp. 416–423. IEEE, Los Alamitos (2014)

42. Pinciroli, C., Bonani, M., Mondada, F., Dorigo, M.: Adaptation and Awareness in Robot Ensembles: Scenarios and Algorithms. In: Wirsing, M., Hölzl, M., Koch, N., Mayer, P. (eds.) Software Engineering for Collective Autonomic Systems. LNCS, vol. 8998, pp. 471–494. Springer, Heidelberg (2015)
43. Plotkin, G.D.: A structural approach to operational semantics. J. Log. Algebr. Program. 60-61, 17–139 (2004)
44. Project InterLink (2007), http://interlink.ics.forth.gr
45. Rossi, F., van Beek, P., Walsh, T.: Handbook of Constraint Programming. Elsevier, Amsterdam (2006)
46. Rowstron, A., Druschel, P.: Pastry: Scalable, Decentralized Object Location, and Routing for Large-Scale Peer-to-Peer Systems. In: Guerraoui, R. (ed.) Middleware 2001. LNCS, vol. 2218, pp. 329–350. Springer, Heidelberg (2001)
47. Salehie, M., Tahvildari, L.: Self-adaptive software: Landscape and research challenges. TAAS 4(2) (2009)
48. Saraswat, V., Rinard, M.: Concurrent constraint programming. In: POPL, pp. 232–245. ACM Press, New York (1990)
49. Schneider, F.B.: Enforceable security policies. ACM Trans. Inf. Syst. Secur. 3(1), 30–50 (2000)
50. Sebastio, S., Amoretti, M., Lluch-Lafuente, A.: A computational field framework for collaborative task execution in volunteer clouds. In: SEAMS, pp. 105–114. ACM, New York (2014)
51. Sebastio, S., Vandin, A.: MultiVeStA: statistical model checking for discrete event simulators. In: Horvath, A., Buchholz, P., Cortellessa, V., Muscariello, L., Squillante, M.S. (eds.) 7th International Conference on Performance Evaluation Methodologies and Tools, ValueTools '13, Torino, Italy, December 10-12, 2013, pp. 310–315. ACM Press, New York (2013), http://dl.acm.org/citation.cfm?id=2631846
52. Sen, K., Viswanathan, M., Agha, G.A.: Vesta: A statistical model-checker and analyzer for probabilistic systems. In: Baier, C., Chiola, G., Smirni, E. (eds.) QEST 2005, pp. 251–252. IEEE Computer Society Press, Los Alamitos (2005)
53. Sommerville, I., Cliff, D., Calinescu, R., Keen, J., Kelly, T., Kwiatkowska, M.Z., McDermid, J.A., Paige, R.F.: Large-scale complex IT systems. Commun. ACM 55(7), 71–77 (2012)
54. Vassev, E., Hinchey, M.: Knowledge Representation for Adaptive and Self-aware Systems. In: Wirsing, M., Hölzl, M., Koch, N., Mayer, P. (eds.) Software Engineering for Collective Autonomic Systems. LNCS, vol. 8998, pp. 221–247. Springer, Heidelberg (2015)

Reconfigurable and Software-Defined Networks of Connectors and Components*

Roberto Bruni[1], Ugo Montanari[1], and Matteo Sammartino[1]

Department of Computer Science, University of Pisa, Italy

Abstract. The diffusion of adaptive systems motivate the study of models of software entities whose interaction capabilities can evolve dynamically. In this paper we overview the contributions in the ASCENS project in the area of software defined networks and of reconfigurable connectors. In particular we highlight: (i) the definition of the Network-conscious pi-calculus and its use in the modeling and verification of the PASTRY protocol, and (ii) the mutual correspondence between different frameworks for defining networks of connectors together with two suitable enhancements for addressing dynamically changing systems.

Keywords: Network-conscious pi-calculus, PASTRY, overlay networks, coalgebraic semantics, HD-automata, BIP, Petri nets with boundaries, algebras of connectors, tile model, reconfigurable connectors, dynamic connectors

1 Introduction

One of the research strands of the ASCENS project is concerned with the study of resource-aware infrastructures and networking middleware modeled in terms of advanced components, glues and connectors which can support different levels of guarantees, reliability, dynamics and integration to heterogeneous components. The study includes the development of foundational models and architectures for network-aware systems with a high degree of dynamism in the communication topology between components. Formal models must allow a separation between the detailed behavior of components and their overall coordination. This paper surveys two approaches to coordination whose focus is on Software-Defined networks and on component-based design, respectively:

- For the former, we have proposed a network-aware extension of classical π-calculus [27], called NCPi, that allows for expressing the creation and the activation of connections, and whose semantics deals with the possible routing paths. We show that NCPi looks more adequate than traditional process calculi to describe Software-Defined and overlay networks, their routing

---

* This research was supported by the European project IP 257414 (ASCENS) and by the Italian MIUR Project CINA (PRIN 2010/11).

M. Wirsing et al. (eds.): Collective Autonomic Systems, LNCS 8998, pp. 73–106, 2015.
© Springer International Publishing Switzerland 2015

mechanisms, and to verify their properties. In particular, we show how NCPi can support the formalization and verification of the PASTRY distributed hash table system of cloud systems.

- For the latter, we have related some of the most notable theories for expressing network of connectors between components, by defining mutual embeddings that reduce the fragmentation in the body of knowledge and the different notions and terminologies involving connectors, and then we have proposed some enhancements to address reconfigurability and dynamism.

Structure of the paper. Section 2 introduces Software-Defined networks and the PASTRY protocol. Section 3 presents the syntax and semantics of NCPi, including an extension with features reflecting real-life routing protocols. Section 4 shows the formalization of the Pastry overlay networks, then used to prove that each message eventually gets to its destination.

Section 5 explains the rationale for software architectures based on (networks of) connectors and components, and surveys some approaches from the literature. Section 6 presents the connection between algebras of connectors and nets with boundaries, a special flavor of Petri nets with interfaces. Section 7 recalls the BIP component framework and relates it with the models in Section 6. Section 8 introduces two enhanced models that allow a higher degree of dynamism.

2   Software-Defined and Overlay Networks

The trend in networking is going towards more "open" architectures, where the infrastructure can be manipulated in software. This trend started in the nineties, when OpenSig [15] and Active Networks [39] were presented, but neither gained wide acceptance due to security and performance problems. More recently, OpenFlow [26,32] or, more broadly, Software-Defined Networking has become the leading approach, supported by Google, Facebook, Microsoft and others. Software-Defined networks (SDNs) allow network administrators to control traffic via software installed on a centralized *controller*. This machine is connected to all switches in the network, and instructs them to install or uninstall forwarding rules and report traffic statistics.

Another important example of programmable infrastructures are peer-to-peer systems. They provide the networking substrate for the execution of distributed applications, such as *Distributed Hash Tables* (DHTs). In peer-to-peer systems, *peers* interact over an application-level *overlay network*, built on top of the physical one. An overlay network is highly dynamic, as peers can join and leave it at any time, and this causes continuous reconfigurations of its topology.

In particular, we consider PASTRY [35], employed in the Science Cloud case-study (see Chapter IV.3 [25]). PASTRY is a peer-to-peer architecture where peers and keys have *identifiers*, regarded as arranged in clockwise order on a *ring*. The main service provided by PASTRY is *routing by key*: given a key k, PASTRY delivers the message to the peer which is *responsible for k*, i.e. the one whose identifier is numerically closest to k than all other peers. Routing is implemented

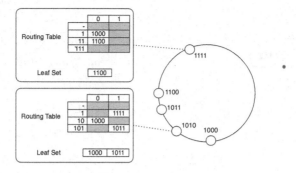

Fig. 1. PASTRY example system

as follows. Each peer with identifier *id* maintains two data structures: a *routing table* and a *leaf-set*. The routing table contains peers that share a prefix with *id*. The leaf-set contains peers (*leaves*) with numerically closest smaller and larger identifiers, relative to *id*. Whenever *id* receives a message with target key *k*, it checks whether *k* belongs to the leaf-set range. If so, the message is forwarded to the leaf numerically closest to *k* (if it is not *id* itself). Otherwise, the routing table is used: the next hop is the peer sharing the longest prefix with *k*.

Example 1. An example system is in Figure 1, where identifiers are binary strings. Consider the peer with identifier 1010 and suppose 1100 is responsible for the key 1101. A message from 1010 with target key 1101 is routed as follows. Since 1101 does not belong to the interval [1000, 1011] spanned by the leaf-set of 1010, the routing table is used: the longest prefix shared by 1010 and 1101 is 1, so the message is forwarded to 1111, the peer in the cell (1, 1). Once 1111 receives the message, it discovers that 1101 is in its leaf-set range (the leaf-set has 1111 itself as upper bound, as no peer has larger identifier), so it forwards the message to the leaf closest to 1101, that is 1100.

3   Network Conscious π-Calculus (NCPi)

Traditional process calculi, such as π-calculus [27], seem inadequate to describe Software-Defined and overlay networks, their routing mechanisms, and to verify their properties. In fact, they abstract away from network details. Complex infrastructural elements, such as network links, could be described in terms of processes, and routing protocols in terms of consecutive step-by-step forwardings. However, end-to-end routing behavior could not be observed in a single transition, e.g. the path of a DHT lookup request through a peer-to-peer overlay. This information can be useful for the analysis of routing algorithms, e.g., to determine whether they are always able to construct a valid/optimal path for given source and destination.

In order to model network architectures in a more explicit way, in [30,36,31] we have introduced the *Network Conscious π-calculus* (NCPi), an extension of

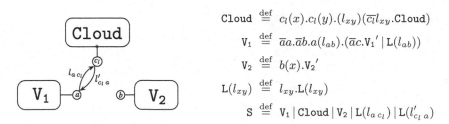

$$\text{Cloud} \stackrel{\text{def}}{=} c_l(x).c_l(y).(l_{xy})(\overline{c_l}l_{xy}.\text{Cloud})$$

$$\text{V}_1 \stackrel{\text{def}}{=} \overline{a}a.\overline{a}b.a(l_{ab}).(\overline{a}c.\text{V}_1' \mid \text{L}(l_{ab}))$$

$$\text{V}_2 \stackrel{\text{def}}{=} b(x).\text{V}_2'$$

$$\text{L}(l_{xy}) \stackrel{\text{def}}{=} l_{xy}.\text{L}(l_{xy})$$

$$\text{S} \stackrel{\text{def}}{=} \text{V}_1 \mid \text{Cloud} \mid \text{V}_2 \mid \text{L}(l_{a\,c_l}) \mid \text{L}(l'_{c_l\,a})$$

Fig. 2. Cloud example system

the π-calculus with a natural notion of network: nodes and links are regarded as computational resources that can be created, passed and used to transmit, so they are represented as names, following the π-calculus methodology.

3.1   Illustrative Example

To have a first look at the calculus, consider the system in Figure 2. It represents the network level of a cloud system, made of (virtual) machines and (virtual) links between them. *Site names* a, b, c_l represent network interfaces; *link names* $l_{a\,c_l}$ and $l'_{c_l\,a}$ represent directed links from a to c_l and viceversa, respectively. We have a *cloud manager* Cloud, capable of creating new links between virtual machines and granting access to them, and two virtual machines V_1 and V_2. We model a situation where the machine V_1 wants to exchange data with V_2, but no links exists between a and b, so V_1 will ask Cloud to create such link.

The formal definition says that Cloud can receive two sites x and y at c_l, create a new link between them and emit it at c_l. The process V_1 can send a and b from a, wait for a link at a and then become the parallel composition of two components: the first one can send c from a; the second one invokes the process L to activate the link l_{ab}. This activation is expressed as the *link prefix* $l_{xy}.-$ in the definition of L: when consumed, it spawns a *transportation service* over l_{xy}, which can be used to forward a datum from x to y. The link prefix expresses a single activation of the link, as input/output prefixes in the π-calculus express a single usage of their subject channel. The recursive definition of L is needed to model a persistent connection. The process V_2 simply waits for a datum at b. Finally, the whole system S is the parallel composition of V_1, V_2, Cloud and two processes modeling a bidirectional persistent connection between V_1 and Cloud.

As in the π-calculus, we have observations representing inputs, output and complete communications. However, since NCPi allows for remote communications, they all include the (possibly empty) sequence of links that are traversed in the communication. For instance, the process V_1 can emit a at a as follows

$$\text{V}_1 \xrightarrow{\bullet;\overline{a}a} \overline{a}b.a(l_{ab}).(\overline{a}c.\text{V}_1' \mid \text{L}(l_{ab}))$$

The label $\bullet;\overline{a}a$ is a zero-length (i.e. with empty sequence of links) *output path*, which can be seen as the π-calculus action $\overline{a}a$. The symbol $\bullet$ is syntactic sugar, indicating where the path starts. In general, there may be a list of links W between $\bullet$ and $\bar{a}a$: $\bullet; W; \bar{a}a$ means that a went through W before being emitted. The syntax also include *bound output paths* of the form $\bullet; W; a(b)$, representing the publication of a previously bound name b (its *extrusion*).

Symmetrically, Cloud can receive a at c_l

$$\text{Cloud} \xrightarrow{c_l a; \bullet} c_l(y)(l_{ay})\overline{c_l}l_{ay}.\text{Cloud}$$

where $c_l a; \bullet$ is an *input path*, analogous to the early π-calculus input action $c_l a$. Input paths always have length zero, as we only allow local receptions (this restriction will be dropped for the concurrent version of NCPi).

Next we introduce *service paths*, which have no counterpart in the π-calculus. A service path has the form $a; W; b$, where W is a sequence of links. It represents a transportation service that can be used to route a datum from a to b. For instance $a; l_{a\,c_l}; c_l$ is a service path from a to c_l over $l_{a\,c_l}$ and we have

$$\text{L}(l_{a\,c_l}) \xrightarrow{a; l_{a\,c_l}; c_l} \text{L}(l_{a\,c_l}).$$

Finally, we have complete communication, denoted by a *complete path* $\bullet; W; \bullet$. Unlike the π-calculus τ-action, this observation is not silent, as the path W of the transmitted datum is observed; the datum itself remains unobservable. Another difference is that a complete path is usually produced by more than one synchronization, each one concatenating a compatible pair of paths. For instance, in order for V_1 to communicate a to Cloud, there must be a first synchronization between V_1 and $\text{L}(l_{ab})$, causing $\bullet; \bar{a}a$ and $a; l_{a\,c_l}; c_l$ to be concatenated

$$V_1 \mid \text{L}(l_{a\,c_l}) \xrightarrow{\bullet; l_{a\,c_l}; \overline{c_l}a} \ldots$$

Here the continuation is the parallel composition of those shown above, and $\bullet; l_{a\,c_l}; \overline{c_l}a$ is an output path where a is emitted at c_l after traversing $l_{a\,c_l}$. A complete path is produced by another, final synchronization:

$$V_1 \mid \text{L}(l_{a\,c_l}) \mid \text{Cloud} \xrightarrow{\bullet; l_{a\,c_l}; \bullet} \ldots$$

meaning that a complete communication over l_{ac_l} has happened.

Now we overview the steps the entire system S can perform:

1. V_1 **communicates to Cloud the endpoints** a **and** b **of the link to be created:** it is observed as two consecutive occurrences of $\bullet; l_{ac_l}; \bullet$. The state of the system after these interactions is

$$a(l_{xy}).(\text{L}(l_{xy}) \mid \bar{a}c.V_1') \mid (l_{ab})(\overline{c_l}l_{ab}.\text{Cloud}) \mid V_2 \mid \text{L}(l_{a\,c_l}) \mid \text{L}(l'_{c_l\,a}) \ .$$

2. $\overline{c_l}l_{ab}.\text{Cloud}$ **communicates** l_{ab} **to** $a(l_{xy}).(\text{L}(l_{xy}) \mid \bar{a}c.V_1')$: we first rearrange the processes using structural congruence

$$(l_{ab})(\, a(l_{xy}).(\text{L}(l_{xy}) \mid \bar{a}c.V_1') \mid \overline{c_l}l_{ab}.\text{Cloud} \mid \text{L}(l'_{c_l\,a})\,) \mid V_2 \mid \text{L}(l_{a\,c_l}) \ .$$

Now the processes within the scope of l_{ab} can interact, and the resulting observation is $\bullet; l'_{c_l\,a}; \bullet$, with continuation

$$(l_{ab})(\mathtt{L}(l_{ab}) \,|\, \bar{a}c.\mathtt{V_1}' \,|\, \mathtt{Cloud} \,|\, \mathtt{V_2}) \,|\, \mathtt{L}(l_{a\,c_l}) \,|\, \mathtt{L}(l'_{c_l\,a}) \ .$$

3. $\bar{a}c.\mathtt{V_1}'$ **communicates** c to $\mathtt{V_2}$: in this case, despite l_{ab} is used for the transmission, only $\bullet; \bullet$ can be observed, because such link is restricted. This is analogous to the π-calculus τ action. The continuation is

$$(l_{ab})(\mathtt{L}(l_{ab}) \,|\, \mathtt{V_1}' \,|\, \mathtt{Cloud} \,|\, \mathtt{V_2}'[c/x]) \,|\, \mathtt{L}(l_{a\,c_l}) \,|\, \mathtt{L}(l'_{c_l\,a}) \ .$$

3.2 Syntax and Semantics

We assume an enumerable set of site names $\mathcal{S}$ (or just sites) and an enumerable set of link names $\mathcal{L}$ (or just links), equipped with two functions $s, t \colon \mathcal{L} \to \mathcal{S}$, telling source and target of each link. We denote by l_{ab} a link l such that $s(l) = a$ and $t(l) = b$. We write $\mathcal{L}_{ab}$ for the set of links of the form l_{ab} and $\mathcal{L}_a$ for the union of all $\mathcal{L}_{ab}$ and $\mathcal{L}_{ba}$, for all b.

As shown in the previous section, the syntax of NCPi processes is an extension of the π-calculus one: prefixes can also express input/output of links, and we have a *link prefix* $l_{ab}.p$, meaning that this process can offer to the environment the service of transporting a datum from a to b through l and then continue as p.

The free names $\mathrm{fn}(p)$ describe the network available to p, in the form of a multigraph made of sites and links. They are defined as expected. For links, if l_{ab} is not the argument of a top-level binder, then $\mathrm{fn}(p)$ includes $\{a, b, l_{ab}\}$; otherwise, for instance in $a(l_{bc}).p$, only l_{bc} is bound, whereas its endpoints are free, namely $\mathrm{fn}(a(l_{bc}).p) := \{a, b, c\} \cup \mathrm{fn}(p) \smallsetminus \{l_{bc}\}$. The interesting cases are:

$$\mathrm{fn}(b(a).p) := \{b\} \cup (\mathrm{fn}(p) \smallsetminus (\{a\} \cup \mathcal{L}_a)) \qquad \mathrm{fn}((a)p) := \mathrm{fn}(p) \smallsetminus (\{a\} \cup \mathcal{L}_a)$$

where a free link in p having a as endpoint is considered bound in $(a)p$ and $b(a).p$. This intuitively means that a global link cannot have private endpoints. Given a name r, we shall write $r \,\#\, p$ to indicate that r is *fresh* w.r.t. p, i.e. $r \notin \mathrm{fn}(p)$; $N \,\#\, p$, with N a set of names, has the expected meaning.

Now we define *renamings* and their extensions to processes. Since names describe graphs, we require renaming to respect their structure, i.e. to be *graph homomorphisms*. In order to define the extension of renamings to processes, we need a notion of α-conversion that establishes how to avoid captures. For reasons that will become clear later, α-conversion can only be defined for processes where bound links are bound explicitly, and not as a side-effect of binding a site. We call such processes *well-formed*. For instance, $a(b).l_{bc}.p$ is not well-formed because l_{bc} is implicitly bound by $a(b)$.

Definition 1 (Well-formed process). *A NCPi process p is* well-formed *if for every subterm q: (i) $q = (a)p'$ implies $\mathrm{fn}(q) = \mathrm{fn}(p') \smallsetminus \{a\}$; (ii) $q = b(a).p'$ implies $\mathrm{fn}(q) = \{b\} \cup \mathrm{fn}(p') \smallsetminus \{a\}$;*

Table 1. Free names, bound names, objects and interaction sites of a path α

path α	fn	bn	obj	is
$a;W;b$	$n(\alpha)$	$\varnothing$	$\varnothing$	$\{a,b\}$
$\bullet;W;\bullet$	$n(\alpha)$	$\varnothing$	$\varnothing$	$\varnothing$
$\bullet;W;\bar{a}r$	$n(\alpha)$	$\varnothing$	$n(r)$	$\{a\}$
$\bullet;W;a(r)$	$n(\alpha) \setminus \{r\}$	$\{r\}$	$n(r) \setminus \{r\}$	$\{a\}$
$ar;\bullet$	$n(\alpha)$	$\varnothing$	$n(r)$	$\{a\}$

Structural congruence axioms for well-formed processes contains the usual commutative monoid laws for $\mid$ and $+$, scope extension and unfolding for process definitions. The interesting case is α-conversion:

$$(a)p \equiv (a')p[^{a'}/a] \qquad b(a).p \equiv b(a').p[^{a'}/a] \qquad a' \# (a)p$$
$$(l_{ab})p \equiv (l'_{ab})p[^{l'_{ab}}/l_{ab}] \qquad c(l_{ab}).p \equiv c(l'_{ab}).p[^{l'_{ab}}/l_{ab}] \qquad l'_{ab} \# (l_{ab})p$$

When α-converting $(a)p$, $[^{a'}/a]$ is never applied to a link l_{ab}, since such link cannot be free in p by well-formedness. Indeed, $[^{a'}/a]$ does not uniquely characterize a renaming if l_{ab} is free; if it is bound, i.e. if $(l_{ab})p'$ is a subprocess of p, then we simply have inductively $((l_{ab})p')[^{a'}/a] \equiv (l'_{a'b})p'[^{l'_{a'b}}/l_{ab}][^{a'}/a]$, for any $l'_{a'b}$ fresh w.r.t. p. The axioms' side conditions guarantee preservation of well-formedness.

We now introduce the operational semantics. As mentioned, observations represent routing paths. We denote them by α. Table 1 introduces some notation for paths: the *interaction sites* of α, written $is(\alpha)$, are those sites where the interaction with another process may happen, similarly to subjects of the π-calculus. We also have free names $fn()$, bound names $bn()$ and objects $obj()$ of α. Given a list of links W, we write W/r for W after removing each occurrence of $r \in \mathcal{L}$, and α/r for α with $/r$ applied to its list of links.

Definition 2 (NCPi transition system). *The* NCPi *transition system is the smallest transition system generated from the rules in Figure 3. We assume that structurally congruent processes have the same transitions.*

We briefly explain the rules. (OUT) and (IN) infer a zero-length path representing, respectively, the beginning and the end of a transmission. As in the early π-calculus, a renaming must be applied to the continuation in the free input case; if the input object is a site a, then we have a substitution between sites, which can be turned into a proper renaming by well-formedness. (LINK) infers a service path made of one link. (INT) infers an internal action, represented as a complete path where everything is unobservable. (RES) computes the paths of a process with an additional restriction (r) from those of the unrestricted process, provided that r is not already bound and is not an object or an interaction site. This side condition reflects that of the corresponding π-calculus rule. (OPEN) treats the case, excluded by (RES), when r is the object of a free output path: such path is turned into a bound output path, again rendering r unobservable when needed. (SUM) and (PAR) are as expected. (ROUTE), (COMP) and (COM) concatenate

(OUT) $\bar{a}r.p \xrightarrow{\bullet;\bar{a}r} p$

(OPEN) $\dfrac{p \xrightarrow{\bullet;W;\bar{a}r} q}{(r)p \xrightarrow{\bullet;W/r;\bar{a}(r)} q}$ $r \neq a$

(IN) $a(r).p \xrightarrow{ar';\bullet} p[r'/r]$

(PAR) $\dfrac{p_1 \xrightarrow{\alpha} q_1}{p_1 \mid p_2 \xrightarrow{\alpha} q_1 \mid p_2}$ bn(α) # p_2

(LINK) $l_{ab}.p \xrightarrow{a;l_{ab};b} p$

(ROUTE) $\dfrac{p_1 \xrightarrow{\bullet;W;\bar{a}x} q_1 \qquad p_2 \xrightarrow{a;W';b} q_2}{p_1 \mid p_2 \xrightarrow{\bullet;W;W';\bar{b}x} q_1 \mid q_2}$ bn(x) # p_2

(INT) $\tau.p \xrightarrow{\bullet;\bullet} p$

(COMP) $\dfrac{p_1 \xrightarrow{a;W;b} q_1 \qquad p_2 \xrightarrow{b;W';c} q_2}{p_1 \mid p_2 \xrightarrow{a;W;W';c} q_1 \mid q_2}$

(SUM) $\dfrac{p \xrightarrow{\alpha} p'}{p+q \xrightarrow{\alpha} p'}$

(COM) $\dfrac{p_1 \xrightarrow{\bullet;W;\bar{a}r} q_1 \qquad p_2 \xrightarrow{ar;\bullet} q_2}{p_1 \mid p_2 \xrightarrow{\bullet;W;\bullet} q_1 \mid q_2}$

(RES) $\dfrac{p \xrightarrow{\alpha} q}{(r)p \xrightarrow{\alpha/r} (r)q}$ $\begin{array}{l} \mathrm{bn}(\alpha) \\ r \notin \cup\,\mathrm{obj}(\alpha) \\ \cup\,\mathrm{is}(\alpha) \end{array}$

Fig. 3. NCPi SOS rules

paths that meet at an interaction site: (ROUTE) extends an output path, provided that the transported name, whenever bound, is fresh w.r.t. the process that offers the transportation service; (COMP) composes two service paths; (COM) completes a communication. It is easy to see that the π-calculus is included in NCPi: we have just to forbid links in processes. The notion of behavioral equivalence is the following one, called *network conscious bisimulation*.

Definition 3 (Network conscious bisimulation). *A binary, symmetric and reflexive relation R is a* network conscious bisimulation *if* $(p,q) \in R$ *and* $p \xrightarrow{\alpha} p'$, *with* bn($\alpha$) $\# q$, *implies that there is* q' *such that* $q \xrightarrow{\alpha} q'$ *and* $(p',q') \in R$. *The bisimilarity is the largest such relation and is denoted by* $\sim^{NC}$.

We have the following closure result for $\sim^{NC}$.

Theorem 1. $\sim^{NC}$ *is closed under all syntactic operators except input prefix and parallel composition.*

Closure under input prefix not holding is expected. Surprisingly, also the parallel composition is problematic. This is because the semantics is transactional, in the sense that paths can involve more than one synchronization. As in the π-calculus, closure under input prefix is achieved by taking the greatest bisimulation closed under all renamings. Closure under parallel composition is discussed in [31].

3.3   Concurrent NCPi(κNCPi)

We now present κNCPi, an extension of NCPi with features reflecting real-life routing protocols. The most important one is that the semantics allows observing simultaneous actions taking place in the network, in the form of *multisets* of paths; this follows the intuition that processes should act in a truly distributed manner, without a central coordinator that imposes an interleaving order to their actions. The technical consequence is that bisimilarity becomes a *congruence*. Examples of real-life protocols exploiting such features can be found in [31], where the *Border Gateway Protocol* [41] is modeled, and in section 4.

The syntax of κNCPi processes is the same as NCPi, with the following exceptions. Arguments of binders, which we denote by s, can be sites or expressions $l_{(ab)}$, meaning that l_{ab} is bound together with a and b. The intuitive meaning of $c(l_{(ab)}).p$ is an atomic, polyadic version of $c(a).c(b).c(l_{ab}).p$. The output primitive also specifies the *destination site*: $\bar{a}br.p$ can emit the datum r, having destination b, at a and continue as p. The definition of fn(p) for the new constructs is

$$\text{fn}(\bar{a}br.p) := \{a,b\} \cup \text{n}(r) \cup \text{fn}(p) \quad \text{fn}(a(l_{(bc)}).p) := \{a\} \cup \text{fn}(p) \smallsetminus (\{b,c\} \cup \mathcal{L}_b \cup \mathcal{L}_c)$$

Well-formed κNCPi processes have to satisfy the requirements of Definition 1 plus the following one: $q = c(l_{(ab)}).p'$ implies fn(q) = $\{c\} \cup$ fn(p') $\smallsetminus \{a,b,l_{ab}\}$. Structural congruence is minimal: we only have α-conversion and unfolding; other axioms are moved to observations or implemented through the rules.

Observations for the concurrent semantics, denoted by Λ, are multisets of paths, called *concurrent paths*. For the purpose of describing a more realistic network behavior, we equip paths α with some additional information:

- both input and output paths include a list of links; in the case of input paths, they are the links that can be traversed in order to reach the destination;
- there is a *bound input path* $ab(s); W; \bullet$, representing the reception of a bound name; this is needed because we introduce an explicit scope closure rule;
- paths always specify a destination site, namely b in $\bullet; W; \bar{a}br$, $abr; W; \bullet$ and $ab(s); W; \bullet$.

We remove extrusion paths: extrusions will be represented by concurrent paths, because we will allow many paths to extrude the same name simultaneously. Concurrent paths can be of the following forms:

- the *empty concurrent path* **1** indicates that no activity is performed;
- the *singleton concurrent path* α is a concurrent path made of a single path;
- the *union* $\Lambda_1 \mid \Lambda_2$ means that the paths in Λ_1 and Λ_2 are being traversed *at the same time*;
- the *extrusion restriction* $(r)\Lambda$ indicates that r is being extruded through one or more paths in Λ.

We impose some axioms on well-formed concurrent paths, telling that they are indeed multisets and that extrusion restrictions can be swapped and grouped at the outermost level.

We now introduce the transition system. Most of the rules are the expected concurrent extensions of Figure 3. The main difference is the synchronization mechanism. This is made of two steps:

(i) paths of parallel processes are collected through the following rule

$$(\text{PAR}) \ \frac{p_1 \stackrel{\Lambda_1}{\Longrightarrow} q_1 \quad p_2 \stackrel{\Lambda_2}{\Longrightarrow} q_2}{p_1 \mid p_2 \stackrel{\Lambda_1 \mid \Lambda_2}{=\!=\!=\!=\!\Longrightarrow} q_1 \mid q_2}$$

where bound names in each concurrent path are require to be fresh w.r.t. the other process and its concurrent path;

(ii) other rules pick two compatible paths from the multiset produced by (i) and replace them with their concatenation, without modifying the source process; in other words, these rules synchronize two subprocesses of the source process. For instance, an output path and a service path with a common interaction site can be joined using the following rule, resulting in an extended output path

$$(\text{SRV-OUT}) \ \frac{p \xrightarrow{(R) \ (\bullet; W; \bar{a}br \mid a; W'; c \mid \Theta)} q}{p \xrightarrow{(R) \ (\bullet; W; W'; \bar{c}br \mid \Theta)} q}$$

where (R) is a sequence of restrictions and Θ is a concurrent path without extrusion restrictions (they have all been brought at the top level using scope extension).

The behavioral equivalence for κNCPi processes is called *concurrent network conscious bisimilarity*, denoted $\sim_\kappa^{NC}$, and is an obvious extension of Definition 3: we require that processes can do the same concurrent paths.

Theorem 2. $\sim_\kappa^{NC}$ *is a congruence with respect to all κNCPi operators.*

This result allows us to equip the π-calculus with a compositional semantics: we can characterize π-calculus processes as κNCPi processes via a syntactic restriction where links are forbidden and emission and destination sites in output prefixes coincide. SOS rules derive all possible paths, non-deterministically. In order to control path construction, e.g. according to a specific routing strategy, we can define a *forwarding predicate*

$$\varphi \colon \mathcal{L} \times \mathcal{S} \times Proc \to \{\texttt{true}, \texttt{false}\}$$

and then use it as an additional side condition for rules achieving step (ii) described above: $\varphi(l_{ab}, c, p)$ tells when a path of p, with destination c, can be extended with l_{ab}. In this way, for instance, we could exclude non-optimal links according to some metric (cost, latency, distance, and others). See [31] for a forwarding predicate modeling BGP.

3.4   Coalgebraic Semantics of NCPi

In [31] we have introduced a presheaf-based coalgebraic semantics for NCPi, in the style of [20]. The basic idea is having a model where we distinguish: (a) a domain of resources, (b) a domain of programs and a (c) domain of "maps" between resources and programs. In NCPi, resources of a process are its free sites and links, describing its communication network. Therefore, (a) is a category **G** of suitable graphs, representing networks, equipped with endofunctors that add new vertices and edges, modeling network resources allocation; (b) is **Set**, where some objects are regarded as sets of NCPi processes; (c) is the category of functors **G** → **Set** (*presheaves on* **C**), associating to each network the set of NCPi processes with such network.

The operational semantics, then, is modeled as a coalgebra with states in a presheaf, thus each state is decorated with its networks: this enables the explicit representation of network resources allocation along transitions. Unfortunately, we still have infinitely many states, because allocated resources may grow indefinitely, even if only a finite portion of them is actually accessible, e.g., in recursive processes performing extrusions. However, our presheaf of states is "well-behaved", so, according to [16], it is always possible to deallocate the unused resources and an equivalent *History Dependent (HD) automaton* [28] can be derived from the NCPi coalgebra. HD-automata are automata with allocation and deallocation along transitions. They admit minimal, possibly finite state, representatives, where all bisimilar states are identified, which can be computed as shown and implemented in [19].

4   Formal Definition and Properties of the PASTRY Distributed Hash Table System

In this section we use κNCPi to model PASTRY overlay networks and DHTs. We will prove the correctness of our model by checking the following property, which says that each message eventually gets to its destination.

Property 1 (Routing convergence). The routing procedure always converges: given a message with target key k and a peer id, either id is responsible for k or it can forward the message to id' numerically closest to k than id.

4.1   Peer Model

The key idea is modeling identifiers as sites, and the routing table and the leaf-set of a peer as two collections of links $\mathcal{L}_{RT}$ and $\mathcal{L}_{LS}$, forming the overlay network. We denote by $a \boxdot b$ a link to b in a's routing table and by $a \boxminus b$ a link to b in a's leaf-set. A peer with identifier a is modeled as the process

$$\mathtt{Peer}(a, \mathcal{L}_{RT}, \mathcal{L}_{LS}) \overset{\text{def}}{=} (\mathcal{O}_{RT})(\mathcal{O}_{LS})\, \mathtt{Control}(a, \mathcal{O}_{RT}, \mathcal{O}_{LS})$$
$$| \, \mathtt{RT}(\mathcal{L}_{RT}, \mathcal{O}_{RT}) \,|\, \mathtt{LS}(\mathcal{L}_{LS}, \mathcal{O}_{LS})$$

$$\mathtt{Control}(a, \mathcal{O}_{RT}, \mathcal{O}_{LS}) \overset{\text{def}}{=} \mathtt{JoinH}(a) + \mathtt{Route}(\mathcal{O}_{RT}, \mathcal{O}_{LS})$$

Processes RT and LS allow other processes to query and modify routing table and leaf-set. These operations are called internally via the names in $\mathcal{O}_{RT}$ and $\mathcal{O}_{LS}$.

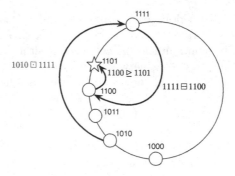

Fig. 4. Routing path from 1010 for the key 1101 in the system of Figure 1

The process **Control** implements the control logic of a peer. **JoinH** executes the distributed protocol for node joins: it updates the peer's own routing data structures and helps populating the joining peer's ones. In [36, Theorem 6.3.1] we show that the reconfiguration of the overlay network due to node joins preserves Property 1. The process **Route** simply activates transportation services over the peer's links. A PASTRY system is modeled as the parallel composition of peer processes. For the system in Figure 1 we have

$$\texttt{Sys} \stackrel{\text{def}}{=} \texttt{Peer}(1000) \,|\, \texttt{Peer}(1010) \,|\, \texttt{Peer}(1011) \,|\, \texttt{Peer}(1100) \,|\, \texttt{Peer}(1111)$$

4.2   DHT Model

Now we want to model routing behavior for a simple Distributed Hash Table, where observations are routing paths of DHT lookups. In order to do this, we introduce a new type of link: $a \trianglerighteq k$ means that the peer with identifier a is responsible for the key k. We can model a Distributed Hash Table over a PASTRY system made of peers $a_1, \ldots, a_n$ as follows. Suppose the DHT has m key-value pairs $\langle k_i, v_i \rangle$, and let a_{k_i} be the identifier of the peer responsible for k_i, i.e. the closest to k_i among $a_1, \ldots, a_n$.

$$\texttt{DHT} \stackrel{\text{def}}{=} \texttt{Peer}(a_1) \,|\, \ldots \,|\, \texttt{Peer}(a_n) \,|\, \texttt{H}$$

$$\texttt{H} \stackrel{\text{def}}{=} \texttt{Entry}(k_1, v_1, a_{k_1}) \,|\, \ldots \,|\, \texttt{Entry}(k_m, v_m, a_{k_m})$$

$$\texttt{Entry}(k, v, a) \stackrel{\text{def}}{=} a \trianglerighteq k \,|\, k(b).\overline{a}bv.\texttt{Entry}(k, v, a)$$

Here H represents the DHT content as the parallel composition of processes that handle the table's entries. The idea is implementing a DHT lookup request for a key k as a message with destination k, carrying the identifier b of the sender. Upon receiving this message, the handler $\texttt{Entry}(k, v, a)$ for $\langle k, v \rangle$ replies to b with a message containing v.

In [36, Section 6.4] we provide an implementation of the the PASTRY routing strategy via a forwarding predicate, and we show that it yields paths satisfying

$$\text{BI(P)} \ \underline{\quad}_{[10]} \ \begin{array}{c}\text{Nets with}\\\text{boundaries}\end{array} \ \underline{\quad}_{[38]} \ \begin{array}{c}\text{Petri}\\\text{Calculus}\end{array} \ \underline{\quad}_{[10]} \ \begin{array}{c}\text{Tile}\\\text{Model}\end{array} \ \underline{\quad}_{[9,11]} \ \text{Reo}$$

Fig. 5. Relation among the different models of connectors & buffers

Property 1. The consequence is that lookup requests always reach the correct peer ([36, Theorem 6.4.2]). As an example, we show how to compute a routing path in the system of Figure 1. For simplicity, let us consider a DHT with only one key-value pair $(1101, v)$ located at 1100:

$$\text{H} \ \overset{\text{def}}{=} \ 1100 \unrhd 1101 \,|\, 1101(a).\overline{1100}\,a\,v.\text{H} \qquad \text{DHT} \ \overset{\text{def}}{=} \ \text{Sys} \,|\, \text{H}$$

Consider the following process, representing a user application running at 1010

$$\text{App} \ \overset{\text{def}}{=} \ \overline{1010} \ 1101 \ 1010.1010(v').\text{App}'(v') \ .$$

This sends a lookup request for the key 1101, receives the result and uses it for some computations. The routing steps for this request are depicted in Figure 4, and correspond to those of Example 1. The corresponding transition is

$$\text{App} \,|\, \text{DHT} \ \xrightarrow{\bullet;1010\boxdot1111;1111\boxminus1100;1100\unrhd1101;\bullet} \ 1010(v').\text{App}'(v') \,|\, \text{Sys} \,|\, 1100\,1010\,v.\text{H}$$

showing the whole routing path from 1010 to 1100.

5   Networks of Connectors and Components

Component-based design is a modular engineering practice that relies on the separation of concerns between coordination and computation. Component-based systems are built from loosely coupled computational entities, the *components*, whose interfaces comprise the number, kind and peculiarities of communication ports. The term *connector* denote entities that glue the interaction of components [33], by imposing suitable constraints on the allowed communications. The evolution of a network of components and connectors (just *network* for short) is as if played in rounds: At each round, the components try to interact through their ports and the connectors allow/disallow some of the interactions selectively. A connector is called *stateless* when the interaction constraints it imposes are the same at each round; *stateful* otherwise. To address composition and modularity of a system, networks are often decorated with (input and output) interfaces: in the simplest case, they consist of ports for network interaction.

Recent years have witnessed an increasing interest about a rigorous modeling of networks. We survey below, following the chronological order in which they were proposed, some formal approaches to the representation, composition and analysis of networks. Although the approaches we shall consider are quite different in spirit, the mutual correspondence results are summarized in Figure 5. All above approaches deal with systems that have static structures, i.e., systems in which the possible interactions among components are all defined at design time and remain unchanged during runtime. Nevertheless, when shifting to connectors for systems that adapt their behavior to changing environments, the situation is less well-understood. In fact, a general and uniform theory for dynamic connectors is still lacking. Some recent progresses are discussed in Section 8.

The algebra of connectors and the tile model. An algebra consisting of five kinds of basic stateless connectors (plus their duals) is presented in [9]. The connectors can be composed in series or in parallel. The operational, observational and denotational semantics of connectors are first formalized separately and then shown to coincide. Moreover, a complete normal-form axiomatization is defined. The *Petri calculus* in Section 6.2 enriches the algebra in [9] with one-place buffers.

The Tile Model [21,8] offers an operational and abstract semantic framework for concurrent systems [29,18,14] and also for suitable classes of connectors, of which the algebra of stateless connectors is just a particular instance. A *tile* $T : s \xrightarrow[\beta]{\alpha} t$ is a rewrite rule stating that the *initial configuration* s can evolve to the *final configuration* t producing the *effect* β; but the step is allowed only if the 'arguments' of s can evolve by providing the *trigger* α. Triggers and effects are called *observations*. Roughly, the semantics of component-based systems can be expressed via tiles when components and connectors are equipped with sequential composition $s; t$ and with a monoidal tensor product $s \otimes t$. Technically, we require that configurations and observations form two *monoidal categories* [24] with the same objects. Tiles express the reactive behaviour of connectors in terms of a Labelled Transition System (LTS) whose labels are pairs ⟨trigger, effect⟩. In this context, the usual notion of equivalence is called *tile bisimilarity*, which is a congruence (w.r.t. ; and ⊗) when a suitable rule format is met [21].

The Reo coordination model. Reo [1] is an exogenous coordination model based on channel-like connectors that mediate the flow of data among components. Notably, a small set of point-to-point primitive connectors is sufficient to express a large variety of interesting interaction patterns, including several forms of mutual exclusion, synchronization, alternation, and context-dependency. Components and primitive connectors can be composed into larger Reo circuits by disjoint union up-to the merging of shared nodes. The semantics of Reo has been formalized in many ways, tile model included [2]. See [22] for a recent survey.

The BIP component framework. BIP [4] is a component framework for constructing systems by superposing three layers of modeling: 1) Behaviour, the lower level, representing the sequential computation of individual components; 2) Interaction, the middle layer, defining the handshaking mechanisms between these components; and 3) Priority, the top level, assigning a partial order of privileges to the admissible synchronizations. The lower layer consists of a set of atomic components with ports, modeled as automata whose arcs are labelled by sets of ports. The second layer consists of connectors that define suitable relations between ports. We name BI(P) the fragment of BIP without priorities (see

Section 7). In absence of priorities, the interaction layer admits the algebraic presentation given in [5]. One key feature of BIP is the so-called *correctness by construction*, which allows the specification of architecture transformations preserving certain properties of the underlying behaviour. For instance it is possible to provide (sufficient) conditions for compositionality and composability which guarantee deadlock-freedom. The BIP component framework has been implemented in a language and a tool-set (cf. Chapter I.3 [17]).

Nets with boundaries and the wire calculus. Nets with boundaries [38] takes inspiration from the open nets of [3]. The idea is to extend Petri nets with interfaces that can be used by transitions to synchronize their firings with the environment. Nets with boundaries can be composed in series and in parallel and come equipped with a labelled transition system operational semantics. The correspondence between BI(P) and nets with boundaries is outlined in Section 7.

The wire calculus [37] shares strong similarities with the tile model, in the sense that it has sequential and parallel compositions and exploits trigger-effect pairs labels as observations. However, it is presented as a process algebra instead of via monoidal categories and it exploits a slightly different kind of vertical composition. Each process comes with an input/output arity typing, written $P : (n, m)$ for a process P with n input ports and m output ports. The usual action prefixes $a.P$ of process algebras are extended in the wire calculus by the simultaneous input of a trigger a and output of an effect b, written $\frac{a}{b}.P$, where a (resp. b) is a string of actions, one for each input port (resp. output port) of the process. In [38,11] a dialect of the wire calculus, called *Petri calculus*, has been used to give an exact characterization of a special class of (stateful) connectors that can be expressed as nets with boundaries. This result is outlined next.

6   Connector Algebras for Petri Nets

In this section we follow the contribution in [38,13]. Roughly, nets with boundaries are first introduced, that come equipped with sequential and parallel composition and with a labelled transition system semantics. Then, the *Petri calculus* is presented, that roughly models circuit diagrams with one-place buffers and interfaces. The first result shows that a Petri calculus process can be defined for each net such that the translation preserves and reflects operational semantics (and thus bisimilarity). The second result provides the converse translation, from Petri calculus to nets. The work in [38] has been recently improved in [11,13] by considering different firing policies for nets and exploiting the tile model to deal with Place/Transition Petri nets with boundaries.

6.1   Petri Nets with Boundaries

Petri nets [34] consist of *places* (i.e. resources types), which are repositories of *tokens* (i.e., resource instances), and *transitions* that remove and produce tokens.

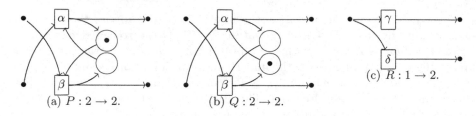

(a) $P : 2 \to 2$.   (b) $Q : 2 \to 2$.   (c) $R : 1 \to 2$.

Fig. 6. Three nets with boundaries

Definition 4 (Net). *A net N is a 4-tuple $N = (S, T, {}^\circ-, -^\circ)$ where S is the (nonempty) set of places, T is the set of transitions, (with $S \cap T = \varnothing$), and the functions ${}^\circ-, -^\circ : T \to 2^S$ assign finite sets of places, called respectively source and target, to each transition.*

Transitions t, u are *independent* when ${}^\circ t \cap {}^\circ u = t^\circ \cap u^\circ = \varnothing$. A set U of transitions is independent when, for all $t, u \in U$, if $t \neq u$ then t and u are independent. Given a set of transitions U, let ${}^\circ U = \cup_{u \in U} {}^\circ u$ and $U^\circ = \cup_{u \in U} u^\circ$.

Definition 5 (Semantics). *Let $N = (S, T, {}^\circ-, -^\circ)$ be a net, $X, Y \subseteq S$ and $t \in T$. Write: $(N, X) \to_{\{t\}} (N, Y) \overset{\text{def}}{=} {}^\circ t \subseteq X \wedge t^\circ \subseteq Y \wedge X \backslash {}^\circ t = Y \backslash t^\circ$.*
    For $U \subseteq T$ a set of independent transitions, write:

$$(N, X) \to_U (N, Y) \overset{\text{def}}{=} {}^\circ U \subseteq X \wedge U^\circ \subseteq Y \wedge X \backslash {}^\circ U = Y \backslash U^\circ.$$

Note that, for any $X \subseteq S$, $(N, X) \to_\varnothing (N, X)$. A pair (N, X) (or just X when N is obvious from the context) is called a *marking*. Sometimes nets comes equipped with an *initial marking* X_0, representing the initial state of the system.
    In the following, given $n \in \mathbb{N}$, we let $\underline{n} \overset{\text{def}}{=} \{0, 1, \dots, n-1\}$.

Definition 6 (Nets with boundaries). *Let $m, n \in \mathbb{N}$. A net with boundaries $N : m \to n$ is a tuple $N = (S, T, {}^\circ-, -^\circ, {}^\bullet-, -^\bullet)$ where $(S, T, {}^\circ-, -^\circ)$ is a net and functions ${}^\bullet- : T \to 2^{\underline{m}}$ and $-^\bullet : T \to 2^{\underline{n}}$ assign transitions to the left and right boundaries of N, respectively.*

The notion of independence of transitions extends to nets with boundaries in the obvious way: $t, u \in T$ are said to be *independent* when

$$ {}^\circ t \cap {}^\circ u = \varnothing \; \wedge \; t^\circ \cap u^\circ = \varnothing \; \wedge \; {}^\bullet t \cap {}^\bullet u = \varnothing \; \wedge \; t^\bullet \cap u^\bullet = \varnothing. $$

Example 2. Figure 6 shows three different nets with boundaries. Places are circles and a marking is represented by the presence or absence of tokens; rectangles are transitions and arcs stand for pre- and post-set relations. The left (resp., right) interface is depicted by points situated on the left (resp., on the right).

    Note that for any $k \in \mathbb{N}$, there is a bijection $\ulcorner\_\urcorner : 2^{\underline{k}} \to \{0, 1\}^k$ with $\ulcorner U \urcorner_i = 1$ if $i \in U$ and $\ulcorner U \urcorner_i = 0$ otherwise. This fact is exploited to define the semantics of a net with boundaries $N : m \to n$ as a double-labelled transition system, where transition labels are pairs of strings in $\{0, 1\}^m \times \{0, 1\}^n$, representing the tokens requested on the left/right boundary by the firing.

Definition 7 (Semantics). *Let $N : n \to n$ be a net and $X, Y \subseteq S$. We write $(N, X) \xrightarrow[\beta]{\alpha} (N, Y)$ iff there exists an independent $U \subseteq T$ such that $(N, X) \to_U (N, Y)$, with $\alpha = \ulcorner {}^\bullet U \urcorner$ and $\beta = \ulcorner U^\bullet \urcorner$.*

Given $N : m \to n$ and $M : k \to l$, their tensor product is the net $N \otimes M : m + k \to n + l$ whose sets of places and transitions are the disjoint union of the corresponding sets in N and M, whose maps ${}^\circ -, -^\circ, {}^\bullet -, -^\bullet$ are defined according to the maps in N and M and whose initial marking is the disjoint union of the initial markings of N and M.

The sequential composition $N; M : m \to k$ of $N : m \to n$ and $M : n \to k$ is slightly more involved and relies on the following notion of synchronization. A synchronization is a pair (U, V) with $U \subseteq T_N$ and $V \subseteq T_M$ independent sets of transitions such that: (1) $U \cup V \neq \varnothing$ and (2) $U^\bullet = {}^\bullet V$.

The set of synchronizations inherits an ordering from the subset relation, i.e. $(U, V) \subseteq (U', V')$ when $U \subseteq U'$ and $V \subseteq V'$. A synchronization is said to be minimal when it is minimal with respect to this order.

The sequential composition $N; M : m \to k$ is defined as the net with boundaries $(S_N \uplus S_M, T_{N;M}, {}^\circ-_{N;M}, -^\circ_{N;M}, {}^\bullet-_{N;M}, -^\bullet_{N;M})$, where:

- $T_{N;M} \stackrel{\text{def}}{=} \{(U, V) | U \subseteq T_N, V \subseteq T_M, (U, V) \text{ a minimal synchronisation}\}$,
- ${}^\circ(U, V)_{N;M} = {}^\circ(U)_N \uplus {}^\circ(V)_M$ and $(U, V)^\circ_{N;M} = (U)^\circ_N \uplus (V)^\circ_M$,
- ${}^\bullet(U, V)_{N;M} = {}^\bullet(U)_N$ and $(U, V)^\bullet_{N;M} = (V)^\bullet_M$.

Intuitively, transitions attached to the left or right boundaries can be seen as transition fragments, that can be completed by attaching other complementary fragments to that boundary. When two transition fragments in N share a boundary node, then they are two mutually exclusive options for completing a fragment of M attached to the same boundary node. Thus, the idea is to combine the transitions of N with that of M when they share a common boundary, as if their firings were synchronized. Of course, only minimal synchronizations are selected. The initial marking of $N; M$ is the disjoint union of X_{0N} and X_{0M}.

Example 3. Consider the nets $P : 2 \to 2$ and $R : 1 \to 2$ in Figure 6. Then, the composed net $P; (R \otimes R) : 2 \to 4$ is shown in Figure 7.

6.2 Petri Calculus

In this section we introduce an algebra of connectors that roughly enriches the algebra of stateless connectors from [9] with one-place buffers along [2]. We call it *Petri calculus* after [38]. The algebra of stateless connectors in [9] can be regarded as a fragment of the Petri calculus where all tiles have identical initial and final connectors, i.e. they are of the form $s \xrightarrow[b]{a} s$. In terms of the wire calculus, this means that only recursive processes of the form $\mathbf{rec}\, X. \frac{a}{b}.X$ are considered.

Terms of the Petri Calculus are defined by the grammar:

$$R ::= \bigcirc \mid \odot \mid \mathsf{I} \mid \mathsf{X} \mid \nabla \mid \Delta \mid \bot \mid \top \mid \wedge \mid \vee \mid \downarrow \mid \uparrow \mid R \otimes R \mid R; R$$

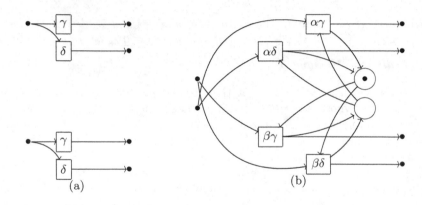

Fig. 7. Nets $R \otimes R$ (a) and $P; (R \otimes R)$ (b)

$\bigcirc : (1,1)$ $\odot : (1,1)$ $\mathsf{I} : (1,1)$ $\mathsf{X} : (2,2)$ $\nabla : (1,2)$ $\Delta : (2,1)$

$\bot : (1,0)$ $\top : (0,1)$ $\wedge : (1,2)$ $\vee : (2,1)$ $\downarrow : (1,0)$ $\uparrow : (0,1)$

$$\frac{R_1 : (k,l) \quad R_2 : (m,n)}{R_1 \otimes R_2 : (k+m, l+n)} \qquad \frac{R_1 : (k,n) \quad R_2 : (n,l)}{R_1 \otimes R_2 : (k,l)}$$

Fig. 8. Sort inference rules

$$\overline{\bigcirc \xrightarrow[0]{1} \odot} \quad \overline{\odot \xrightarrow[1]{0} \bigcirc} \quad \overline{\odot \xrightarrow[1]{1} \odot} \quad \overline{\mathsf{I} \xrightarrow[1]{1} \mathsf{I}} \quad \overline{\nabla \xrightarrow[11]{1} \nabla} \quad \overline{\Delta \xrightarrow[1]{11} \Delta} \quad \overline{\bot \xrightarrow[]{1} \bot} \quad \overline{\top \xrightarrow[1]{} \top}$$

$$\overline{\mathsf{X} \xrightarrow[yx]{xy} \mathsf{X}} \quad \overline{\wedge \xrightarrow[x\overline{x}]{1} \wedge} \quad \overline{\vee \xrightarrow[1]{x\overline{x}} \vee} \quad \frac{R_1 \xrightarrow{\alpha} R_2 \quad R_1' \xrightarrow[\beta]{\sigma} R_2'}{R_1; R_1' \xrightarrow[\beta]{\alpha} R_2; R_2'} \quad \frac{R_1 \xrightarrow[\beta]{\alpha} R_2 \quad R_1' \xrightarrow[\sigma]{\rho} R_2'}{R_1 \otimes R_1' \xrightarrow[\beta\sigma]{\alpha\rho} R_2 \otimes R_2'} \quad \frac{R : (m,n)}{R \xrightarrow[0^n]{0^m} R}$$

Fig. 9. Operational semantics for the Petri Calculus

It consists of the following constants plus parallel and sequential composition: the empty place $\bigcirc$, the full place $\odot$, the identity wire I, the twist X, the duplicator ∇ and its dual Δ, the mutex $\wedge$ and its dual $\vee$, the hiding $\bot$ and its dual $\top$, the inaction $\downarrow$ and its dual $\uparrow$. Any term R has a unique associated *sort* (k,l) with $k, l \in \mathbb{N}$, that fixes the size k of the left (input) interface and the size l of the right (output) interface of P (see Fig. 8).

The operational semantics is defined by the rules in Fig. 9, where $x, y \in \{0,1\}$ and we let $\overline{x} = 1 - x$. The labels $\alpha, \beta, \rho, \sigma$ of transitions are binary strings, all transitions are sort-preserving, and if $R \xrightarrow[\beta]{\alpha} R'$ with $R, R' : (n,m)$, then $|\alpha| = n$ and $|\beta| = m$. Notably, the induced bisimilarity is a congruence.

Example 4. For example, let $R_1 \stackrel{\text{def}}{=} (\nabla \otimes \nabla); (\odot \otimes \mathsf{X} \otimes \bigcirc); (\Delta \otimes \Delta); \mathsf{X}$ and $R_2 \stackrel{\text{def}}{=} (\nabla \otimes \nabla); (\bigcirc \otimes \mathsf{X} \otimes \odot); (\Delta \otimes \Delta); \mathsf{X}$. It is immediate to check that both $R_1 : (2,2)$

and $R_2 : (2,2)$, in fact: $\nabla \otimes \nabla : (2,4)$, $\odot \otimes \times \otimes \bigcirc : (4,4)$, $\bigcirc \otimes \times \otimes \odot : (4,4)$, $\triangle \otimes \triangle : (4,2)$, and $\times : (2,2)$. The only moves for R_1 are $R_1 \xrightarrow[00]{00} R_1$ and $R_1 \xrightarrow[10]{01} R_2$ while for R_2 are $R_2 \xrightarrow[00]{00} R_2$ and $R_2 \xrightarrow[01]{10} R_1$. It is immediate to note that R_1 and R_2 are terms analogous to the nets in Fig. 6 and that R_1 is bisimilar to $\times; R_2; \times$.

A close correspondence between nets with boundaries and Petri calculus terms is established in [13], by providing mutual encodings with tight semantics correspondence. First, it is shown that any net $N : m \to n$ with initial marking X can be associated with a term $R_{N,X} : (m,n)$ that preserves and reflects the semantics of N. Conversely, for any term $R : (m,n)$ of the Petri calculus there exists a bisimilar net $N_R : m \to n$. We refer the interested reader to [13].

7 From BI(P) to Petri Nets and Vice Versa

This section surveys the correspondence between BI(P) systems and nets (and with the Petri calculus, by transitivity) as studied in [10]. First, a composition operation for BI(P) systems is introduced that enables the structured definition of larger systems. Intuitively, the places of the net are in one-to-one correspondence with the states of the components, while the transitions of the net represent the synchronized execution of the transitions of the components. Then, this compositional version of BI(P) systems is used to define a compositional mapping of BI(P) systems to bisimilar nets with boundaries (see Section 7.2). Finally, it is shown that any net with boundaries with vacuous left interface can be encoded as a BI(P) system (see Section 7.3).

7.1 BI(P): BIP Without Priorities

This section reports on the formal definition of BIP as presented in [6]. Since we disregard priorities, we call BI(P) the framework presented here.

Given a set of ports P, an *interaction* over P is a non-empty subset $a \subseteq P$. We write an interaction $\{p_1, p_2, \ldots, p_n\}$ as $p_1 p_2 \ldots p_n$ and $a \downarrow_{P_i}$ for the projection of an interaction $a \subseteq P$ over the set of ports $P_i \subseteq P$, i.e., $a \downarrow_{P_i} = a \cap P_i$. Projection extends to sets of interactions by $\gamma \downarrow_P = \{a \downarrow_P \mid a \in \gamma \wedge a \downarrow_P \neq \varnothing\}$.

Definition 8 (Component). *A component $B = (Q, P, \to)$ is a triple where Q is a set of states, P is a set of ports, and $\to \subseteq Q \times 2^P \times Q$ is the set of transitions.*

As usual, we write $q \xrightarrow{a} q'$ to denote the transition $(q, a, q') \in \to$. We let q_a_q' be the *name* of the transition $q \xrightarrow{a} q'$. Given a transition $t = q\_a\_q'$, we let $°t$, $t°$ and $\lambda(t)$ denote respectively its source q, its target q' and its label a. An interaction a is enabled in q, denoted $q \xrightarrow{a}$, iff there exists q' s.t. $q \xrightarrow{a} q'$. By abusing notation, we will also write $q \xrightarrow{\varnothing} q$ for any q.

Definition 9 (BI(P) system). *A BI(P) system $BS = \gamma(B_1, \ldots, B_n)$ is the composition of a finite set $\{B_i\}_{i=1}^n$ of transitions systems $B_i = (Q_i, P_i, \to_i)$*

such that their sets of ports are pairwise disjoint, i.e., $P_i \cap P_j = \varnothing$ for $i \neq j$ parameterized by a set $\gamma \subset 2^P$ of interactions over the set of ports $P = \biguplus_{i=1}^n P_i$. We call P the underlying set of ports of BS, written $\iota(BS)$.

The semantics of a BI(P) system $\gamma(B_1, \ldots, B_n)$ is given by the transition system $(Q, P, \to_\gamma)$, where $Q = \Pi_i Q_i$, $P = \biguplus_{i=1}^n P_i$ and $\to_\gamma \subseteq Q \times 2^P \times Q$ is the least set of transitions satisfying the following inference rule

$$\frac{a \in \gamma \qquad \forall i \in 1..n : q_i \xrightarrow{a \downarrow P_i} q_i'}{(q_1, \ldots, q_n) \xrightarrow{a}_\gamma (q_1', \ldots, q_n')}$$

Definition 10 (Coherent interaction extension). *A set of interactions γ' is a coherent extension of γ over the set of ports P, written $\gamma \rhd_P \gamma'$, iff $\gamma' \downarrow_P \subseteq \gamma$.*

The idea underlying coherent extension is that the extended set of interactions γ' does not allow more interactions (in P) than those specified by γ.

Definition 11 (cBI(P) system). *A composite BI(P) system C, cBI(P) for short, is either a BI(P) system $\gamma(B_1, \ldots, B_n)$ or a composition $\gamma(C_1, \ldots, C_n)$ where $\{C_i = \gamma_i(C_{i,1}, \ldots, C_{i,n_i})\}_{i=1}^n$ is a family of cBI(P) systems such that their sets of underlying ports are pairwise disjoint, i.e., $\iota(C_i) \cap \iota(C_j) = \varnothing$ for $i \neq j$, and γ a set of interactions over $\biguplus_{i=1}^n \iota(C_i)$ s.t. $\gamma_i \rhd_{\iota(C_i)} \gamma$.*

The semantics of cBI(P) systems is defined analogously to that of BI(P) systems by viewing each subsystem as a component. Next result states that any BI(P) system can be seen as a cBI(P) system of exactly two components. We will use this property when defining the compositional encoding of BI(P) systems.

Lemma 1. *Let $BS = \gamma(B_1, \ldots, B_n)$ be a BI(P) system. Then, for any $i < n$, BS is bisimilar to the cBI(P) system $C = \gamma(\gamma \downarrow_{P_{1..i}} (B_1, \ldots, B_i), \gamma \downarrow_{P \setminus P_{1..i}} (B_{i+1}, \ldots, B_n))$ where $P = \iota(BS)$ and $P_{1..i} = \biguplus_{j \leq i} \iota(B_j)$.*

7.2 Structural Mapping from BI(P) to Nets with Boundaries

Given a finite set S with $k = |S|$, we use w_S to denote an injective function $w_S : S \to \underline{k}$ that orders elements of S. By abuse of notation, we write also w_S to denote its extension $w_S : 2^S \to 2^{\underline{k}}$.

Definition 12. *Let $B = (Q, P, \to)$ be a transition system. The corresponding net with boundaries $[\![B]\!] : 0 \to |P|$ is $[\![B]\!] = (Q, T, {}^\circ-, -^\circ, {}^\bullet-, -^\bullet)$ where:*

- $T = \{q\_a\_q' \mid q \xrightarrow{a} q'\}$.
- ${}^\circ(q\_a\_q') = \{q\}$ and $(q\_a\_q')^\circ = \{q'\}$.
- ${}^\bullet(q\_a\_q') = \varnothing$ and $(q\_a\_q')^\bullet = w_P(a)$.

Lemma 2. *Let $B = (Q, P, \to)$ be a transition system. Then, $q \xrightarrow{a} q'$ if and only if $([\![B]\!], \{q\}) \xrightarrow[\ulcorner w_P(a) \urcorner]{} ([\![B]\!], \{q'\})$.*

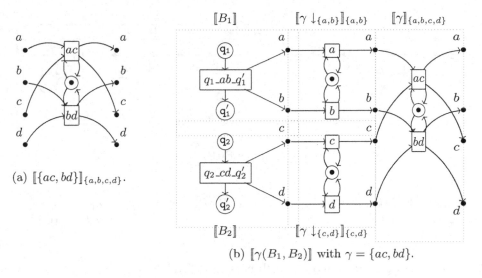

(a) $[\![\{ac, bd\}]\!]_{\{a,b,c,d\}}$.

(b) $[\![\gamma(B_1, B_2)]\!]$ with $\gamma = \{ac, bd\}$.

Fig. 10. Compositional encoding

Next definition introduces the encoding of a set of synchronizations glueing components as a marked net with boundaries.

Definition 13. *Let γ be a set of synchronizations over P. The corresponding marked net with boundaries $[\![\gamma]\!]_P : |P| \to |P|$ is $(\{P_\gamma\}, \gamma, {}^\circ-, -^\circ, {}^\bullet-, -^\bullet, \{P_\gamma\})$ with: ${}^\circ a = a^\circ = \{P_\gamma\}$ and ${}^\bullet a = a^\bullet = w_P(a)$.*

Note that the place P_γ guarantees that all interactions are mutually exclusive.

Example 5. Consider the set of interactions $\gamma = \{ac, bd\}$ and assume $w_{\{a,b,c,d\}}$ coincides with alphabetical order. The corresponding net is shown in Fig. 10(a).

Lemma 3. $[\![\gamma]\!]_P \xrightarrow[\ulcorner w_P(a)\urcorner]{\ulcorner w_P(a)\urcorner} [\![\gamma]\!]_P$ *iff $a \in \gamma$.*

Next definition introduces the compositional encoding of BI(P) systems.

Definition 14. *Let $C = \gamma(C_1, \ldots, C_n)$ be a cBI(P) system. The net with boundaries $[\![C]\!] : 0 \to |P|$ with $P = \iota(C)$ is recursively defined as*

$$[\![\gamma(C_1)]\!] = [\![C_1]\!]; [\![\gamma]\!]_P$$
$$[\![\gamma(C_1, \ldots, C_n)]\!] = (\gamma \downarrow_{\iota(C_1)} [\![C_1]\!] \otimes [\![\gamma \downarrow_{P\setminus\iota(C_1)} (C_2, \ldots, C_n)]\!]); [\![\gamma]\!]_P$$

Example 6. Consider the BI(P) system $\{ac, bd\}(B_1, B_2)$ where B_1 has just one transition $q_1 \xrightarrow{ab} q_1'$ and B_2 has only $q_2 \xrightarrow{cd} q_2'$. The encoded net is in Figure 10(b). Note the necessity of considering all transitions in the encoding of $\{ac, bd\}$ to be mutual exclusive. Otherwise, the encoded form will also allow behaviors like $([\![B]\!], \{q_1, q_2\}) \xrightarrow{\ulcorner abcd\urcorner} ([\![B]\!], \{q_1', q_2'\})$, where $abcd \notin \{ac, bd\}$.

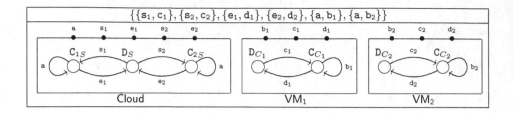

Fig. 11. A simple BI(P) system

Theorem 3. *Let* $C = \gamma(C_1, \ldots, C_n)$ *be a cBI(P) system. Then,* $(q_1, \ldots, q_n) \xrightarrow{a}_\gamma$ $(q_1', \ldots, q_n')$ *iff* $(\llbracket C \rrbracket, \{q_1, \ldots, q_n\}) \xrightarrow[\ulcorner wP(a) \urcorner]{} (\llbracket C \rrbracket, \{q_1', \ldots, q_n'\})$ *with* $P = \iota(C)$.

7.3   Encoding Nets with Boundaries into BI(P)

This section shows that any net with boundaries without left interface can be seen as a BI(P) system consisting on just one component. The correspondence is stated by showing that there exists a straightforward encoding that maps states and transitions of the net to states and transitions of the unique component.

Definition 15. *Let* $N : 0 \to n$ *with* $N = (S, T, {}^\circ-, -^\circ, {}^\bullet-, -^\bullet)$ *be a net with boundaries. Then, the corresponding BI(P) system* $BS_N = \gamma(B)$ *is defined as follows:* $\gamma = 2^{\underline{n}}$ *and* $B = (2^S, 2^{\underline{n}}, \to)$ *with* $\to = \{X \xrightarrow{a} Y \mid (N, X) \xrightarrow[\ulcorner a \urcorner]{} (N, Y)\}$.

Note that $N : 0 \to n$ corresponds to a component that has $2^{\underline{n}}$ ports, i.e., one port for any possible combination of the ports on the interface.

8   Reconfigurable and Dynamic BIP

In order to contribute to the development of a general theory for dynamic connectors, in this section we present two other extensions of the BI(P) framework with different degrees of "dynamism" that allow enhanced conciseness, modularity and expressiveness. A *reconfigurable* BI(P) system allows for the dynamic modification of interactions among components. A *dynamic* BI(P) system supports the runtime creation / elimination of ports and components.

Example 7. Consider the BI(P) system shown in Fig. 11, which contains a cloud manager component Cloud that interacts with two virtual machines VM_1 and VM_2. The Cloud starts a connection with VM_i via the interaction $s_i c_i$. After the session is started, the manager and the clients can interact on ab_i. The session ends when $e_i d_i$ is performed. Note that the manager has dedicated ports (s_i, e_i) for handling the connections of different machines. Next, we introduce two enhancements that allows for a more compact description of this system.

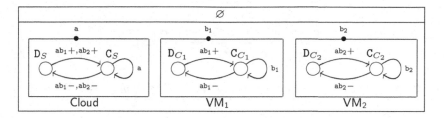

Fig. 12. A simple reconfigurable BI(P) system

8.1   Reconfigurable BI(P)

Our first extension is concerned with the possibility of enabling and disabling specific interactions dynamically. An interaction a can be enabled / disabled when all components involved in the interaction a agree to do so. After a is enabled, it can be used as an ordinary interaction until it gets disabled.

Our first result proves that any reconfigurable BI(P) system is equivalent to an ordinary BI(P) system where a "controller" component is introduced for each interaction that can be added or removed at run-time. Thus, reconfigurable BI(P) only provides a more compact representation of ordinary systems, while ordinary BI(P) representations may require an exponential blow up in the number of controllers (interactions are subsets of ports). The crux of the proof is the fact that the set of controller components can be defined statically.

Transitions in a reconfigurable BI(P) component have a decoration ρ that can be either (i) ϵ for ordinary interactions, (ii) $+$ to add a new interaction, and (iii) $-$ to remove an interaction.

Definition 16 (Reconfigurable component). *Let $\mathcal{P}$ be a set of ports. A reconfigurable component $R = (Q, P, \rightarrowtail)$ is a transition system where Q is a set of states, $P \subset \mathcal{P}$ is a finite set of ports, and $\rightarrowtail \subseteq Q \times 2^{P} \times \{+, -, \epsilon\} \times Q$ is the set of labelled transitions such that $(q, a, \epsilon, q') \in \rightarrowtail$ implies $a \in 2^{P}$ and $(q, a, \rho, q') \in \rightarrowtail$ with $\rho \in \{+, -\}$ implies $a \cap P \neq \varnothing$.*

We write $q \xrightarrow{a\rho} q'$ for $(q, a, \rho, q') \in \rightarrowtail$. We say that a is enabled in q, denoted $q \xrightarrow{a}$, iff there exists q' s.t. $q \xrightarrow{a\epsilon} q'$. We assume that for all q, q' it holds $q \xrightarrow{\varnothing\epsilon} q'$ iff $q = q'$. Given a set of ports P, we write $a \# P$ if $a \cap P = \varnothing$.

Definition 17 (Reconfigurable BI(P) system). *A reconfigurable BI(P) system $RS = \gamma(R_1, \ldots, R_n)$ is the composition of a finite set $\{R_i\}_{i=1}^{n}$ of reconfigurable components $R_i = (Q_i, P_i, \rightarrowtail_i)$ such that their sets of ports are pairwise disjoint, i.e., $P_i \cap P_j = \varnothing$ for $i \neq j$, parametrized by a set $\gamma \subset 2^{\mathcal{P}}$. We call $P = \biguplus_{i=1}^{n} P_i$ the underlying set of ports of RS, written $\iota(RS)$.*

Example 8. The scenario in Example 7 can be modeled as the reconfigurable BI(P) system in Fig. 12, where for simplicity we represented multiple transitions

$$\frac{a \in \gamma \quad \forall i \in 1..n : q_i \xrightarrow{\ a \downarrow_{P_i} \epsilon\ } q_i'}{\gamma(q_1, \ldots, q_n) \xrightarrow{\ a\ } \gamma(q_1', \ldots, q_n')} [\text{INT}]$$

$$\frac{a \in 2^P \smallsetminus \gamma \quad \neg(a\#P_i) \implies q_i \xrightarrow{\ a+\ } q_i' \quad (a\#P_i) \implies q_i' = q_i \quad \gamma' = \gamma \cup \{a\}}{\gamma(q_1, \ldots, q_n) \xrightarrow{\ a\ } \gamma'(q_1', \ldots, q_n')} [\text{ADD}]$$

$$\frac{a \in \gamma \quad \neg(a\#P_i) \implies q_i \xrightarrow{\ a-\ } q_i' \quad (a\#P_i) \implies q_i' = q_i \quad \gamma' = \gamma \smallsetminus \{a\}}{\gamma(q_1, \ldots, q_n) \xrightarrow{\ a\ } \gamma'(q_1', \ldots, q_n')} [\text{DEL}]$$

Fig. 13. Operational semantics of reconfigurable BI(P) systems

with the same source and target (but different labels) with a single arc with multiple labels (e.g., $\text{ab}_1+, \text{ab}_2+$). Now, the transitions ab_i+ and ab_i- respectively allow for the dynamic enabling / disabling of the interaction ab_i.

The semantics of a reconfigurable BI(P) system $RS = \gamma(R_1, \ldots, R_n)$ with $\iota(RS) = P$ and $\gamma \subseteq 2^P$ is given by the transition system $(Q, \rightarrow)$ where

- $Q = 2^P \times \Pi_i Q_i$ (we write $\gamma(q_1, \ldots, q_n)$ for $\langle \gamma, \langle q_1, \ldots, q_n \rangle \rangle \in Q$), and
- $\rightarrow \subseteq Q \times 2^P \times Q$ is the least set of transitions given by the rules in Fig. 13.

Each state of the transition system keeps, not only the states of all components but also, the set γ of all enabled interactions. Rule [INT] stands for ordinary interactions. Rule [ADD] accounts for the addition of a new global interaction a to the set of enabled interactions γ. Rule [DEL] specifies the removal of an enabled interaction and is analogous to [ADD].

Example 9. Consider the reconfigurable BI(P) system in Example 8. The initial state in which no connection has been established is given by the term $\varnothing(D_S, D_{C_1}, D_{C_2})$. In this state, the system can start a session between the Cloud and either VM_1 or VM_2. Assuming that a session with VM_1 is established, then the system can move as follows (where $s = \{\text{ab}_1\}(C_S, C_{C_1}, D_{C_2})$):

$$\varnothing(D_S, D_{C_1}, D_{C_2}) \xrightarrow{\ \text{ab}_1+\ } s \xrightarrow{\ \text{ab}_1\ } \ldots \xrightarrow{\ \text{ab}_1\ } s \xrightarrow{\ \text{ab}_1-\ } \varnothing(D_S, D_{C_1}, D_{C_2})$$

Let $\mathcal{R}(R) = \{a \mid (q, a, \rho, q') \in \rightarrow \text{ and } \rho \neq \epsilon\}$ be the set of reconfigurable interactions of a reconfigurable component $R = (Q, P, \rightarrow)$. For any $a \in \mathcal{R}(R)$ we add two additional ports $\widetilde{a}^R+$ and $\widetilde{a}^R-$ in the encoded component, where $\widetilde{a}^R = (a \cap P) \cup \{\widetilde{p} \mid p \in a \smallsetminus P\}$ (decorations $\widetilde{\ }$ are needed to guarantee uniqueness of ports in different components). We let $\widetilde{\mathcal{R}(R)} = \{\widetilde{a}^R \mid a \in \mathcal{R}(R)\}$. For example, $\widetilde{\mathcal{R}(\text{Cloud})} = \{\widetilde{\text{ab}}_1, \widetilde{\text{ab}}_2\}$. The function $\mathcal{R}(\cdot)$ is extended to reconfigurable BI(P) systems $RS = \gamma(R_1, \ldots, R_n)$ by letting $\mathcal{R}(RS) = \bigcup_{1 \leq i \leq n} \mathcal{R}(R_i)$.

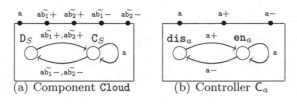

(a) Component Cloud   (b) Controller C_a

Fig. 14. Encoding reconfigurable BI(P) in BI(P)

Definition 18. *Let $R = (Q, P, \twoheadrightarrow)$ be a reconfigurable component. The corresponding BI(P) component $[\![R]\!]$ is $(Q, P \cup (\widetilde{\mathcal{R}(R)} \times \{+, -\}), \to)$ with $(q, a, q') \in \to$ iff $(q, a, \epsilon, q') \in \twoheadrightarrow$ or $(q, a', \rho, q') \in \twoheadrightarrow$, $\rho \neq \epsilon$ and $a = (\widetilde{a'}^R, \rho)$.*

Figure 14(a) shows the BI(P) component corresponding to the reconfigurable component `Cloud` depicted in Fig. 12.

Next, we associate any reconfigurable interaction a with a new BI(P) component $C_a = (Q_{C_a}, P_{C_a}, \to)$, called *controller*: it models the dynamic enabling / disabling of a (see Fig. 14(b)).

Definition 19. *Let $RS = \gamma(R_1, \ldots, R_n)$ be a reconfigurable BI(P) system with $\mathcal{R}(RS) = \{a_0, \ldots, a_j\}$. The corresponding BI(P) system is defined by*

$$[\![\gamma(R_1, \ldots, R_n)]\!] = [\![\gamma]\!]([\![R_1]\!], \ldots, [\![R_n]\!], C_{a_0}, \ldots, C_{a_j})$$

where $[\![\gamma]\!] = (\gamma \smallsetminus \mathcal{R}(RS)) \cup (\bigcup_{a \in \mathcal{R}(RS), \rho \in \{\epsilon, +, -\}} \{[\![a]\!]_\rho\})$ with

$$[\![a]\!]_\rho = \begin{cases} \{a\rho\} \cup \{\widetilde{a}^{R_i}\rho \mid 1 \leq i \leq n \text{ and } a \in \mathcal{R}(R_i)\} & \text{if } \rho \in \{+, -\} \\ \{a\} \cup \{p \mid 1 \leq i \leq n \text{ and } p \in a \downarrow_{P_i}\} & \text{if } \rho = \epsilon \end{cases}$$

Finally, any state $\gamma(q_1, \ldots, q_n)$ of RS is associated with a state $[\![\gamma(q_1, \ldots, q_n)]\!] = (q_1, \ldots, q_n, s_0, \ldots, s_j)$ of $[\![RS]\!]$ where $s_i = en_{a_i}$ if $a_i \in \gamma$, and $s_i = dis_{a_i}$ if $a_i \notin \gamma$.

Example 10. The reconfigurable system introduced in Example 8 is encoded as the BI(P) system shown in Fig. 15.

Theorem 4. *Given $RS = \gamma(R_1, \ldots, R_n)$, we have $\gamma(q_1, \ldots, q_n) \xrightarrow{a} \gamma'(q_1', \ldots, q_n')$ iff $\exists b \in \{a, \gamma_a, \gamma_{a+}, \gamma_{a-}\}$ s.t. $[\![\gamma(q_1, \ldots, q_n)]\!] \xrightarrow{b}_{[\![\gamma]\!]} [\![\gamma'(q_1', \ldots, q_n')]\!]$.*

8.2 Dynamic BI(P)

In this section we further extend BI(P) by allowing the dynamic replication of components. In the case of dynamic BI(P) we can define systems that are possibly infinite state and more expressive than ordinary BI(P) systems. We take as an inspiring example the notion of correlation sets in web services [40,23]. In these cases, when a service call is made, then an instance of the session is initialized with suitable correlation data (e.g., specific message fields) gathered

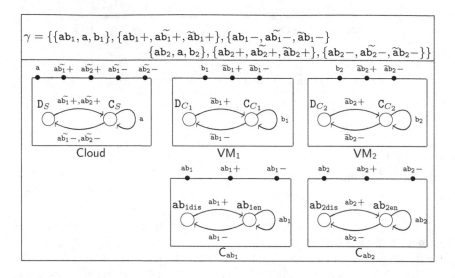

Fig. 15. A simple reconfigurable BI(P) system encoded in ordinary BI(P)

for the partner. To this aim we exploit *colored* tokens, where the colors are freshly created session identifiers. This way, we do not need to replicate the ports and structure of components, instead we keep all the coloured tokens within the same instance of the component, then it can happen that two or more coloured tokens mark the same state at the same time. An interaction is possible only when all the involved components carry correlated colors, i.e., identifiers for the same session. In fact, while session identifiers are created locally to each component (e.g., s_1 in a first component and s_2 in a second component), a new interaction is also created that correlates them (e.g., $s_1 s_2$). Possibly many sessions are opened with the same partners involved. In subsequent interactions, correlation tokens are then exploited to identify the session that interaction is part of. When the session ends, the correlation tokens are discarded. At the beginning, when the system is initialized, we assume that all components carry correlated tokens, i.e., that they are all part of the same session. Notably, reachability is decidable for dynamic BI(P). This is achieved by tracing a correspondence between dynamic BI(P) systems and Place/Transition (P/T) Petri nets.

We assume an infinite set of port names $\mathcal{P}$ ranged over by $a, b, \ldots$, an infinite set of port variable names $\mathcal{X}$ ranged over by $x, y, \ldots$, and an infinite set of state names $\mathcal{Q}$ ranged over by $p, q, \ldots$, such that $\mathcal{P}$, $\mathcal{Q}$ and $\mathcal{X}$ pairwise disjoint. As in general an interaction is related to a specific session, we sometimes decorate ports and interactions with specific correlation tokens as their subscripts. For example, for $a = ab$ we write a_c for $a_c b_c$.

Definition 20 (Dynamic component). *A dynamic component is a tuple $D = (Q, P, \rightarrow)$ where $Q \subset \mathcal{Q}$ is a set of places, $P \subset \mathcal{P}$ is a set of ports, and $\rightarrow$ is a finite set of transitions, each having one of the following shapes:*

$$\frac{q(x) \xrightarrow{\alpha} q'(x) \qquad a \in \delta(P) \qquad \alpha \in \{a_x, x\}}{\langle P, q(a) \oplus f \rangle \xrightarrow{\alpha[x/a]} \langle P, q'(a) \oplus f \rangle} [\text{CINT}]$$

$$\frac{q(x) \xrightarrow{a_x y+} q'(x) \oplus q''(y) \qquad a \in \delta(P) \qquad b \notin P}{\langle P, q(a) \oplus f \rangle \xrightarrow{a_a b+} \langle P \cup \{b\} \cup P_b, q'(a) \oplus q''(b) \oplus f \rangle} [\text{COPEN}]$$

$$\frac{q(x) \xrightarrow{x-} \varnothing \qquad a \in \delta(P)}{\langle P, q(a) \oplus f \rangle \xrightarrow{a-} \langle P \smallsetminus (\{a\} \cup P_a), f \rangle} [\text{CCLOSE}]$$

Fig. 16. Operational semantics of dynamic components

- $q(x) \xrightarrow{a_x} q'(x)$, i.e., (a coloured version of) a BI(P) transition;
- $q(x) \xrightarrow{a_x y+} q'(x) \oplus q''(y)$, i.e., a port creation;
- $q(x) \xrightarrow{x-} \varnothing$, i.e., a port removal;
- $q(x) \xrightarrow{x} q'(x)$, i.e., an interaction over a dynamically created port.

Ports that appear in labels of the form a_x are parametric to the correlation token and are called *static* ports; the other ports are called *dynamic*. We assume static ports cannot be used as correlation tokens. In the following we denote by P_x the set of static ports of P, by P_a the set of static ports in P parametrized by the token a and by $\delta(P)$ the set of dynamic ports. For example, if $P = \{a, b\}$ with a static and b dynamic, then $P_c = \{a_c\}$. Note that if all transitions have the form $q(x) \xrightarrow{a_x} q'(x)$ then D is essentially an ordinary BI(P) component.

The current state of a dynamic component $D = (Q, \mathcal{P}, \rightarrow)$ takes the form $\langle P, f \rangle$ with $P \subset \mathcal{P}$ defining the current ports of the component (that includes opened sessions) and $f : Q \rightarrow 2^P$ such that $f(q_1) \cap f(q_2) = \varnothing$ for $q_1 \neq q_2$. The function f represents the current internal state of the component replicas. For example, if $f(q) = \{a, b\}$ then there are two replicas of the component, one involved in session a and one in b both with current state q. The condition $f(q_1) \cap f(q_2) = \varnothing$ for $q_1 \neq q_2$ guarantees that each replica is associated with a different session and that to each session corresponds exactly one state.

As a matter of notation we denote $f \oplus p(a)$ the function defined as

$$(f \oplus p(a))(q) = \begin{cases} f(q) & \text{if } q \neq p \\ f(q) \cup \{a\} & \text{if } q = p \end{cases}$$

Remark 1. Initially there is only one session opened for each component. To shorten the notation but without loss of generality, we shall assume that such initial session identifier is void, i.e. $f(p) = \{\bullet\}$ and omit the corresponding port $\bullet$ from the drawing of components (in the initial and subsequent states).

The operational semantics of components is given by the three rules in Fig. 16. The first rule ([CINT]) deals with both: i) the case of an ordinary interaction a_a (here coloured by the token a); and ii) the case of a dynamic interaction over the session associated with a. The rule ([COPEN]) is the most complex one, as

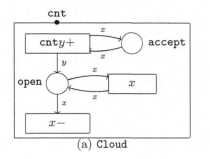
(a) Cloud

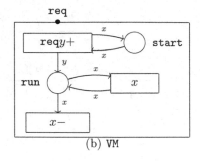
(b) VM

Fig. 17. Two dynamic components

it deals with component spawning and port creation. Here the freshly created session identifier is b, which is then used as a fresh dynamic port, together with suitable instances P_b of the static ports of the component. The spawned instance of the component has initial state $q''(b)$. Ports in P_b will allow the spawned instance of the component to interact on static ports with some other spawned components that are part of the same session. Moreover, the spawned instance of the component will be able to interact on the port b by synchronizing with all the other spawned components that are part of the same session. Note that although the token b has been created within the session a, such information is not maintained in the state, i.e., sessions a and b will run independently. Finally, the rule ([CCLOSE]) deals with session closure, where the token a and all the ports $\{a\} \cup P_a$ associated with the closed session a are discarded.

Example 11. Consider a cloud manager that interacts with a possibly unbounded number of clients. This behaviour can be modeled as the component depicted in Fig. 17(a), where arcs are decorated with the colors of the involved tokens. (The analogous client is in Fig. 17(b).) The component in Fig. 17(a) has one static port cnt, two places accept and open with the following three transitions:

- $t_0 = \texttt{accept}(x) \xrightarrow{\texttt{cnt}_x\, y+} \texttt{accept}(x) \oplus \texttt{open}(y)$: the action cnt opens a new session (whose id is stored in place open).
- $t_1 = \texttt{open}(x) \xrightarrow{x} \texttt{open}(x)$: for any open session, an action on the corresponding dynamic port can be repeatedly performed.
- $t_2 = \texttt{open}(x) \xrightarrow{x-} \varnothing$: An already opened session x is closed by synchronizing all participants to that session on the interaction $x-$.

Definition 21 (Dynamic BI(P) system). *A dynamic BI(P) system $DS = \gamma(D_1, \ldots, D_n)$ is the composition of a finite set $\{D_i\}_{i=1}^{n}$ of dynamic BI(P) components $D_i = (Q_i, P_i, \rightarrow_i)$ such that their sets of ports are pairwise disjoint, parametrized by a set $\gamma \subset 2^P$ of interactions over the set of ports $P = \biguplus_{i=1}^{n} P_i$.*

Without loss of generality, we assume that for any $a \in \gamma$ it is either the case that a contains static ports only and we call it *static* or it contains no static port

$$\frac{a \in \gamma \qquad \forall i.s_i \xrightarrow{a \downarrow P_i} s_i'}{\gamma(s_1, \ldots, s_n) \xrightarrow{a} \gamma(s_1', \ldots, s_n')} \text{[SINT]}$$

$$\frac{\begin{array}{c} a \in \gamma \quad i \in I(a) \implies s_i \xrightarrow{a \downarrow P_i \mathbf{b}_i +} s_i' \quad \mathbf{b}_i \text{ fresh} \quad \sigma = [^{ids_i(a)}/_{\mathbf{b}_i}]_{i \in I(a)} \\ i \in \overline{I(a)} \implies s_i' = s_i \qquad b = \{\mathbf{b}_i\}_{i \in I(a)} \end{array}}{\gamma(s_1, \ldots, s_n) \xrightarrow{a} (\gamma \cup \{b\} \cup \gamma_\sigma)(s_1', \ldots, s_n')} \text{[SOPEN]}$$

$$\frac{a \in \gamma \quad i \in I(a) \implies s_i \xrightarrow{a \downarrow P_i -} s_i' \quad i \in \overline{I(a)} \implies s_i' = s_i}{\gamma(s_1, \ldots, s_n) \xrightarrow{a} (\gamma \ominus a)(s_1', \ldots, s_n')} \text{[SCLOSE]}$$

Fig. 18. Operational semantics of dynamic BI(P) systems

at all and we call it *dynamic*. Moreover, if $a \downarrow_{P_i}$ is made of static ports, then $a \downarrow_{P_i} = a_{\mathbf{a}_i}'$ for some a' and $\mathbf{a}_i \in P_i$, i.e., all static ports in $a \downarrow_{P_i}$ are parametrized by the same session identifier $\mathbf{a}_i$. In such case, we let $ids_i(a)$ denote $\mathbf{a}_i$ We write $I(a)$ to denote the set of indices $\{i \mid \neg(a\#P_i)\}$ of the components involved in a and $\overline{I(a)}$ to denote its complement $[1, n] \smallsetminus I(a) = \{i \mid a\#P_i\}$. If a is static, we denote by $ids(a)$ the set $\{ids_i(a) \mid i \in I(a)\}$, otherwise we let $ids(a) = \varnothing$.

Given a substitution $\sigma = [^{\mathbf{a}_i}/_{\mathbf{b}_i}]_{i \in I}$ and a static interaction $a \in \gamma$ such that $ids(a) \subseteq \{\mathbf{a}_i\}_{i \in I}$ we write a_σ for the interaction obtained by replacing in a each parameter $\mathbf{a}_i$ by the corresponding parameter $\mathbf{b}_i$. Moreover, we write γ_σ for the set of renamed static interactions $\{a_\sigma \mid a \in \gamma \wedge ids(a) \subseteq \{\mathbf{a}_i\}_{i \in I}\}$. Finally, given a dynamic interaction a we let $\gamma \ominus a = \{a' \in \gamma \mid a' \cap a = \varnothing \wedge ids(a') \cap a = \varnothing\}$ be the set of interactions in γ where the ports in a do not appear.

Let s_i range over $2^{P_i} \times P_i^{Q_i}$ representing a generic state of the component D_i. The semantics of a dynamic BI(P) system $\gamma(D_1, \ldots, D_n)$ is defined by the three rules in Fig. 18. Rule [SINT] deals with the usual synchronization. Rule [SOPEN] represents the opening of a session: local fresh session identifiers $\mathbf{b}_i$ are created (that are used in s_i') and the set of interactions is enriched with the new session synchronization $b = \{\mathbf{b}_i\}_{i \in I(a)}$ and a renamed instance γ_σ of the static interactions in γ (for the new session). Finally, rule [SCLOSE] deals with the synchronized closing of a session: note that the set of interactions is updated by removing the interactions concerned with the closed session.

Example 12. Consider the dynamic BI(P) components introduced in Example 11. We illustrate one possible run of the server with two clients in Fig. 19. Roughly, it corresponds to the series of transitions in Fig. 20, where $\gamma, \gamma', \gamma''$ are the ones indicated in Fig. 19. Note that suitable replicas $\mathtt{cnt_v}$, $\mathtt{cnt_w}$, $\mathtt{req_{1m}}$, $\mathtt{req_{2n}}$ of the static ports $\mathtt{cnt}$, $\mathtt{req_1}$, $\mathtt{req_2}$ have been created locally to each component, and that the set of interactions has been enriched with suitable replicas $\mathtt{cnt_v\,req_{1m}}$ and $\mathtt{cnt_w\,req_{2n}}$ of the static interactions $\mathtt{cnt\,req_1}$ and $\mathtt{cnt\,req_2}$ together with freshly created dynamic interactions $\mathtt{v\,m}$ and $\mathtt{w\,n}$. Let s denote the last state reached. Then, the server can interact with the clients by performing the inter-

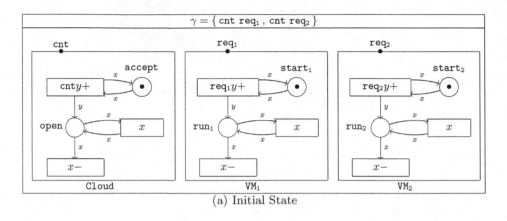

(a) Initial State

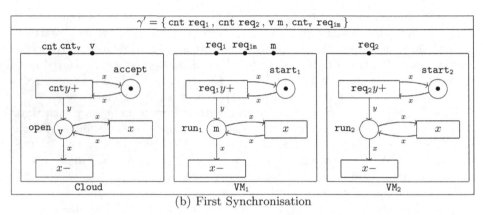

(b) First Synchronisation

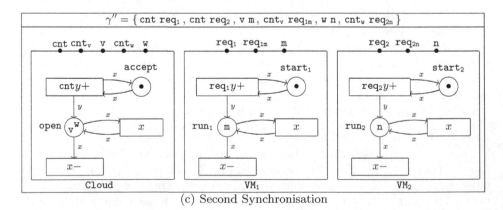

(c) Second Synchronisation

Fig. 19. A run of the server with two clients

$$\gamma \left(\begin{array}{l} \langle\{\texttt{cnt}\}, \texttt{accept}(\bullet)\rangle, \\ \langle\{\texttt{req}_1\}, \texttt{start}_1(\bullet)\rangle, \\ \langle\{\texttt{req}_2\}, \texttt{start}_2(\bullet)\rangle \end{array} \right) \xrightarrow{\texttt{cnt req}_1} \gamma' \left(\begin{array}{l} \langle\{\texttt{cnt}, \texttt{cnt}_v, v\}, \texttt{accept}(\bullet) \oplus \texttt{open}(v)\rangle, \\ \langle\{\texttt{req}_1, \texttt{req}_{1m}, m\}, \texttt{start}_1(\bullet) \oplus \texttt{run}_1(m)\rangle, \\ \langle\{\texttt{req}_2\}, \texttt{start}_2(\bullet)\rangle \end{array} \right)$$

$$\xrightarrow{\texttt{cnt req}_2} \gamma'' \left(\begin{array}{l} \langle\{\texttt{cnt}, \texttt{cnt}_v, v, \texttt{cnt}_w, w\}, \texttt{accept}(\bullet) \oplus \texttt{open}(v) \oplus \texttt{open}(w)\rangle, \\ \langle\{\texttt{req}_1, \texttt{req}_{1m}, m\}, \texttt{start}_1(\bullet) \oplus \texttt{run}_1(m)\rangle, \\ \langle\{\texttt{req}_2, \texttt{req}_{2n}, n\}, \texttt{start}_2(\bullet) \oplus \texttt{run}_2(n)\rangle \end{array} \right)$$

Fig. 20. Transitions representing a run of the server with two clients

actions vm and wn as many times as needed, with the system remaining in the same state s: $s \xrightarrow{v\,m} s \xrightarrow{w\,n} s \cdots$ Finally, we illustrate the case when the session between the server and the second client is closed:

$$s \xrightarrow{w\,n} \gamma' \left(\begin{array}{l} \langle\{\texttt{cnt}, \texttt{cnt}_v, v\}, \texttt{accept}(\bullet) \oplus \texttt{open}(v)\rangle, \\ \langle\{\texttt{req}_1, \texttt{req}_{1m}, m\}, \texttt{start}_1(\bullet) \oplus \texttt{run}_1(m)\rangle, \\ \langle\{\texttt{req}_2\}, \texttt{start}_2(\bullet)\rangle \end{array} \right)$$

The above transition is obtained by combining a closing transitions of the server (label $w-$) with a closing transition of the second client (label $n-$).

Unlike reconfigurable BI(P) systems, dynamic BI(P) systems are strictly more expressive than ordinary BI(P) systems. This can be immediately seen by noting that BI(P) systems are finite state, while this is not the case for dynamic BI(P) systems (see, e.g., Example 12).

In [12] we have defined a correspondence between dynamic BI(P) systems and Place/Transition Petri nets. This is interesting because: i) it shows that properties like reachability remains decidable and ii) it draws a nice analogy with the correspondence between ordinary BI(P) systems and Petri nets in [10].

Roughly, given a dynamic BI(P) system $DS = \gamma(D_1, ..., D_n)$ we define a P/T Petri net $N(DS)$ whose places are tuples of states from components $D_1, ..., D_n$ and whose transitions represent the possible interactions. Note that $N(DS)$ is determined statically and although it may contain more places and transitions than those strictly necessary, it is finite.

Another dynamic extension of BIP is Dy-BIP [7]. With respect to Dy-BIP, we think dynamic BI(P) has some advantages. While Dy-BIP imposes ad hoc restrictions (e.g., transitions of atomic components are labelled with only one single local port instead of a set of local ports) and extensions (e.g. transitions of atomic components are decorated with non-local architecture constraints that may involve port names of other components, thus compromising the modularity of the specification and moreover history variables are introduced to store the identity of interacting components), this is not necessary for dynamic BI(P). Furthermore, the number of component instances cannot change in Dy-BIP, contrary to dynamic BI(P). Finally, the definition of Dy-BIP systems can be error-prone or lead to incomplete specifications unless the design methodology outlined in [7] is adopted.

9   Concluding Remarks

One of the main limitations of the state-of-the-art theories of component-based system is the lack of a reference paradigm for describing and analyzing their highly dynamic interactions. In this paper we have overviewed some recent proposals for addressing this limitation that emerged within the ASCENS project, i.e., the Network-Conscious pi-calculus and possible BI(P) enhancements.

References

1. Arbab, F.: Reo: a channel-based coordination model for component composition. Math. Struct. in Comp. Sci. 14(3), 329–366 (2004)
2. Arbab, F., Bruni, R., Clarke, D., Lanese, I., Montanari, U.: Tiles for reo. In: Corradini, A., Montanari, U. (eds.) WADT 2008. LNCS, vol. 5486, pp. 37–55. Springer, Heidelberg (2009)
3. Baldan, P., Corradini, A., Ehrig, H., Heckel, R.: Compositional semantics for open Petri nets based on deterministic processes. Mathematical Structures in Computer Science 15(1), 1–35 (2005)
4. Basu, A., Bozga, M., Sifakis, J.: Modeling heterogeneous real-time components in BIP. In: SEFM'06, pp. 3–12. IEEE Computer Society Press, Los Alamitos (2006)
5. Bliudze, S., Sifakis, J.: The algebra of connectors - structuring interaction in BIP. IEEE Trans. Computers 57(10), 1315–1330 (2008)
6. Bliudze, S., Sifakis, J.: Causal semantics for the algebra of connectors. Formal Methods in System Design 36(2), 167–194 (2010)
7. Bozga, M., Jaber, M., Maris, N., Sifakis, J.: Modeling dynamic architectures using Dy-BIP. In: Gschwind, T., De Paoli, F., Gruhn, V., Book, M. (eds.) SC 2012. LNCS, vol. 7306, pp. 1–16. Springer, Heidelberg (2012)
8. Bruni, R.: Tile Logic for Synchronized Rewriting of Concurrent Systems. Ph.D. thesis, Computer Science Department, University of Pisa (1999)
9. Bruni, R., Lanese, I., Montanari, U.: A basic algebra of stateless connectors. Theor. Comput. Sci. 366(1-2), 98–120 (2006)
10. Bruni, R., Melgratti, H., Montanari, U.: Connector algebras, Petri nets, and BIP. In: Clarke, E., Virbitskaite, I., Voronkov, A. (eds.) PSI 2011. LNCS, vol. 7162, pp. 19–38. Springer, Heidelberg (2012)
11. Bruni, R., Melgratti, H., Montanari, U.: A connector algebra for P/T nets interactions. In: Katoen, J.-P., König, B. (eds.) CONCUR 2011 – Concurrency Theory. LNCS, vol. 6901, pp. 312–326. Springer, Heidelberg (2011)
12. Bruni, R., Melgratti, H.C., Montanari, U.: Behaviour, interaction and dynamics. In: Iida, S., Meseguer, J., Ogata, K. (eds.) Specification, Algebra, and Software. LNCS, vol. 8373, pp. 382–401. Springer, Heidelberg (2014)
13. Bruni, R., Melgratti, H.C., Montanari, U., Sobocinski, P.: Connector algebras for C/E and P/T nets' interactions. Logical Methods in Computer Science 9(3) (2013)
14. Bruni, R., Montanari, U.: Dynamic connectors for concurrency. Theor. Comput. Sci. 281(1-2), 131–176 (2002)
15. Campbell, A.T., Katzela, I., Miki, K., Vicente, J.B.: Open signaling for ATM, internet and mobile networks (OPENSIG'98). Computer Communication Review 29(1), 97–108 (1999)

16. Ciancia, V., Kurz, A., Montanari, U.: Families of symmetries as efficient models of resource binding. ENTCS 264(2), 63–81 (2010)
17. Combaz, J., Bensalem, S., Tiezzi, F., Margheri, A., Pugliese, R., Kofron, J.: Correctness of Service Components and Service Component Ensembles. In: Wirsing, M., Hölzl, M., Koch, N., Mayer, P. (eds.) Software Engineering for Collective Autonomic Systems. LNCS, vol. 8998, pp. 107–159. Springer, Heidelberg (2015)
18. Ferrari, G.L., Montanari, U.: Tile formats for located and mobile systems. Inf. Comput. 156(1-2), 173–235 (2000)
19. Ferrari, G.L., Montanari, U., Tuosto, E.: Coalgebraic minimization of HD-automata for the pi-calculus using polymorphic types. Theor. Comput. Sci. 331(2-3), 325–365 (2005)
20. Fiore, M.P., Turi, D.: Semantics of name and value passing. In: LICS 2001, pp. 93–104. IEEE Computer Society Press, Los Alamitos (2001)
21. Gadducci, F., Montanari, U.: The tile model. In: Proof, Language, and Interaction, pp. 133–166. MIT Press, Cambridge (2000)
22. Jongmans, S.-S.T.Q., Arbab, F.: Overview of thirty semantic formalisms for Reo. Scientific Annals of Computer Science 22(1), 201–251 (2012), doi:10.7561/SACS.2012.1.201
23. Lapadula, A., Pugliese, R., Tiezzi, F.: A formal account of WS-BPEL. In: Lea, D., Zavattaro, G. (eds.) COORDINATION 2008. LNCS, vol. 5052, pp. 199–215. Springer, Heidelberg (2008)
24. MacLane, S.: Categories for the Working Mathematician. Springer, Heidelberg (1971)
25. Mayer, P., Velasco, J., Klarl, A., Hennicker, R., Puviani, M., Tiezzi, F., Pugliese, R., Keznikl, J., Bureš, T.: The Autonomic Cloud. In: Wirsing, M., Hölzl, M., Koch, N., Mayer, P. (eds.) Software Engineering for Collective Autonomic Systems. LNCS, vol. 8998, pp. 495–512. Springer, Heidelberg (2015)
26. McKeown, N., Anderson, T., Balakrishnan, H., Parulkar, G.M., Peterson, L.L., Rexford, J., Shenker, S., Turner, J.S.: Openflow: enabling innovation in campus networks. Comput. Commun. Rev. 38(2), 60–74 (2008)
27. Milner, R., Parrow, J., Walker, D.: A calculus of mobile processes, I–II. Inf. Comput. 100(1), 1–77 (1992)
28. Montanari, U., Pistore, M.: Structured coalgebras and minimal hd-automata for the π-calculus. Theor. Comput. Sci. 340(3), 539–576 (2005)
29. Montanari, U., Rossi, F.: Graph rewriting, constraint solving and tiles for coordinating distributed systems. Applied Categorical Structures 7(4), 333–370 (1999)
30. Montanari, U., Sammartino, M.: Network conscious π-calculus: A concurrent semantics. ENTCS 286, 291–306 (2012)
31. Montanari, U., Sammartino, M.: A network-conscious π-calculus and its coalgebraic semantics. Theor. Comput. Sci. 546(0), 188–224 (2014), doi:10.1016/j.tcs.2014.03.009
32. Openflow foundation website, http://www.openflow.org/
33. Perry, D.E., Wolf, E.L.: Foundations for the study of software architecture. ACM SIGSOFT Software Engineering Notes 17, 40–52 (1992)
34. Petri, C.: Kommunikation mit Automaten. Ph.D. thesis, Institut für Instrumentelle Mathematik, Bonn (1962)
35. Rowstron, A.I.T., Druschel, P.: Pastry: Scalable, decentralized object location, and routing for large-scale peer-to-peer systems. In: Middleware, pp. 329–350 (2001)
36. Sammartino, M.: A Network-Aware Process Calculus for Global Computing and its Categorical Framework. Ph.D. thesis, University of Pisa (2013)

37. Sobocinski, P.: A non-interleaving process calculus for multi-party synchronisation. In: ICE'09. EPTCS, vol. 12, pp. 87–98 (2009)
38. Sobociński, P.: Representations of Petri net interactions. In: Gastin, P., Laroussinie, F. (eds.) CONCUR 2010. LNCS, vol. 6269, pp. 554–568. Springer, Heidelberg (2010)
39. Tennenhouse, D.L., Wetherall, D.J.: Towards an active network architecture. Comput. Commun. Rev. 26, 5–18 (1996)
40. Viroli, M.: A core calculus for correlation in orchestration languages. J. Log. Algebr. Program. 70(1), 74–95 (2007)
41. Rekhter, Y.: A border gateway protocol 4 (bgp-4). (March 1995), http://www.ietf.org/rfc/rfc1771.txt

CHAPTER I.3

Correctness of Service Components and Service Component Ensembles*

Jacques Combaz[1], Saddek Bensalem[1], Francesco Tiezzi[2], Andrea Margheri[3], Rosario Pugliese[3], and Jan Kofroň[4]

[1] UJF-Verimag, Grenoble, France
[2] IMT Institute for Advanced Studies Lucca, Italy
[3] Università degli Studi di Firenze, Italy
[4] Charles University, Prague, Czech Republic

Abstract. Nowadays, cyber-physical systems consist of a large and possibly unbounded number of nodes operating in a partially unknown environment to which they need to adapt. They also have strong requirements in terms of performances, resource usage, reliability, or security. To face this inherent complexity it is crucial to develop adequate tools and underlying models to analyze these properties at design time. Proposed models must be able to capture essential aspects of the behavior (e.g. interactions between the components, adaptive behavior, uncertain or changing environments), and the corresponding analysis techniques can only succeed if they exploit as much as possible the specific structure of the considered systems (e.g. large replication of the same component, hierarchical compositions). We consider *qualitative* analyses targeting boolean properties stating that the system behaves without any flaw, as well as *quantitative* analyses that evaluate expected performances according to predefined metrics (energy/memory consumption, average/maximum time to accomplish a task, probability to fulfil a goal, etc.). We also address security specific issues such as control policies and information flow.

Keywords: Formal methods, Verification, Model-Checking

1 Introduction

There are several reasons for checking the design of a system before its real-life deployment. One of them is saving cost and time: finding misconceptions very early in a design flow very often shortens the iterative trial and error process required to obtain the desired properties. For some systems, it is even practically inconceivable to modify them a posteriori (e.g. hardware systems, autonomous rovers for space missions). Formal guarantees can be also required prior to the

---

* This research was supported by the European project IP 257414 (ASCENS).

M. Wirsing et al. (eds.): Collective Autonomic Systems, LNCS 8998, pp. 107–159, 2015.
© Springer International Publishing Switzerland 2015

deployment for safety reasons, e.g. for critical systems. Verification approaches rely on solid mathematical foundations to establish properties of a system at design time. They are model-based, that is, they represent the system (and its environment) using mathematical models. Therefore, they analyze properties under the assumption that the real system behaves according to its model.

System design differs radically from pure software design in that it must account not only for functional requirements but also for extra-functional requirements regarding the use of execution platform resources, such as time, memory, and energy. This is especially true for cyber-physical systems, for which strong requirements in terms of performances, resource usage, reliability, or even security, are considered. Meeting extra-functional requirements needs the evaluation of how design choices affect overall system behavior. It also implies a deep understanding of how components of the system are interrelated, and how they interact with the underlying execution platform. Yet system designers currently lack rigorous techniques for deriving global models of a given system from software specifications and the execution platform. The inherent system complexity, and in particular the number of components they involve, can easily lead to non-tractable models. As a results, one of the main challenges in building system models is not only to come up with faithful representations but also to develop efficient analysis techniques so as to validate system properties. Usually, system properties can be classified into two main categories:

- *qualitative* properties which are boolean properties stating that the system operate without any flaw,
- and *quantitative* properties that refers to the evaluation of system performance according to predefined metrics (energy/memory consumption, average/maximum time to accomplish a task, probability to fulfill a goal, etc.).

Our approach for dealing with qualitative properties is to use so called formal verification techniques, e.g. model-checking [10]. When successful, such techniques provide formal guaranties that the system satisfies the target property, by establishing a mathematical proof of it. However, they often face state-space explosion issues which makes them practically not scalable to large systems [30]. We advocate the use of compositional verification methods, in which global properties of the whole system are established based on local characterizations of its components and their interactions, which avoids building explicitly the composition of components which is the source of the exponential grow of the state-space. They also permit incrementality, that is, to profit from properties established for sub-part of the system when verifying the whole system. For instance, this may avoid to redo from scratch the verification process after adding a few components to an existing system.

Concerning quantitative properties and system performance, one can notice that they are in general strongly related to the environment in which the system is immersed: a design may perform well in some contexts, but poorly in others. As a result, we need models for the environment behavior that can capture a large spectrum of possible situations that the system may face. Including stochasticity in our models permits us to quantify the degrees of likelihood for each scenario. We not only worked on the development of stochastic models and corresponding framework for the evaluation of quantitative properties, but also on their application to several realistic case studies showing their practicability.

Security aspects are addressed specifically according two working directions. To address confidentiality issues we develop a model-driven framework for information flow analysis which is suited for checking *non-interference*, a system property stating that information about higher security levels cannot be inferred from lower security levels. We also propose the framework FACPL for the development and the enforcement of security policies.

The rest of the chapter is structured as follows. Section 2 presents verification techniques having in common a single semantic model and corresponding tool-chain, namely BIP [24]. This includes compositional verification targeting qualitative properties (Section 2.1), statistical model-checking which is suited for quantitative properties (Section 2.2), and information flow analysis for confidentiality properties (Section 2.3). Additional and complementary verification techniques based on alternative models are also presented in Section 3. Finally, Section 4 gives a summary of the contributions of this chapter and provides future working directions.

2   Verification Techniques for BIP Models

In this Section we present three verification techniques developed specifically for BIP models [24]. BIP was the main model considered in the ASCENS project to perform formal verification of systems. A connection between SCEL (used in ASCENS for specifying systems and presented in Chapter I.1 [33]) and BIP has also been made but its presentation is beyond the scope of this chapter.

In BIP there exists a clear separation between computation and coordination (expressed in terms of interactions and priorities), which allows to check safety properties compositionally by a separate analysis of components behavior and system architecture, as explained in Section 2.1. Two extensions of BIP have also been considered for verification of other types of properties: one adds stochasticity in BIP systems for quantitative properties (Section 2.2), the other one assigns security domains for non-interference of the information flow (Section 2.3).

2.1   Compositional Verification

Component-based design confers numerous advantages, in particular, increased productivity through reuse of existing components. Nonetheless, establishing the correctness of ensembles of components remains an open issue. In contrast to other engineering disciplines, software and system engineering badly ensures predictability at design time. Consequently, a posteriori verification as well as empirical validation are essential for ensuring correctness. Monolithic verification [58,31] of component-based systems is a challenging problem. It often requires computing the product of the components by using both interleaving and synchronization. The complexity of the product system is often prohibitive due to state explosion. Compositional methods in verification have been developed to cope with state explosion. Generally based on divide-and-conquer principles, compositional methods attempt to break monolithic verification problems into smaller sub-problems by exploiting either the structure of the system or of the property to verify, or both. Compositional reasoning can be used in different flavors, e.g. deductive verification, assume-guarantee reasoning [53,42,57], contract-based verification [32,47], compositional generation, etc.

In a series of recent works [14,21,16], we proposed novel approaches and the DFINDER tool [19] which rely on compositional generation of invariants for systems described in the BIP framework [24]. We observed that most of the existing work on generating invariants for component-based systems are too general and do not strongly exploit the structure of the system and the algebra that defines the interactions between its components. Moreover, only few attempts have been made for exploiting compositionality principles in timed systems and they remain marginal in the research literature. Our techniques start by building invariants for individual components, which can be done with any existing approach for invariant generation on sequential programs. The novel concept in DFINDER is that the invariant for the overall system is then obtained by glueing this set of individual invariants with another one that is an abstraction of the algebra used to define the interactions between the components. By doing so, one avoids building huge parts of the state-space before generating the invariant. One of the major advantages of our approach is that it allows for the development of incremental techniques such as [16], capable of reusing invariants that have already been computed on subparts of the model. The incremental approach is particularly useful when multiple instances of the same component (atomic or composite) are used in the system. In such cases, it allows to factorize the analysis. Thus, local invariants established on a subpart of the system can be automatically lifted to all similar subparts within the system.

DFINDER originally implements efficient symbolic techniques for computing invariants [19]. It relies on the external third party tools Omega for constraints manipulation, Yices for SAT solving, and JavaBDD for BDD operations. As shown in Figure 1, DFINDER combines several invariants obtained from system components and system architecture, into a global invariant GI for the complete system [20]. Given a target safety property expressed as a predicate Φ on the state of the system (e.g. deadlock freedom is obtained $\Phi = \neg DIS$, where DIS is a predicate characterizing the deadlock states), if the formula $GI \wedge \neg \Phi$ (i.e. $GI \wedge DIS$ for deadlock freedom) is unsatifiable then the system satisfies Φ. In the other case, the solutions denote some suspicious counter examples that can be reused by the tool to automatically refine the analysis.

Regarding verification of timed systems it is generally admitted that the difficulty for using compositional reasoning is inherently due to the synchronous model of time. Time progress hides continuous synchronization of all the components of the system. Getting rid of such synchronization is necessary for analyzing independently different parts of the system (or of the property) but also extremely problematic when attempting to re-compose the partial verification

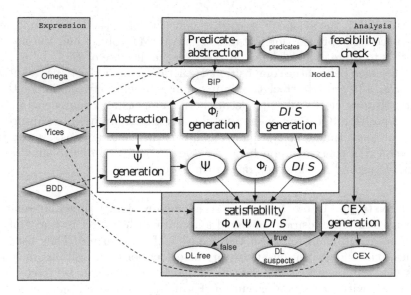

Fig. 1. Structure of the DFINDER tool

results. We developed a novel compositional method for the generation of invariants for timed systems. In contrast to exact reachability analysis, invariants are symbolic approximations of the set of reachable states of the system. The main challenge for timed systems was capture the relations between the local timing of the components induced by their interactions Without them the proposed compositional analysis proved to be too weak for verifying even simple systems. The proposed relations take the shape of equalities between the clocks of components used for expressing their timing constraints. We proved the soundness of the proposed approach, and successfully applied it to academic examples and non trivial case studies. However, the method is not complete, that is, it may be not able to prove certain properties even if they are satisfied by the system.

Our Compositional Verification Method. The compositional method we propose here is based on the verification rule (VR) from [18]. Assume that a system consists of n components B_i interacting by means of an interaction set γ, and that the system property of interest is Φ. If components B_i, respectively interactions γ, can be locally characterized by means of invariants $CI(B_i)$, respectively $II(\gamma)$, and if Φ can be proved to be a logical consequence of the conjunction of the local invariants, then Φ is a global invariant. This is what the rule below synthesizes.

$$\frac{\vdash \bigwedge_i CI(B_i) \wedge II(\gamma) \rightarrow \Phi}{\|_\gamma B_i \models \Box\Phi} \quad \text{(VR)}$$

In the rule (VR), the symbol $\vdash$ is used to underline that the logical implication can be effectively proved (for instance with an SMT solver) and the notation $B \models \Box \Phi$ is to be read as "Φ holds in every reachable state of B".

The key idea behind the compositional generation method is to use additional *history clocks* in order to track the timing of interactions between different components. History clocks allow to decouple the analysis for components and for their composition. On component level, history clocks are used to capture and expose the local timing constraints relevant to their interactions. At composition level, extra constraints on history clocks are enforced due to simultaneity of interactions and to the synchrony of time progress.

Timed Systems. In our framework, the components are timed automata [8] and systems are compositions of timed automata with respect to n-ary interactions. Timed automata represent the behavior of components. They have control locations and transitions between these locations. Transitions may have timing constraints, which are defined on clocks. Clocks can be reset and/or tested along with transition execution. Formally, a timed automaton is a tuple $(L, l_0, A, T, X, \mathsf{tpc})$ where L is a finite set of control locations, l_0 is an initial control location, A is a finite set of actions, X is a finite set of clocks, $T \subseteq L \times (A \times C \times 2^X) \times L$ is finite set of transitions labeled with actions, guards, and a subset of clocks to be reset, and $\mathsf{tpc} : L \to C$ assigns a time progress condition to each location. C is the set of timing constraints which are predicates on the clocks X defined by the following grammar:

$$C ::= true \mid false \mid x \# ct \mid x - y \# ct \mid C \wedge C$$

with $x, y \in X$, $\# \in \{<, \leq, =, \geq, >\}$ and $ct \in \mathbb{Z}$. Time progress conditions are restricted to conjunctions of constraints as $x \leq ct$. For simplicity, we assume that at each location l the guards of the outgoing transitions imply the time progress condition $\mathsf{tpc}(l)$ of l.

A timed automaton is a syntactic structure whose semantics is based on continuous and synchronous time progress. That is, a state is given by a control location paired with real-valued assignments of the clocks. From a given state, a timed automaton can let time progress when permitted by the time progress condition of the corresponding location, or execute a (discrete) transition if its guard evaluates to true. The effect of time progress of $\delta > 0$ is to increase synchronously all the clocks by the real value δ. Executions of transitions are instantaneous, that is, they keep values of clocks unchanged except the ones that are reset (i.e. assigned to 0). Because of their continuous semantics, timed automata have in general infinite state spaces. However, they admit finite symbolic representations of their state spaces called zone graph [7,6,40,66], in which equivalent assignments of clocks are grouped in a single (symbolic) state called *zone* having the shape of timing constraints defined previously. That is, the reachable states of a timed automata corresponds to a finite number of configurations (l_j, ζ_j), $1 \leq j \leq m$, where for all j, l_j is a control location and ζ_j is a timing constraint.

Examples of timed automata are provided by Figure 2. For instance, compo-nents $Worker_i$, $i \in \{1,2\}$, are implemented by similar timed automata, consist-ing of two control locations l_1^i and l_2^i and two transitions: a transition from l_1^i to l_2^i labelled by action b_i and having timing constraint $y \geq 8$, and a transition from l_2^i to l_1^i having action d_i and resetting clock y. By convention non displayed guards of transitions and time progress conditions of locations are *true*.

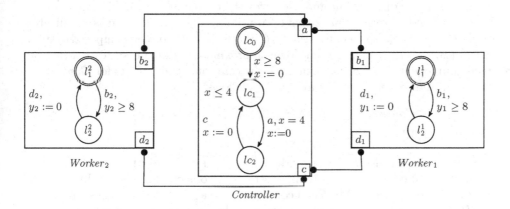

Fig. 2. A composition of three timed automata

In our framework, components interact by means of strong synchroniza-tion between their actions. The synchronizations are specified in the so called *interactions* as sets of actions. An interaction can involve at most one ac-tion of each component. Given n components (i.e. timed automata) $B_i = (L^i, l_0^i, A^i, T^i, X^i, \mathsf{tpc}^i)$, $1 \leq i \leq n$, and a set of interactions γ, we denote by $\gamma(B_1, \ldots, B_n)$ the composition of components B_i with respect to interactions γ. States of the composition $\gamma(B_1, \ldots, B_n)$ are combinations of the states of the components B_i. In $\gamma(B_1, \ldots, B_n)$, a component B_i can execute an action a_i only as part of an interaction $\alpha \in \gamma$, $a_i \in \alpha$, that is, along with the execution of all the actions participating to α, which corresponds to the usual notion of multi-party interaction. Notice that for a component B_i of a composition $\gamma(B_1, \ldots, B_n)$, the application of interactions γ can only restrict its reachable states. That is, the reachable states of B_i when executed in the composition $\gamma(B_1, \ldots, B_n)$ are included in the reachable states of B_i executed alone (i.e. as a single timed au-tomata). This property is essential for building our compositional verification method, presented below.

Components and Interaction Invariants. To give a logical characterization of a system $S = \gamma(B_1, \ldots, B_n)$ we use invariants. An invariant Φ is a state property which holds in every reachable state of S, in symbols, $S \models \Box \Phi$.

Component invariants $CI(B_i)$ characterize the reachable states of components B_i when considered alone. Such invariants can easily be computed from the zones of the corresponding timed automata. More precisely, given the reachable (symbolic) states (l_j, ζ_j), $1 \leq j \leq m$, of component B_i, the invariant for B_i is defined by:

$$\bigvee_{1 \leq j \leq m} l_j \wedge \zeta_j,$$

where we abuse of notation and use l_j for the predicate that holds whenever B_i is at location l_j. Notice that zones ζ_j are timing constraints, that is, predicates on clocks. Notice also that invariants $CI(B_i)$ still hold for the composed system $S = \gamma(B_1, \ldots, B_n)$, but are only over approximations of the states reached by each component B_i in S. For example, the component invariants for *Controller*, *Worker*$_1$ and *Worker*$_2$ of Figure 2 are as follows:

$$CI(Controller) = (lc_0 \wedge x \geq 0) \vee (lc_1 \wedge x \leq 4) \vee (lc_2 \wedge x \geq 0)$$

$$CI(Worker_i) = (l_1^i \wedge y_i \geq 0) \vee (l_2^i \wedge y_i \geq 8).$$

Interaction invariants $II(\gamma)$ are induced by the synchronizations and have the form of global conditions involving control locations of components. In previous work, we have considered boolean conditions [18] as well as linear constraints [15] for $II(\gamma)$. For instance, such invariants exclude configurations such that $lc_1 \wedge l_2^i$, that is, they establish $\neg(lc_1 \wedge (l_2^1 \vee l_2^2))$. Interaction invariants are not the main purpose of this work, interested readers should refer to [18] and [15] for detailed presentations.

A safety property of interest for example of Figure 2 is absence of deadlocks. A necessary condition for deadlock freedom is that a can synchronize with b_1 or b_2 when the controller is at lc_1 and the workers are at l_1^i, that is, $\Phi = lc_1 \wedge l_1^1 \wedge l_1^2 \implies y_1 - x \geq 4 \vee y_2 - x \geq 4$. Even if Φ holds in S, it cannot be proved by applying (VR) using only component invariants $CI(B_i)$ and interaction invariant $II(\gamma)$. A counter example is given by $lc_1 \wedge l_1^1 \wedge l_1^2$ and $x = y_1 = y_2 = 0$, which satisfies the invariant $CI(Controller) \wedge CI(Worker_1) \wedge CI(Worker_2) \wedge II(\gamma)$[5] but violate property Φ, that is, $CI(Controller) \wedge CI(Worker_1) \wedge CI(Worker_2) \wedge II(\gamma) \not\Longrightarrow \Phi$. One problem is that the proposed invariants cannot relate values of clocks of different components according to their synchronizations (e.g. synchronous reset of clocks).

Adding History Clocks. To strengthen computed invariants, we proposed to equip each component B_i (and later, interactions) with *history clocks*: one clock h_{a_i} per action of a_i of B_i. A history clock h_{a_i} is reset on all transitions executing a_i. Notice that since there is no timing constraint involving history clocks, the behavior of the components remain unchanged after the addition of the history clocks, which is shown in [9]. They are only introduced for establishing properties. Each time an interaction $\alpha \in \gamma$ is executed, all the history clocks

---

[5] Notice that interaction invariants cannot exclude $lc_1 \wedge l_1^1 \wedge l_1^2$ since it is a reachable configuration.

corresponding to the actions participating in α are reset synchronously, and then become identical at the next state (until another interaction is executed). Moreover, history clocks of actions of the last executed interaction α are necessarily lower than the ones of actions not participating in α, since they are the last being reset. That is, at each state of the system there exists an interaction α (i.e. the last executed interaction) for which $h_{a_i} = h_{a_j}$ for all $a_i, a_j \in \alpha$, and $a_i \le a_k$ for all $a_k \notin \alpha$. Notice that actions that are not part of α are subject to the same type of constraint depending on the interaction executed right before α. This is captured by the recursive definition of the following invariant:

$$\mathcal{E}(\gamma) = \bigvee_{\alpha \in \gamma} \left(\left(\bigwedge_{\substack{a_i, a_j \in \alpha \\ a_k \notin \alpha}} h_{a_i} = h_{a_j} \le h_{a_k} \right) \wedge \mathcal{E}(\gamma \ominus \alpha) \right),$$

where $\gamma \ominus \alpha = \{\beta \setminus \alpha \mid \beta \in \gamma \wedge \beta \nsubseteq \alpha\}$. It can be shown that $\mathcal{E}(\gamma)$ is an invariant of the system [9]. For example of Figure 2, invariant $\mathcal{E}(\gamma)$ is given by:

$$\mathcal{E}(\gamma) = (h_a = h_{b_1} \le h_{b_2} \vee h_a = h_{b_2} \le h_{b_1}) \wedge (h_c = h_{d_1} \le h_{d_2} \vee h_c = h_{d_2} \le h_{d_1}).$$

Component invariants for example of Figure 2 including the history clocks are as follows:

$$CI(Controller^h) = lc_0 \vee (lc_1 \wedge x \le 4 \wedge (h_a = h_c \ge 8 + x \vee x = h_c \le h_a)) \vee$$
$$(lc_2 \wedge x = h_a \wedge (h_c \ge h_a + 12 \vee h_c = h_a + 4))$$
$$CI(Worker_i^h) = (y = h_{d_i} \wedge l_1^i \wedge h_{d_i} \le h_{b_i}) \vee (l_2^i \wedge h_{d_i} \ge 8 + h_{b_i}).$$

Such invariants proved to be sufficient for stating deadlock-freedom for a similar example involving only one worker, but are too weak for establishing deadlock-freedom with two workers. When interactions are conflicting on shared action a_i, the proposed invariants for history clock h_{a_i} always consider that any of these interactions can execute. For instance, in example of Figure 2 our invariants cannot capture the fact that if action a of Controller synchronizes with b_1 of $Worker_1$, then the following execution of action c of Controller can only synchronize with d_1 of $Worker_1$ (it cannot synchronize with d_2 of $Worker_2$).

Handling Conflicting Interactions. We developed a general way for computing stronger invariants relating execution of the interactions. The principle is to add again history clocks h_α for each the interaction α of γ, and to reset h_α each time α is executed by the means of an additional component and adequate synchronizations. A full description of this approach can be found in [9]. For an action a_i of component B_i, we define the separation constraint $\mathcal{S}(\gamma, a_i)$ as:

$$\mathcal{S}(\gamma, a_i) = \bigwedge_{\substack{\alpha, \beta \in \gamma \mid a_i \in \alpha, \beta \\ \alpha \ne \beta}} \mid h_\alpha - h_\beta \mid \ge \delta_{a_i},$$

where δ_{a_i} is a lower bound of the time elapsed between two consecutive executions of a_i in B_i, which can be statically computed from the timed automata of

B_i. It can be shown [9] that separation constraints $\mathcal{S}(\gamma, a_i)$ are invariants of the system, that is, the following is an invariant of the system:

$$\mathcal{S}(\gamma) = \bigwedge_{1 \leq i \leq n} \bigwedge_{a_i \in A_i} \mathcal{S}(\gamma, a_i).$$

Invariant $\mathcal{E}(\gamma)$ can be rewritten using additional history clocks as follows:

$$\mathcal{E}(\gamma) = \bigwedge_{1 \leq i \leq n} \bigwedge_{a_i \in A_i} h_{a_i} = \min_{\alpha \ni a_i} h_\alpha.$$

This corresponds to the intuition that the history clock of an action a_i equals the history clock of the last executed interaction α involving a_i, which is the one having h_α minimal.

Experiments. We have developed a prototype in Scala implementing the approach. It takes as input components B_i, interactions γ, and a global safety property Φ, and checks whether the system satisfies Φ. To this end, it first computes the invariants proposed above, using PPL [2]. Then it generates Z3 [4] Python code to check the satisfiability of the following formula:

$$\bigwedge_{1 \leq i \leq n} CI(B_i) \wedge II(\gamma) \wedge \mathcal{E}(\gamma) \wedge \mathcal{S}(\gamma) \wedge \neg \Phi. \tag{1}$$

Notice that when γ has no conflicting interactions we can simply use the initial form for $\mathcal{E}(\gamma)$ and discard $\mathcal{S}(\gamma)$. If (1) is not satisfiable then the system is guaranteed to satisfy Φ (i.e. our approach is sound). Otherwise, Z3 returns an assignment of the variables satisfying (1) and corresponding to a global state of the system that violates property Φ. Since we use over-approximations (i.e. invariants) instead of the exact behavior of the system, this state may be not reachable and Φ may actually hold in the system.

We experimented the approach on several classical examples, namely the *Train-Gate-Controller* (*TGC*), the *Fischer* mutual exclusion protocol, and the *Temperature-Control-System* (*TCS*). We compared our prototype implementation with Uppaal [3]. Uppaal is a widely used model-checker for timed systems implementing symbolic reachability of parallel composition of timed automata using zones. We measured execution times for verifying properties of interest for these examples, i.e. mutual exclusion for *TGC* and *Fischer* and deadlock-freedom for *TCS* (see Table 1). Experimental results shown that Uppaal is subject to state-explosion when increasing the number of components, which happened with *TCS* for 16 components or more, and with *Fischer* for 14 components or more. In contrast, our prototype managed to verify *TCS* even for 124 components in less than 20 seconds. We believe that such compositional approach is very interesting for systems composed of large number of identical components (e.g. swarms of robots) since in this case we reuse already computed invariants following incremental approaches of [19].

Table 1. Experimental results for model-checking tool Uppaal and our prototype tool

| Model & | Size | Time/Space | |
Property		Our prototype	Uppaal
	1	0m0.156s/2.6kB+140B	0ms/8 states
Train Gate Controller &	2	0m0.176s/3.2kB+350B	0ms/13 states
mutual exclusion	64	0m4.82s/530kB+170kB	0m0.210s/323 states
	124	0m17.718s/700kB+640kB	0m1.52s/623 states
	2	0m0.144/3kB	0m0.008s/14 states
Fischer &	4	0m0.22s/6.5kB	0m0.012s/156 states
mutual exclusion	6	0m0.36s/12.5kB	0m0.03s/1714 states
	14	0m2.840s/112kB	no result in 4 hours
	1	0m0.172s/840B+60B	0m0.01s/4 states
Temperature Controller &	8	0m0.5s/23kB+2.4kB	11m0.348s/57922 states
absence of deadlock	16	0m2.132s/127kB+9kB	no result in 6 hours
	124	0m19.22s/460kB+510kB	no result in 6 hours

Case Study. To illustrate the applicability of our approach, we also applied it to a robotics scenario provided by the ASCENS partner EPFL. It consists of cooperating robots used in a child's bedroom for home automation, automatic cleaning, or child assistance in tidying up. We considered the following types of robots/devices in the room, all capable of wireless communications.

Cleaning Robot. We assume the presence of an autonomous vacuum cleaner. This kind of domestic robot is nowadays widely used and working well, e.g. Roomba Vacuum Cleaning Robot. The distinguishing feature we consider in our setting is its ability to cooperate with other types of robots.

Toy Case Robot. The toy case robot—called Ranger—is currently developed in a research project of EPFL [1]. Its goal is to encourage the child to put away the toys in the case. To this end, it interacts with the child and produces pleasing sound and light each time the child takes toys from the floor and puts them in the case. The effectiveness of such robot has already been shown in previous studies. We also assume that this robot has sensors able to detect the presence of the child when he is close enough.

Bed and desk chair. We assume that the bed and the desk chair are equipped with sensors allowing to detect when the child seats on.

Door. We assume that the bedroom door is equipped with an electric closing and locking system. A safety mechanism stops any closing procedure if the child tries to enter the bedroom while the door is closing.

Ceiling Camera. A camera located on the ceiling can take pictures that can be analyzed to detect whether the child is in the bedroom. The shape of the child can be tracked in these pictures only if it is not too close to other shapes, i.e. if the child is not playing with the toy case and not on the bed or the chair. For energy consumption reasons, we assume that the pictures are shot and analyzed only once a while, e.g. at a given period P.

In this scenario we focused on a safety property stating that the child should not be in the bedroom while the cleaning robot is cleaning. To achieve this property, we designed a protocol in which the cleaning robot (1) checks if the child is outside the bedroom by correlating information from all the other robots / devices, (2) if so, closes and locks the door to keep the child outside, and (3) cleans the bedroom. To accomodate with the delays induced by the communication amongst the distributed robots, our protocol also relies on time measured by timers. A picture is considered fresh if it was shot by the camera less than F time units before. Similarly, the child is considered not detected by the chair, the case or the bed if he was not there for more than R time units.

We used our compositional verification method to prove that our protocol satisfies that the child is not in the bedroom while the robot is cleaning, for any value of the parameters such that $R \geq F$. In the BIP model we built (Figure 3), this property boils down to checking that if the cleaning robot is in control state C, then the child must be in state 0 (which are the blue states of Figure 3). This property is non trivial as it strongly depends on the individual behavior of all the devices and in particular their timings, and it can be tricky to ensure for the system. Notice that the model proposed here is far too abstract to be used directly for implementing the devices. It uses primitives such as atomic synchronizations between two or more components (i.e. multi-party interactions) that should be translated into simpler interactions (e.g. messages passing). To get correct-by-construction implementations we could transform the proposed BIP model into a Send/Receive BIP model using techniques developed for generating distributed implementations from BIP [25].

Conclusion. We have presented a compositional verification method for systems subject to timing constraints. It relies on invariants computed separately from system components and their interactions. This method is sound for verification of safety properties, that is, it can be used to prove that the system cannot reach an undesirable configuration. We believe that it is suited to check correctness of coordinations within distributed systems, usually implemented by communication protocols relying on time, as shown by the case robotics case study.

2.2 Application of SMC-BIP to a Robotics Scenario

We applied the statistical model-checking tool SMC-BIP to the robotics case study of the ASCENS project which is described in Chapter IV.2 [55]. The scenario consists in (1) deploying a swarm of marXbot [26] robots—the explorers—to find victims (which are other marXbots) distributed all over an arena shown in Figure 7, and (2) to rescue the victims. We focused on the deployment phase only whose goal is not only to deploy the swarm and to find the victims, but

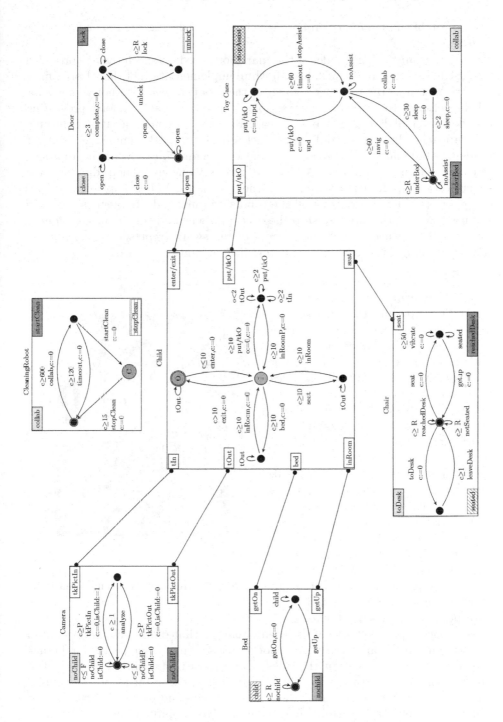

Fig. 3. BIP model of the cooperating robots example

also to establish "landmark" robots which are used during the rescued phase as routers.

We first built a BIP model of the marXbot based on specifications provided by ASCENS partners. It includes a faithful implementation of the 24 proximity sensors as well as the rotating scanner of the robot, considering noisy values for all the sensors. To keep our model simple, we used abstractions for representing the detection of landmarks by the camera and the communications through the range-and-bearing module. The skeleton of the BIP component used for modelling the marXbot behavior is provided in Figure 5. Following the approach implemented in the simulator ARGoS [56], we rely on synchronous discrete time execution with a duration of 10 ms for the time steps. This is implemented by a connector (*tick*) synchronizing all the robots (victims and explorer) as shown in Figure 4. Notice that we also stop the execution when all the victims are found, by disabling connector *tick*. The model of the swarm represents 1500 lines of BIP code along with 1200 lines of external C++ code.

Single Robot Behavior. We started by experimenting with several behavioral strategies for a single robot: straight walk, random walk, and random walk improved using the rotating scanner. All includes basic obstacle avoidance so as not to bump into walls and/or other robots. Figures 6 and 8 show examples of simulations obtained for different strategies and corresponding delays for finding the victims. In Figure 6, victims are the five small circles (three at the top and two at bottom) in the arena, and the path followed by the explorer is represented by drawings inside the arena. Using straight walk minimizes the distance for travelling from one location to another. However, it resulted in a very poor coverage since the explorer

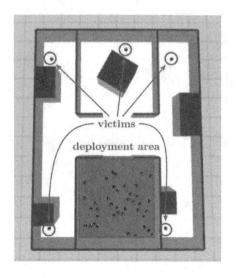

Fig. 7. Arena of the rescue scenario

was trapped on the left side of the arena from which it did not escape even after a long time. Random walk led to good coverage but longer delays for finding the first three victims than the ones obtained with straight walk. From this observation, we improved random walk by using the rotating scanner which allows the explorer to track long distances obstacles and to follow corridors and walls, which is clearly visible on simulations (see Figures 6 and 8). All these observations are confirmed by the analysis performed by SMC-BIP with which we computed the expected time for finding the 1st and the 5th considering

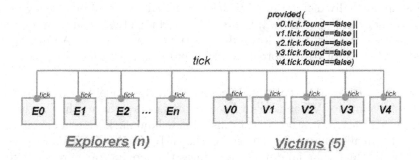

Fig. 4. Architecture of the BIP model built for the whole system

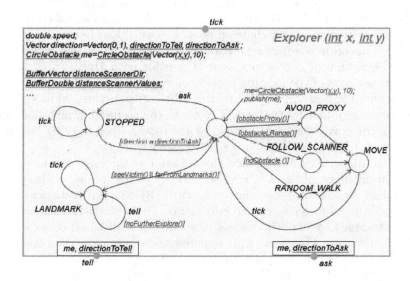

Fig. 5. BIP model for the behavior of a single robot

probability 0.85, provided in Figure 9. Parameters α, β and δ in table of Figure 9 correspond to the target degree of confidence for SMC-BIP. The lower these parameters are, the lower the probability to obtain an incorrect answer is. They are formally defined in [17]. Using SMC-BIP we also managed to show that increasing the number of explorers (we tested for 11, 21, and then 31) tends to reduce the expected delays for finding victims (see Figure 9). An example of simulations traces for 31 explorers can be found in Figure 10(a).

Cooperation Between Robots. We completed the model by including landmarking mechanisms. When a robot become too far away from other landmarks, or if it finds a victim, it stops to establish a new landmark. Landmarking alone reduced drastically the performances, as shown by Figure 11. This can be explained by the fact that landmarking reduces the moving range of the explorers and decreases the number of active robots, sometimes to the point where all robots were stopped (i.e. were landmarks) whereas victims remained to be found. An example of such situation can be observed in Figure 10(b).

The actual goal of landmarking is to prevent explorers/rescuers from going to uninteresting areas, which is essentially useful for the rescue part of the scenario. For this, landmarks must communicate with active robots to route them for achieving their goal (exploring, rescuing, etc.). We included basic communication capabilities in the model allowing landmarks to route robots back if there is no need for exploration in their given direction (e.g. presence of a dead end). These communications were implemented by simple connectors between the robots (see Figure 12). By the way, this shows limitations of (static) BIP representations as we had to include all possible connections between the robots, that is, n^2 connectors when using n explorers. It would have been better to use dynamic description of connectors as it is possible with DyBIP [27], but this feature was not part of the existing tool-chain we used. Adding communications allowed acceptable performance for finding all the five victims, while establishing landmarks required by the second phase of the scenario. Simulation traces clearly show the switchbacks performed by the robots when meeting landmarks from which no further exploration is needed (see Figure 10(c)).

SMC-BIP allowed us to fine-tune the behavior of the marXbot to optimize the deployment phase of the ASCENS scenario. Such fine-tuning is also possible with standard simulation techniques (e.g. with ARGoS), but statistical model-checking permits us to have reliable information about the performances of the swarm, guaranteed by explicit degrees of confidence and based on exploration of possible behaviors. For example, it required sometimes more than 20000 simulations for SMC-BIP to conclude on a single delay value. The BIP model we developed can also be a basis for computing stochastic abstractions and/or for applying verification techniques and tools.

2.3   Model-Driven Information Flow Security for SCEs

Systems and software conceived nowadays know a continuous increase of their complexity. Information protection and secure information flow between these

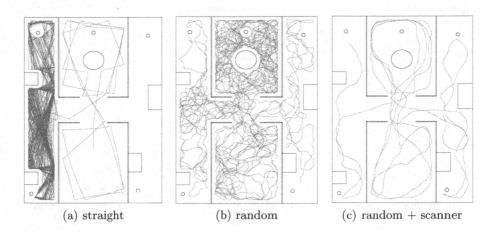

(a) straight   (b) random   (c) random + scanner

Fig. 6. Simulation of a single robot and various moving strategies

strategy:	straight	random	random + scanner			
number of explorers:	1	1	1	11	21	31
1st victim	207	1243	556	175	149	154
2nd victim	2265	5619	790	329	220	176
3rd victim	2983	12675	1231	551	481	273
4th victim	timeout	16053	3075	964	638	500
5th victim	timeout	16883	3358	1134	645	540

Fig. 8. Delays in seconds for finding victims corresponding to simulations of Figures 6 and 10(a)

strategy:	straight	random	random + scanner		
number of explorers:	1	1	1	11	21	31
1st victim ($\alpha=\beta=\delta=0.05$)	343	2996	892	211	188	152
5th victim ($\alpha=\beta=\delta=0.01$)	timeout	41250	11562	1171	820	742

Fig. 9. Delays in seconds computed by SMC-BIP for finding victims with probability $P=0.85$

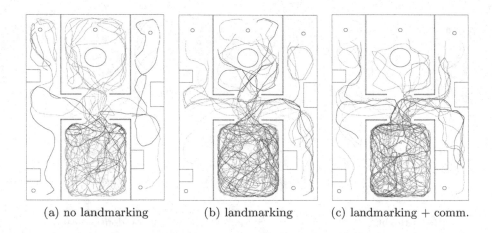

(a) no landmarking   (b) landmarking   (c) landmarking + comm.

Fig. 10. Simulation of landmarking strategies for 31 explorers

strategy:	landmarking	landmarking + communication
1st victim ($\alpha=\beta=\delta=0.05$)	380	375
5th victim ($\alpha=\beta=\delta=0.01$)	timeout	1797

Fig. 11. Delays in seconds computed by SMC-BIP for finding victims with probability $P=0.85$

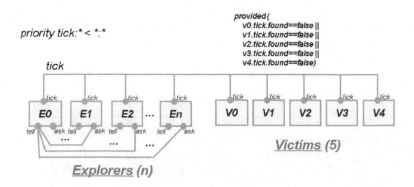

Fig. 12. Architecture of the BIP model including communications explorers and landmarks

systems is paramount and represent a great design challenge. Model driven security (MDS) [11] is an innovative approach that tend to solve system-level security issues by providing an advanced modeling process representing security requirements at a high level of abstraction. Indeed, MDS guarantees separation of concerns between functional and security requirements, from early phases of the system development till final implementation.

Information flow security can be ensured using various mechanisms. Amongst the first approaches considered, ones find access control mechanisms [62,45] that allow protecting data confidentiality by limiting access to data to be read or modified only by authorized users. Unfortunately, these mechanisms have been proven incomplete and limited since only by preventing the direct access to data, indirect (implicit) information flows are still possible given rise to the so called covert channels [63]. As an alternative, non-interference has been studied as a global property to characterize and to develop techniques ensuring information flow security. Initially defined by Goguen and Meseguer [39], non-interference ensures that the system's secret information does not affect its public behavior.

In this work, we adapt the Model driven security (MDS) [11] approach to develop a component-based framework, named *secBIP*, that guarantees automated verification and implementation of secure information flow systems with respect to specific definition of non-interference. In general, component-based frameworks allow for the construction of complex systems by composition of atomic components with communication and coordination operators. That is, systems are obtained from unitary atomic components that can be independently deployed and composed with other components. Component-based frameworks are usually well adopted for managing key issues for functional design including heterogeneity of components, distribution aspects, performance issues, etc. Nonetheless, the use of component-based frameworks is also beneficial for establishing information flow security. Particularly, the explicit system architecture allows tracking easily intra and inter-components information flow.

The *secBIP* framework is built as an extension of the *BIP* [12] framework encompassing information flow security. *secBIP* allows to create systems that are secure by construction if certain local conditions hold for composed components. The *secBIP* extension includes specific annotations for classification of both data and events. Thanks to the explicit use of composition operators in *BIP*, the information flow is easily tracked within models and security requirements can be established in a compositional manner, first locally, by checking the behavior of atomic components and then globally, by checking the communication and coordination inter-components.

Information flow security has been traditionally studied separately for language-based models [61,64] (see also the survey [60]) and trace-based models [51,52,67,48]. While the former mostly focus on verification of data-flow security properties in programming languages, the latter is treating security in event-based systems. In *secBIP*, we achieve a useful combination between both aspects, data-flow and event-flow security, in a single semantics model. We introduce and distinguish two types of non-interference, respectively *event non-interference* and *data non-interference.* For events, non-interference states that the observation of public events should not allow to deduce any information about the occurrence of secret events. For data, it states that there is no leakage of secret data into public ones.

The rest of our contribution is structured as follows. First, we introduce the security extension and we provide the two associated definitions of non-interference, respectively for data flows and event flows. Next, we formally establish non-interference based on unwinding relations and we provide sufficient conditions that facilitate its automatic verification. Finally we illustrate the approach on a use-case, and we conclude.

Information Flow Security. We explore information flow policies [34,13,39] with focus on the non-interference property. In order to track information we adopt the classification technique and we define a classification policy where we annotate the information by assigning security levels to different parts of *secBIP* model (data variables, ports and interactions). The policy describes how information can flow from one classification with respect to the other.

As an example, we can classify public information as a Low (L) security level and secret (confidential) information as High (H) security level. Intuitively High security level is more restrictive than Low security level and we denote it by $L \subseteq H$. In general, security levels are elements of a security domain, defined as follows:

Definition 1 (security domain). *A security domain is a lattice of the form $\langle S, \subseteq, \cup, \cap \rangle$ where:*

- *S is a finite set of security levels.*
- *$\subseteq$ is a partial order "can flow to" on S that indicates that information can flow from one security level to an equal or a more restrictive one.*
- *$\cup$ is a "join" operator for any two levels in S and that represents the upper bound of them.*
- *$\cap$ is a "meet" operator for any two levels in S and that represents the lower bound of them.*

As an example we consider the set $S = \{L, M_1, M_2, H\}$ of security levels that are governed by the "can flow to" relation $L \subseteq M_1$, $L \subseteq M_2$, $M_1 \subseteq H$ and $M_2 \subseteq H$. M_1 and M_2 are incomparable and we note $M_1 \not\subseteq M_2$ and $M_1 \not\supseteq M_2$. This security domain is graphically illustrated in figure 13.

We briefly recall the definition of BIP models. For a detailed description the reader can refer to [12]. We assume that the system is represented by a set of atomic components B_i, $1 \leq i \leq n$, interacting through multiparty interactions (i.e. synchronizations between two or more components). Each component B_i defines an interface consisting of communication ports associated with variables, and its behavior is given by an automaton whose transitions τ are labelled by ports, are guarded by boolean expressions g_τ on variables, and updates values of variables according to functions f_τ. An interaction a between components B_i,

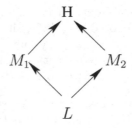

Fig. 13. Security domain

$i \in I \subseteq \{1, \ldots, n\}$, is defined as a subset of ports such that it has at most one
port of each components, i.e. $a = \{p_i\}_{i \in I}$. Moreover, an interaction a can be
guarded by a boolean condition G_a on the variables associated to its ports, and
may assign new values to these variables according to a function F_a. Given a set
of interactions γ, we denote by $C = \gamma(B_1, \ldots B_n)$ the composition of B_1, $\ldots$,
B_n with respect to interactions γ. In the composite component C, transitions of
atomic components B_i are executed synchronously according to interactions γ.
That is, if for an interaction $a = \{p_i\}_{i \in I}$ of γ the guard G_a evaluates to true,
and if all components B_i enable transitions τ_i labelled by p_i, then a can execute
if C which corresponds to the synchronous execution of all transitions τ_i after
execution of transfer function F_a. A detailed formalization of the model provided
in [12]. In the following, we write X (resp. P) for the set of all variables (resp.
ports) defined in all atomic components $(B_i)_{i=1,n}$ of C. We also write Q_C (resp.
Q_C^0) for the set of states of C (resp. initial states of C). A security assignment
for C with respect to a security domain $\langle S, \subseteq, \cup, \cap \rangle$ assigns security levels to
variables, ports and interactions in a consistent way. It is defined as follows.

Definition 2 (security assignment). *A security assignment for component
C is a mapping $\sigma : X \cup P \cup \gamma \to S$ that associates security levels to variables,
ports and interactions such that the security levels of ports match the security
levels of interactions, that is, for all $a \in \gamma$ and for all $p \in a$ it holds $\sigma(p) = \sigma(a)$.*

In atomic components, the security levels considered for ports and variables allow
to track intra-component information flows and control the intermediate computation steps. Moreover, inter-components communication, that is, interactions
with data exchange, are tracked by the security levels assigned to interactions.

Let σ be a security assignment for C.

For a security level $s \in S$, we define $\gamma \downarrow_s^\sigma$ the restriction of γ to interactions
with security level at most s that is formally, $\gamma \downarrow_s^\sigma = \{a \in \gamma \mid \sigma(a) \subseteq s\}$.

For a security level $s \in S$, we define $w|_s^\sigma$ the projection of a trace $w \in \gamma^*$
to interactions with security level lower or equal to s. Formally, the projection
is recursively defined on traces as $\epsilon|_s^\sigma = \epsilon$, $(aw)|_s^\sigma = a(w|_s^\sigma)$ if $\sigma(a) \subseteq s$ and
$(aw)|_s^\sigma = w|_s^\sigma$ if $\sigma(a) \not\subseteq s$. The projection operator $|_s^\sigma$ is naturally lifted to sets
of traces W by taking $W|_s^\sigma = \{w|_s^\sigma \mid w \in W\}$.

For a security level $s \in S$, we define the equivalence $\approx_s^\sigma$ on states of C. Two states q_1, q_2 are equivalent, denoted by $q_1 \approx_s^\sigma q_2$ iff (1) they coincide on variables having security levels at most s and (2) they coincide on control locations having outgoing transitions labeled with ports with security level at most s.

We are now ready to define the two notions of non-interference.

Definition 3 (event non-interference). *The security assignment σ ensures event non-interference of $\gamma(B_1, \ldots, B_n)$ at security level s iff,*

$$\forall q_0 \in Q_C^0 : \text{TRACES}(\gamma(B_1, \ldots, B_n), q_0)|_s^\sigma = \text{TRACES}((\gamma \downarrow_s^\sigma)(B_1, \ldots, B_n), q_0),$$

where $\text{TRACES}(\gamma(B_1, \ldots, B_n))$ *denotes the set of execution traces of the system* $\gamma(B_1, \ldots, B_n)$ *(see [28] for a formal definition of traces of BIP systems).*

Event non-interference ensures isolation/security at interaction level. The definition excludes the possibility to gain any relevant information about the occurrences of interactions (events) with strictly greater (or incomparable) levels than s, from the exclusive observation of occurrences of interactions with levels lower or equal to s. That is, an external observer is not able to distinguish between the case where such higher interactions are not observable on execution traces and the case these interactions have been actually statically removed from the composition. This definition is very close to Rushby's [59] definition for transitive non-interference. But, let us remark that event non-interference is not concerned about the protection of data.

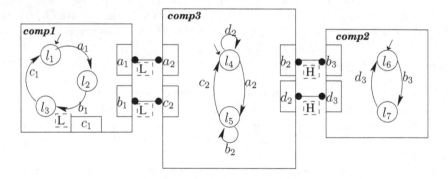

Fig. 14. Example for event non-interference

Example 1. Figure 14 presents a simple illustrative example for event non-interference. The model consists of three atomic components $comp_{i,i=1,2,3}$. Different security levels have been assigned to ports and interactions: $comp_1$ is a low security component, $comp_2$ is a high security component, and $comp_3$ is mixed security component. The security levels are represented by dashed squares related to interactions, internal ports and variables. As a convention, we apply high (H)

level for secret data and interactions and low(L) level for public ones. The set
of traces is represented by the automaton in figure 15 (a). The set of projected
execution traces at security level L is represented by the automaton depicted in
figure 15 (b). This set is equal to the set of traces obtained by restricted composition, that is, using interaction with security level at most L and depicted in
figure 15 (c). Therefore, this example satisfies the event non-interference condition at level L.

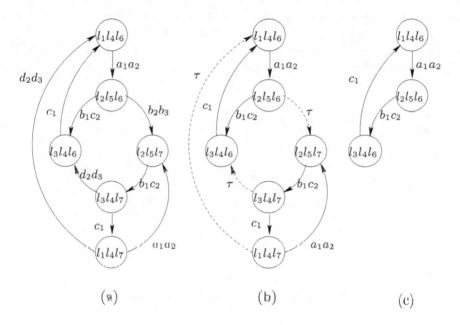

$$(a) \qquad\qquad (b) \qquad\qquad (c)$$

Fig. 15. Sets of traces represented as automata

Definition 4 (data non-interference). *The security assignment σ ensures
data non-interference of $C = \gamma(B_1, \ldots, B_n)$ at security level s iff,*

$$\forall q_1, q_2 \in Q_C^0 : q_1 \approx_s^\sigma q_2 \Rightarrow$$
$$\forall w_1 \in \text{TRACES}(C, q_1), w_2 \in \text{TRACES}(C, q_2) : w_1|_s^\sigma = w_2|_s^\sigma \Rightarrow$$
$$\forall q_1', q_2' \in Q_C : q_1 \xrightarrow[C]{w_1} q_1' \land q_2 \xrightarrow[C]{w_2} q_2' \Rightarrow q_1' \approx_s^\sigma q_2'$$

Data non-interference provides isolation/security at data level. The definition
ensures that, all states reached from initially indistinguishable states at security level s, by execution of arbitrary but identical traces whenever projected at
level s, are also indistinguishable at level s. That means that observation of all
variables and interactions with level s or lower excludes any gain of relevant information about variables at higher (or incomparable) level than s. Compared to

event non-interference, data non-interference is a stronger property that considers the system's global states (local states and valuation of variables) and focus on their equivalence along identical execution traces (at some security level).

Example 2. Figure 16 presents an extension with data variables of the previous example from figure 14. We consider the following two traces $w_1 = \langle a_1a_2, b_2b_3,$ $c_2b_1, d_2d_3, c_1, a_2a_1 \rangle$ and $w_2 = \langle a_1a_2, b_2b_3, c_2b_1, c_1, a_2a_1 \rangle$ that start from the initial state $((l_1, u = 0, v = 0), (l_4, x = 0, y = 0), (l_6, z = 0, w = 0))$. Although the projected traces at level L are equal, that is, $w_1|_L^\sigma = w_2|_L^\sigma = \langle a_1a_2, c_2b_1, c_1, a_1a_2 \rangle$, the reached states by w_1 and w_2 are different, respectively $((l_2, u = 4, v = 2), (l_5, x = 3, y = 2), (l_6, z = 1, w = 1))$ and $((l_2, u = 4, v = 2), (l_5, x = 2, y = 2), (l_7, z = 1, w = 0))$ and moreover non-equivalent at low level L. Hence, this example is not data non-interferent at level L.

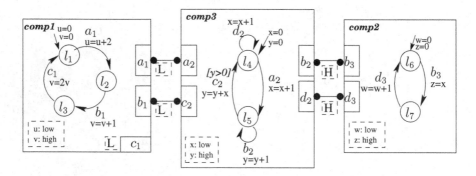

Fig. 16. Example for data non-interference

Definition 5 (secure component). *A security assignment σ is secure for a component $\gamma(B_1, \ldots, B_n)$ iff it ensures both event and data non-interference, at all security levels $s \in S$.*

Verification. The verification technique of non-interference proposed for *secBIP* models is using the so-called unwinding conditions. This technique was first introduced by Goguen and Meseguer for the verification of transitive non-interference for deterministic systems [39]. The unwinding approach reduces the verification of information flow security to the existence of certain unwinding relation. This relation is usually an equivalence relation that respects some additional properties on atomic execution steps, which are shown sufficient to imply non-interference. In the case of *secBIP*, the additional properties are formulated in terms of individual interactions/events and therefore easier to handle.

Let $C = \gamma(B_1, \ldots, B_n)$ be a composite component and let σ be a security assignment for C.

Definition 6 (unwinding relation). *An equivalence $\sim_s$ on states of C is called an unwinding relation for σ at security level s iff the two following conditions hold:*

1. *local consistency*
   $$\forall q, q' \in Q_C : \forall a \in \gamma : q \xrightarrow[C]{a} q' \Rightarrow \sigma(a) \subseteq s \vee q \sim_s q'$$
2. *output and step consistency*
   $$\forall q_1, q_2, q_1' \in Q_C : \forall a \in \gamma :$$
   $$q_1 \sim_s q_2 \wedge q_1 \xrightarrow[C]{a} q_1' \wedge \sigma(a) \subseteq s \Rightarrow$$
   $$\exists q_2' \in Q_C : q_2 \xrightarrow[C]{a} q_2' \wedge$$
   $$\forall q_2' \in Q_C : q_2 \xrightarrow[C]{a} q_2' \Rightarrow q_1' \sim_s q_2'$$

The existence of unwinding relations is tightly related to non-interference. The following two theorems formalize this relation for the two types of non-interference defined. Let C be a composite component and σ a security assignment.

Theorem 1 (event non-interference). *If an unwinding relation $\sim_s$ exists for the security assignment σ at security level s, then σ ensures event non-interference of C at level s.*

Theorem 2 (data non-interference). *If the equivalence relation $\approx_s^\sigma$ is also an unwinding relation for the security assignment σ at security level s, then σ ensures data non-interference of C at level s.*

The two theorems above can be used to derive a practical verification method of non-interference using unwinding. We provide hereafter sufficient syntactic conditions ensuring that indeed the unwinding relations $\sim_s$ and $\approx_s$ exist on the system states. These conditions aim to efficiently simplify the verification and reduce it to local constrains check on both transitions (inter-component verification) and interactions (intra-component verification). Especially, they give an easy way to automate the verification.

Definition 7 (security conditions). *Let $C = \gamma(B_1, \ldots, B_n)$ be a composite component and let σ be a security assignment. We say that C satisfies the security conditions for security assignment σ iff:*

(i) *the security assignment of ports, in every atomic component B_i is locally consistent, that is:*
   - *for every pair of causal transitions:*
     $$\forall \tau_1, \tau_2 \in T_i : \tau_1 = \ell_1 \xrightarrow{p_1} \ell_2, \tau_2 = \ell_2 \xrightarrow{p_2} \ell_3 \Rightarrow$$
     $$\ell_1 \neq \ell_2 \Rightarrow \sigma(p_1) \subseteq \sigma(p_2)$$
   - *for every pair of conflicting transitions:*
     $$\forall \tau_1, \tau_2 \in T_i : \tau_1 = \ell_1 \xrightarrow{p_1} \ell_2, \tau_2 = \ell_1 \xrightarrow{p_2} \ell_3 \Rightarrow$$
     $$\ell_1 \neq \ell_2 \Rightarrow \sigma(p_1) \subseteq \sigma(p_2)$$

(ii) all assignments $x := e$ occurring in transitions within atomic components and interactions are sequential consistent, in the classical sense:

$$\forall y \in use(e): \ \sigma(y) \subseteq \sigma(x),$$

where $use(e)$ denotes the set of variables involved in an expression e

(iii) variables are consistently used and assigned in transitions and interactions, that is,

$$\forall \tau \in \cup_{i=1}^{n} T_i \ \ \forall x, y \in X \ : x \in def(f_\tau), y \in use(g_\tau) \ \Rightarrow$$
$$\sigma(y) \subseteq \sigma(p_\tau) \subseteq \sigma(x)$$
$$\forall a \in \gamma \ \ \forall x, y \in X \ : x \in def(F_a), y \in use(G_a) \ \Rightarrow$$
$$\sigma(y) \subseteq \sigma(a) \subseteq \sigma(x),$$

where $def(F)$ denotes the set of variables modified by a function F.

(iv) all atomic components B_i are port deterministic:

$$\forall \tau_1, \tau_2 \in T_i: \ \tau_1 = \ell_1 \xrightarrow{p} \ell_2, \tau_2 = \ell_1 \xrightarrow{p} \ell_3 \ \Rightarrow$$
$$(g_{\tau_1} \wedge g_{\tau_2}) \text{ is unsatisfiable}$$

The first family of conditions (i) is similar to Accorsi's conditions [5] for excluding causal and conflicting places for Petri net transitions having different security levels. Similar conditions have been considered in [36,38] and lead to more specific definitions of non-interferences and bisimulations on annotated Petri nets. The second condition *(ii)* represents the classical condition needed to avoid information leakage in sequential assignments. The third condition *(iii)* tackles covert channels issues. Indeed, *(iii)* enforces the security levels of the data flows which have to be consistent with security levels of the ports or interactions (e.g., no low level data has to be updated on a high level port or interaction). Such that, observations of public data would not reveal any secret information. Finally, condition *(iv)* enforces deterministic behavior on atomic components.

The relation between the syntactic security conditions and the unwinding relations is precisely captured by the following theorem.

Theorem 3 (unwinding theorem). *Whenever the security conditions hold, the equivalence relation $\approx_s^\sigma$ is an unwinding relation for the security assignment σ, at any security level s.*

The following corollary is the immediate consequence of theorems 1, 2 and 3.

Corollary 1. *Whenever the security conditions hold, the security assignment σ is secure for the component C.*

Application. We illustrate the *secBIP* framework to handle information flow security issues for a typical example, the web service reservation system introduced in [41]. A businessman, living in France, plans to go to Berlin for a private and secret mission. To organize his travel, he uses an intelligent web service who contacts two travel agencies: The first agency, *AgencyA*, arranges flights in Europe and the second agency, *AgencyB*, arranges flights exclusively to Germany. The reservation service obtains in return specific flight information and their corresponding prices and chooses the flight that is more convenient for him.

In this example, there are two types of interference that can occur, (1) data-interference since learning the flight price may reveal the flight destination and (2) event interference, since observing the interaction with *AgencyB* can reveal the destination as well. Thus, to keep the mission private, the flight prices and interactions with *AgencyB* have to be kept confidential.

The modeling of the system using *secBIP* involves two main distinct steps: first, functional requirements modeling reflecting the system behavior, and second, security annotations enforcing the desired security policy. The model of the system has four components denoted: *Travel_A* and *Travel_B* who are instances from the same component and correspond respectively to AgencyA and AgencyB, and components *Reservation* and *Payment*. To avoid figure 17 cluttering, we did not represent the interactions with *Travel_A* component. Search parameters are supplied by a user through the *Reservation* component ports *dests* and *dates* to which we associate respectively variables (*from*, *to*) and *dates*. Next, through search interaction, *Reservation* component contacts *Travel_B* component to search for available flights and obtains in return a list L of specific flights with their corresponding prices. Thereafter, *Reservation* component selects a ticket t_i from the list L and requests the *Payment* component to perform the payment.

All the search parameters *from*, *to*, *dates*, as well as the flights list L are set to low since users are not identified while sending these queries. Other sensitive data like the selected flight t_i, the price variable p and the payment parameters (identity *id*, credit card variable *cna* and code number *cno*) are set to high. Internal ports *dests* and *dates* as well as *search*, *fly_list*, *accept* interactions are set to low since these interactions (events) do not reveal any information about the client private trip. However, the *select_fly* interaction must be set to high since the observation of the selection event from *AgencyB* allow to deduce the client destination. In the case of a selected flight from *AgencyA*, the *select_fly* interaction could be set to low since, in this case, the destination could not be deduced just from the event occurrence.

We recall that any system can be proven non-interferent iff it satisfies the syntactic security conditions from definition 7. Indeed, these conditions hold for the system model depicted in Figure 17. In particular, it can be easily checked that all assignments occurring in transitions within atomic component as well as within interactions are sequentially consistent. For example, at the *select_fly* interaction we assign a low level security item from the flight list L to a high security level variable ti, formally $t_i = L[i]$. Besides, the security levels assignments to ports exclude inconsistencies due to causal and conflicting transitions, in all atomic components.

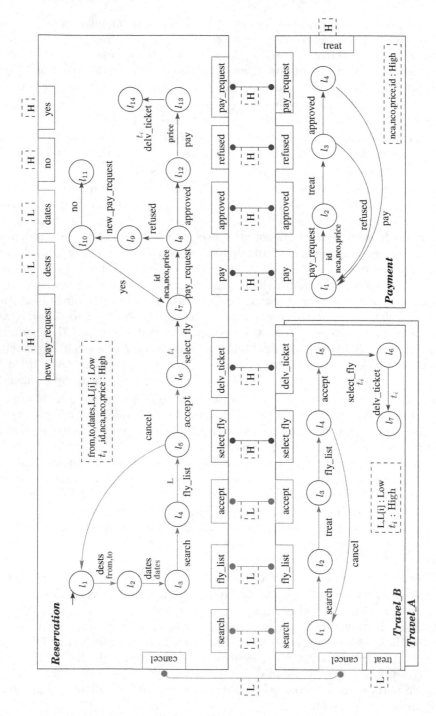

Fig. 17. Reservation Web Service composition

Conclusion. We presented a model driven security framework to secure component-based systems. We formally defined two types of non-interference, respectively event and data non-interference. We provided a set of sufficient syntactic conditions formulated to simplify non-interference verification. These conditions are extensions of security typed language rules applied to our model. The use of our framework has been demonstrated to secure a web service application.

3   Alternative Approaches to Ensure System Correctness

In addition to verification techniques developed for BIP models and detailed in the previous section, we present here complementary methods for checking system correctness. We developed a fully integrated Java-based framework in which it is possible to perform in concert control synthesis and formal verification (Section 3.1). Security is also addressed in Section 3.2 via a framework for the expression and the enforcement of policies in systems. Finally, Section 3.3 gives an overview of the work we made towards the verification of the code implementing system components.

3.1   Quantitative Synthesis and Verification Framework

We developed a framework that integrates various recent and more classic algorithms for quantitative verification and synthesis. To our best knowledge, this is the first time that verification and synthesis work in tandem in the same framework. Figure 18 gives a general overview of our framework.

At the core lies a Java Embedded Domain Specific Language for describing continuous models. We provide, hidden from the user, means for deriving a discretized from the continuous model. The user has full access to this derived model and can use it in his own programs. Our framework provides several algorithms to effectively find optimal controllers for the discretized model. We also provide several ways to use these discretized controllers as controllers in the original continuous model.

In addition we provide two means of controller validation and verification. First, Probabilistic Model Checking checks the performance of the continuous controller against a discretized model. This discretized model does not have to be (and should not be) the same as the discretized model from which we generated the controller. Instead, we should use different parameters for discretization as well as different parameters in the model itself to check the model for robustness and over-fitting. Second, we have implemented Bayesian Stochastic Model checking which allows to validate and verify the controller in a continuous environment. This allows us to check the controller against models with different parameters, as well as to check errors induced by the discretization.

For an example of a controller our system generates and validates, consider an Adaptive Cruise Control (ACC) system. ACCs are now built into luxury cars and are responsible for automatically maintaining a fixed distance to the car

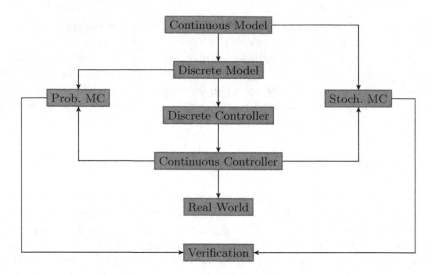

Fig. 18. Framework Overview

in front of it. Such a system senses (1) the current distance between the car it equips and the car in front of it, and (2) their relative velocity, i.e,. by calculating how much the distance shrinks or grows per second. On the one hand, the goal of this system is to reach and maintain the desired distance quickly. On the other hand, the controller is also responsible for pleasant driving. That is, it should not unnecessarily or suddenly accelerate or jerk (where jerk is the change of acceleration over time). There is an obvious trade-off between these two criteria, and our framework allows study of trade-offs like these. An additional concern is that the relative velocity is not exclusively under the control of the system. Instead, since we do not know and cannot predict the other driver's intentions, we assume that she is going to behave randomly.

We support various algorithms for finding such optimal controllers, and we also support analyzing the controller we generate. The analysis is necessary for the following reasons.

1. Controllers are generated under certain assumptions; we need to know what happens if these assumptions are not met by the real world.
2. Controllers are optimized with regard to a certain set of criteria; we might be interested in other criteria as well.
3. Continuous state space makes it necessary that we use discretization techniques; we have to study the influence discretization has on the controller.
4. Behavior of the environment is modelled as probabilistic; we want to know the worst-case behavior of the controller under all possible behaviors of the environment.

Formally, we use Markov Decision Processes (MDPs) as models. A Markov Decision Process is a probabilistic model with a finite set of states S. In each state, there is at least one active action from the finite set of possible actions A. Function $\alpha : S \rightarrow 2^A \setminus \{\emptyset\}$, defines what actions are active in what state. For each pair of states and active actions, there is a probability distribution defining how likely it is that we go to some state from a state with that action, i.e., $p : S \times A \rightarrow D(S)$. Lastly, we want to evaluate the costs/rewards of each decision. To that end, we define a vector of functions $R = (S \rightarrow \mathbb{R})^n$. A MDP is then a tuple $M = (S, A, \alpha, p, R)$.

Specification. Our framework supports various input formats defining MDPs. Here, we will concentrate on a novel format based on Java programs. In this format, models inherit from a class `Model`, with a few abstract methods. Before we define the exact semantics of the abstract model, we will consider the ACC model as an example.

```java
public class ACC extends Model<ACC> {
  // Distance from car in front
  @CVAR(min=0, max=100)
  public double distance;

  // Relative velocity
  @CVAR(min=-14, max=14)
  public double velocity;

  // Distance we desire
  public double desiredDistance = 50;

  // Updates per second
  public int ticks = 10;

  @Override
  public void next(double acceleration, ACC target) {
    double random_acceleration = normal.sample(0, 4.0);
    double nextVelocity = velocity +
                (acceleration + random_acceleration) / ticks;
    double nextDistance = distance -
                (0.5 * velocity + 0.5 * nextVelocity) / ticks;
    target.velocity = nextVelocity;
    target.distance = nextDistance;
  }

  @Override
  public double[] rewards(double acceleration) {
    double[] rewards = new double[2];
    rewards[0] = -Math.abs(desiredDistance - distance);
    rewards[1] = -acceleration* acceleration;
    return rewards;
  }
}
```

A few features here are noteworthy. Variables that are part of the model are annotated with `@CVAR`. A variable should be part of a model if (1) it influences the probability distribution and (2) it changes over time. In our case, variables `distance` and `velocity` are part of the model, while `desiredDistance` and `ticks` are not part of the model (because they are constant). Method `void next(double acceleration, ACC target)` defines a distribution over the next states, given the current state. We first sample a random acceleration for the other car, with mean zero and standard deviation 4. Next, we calculate the velocity of the next state, based on the current velocity, the random acceleration and the acceleration we got as input. Lastly, based on old velocity and distance and on the new velocity, we calculate the distance of the next state. Note that our framework supports both loops and branching, although they are not present in this example. Additionally, we define the rewards the controller gets for its decisions in method `double[] rewards(double acceleration)`. In the case of `ACC`, it receives a cost (negative reward) depending on how far the current distance is from the desired distance (`rewards[0]`), and a cost depending on how much it accelerates (`rewards[1]`). Note that these two define exactly the trade-off mentioned before. On the one hand, we want to minimize both `rewards[0]` and `rewards[1]`, but applying less acceleration will lead to a greater deviation from our desired distance. On the other hand, being stricter about staying close to the desired distance requires more acceleration.

A class like `ACC` (defined above) by itself defines a continuous Markov Decision Process, i.e., a MDP with infinite sets of states and actions. It describes how a system evolves over time. For example, if we are in a state in which distance is 50 and velocity is -4, then we first have to draw a random sample from a normal distribution to determine how much the car in front of us accelerates or brakes. In our example, we assume that we draw a zero. Therefore, only our own acceleration counts. Since we are already at the desired distance, we can assume that a sensible controller will brake to catch the negative relative velocity. Let us assume that the controller gives us an acceleration of $4m/s^2$. Then the next velocity is going to be $-4 + (4 + 0)/10 = -3.6$. The next distance is defined by the current distance plus the average of old and new distance, i.e. $50 + (-3.6 + -4.0)/2/10 = 49.62$ meters. So now we are in state $(49.62, -3.6)$. Notice how we left the desired distance, but we also decreased our velocity. Presumable, the controller will continue in this way until we have removed all our access velocity, producing more points on the way (e.g., $(49.28, -3.2), (48.89, -2.8), \ldots, (48, 0)$. At this point, the controller will continue braking so that the other car gains distance again, e.g., we will now see points $(48.02, 0.4), (48.08, 0.8) \ldots$. After that (at around distance $49m$) we might see acceleration again such that we reach relative velocity 0 once we reach the desired distance. Note that in this example we assumed that the car in front of the controlled car will maintain its own velocity. In the real model, though, the controller has to cope with the other car's random behavior.

In the trace above, the controller gets rewards at each instant. For example, in the transition between the second two points (from $(49.28, -3.2)$ to $(48.89, -2.8)$), the controller gets two scores: 1. 0.72 for the deviation from the desired distance, and 2. -9 for the applied acceleration. We will discuss later how we combine these instantaneous rewards to rewards over infinite traces and how to combine rewards over traces to rewards for controllers (which define probability measures of infinite sets of infinite traces).

Synthesis. In general, finding perfect controllers for these continuous, probabilistic sequential models is impossible. We still have to deal with them since they are very useful for modelling real world physics. Further, once we decide what action to take in what state, we can use a model like the above for simulation and continuous analysis[6]. In fact, we will use models like ACC for Bayesian Model Checking of synthesized controllers later.

Discretization. To fit such a continuous, infinite state model into our framework, (i.e., finite set of states and actions), we employ sigma point sampling [23] and linear interpolation. This is a non-trivial process, but happens transparently for the user. All that is necessary for him is to add an annotated class like in the following.

```
@Discretize(model=ACC.class)
public static class DModel extends ACC {};
```

DModel is now a discretized version of ACC and describes a MDP as formally defined above. The specific details of discretization (like number of discrete states used) and sampling are configurable. Note that discretized classes like this one are not part of the hidden internals of the framework but are fully accessible to the engineer.

Algorithms. We support various algorithms for finding optimal controllers. They differ in how they treat the sequence of rewards the evolution of the process presents. Let $r_1, r_2, r_3 \ldots$ be a sequence of vectors. Then the aggregated reward is defined in one of the following ways.

- Total Sum: $r_1 + r_2 + r_3 + \ldots$
- Discounted: $r_1 + \lambda r_2 + \lambda^2 r_3 \ldots$
- Average Payoff: $\lim_{n \to \infty} 1/n \sum_{i=0}^{n} r_i$

When we fix a controller, a model gives us a vector of expected rewards for each state of the model. Together with a distribution over the states, these rewards can be combined into a single vector, which serves as an overall *quality measure*. For two different controllers with rewards $r_1, r_2 \in \mathbb{R}^n$, we say that the controller generating r_1 is better than the controller generating r_2 if $r_1 > r_2$. In a recent publications [37], the authors showed that all possible quality measures form a convex set for Total Sum and Discounted aggregators. This allows us to effectively approximate the shape of all possible quality measures in form of a Pareto Curve. One example of such a curve is shown in Figure 19(a). The curve clearly shows the trade-offs between the two rewards. An engineer might select a region for further refinement, or ask us to analyze all controllers in a certain region of the curve (all of this is supported by our framework). From the extreme right of this curve we can conclude that even small reductions in the importance of the deviation from distance over time leads to massive decreases in applied acceleration in this area. Analogously, the left extreme of the curve shows us that that small reductions in applied acceleration lead to big gains in time spend far away from the desired distance. Using these conclusions, an engineer can pick a quality measure and therefore a controller he desires.

---

[6] Note that this is indeed the way simulations are usually written

We show the actions of a controller generated with weight $(0.9788, 0.0211)$ by our framework in Plot 20(a). On the x-axis we present the distance to the car in front, while we present the relative velocity on the y-axis. The color indicates the applied acceleration. For example, where the distance is as desired (50 m), and the relative velocity is 0, no further acceleration is applied. Going through this point is a diagonal going from roughly (35, -15) to (65, 15) where applied acceleration equals zero. In this area, the controller judges the relative velocity just right to reach the desired distance quickly enough. As we move horizontally outwards from this narrow band, the acceleration the controller applies rises sharply. Especially, as either distance or relative velocity decreases, the controller increases the applied acceleration.

Plot 19(b) shows one trace of the interplay between controller and environment as it happens in the continuous environment (i.e., we run the program defined above as it is). It starts out in position (50,10), i.e., where the distance is as desired but we are closing in too fast. As we follow the trace, we see that the car equipped with an ACC gains on the car in front (as its velocity is greater than that of the other car). The color of the trace shows the applied braking force in each particular moment. As we can see, the controller brakes the car harshly until he reaches a relative velocity of -3 m/s. At this point it slowly decreases the de-acceleration until a relative velocity of about -5 m/s is reached. It now maintains speed until we reach a distance of about 47 m (i.e., the car is 3 meters too close). Would the controller maintain speed here, then it would overshoot the desired distance. Instead, it gently accelerates the car again until it reaches a relative velocity of 0 and is very close to the desired distance. The "ball" region around the desired distance and relative velocity 0 shows how the controller reacts to the random behavior of the car in front.

In Plot 20(b), we present a controller generated with weight $(0.9588, 0.0411)$. In comparison to the weight above, we have decreased the importance of `rewards[0]`, and increased the importance of `rewards[1]`. This decreases the importance of the distance to the other car and increases the importance of not applying too much acceleration. This has the effect of growing the band where relative velocity is judged adequate, and also moving the area of increased acceleration further out.

These two examples show that the weight chosen when optimizing a controller can have a strong influence on the one hand, and that choosing weights is not intuitive on the other hand, especially as the number of dimension increases. We therefore consider the easy availability of Pareto Curves an asset of our framework.

Verification. Once a controller has been selected, we can turn to verification and validation. To that end, we support two systems that complement each other: (1) a classical probabilistic model checking algorithm, and (2) a Bayesian probabilistic model checking algorithm.

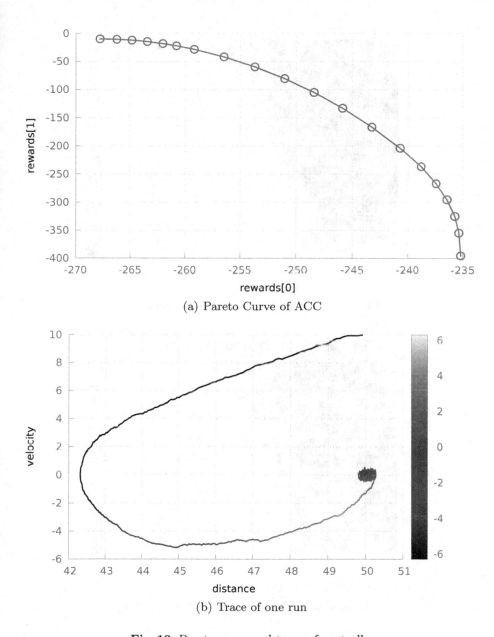

(a) Pareto Curve of ACC

(b) Trace of one run

Fig. 19. Pareto curve and trace of controller

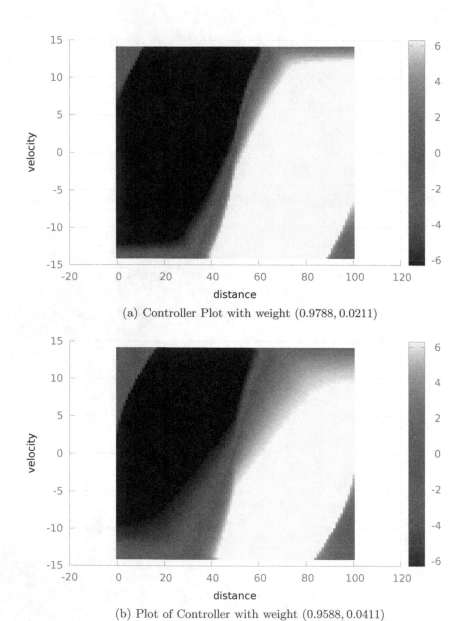

(a) Controller Plot with weight $(0.9788, 0.0211)$

(b) Plot of Controller with weight $(0.9588, 0.0411)$

Fig. 20. Two controller plots for different weights

Classical Probabilistic Model Checking. We use both systems to judge how the controller behaves if assumptions we made about the environment are not met and how the controller behaves with regard to properties that were not used for its construction. As an example of the latter, we can consider the stability of the system. In control theory, stability is the property of a system to reach a bounded set of states and never leave it. In our case, we define this set as a bound on the deviation of the distance of the two cars from the desired distance. We can easily state a desired bounded set of states via PCTL formula: $P_{=?}[\mathsf{G}(|d - 50| < c)]$, where d denotes the distance between the two cars and c is a constant. This formally asks "what is the probability of from now on always (denoted by G) seeing states whose deviation from 50 meters is less than c. Our framework takes this formula as input and calculates the probability of being in a stable (i.e., in a state from which only other stable states can be reached) for each state. In Plot 21(a) we plot the probability of being in a stable state, where we arbitrarily judge a state stable if $c = 5$. Note, first, that any state with a distance not within 5 meters of the desired distance cannot be stable. Note second, that as the relative velocity becomes more extreme, the probability of a state being stable goes towards zero. At the very extreme ends, the controller is unable to maintain control over the relative velocity in a way that guarantees that the distance will stay within 5 meters of the desired distance. Closer to the area where relative velocity is 0, the probability lies between 0 and 1. The reason that there is no sharp threshold between probability 0 and 1 lies in the random acceleration of the car in front. With a certain probability, the car in front will contribute to moving the distance towards the desired distance (braking where the controller needs to accelerate and vice versa). With a certain probability, the car will work against our controller (accelerating where we need to accelerate, braking where the controllers needs to brake as well).

Judging the probability of reaching a stable state is an additional task. This can be easily done in our framework by checking the controller against formula $P =?(\mathsf{F}P_{=1}[\mathsf{G}(|d - 50| < c)))$. Verbally, this means "what is the probability of reaching a state such that the state is stable almost surely?". As it turns out, the probability is 1 for all states of our model, i.e., under the given assumptions the controller is able to reach and maintain a low deviation from the desired distance to the other car almost surely.

We can now modify certain parameters of the system, and judge its behavior under these modified assumptions. For example, consider very rainy weather, where we assume that acceleration only works at 70% efficiency of what the controller expects[7]. In this case, the probability of a state being stable is only about at most 40% (see Plot 21(b))[8].

Lastly, our framework also allows us to easily turn the tables around and choose actions for the car in front. In this new model, the braking force applied

---

[7] This assumes that we use the same controller in bad weather, and that we cannot compensate

[8] Note that there are techniques for dealing with uncertain parameters(e.g., Robust Markov Decision Processes

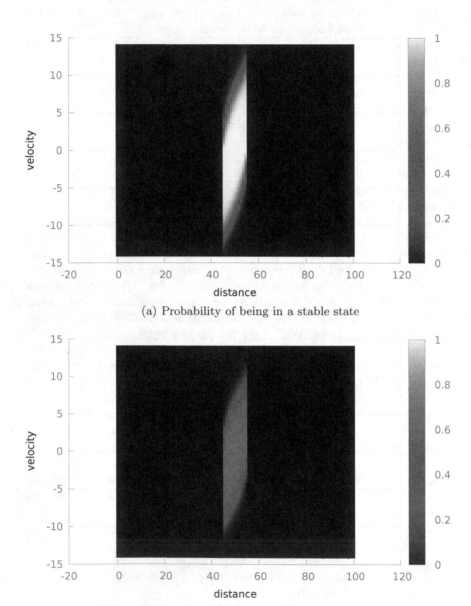

(a) Probability of being in a stable state

(b) Probability of being in a stable state with 70% acceleration effectiveness

Fig. 21. Statibilty of the controller

by the ACC is determined by a controller we previously generated, and we now synthesize worst-case accelerations for the car in front. This is easily achieved by replacing the function **next** of the Java class **ACC** (defined previously) by the following implementation.

```
public void next(double acceleration2, ACC target) {
  double acceleration = controller.get(this);
  double nextVelocity = velocity +
    (accleration + acceleration2) / ticks;
  double nextDistance = distance -
    (0.5 * velocity + 0.5 * nextVelocity) / ticks;
  target.velocity = nextVelocity;
  target.distance = nextDistance;
}
```

Now we can apply the very same techniques we used above to compute the worst-case probability of a state being stable.

Bayesian Probabilistic Model Checking. As we have noted before, the models described in Java lend themselves directly to continuous state space simulation. In general, we cannot check PCTL formulas since they may express properties over infinite runs. Instead we have to give time-bound formulas. As an example, we consider a formula expressing the property "What is the probability that we reach a state inside 5 meters around the desired distance in 1000 steps (where 1 step is 10 milliseconds long), and stay inside this area for the next 1000 steps." Bayesian probabilistic model checking allows us to make statements like "given the set of samples generated, the probability that this formula is true lies in the interval $[a, b]$ with probability c". In this framework, the width of the interval $b - a$ and confidence c are configurable. In our case it turns out, that with 95% confidence the formula holds with probability $[0.98, 1.00]$ from some randomly generated state. We assume that the remaining cases will require longer runs. For comparison, we decreased the efficiency of the applied acceleration to 70%. In this case, we get an interval $[0.971297, 0.991297]$, which shows us that the controller performs well even under adverse conditions.

Conclusion. We believe that our framework is the first time that verification and synthesis are present in a loop in the same tool. It allows engineers to (1) quickly model probabilistic environments for controllers in a language they know, (2) study the trade-offs their model possesses and pick a controller that is to their liking, (3) study the robustness of their controller with respect to environment assumptions, (4) study the performance of the controller in criteria for which the controller was not optimized, (5) allow efficient specification of latter criteria via a formal language, (6) judge the effect of discretization on the same criteria via the simulation engine we contribute. (7) effectively compare the influence discretization resolution has on the controllers.

In addition to what we presented here, our framework is developer-friendly and open and allows for quick addition of new synthesis and analysis algorithms. It also allows the easy consumption of new input formats. For example, to judge the correctness of our PCTL model checking algorithm, we imported PRISM [46] models and compared results.

Lastly, the implementation uses parallel algorithms in all performance relevant parts of the system. Speedup is linear in the number of processors, up to 12 processors we checked.

3.2   Access Control, Resource Usage, and Adaptation Policies for a Cloud Scenario

In this section, we briefly present a development methodology for policy-based systems and its application to a Cloud IaaS scenario. This methodology is based on the policy language FACPL [50], whose simplified variant is presented in Chapter I.1 [33] (Section 4). FACPL is capable of dealing with different systems' aspects through a user-friendly, uniform, and comprehensive approach. Indeed, FACPL can express access control policies as well as policies dealing with other systems' aspects, as e.g. resource usage and adaptation.

FACPL intentionally takes inspiration from XACML [54], the OASIS standard language for defining access control policies, but is much simpler and usable. Differently from XACML, FACPL has a compact and intuitive syntax and is endowed with a formal semantics based on solid mathematical foundations, which make it easy to learn and, most of all, paves the way to reasoning about policies. Moreover, in FACPL policies can be written at a higher abstraction level than XACML.

The development and the enforcement of FACPL policies is supported by practical software tools: a powerful Eclipse-based development environment and a Java library supporting the policy evaluation process. The policy designer can use the dedicated environment for writing the desired policies in FACPL syntax, by taking advantage of the supporting features provided by the tool. Then, according to the rules defining the language's semantics, the tool automatically produces a set of Java classes implementing the FACPL policies. The generated policy code can be integrated as a module into the enclosing application and can be used to compute a policy decision by executing it with the request code passed as parameter.

A Cloud IaaS Scenario. We consider here a scenario from the Cloud computing domain, in which a small-size IaaS provider offers to customers a range of pre-configured *virtual machines* (VMs), providing different amounts of dedicated computing capacity in order to meet different computing needs. Each type of VM features a specific *Service Level Agreement* (SLA) that the provider commits to guarantee. Thus, the allocation of the right amount of resources needed to instantiate new VMs (while respecting committed SLAs) is a key aspect of the considered IaaS provider. As is common for Cloud systems, virtualisation is accomplished using an *hypervisor*, i.e., a software entity managing the execution of VMs.

For the sake of simplicity, the considered IaaS provider relies only on two hypervisors (i.e., HYPER_1 and HYPER_2) running on top of two physical machines.

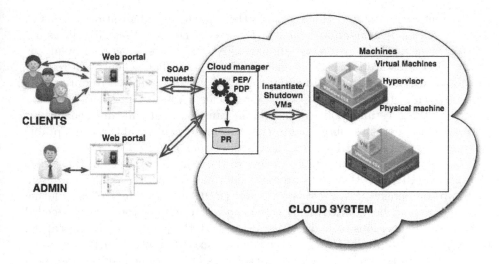

Fig. 22. IaaS provider scenario

The provider offers strongly defined types of VMs, like most of popular IaaS providers (consider, e.g., the instance types *M1 Small* and *M1 Medium* provided by Amazon EC2). Two types of VMs, namely TYPE_1 and TYPE_2, are in the provider's service portfolio. Each type of VM has an associated SLA describing the hardware resources needed to instantiate the VM (e.g., CPU performance, size of memory and storage) by means of an aggregated measure: TYPE_1 requires the allocation of one *unit of resources*, while TYPE_2 requires two units.

The two types of VMs have different guarantees when the system is highly loaded. Specifically, if the system does not have enough resources for allocating a new TYPE_2 VM, an appropriate number of TYPE_1 VMs already instantiated will be frozen and moved to a queue of suspended VMs. This queue is periodically checked with the aim of trying to reactivate suspended VMs. When a VM is frozen, according to the *Insurance* [65] SLA approach for resource provisioning in Cloud computing systems, the VM's owner will receive a credit that can be used, e.g., for activating new VMs or for paying computational time.

Policy-Based Implementation. A graphical representation of the data-flow in our implementation of the scenario is shown in Figure 22. Clients interact with the Cloud system via a Web portal that, following a multi-tenancy architecture, sends VM instantiation requests to the *Cloud manager* through SOAP messages. This means that the manager exposes its functionalities to users by means of a Web service. Then, the manager evaluates the received requests with respect to a set of policies defining the logic of the system. In particular, such policies specify the credentials the clients have to provide in order to access the service (*access control policies*), the resource allocation strategy (*resource-usage policies*), and the actions to be performed to fulfill the requests by also taking into account the current system state, which include the system re-configuration actions in case of high load (*adaptation policies*). It is worth noticing that all policies are written by using the same policy language, FACPL, and are enforced by means of the same software tool. By means of a similar workflow, clients can request the shutdown of VMs, which involves the release of the allocated resources.

The administrator of the Cloud system can access a dedicated panel for managing the governing policies. Indeed, he can change at run-time the current policies with other ones, obtaining in this way a fully configurable and adaptable system. The core of the Cloud manager is the *Policy Enforcement Point* (PEP), which evaluates client requests according to the available policies in the *Policy Repository* (PR) and the environmental information about the Cloud system. The sub-component *Policy Decision Point* (PDP) has the duty of calculating if a request can be granted or rejected, and determining the actions needed to enforce the decisions (called *obligations* in FACPL jargon), such as creation, freezing and shutdown of VMs. The enforcing is executed by the PEP by sending to the hypervisors the commands corresponding to the obtained actions. Notably, policies are independent from the specific kind of hypervisors installed on the system, such as XEN or Linux-KVM, i.e., the actions returned by the PDP are converted by the PEP into the appropriate commands accepted by the used hypervisors. Thus, in principle, the policy engine we have developed could be integrated with any IaaS system provided that the adequate action translation is also defined.

We have developed two different approaches for managing, instantiating and releasing requests. The first one concentrates the workload on hypervisor HYPER_1, while hypervisor HYPER_2 is only used when the primary one is fully loaded. Thus, by keeping the secondary hypervisor in stand-by mode until its use becomes necessary, energy can be saved. The second approach, instead, balances the workload between the two hypervisors.

An excerpt of the *energy saving* policies is presented below (we refer the interested reader to [49] for a complete account). This specification defines a PEP using the enforcing algorithm deny-biased[9] and a PDP using the combining algorithm permit-overrides[10], and includes a policy set, for supervising VMs instantiation requests (specifying action CREATE), and a policy, for supervising release requests (specifying action RELEASE). Such policies are included through a cross name reference, which simplifies code organisation.

```
{
 pep:  deny-biased;
 pdp:  permit-overrides
       include Create_Policies
       include Release_Policies
```

[9] The algorithm deny-biased states: if the PDP decision is permit and all obligations are successfully discharged, then the PEP grants access, otherwise it forbids access.
[10] The algorithm permit-overrides states: if any policy among the considered ones evaluates to permit, then the decision is permit; otherwise, if all policies are found to be not-applicable, then the decision is not-applicable; in the remaining cases, the decision is deny or indeterminate according to specific error situations (see [49]).

```
}
```

The policy set **Create_Policies** uses the combining algorithm **permit-overrides** and specifies a policy for each type of VM, namely **SLA_Type1** and **SLA_Type2**, and a *target* determining the requests to which the policy set applies, i.e. all requests having attribute **action/action-id** set to **CREATE**.

```
PolicySet Create_Policies { permit-overrides
    target:
        equal("CREATE",action/action-id)
    policies:
        Policy SLA_Type1 < ... >
        Policy SLA_Type2 < ... >
}
```

The enclosed policies achieve the prioritized choice between the two hypervisors by specifying the combining algorithm **deny-unless-permit** and by relying on the rules order. As an example, we report below the policy managing the instantiation of **TYPE_1** VMs. The policy's target indicates that instantiation of **TYPE_1** VMs can be required by clients having **P_1** or **P_2** as profile. The policy's combining algorithm evaluates the enclosed rules according to the order they occur in the policy; then, if one of them evaluates to **permit**, the evaluation terminates. Rule **hyper_1** evaluates to **permit** only if the hypervisor **HYPER_1** has at least one unit of available resources and, in this case, returns an obligation requiring the PEP to create a VM in this hypervisor. Rule **hyper_2**, governing VMs creation on **HYPER_2**, is similar. If no rule evaluates to **permit**, then the combining algorithm returns **deny** and, hence, the policy's (optional) obligation will be executed by the PEP to notify the Cloud administrator that there are not enough resources in the system to instantiate a new **TYPE_1** VM. In this way, the administrator can decide to upgrade the system by adding new resources (e.g., a new physical machine).

```
Policy SLA_Type1 < deny-unless-permit
    target:
        (equal("P_1", subject/profile-id)||equal("P_2", subject/profile-id))
        & & equal("TYPE_1", resource/vm-type)
    rules:
        Rule hyper_1 (permit
            target:
                less-than-or-equal(1, system/hyper1.availableResources)
            obl:
                [permit M create("HYPER_1", system/vm-id, "TYPE_1")]
        )
        Rule hyper_2 ( ... )
    obl:
        [deny O warning("Not enough available resources for TYPE_1 VMs")]
>
```

The policies for the *load balancing* approach are the same as before except that a condition on the hypervisors' load is added to each instantiation rule. This condition permits applying a rule for a certain hypervisor only if its amount of available resources is greater than or equal to the amount of available resources of the other hypervisor. For example, the rule **hyper_1** is extended as follows:

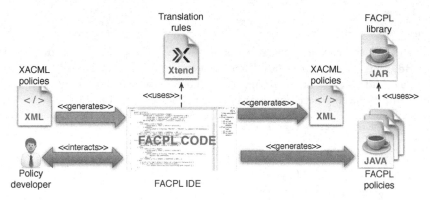

Fig. 23. FACPL toolchain

```
Rule hyper_1 ( permit
   target: ...
   condition: less-than-or-equal(system/hyper2.availableResources,
                                 system/hyper1.availableResources)
   obl: ... )
```

Supporting Tools. We have seen so far how the FACPL language can be used to define policies for the considered Cloud scenario. We conclude by briefly describing the software tools we have used to develop and enforce FACPL policies (we refer to [35] for a more complete account of these tools).

Figure 23 shows the toolchain supporting the use of FACPL. The FACPL Integrated Development Environment (IDE) allows the policy developer to specify the system policies in FACPL. In addition to policies, the IDE permits also specifying user requests in order to test and validate the policies. The specification task is facilitated both by the high level of abstraction of FACPL and by the graphical interface provided by our IDE. Furthermore, the developer can automatically create FACPL code starting from XACML policies. Obviously, the tool just accepts XACML inputs that only contain the supported elements.

By exploiting some translation rules, written using the Xtend language, which provides facilities for defining code generators, the IDE generates the corresponding low-level policies both in Java and in XML. The latter format obeys the XACML 3.0 syntax and can be used to connect our toolchain to external XACML tools (as, e.g., the test cases generator X-CREATE [22]). The former format relies on a Java library specifically designed for compile- and run-time supporting FACPL code. Once these Java classes are compiled, they can be used by the enclosing main application (i.e., the Cloud manager in our scenario) for evaluating client requests, simply by means of standard method invocation. Whenever new policies are introduced, new Java classes will be generated and compiled.

As an example of Java code generation, we report below an excerpt of the code corresponding to the policy SLA_Type1:

```
public class Policy_SLA_Type1 extends Policy {
    public Policy_SLA_Type1() {
        addId("SLA_Type1");
        addCombiningAlg(it.unifi.facpl.lib.algorithm.DenyUnlessPermit.class);
        addTarget(new TargetTree(Connector.AND,
            new TargetTree(...), new TargetTree(...)));
        addRule(new hyper_1());
        addRule(new hyper_2());
        addObligation(new ObligationExpression("warning",Effect.DENY,
            TypeObl.O,"Not enough available resources for TYPE_1 VMs"));
    }
    private class hyper_1 extends Rule {
        hyper_1 (){
            addId("hyper_1");
            addEffect(Effect.PERMIT);
            addTarget( ... );
            addConditionExpression(null);
            addObligation(new ObligationExpression ("create",Effect.PERMIT,
                TypeObl.M,"HYPER_1",new StructName("system","vm-id"), "TYPE_1"));
        }
    }
    private class hyper_2 extends Rule { ... }
}
```

Policy evaluation is coordinated by the class implementing the combining algorithm (i.e., `DenyUnlessPermit.class`). The expression corresponding to the policy target is structured as nested expressions organised according to the structure of the original FACPL target. Since rules are only used inside their enclosing policy, for each of them the policy class contains an inner class. In the code above, these are the classes `hyper_1` and `hyper_2`.

In order to experiment with the Java code generated from the complete FACPL specification of the Cloud manager behaviour, we have integrated such code with a mock-up application and then with a more realistic application managing XEN hypervisors. Both applications provide a front-end for the administrator, from where he can manage the policies governing the hypervisors, and a front-end for the clients, from where they can submit requests for the creation or the shutdown of VMs. The two applications expose the same behavior to users and only differ in their back-end, as the cloud manager in the mock-up application interacts with a simple emulator of the hypervisors, while the manager in the XEN-based one interacts with real hypervisors. Notably, the mock-up application allows different users to independently experiment with the cloud system by creating a dedicated session for each of them. Instead, users of the XEN-based application interacts with the same servers and, as it happens in real cloud platforms, they share the same servers loading.

The two applications have been implemented by using the Java code automatically generated from the same FACPL policies. This gives a practical evidence of the interoperability and composability of the Java code generated from FACPL code. Indeed, such classes are decoupled from their working environment, hence no changes are needed to embed them in a real-world application rather than a mock-up one, apart from the implementation of the context handler.

For both applications, the server-side implementation is a Tomcat server that, by integrating FACPL and Xtext libraries, is able to accept FACPL polices, parse and compile these policies, and finally enforce the corresponding decisions for adapting hypervisors' state to client requests.

3.3 jDEECo Verification

jDEECo is a Java-based implementation of the DEECo component model [29] runtime framework. It allows for convenient management and execution of jDEECo components and ensemble knowledge exchange. DEECo is, in turn, a software-engineering refinement of the SCEL concepts (see Chapter I.1 [33] for a detailed presentation of SCEL).

The main tasks of the jDEECo runtime framework are providing access to the knowledge repository, storing the knowledge of all the running components, scheduling execution of component processes (either periodically or when a triggering condition is met), and evaluating membership of the running ensembles and, in the positive case, carrying out the associated knowledge exchange (also either periodically or when triggered). In general, the jDEECo runtime framework allows both local and distributed execution; currently, the distribution is achieved on the level of knowledge repository.

We designed and implemented support for automated verification of jDEECo applications with the Java Pathfinder model checker (JPF) [43]. This work consists of two main steps: (1) making the jDEECo runtime framework amenable to practical verification with JPF and (2) implementing support for checking specific properties relevant to jDEECo applications. First we provide a brief introduction to JPF and then we describe the two main steps.

Java Pathfinder (JPF) is a highly customizable verification framework for Java programs. The core of JPF is a special JVM that supports non-deterministic thread scheduling choices, non-deterministic data choices (for input values), backtracking, and state matching. Using these mechanisms, JPF systematically explores the state space of a given program, in particular all possible thread interleavings, and looks for specific errors such as assertion violations and deadlocks. During the state space traversal, JPF makes thread scheduling non-deterministic choices at (i) bytecode instructions that access global data (e.g., fields of shared heap objects) and (ii) synchronization primitives (locking, calls of the wait() method, etc). JPF has limited support for Java reflection and other library classes that use native methods (e.g., file I/O and networking).

The main goal in our effort to make the jDEECo framework (Fig. 24) amenable to verification with JPF was to enable systematic traversal of all possible interleavings of sessions executed by component processes, while at the same time mitigating state explosion, i.e. limit the number of unnecessary thread scheduling choices in the state space. We apply JPF to a local version of the jDEECo runtime framework, whose development started in the previous year, in order to precisely verify the concrete behavior of jDEECo. We do not perform abstraction of any kind. The architecture of the local version being subject to verification is in Fig. 25. Due to the fact that JPF has limited support for native methods (especially reflection), the verification process works as follows. First, all components and ensembles forming the jDEECo application that are

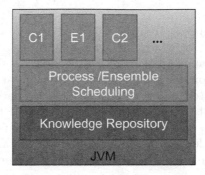

Fig. 24. jDEECo: Look inside

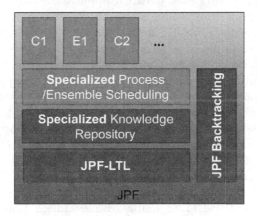

Fig. 25. jDEECo + JPF

subject to verification are serialized into a file. Then, JPF is run on the program consisting of the local version of the jDEECo runtime framework and the given application. Runtime loads all the components and ensembles from the file without the use of reflection, and then starts all the component processes. Note that JPF interprets every action performed by the runtime, starting with the loading of components from the file, up to the finish of the application, and searches for errors. To mitigate state explosion, we configured JPF such that it makes thread scheduling choices at the beginning of each session. This is sufficient in order to let JPF check all interleavings of sessions, because each session makes only a single atomic modification of the knowledge. Components interact only through modifications of the global knowledge. We disabled thread choices at all other places inside the jDEECo framework (e.g., field accesses in classes that implement the knowledge repository). Even though component processes are periodic, JPF does not have to model the periods (real time), because it just has to explore all interleavings of actions that may influence the future behavior of multiple threads. Our solution is to use a thread scheduler that ignores periods and limit the number of iterations of each process by $(N*H)/P + 1$, where P is the period of a given process, H is the length of one hyperperiod, and N is the number of hyperperiods for which the given application should be tested. The user has to define the number of hyperperiods because this value is typically application-specific. Upon reaching an error state (e.g., an assertion violation), JPF prints the full counterexample, which includes the path leading to the error state and snapshot of the current state. A limitation of this approach is that JPF explores an over-approximation of the set of possible thread interleaving because it does not model periods, and therefore it may report spurious errors that cannot happen in any feasible interleaving of the processes with respect to specific periods.

In the second step of our work, we focused on checking properties of two kinds: temporal behavior of jDEECo applications and data consistency. This includes assertions over values stored in the knowledge repository (e.g., the assertion "*battery.level* > 0" for a component representing a car) and LTL formulas. An example of a LTL formula is "G(follower_near_leader => F follower_at_destination)" for the Convoy demo application, which is a part of the jDEECo distribution. Temporal behavior of the jDEECo applications is interesting because component processes make small steps and it is not clear whether the process will reach the goal state. Atomic propositions in LTL formulas may contain path expressions, arithmetic operators, and logical operators. JPF can search for assertion violations out of the box, so we just had to implement checking of the LTL formulas using JPF. Our solution is based on JPF-LTL [44], which is a third-party extension to JPF that supports checking of LTL formulas. In order to support checking LTL formulas over jDEECo applications, we modified the implementation of JPF-LTL to enable seamless integration into the jDEECo framework and created a new module for jDEECo. The module evaluates atomic propositions based on the content of knowledge repository and stores the current value of each proposition. LTL formulas are checked on-the-fly during the state space traversal by JPF. The process works as follows. When the knowledge repository is updated by some process, our module at the jDEECo side evaluates all atomic propositions and gives the list of satisfied propositions to JPF. At the JPF side, it is then checked whether the LTL formula still holds.

4   Conclusion

System designers deal with two types of hardly reconcilable requirements: trustworthiness requirements and optimization requirements. The former characterize properties whose violation may disrupt system availability with more or less severe consequences. The latter are constraints applied to resources dealing with performance, cost or tradeoffs between them. As a rule, improving trustworthiness entails non-optimized use of resources. Conversely, resource optimization may jeopardize trustworthiness.

A key issue is ensuring trustworthiness without disregarding optimization. In this chapter we proposed methods to help designers for choosing amongst different equally trustworthy designs those better fitting the resources of the computing infrastructure. For the analysis of optimization requirements we proposed statistical model-checking approaches and corresponding tools, e.g. the statistical-based verification tool SBIP for stochastic systems that enrich BIP tool-set. SBIP provides two major extensions to the BIP framework: (1) a probabilistic semantics that expands BIP modeling capabilities for stochastic systems, and (2) a set of statistical algorithms for verification of qualitative and quantitative properties. The SBIP tool has been used to verify a set of large scale real life systems such as Avionics Full-DupleX switched ethernet, Precision Time Protocol IEEE 1588, MPEG2 Decoder, and Controller Area Network (CAN)/CAN Open.

Regarding security policies, we proposed a framework for information flow security in component ensembles, in which the security policies are checked early in the design following a model-based approach. We introduced a compositional verification method for non-interference properties. This work can be extended to investigate additional security conditions allowing to relax the non-interference property and control where downgrading can occur. Second, it will be interesting to work on the implementation of a complete design flow for secure systems based on secBIP. As a first step, we shall implement the verification method presented for annotated secBIP models. Then, we will use these models for generation of secure implementations, that is, executable code where the security properties are enforced by construction, at the generation time.

In addition to security, we also completed the verification techniques proposed for the verification of ensembles as explained as follows. We first focused on systems with bounded and static architectures. We proposed a verification method that encompasses timing constraints of components. As shown by the experimental results, and due to its compositional nature, the proposed method scales better to large systems than existing symbolic exploration algorithms such as the ones used in the tool Uppaal [3].

Finally, we presented a method towards the verification of service component implementation code by adding a support for jDEECo applications to the Java Pathfinder model checker. The current approach does not scale well, because each transition in the program state space between two thread choices consists of many bytecode instructions (up to hundreds of thousands), and therefore it takes JPF a very long time to interpret all these instructions (and process such a long transition). A new direction of work is to improve scalability of the verification process.

References

1. Intelligent robots for improving the quality of life, http://www.nccr-robotics.ch
2. PPL, http://bugseng.com/products/ppl/
3. Uppaal, http://www.uppaal.org/
4. Z3, http://research.microsoft.com/en-us/um/redmond/projects/z3/

5. Accorsi, R., Lehmann, A.: Automatic information flow analysis of business process models. In: Barros, A., Gal, A., Kindler, E. (eds.) BPM 2012. LNCS, vol. 7481, pp. 172–187. Springer, Heidelberg (2012)
6. Alur, R.: Timed automata. In: Halbwachs, N., Peled, D.A. (eds.) CAV 1999. LNCS, vol. 1633, pp. 8–22. Springer, Heidelberg (1999)
7. Alur, R., Courcoubetis, C., Dill, D.L., Halbwachs, N., Wong-Toi, H.: An implementation of three algorithms for timing verification based on automata emptiness. In: RTSS, pp. 157–166 (1992)
8. Alur, R., Dill, D.L.: A theory of timed automata. Theor. Comput. Sci. 126(2), 183–235 (1994)
9. Astefanoaei, L., Rayana, S.B., Bensalem, S., Bozga, M., Combaz, J.: Compositional invariant generation for timed systems. Tech. Rep. TR-2013-5, Verimag Research Report
10. Baier, C., Katoen, J.P.: Principles of Model Checking (Representation and Mind Series). MIT Press, Cambridge (2008)
11. Basin, D., Doser, J., Lodderstedt, T.: Model driven security: from uml models to access control infrastructures. ACM Transactions on Software Engineering and Methodology 15 (2006)
12. Basu, A., Bensalem, S., Bozga, M., Combaz, J., Jaber, M., Nguyen, T.H., Sifakis, J.: Rigorous component-based design using the BIP framework. IEEE Software Special Edition – Software Components beyond Programming – from Routines to Services 28(3), 41–48 (2011)
13. Bell, E.D., La Padula, J.L.: Secure computer system: Unified exposition and multics interpretation (1976)
14. Bensalem, S., Bozga, M., Sifakis, J., Nguyen, T.-H.: Compositional verification for component-based systems and application. In: Cha, S(S.), Choi, J.-Y., Kim, M., Lee, I., Viswanathan, M. (eds.) ATVA 2008. LNCS, vol. 5311, pp. 64–79. Springer, Heidelberg (2008)
15. Bensalem, S., Boyer, B., Bozga, M., Legay, A.: Incremental generation of linear invariants for component-based systems. Tech. Rep. TR-2012-15, Verimag Research Report (2012), http://www-verimag.imag.fr/TR/TR-2012-15.pdf
16. Bensalem, S., Bozga, M., Legay, A., Nguyen, T.H., Sifakis, J., Yan, R.: Incremental component-based construction and verification using invariants. In: FMCAD'10 (2010)
17. Bensalem, S., Bozga, M., Delahaye, B., Jegourel, C., Legay, A., Nouri, A.: Statistical model checking qoS properties of systems with SBIP. In: Margaria, T., Steffen, B. (eds.) ISoLA 2012, Part I. LNCS, vol. 7609, pp. 327–341. Springer, Heidelberg (2012)
18. Bensalem, S., Bozga, M., Sifakis, J., Nguyen, T.H.: Compositional verification for component-based systems and application. In: Cha, S(S.), Choi, J.-Y., Kim, M., Lee, I., Viswanathan, M. (eds.) ATVA 2008. LNCS, vol. 5311, pp. 64–79. Springer, Heidelberg (2008)
19. Bensalem, S., Griesmayer, A., Legay, A., Nguyen, T.-H., Sifakis, J., Yan, R.: D-finder 2: Towards efficient correctness of incremental design. In: Bobaru, M., Havelund, K., Holzmann, G.J., Joshi, R. (eds.) NFM 2011. LNCS, vol. 6617, pp. 453–458. Springer, Heidelberg (2011)
20. Bensalem, S., Legay, A., Nguyen, T.H., Sifakis, J., Yan, R.: Incremental invariant generation for compositional design. In: TASE (2010)
21. Bensalem, S., Bozga, M., Nguyen, T.-H., Sifakis, J.: D-Finder: A tool for compositional deadlock detection and verification. In: Bouajjani, A., Maler, O. (eds.) CAV 2009. LNCS, vol. 5643, pp. 614–619. Springer, Heidelberg (2009)

22. Bertolino, A., Daoudagh, S., Lonetti, F., Marchetti, E.: The X-CREATE Framework - A Comparison of XACML Policy Testing Strategies. In: WEBIST, pp. 155–160. SciTePress (2012)
23. Bertuccelli, L.F., How, J.P.: Robust Markov decision processes using sigma point sampling. In: American Control Conference (ACC), 11-13 June 2008, pp. 5003–5008 (2008)
24. BIP – incremental component-based construction of real-time systems, www.bip-components.com
25. Bonakdarpour, B., Bozga, M., Quilbeuf, J.: Model-based implementation of distributed systems with priorities. Design Autom. for Emb. Sys. 17(2), 251–276 (2013), doi:10.1007/s10617-012-9091-0
26. Bonani, M., Longchamp, V., Magnenat, S., R\'etornaz, P., Burnier, D., Roulet, G., Vaussard, F., Bleuler, H., Mondada, F.: The MarXbot, a Miniature Mobile Robot Opening new Perspectives for the Collective-robotic Research. In: International Conference on Intelligent Robots and Systems (IROS), 2010 IEEE/RSJ, pp. 4187–4193. IEEE Press, Los Alamitos (2010), http://mobots.epfl.ch/
27. Bozga, M., Jaber, M., Maris, N., Sifakis, J.: Modeling dynamic architectures using dy-bip. In: Gschwind, T., De Paoli, F., Gruhn, V., Book, M. (eds.) SC 2012. LNCS, vol. 7306, pp. 1–16. Springer, Heidelberg (2012)
28. Bozga, M., Jaber, M., Sifakis, J.: Source-to-source architecture transformation for performance optimization in BIP. IEEE Trans. Industrial Informatics 6(4), 708–718 (2010), doi:10.1109/TII.2010.2069102
29. Bures, T., Gerostathopoulos, I., Horky, V., Keznikl, J., Kofron, J., Loreti, M., Plasil, F.: Language Extensions for Implementation-Level Conformance Checking. In: ASCENS Deliverable D1.5 (2012)
30. Clarke, E.M., Klieber, W., Nováček, M., Zuliani, P.: Model checking and the state explosion problem. In: Meyer, B., Nordio, M. (eds.) LASER 2011. LNCS, vol. 7682, pp. 1–30. Springer, Heidelberg (2012), doi:10.1007/978-3-642-35746-6_1
31. Clarke, E., Grumberg, O., Peled, D.: Model checking. MIT Press, Cambridge (1999)
32. David, A., Larsen, K.G., Legay, A., Møller, M.H., Nyman, U., Ravn, A.P., Skou, A., Wasowski, A.: Compositional verification of real-time systems using Ecdar. STTT (2012)
33. De Nicola, R., Latella, D., Lafuente, A.L., Loreti, M., Margheri, A., Massink, M., Morichetta, A., Pugliese, R., Tiezzi, F., Vandin, A.: The SCEL Language: Design, Implementation, Verification. In: Wirsing, M., Hölzl, M., Koch, N., Mayer, P. (eds.) Software Engineering for Collective Autonomic Systems. LNCS, vol. 8998, pp. 3–71. Springer, Heidelberg (2015)
34. Denning, D.E., Denning, P.J.: Certification of programs for secure information flow. Commun. ACM pp. 504–513 (1977)
35. FACPL Website (2013), http://rap.dsi.unifi.it/facpl/
36. Focardi, R., Gorrieri, R., Martinelli, F.: Classification of security properties. In: Focardi, R., Gorrieri, R. (eds.) FOSAD 2001. LNCS, vol. 2946, pp. 139–185. Springer, Heidelberg (2004)
37. Forejt, V., Kwiatkowska, M., Parker, D.: Pareto curves for probabilistic model checking. In: Chakraborty, S., Mukund, M. (eds.) ATVA 2012. LNCS, vol. 7561, pp. 317–332. Springer, Heidelberg (2012)
38. Frau, S., Gorrieri, R., Ferigato, C.: Petri net security checker: Structural noninterference at work. In: Degano, P., Guttman, J.D., Martinelli, F. (eds.) FAST 2008. LNCS, vol. 5491, pp. 210–225. Springer, Heidelberg (2009)

39. Goguen, J.A., Meseguer, J.: Security policy and security models. In: Proceedings of 1982 Symposium on Security and Privecy, pp. 11–20. IEEE Computer Society Press, Los Alamitos (1982)

40. Henzinger, T.A., Nicollin, X., Sifakis, J., Yovine, S.: Symbolic model checking for real-time systems. Inf. Comput. 111(2), 193–244 (1994), doi:10.1006/inco.1994.1045

41. Hutter, D., Volkamer, M.: Information flow control to secure dynamic web service composition. In: Clark, J.A., Paige, R.F., Polack, F.A.C., Brooke, P.J. (eds.) SPC 2006. LNCS, vol. 3934, pp. 196–210. Springer, Heidelberg (2006)

42. Jones, C.B.: Specification and design of (parallel) programs. pp. 321–332 (1983)

43. Java PathFinder, http://babelfish.arc.nasa.gov/trac/jpf/

44. JPF-LTL: An extension to JPF for checking LTL, https://bitbucket.org/michelelombardi/jpf-ltl

45. Kuhn, D.R.: Role based access control on mls systems without kernel changes. In: Proceedings of the ACM Workshop on Role Based Access Control, pp. 25–32 (1998)

46. Kwiatkowska, M., Norman, G., Parker, D.: PRISM 4.0: Verification of probabilistic real-time systems. In: Gopalakrishnan, G., Qadeer, S. (eds.) CAV 2011. LNCS, vol. 6806, pp. 585–591. Springer, Heidelberg (2011)

47. Lin, S.-W., Liu, Y., Hsiung, P.-A., Sun, J., Dong, J.S.: Automatic generation of provably correct embedded systems. In: Aoki, T., Taguchi, K. (eds.) ICFEM 2012. LNCS, vol. 7635, pp. 214–229. Springer, Heidelberg (2012)

48. Mantel, H.: Possibilistic definitions of security - an assembly kit. In: Proceedings of the 13th IEEE workshop on Computer Security Foundations (CSFW '00), p. 185. IEEE Computer Society Press, Los Alamitos (2000)

49. Margheri, A., Masi, M., Pugliese, R., Tiezzi, F.: Developing and enforcing policies for access control, resource usage, and adaptation. In: Tuosto, E., Chun, O. (eds.) WS-FM 2013. LNCS, vol. 8379, pp. 85–105. Springer, Heidelberg (2014)

50. Margheri, A., Pugliese, R., Tiezzi, F.: Linguistic Abstractions for Programming and Policing Autonomic Computing Systems. In: UIC/ATC, pp. 404–409. IEEE Computer Society Press, Los Alamitos (2013)

51. McCullough, D.: Noninterference and the composability of security properties. In: Proceedings of the 1988 IEEE conference on Security and privacy (SP'88), pp. 177–186. IEEE Computer Society Press, Los Alamitos (1988)

52. McLean, J.: A general theory of composition for trace sets closed under selective interleaving functions. In: Proceedings of the 1994 IEEE Symposium on Security and Privacy (SP '94), p. 79. IEEE Computer Society Press, Los Alamitos (1994)

53. Misra, J., Chandy, K.M.: Proofs of networks of processes. IEEE Transactions on Software Engineering 7(4), 417–426 (1981)

54. OASIS XACML TC: eXtensible Access Control Markup Language (XACML) version 3.0 - Candidate OASIS Standard (September 2012)

55. Pinciroli, C., Bonani, M., Mondada, F., Dorigo, M.: Adaptation and Awareness in Robot Ensembles: Scenarios and Algorithms. In: Wirsing, M., Hölzl, M., Koch, N., Mayer, P. (eds.) Software Engineering for Collective Autonomic Systems. LNCS, vol. 8998, pp. 471–494. Springer, Heidelberg (2015)

56. Pinciroli, C., Trianni, V., O'Grady, R., Pini, G., Brutschy, A., Brambilla, M., Mathews, N., Ferrante, E., Caro, G.D., Ducatelle, F., Birattari, M., Gambardella, L.M., Dorigo, M.: Argos: a modular, parallel, multi-engine simulator for multi-robot systems. Swarm Intelligence 6(4), 271–295 (2012)

57. Pnueli, A.: In transition from global to modular temporal reasoning about programs. In: Apt, K. (ed.) Logics and Models of Concurrent Systems, pp. 123–144. Springer, New York (1984)
58. Queille, J.P., Sifakis, J.: Specification and verification of concurrent systems in CESAR. In: Dezani-Ciancaglini, M., Montanari, U. (eds.) Programming 1982. LNCS, vol. 137, pp. 337–351. Springer, Heidelberg (1982)
59. Rushby, J.: Noninterference, transitivity, and channel-control security policies. Tech. rep. (December 1992), http://www.csl.sri.com/papers/csl-92-2/
60. Sabelfeld, A., Myers, A.C.: Language-based information-flow security. IEEE Journal on selected areas in communications 21(1) (2003)
61. Sabelfeld, A., Sands, D.: A per model of secure information flow in sequential programs. Higher Order Symbol. Comput. 14(1), 59–91 (2001)
62. Sandhu, R., Munawer, Q.: How to do discretionary access control using roles. In: RBAC '98 Proceedings of the third ACM workshop on Role-based access control, pp. 47–54. ACM Press, New York (1998)
63. Shen, J.-j., Qing, S., Shen, Q., Li, L.: Covert channel identification founded on information flow analysis. In: Hao, Y., Liu, J., Wang, Y.-P., Cheung, Y.-m., Yin, H., Jiao, L., Ma, J., Jiao, Y.-C. (eds.) CIS 2005. LNCS (LNAI), vol. 3802, pp. 381–387. Springer, Heidelberg (2005)
64. Smith, G., Volpano, D.: Secure information flow in a multi-threaded imperative language. In: Proceedings of the 25th ACM SIGPLAN-SIGACT symposium on Principles of programming languages (POPL '98), pp. 355–364. ACM Press, New York (1998)
65. Verma, D.C.: Service level agreements on IP networks. Proceedings of the IEEE 92(9), 1382–1388 (2004)
66. Yi, W., Pettersson, P., Daniels, M.: Automatic verification of real time communicating systems by constraint-solving. In: FORTE, pp. 243–258 (1994)
67. Zakinthinos, A., Lee, E.S.: A general theory of security properties. In: Proceedings of the 1997 IEEE Symposium on Security and Privacy (SP '97), p. 94. IEEE Computer Society Press, Los Alamitos (1997)

Part II:
Modeling and Theory of Adaptive and Self-aware Systems

Ensembles face several challenges related to adaptation that are not present for simpler software systems. The second part of the book is therefore devoted to models and theories for self-aware and adaptive systems.

The first chapter reconciles two perspectives on adaptation, black-box adaptation which only takes into account the performance of a system in particular environments and white-box adaptation which classifies the system's data or actions into basic or adaptive activities. The second chapter is concerned with the distribution of knowledge between the components of an ensemble, and in particular the deduction of global knowledge from local representations. It includes a representation for soft-constraint satisfaction problems that can express dynamic programming strategies, which is applied to various optimization problems. The second part of the chapter shows how the techniques can be generalized to problems that are not straightforward optimization problems.

To operate in difficult, changing conditions it is often useful for a component to have knowledge about the environment, the other actors present in the environment, and the ensemble itself. The third chapter introduces KnowLang, a language for knowledge representation. KnowLang provides a comprehensive set of operators to specify logical and stochastic knowledge, to describe the update of knowledge bases and to describe reasoning processes. The chapter introduces the pyramid of awareness and the awareness control loop. The fourth chapter continues the discussion of awareness with a multi-dimensional classification of awareness mechanisms and then focuses on reasoning and learning techniques for achieving awareness and adaptation. It introduces extended behavior trees (XBTs), a graphical language for modeling behavior strategies that include hierarchical reasoning and learning and shows how a novel method for reinforcement learning in cooperative ensembles can be expressed using XBTs. Additionally, mechanisms for integrating on-line and off-line learning in an approach called teacher-student learning are described.

The fifth and final chapter in this part is focused on one particular aspect of awareness that is highly relevant for ensembles consisting of many, often small and energy-constrained, devices: performance. Performance monitoring, measurement evaluation, performance modeling, adaptation and design are described in the context of the ASCENS cloud case study.

M. Wirsing et al. (eds.): Collective Autonomic Systems, LNCS 8998, p. 161, 2015.
© Springer International Publishing Switzerland 2015

CHAPTER II.1

Reconciling White-Box and Black-Box Perspectives on Behavioral Self-adaptation⋆

Roberto Bruni[1], Andrea Corradini[1], Fabio Gadducci[1], Matthias Hölzl[2],
Alberto Lluch Lafuente[3], Andrea Vandin[4], and Martin Wirsing[2]

[1] Department of Computer Science, University of Pisa, Italy
[2] Ludwig-Maximilians-Universität München, Germany
[3] DTU Compute, Technical University of Denmark, Denmark
[4] Electronics and Computer Science, University of Southampton, UK

Abstract. This paper proposes to reconcile two perspectives on behavioral adaptation commonly taken at different stages of the engineering of autonomic computing systems. Requirements engineering activities often take a *black-box* perspective: A system is considered to be adaptive with respect to an environment whenever the system is able to satisfy its goals irrespectively of the environment perturbations. Modeling and programming engineering activities often take a *white-box* perspective: A system is equipped with suitable adaptation mechanisms and its behavior is classified as adaptive depending on whether the adaptation mechanisms are enacted or not. The proposed approach reconciles black- and white-box perspectives by proposing several notions of coherence between the adaptivity as observed by the two perspectives: These notions provide useful criteria for the system developer to assess and possibly modify the adaptation requirements, models and programs of an autonomic system.

Keywords: Autonomic Computing, Behavioral Adaptation, Requirements Engineering, Software Engineering, Linear-time Properties, Games

1 Introduction

Autonomic systems operating in highly variable, even unpredictable, environments must be *self-adaptive*. Unfortunately, there is not a widely accepted agreement on a foundational model for adaptivity. Already in the early Sixties Lofti Zadeh [27] claimed that *"it is very difficult – perhaps impossible – to find a way of characterizing in concrete terms the large variety of ways in which adaptive behavior can be realized"* and was pessimistic regarding the possibility to obtain a unifying definition due to the inherent difficulty of subsuming under the same

⋆ This research was supported by the European project IP 257414 (ASCENS) and by the Italian project PRIN 2010LHT4KM (CINA).

M. Wirsing et al. (eds.): Collective Autonomic Systems, LNCS 8998, pp. 163–184, 2015.
© Springer International Publishing Switzerland 2015

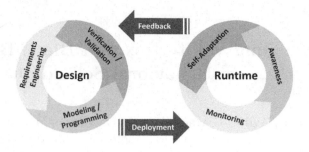

Fig. 1. The ASCENS life cycle for autonomic software component ensembles

hood both the *external* manifestations of adaptive systems (*black-box* adaptivity) and the *internal* mechanisms by which adaptation is achieved (*white-box* adaptivity).

These two perspectives persist today. Often, requirements engineering activities take the black-box one, by expressing requirements as goals to be achieved in some environments (cf. Chapter III.3 [26]). The system is adaptive to an environment if it may satisfy the goal in that environment. Sometimes, pairs of environments and goals are considered, if it makes sense to consider different goals in different environments. An example of these approaches is in the ASCENS [4] methodology (cf. Chapter III.1 [14]) to the engineering of autonomic systems (cf. Fig. 1): The *General Ensemble Model* (GEM) [15], a formalisation of the SOTA [1] approach to requirements engineering, takes a black-box perspective.

Later design activities such as modeling and programming tend to take the white-box perspective by focusing on the realisation of adaptation mechanisms, often based on linguistic or architectural techniques. A widely used approach is to clearly separate the functional and adaptation logics when structuring the behavior of a system. Thus, computations are classified according to the presence of normal steps aimed at realising the functional logic and adaptation steps aimed at adapting the system's behavior. An archetypal approach are Adaptable Interface Automata (AIAs) [6], a formalisation of white-box perspectives for autonomic systems like CODA [7] developed within ASCENS [4].

Contribution. Clearly, adaptation remains a subjective concept in both perspectives. The fundamental difference lies in who is responsible of declaring whether a system is adaptive or not: the requirements engineer (black-box) or the system engineer (white-box). Ideally, both perspectives should be coherent. This paper proposes an approach to reconcile black- and white-box approaches to behavioral adaptation in autonomic systems and to assess their coherence.

The key idea is that the white-box perspective allows to classify and quantify the behaviors of the system in an environment according to the presence of actual adaptations. Mismatches between black- and white-box perspectives may arise, e.g. if the system satisfies its goals in an environment, but no adaptation is observed. Mismatches can be used to improve the system, e.g. by disabling computationally expensive adaptation mechanisms based on monitoring and awareness (cf. Fig. 1). Moreover, mismatches may provide information to requirements and system engineers, since they can help to assess and modify specifications.

Our presentation focuses on the above mentioned approaches developed within the ASCENS project [4], respectively GEM and AIAs. However, the methodology we introduce is general enough to be applicable in a wide range of approaches to the engineering of autonomic systems.

Structure of the Paper. Section 2 briefly presents a case study from the AS-CENS project that we use for illustrative purposes throughout the paper. Section 3 recalls two archetypal approaches to adaptation based on black-box and white-box perspectives, namely GEM (Section 3.1) and AIAs (Section 3.2). Section 4 presents our approach to reconcile them. Section 5 discusses related works. Section 6 concludes the paper and outlines opportunities for future research.

2   A Robot Rescue Case Study

We shall use the *robot rescue scenario* (cf. Chapter IV.2 [21]) from the ASCENS case studies (cf. Chapter IV.1 [25]) as a running example throughout the paper. Fig. 2 illustrates this scenario, where a swarm of rescuer robots (represented as black circles with a grip) has to rescue victims (represented as stars) of a natural or industrial disaster (toxic waves in the figure), possibly cooperating to secure the area first (building a protection barrier in the figure) and then pulling the victim with the grippers until a safe place (e.g. Home in the figure) is reached.

To keep the scenario as simple as possible we limit us in some cases to a single rescuer robot and a single victim that has to be rescued. We assume that the locations of the victim and the robot are expressed as Cartesian coordinates: The robot can navigate the environment with constraints specified by kinematic equations and pick up objects in the environment according to certain physical constraints. The main requirement of the system is that the robot transports the victim to a rescue zone, but often a purely goal-based description is not sufficient to capture the real requirements.

We assume that one of the main question of interest is to determine whether the rescuer robot is capable of rescuing the victim under certain conditions on the environment. This is, as we shall see in Section 3.1, precisely a question about the adaptivity properties from

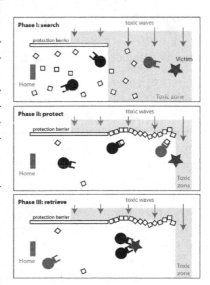

Fig. 2. Robot Rescue Scenario

the black-box perspective. For instance, if the victim has a weight of 80 Kg and the robot is capable of lifting only 20 Kg, then it is simply not possible for the robot to complete the rescue mission, given reasonable assumptions about the operating environment. However, an autonomic robot with these specifications operating on the moon would be able to lift the victim, and likewise a subaqueous robot.

The interplay between system and environment is not only important for the general structure of the system, it remains relevant as designers progress to more and more detailed system designs and their inherent trade-offs: A biped robot that is in principle capable of lifting a victim might not be able to do so in a marsh whereas a tracked vehicle might be able to. On the other hand, a tracked vehicle might not be capable of navigating stairs that pose no problem for the biped. A quadcopter might be able to lift a victim if the location is at sea level, but not if it is high in the mountains. Of course, given a specification of the problem the system designers and programmers have to decide how to actually solve the problem from an architectural and algorithmic point of view. This very same scenario has been tackled in the ASCENS project with a variety of techniques, from aspect-oriented programming to high-level policies, to meta-programming techniques (see e.g. the long discussion in [10] and the references therein).

3   Black-Box and White-Box Adaptation

This section offers a gentle introduction to two archetypal examples of black-box and white-box approaches to adaptation in autonomic computing systems, namely GEM (Section 3.1) and AIAs (Section 3.2). The presentation of both approaches has been simplified to focus on their essential features.

3.1   A Black-Box Perspective on Adaptive Systems

GEM [15], the *General Ensemble Model*, is a formalisation of the state space-based SOTA approach to requirements engineering [1]. GEM models describe the possible behaviors of a system as trajectories through its phase space[5] while the system is interacting with an environment, i.e., a system consists of a preordered *time structure* T, a phase space X and a set of trajectories in $T \to X$.[6] T might be as simple as the natural numbers with the usual order, while in our example the state space might be the position of each robot. Since they are used during the analysis or the high-level design of a system, the initial GEM models of a system typically have very little information about its internal structure. Chapter III.3 [26] in this volume discusses the Ensemble Development Life Cycle (EDLC) and the role that SOTA plays in the overall development process.

We illustrate the kind of GEM models that might be built during the development of a system like our scenario in Section 2, with some examples: The

---

[5] In this section we use the terms phase space and state space interchangeably.

[6] GEM actually allows the definition of more general types of systems, and ensembles in GEM are defined in a manner that is isomorphic but not identical to the one given here. The definition given above corresponds to *time ensembles*.

developer might start the initial system inception by defining simple and abstract requirements in the form of GEM models that are meant to analyse whether the proposed system is feasible at all. These models can be either discrete-state or continuous. For instance, for large ensembles we might approximate the number r of rescue robots that are still properly working after time t by the differential equation $\dot{r}(t) = -\alpha r(t) + c$, where α is the rate at which robots can be damaged (e.g. by toxic waves), c is a constant rate of newly produced robots, and $\dot{r}$ is the derivation dr/dt. After the feasibility of the system has been determined, a high-level GEM model for the rescue scenario might describe the state of the system in an abstract manner, e.g. by specifying the aforementioned Cartesian locations and movement constraints.

In general the phase space X becomes unwieldy as the systems become larger, therefore GEM allows developers to define individual components of a system on their own, and to combine them using *combination operators* that construct a new state space from the state spaces of the components. Those operators are denoted by $\otimes$. In the example, the system's designers might define two components, the robot S_r and the victim S_v, to investigate whether a robot can transport victims under the given environment conditions. To be useful the state of these components has to be sufficiently complete to allow a full description of the relevant aspects of the system behavior. The state X_r of the robot would probably include state variables for the robot's velocity and orientation, its position, the configuration of its gripper, its carrying capacity and so on. Similarly, the state of a victim would contain information about its physical properties, e.g., weight and how the victim's body behaves when it is picked up by the robot. By applying a suitable combination operator, designers can build a component $S_r \otimes S_v$ that represents a robot carrying a victim. In the combined system, state variables of the individual components that are no longer necessary to describe the combined system can be suppressed and new state variables that result from the combination can be introduced. For example, the configuration of the robot's gripper and the physical properties of the victim's body may be replaced in $S_r \otimes S_v$ by state parameters that specify the manoeuvrability of the robot while it is carrying the victim.

In a simple version of the rescue scenario, the main requirement for each rescuer robot can be described in a purely goal-based manner: Transport the victim to a safe zone. On the other hand, such a purely goal-based description is often not sufficient to capture the real requirements. Therefore, GEM allows developers to describe the quality of a solution (called its *utility* in GEM) using real numbers. For example, the utility of the robot might be defined as the time it needs to rescue the victim, possibly taking into account factors such as the exposure of the victim to environmental hazards during the transport phase.

The GEM *Approach to Black-Box Adaptation.* GEM defines a notion of adaptation, which we call *black-box adaptation*, that is applicable to models in the early stages of requirements engineering of autonomic computing systems (cf. the leftmost cycle in Fig 1). It is clear that at those stages the focus of the definition has to rely on the "circumstances" aspect of adaptation and not on the "change of the system", since little or no information about the system's internal structure is usually available at this stage of the development process. Nevertheless there are some interesting adaptation-related questions that can be answered by looking at the intrinsic capabilities of a *system S* and its *environment η*.

As we already advanced in the previous section, the most obvious question is perhaps "Is the system in principle capable of satisfying the requirements?". More precisely, it is mandatory to specify the range of environments $\mathcal{E}$ under consideration and ask for which environments in $\mathcal{E}$ a given system can fulfill the requirements. This is the basic idea underlying black-box adaptation.

While focusing on systems and environments would be sufficient from a theoretical point of view, models are often not detailed enough to contain all the information required to analyse the behavior of the combination. For example, the ability to recognise robots might be reduced because of lighting conditions in the environment; however the robot's model might not contain sufficient detail to represent this when combining it with an environment. GEM therefore introduces a third component into the ensemble model that describes the interaction of the system with the environment. In GEM this component is called the *network ν*, although in the rescue example "system/environment fit" might better describe the role of *ν*. For example, the performance of a robot's camera obviously depends on the lighting conditions, but in many cases the modelers do not want to specify the system in enough detail to compute the effect of lighting on the camera. To model the decreased camera quality under the expected lighting condition, the camera can instead be combined with the environment using a noisy or lossy communication channel in *ν*, without adjusting the models of the system or the environment themselves.

The GEM *Formalisation of Black-Box Adaptation.* We can now describe blackbox adaptation in slightly more detail.

Definition 1 (adaptation domain and requirements). *Given a set of environments $\mathcal{E}$, networks $\mathcal{N}$ and goals $\mathcal{G}$, an* adaptation domain $\mathcal{A}$ *is a subset of* $\mathcal{E} \times \mathcal{N} \times \mathcal{G}$, *i.e., a set of triples (η, ν, γ) called an* adaptation requirements.

An adaptation domain is therefore a package consisting of environments, networks and goals that are of interest to the system designer. Adaptation domains provide a basic signature for adaptation requirements that can be instantiated in several ways as we shall see further in this paper. A concrete example of this is the requirements specification language SOTA [1].

Concrete GEM models where adaptation domains are given a precise semantics can be subject to different kinds of analysis. A typical example is requirements satisfiability. For instance, the adaptation domain $\mathcal{A} = \{(\eta, \nu, \gamma), (\eta, \nu, \neg\gamma)\}$ is unlikely to be satisfiable under any reasonable semantics for $\neg$.

Of course, given a satisfiable adaptation domain, the question remains whether a given system can adapt to it. This concept is formalised as follows.

Definition 2 (adaptation to a domain). *Let* $S \otimes \eta \otimes \nu \models \gamma$ *denote that a system* S *fulfills a goal* γ *when in environment* η *with network* ν. *We say a system* S *can adapt to an adaptation domain* $\mathcal{A}$, *written* $S \Vdash \mathcal{A}$, *iff* $\forall (\eta, \nu, \gamma) \in \mathcal{A} . S \otimes \eta \otimes \nu \models \gamma$.

Again some of the concepts such as goal fulfillment $\models$ and composition $\otimes$ are left underspecified on purpose. They can be instantiated in many different ways. For instance, in this paper we shall see a trace-based semantics for $\models$ and automata synchronisation semantics for $\otimes$, which turn out to be very useful for reconciling black- and white-box perspectives.

Very often, one needs to compare the adaptation ability of different systems, which may correspond to different early designs of the same system. Recall, for instance, our case study (cf. Section 2) and the example of biped and tracked robots, where systems may make different trade-offs and therefore be able to deal with different adaptation requirements or domains. For instance, given a fixed adaptation domain $\mathcal{A}$, a system S_1 may be able to satisfy *every* adaptation requirement system in $\mathcal{A}$ that S_2 can satisfy; in that case we say S_1 is *at least as adaptive to* $\mathcal{A}$ *as* S_2. But it can be also the case that a system S_1 may be able to operate in *every* adaptation domain of interest in which system S_2 can operate; in that case we say S_1 is *at least as adaptive* as S_2. If S_1 can additionally adapt to at least one adaptation domain to which S_2 cannot adapt we call S_1 *more adaptive* than S_2. More formally, we define an adaptation space $\mathfrak{A}$ as a family of adaptation domains, $\mathfrak{A} \subseteq \mathfrak{P}(\mathcal{E} \times \mathcal{N} \times \mathcal{G})$. For any adaptation space we define a pre-order of adaptivity for systems as follows.

Definition 3 (adaptation pre-orders). *Let* $\mathfrak{A}$ *be an adaptation space and let* $\mathcal{A} \in \mathfrak{A}$ *be one of its adaptation domains. The* $\mathcal{A}$-*adaptation pre-order* $\sqsubseteq_{\mathcal{A}} \in S \times S$ *is the relation among systems defined by*

$$S \sqsubseteq_{\mathcal{A}} S' \longleftrightarrow \forall (\eta, \nu, \gamma) \in \mathcal{A} . S \otimes \eta \otimes \nu \models \gamma \implies S' \otimes \eta \otimes \nu \models \gamma$$

The adaptation pre-order $\sqsubseteq_{\mathfrak{A}} \in S \times S$ *is the relation among systems defined by*

$$S \sqsubseteq_{\mathfrak{A}} S' \Longleftrightarrow \forall \mathcal{A} \in \mathfrak{A} : S \Vdash \mathcal{A} \implies S' \Vdash \mathcal{A}$$

It is worth to remark that $S \sqsubseteq_{\mathfrak{A}} S'$ implies $\forall \mathcal{A} \in \mathfrak{A} . S \sqsubseteq_{\mathcal{A}} S'$ but the contrary is not true. A trivial example is one in which the adaptation space $\mathfrak{A}$ is just $\{\mathcal{A}\}$, neither S nor S' adapt to $\mathcal{A}$ but $S \sqsubseteq_{\mathcal{A}} S'$, i.e. S' can satisfy more requirements than S but they both adapt to the same set of domains, namely none.

It is easy to extend those relations to the case of utility-based systems; intuitively a system S' is more adaptive than a system S given an adaptation domain $\mathcal{A}$ if the utility of S' is at least as high as that of S for every element of $\mathcal{A}$, and higher for at least one element of $\mathcal{A}$. This definition is extended to adaptation spaces in the obvious way.

All in all, GEM's approach to adaptation requirements engineering from a black-box perspective provides a simple yet useful tool for designers to analyse various aspects of early system specifications. For instance, GEM models can be used to compare various early systems designs in terms of their adaptation abilities to cope with the desired requirements; adaptation spaces can also be used to check whether it is at all possible to satisfy all adaptation requirements, or whether certain requirements are expensive to implement.

3.2   A White-Box Perspective on Adaptive Systems

White-box perspectives on adaptation shift the attention to later stages of system design (e.g. Modeling and Programming in Fig. 1) and allow one to specify or inspect (part of) the internal structure of a system in order to offer a clear *separation of concerns* to distinguish changes of behavior that are part of the application or functional logic from those which realise the adaptation logic. This section summarises the CODA approach to adaptation and one of its formalisations, namely *Adaptable Transition Systems* [6].

The CODA *Approach to White-Box Adaptation.* In general, the behavior of a system is governed by a program and according to the traditional, basic view, a program is made of *control* (i.e. algorithms) and *data*. The conceptual notion of adaptation proposed in [7] requires to identify *control data* which can be changed to *adapt* the system behavior. *Adaptation* is, hence, the run-time modification of such control data. According to this notion, a system is *adaptable* if it has a distinguished collection of control data that can be modified at run-time, *adaptive* if it is adaptable and its control data are modified at run-time, at least in some of its executions, and *self-adaptive* if it modifies its own control data at run-time. So, essentially, the CODA approach to measure the adaptation ability of a system is to identify control data and observe its modification in the system's behaviors. For example, the adaptation mechanisms of robots like the ones in our scenario are sometimes based on the use of operation modes. Each mode of operation is tailored to some specific class of situation and a high-level controller adapts the behavior of the robot by switching between modes of operation. In this case, the control data is precisely the data defining the current mode of operation.

Several programming paradigms and reference models have been proposed for adaptive systems. A notable example is the Context Oriented Programming paradigm, where the contexts of execution and code variations are first-class citizens that can be used to structure the adaptation logic in a disciplined way [24]. This paradigm has also influenced the many programming and modeling approaches developed within the ASCENS project [4] among which we cite the *Service Component Ensemble Language* (see [12] and also Chapter I.1 [11]) and the architectural approach of [9]. Nevertheless, it is not the choice of the programming language what makes a program adaptive: any computational model or programming language can be used to implement an adaptive system, just by identifying the part of the data that governs the adaptation logic, that is the control data. Consequently, the nature of control data can vary considerably, including all possible ways of encapsulating behavior: from simple configuration parameters to a complete representation of the program in execution that can be modified at run-time, as it is typical of computational models that support meta-programming or reflective features.

Adaptable Transition Systems: A Foundational Model for CODA. Adaptable Interface Automata (AIAs) are a model of adaptive component-based systems built upon *interface automata* [2,3]. AIAs are an incarnation of the more general concept of adaptable transition systems. The key feature of AIAs are *control propositions* evaluated on states, the formal counterpart of control data. The choice of such propositions is arbitrary but it imposes a clear separation between ordinary behaviors and adaptive ones.

Interface automata were introduced in [3] as a framework for component-based design and verification. Following [2], an interface automaton P is a tuple $\langle V, V^i, \mathcal{A}^I, \mathcal{A}^O, \mathcal{T} \rangle$, where V is a set of states; $V^i \subseteq V$ is the set of initial states, which contains at most one element (if V^i is empty then P is called *empty*); $\mathcal{A}^I$ and $\mathcal{A}^O$ are two disjoint sets of *input* and *output actions* (we denote by $\mathcal{A} = \mathcal{A}^I \cup \mathcal{A}^O$ the set of all actions); and $\mathcal{T} \subseteq V \times \mathcal{A} \times V$ is a deterministic set of *transitions* (also called *steps*), i.e. for any two transitions $(u, a, v) \in \mathcal{T}$ and $(u, a, v') \in \mathcal{T}$ we have that $v = v'$. An interface automaton can represent, for instance, the behavioral model of one of our robots, where actions represent interactions with the environment and the distinction between input and output reflects the flow of information between them.

As usual, a transition (u, a, v) can be denoted by $u \xrightarrow{a} v$. The absence of non-determinism is not essential for the purposes of this paper, but it plays a fundamental role for the feasibility of control synthesis. Given $\mathcal{B} \subseteq \mathcal{A}$, we sometimes use $P_{|\mathcal{B}}$ to denote the automaton obtained by restricting the set of steps to those whose action is in $\mathcal{B}$. Also, the set of actions in $\mathcal{B}$ labelling the outgoing transitions of a state u is denoted by $\mathcal{B}(u)$. A *computation* ρ of an interface automaton P is a finite or infinite sequence of consecutive transitions $\{u_i \xrightarrow{a_i} u_{i+1})\}_{i<n}$ from $\mathcal{T}$ (thus n can be ω).

In our case study, an interface automaton could represent the overall behavior of a robot, possibly obtained as the result of composing different components such as controllers and sensors. The main idea of AIAs is to exhibit the minimal amount of information that allows one to distinguish the ordinary behaviors aimed at realising the application logic of the system (e.g. a robot) from the behaviors aimed at realising the system's adaptation. AIAs extend interface automata with atomic propositions (state observations), some of which are called *control propositions* and play the role of the control data of [7].

Definition 4 (adaptable interface automata). *An* adaptable interface automaton *(*AIA*) is a tuple* $\langle P, \Phi, l, \Phi^c \rangle$ *such that* $P = \langle V, V^i, \mathcal{A}^I, \mathcal{A}^O, \mathcal{T} \rangle$ *is an interface automaton;* Φ *is a set of atomic propositions,* $l : V \to 2^{\Phi}$ *is a labelling function mapping states to sets of propositions; and* $\Phi^c \subseteq \Phi$ *is a distinguished subset of* control propositions.

We call P an AIA with underlying interface automaton P, whenever this introduces no ambiguity. Most of the ingredients of Interface Automata are trivially lifted to AIAs. This includes the notion of computation. Furthermore, we shall consider as well the usual notion of trace, denoting with $Traces(P)$ the set of traces of an AIA P, i.e. the projection of all computations of P on the state observation Φ. More precisely, if $u \xrightarrow{a} v$ is a transition of a computation, its projection on a trace will be the trace transition $l(u) \xrightarrow{a} l(v)$. Additional lifted concepts are those of compatibility and composition among AIAs. Indeed, AIAs come equipped with a suitable composition operator, denoted $\otimes$, which essentially corresponds to lifting the composition operator on the underlying Interface Automata structure. We refer the interested reader to [6]. The choice of symbol $\otimes$ is not an accident: interpreting composition in GEM models as composition of AIAs is indeed part of our approach to reconcile both views on adaptation, as we shall explain later in Section 4.

The AIA Approach To White-Box Adaptation. A transition $u \xrightarrow{a} u' \in T$ is called an *adaptation* if it changes the control data, i.e. if there exists a proposition $\phi \in \Phi^c$ such that either $\phi \in l(u)$ and $\phi \notin l(u')$, or vice versa. Otherwise, it is called a *basic* transition. Consider for instance an AIA modeling one of the robots of our case study. Let us assume that its control propositions allow one to observe the robot's mode of operation, whose change is the way of implementing adaptive behaviors. Then the adaptive transitions will exactly correspond to those adaptive behaviors, i.e. switching between modes of operation. The basic behaviors would be the ordinary behavior within a mode of operation. Clearly, the concept trivially lifts to trace transitions. An action $a \in A$ is called a *control action* if it labels at least one adaptation. The set of all control actions of an AIA P is denoted by $\mathcal{A}_P^C$.

Computations are classified according to the presence of adaptation steps.

Definition 5 (adaptive computations). *Let P be an AIA and ρ a computation in P. We say that ρ is basic if it contains no adaptive transition, and it is adaptive otherwise.*

We will also use the concepts of *basic computation* starting at a state u and of *adaptation phase*, i.e. a maximal computation made of adaptive steps only. Again, this concept can be trivially lifted to traces.

The concept of adaptive trace can be formalised in temporal logics such as LTL as follows, $\psi_{adaptive} \equiv \neg \bigwedge_{\phi \in \Phi^c}(\phi \leftrightarrow \mathbf{G}\phi)$, i.e. it is not the case that all observable control data remain the same forever. This clearly enables the use of standard model checking techniques to analyse properties of adaptive systems (see e.g. the references and the discussion in [6]).

It is worth to remark that what distinguishes adaptive computations and adaptation phases are not the actions, because control actions may also label transitions that are not adaptations. However, very often an AIA has *coherent control*, meaning that the choice of control propositions is coherent with the induced set of control actions, in the sense that all the transitions labelled with control actions are adaptations. In the rest of the paper we assume that every system under consideration has coherent control.

The relationship between the set of control actions $\mathcal{A}_P^C$ and the alphabets $\mathcal{A}_P^I$ and $\mathcal{A}_P^O$ is arbitrary in general, but it could satisfy some pretty obvious constraints for specific classes of systems. Let P be an AIA. We say that P is *adaptable* if $\mathcal{A}_P^C \neq \emptyset$; *controllable* if $\mathcal{A}_P^C \cap \mathcal{A}_P^I \neq \emptyset$; *self-adaptive* if $\mathcal{A}_P^C \cap \mathcal{A}_P^O \neq \emptyset$. Intuitively, an AIA is *adaptable* if it has at least one control action, which means that at least one transition is an adaptation. An adaptable AIA is *controllable* if control actions include some input actions and *self-adaptive* if control actions include some output actions (which are under the control of the AIA). From these notions we can derive others. For instance, we can say that an adaptable AIA is *fully self-adaptive* if $\mathcal{A}_P^C \cap \mathcal{A}_P^I = \emptyset$ (the AIA has full control over adaptations). Note that hybrid situations are possible as well, when control actions include both input actions (i.e. actions in $\mathcal{A}_P^I$) and output actions (i.e. actions in $\mathcal{A}_P^O$). In this case we have that P is both *self-adaptive* and *controllable*. In our case study we could expect to have fully self-adaptive ground rescue robots or partially adaptive ones that can be influenced from supervisor quadcopter robots.

Those notions can be lifted to computations in the obvious way.

Definition 6 (adapted computations). *Let P be an AIA and ρ a computation in P. We say that ρ is* controlled *if it contains a transition which is an adaptation and corresponds to an input action, and it is* fully self-adapted *if all its adaptation transitions correspond to output actions.*

Such concepts may be formalised as well with modal logics. Of course, LTL cannot be directly applied since it is a pure state-based logic and here we need to observe actions, but one may use logics for double-labelled transition systems or standard encodings between action-labelled transitions systems (e.g. automata) and state-labelled transitions systems (e.g. Kripke structures).

4   Reconciling Black-Box and White-Box Adaptation

We present here our approach to reconcile white-box and black-box perspectives on adaptation. We assume that the black-box perspective on the systems under study is formalised by GEM models whose systems, environments and networks are suitably represented by AIAs, our reference model for white-box perspective. One of the key observations regarding the different treatments of adaptation on black-box and white-box perspectives is that adaptation in the former case is "asymmetric" in that it considers various environments in which a system may operate, but the system is defined by all its possible behaviors, irrespectively of whether they require internal changes or not. Tackling this asymmetry is one of the issues in the conciliation. We propose here two ways of reconciling white-box and black-box perspectives on adaptation. A first, simple one is based on a trace-based semantics of GEM and AIAs (cf. Section 4.1). The second one (cf. Section 4.2) is based on game semantics.

4.1   Trace-Based Reconciliation

A key assumption to combine GEM and AIA concepts is to assume that GEM notion of property satisfaction is based on semantic relations on computations. For the sake of illustration, we consider the well-studied and popular notion of property satisfaction based on trace inclusion.

Definition 7 (trace-based adaptation). *Let S be a system and (η, ν, γ) a requirement. We instantiate the fulfillment by S of a goal γ in an environment η with network ν as*

$$S \otimes \eta \otimes \nu \models \gamma \quad \textit{iff} \quad \textit{Traces}(S \otimes \eta \otimes \nu) \subseteq \textit{Traces}(\gamma)$$

Recall that trace inclusion amounts to the satisfaction relation of model checking linear-time temporal logics. This means that if goals are expressed as LTL properties (as SOTA requirements essentially are), checking the fulfillment of requirements can be done with efficient state-of-the art model checking techniques.

A consequence of our choice of trace based semantics is that we are instantiating the adaptation of a system S to an adaptation domain $\mathcal{A}$ as $S \Vdash \mathcal{A}$ iff $\forall(\eta, \nu, \gamma) \in \mathcal{A}. \textit{Traces}(S \otimes \eta \otimes \nu) \subseteq \textit{Traces}(\gamma)$. This trace-based notion is not only interesting from the theoretical point, but it allows us to re-use all the useful machinery of linear-time properties, including model checking. For instance, we may assume goals γ to be suitably specified in languages with linear-time semantics such as ω-regular expressions, linear-time temporal logic, and various forms of automata or transition systems. Moreover, the SOTA approach to requirements engineering for autonomic systems, for which GEM provides a formalisation, is indeed based on trace semantics and inclusion relations.

More interestingly, the trace-based semantics offers a common ground to compare and reason about properties of systems and their computations from both the black-box and white-box perspectives. The first interesting question we address to reconcile the two perspectives on a system is the following. Let S be a system that is adaptive to an adaptation domain $\mathcal{A}$ (i.e. $S \Vdash \mathcal{A}$). Are the behaviors of S that witness adaptation to $\mathcal{A}$ adaptive from the white-box point of view? This leads us to the concept of *coherent adaptation*.

Definition 8 (coherent adaptation). *Let S be a system and $\mathcal{A}$ be an adaptation domain. We say that S is* coherently adaptive *to $\mathcal{A}$ if $S \Vdash \mathcal{A}$ implies that for all $(\eta, \nu, \gamma) \in \mathcal{A}$ there is at least one trace $\rho \in \textit{Traces}(S \otimes \eta \otimes \nu)$ that is adaptive.*

It is worth to remark once more that coherence can be boiled down to a standard model checking problem. Note that if a system S is not coherently adaptive to an adaptation domain $\mathcal{A}$ then the system is able to satisfy one goal in $\mathcal{A}$ without performing any transition observationally identified as adaptation (from the white-box perspective). This implies a certain mismatch between what is considered to be a normal operation environment from the system design point of view (i.e. the system S as an AIA) and from the requirements point of view (i.e. the adaptation domain $\mathcal{A}$). The system designer can then exploit this information for improving the design of the system. For instance, in the case of our case study, a lack of coherent adaptation could help the designer decide that the components of the robot software realising its adaptive behavior are not necessary, so that robots can be deployed with a light-weight version of the software, possibly consuming less computational resources and battery.

Further distinctions can be done by considering the presence/absence of adaptation transitions controlled by the environment: if all adaptation transitions correspond to output control actions of S, the system is *fully self-adaptive* to $\mathcal{A}$, even if it may not necessarily be *fully self-adaptive* in general.

Ideally, one would like to have a system S that is *coherently adaptive* and *fully self-adaptive* with respect to the adaptation domain $\mathcal{A}$ under consideration. That is, a system that has full control over its adaptation actions when operating in $\mathcal{A}$ and whose adaptation mechanisms are actually enacted in all the situations identified in the adaptation domain $\mathcal{A}$. When this is not the case the system designer can take the necessary actions as we exemplified above.

4.2 A Game-Based Reconciliation

The last section introduced the notion of coherent adaptation for systems represented by AIAs. This definition can be generalised to arbitrary SOTA/GEM models if we define control propositions Φ^c (see Section 3.2) as propositions in a suitable logic over the state space X. These propositions define a subset $X^c \subseteq X$ that we call the *control space* of the system. The notion of adaptive computation from Definition 5 can then be applied to segments of SOTA/GEM traces: Let T be the time domain of the model, $\theta : T \to X$ a trajectory in X, and $t_1, t_2 \subset T$. We say that θ *is adaptive* in the interval $[t_1, t_2]$ if it intersects the control space in that interval, i.e., $\{\theta(t) \mid t \in [t_1, t_2]\} \cap X^c \neq \emptyset$; it is *purely adaptive* if it is contained in X^c, i.e., $\{\theta(t) \mid t \in [t_1, t_2]\} \subseteq X^c$; and it is *basic* if it is not adaptive. Definition 8 can be applied to arbitrary SOTA/GEM models in a similar manner.

An environment that reacts to the system behaviors but does not pursue its own goals is sometimes called (purely) *parametric* or *stochastic*; an environment in which other agents pursue their own goals (and thus may actively work to inhabit the ensemble goals) is called *game-theoretic* or *strategic*. Many interesting and practically occurring environments are strategic; in these environments it is useful to regard black-box adaptation as a game between two players *System* and *Environment*, moderated by a *Network* that determines properties such as the information available to each player during the game.

The structure of this game (e.g., whether the players move simultaneously or in an alternating manner) and the features of the combined state space X are given by a combination operator between the models of the *System* S, the *Environment* η and the *Network* ν. The moves of *System* and *Environment* are given by the models S and η, and their effect is described by the change to the combined state space X. The information about the moves of the other player is provided by ν (which may also contribute to the shared state space). Roughly speaking, S and η determine the moves in the game, whereas ν describes the information sets and thus, together with the combination operator, determines whether the game is one with concurrent or sequential moves and whether it is one of perfect or imperfect information. We call this way of specifying a GEM model M a *game-based presentation* (of M). In a game-based presentation we may say "M_1 wins against more opponents (from an adaptation domain $\mathcal{A}$) than M_2" instead of "M_1 is more adaptive than M_2."

SOTA/GEM themselves impose no specific organization on models, and many SOTA/GEM models have a continuous time structure and large state spaces; therefore writing a game-based presentation of a model does not imply that the model becomes amenable to game-theoretic analysis. However, typical models are often structured in a particular way: The model is represented as a hierarchy of components, and components interact mostly in a local manner between themselves and with the environment. The temporal structure of a model can often be divided into several concurrent threads, where in each thread components of the system interact in "episodes" that can themselves be regarded as a discrete unit. Control propositions can then provide additional structure by classifying each episode either as "adaptive" or "performative". In this manner we can often apply game-theoretic techniques to discrete abstractions of parts of the overall model, and this analysis is often particularly useful to investigate the adaptation strategies of a system. The following example will illustrate this in more detail.

To obtain more interesting adaptation concerns we focus on a slightly more complex variant of the rescue scenario presented in Section 2. We assume that the rescue mission is performed by an ensemble E (for *ensemble* or, as we see shortly, *evaders*) consisting of a large number of robots E_i. To keep the kinematics simple we assume that each robot can instantaneously change direction, but that its speed is limited by v_{max}. We can describe its position in a cartesian coordinate system at each instant with two state variables x_i and y_i. Its velocity is given by the derivations $v_i = \dot{x}_i$ and $w_i = \dot{y}_i$ with the constraint that $\sqrt{v_i^2 + w_i^2} \leq v_{max}$.

We assume that each robot has three ingress routes into the environment on which it encounters different amounts of toxic waste. Route ρ_1 is mostly free of waste and therefore does not damage the robot; on route ρ_2 the robot incurs a 10% chance of suffering debilitating damage that causes it to fail its mission, on route ρ_3 this chance is 20%.

To obtain more interesting adaptive behaviors, we now suppose that there is a party actively opposing the rescue ensemble, either because there are raptors in the area that mistake the robot for prey, or because the rescue mission takes place in a conflict zone in which an enemy is shooting at the robot. We call this opponent H (for *hunters*) and assume that each H_j moves at constant speed v_H where supposedly $v_H > v_{max}$, but where H_j cannot instantaneously change direction but only turn with a minimum radius τ_{min}. Its cartesian coordinates ξ and χ are thus described by the following equations

$$\dot{\xi} = v_H \cos\theta \qquad \dot{\chi} = v_H \sin\theta \qquad \dot{\theta} = u \cdot v_H / \tau_{min}, \quad 0 \leq u \leq 1$$

where θ is the angle between H_j and the x-axis. It is easy to see that if the speed v_H of H_j is only slightly larger than v_{max} and if its turning radius τ_{min} is large, then it is impossible for H_j to catch any E_i. On the other hand, if v_H is much larger than v_{max} and τ_{min} is small, then a E_i that finds itself close to H_j has no hope of escaping. What might perhaps not be obvious is that even this simple hunter/evader dynamics, known under the name "homicidal chauffeur" problem generates a rich solution space that gives rise to multiple different strategies, depending on the initial conditions and parameters [20].

The rescue scenario now unfolds in the following way: Each hunter H_j chooses a route ρ_κ to guard and each evader E_i chooses a route ρ_μ to take. The hunters that have chosen to guard a given route then attack the evaders taking that route. If E_i can successfully evade all attacks and it is not damaged by the waste, it completes its rescue mission and receives a reward of 1, otherwise it receives a reward of 0; if a hunter H_j captures an evader it receives a reward of 1 otherwise of 0. If an evader E_i is disabled by toxic waves this results in a reward of 1 for the ensemble H that is not attributed to any H_j.

Both E and H try to optimise their respective rewards; for each trip of an evader E_i one of the players receives reward 1 and the other 0, therefore the players will always try to obtain opposite outcomes. Obviously the rewards obtained by E depend on the strategy chosen by H, and vice versa. Even for this relatively simple scenario, finding the optimal behavior for the rescue robots is a non-trivial task. Therefore we have to divide the model into smaller components that are more amenable to analysis, and then further refine our initial analysis steps once we have gained a better understanding of the problem. To this end we will first focus on the choices of single agents.

When looking at the trajectory of an evader E_i through the state space, we see that it repeatedly moves through the following segments: (1) first it picks a route ρ_μ without modifying other parameters in the state space; (2) then it moves through the other dimensions of the state space without modifying its choice of route. If we choose Φ^c so that X^c contains (1) the choice of a route ρ_μ when all other parameters are kept constant and (2) the evasive manoeuvring of an evader when avoiding a hunter, we see that the trajectory for E_i repeatedly traverses the following stages: (i) a purely adaptive segment of the trace in which E_i chooses the route it takes (the "adaptation stage"); (ii) a basic segment of the trace in which E_i performs a rescue mission, possibly interrupted by E_i evading a hunter (the "performance stage"), the evasion being an adaptive segment of E_i's trajectory that is not purely adaptive. This structure supports the design of the ensemble relatively well: The non-adaptive behaviors that are required in the basic segment (navigation, picking up the victim, etc.) can be implemented using established methods. The adaptation in the performance stage depends only on the local interaction of an evader and a hunter, and it can be solved for different initial configurations of E_i and H_j. If the developers of the evaders know the control strategies that are used by the hunters, the designers of the evaders can exploit this model to develop efficient strategies to counter them, or determine that no such strategies exist.

	ρ_1	ρ_2	ρ_3
ρ_1	0, 1	1, 0	1, 0
ρ_2	0.9, 0.1	0, 1	0.9, 0.1
ρ_3	0.8, 0.2	0.8, 0.2	0,1

Fig. 3. Payoff matrix for the choice of route

The adaptive segment is, in some respects, the most challenging part: It cannot be locally solved since it depends crucially on the distribution of hunters between the different routes, and on the expected outcomes of the "homicidal chauffeur" game between hunters and evaders. In order to restrict the amount of required game-theoretic background, we study a greatly simplified version of this question. We assume, for now, that a single hunter $H = H_1$ is matched against a single evader $E = E_1$ and that the hunter always manages to capture the evader when they choose the same route. Fig. 3 shows the payoff matrix for this game. The rows of this matrix represent the route choices of E, the columns the choices of H. In each cell of the table, the first number gives the reward obtained by E if this pair of strategies is played, the second number gives the reward of H. For example, if H and E both choose route ρ_1 then H receives a reward of 1 since we assume that it always captures E, and E receives a reward of 0. If, however, E chooses ρ_2 while H chooses ρ_1, then 90% of the time E receives a reward of 1, whereas 10% of the time it is disabled by toxic waves, and therefore H receives the reward even though the two players do not encounter each other. See [19] for more information on utility theory and values of lotteries.

Given this payoff matrix, how should E choose its routes? It is clear that no choice of route of E is a best reply against all possible choices of H, since the pair of routes ρ_i, ρ_i always results in a loss for H. The solution for robot E is therefore to mix the routes it chooses, so that H cannot predict the route that it should guard. Closer investigation of the game results in the observation that to prevent H from exploiting its choices E has to pick the probability p_i of choosing route ρ_i so that its probability of survival times the probability of choosing the route is the same for all routes [22]: $1 \times p_1 = 0.9 \times p_2 = 0.8 \times p_3$. This results in the approximate probabilities $p_1 = 30\%$, $p_2 = 33\%$ $p_3 = 37\%$. Therefore, perhaps slightly counter-intuitively, E has to choose the most dangerous route most frequently to maximise its guaranteed reward. To refine this analysis we need to compute the expected outcomes of the "homicidal chauffeur" (HC) game between E and H. Whereas the choice of route could be cast in terms of a traditional competitive game this is not possible for the HC game; here the continuous time and the dynamics generated by the system of differential equations are essential. We are therefore in the realm of differential games [16].

The HC game generates a rich and varied solution space that we only describe qualitatively and in general terms: If the hunter H arrives in a position behind and only slightly offset to the evader E as shown in Fig. 4(a), the best solution for E is to move away from H in a straight line, and H will follow this line until

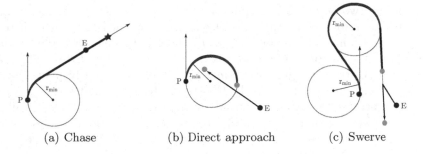

(a) Chase   (b) Direct approach   (c) Swerve

Fig. 4. Strategies for initial configurations: evader in back front (a) and back (b,c)

it captures E (indicated by the star). If the HC game continues indefinitely long, the velocity of H is much higher than the maximal velocity v_{max} of E and the turn radius τ_{min} of H is sufficiently small this capture will always occur and the strategy employed by E does not actually matter given the reward structure of our model. But if H has only a limited range (e.g., due to a small fuel supply), and the initial position of E is far enough away, E may successfully evade H. The goal of E in the HC game is therefore to maximise the distance that H has to cover before capture can no longer be avoided.

If the initial configuration is slightly different, with E behind H, a different situation may arise: E may navigate *towards* H in order to arrive inside the circle described by the turn of H, as shown in Fig. 4(b). Once E is inside the turning circle of H, the hunter cannot reach the evader by continuing to turn in the same direction. But this does not mean that E will necessarily escape H: the hunter can "swerve" away from E, i.e., turn in the opposite direction, then continue straight to gain some distance and, once it has gained enough separation, turn back towards E as shown in Fig. 4(c). In this case the correct strategy for E is to first turn towards H in order to force H into as big a swerve as possible, and then to turn away from H once the chase situation of Fig. 4(a) has been reached. By formalising these observations we can compute the probability that E can escape H for a given distribution of initial configurations. It is thus possible to use this estimate to improve the choice of ingress route by inserting these values into the payoff matrix in Fig. 3.

So far the analysis has only taken into account the interaction between two players. This is not a problem for the HC game, since the pursuit dynamics of the system consists of a number of independent two-player HC games. But for the choice of route, the relative sizes of the ensembles E and H can greatly influence the validity of the analysis: If the cardinalities of H and E are similar then the analysis remains at least approximately valid for many reasonable strategies. If however there are three times as many members in H than in E, then the system H has a strategy that prevents E from completing any rescue mission at all (guard each route with one third of H's members) and the analysis for the single-robot case cannot be transferred.

There are two additional complications when considering the adaptation of competing ensembles consisting of multiple members each: (1) When there are multiple players in each "team" E and H, there is no guarantee that a stable equilibrium of strategies will emerge; instead, at each point of time E is trying to find a best strategy against the mix of strategies currently played by the members of H while simultaneously H is trying to find a best strategy against the mix of strategies currently played by the members of E. This results in a dynamical system that may exhibit stable behavior, periodic cycles between different strategy mixes, or even chaotic changes in the strategy mixes of E and H. (2) The previous analysis relies on the assumption that both players play optimal strategies. This is not necessarily the case when a system is deployed in a real environment, and assuming that opponents play optimally when this is not often the case leads to less than optimal performance.

For these reasons, systems will rarely be developed with fixed adaptation rules; instead, members of an ensemble will often observe which strategies (used either by themselves or by other members) are particularly successful and use these strategies more frequently in the future. The effects of these kinds of adaptations can also be modelled and analysed in a game-theoretic setting: Since it is possible to compute the reward obtained by different strategy combinations in the basic segment of our example, we can compute the expected reward for a strategy used by a rescue robot E_i against a distribution of strategies for H. If we have large numbers of evaders and hunters, we can regard the sequence of adaptations as an evolutionary game: We abstract from the detailed interleaving of the segments of individual agents and assume that adaptation is a continuous game played between randomly chosen evaders and hunters. We assign a probability of being chosen to each of the paths ρ_μ for $E_i \in E$ and for $H_j \in H$: The expected value of a choice of ρ_μ against the distribution of H (respectively E) in the adaptation stage can be computed using the corresponding performance stages. The probabilities in the next round of the game are adjusted using these values: strategies with high values in the previous stage are played more frequently in the next stage; strategies with low values are played less frequently.

Chapter II.4 [13] in this volume goes into more details about evolutionary games and the methods to solve them. Note that the separation of behaviors into adaptive and base behaviors allowed us to reduce the analysis task into the pairwise evaluation of configurations (which depends on the number of configurations but not on the number of agents), and an evolutionary game between two populations of configurations (which, again, depends on the number of configurations but not the size of the ensembles). Since neither part of the analysis depends on the size of the ensembles, they scale to ensembles of arbitrary size. Furthermore, while the computation of the values of the performance stages is rather involved, this computation can be performed offline; for a moderate number of configurations the computation of an adaptation strategy via the evolutionary game becomes viable at run time. This is important if the evaders need to dynamically adjust their adaptation strategy (e.g., because there is uncertainty about the distribution of strategies used by the hunters).

We conclude this section by returning to the connection between black-box and white-box adaptation mentioned in Section 4.1: Suppose that we start with a simple system that supports neither the choice of route nor the evasive manoeuvring described in this section. By adding either of these features to the implementation we allow the system to move along trajectories through its control space X^C that were not present in the original system. The new trajectories in turn allow the system to operate in adaptation spaces in which it previously could not reach its goals, i.e., they increase its black-box adaptivity. Similarly, if we want to increase the system's black-box adaptivity so that it can operate in new environments, we have to add new trajectories through its phase space. Since these trajectories serve the express purpose of adapting the system to novel situations it is sensible that the parts of the phase space traversed by these trajectories belong to the control space X^C. This shows again that black-box and white-box adaptation are closely connected when the control propositions of the system are appropriately defined.

5   Related Work

The notion of behavioral adaptation has been studied in several works. The interested reader is referred to [7,10,23]. For a discussion of work related to the main formalisms used in this paper like GEM [15] and AIAs [6] we refer to the corresponding publications. We briefly discuss here some works related to properties of adaptive systems, a key notion in the presented contribution.

Several proposals follow a black-box perspective that aims at somehow measuring or expressing requirements on how a software system changes its ability to reach a goal under specific context variations. An interesting contribution of this kind is represented by [18], which analyses the notion of adaptation in a very general sense and identifies the main concepts around adaptation drawn from several different disciplines, including evolution theory, biology, psychology, business, control theory and cybernetics. Furthermore, it provides some general guidelines on the essential features of adaptive systems in order to support their design and understanding. The author claims that *"in general, adaptation is a process about changing something, so that it would be more suitable or fit for some purpose that it would have not been otherwise"*. Accordingly, the term *adaptability* is then used to denote the capacity of enacting adaptation, and *adaptivity* for the degree or extent to which adaptation is enacted. The author concludes by suggesting that *"due to the relativity of adaptation it does not really matter whether a system is adaptive or not (they all are, in some way or another), but with respect to what it is adaptive"*.

A formal black-box definition is proposed in [5]. If a system reacts differently to the same input stream provided by the user at different times, then the system is considered to be adaptive because ordinary systems should exhibit a deterministic behavior. Thus, a non-deterministic reaction is interpreted as an evidence of the fact that the system adapted its behavior after an interaction with the environment. For example, a system where a change of behavior is triggered by an interaction with the user would not be classified as adaptive, which we think is too strong a requirement.

A different line of research studies the properties of adaptive systems and their classification according to the kind of computations that are concerned with, so that the usual adaptation analysis $S \Vdash \mathcal{A}$ is instantiated in some of the computations of S depending of the class of goals in $\mathcal{A}$. We have seen this in the trace-based semantics of GEM presented here.

Some authors [29,28,17] distinguish the following three kinds of properties. *Local* properties are *"properties of one [behavioral] mode"*, i.e. properties that must be satisfied by basic computations only. *Adaptation* properties are to be *"satisfied on interval states when adapting from one behavioral mode to another"*, i.e. properties of adaptation phases. *Global* properties *"regard program behavior and adaptations as a whole. They should be satisfied by the adaptive program throughout its execution, regardless of the adaptations."*, i.e. properties about the overall behavior of the system.

The authors of [6] consider also the class of *adaptability* properties, i.e. properties that may fail for local (i.e. basic) computations, and that need the adapting capability of the system to be satisfied. We refer to [6] for a presentation of some such properties in the context of AIAs.

6   Conclusion

The development of reliable autonomic computing systems poses many challenges for the software engineer. Several approaches have been proposed to tackle those challenges at different stages of system development and regarding the various aspects of those systems. In this paper we focused on behavioral adaptation aspects as tackled in requirements engineering, modeling and programming activities within development methodologies such as the one of ASCENS (cf. Fig.1).

We have reconciled two foundational approaches to behavioral adaptation, each taking a different perspective: GEM which provides a black-box perspective, useful to reason about adaptivity from the requirements point of view, and AIAs, which provide a white-box perspective, useful to reason about adaptivity from the modeling and programming point of view. A first common ground to relate both approaches is a trace-based semantics. First, GEM is instantiated on a trace inclusion-based notion of property satisfaction (i.e. adaptation in the GEM approach). Second, the AIA approach allows us to distinguish adaptations from normal behaviors within traces. A notion of coherence is then defined which can be used to identify mismatches between requirements and models in the design of an autonomic system. A second, more sophisticated approach has been presented as well, built on a game-based semantics of adaptive systems, as advocated in [8].

An interesting line of research is to investigate quantitative notions of the hereby proposed notion of adaptation coherence, e.g. to measure the influence of adaptation mechanisms to achieve certain goals that would provide system developers with further tools to assess and analyse their designs.

References

1. Abeywickrama, D.B., Bicocchi, N., Zambonelli, F.: SOTA: Towards a general model for self-adaptive systems. In: Reddy, S., Drira, K. (eds.) WETICE 2012, pp. 48–53. IEEE Computer Society Press, Los Alamitos (2012)
2. de Alfaro, L.: Game models for open systems. In: Dershowitz, N. (ed.) Verification: Theory and Practice. LNCS, vol. 2772, pp. 269–289. Springer, Heidelberg (2004)
3. de Alfaro, L., Henzinger, T.A.: Interface automata. ACM SIGSOFT Software Engineering Notes, vol. 26(5), ESEC/SIGSOFT FSE 2001, pp. 109–120 (2001)
4. Autonomic Service Component Ensembles (ASCENS), http://www.ascens-ist.eu
5. Broy, M., Leuxner, C., Sitou, W., Spanfelner, B., Winter, S.: Formalizing the notion of adaptive system behavior. In: Shin, S.Y., Ossowski, S. (eds.) SAC 2009, pp. 1029–1033. ACM Press, New York (2009)
6. Bruni, R., Corradini, A., Gadducci, F., Lluch Lafuente, A., Vandin, A.: Adaptable transition systems. In: Martí-Oliet, N., Palomino, M. (eds.) WADT 2012. LNCS, vol. 7841, pp. 95–110. Springer, Heidelberg (2013)
7. Bruni, R., Corradini, A., Gadducci, F., Lluch Lafuente, A., Vandin, A.: A conceptual framework for adaptation. In: de Lara, J., Zisman, A. (eds.) FASE 2012. LNCS, vol. 7212, pp. 240–254. Springer, Heidelberg (2012)
8. Bruni, R., Corradini, A., Gadducci, F., Lluch-Lafuente, A., Vandin, A.: Adaptation is a game. TinyToCS 2 (2013)
9. Bruni, R., Corradini, A., Gadducci, F., Lluch-Lafuente, A., Vandin, A.: Modelling and analyzing adaptive self-assembly strategies with Maude. Science of Computer Programming 99(1), 75–94 (2015)
10. Bruni, R., Corradini, A., Gadducci, F., Lluch Lafuente, A., Vandin, A.: A white box perspective on adaptation. In: De Nicola, R., Hennicker, R. (eds.) Software, Services and Systems. LNCS, vol. 8950, Springer, Heidelberg (2015)
11. De Nicola, R., Latella, D., Lafuente, A.L., Loreti, M., Margheri, A., Massink, M., Morichetta, A., Pugliese, R., Tiezzi, F., Vandin, A.: The SCEL Language: Design, Implementation, Verification. In: Wirsing, M., Hölzl, M., Koch, N., Mayer, P. (eds.) Software Engineering for Collective Autonomic Systems. LNCS, vol. 8998, pp. 3–71. Springer, Heidelberg (2015)
12. De Nicola, R., Loreti, M., Pugliese, R., Tiezzi, F.: A formal approach to autonomic systems programming: The SCEL language. ACM Transactions on Autonomous and Adaptive Systems 9(2), 7:1–7:29 (2014)
13. Hölzl, M., Gabor, T.: Reasoning and Learning for Awareness and Adaptation. In: Wirsing, M., Hölzl, M., Koch, N., Mayer, P. (eds.) Software Engineering for Collective Autonomic Systems. LNCS, vol. 8998, pp. 249–290. Springer, Heidelberg (2015)
14. Hölzl, M., Koch, N., Puviani, M., Wirsing, M., Zambonelli, F.: The Ensemble Development Life Cycle and Best Practices for Collective Autonomic Systems. In: Wirsing, M., Hölzl, M., Koch, N., Mayer, P. (eds.) Software Engineering for Collective Autonomic Systems. LNCS, vol. 8998, pp. 325–354. Springer, Heidelberg (2015)
15. Hölzl, M., Wirsing, M.: Towards a system model for ensembles. In: Agha, G., Danvy, O., Meseguer, J. (eds.) Formal Modeling: Actors, Open Systems, Biological Systems. LNCS, vol. 7000, pp. 241–261. Springer, Heidelberg (2011)
16. Isaacs, R.: Differential Games. Dover, New York (1965)

17. Kulkarni, S.S., Biyani, K.N.: Correctness of component-based adaptation. In: Crnković, I., Stafford, J.A., Schmidt, H.W., Wallnau, K. (eds.) CBSE 2004. LNCS, vol. 3054, pp. 48–58. Springer, Heidelberg (2004)
18. Lints, T.: The essentials in defining adaptation. Aerospace and Electronic Systems 27(1), 37–41 (2012)
19. Maschler, M., Solan, E., Zamir, S.: Game Theory. Cambridge University Press, Cambridge (2013)
20. Patsko, V.S., Turova, V.L.: Homicidal chauffeur game: History and modern studies. In: Breton, M., Szajowski, K. (eds.) Advances in Dynamic Games. Annals of the International Society of Dynamic Games, vol. 11, pp. 227–252. Birkhäuser, Basel (2011)
21. Pinciroli, C., Bonani, M., Mondada, F., Dorigo, M.: Adaptation and Awareness in Robot Ensembles: Scenarios and Algorithms. In: Wirsing, M., Hölzl, M., Koch, N., Mayer, P. (eds.) Software Engineering for Collective Autonomic Systems. LNCS, vol. 8998, pp. 471–494. Springer, Heidelberg (2015)
22. Ross, D.: Game theory. In: Zalta, E.N. (ed.) The Stanford Encyclopedia of Philosophy. Stanford University, Winter 2014 edn. (2014), http://plato.stanford.edu/archives/win2014/entries/game-theory/
23. Salehie, M., Tahvildari, L.: Self-adaptive software: Landscape and research challenges. ACM Transactions on Autonomous and Adaptive Systems 4(2), 14:1–14:42 (2009)
24. Salvaneschi, G., Ghezzi, C., Pradella, M.: Context-oriented programming: A programming paradigm for autonomic systems (v2). CoRR abs/1105.0069 (2012)
25. Šerbedžija, N.: The ASCENS Case Studies: Results and Common Aspects. In: Wirsing, M., Hölzl, M., Koch, N., Mayer, P. (eds.) Software Engineering for Collective Autonomic Systems. LNCS, vol. 8998, pp. 451–469. Springer, Heidelberg (2015)
26. Vassev, E., Hinchey, M.: Engineering Requirements for Autonomy Features. In: Wirsing, M., Hölzl, M., Koch, N., Mayer, P. (eds.) Software Engineering for Collective Autonomic Systems. LNCS, vol. 8998, pp. 379–403. Springer, Heidelberg (2015)
27. Zadeh, L.A.: On the definition of adaptivity. Proceedings of the IEEE 51(3), 469–470 (1963)
28. Zhang, J., Goldsby, H., Cheng, B.H.C.: Modular verification of dynamically adaptive systems. In: Moreira, A., Schwanninger, C., Baillargeon, R., Grechanik, M. (eds.) AOSD 2009, pp. 161–172. ACM Press, New York (2009)
29. Zhao, Y., Ma, D., Li, J., Li, Z.: Model checking of adaptive programs with mode-extended linear temporal logic. In: EASe 2011, pp. 40–48. IEEE Computer Society Press, Los Alamitos (2011)

CHAPTER II.2

From Local to Global Knowledge and Back*

Nicklas Hoch[1], Giacoma Valentina Monreale[2], Ugo Montanari[2],
Matteo Sammartino[2], and Alain Tcheukam Siwe[3]

[1] Volkswagen AG, Corporate Research Group, Wolfsburg, Germany
[2] Dipartimento di Informatica, Università di Pisa, Pisa, Italy
[3] IMT Institute for Advanced Studies, Lucca, Italy

Abstract. Two forms of knowledge are considered: declarative and procedural. The former is easy to extend but it is equipped with expensive deduction mechanisms, while the latter is efficiently executable but it can hardly anticipate all the special cases. In the first part of this chapter (Sections 2 and 3), we first define a syntactic representation of Soft Constraint Satisfaction Problems (SCSPs), which allows us to express dynamic programming (DP) strategies. For the e-mobility case study of ASCENS, we use Soft Constraint Logic Programming (SCLP) to program (in CIAO Prolog) and solve local optimization problems of single electric vehicles. Then we treat the global optimization problem of finding optimal parking spots for all the cars. We provide: (i) a Java orchestrator for the coordination of local SCLP optimizations; and (ii) a DP algorithm, which corresponds to a local to global propagation and back. In the second part of this chapter (Section 4) we assume that different subjects are entitled to decide. The case study concerns a *smart grid* model where various prosumers (producers-consumers) negotiate (in real time, according to the DEZENT approach) the cost of the exchanged energy. Then each consumer tries to plan an optimal consumption profile (computed via DP) where (s)he uses less energy when it is expensive and more energy when it is cheap, conversely for a producer. Finally, the notion of an *aggregator* is introduced, whose aim is to sell flexibility to the market.

Keywords: service component ensembles, local knowledge, global knowledge, declarative knowledge, procedural knowledge, constraint programming, soft constraint, soft constraint satisfaction problem, soft constraint logic programming, hierarchical soft constraint satisfaction problem, dynamic programming, e-mobility, prolog, ciao prolog, optimization, electric car, parking optimization problem, smart grid, prosumer, dezent, address project, power, energy, aggregator, java, constraint semiring, reinforcement learning.

* This research was supported by the European project IP 257414 (ASCENS).

M. Wirsing et al. (eds.): Collective Autonomic Systems, LNCS 8998, pp. 185–220, 2015.
© Springer International Publishing Switzerland 2015

1   Introduction

Service Component ensembles are usually distributed, open systems. The requirements of self-awareness, self management and autonomicity imply the existence of convenient knowledge representation and deduction mechanisms. Typically, information is distributed in the various components of the system, which on the other hand can appear and disappear, making the structure of the ensemble quite variable in time.

As a consequence, it is not efficient to keep a full representation of the global knowledge of the system. Rather, it is better to start from the local knowledge of components and to derive the required conclusions by need (forward propagation). Conversely, the discovery of certain global properties may imply important knowledge acquisitions and state changes by the components (backward propagation). However, the deduction of global knowledge from local information may be a complex procedure, typically of exponential complexity, similar to the process of solving partial differential equations. Thus we expect to be impossible to derive an exact/complete global knowledge and we are ready to accept various forms of approximation.

Two rather different forms of knowledge exist, *declarative* and *procedural*, which have been compared and contrasted since the beginning of the studies of knowledge representation in artificial intelligence [20].

Declarative knowledge is typically (i) symbolic; (ii) equipped with deduction procedures which define its (usually much larger) closure; (iii) easy to extend; but (iv) deduction steps may require exhaustive "British museum" search, and thus often inacceptable amounts of space and time. Procedural knowledge is instead efficiently accessible (executable), but rather boring, in the sense that all the special cases must be anticipated, rigid and difficult to modify.

As a consequence, the process of forward propagation is rather different for declarative and procedural knowledge: the former corresponds to proof discovery in some formal system, while the latter can be obtained via coordination of executable processes in some procedural language. The most convenient approach is thus to employ a declarative formalism for local deductions (possibly concerning a small number of components) and a procedural formalism for forward propagation.

In the applications ASCENS is considering, both kinds of knowledge are needed, with independent roles. That is, none of them should be fully controlled by the other. For instance, it should not be the case that the declarative part synthesizes the code for the procedural knowledge and deploys it. In fact, to do so the declarative part should be fully aware of the operational semantics of the programs/machines/networks and able to reason about it, which seems unfeasible. Conversely, branching procedures of the procedural part should be simple and should query the declarative part for issues related, e.g., to the ontology of the application area.

The interaction/coordination primitives between the two kinds of knowledge are thus the critical choice, since they should have a clear meaning on both sides and a reasonable correspondence, even if the two semantics have just a limited overlapping. In general, the main difference between the two knowledge forms is that disjunctive expressions in the declarative case, which are essential for expressiveness, correspond to nondeterminism in the procedural case, which is usually present only in very restricted forms. For instance, process description languages and logic languages resolve nondeterminism at the first move. A significant extension would be introducing nondeterminism in a more explicit, useful form. We remind that AND-OR semantics of logic programming has been extensively studied in the Fifth Generation period, to take advantage of both AND and OR parallelism e.g. in the Andorra Kernel Language (AKL). Here we can envisage a complex state in the procedural component, where suitable mutual exclusion relations hold between processes, e.g. in the style of Petri net nonsequential, nonderministic processes. However, we will not examine this issue further in this chapter.

Among the existing formalisms, a good example of combination of declarative and procedural knowledge is offered by *constraint programming* [32], where a *constraint system*, able to represent declarative knowledge, coexists with some imperative/functional/process description language. Also, while classical constraints have a crisp, logical interpretation (they either hold or do not hold), it is convenient to interpret *soft* constraints in a *constraint semiring*, where the values may represent partial validity (e.g. fuzzy constraints) or costs in an optimization problem. Constraint semirings are equipped with *multiplicative* and *additive* operations, expressing constraint combination and constraint choice respectively. For the optimization case, the costs are real numbers plus infinity, while the multiplicative and additive operations are sum and min, respectively.

In Section 2, we shortly introduce constraint semirings, Soft Constraint Satisfaction Problems (SCSP) and Soft Constraint Logic Programming (SCLP). We define a syntactic representation of SCSPs which allows one to express dynamic programming solution strategies. Such strategies, for large problems, correspond to forward propagation, and we hint at convenient approximation methods for limiting the computational complexity. Then in Section 3 we present our contributions to the e-mobility case study of ASCENS. The first contribution is about using SCLP for solving some optimization problems of an electrical vehicle at trip level and at journey level. Since the problem concerns a single vehicle at a time, and the solution is exact, we can consider it as applying a declarative approach to a local problem. We implemented the SCLP program on a CIAO Prolog system, where the soft primitives are separately realized on the same system. The second contribution is about a parking problem, where the best global allocation must be found of all the cars to the available parking slots. For each car, the considered cost includes driving distance from the car to the chosen parking lot, walking distance from the parking lot to the destination address, and the cost of the parking. Being the problem global, its solution is expected to be unfeasible (both for our SCLP implementation and for state-of-the-art optimization packages). Thus the approach is proposed of finding the optimal slot for each car separately (local knowledge) and to combine them heuristically using a procedural programming language (forward propagation). In the actual implementation, a Java program checks that the constraints on the capacity of parking lots are satisfied by the tentative allocation based only on optimal, local, independent choices of the single cars. If there are parking lots with too many cars, their costs is increased, and the local optimization procedure is repeated, in the hope that the number of cars choosing the critical lots is adequately reduced.

In Section 4 we consider the more complex case where the computation process cannot be expressed as an optimization problem, since there are different subjects entitled to decide. The case study concerns a smart grid model where various prosumers (producers-consumers) negotiate (in real time, according to the DEZENT approach) the cost of the exchanged energy. The parameters of the negotiation (implying, e.g., a slow or fast increase/decrease in the offer) are determined using a reinforcement learning approach. Each consumer tries to plan an optimal consumption profile (computed via dynamic programming) where (s)he uses less energy when it is expensive and more energy when it is cheap, conversely for a producer. Variations of energy requirements are possible using an energy storage, with limited capacity and charging speed. Extensive experimental results using the DEZENT simulator allow to establish the conditions under which the gain is maximal with respect to a neutral prosumer which does not modify the basic consumption profile. Finally, the notion of *aggregator* is introduced, whose aim is to sell flexibility in its market, and its realization in the EU project ADDRESS is compared with our DEZENT version.

2   Constraints Programming

2.1   Constraint Satisfaction Problems

Classical constraint satisfaction problems (CSPs) [35] represent an expressive and natural formalism useful to specify different types of real-life problems. A CSP can be described as a set of variables with their domains, and a set of constraints. A constraint is a limitation of the possible combinations of the values of some variables. So, solving a CSP consists in finding an assignment of values to all its variables guaranteeing that all constraints are satisfied.

Despite their applicability, the main limit is the ability of just stating if a certain assignment to the variables is allowed or not. This is indeed not enough to model scenarios where the knowledge is either not entirely available or not crisp. In these cases constraints are preferences and, when the problem is over-constrained, one would like to find a solution that is not so bad, i.e., the best solution according to the levels of preference. For this reason, in [9,10], the *soft CSP* framework has been proposed. It extends classical constraints by adding to the usual notion of CSP the concept of a structure expressing the levels of satisfiability or the costs of a constraint. Such a structure is represented by a semiring, that is, a set with two operations: one (usually denoted by $+$) is used to generate an ordering over the levels, while the other one (denoted by $\times$) is used to define how two levels can be combined and which level is the result of such a combination.

2.2   CSP and Dynamic Programming

In this section we shortly illustrate an approach to SCSPs based on dynamic programming, understood as the decoupling of declarative and procedural knowledge. Here SCSPs are represented as distributed systems where constraints are deployed in different locations, connected via their shared variables. The procedural part consists in decomposing the problem into subproblems, each depending on a small set of variables. The declarative part then consists in optimizing subproblems with respect to their variables, which then can be eliminated. The global solution is then reconstructed. The problem of finding the optimal strategy of variable elimination, here solved heuristically, is called the *secondary optimization problem* of dynamic programming [8]. It affects in an essential way the computational costs of solutions. Details and proofs can be found in [21].

An Algebraic Specification for SCSPs. Let $\mathbb{V} = \{x, y, \dots\}$ a set of variables and $\mathbb{C} = \{A, B, \dots\}$ a set of atomic constraints, equipped with an arity function $ar : \mathbb{C} \to \mathbb{N}$ telling how many variables each constraint involves. We assume an *empty constraint nil*, with $ar(nil) = 0$. The *SCSP signature* is given by

$$p, q := p \parallel q \mid (x)p \mid A(\tilde{x}) \mid nil$$

where: the *parallel composition* $p \parallel q$ consists of two subproblems p and q, possibly sharing some variables; the *restriction* $(x)p$ is p where the assignment for x has already been determined; the *atomic problem* $A(\tilde{x})$ represents a problem that only involves the constraint A over variables $\tilde{x}$; *nil* represents the *empty problem*. The variable x is said to be bound in $(x)p$. The free variables of p, $fv(p)$, are those variables that have an occurrence in p that is not inside a subterm of p of the form $(x)q$.

We consider terms up to structural congruence. The operator $\parallel$ (with *nil*) forms a commutative monoid, meaning that problems in parallel can be solved in any order. Restrictions can be α-converted, i.e., names of assigned variables are irrelevant, and they can also be swapped, i.e., assignments can happen in any order, and can be removed, whenever restricted variables do not appear in their scope. The most important axiom is *scope extension*

$$(x)(p \parallel q) = (x)p \parallel q \qquad x \notin fv(q)$$

The intuition is that, instead of assigning x when solving the whole $p \parallel q$, the assignment can happen *earlier*, when solving p, if q does not involve x. SCSP specifications without scope extension are called *hierarchical*, because the order in which variables are assigned w.r.t. subproblems cannot be changed.

We include *permutations* in the signature, that are operations representing bijective functions over variables. The importance of permutations for representing signatures with variables and variable binding has long been recognized. In particular, through permutation we can define the *support* of an element in a model of the SCSP signature, that is the set of "relevant" variables. For instance, the support of a term p is $fv(p)$.

Every non-hierarchical term has a *normal form*, with all restrictions at the top level

$$(\tilde{x})(A_1(\tilde{x}_1) \parallel A_2(\tilde{x}_2) \parallel \cdots \parallel A_n(\tilde{x}_n)) \ ,$$

which can be obtained via structural congruence. A term in normal form is intuitively closer to a typical SCSP: $\tilde{x}$ specifies which variables should be assigned, and the term in its scope represents constraints and their connections. Non-hierarchical terms also admit *canonical forms*, dual to normal forms: every restriction (x) is as close as possible to the atomic problems where x occurs. They are produced by the repeated application of the scope extension axiom from left to right, until termination. A term may have more than one canonical form, each of them being a hierarchical term. For instance the term

$$(x_1)(x_2)(x_3)(A(x_1, x_2) \parallel B(x_2, x_3) \parallel C(x_3))$$

has exactly the following four canonical forms

$$(x_1)((x_2)(A(x_1, x_2) \parallel (x_3)(B(x_2, x_3) \parallel C(x_3))))$$
$$(x_1)((x_3)((x_2)(A(x_1, x_2) \parallel B(x_2, x_3)) \parallel C(x_3)))$$
$$(x_2)((x_1)A(x_1, x_2) \parallel (x_3)(B(x_2, x_3) \parallel C(x_3)))$$
$$(x_3)((x_2)((x_1)A(x_1, x_2) \parallel B(x_2, x_3)) \parallel C(x_3))$$

Notice that

$$(x_2)((x_1)A(x_1, x_2) \parallel (x_3)(B(x_2, x_3) \parallel C(x_3)))$$
$$(x_2)((x_3)(B(x_2, x_3) \parallel C(x_3)) \parallel (x_1)A(x_1, x_2))$$

and

$$(x_1)((x_3)((x_2)(A(x_1, x_2) \parallel B(x_2, x_3)) \parallel C(x_3)))$$
$$(x_3)((x_1)((x_2)(A(x_1, x_2) \parallel B(x_2, x_3)) \parallel C(x_3)))$$

are structurally congruent as hierarchical terms, so they correspond to the same canonical forms.

Evaluation of SCSP Terms. SCSP terms can be evaluated in a model of the SCSP specification, that is: a set of values, equipped with interpretations of syntactic operators complying with the axioms. It can be shown that structurally congruent terms have the same evaluation. However, evaluations may be computed in different ways, each possibly with a different computational cost. One can consider a notion of complexity for a SCSP term p, similar to the one of [8], estimating the cost of computing its evaluation $[\![p]\!]$. This is given by the function with greatest "size" of subterms q of p encountered while inductively constructing $[\![p]\!]$, the size being given by $|fv(q)|$. It can be shown that any canonical form of a term has complexity lower or equal than the normal form.

Computation of Cost Functions via Dynamic Programming. In the context of optimization problems, we can evaluate a SCSP term p as a cost function

$$[\![p]\!] : (\mathbb{V} \to \mathbb{D}) \to \mathbb{R}_\infty$$

giving a cost to each assignment to the free variables of p (discarding assignments to other variables). Typically, parallel composition and restriction are interpreted on cost functions as sum of costs and minimization w.r.t. the restricted variable, respectively. We will see an example of another interpretation in a later section.

In order to compute $[\![p]\!]$, one has to choose a particular hierarchical term for p, which amounts to choosing the order of variable elimination, i.e., a solution of the secondary optimization problem. Then, $[\![p]\!]$ can be computed using dynamic programming with tabling. In fact, since $[\![p]\!]$ is only determined by $fv(p)$, it admits a *finite* representation as a table associating values to all assignments to $fv(p)$. More precisely, $[\![p]\!]$ is computed, following a bottom-up order, from atomic subterms to increasingly complex terms. [4] This allows computing and storing tabular representations of cost functions the first time they are encountered, once and for all. Notice that the algorithm is parametric w.r.t. the interpretation of syntactic operators on cost functions. We emphasize that each hierarchical term, structurally congruent to p, corresponds to a different solution algorithm with its own computational complexity, even if all such terms compute the same cost function $[\![p]\!]$. Therefore, the notion of hierarchical term is meaningful by itself.

2.3 Constraint Logic Programming

Constraint logic programming (CLP) [24] extends logic programming (LP) by embedding constraints in it: term equalities are replaced with constraints and the basic operation of LP languages, the unification, is replaced by constraint handling in a constraint system. It therefore inherits the declarative approach of LP, according to which the programmer specifies what to compute while disregarding how to compute it, by also offering efficient constraint-solving algorithms.

However, only classical constraints can be handled in the CLP framework. So, in [11], CLP has been extended to also handle soft constraints. This has led to a high-level and flexible declarative programming formalism, called *Soft CLP* (SCLP), allowing to easily model and solve real-life problems involving constraints of different types. Roughly speaking, SCLP programs are logic programs where constraints are represented by predicates which are defined by clauses whose body is a value of the semiring modeling the levels of satisfiability or the costs of the constraints. The flexibility of the approach is due to the fact that the same framework can be used to handle different kinds of soft constraints by simply choosing different semirings. It can indeed be used to handle fuzzy, probabilistic, prioritized and optimization problems, as well as classical constraints.

---

[4] Actually, thanks to structural congruence, we can compute the cost function of many parallel terms at once, and we can optimize w.r.t. a set of restrictions, i.e., a sequence of restrictions at the same level. We will see an example in a later section.

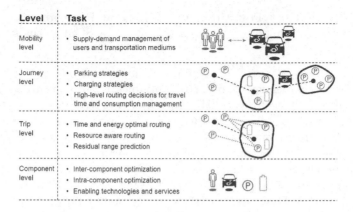

Level	Task
Mobility level	• Supply-demand management of users and transportation mediums
Journey level	• Parking strategies • Charging strategies • High-level routing decisions for travel time and consumption management
Trip level	• Time and energy optimal routing • Resource aware routing • Residual range prediction
Component level	• Inter-component optimization • Intra-component optimization • Enabling technologies and services

Fig. 1. Levels of mobility in the e-mobility framework

3   E-mobility Optimization Problems

In the e-mobility case study, a user is positioned in a location and has a set of appointments. Each of them is in a location and has a starting time and a duration. The user makes a series of decisions regarding the sequences of trips from an appointment to another one. For example, he decides which route he wants to follow, where to park and if and how to charge the Electric Vehicle (EV hereafter) at the appointment location. All possible combinations of travel choices form the choice set. A travel choice is optimal if it minimizes the user' cost criteria.

In [22], the authors propose a hierarchical presentation of the e-mobility framework, which they exploit to decompose the optimization problem in sub-optimization problems. In particular, they identify four levels of mobility, described in Figure 1: the *component level*, whose main tasks are the inter- and intra-component coordination; the *trip level*, whose main task is the time and energy optimal routing; the *journey level*, which handles sequences of trips together with charging and parking strategies; and the *mobility level*, which handles mobility services, such as car and ride service. Each level offers different optimization problems and the results of the lower level can be employed as inputs of the higher level. However, since, in general, the best solution of the lower level could be not optimal for the higher one, the results of the lower level could contain several solutions and not only the best one.

Besides optimizing local resources, the e-Mobility case study aims at solving global problems, involving large ensembles of different vehicles. Such large problems tend to be complex and often a globally optimal solution may be impossible to find. For this reason specific strategies are needed to solve them. In particular, we are interested in the *parking optimization problem* [4], consisting in finding the best parking lot for each vehicle of an ensemble. The best parking lot is chosen by considering: the distance from the current location of the vehicle to the parking lot, the distance from the parking lot to the appointment location and the cost of the parking lot.

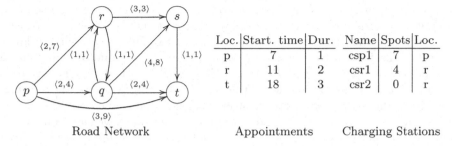

Loc.	Start. time	Dur.	Name	Spots	Loc.
p	7	1	csp1	7	p
r	11	2	csr1	4	r
t	18	3	csr2	0	r

Road Network   Appointments   Charging Stations

Fig. 2. The road network, the user's appointments and the charging stations

3.1 Trip Level and Journey Level Optimization Problems

Here we consider the trip level and journey level optimization problems. Finding a single optimal trip is the classical shortest path problem. Only, when there are different, two or more, incomparable costs for the same path (e.g., travel time and fuel consumption), the Pareto solution should be found, namely the set of tuples of costs not worse in all components than any other tuple. Which solution will actually be taken will be left to further steps, taking into account additional requirements by the user. Finding instead the optimal journey, that is, the optimal sequence of coupled trips, consists in finding the best journeys not only in terms of travel time and energy consumption, but also in terms of other important criteria for the user, such as the charging cost, the number of charging events, etc. However, the solution needs to guarantee that the user reaches each appointment in time and that the state of charge (SoC) of the vehicle never falls below a predefined threshold.

The trip level problem substantially coincides with the multicriteria version of the shortest path problem modeled in [14] as an SCLP program. So, starting from a slightly different specification of this problem, we propose an SCLP program modeling the journey problem. In order to also actually execute both SCLP programs, we propose CIAO Prolog [15], a system supporting constraint logic programming. We therefore explicitly implement the soft framework, by defining two predicates, the *plus* and the *times* ones, which respectively model the additive and the multiplicative operations of the semiring. More details can be found in [27].

Models. In the trip level optimization problem, the road network is indeed represented by a directed graph $G := (N, E)$, where each arc $e \in E$ from a node p to a node q has associated a label $\langle c_T, c_E \rangle$, that is, a pair whose elements represent the costs, respectively in terms of time and energy consumption, of the arc from p to q.

So, given the road network G, such as the one on the left of Figure 2, a source node n_s and a destination node n_d, the problem consists in finding all the best paths between n_s and n_d in terms of time and energy consumption. Note that, since the costs of the arcs are elements of a partially ordered set, the solution can contain several paths, that is, all paths which are not dominated by others, but which have different incomparable costs. For example, if we want to know the best paths from p to t in the graph of Figure 2, the solution will contain both the paths $\{p, t\}$ with cost $\langle 3, 9 \rangle$ and $\{p, q, t\}$ with cost $\langle 4, 8 \rangle$. The former is indeed better in terms of time while the latter in terms of energy consumption.

As far as the journey level optimization problem is concerned, we use the formalization presented in [22]. Actually, we consider a simpler version of it, which avoids to consider car parks and the time that the users would take to go from either the car park or the charging station to the location of the appointment. Moreover, we consider only the time and energy consumption as cost criteria to be minimized. All these simplifications allow a slender and more readable presentation of the SCLP program modeling the problem.

Let $A = \{A_1, \ldots, A_n\}$ be the set of the user's appointments. In order to describe the problem, we use different time variables. All of them have the shape $_it_Z^Y$, where i denotes the appointment, $Y \in \{D, A\}$ (D stands for drive and A for appointment), and $Z \in \{S, E\}$ (S stands for start and E for end).

Each appointment is defined by a location L_i, a starting time $_it_S^A$, an end time $_it_E^A$ and therefore a duration $_id^A$. In order to go from an appointment A_i to the next one A_{i+1}, the user leaves with an EV from the location L_i at time $_it_S^D$ and drive to location L_{i+1}. The user travels along the route alternative iR^D (computed by the trip level problem), which consumes energy and hence reduces the SoC. Obviously, the chosen route must allow the user to arrive to destination with the SoC of his EV. We assume that the SoC always decreases during driving and increases during charging events[5]. The user arrives at $_it_E^D$ and the appointment starts at $_it_S^A$. The user must arrive in time to the appointment, so it is required that $_it_E^D \leq _it_S^A$. During the appointment, it is also possible to schedule a charging event if the SoC of the EV is not enough to continue the journey. We assume to have a set of charging stations. Each of them is simply defined by its name $CSname$, the number of available charging spots $SpotsNum$, and the location L where it is.

Therefore, given the road network G, a set of appointments, as the ones described in the table in the middle of Figure 2, and a set of charging stations, as the ones in the rightmost table of Figure 2, the problem consists in finding all the best journeys through all the appointment locations in terms of time and energy consumption. As for the travel optimization problem, also here the solution can contain several journeys, that is, all the non-dominated ones.

SCLP Programs. In the following, we show how the SCLP framework can be used to solve the two optimization problems presented.

As far as the trip level optimization problem, we propose a slightly different version of the model proposed in [14] for the multi-criteria shortest path problem. So, as there, we consider an SCLP program over the c-semiring denoted $P^H(S)$

---

[5] This is the typical behaviour of EVs, however, as explained in [22], in particular cases it might also increase during driving and decreases during charging.

which, given a source node n_s and a target node n_d, allows us to obtain the set of the costs of all non-dominated paths from n_s to n_d.

The semiring $P^H(S)$ is obtained starting from a semiring $S = \langle A, +, \times, 0, 1 \rangle$, which in our case is the one modeling the costs associated to each edge, i.e, $S = \langle N^2, min', +', \langle \infty, \infty \rangle, \langle 0, 0 \rangle \rangle$, where min' and $+'$ are the min and $+$ operations extended to pairs. Indeed, in general we want to minimize the sum of each cost, but, since we want to obtain all the non dominated paths, we consider $P^H(S)$.

Given a semiring S, we define $P^H(S) = \langle P^H(A), \uplus, \times^*, \emptyset, A \rangle$, where $P^H(A)$ is the Hoare Power Domain of A, that is, $P^H(A) = \{S \subseteq A | x \in S, y \leq_S x$ implies $y \in S\}$. In the finite case, these sets are isomorphic to those containing just the non-dominated values, thus, in the following, we will use this more compact and efficient representation, where each element of $P^H(A)$ will represent the costs of all non-dominated paths from a node to another one. The top element of the semiring is the set A (its compact form is $\{1\}$, which in our example is $\{\langle 0, 0 \rangle\}$); the bottom element is the empty set; $\uplus$ is the formal union that takes two sets and gives their union; $\times^*$ takes two sets and produces another one obtained by multiplying (using the multiplicative operation of the original semiring, in our case $+'$) each element of the first set with each element of the second one.

Note that, in the partial order induced by the additive operation of this semiring, $a \leq_{P^H(S)} b$ intuitively means that for each element of a, there exists an element of b which dominates it (in the partial order of the original semiring).

Following [14], in order to also really execute the SCLP program, we model the problem with a program in CIAO Prolog, shown in Figure 3.

Here we consider the road network presented in Figure 2, so we have a set of clauses modeling it. In particular, we have a set of facts modeling all the edges of the graph. Each fact has the shape $edge(n_s, n_d, [c_T, c_E])$, where n_s represents the source node, n_d represents the destination node and the pair $[c_T, c_E]$ represents the costs of the edge in term of time and energy. Note that, differently from what would happen in the pure SCLP framework, these facts (representing constraints) have the cost in the head of the clauses and not in the body. This is needed for implementing the soft framework, and in particular the two operations of the semiring.

Moreover, there are two clauses *path* describing the structure of paths: the upper one models the base case, where a path is simply an edge, while the lower one represents the recursive case, where a path is an edge plus another path. The head of the path clauses has the following shape $path(n_s, n_d, L_N, L_V, [c_T, c_E], Lim)$, where n_s and n_d are respectively the source and destination nodes, L_N is the list needed to remember, at the end, all the visited nodes of the path in the ordering of the visit, L_V is the list of the already visited nodes needed to avoid infinite recursion where there are graph loops, $[c_T, c_E]$ is used to remember the cost of the path in terms of time and energy, and finally, Lim represents the maximum amount of energy that the EV can consume. It is used to retrieve only the paths with a total cost in terms of energy equal to or less than the passed value.

The *times* and *plus* clauses are useful to model the soft framework. In particular, the first clause is useful to model the multiplicative operation of the

```
:-module(paths,_,_).
:-use_module(library(lists)).
:-use_module(library(aggregates)).

minPair([T,E],[T1,E1]):-          edge(p,q,[2,4]).   edge(q,t,[2,4]).
  T < T1,                          edge(p,r,[2,7]).   edge(r,s,[3,3]).
  E < E1.                          edge(p,t,[3,9]).   edge(r,q,[1,1]).
                                   edge(q,r,[1,1]).   edge(s,t,[1,1]).
                                   edge(q,s,[4,8]).
times([T1,E1],[T2,E2],[T3,E3]):-
  T3 = T1 + T2,
  E3 = E1 + E2.                    path(X,Y,[X,Y],_,[T,E],Lim):-
                                     edge(X,Y,[T,E]),
                                     E =< Lim.
plus([],L,[]).
plus([[P,T,E]|RestL],L,
  [[P,T,E]|BestPaths]):-           path(X,Y,[X|L],V,[T,E],Lim):-
  nondominated([T,E],L),             edge(X,Z,[T1,E1]),
  plus(RestL,L,BestPaths).           nocontainsx(V,Z),
plus([[P,T,E]|RestL],L,BestPaths):-  path(Z,Y,L,[Z|V],[T2,E2],Lim),
  \+nondominated([T,E],L),           times([T1,E1],[T2,E2],[T,E]),
  plus(RestL,L,BestPaths).           E =< Lim.


                                   paths(X,Y,Lim,BestPaths):-
nondominated([T,E],[]).              findall([P,T,E],path(X,Y,P,[X],
nondominated([T,E],[[P,T1,E1]|L]):-  [T,E],Lim),ResL),
  \+minPair([T1,E1],[T,E]),          plus(ResL,ResL,BestPaths).
  nondominated([T,E],L).
```

Fig. 3. The CIAO program modeling the trip level optimization problem

semiring allowing us to compose the global costs of the edges together, time with time and energy with energy. The *plus* predicate instead mimics the additive operation and it is useful to find the best, i.e. non-dominated, paths among all the possible solutions. The *plus* predicate is indeed used in the body of the *paths* clause, which collects all the paths from a given source node to a given destination node and returns the best solutions chosen with the help of the *plus* predicate. So, if we want to know the best paths, in the graph of Figure 2, from p to t with a total cost in terms of energy consumption less than or equal to 10, we have to perform the CIAO query $paths(p, t, 10, BestPaths)$, where the *BestPaths* variable will be instantiated with the list containing all the non-dominated paths. In particular, for each of them, the list will contain the sequence of the nodes in the path and the total cost of the path in terms of time and energy. The output of the CIAO program for this query is shown in Figure 4.

Now, by using the SCLP program modeling the travel optimization problem, we can also show the one modeling the journey level problem. Also in this case, as before, we consider the $P^H(S)$ semiring and we propose a CIAO program, where we also model the soft framework. The CIAO program modeling the journey optimization problem is presented in Figure 5.

```
Ciao 1.14.2-13646: Mon Aug 15 10:49:59 2011

?-    paths(p,t,10,BestPaths).

BestPaths = [[[p,t],3,9],[[p,q,t],2+2,4+4]]  ?.
no
?-
```

Fig. 4. The output for the query $paths(p, t, 10, BestPaths)$

```
:-module(journey,_,_).                journey([X,Y],[P],[],[T,E],SoC):-
:-use_module(paths).                     appointment(X,Tx,Dx), appointment(Y,Ty,Dy),
                                         path(X,Y,P,[X],[T,E],SoC),
plus([],L,[]).                           timeSum(Tx,Dx,T,ArrT), ArrT=<Ty.
plus([[P,T,E,ChEv]|RestL],L,
     [[P,T,E,ChEv]|BestPaths]):-      journey([X,Y],[P],[[X,ID]],[T,E],SoC):-
  nondominated([P,T,E],L),               appointment(X,Tx,Dx), appointment(Y,Ty,Dy),
  plus(RestL,L,BestPaths).               \+path(X,Y,P,[X],[T,E],SoC),
plus([[P,T,E,ChEv]|RestL],L,             chargingStation(ID,Spots,X),Spots>0,
                  BestPaths):-           newSoC(SoC,Dx,NewSoC),
  \+nondominated([P,T,E],L),             path(X,Y,P,[X],[T,E],NewSoC),
  plus(RestL,L,BestPaths).               timeSum(Tx,Dx,T,ArrT), ArrT=<Ty.

                                      journey([X|[Y|Z]],[P|LP],ChEv,[T,E],SoC):-
nondominated([P,T,E],[]).                appointment(X,Tx,Dx), appointment(Y,Ty,Dy),
nondominated([P,T,E],                     path(X,Y,P,[X],[T1,E1],SoC),
          [[P1,T1,E1,ChEv1]|L]):-        timeSum(Tx,Dx,T1,ArrT), ArrT=<Ty,
  \+minPair([T1,E1],[T,E]),              journey([Y|Z],LP,ChEv,[T2,E2],(SoC-E1)),
  nondominated([P,T,E], L).              times([T1,E1],[T2,E2],[T,E]).

                                      journey([X|[Y|Z]],[P|LP],[[X,ID]|ChEv],[T,E],SoC):-
appointment(p,7,1).                      appointment(X,Tx,Dx), appointment(Y,Ty,Dy),
appointment(r,11,2).                     \+path(X,Y,P,[X],[T1,E1],SoC),
appointment(t,18,3).                     chargingStation(ID,Spots,X), Spots>0,
                                         newSoC(SoC,Dx,NewSoC),
chargingStation(csp1,7,p).               path(X,Y,P,[X],[T1,E1],NewSoC),
chargingStation(csr1,4,r).               timeSum(Tx,Dx,T1,ArrT), ArrT=<Ty,
chargingStation(csr2,0,r).               journey([Y|Z],LP,ChEv,[T2,E2],(NewSoC-E1)),
                                         times([T1,E1],[T2,E2],[T,E]).

journeys(Places,EV,BestJourneies):-
findall([P,T,E,ChEv],journey(Places,P,ChEv,[T,E],SoC),ResL),
plus(ResL,ResL,BestJourneies).
```

Fig. 5. The CIAO program modeling the journey optimization problem

We have a set of facts modeling the user's appointments and the charging stations. In particular, for each appointment A_i, there is a clause

$$appointment(L_i, {}_it^A_S, id^A),$$

while for each charging station we have a clause

$$chargingStation(CSname, SpotsNum, L).$$

Moreover, there are four *journey* clauses describing the structure of journeys. The upper two represent the base case, while the other two represent the recursive case. The first clause models the case where a journey is simply a path with a cost in terms of energy less than or equal to the SoC of the EV. The second clause models the case where the SoC of the EV is not enough to do any path and so a charging event, incrementing the energy level, must be scheduled. The third *journey* clause represents the case where a journey is a path with a cost in terms of energy less than or equal to the SoC of the EV, plus another journey. Finally, the last clause models the recursive case where a charging event is needed. In all cases we check that the paths allow the user to arrive in time.

The head of the journey clauses has the shape

$$journey(L_L, L_P, L_{ChEv}, [C_T, C_E], SoC),$$

where L_L is the list of the locations of the appointments, L_P is the list needed to remember, at the end, all the paths of the journey in the correct ordering, L_{ChEv} is the list needed to remember all the charging events needed to complete the journey, $[C_T, C_E]$ represents the cost of the journey in terms of time and energy, and finally, SoC represents the current energy level of the EV.

To make the program as readable as possible, we omit the predicates *newSoC* and *timeSum*, useful to respectively compute the new energy level of the EV after a charging event and the arriving time of the user to an appointment.

The *plus* clauses are useful to model the soft framework and they are very similar to the ones of the trip level problem. The only difference is that here we have to consider the charging events. Moreover, note that we reuse the *times* predicate defined in the CIAO program in Figure 3.

The *journeys* clause collects all the journeys through a set of locations (the ones of the user's appointments) and returns the best solutions chosen with the help of the *plus* predicate. So, if we want to know the best journeys, in the graph of Figure 2, through the locations where the user has the appointments, with an EV having an energy level equal to 10, we have to perform the CIAO Prolog query

$$journeys([p, r, t], 10, BestJourneys),$$

where p, r, t are the locations of the appointments and the *BestJourneys* variable will be instantiated with the list containing all the non-dominated journeys. In particular, for each of them, the list will contain the sequence of the paths of the journey, the total cost of the journey in terms of time and energy, and the list of the charging events, each of them described by the name of the charging station and its location.

The output of the CIAO program for this query is shown in Figure 6.

3.2   Coordination of Local and Global Optimization: The Parking Problem

In order to solve the parking problem, we propose a technique based on the coordination of declarative and procedural knowledge. It consists in decomposing

```
Ciao 1.14.2-13646: Mon Aug 15 10:49:59 2011

?- journeys([p,r,t],10,BestJourneys).

BestJourneys = [
                [[[p,r],[r,s,t]],2+(3+1),7+(3+1),[[r,csr1]]],
                [[[p,r],[r,q,t]],2+(1+2),7+(1+4),[[r,csr1]]],
                [[[p,q,r],[r,s,t]],2+1+(3+1),4+1+(3+1),[]],
                [[[p,q,r],[r,q,t]],2+1+(1+2),4+1+(1+4),[]]
              ] ?.
no
?-
```

Fig. 6. The output for the query $journeys([p, r, t], 10, BestJourneys)$

the global optimization problem in many local problems which can be separately solved by a SCLP implementation and which are coordinated by suitable procedural strategies acting at run time on the declarative optimization environment to guarantee an acceptable global solution. Here the use of SCLP is convenient for two reasons: (1) it allows one to naturally model and solve local optimization problems (see for example [27]); (2) a fact/clause-based declarative implementation is more flexible and easier to modify than an ordinary imperative module structure.

In particular, we consider the parking optimization problem. The application of the coordination technique described above to this problem leads to several local optimization problems, one for each vehicle of the ensemble, consisting in determining the best parking lot for it. All these local problems are solved separately by using a SCLP implementation. The orchestrator implementing the coordination strategy then receives the results of all the local optimization solutions and verifies if the local solutions all together form an admissible global solution, i.e., if local optimal choices can be satisfied by the parking lots. If it is so, the problem is solved, otherwise the orchestrator queries the declarative knowledge again, but now by increasing the costs of the parking lots which received too many requests. The procedure is repeated, with suitable variations, until a global solution is found. Notice that in this way the orchestrator has a hypothetical, transactional behavior, with the options of committing (a solution is found) or partially backtracking (on the parkings which are overfull).

The solution is guaranteed to be just an acceptable global solution: it may or may not be globally optimal. However, sub-optimality is in general needed to solve the problem in reasonable time.

The coordination technique has been implemented in a demo application. We used Java for the orchestrator and CIAO to model and solve the local problems. Figure 7 shows one phase of this execution. There, four vehicles, represented by the markers A, B, C and D, are finding a parking lot. Parking lots are represented by circles and each has a capacity of two vehicles. Each vehicle has autonomously computed the best parking lot for it and has sent its local solution to the Java orchestrator. Therefore, the vehicles A, B and D would like to

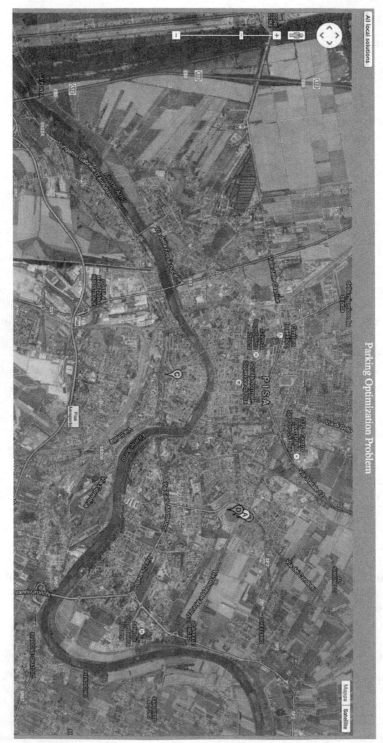

Fig. 7. Demo application for the parking optimization problem

park in the rightmost parking lot, while C prefers the parking lot at the lower part of the map. The orchestrator checks if each parking lot is able to satisfy the requests of the vehicles. In this case, since there are too many requests for the rightmost parking lot, the orchestrator increases the cost of it and asks to the vehicles to recompute new local solutions.

3.3   Dynamic Programming

We show how the parking optimization problem can be represented and solved in the style of Section 2.2. We consider the following formalization of the problem. Assume a set of parking zones $\mathbb{C} = \{A, B, \dots\}$ and of car variables $\mathbb{V} = \{x, y, \dots\}$, and two functions:

 - $c \colon \mathbb{C} \to \mathbb{N}$, assigning a *capacity* to every zone;
 - $F \colon \mathbb{V} \to \mathbb{C} \to \mathbb{R}_\infty$, speciyfing the cost $F(x)(A)$ for x to park in A.

Given an assignment $\rho \colon \mathbb{V} \to \mathbb{C}$ of cars to zones, let $\rho_A = \{x \mid \rho(x) = A\}$. We want to find an assignment ρ such that $|\rho_A| \leq c(A)$, for all $A \in \mathbb{C}$, minimizing

$$\sum_{x \in \mathbb{V}} F(x)(\rho(x))$$

Here a term p of the SCSP specification is intended to represent a parking system: $A(x_1, \dots, x_n)$ means that x_i might be parked in A; $(x)p$ means that car x cannot be parked outside of p, so it must have a parking spot in one of the zones of p. In general, a term p represents a part of the system made of one or more parking zones.

To each parking system p we associate a cost function

$$[\![p]\!] : \mathscr{P}(fv(p)) \to \mathbb{R}_\infty$$

The intended meaning of $[\![p]\!]X$ is the cost of actually parking cars $X \subseteq fv(p)$ in p. Any subset of $fv(p)$ can be seen as a boolean vector $\{\checkmark, -\}^{|fv(p)|}$, where $\checkmark$ marks a variable in the subset, so $[\![p]\!]$ can be represented as a finite table associating a value to all such vectors.

Solution Algorithm. We present a solution algorithm, based on dynamic programming. The computation of $[\![p]\!]$ is performed as follows.

Atomic terms. if p is an atom $A(\tilde{x})$ then we have

$$[\![A(\tilde{x})]\!]X = \begin{cases} \sum_{x \in X} F(x)(A) & |X| \leq c(A) \\ \infty & \text{otherwise} \end{cases}$$

Variable elimination. if $p = (\tilde{x})(q_1 \parallel \cdots \parallel q_n)$, where q_i are canonical terms without parallel composition as top operator, then we assume to have already computed tables $[\![q_i]\!]$. We consider each $X \subseteq fv(p)$, and all collections of n sets $X_1 \subseteq fv(q_1), \dots, X_n \subseteq fv(q_n)$ that form a partition of $X \cup \tilde{x}$ ($\tilde{x}$ and X are disjoint, as so are $\tilde{x}$ and $fv(p)$). Then we compute $[\![q_1]\!]X_1 + \cdots + [\![q_n]\!]X_n$, for every such collection of sets, and we set $[\![p]\!]X$ as the smallest among these values.

Table 1. Example tables. Parameters of atomic subterms are often omitted

(a) $[\![A(x_1, x_3)]\!]$

x_1	x_3	$cost$
✓	✓	7
✓	–	3
–	✓	4
–	–	0

(b) $[\![B(x_2, x_3)]\!]$

x_2	x_3	$cost$
✓	✓	10
✓	–	4
–	✓	6
–	–	0

(c) $[\![C(x_2)]\!]$

x_2	$cost$
✓	1
–	0

(d) $[\![(x_1)A(x_1, x_3)]\!]$

x_3	$cost$
✓	7
–	3

(e) $[\![(x_2)(\, B(x_2, x_3) \parallel C(x_2)\,)]\!]$

x_3	$[\![B]\!]$ x_2	$[\![C]\!]$ x_3	$[\![B]\!]+[\![C]\!]$ x_2	$cost$
✓	✓	✓	–	10
	–	✓	✓	7	7
–	✓	–	–	4
	–	–	✓	1	1

(f) $[\![(x_3)(\, (x_1)A(x_1, x_3) \parallel (x_2)(\, B(x_2, x_3) \parallel C(x_2)\,)\,)]\!]$

$[\![(x_1)A]\!]$ x_3	$[\![(x_2)(B \parallel C)]\!]$ x_3	$[\![(x_1)A]\!]+[\![(x_2)(B \parallel C)]\!]$	$cost$
✓	–	8	
–	✓	10	8

Example. Consider the scenario with three possible parking zones A, B, C and three cars x_1, x_2 and x_3. The following table shows, for each zone, the cost of parking a car in it and its capacity.

	$F(x_1)$	$F(x_2)$	$F(x_3)$	c
A	3	∞	4	2
B	∞	4	6	2
C	∞	1	∞	2

The term in normal form modeling the system is

$$(x_1)(x_2)(x_3)(A(x_1, x_3) \parallel B(x_2, x_3) \parallel C(x_2))$$

while we consider its canonical form

$$p = (x_3)((x_1)A(x_1, x_3) \parallel (x_2)(B(x_2, x_3) \parallel C(x_2))).$$

because, as mentioned, it has lower computational complexity.

In order to compute the solution, the dynamic programming algorithm starts from the cost functions for each zone. These are shown in Table 1 where the leftmost columns indicates whether a car is parked inside (✓) or outside (–) the subsystem described by the term. Then, the algorithm eliminates all the variables in the order they appear in p, from the inmost to the outmost one:

1. *Elimination of x_1*: Table $[\![(x_1)A(x_1,x_3)]\!]$ (1d), with only one column x_3, is computed by forcing x_1 to be inside A;
2. *Elimination of x_2*: the table

$$[\![(x_2)(B(x_2,x_3) \| C(x_2))]\!]$$

   is computed: Table 1e shows values for x_3, the partitions considered when computing the output cost, and the final cost. Notice that this and the previous step could be executed in parallel. This fact comes immediately from terms $(x_1)A(x_1,x_3)$ and $(x_2)(B(x_2,x_3) \| C(x_2))$ being composed in parallel in $(x_1)A(x_1,x_3) \| (x_2)(B(x_2,x_3) \| C(x_2))$.
3. *Elimination of x_3*: finally, the Table $[\![p]\!]$ (1f) is computed, by comparing costs of parking x_3 inside either $(x_1)A(x_1,x_3)$ or $(x_2)(B(x_2,x_3) \| C(x_2))$.
4. *Optimal variable assignment*: tracking back through the Tables we find:
   - x_3 inside $(x_1)A(x_1,x_3) \| (x_2)(B(x_2,x_3) \| C(x_2))$;
   - x_3 inside $(x_1)A(x_1,x_3)$;
   - x_3 inside $A(x_1,x_3)$ with cost 4;
   - x_1 inside $A(x_1,x_3)$ with cost 3;
   - x_2 inside $B(x_2,x_3) \| C(x_2)$;
   - x_2 inside $C(x_2)$ with cost 1.

4   Smart GRIDS for Renewable Electrical Power Production/Consumption

The electricity is a vital asset and a priority for the social and economic development of today's world. Building energy infrastructures with high efficiency and renewable energy sources is an important yet challenging task for a sustainable future. Smart grid is a term referring to a modernized electrical grid that uses information and communications technology to gather and act on information, such as information about the behaviors of suppliers and consumers, in an automated fashion to improve the efficiency, reliability, economics, and sustainability of the production and distribution of electricity. The power grid operation can be subdivided into three main tasks:

- *Centralized power generation*: where electricity is produced by large size energy source generators as coal plants, nuclear plants, natural gas plants and hydroelectric plants. Generally, electricity is produced at an extra high voltage, in the order of 265 to 275 KV.
- *Power transmission*: it is a high voltage electric transmission in the order of 110 KV or above, from generating power plants to substations located near to population centers. The electricity is transmitted at high voltages to reduce the energy loss in long distance transmission. It is usually transmitted through overhead power lines.
- *Electricity distribution*: it is the final stage in the delivery of electricity to end users or consumers. It works typically at medium-voltage (less than 50 KV) and low-voltage (less than 1 KV).

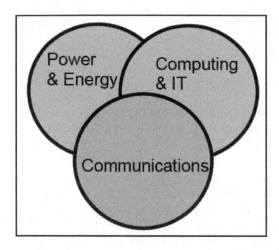

Fig. 8. Smart grid foundational layers

The increasing cost of the electricity along with the need to reduce greenhouse gas emissions to protect the environment, have made energy efficiency one of the technological challenges of our century. The purpose is to optimize the grid operation and the electricity usage worldwide. We can refer to the EU's 20-20-20 climate change objectives, whose target for the year 2020 includes: 20% reduction in greenhouse gas emissions, 20% EU renewables share and 20% savings in consumption by improving energy efficiency [1]. These goals require new solutions and management strategies at the (see Figure 8):

 — power and energy layer;
 — communications layer;
 — computing and information technology layer.

At the power and energy layer there is a need to integrate renewable energy sources, such as solar and wind, in the electricity production chain, in order to reduce the peak of energy consumption and transmission losses. This may lead to a decentralization of the power grid due to the electricity production from the medium and low voltage layers of the grid; and to the need to take into account the intermittence of renewable energy sources during the electricity production. In the communication layer, and in the computing and information technology layer, both electric power and information flows will be distributed. The need to reduce energy demand imbalances will require tackling the optimization of the electricity generation, transportation and distribution. This will be possible by controlling the real-time collection of data on the status of systems and on the network, and by using advanced technologies of communication and elaboration of data based on models of distributed computing and on adaptive algorithms.

In the smart power grid context we can distinguish between two types of electricity power management systems: (i) the centralized [5] power management system which is a model in which at the physical layer, the grid is designed for a one-way flow of the electricity; and (ii) the decentralized [37] power management system. Hereafter we present a power grid scenario based on the ADDRESS project [6,30,7].

4.1   ADDRESS: An Integrated Power Management System

ADDRESS [6,30,7] is a large-scale integrated R&D project co-founded by the European Commission under the 7th Framework Programme, in the energy area for the "Development of Interactive Distribution Energy Networks". ADDRESS stands for Active Distribution network with full integration of Demand and distributed energy RESourceS and has been carried out by a Consortium of 25 partners from 11 European countries. The main goal of the ADDRESS project was to enable the active participation of domestic and small commercial consumers to electricity system markets and the provision of services to the different electricity system participants (see Figure 9, Figure 10 coming from [30]). More specifically, the active participation of domestic and small commercial consumers is suggested to be managed by a new market player called "aggregator" whose objective is to exploit the flexibility of power consumers for building active demand services to the power market. Figure 9 represents the ADDRESS architecture, with the main players and the relationships between them. Other important components of the ADDRESS architecture are: consumers, Distribution System Operators (DSO), markets and contracts. In ADDRESS, consumers are the providers of flexibility and they are directly connected to the low voltage distribution network. The aggregator, see Figure 10, is the key mediator between consumers, markets and other power system participants. Its main function is to gather (aggregate) the flexibility of consumers for building Active Demand (AD) services; to offer the AD services to the power system participants via the markets; to manage the risks associated with uncertainties in the markets; and finally to maximize the value of consumers' flexibility.

4.2   Decentralized Prosumer Based Solution for Smart Energy Production/Consumption

Decentralized power management systems will play a key role in reducing greenhouse gas emissions and increasing electricity production through alternative energy sources. A particular attention will be placed on end-users. They will now play different roles acting as producer or consumer and thus they will contribute to energy saving in the network. The term prosumer (producer-consumer) will refer to a user that not only consumes electricity, but can also produce and store electricity.

In the next section, we focus on power market models in which prosumers interact in a distributed environment during the purchase or sale of electric power. We have chosen to follow the distributed power market model DEZENT. In Section 4.6 we extend [28] and, following [33], we define the optimization algorithm used by the prosumer during the planning phase of the electricity consumption/production. Finally, in Section 4.7 we propose [29] an aggregator in the DEZENT power market model and in Section 4.8 we compare the results with that of the aggregator of the ADDRESS project.

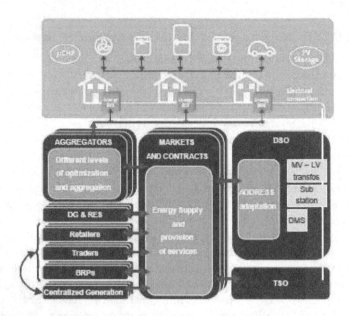

Fig. 9. ADDRESS conceptual architecture

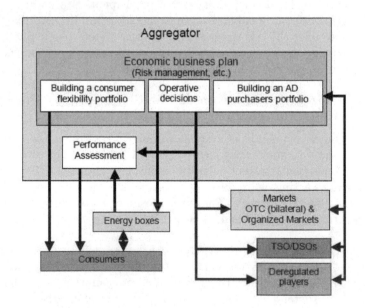

Fig. 10. ADDRESS project architecture

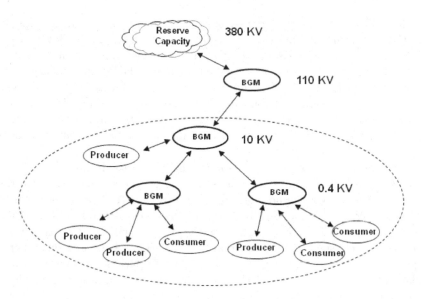

Fig. 11. Power grid and associated agents

4.3 The DEZENT Electrical Market Model and Its Reinforcement Learning Adaptation Model

DEZENT [37,36] is the result of a R&D project between the School of Computer Science and the College of Electrical Engineering of Dortmund University, the E.ON Energy and the German research foundation (DFG). The DEZENT project was devoted to decentralized and adaptive electric power management through a distributed real-time multi-agent architecture. DEZENT power management system focuses on a regional grid where there is a predominant use of renewable energy sources. The power grid architecture (see Figure 11 coming from [36]) is subdivided into four levels. The first level (0.4 kV) is a low-range network covering subdivisions (a neighborhood). The second level (10 kV) is a medium-range area network covering a suburb (regional grid). The third level (110 kV) is a long-distance energy transport network. Finally in the fourth level (380 kV) the electricity is produced from large power plants (coal, gas or nuclear). Power needs of prosumers are covered through alternative energy sources within the first 2 layers and additional power needs will be covered at the latest by the fourth level.

At the negotiation layers, the balancing of demand and supply between participants is carried out through balancing group managers (BGMs), which are located in different network layers and operate in parallel on each grid. A BGM is a financial instrument which balances the supply and the demand of electricity between a producer and a consumer who have submitted a similar bid. A day is discretized, resulting in a set of consecutive slots, and negotiation takes place in each slot. Slot duration must be longer than the time needed for stabilizing power flow. The latter time depends on the size of the balancing groups. The negotiation will start independently for the groups on the lowest level (a small subdivision). If a balance cannot be found for all customer agent in a group, then unsatisfied customers are sent to the next-higher BGM and the negotiation scope is extended to that new group of customers. A slot in DEZENT consists of 3 cycles of negotiation and the sale or purchase of the electricity (at a fixed cost) to/from the main production facilities. Each cycle consists of 10 rounds of negotiation in which bids and offers of customer agents are adjusted according to their own negotiation strategies.

In the case of a consumer, let $[A_k, B_k]$ be the price frame of negotiation for level k ($1 \leq k \leq 3$). Here A_k represents the lower bound of the electricity cost and B_k the upper bound. Let S_C be a finite set of real values. The negotiation strategy set by a consumer agent C is characterized by a pair of the form $(s_1, \text{bid}(0))$. Here s_1 is chosen from the set S_C, while $\text{bid}(0)$ is the opening bid and it is chosen from the interval $[A_k, 1/2(B_k + A_k)]$. The consumer will also specify a device-specific urgency urg_0. All these parameters characterize the gradient of the bidding curves of the consumer. After round n, $n \in [0 - 9]$, the unsatisfied consumer will increase his bid according to the function :

$$\text{bid}(n) = -\frac{1}{e^{\frac{urg_0 \cdot n}{s_1} + s_2}} + B_k \tag{1}$$

where the parameter s_2 is determined by the opening bid: $s_2 = -\log(B_k - \text{bid}(0))$. This consumer will participate to the next negotiation round n by using the new value of his bid ($\text{bid}(n)$).

Conversely, in the case of a producer, let $[A_k, B_k]$ be the price frame of negotiation for level k ($1 \leq k \leq 3$). Let T_P be a finite set of real values. A negotiation strategy set by a producer agent P is characterized by a pair of the form $(t_1, \text{offer}(0))$. Here t_1 is chosen from the set T_P, while $\text{offer}(0)$ is the opening offer and it is chosen from the interval $[1/2(B_k + A_k), B_k]$. The producer will also specify a device-specific urgency urg_0. All these parameters characterize the gradient of the bidding curves of the producer. After round n, $n \in [0 - 9]$, the unsatisfied producer will decrease his offer according to the function :

$$\text{offer}(n) = \frac{1}{e^{\frac{urg_0 \cdot n}{t_1} + t_2}} + A_k \tag{2}$$

where the parameter t_2 is determined by the opening offer: $t_2 = -\log(\text{offer}(0) - A_k)$. Finally, this producer will participate to the next negotiation round n by using the new value of his offer ($offer_P(n)$). At the end of each slot, each consumer/producer will adapt his own negotiation strategy in DEZENT and this adaptation process will be made by using reinforcement learning techniques.

4.4 Background on Reinforcement Learning

In computer science, reinforcement learning [25] is the problem faced by an agent that must learn the behavior through trial-and-error interactions with a

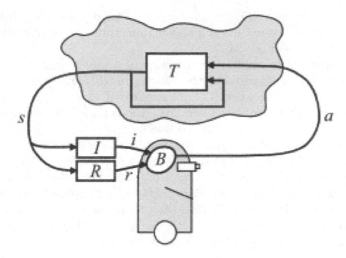

Fig. 12. The standard reinforcement-learning model

dynamic environment. There are two main strategies for solving reinforcement-learning problems: the first is to search in the space of behaviors in order to find one that performs well in the environment and this approach has been taken by work in genetic algorithms and genetic programming; the second is to use statistical techniques and dynamic programming methods to estimate the utility of taking actions in states of the world. Hereafter we are focusing on statistical techniques because they take advantage of the special structure of reinforcement-learning problems, which is not available in optimization problems in general [25]. In the standard reinforcement learning model, an agent is connected to its environment via perception and action, as depicted in Figure 12. On each step of interaction the agent receives as input i some indication of the current state s of the environment; the agent then chooses an action, a, as output. The action changes the state of the environment, and the value of this state transition is communicated to the agent through a scalar reinforcement signal, r. The agent's behavior, B, should choose actions that tend to increase the long-run sum of values of the reinforcement signal. It can learn to do this over time by systematic trial and error, guided by a wide variety of algorithms. The reinforcement learning approach is similar to the El Farol bar problem [38] in economics and the minority game in statistical physics [17]. Chapter II.4 [23] in this volume contains further background material on reinforcement learning and dynamic programming.

4.5   Periodic Reinforcement Learning in DEZENT

In DEZENT, prosumers adapt their negotiation strategy at the end of each slot. Each customer has a set of strategy bids (user acting as a consumer) and offers (user acting as a producer). The selection of the negotiation strategy of the

next slot is made probabilistically according to a fixed probability distribution
defined in DEZENT. The reward of a negotiation strategy is computed by using
the Sutton's update method [34].

More specifically, the negotiation function of a user acting as a consumer
(see Equation 1) is characterized by the pair $(s_1, \text{bid}(0))$ and that of a user acting as a producer (see Equation 2) is characterized by the pair $(t_1, \text{offer}(0))$.
Moreover, the parameter s_1 is chosen from the set S_C, the parameter t_1 is
chosen from the set T_P, the opening consumer bid is chosen from the interval $[A_0, 1/2(B_0 + A_0)]$ and finally, the opening producer offer is chosen from the
interval $[1/2(B_0 + A_0), B_0]$. Let us denote the set of feasible bids for a consumer
C by O_C and the set of feasible offers for a producer P by O_P. Each element of
the set O_C belongs to the interval $[A_0, 1/2(B_0 + A_0)]$ and each element of the
set O_P belongs to the interval $[1/2(B_0 + A_0), B_0])$. The strategy space of a pro-
sumer is defined by: $\mathcal{A} := (\mathcal{A}_C, \mathcal{A}_P) = (S_C \times O_C, T_P \times O_P)$. Here the strategy
spaces $\mathcal{A}_C$ and $\mathcal{A}_P$ are used when the prosumer acts as a consumer and as a
producer respectively.

For the selection of the negotiation strategy of the next slot, 3 modes have
been defined in DEZENT: *Exploitation*, *Explore1* and *Explore2*. *Exploitation*
selects the action with the maximum reward. *Explore1* randomly picks a strategy which is in the neighborhood of the action with the maximum reward. Finally, *Explore2* randomly picks any strategy. One mode is randomly determined
according to a fixed probability distribution. Then a strategy is selected and
executed through the determined mode. The learning process is applied to the
selection of the strategies and not of the modes. Otherwise, the size of the matrix encoding the learning space and the convergence time of the learning process
would have grown unacceptably.

At the end of a negotiation, the final achieved price is normalized according
to the frame size of the negotiation of DEZENT. Then, the temporal difference
method of Sutton[34] is used to derive the reward of the negotiation strategy
currently executed. More specifically, let a be a negotiation strategy and $P(t, a)$
be the value of the reward at the beginning of the slot t. Suppose that the
strategy a has been executed and let $r'(t)$ be the normalized prices negotiated
under strategy a. The reward $P(t+1, a)$ of the strategy a at the end of slot t is
computed by using Sutton's update formula [34]:

$$P(t+1, a) := P(t, a) + \alpha(r'(t) - P(t, a)); \ 0 < \alpha \leq 1 \qquad (3)$$

4.6 Optimal Prosumer Profiling via Dynamic Programming

In this section we propose a strategy which helps prosumers to optimize their
consumption (production) and to better manage their own electricity costs. The
challenge is to make elastic the demand for, and the supply of, electricity of prosumers in order to optimize their energy cost based on power market conditions
and on suitable constraints on their power consumption. A prosumer is characterized by the class of energy variation profiles (s)he can adopt during the day. If
the energy variation is positive, then the prosumer acts as a producer, otherwise

(s)he acts as a consumer. In our model, the allowed profiles must satisfy the following constraints: (i) the energy variation in a slot has a lower and an upper bound; (ii) the sum of all the energy variations in the whole day is zero, i.e. if in some slot the variation is positive, in some other slot it must be negative. (iii) summing up all the variations from the beginning of the day to any time, we cannot exceed a lower and an upper bound. This constraint accounts for available energy storage media, like electric vehicle batteries or thermic accumulations due to anticipated heating, or delayed air conditioning. Given the class of consumption profiles, the prosumer will choose the optimal profile on the basis of the information (s)he has on the unit cost of the energy which resulted by the DEZENT negotiation in each slot of the previous day. In fact, if we assume that the free market cost in the same slot of the previous day is the same, that the prosumer environment is the same and that the reinforcement learning algorithm of DEZENT is close to convergence, we can safely rely on the costs (result of the negotiation) of the previous day. The aim of the prosumer is to find an allowed profile assigning to each slot an energy consumption (production) of optimal total cost. Moreover, whenever the prosumer acts as a producer, an additional cost is added in the control algorithm. The additional cost is due to the fact that a part of the electricity stored will be lost by the Joule effect or some kind of loss in energy transformations. We term it "overhead" and it characterizes the inefficiency of the prosumer energy store. The prosumers use a dynamic programming algorithm for planning their energy consumption (production). The control algorithm of the prosumers has two inputs: (i) the definition of the class of allowed consumer profiles; and (ii) the cost of a unit of energy which resulted by the DEZENT negotiation in each slot of the previous day. Hereafter, the optimization problem and the proposed dynamic programming algorithm used to solve it are defined.

Notations: some definitions and notations are listed below ($\mathbf{N}$ are the natural numbers).

Discretized energy : $s_1, \ldots, s_n$ slots in a day, $n : \mathbf{N}$

$\quad\quad\quad\quad\quad : e : \mathbf{R}$ basic energy level, $e > 0$

$\quad\quad\quad\quad\quad : ae$ average consumption, $a : \mathbf{N}$

$\quad\quad\quad\quad\quad : re$ maximal energy reserve, $r : \mathbf{N}$

$\quad\quad\quad\quad\quad : r_0 e$ initial energy reserve, $r_0 : \mathbf{N}$

$\quad\quad\quad\quad\quad : \pm ke$ maximal variation in energy

$\quad\quad\quad\quad\quad$ consumption, $k : \mathbf{N}, \; k \leq a/2$

$\quad\quad\quad\quad\quad : o : \mathbf{Z} \to \mathbf{R}$ overhead,

$\quad\quad\quad\quad\quad$ if $0 \leq x$ then $o(x) = x$ else $x \leq o(x) \leq 0$.

Unitary energy cost : $c_i : \mathbf{R}$ in slot s_i, $\;\; i = 1, 2, \ldots, n$ $\;\; c_i \geq 0$.

Notice that the decision variables are discretized, despite the fact that the calculations are made on the reals. Moreover the number $2k + 1$ of possible values of the decision variables determine the precision of the algorithm.

Optimization problem: the optimization problem is then defined by the decision variables, the function to be minimized and the constraints on the energy consumption.

$$\text{Decision variables} : -k \leq x_i \leq +k, \ x_i : \mathbf{N} \text{ where } x_i \quad (4)$$
$$\text{is the variation for slot } s_i,$$
$$i = 1, 2, \ldots, n.$$

$$\text{Cost function to be minimized} : f(x_1, \ldots, x_n) = \sum_{i=1}^{n} (o(x_i) + a)c_i \quad (5)$$

$$\text{Optimal cost} : C = \min_{x_1, \ldots, x_n} \sum_{i=1}^{n} (o(x_i) + a)c_i \quad (6)$$

$$\text{Constraints} : \forall \ 0 \leq j \leq n. \ 0 \leq r_0 + \sum_{i=1}^{j} x_i \leq r \quad (7)$$

$$: \sum_{i=1}^{n} x_i = 0 \quad (8)$$

Algorithm: the proposed solution algorithm decomposes the problem into subproblems, so that an efficient dynamic programming approach can be employed. Let $C_j(y_j) : \mathbf{R} \cup \{\infty\}$, $j = 0, \ldots, n$, $0 \leq y_j \leq r$ be the optimal energy costs for slots $s_1, \ldots, s_j$, when the final energy reserve at slot s_j is $y_j e$. Here $C_j(y_j) = \infty$ if energy reserve $y_j e$ cannot be achieved at slot j. Thus $C_0(y_0)$ (no slot has elapsed yet) is everywhere ∞ except for $C_0(r_0) = 0$.

$$\text{Subproblems} : C_j(y_j) = \min_{x_1, \ldots, x_j} \sum_{i=1}^{j} (o(x_i) + a)c_i, j = 1, 2, \ldots, n. \quad (9)$$

$$: \forall i'. \ 1 \leq i' \leq j, \quad 0 \leq r_0 + \sum_{i=1}^{i'} x_i \leq r \quad (10)$$

$$: r_0 + \sum_{i=1}^{j} x_i = y_j \quad 0 \leq y_j \leq r. \quad (11)$$

$$\text{Dynamic programming} : \quad (12)$$
$$C_j(y_j) = \min_{\substack{-k \leq x_j \leq k \\ 0 \leq y_j - x_j \leq r}} C_{j-1}(y_j - x_j) + (o(x_j) + a)c_j,$$

$$: C_0(y_0) = \text{ if } y_0 = r_0 \text{ then } 0 \text{ else } \infty \quad (13)$$
$$: C_n(r_0) = C \quad (14)$$

The value of C_j at slot j can be computed sequentially in terms of C_{j-1} by looking backwards for $C_j(y_j)$ to the optimal energy costs at slot $j-1$ for eligible values $y_j - x_j$ of the energy reserve. Finally, an *optimal strategy* S is any sequence $S = (\widehat{x_1}, \widehat{y_1}), \ldots, (\widehat{x_n}, r_0)$ such that the values of $\widehat{x_j}$ and of $\widehat{y_{j-1}}$ are computed backwards from $\widehat{y_j}$, $j = n \ldots, 1$, by letting $\widehat{y_n} = r_0$, the final reserve being r_0. Formally:

$$\text{Optimal strategies}: C_j(\widehat{y_j}) = C_{j-1}(\widehat{y_j} - \widehat{x_j}) + (o(\widehat{x_j}) + a)c_j, \tag{15}$$
$$j = 1, 2, \ldots, n$$
$$: \widehat{y_{j-1}} = \widehat{y_j} - \widehat{x_j} \tag{16}$$
$$: \widehat{y_n} = r_0 \tag{17}$$

The time and space complexity of the algorithm are $O(nrk)$ and $O(nr)$ respectively.

4.7   BGM as Prosumers in DEZENT

In this section the operation of the balancing group managers (BGM) previously defined in DEZENT work will be extended. In a decentralized way, the concept of aggregator is introduced. A new agent called aggregator is characterized by a set of virtual prosumers. Each virtual prosumer exploits the control model defined in Section 4.6. In the proposed approach, each prosumer is neutral in the sense that it essentially neither consumes nor produces energy, as it can only sell in the power market the energy previously bought and stored. Actually, a virtual prosumer consumes a little amount of energy, due to the overhead of the energy storing processes. Thus the behavior of the virtual prosumer is similar to that of a rechargeable battery. Only, a real prosumer could combine the effect of a virtual prosumer with that of a producer and a consumer.

The aim of the aggregator in this model is twofold: (i) to reduce the energy cost of the consumer's population during peak energy consumption; and (ii) to maximize its profit. In order to evaluate the impact of our aggregator, we compare two types of power market situations: (i) a neutral situation in which there is no aggregator in the power market; and (ii) the active situation in which an aggregator is present. Each simulation (wrt. the type of the power market situations) is run separately and in the same conditions.

The space of the experiments is based on the available DEZENT simulator and on the implementation of the introduced aggregator. It depends essentially on three parameters: (i) the free market power cost, which can exhibit high or low variance: for this we chose real data from the day ahead market prices of Switzerland (date: March 9, 2013) [2] and Italy (date: June 18, 2013) [3] respectively; (ii) the prosumers environment, namely heavy production or heavy consumption, in which the total amount of the electricity produced in the subnet is respectively greater than or less than the total amount needed in the subnet. In the heavy consumption situations, the additional, needed power is made available at the large power plant level, at a price which depends on the time of the day.

Analogously for the heavy production situations. In all these cases, the profile cost of the electricity at the global level (namely at the large power plant level) was the same for all days; (iii) the available energy reserve capacity of the virtual prosumers characterizing the aggregator; it is either finite or infinite.

The experiments were conducted on the IMT cluster at the IMT Institute of Advanced Studies Lucca, simulating a 3 days service period (see Table 2) and our comparative studies were based on the total cost of the electricity paid at the end of the last day by the consumer population and on the profit realized by the aggregator. Here the last day has been considered, since in this way transitory effects are minimized. The performance of the aggregator relies on the performance of the combination of the reinforcement learning mechanism at DEZENT level and of the control mechanism used for profile optimization of virtual prosumers characterizing the aggregator.

Figure 13 concerns the best case of the simulations: larger differences in energy global cost (day ahead power market: Switzerland, March 9, 2013) in the presence of undersupply conditions and infinite reserve capacity of virtual prosumers in the case in which the aggregator is active.

Figure 13 (a) shows the behavior of the optimal controller of one of the virtual prosumers of the aggregator. The two upper curves of Figure 13 (a) represent the unitary cost of energy as resulting from the negotiation phase at day 2 (solid curve) and at day 3 (dashed curve). The difference between the two upper curves gives an idea of the possible variations between the outcomes of different negotiations. Notice that the profile of the global energy cost and the context of competing prosumers is the same in both days. The lower dashed curve (respectively lower solid curve) represents the result of the optimization algorithm applied to the curve of day 2 (respectively of day 3). The curves plot the sum (from the beginning of the day) of the suggested variations: according to the constraints we assumed on the virtual prosumers profiles, the sum of the variation must be not greater than 0 and should start and end up at 0. Notice that the controller correctly suggests variations which are opposite wrt. the negotiated cost.

Figure 13 (b) reports the result of the placebo test on the behavior of the consumer population. In Figure 13 (b), the dashed curve represents the energy cost achieved in each hour by the entire population when there is no aggregator in the power market. Analogously, the solid curve represents the case in which the aggregator is active. The observation we have is that the consumer's population when the aggregator is active has spent less during peak energy consumption period.

In Figure 13 (c) the final cost achieved at the end of day 3 by the population of consumers in which the aggregator was active (solid curve) is less than the case in which there was no aggregator (dashed curve). This positive effect is due to the introduction of our aggregator.

In Figure 13 (d) the solid curve reports the energy cost (actual profit) realized by the aggregator in the power market. The profit is given by the sum of the entire profit realized by the 4 virtual prosumers characterizing the aggrega-

Table 2. Experimental setup of the placebo test

	Negotiation Level	1
	BGM on Level 1	1
Architecture	Clients	15
	Producers (50 − 200 KW)	10
	Consumers (200 KW)	5
Electricity price	Day duration: 60 slots (24 hours)	
	Profile cost of the electricity (free market)	
prosumers environment	Heavy consumption	
	Heavy production	
Energy reserve	Infinite	
	Finite: 0 to 40	
Controller	Class of consumption profiles	
	Planning phase: optimization	
aggregator	Collection of 4 prosumers	
Simulations	Duration: 3 days	
	Test 1: without aggregator	
	Test 2: with aggregator	

tor. The dashed curve, of the same figure, represents the expected profit of the aggregator at the end of day 3, computed by assuming known in advance the energy cost. That curve has been obtained by summing up all the energy costs of the optimal profile of day 3 of the prosumers. As mentioned above, Figure 13 concerns the best case. In the worst case, the gain is low; but in any case there is no loss, neither from the side of the aggregator nor from that of prosumers.

4.8   Comparison: DEZENT's Aggregator versus ADDRESS's Aggregator

Four key factors have been considered for assessing the impact of the aggregator introduced in the ADDRESS project: the general weather conditions of the area, the consumer density and characterization, the electricity industry infrastructure and the technological context. The success of the aggregator has been evaluated according to the global welfare improvements of the power grid management systems and to the profit maximization of the aggregator. The positive impact of the aggregator was observed in two scenarios: Southern City and Mid-Latitude High-Rise Community [30].

Both scenarios were characterized by a significant number of domestic and small business consumers whose demand for electricity is driven primarily by cooling needs, space heating and air conditioning. The suggested result of the ADDRESS project is that the potential supply of active demand by the aggregator within the areas of the scenarios is quite high and this is due to high consumer density and high demand for electricity, the latter driven chiefly by the needs for space cooling, which is inherently flexible. Conversely, a limited

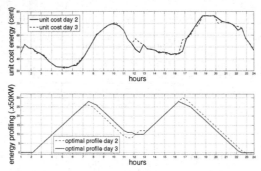

(a) best case: controller operation of one prosumer

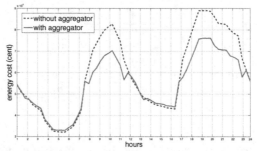

(b) best case: consumer population, aggregated energy cost

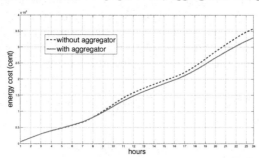

(c) best case: consumer population, final energy cost

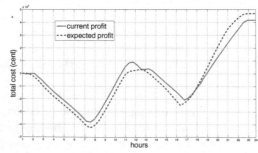

(d) best case: aggregator, profit realized

Fig. 13. Simulation studies

effect of the aggregator was observed in two scenarios: Southern Countryside and Northern Suburban Village [30]. In both cases the density of the consumers was sparse and their demands for electricity were dominated by lighting.

In light of the result of the four ADDRESS scenarios mentioned above, it is clear that an aggregator potential success depends on the flexibility of power consumption in the area and on convenient power exchange in the power market. The main difference on the use of active demand between the ADDRESS approach and the approach we introduce in DEZENT is that ADDRESS focuses on an integrated power management system while DEZENT focuses on a completely decentralized and real time power management system.

The results we obtained in the simulation studies in Section 4.7 are similar to those obtained in the ADDRESS approach. The best case scenario we simulated (in Section 4.7) in our approach corresponds to the best case scenarios simulated also in the ADDRESS approach. Namely, they represent the situation in which the aggregator can maximize its profit at the power market while lowering peak energy consumption at the power grid layer. This is thanks to the flexibility of consumers and of the power market situation. Similarly, in the worst case scenarios of the two approaches, the gain of the aggregator is low and its impact on the power market is almost neutral.

5   Conclusion and Future Work

In the chapter, we considered two related issues, both quite relevant for service component ensembles. On the one hand we have local vs. global knowledge, where the distinction is made more significant by the variability of ensembles, due to their open ended and autonomic nature. On the other hand we distinguish declarative from procedural knowledge. Here declarative knowledge is typically symbolic, equipped with deduction procedures and easy to extend. However, deduction steps may require exhaustive search, and thus often unacceptable amounts of space and time. Procedural knowledge is instead efficiently executable, but rigid and difficult to modify. The two issues are related in the sense that the process of forward propagation typically proceeds from local-declarative towards global-procedural knowledge: deduction/coordination mechanisms vary accordingly.

In the chapter we present two case studies of the above framework, the first about an application of SCLP and SCSP programming to the e-mobility case study of ASCENS, the second about reinforcement learning and dynamic programming for global negotiation and local prosumer profile optimization, respectively, for a smart grid application. In both cases we take advantage of the ability of constraint programming and reinforcement learning of addressing both declarative and procedural issues.

5.1   Related Work

The literature on SCSPs and on their solution using dynamic programming techniques is vast. The following lines of research are relevant to us. Bistarelli, Montanari and Rossi deal with SCSP [10] and its combination with logic programming [11,12] and concurrency [13]. Their approach is too restrictive, and does not easily accommodate the example of Section 3.3. Dechter in [18] introduces bucket elimination as a general solution technique for a variety of problems: it consists in a strategy of problem reduction employing a convenient elimination ordering of variables and constraints. Kohlas and Pouly in [26] suggest *valuation algebras* as a foundation for a general view of information processing. Our approach is similar, being based on a simple, process calculus-like algebraic specification. The main advantage of our presentation is that it benefits from the well-established machinery of permutation algebras [31,19]. The analogy with process algebras is useful when providing a uniform language for supporting both the declarative and the procedural parts of our approach. A first approximation of such a language is cc-pi [16], which combines concurrent constraint programming and pi-calculus.

The SCLP approach presented in Section 3 is mainly related to [14], dealing with the multicriteria version of the shortest path problem. However, we consider a different semiring (namely the one based on Hoare Power Domain operator), which allows us to obtain only the best routes. In [22] a form of approximation is introduced, by considering an aggregated cost function to be optimized, whereas we consider two criteria, and we return all optimal journeys considered equivalently feasible.

Finally, Section 4 is mainly related to the ADDRESS project [6]. Details can be found in [33].

5.2   Future Work

Future work in the above line could concern the definition of formalisms and programming languages flexible enough to express both local-declarative and global-procedural aspects at the same time, but with varying degrees of expressiveness. Language SCEL, proposed by ASCENS, addresses this issue. A recent development where SCEL is extended with constraint programming primitives which do not require global consistency, but which can impose it locally, if needed, are first results in this direction.

References

1. http://www.twenties-project.eu
2. European power exchange, http://www.epexspot.com
3. Gestore mercati elettrici, http://www.mercatoelettrico.org
4. ASCENS: Requirement specification and scenario description of the ascens case studies, deliverable 7.1 (2011)
5. Barroso, L.A., Cavalcanti, T.H., Giesbertz, P., Purchala, K.: Classification of electricity market models worldwide. In: IEEE PES, International Symposium, pp. 9–16. IEEE, Los Alamitos (2005)
6. Belhomme, R., Real de Asua, R.C., Valtorta, G., Paice, A., Bouffard, F., Rooth, R., Losi, A.: Address - active demand for the smart grids of the future. In: CIRED Seminar: Smart Grids for Distribution, pp. 1–4.

7. Belhomme, R., Sebastian, M., Diop, A., Entem, M., Bouffard, F., Valtorta, G., De Simone, A., Cerero, R., Yuen, C., Karkkainen, S., Fritz, W.: Address technical and commercial architecture, deliverable ADDRESS D1.1 (2010), http://www.addressfp7.org/

8. Bertelé, U., Brioschi, F.: On non-serial dynamic programming. Journal of Combinatorial Theory, Series A 14(2), 137–148 (1973)

9. Bistarelli, S., Montanari, U., Rossi, F.: Constraint solving over semirings. In: IJCAI, pp. 624–630 (1995)

10. Bistarelli, S., Montanari, U., Rossi, F.: Semiring-based constraint satisfaction and optimization. J. ACM 44(2), 201–236 (1997)

11. Bistarelli, S., Montanari, U., Rossi, F.: Semiring-based contstraint logic programming: syntax and semantics. ACM Trans. Program. Lang. Syst. 23(1), 1–29 (2001)

12. Bistarelli, S., Montanari, U., Rossi, F.: Soft constraint logic programming and generalized shortest path problems. J. Heuristics 8(1), 25–41 (2002)

13. Bistarelli, S., Montanari, U., Rossi, F.: Soft concurrent constraint programming. ACM Trans. Comput. Log. 7(3), 563–589 (2006)

14. Bistarelli, S., Montanari, U., Rossi, F., Santini, F.: Unicast and multicast qos routing with soft-constraint logic programming. ACM Trans. Comput. Log. 12(1), 5 (2010)

15. Bueno, F., Cabeza, D., Carro, M., Hermenegildo, M.V., López-García, P., Puebla, G.: The ciao prolog system. Reference manual. Tech. Rep. CLIP3/97.1, School of Computer Science, Technical University of Madrid, UPM (1997)

16. Buscemi, M.G., Montanari, U.: CC-pi: A constraint-based language for specifying service level agreements. In: De Nicola, R. (ed.) ESOP 2007. LNCS, vol. 4421, pp. 18–32. Springer, Heidelberg (2007)

17. Challet, D., Zhang, Y.C.: Emergence of cooperation and organization in an evolutionary game. Physica A: Statistical Mechanics and its Applications 246(3–4), 407–418 (1997)

18. Dechter, R.: Bucket elimination: A unifying framework for reasoning. Artif. Intell. 113(1-2), 41–85 (1999)

19. Gadducci, F., Miculan, M., Montanari, U.: About permutation algebras (pre)sheaves and named sets. Higher-Order and Symbolic Computation 19(2-3), 283–304 (2006)

20. Hewitt, C.: PLANNER: A language for proving theorems in robots. In: IJCAI, pp. 295–302 (1969)

21. Hoch, N., Monreale, V., Montanari, U., Sammartino, M.: Declarative vs procedural approach for scsp with an application to an e-mobility optimization problem. Internal Report (2014)

22. Hoch, N., Zemmer, K., Werther, B., Siegwart, R.: Electric vehicle travel optimization-customer satisfaction despite resource constraints. In: 2012 IEEE Intelligent Vehicles Symposium, pp. 172–177 (2012)

23. Hölzl, M., Gabor, T.: Reasoning and Learning for Awareness and Adaptation. In: Wirsing, M., Hölzl, M., Koch, N., Mayer, P. (eds.) Software Engineering for Collective Autonomic Systems. LNCS, vol. 8998, pp. 249–290. Springer, Heidelberg (2015)

24. Jaffar, J., Lassez, J.: Constraint logic programming. In: POPL, pp. 111–119 (1987)

25. Kaelbling, L.P., Littman, M.L., Moore, A.W.: Reinforcement learning: A survey. J. Artif. Intell. Res. (JAIR) 4, 237–285 (1996)

26. Kohlas, J., Pouly, M.: Generic Inference: A Unifying Theory for Automated Reasoning. John Wiley, Chichester (2011)

27. Monreale, G.V., Montanari, U., Hoch, N.: Soft constraint logic programming for electric vehicle travel optimization. In: 26th Workshop on Logic Programming (2012)
28. Montanari, U., Siwe, A.T.: Real time market models and prosumer profiling. In: IEEE INFOCOM Workshops. pp. 7–12 (2013)
29. Montanari, U., Siwe, A.T.: Prosumers as aggregators in the dezent context of regenerative power production. In: IEEE SASO Workshops (2014)
30. Peters, E., Belhomme, R., Battle, C., Bouffard, F., Karkkainen, S., Six, D., Hommelberg, M.: Address: Scenarios and architecture for the active demand development in the smart grids of the future. In: CIRED 20th International Conference on Electricity Distribution, pp. 1–4 (2009)
31. Pitts, A.M.: Nominal Sets: Names and Symmetry in Computer Science. Cambridge Tracts in Theoretical Computer Science, vol. 57. Cambridge University Press, Cambridge (2013)
32. Rossi, F., van Beek, P., Walsh, T.: Handbook of Constraint Programming. Foundations of Artificial Intelligence. Elsevier, Amsterdam (2006)
33. Siwe, A.T.: Prosumer planning in the DEZENT context of regenerative power production. Ph.D. thesis (2013)
34. Sutton, R.S.: Learning to predict by the methods of temporal differences. Machine Learning 3, 9–44 (1988)
35. Tsang, E.P.K.: Foundations of constraint satisfaction. Computation in cognitive science. Academic Press, London (1993)
36. Wedde, H.F., Lehnhoff, S., Moritz, K.M., Handschin, E., Krause, O.: Distributed learning strategies for collaborative agents in adaptive decentralized power systems. In: IEEE International Conference and Workshop on the Engineering of Computer Based Systems (ECBS '08), pp. 26–35 (2008)
37. Wedde, H.F., Lehnhoff, S., Rehtanz, C., Krause, O.: Bottom-up self-organization of unpredictable demand and supply under decentralized power management. In: IEEE International Conference on Self-Adaptive and Self-Organizing Systems (SASO '08), pp. 74–83 (2008)
38. Whitehead, D.: The el farol bar problem revisited: Reinforcement learning in a potential game. ESE Discussion Papers 186, Edinburgh School of Economics, University of Edinburgh (2008)

Knowledge Representation for Adaptive and Self-aware Systems*

Emil Vassev and Mike Hinchey

Lero–the Irish Software Engineering Research Center, University of Limerick, Limerick, Ireland

Abstract. This chapter presents the ASCENS approach to knowledge representation and reasoning for self-adaptive systems. The approach targets both the integration and promotion of autonomy and self-adaptation in software-intensive systems by providing a mechanism and methodology for specification and operation of knowledge for self-adaptive behavior. The approach is based on the KnowLang Framework, a formal approach to knowledge representation and reasoning developed within the ASCENS Project mandate. With KnowLang we build special knowledge bases meant to be integrated in software-intensive systems to establish the vital connection between knowledge, perception, and actions realizing self-adaptive behavior. At runtime, the knowledge is used against the perception of the world to generate appropriate actions in compliance to the system goals and beliefs.

Keywords: self-adaptive systems, knowledge representation, reasoning, adaptive behavior, awareness

1 Introduction

One of the significant scientific contributions that we achieved with the ASCENS Project is related to *knowledge representation and reasoning* (KR&R) for self-adaptive systems. Note that self-adaptive systems must be aware of their physical environment and whereabouts, as well as of their current internal status. This ability helps software intensive systems sense, draw inferences, and react by exhibiting self-adaptation. A common understanding about the process of self-adaptation is the ability of a system to autonomously monitor its behavior and eventually modify the same according to changes in the operational environment, or in the system itself. The paradigm requires that the system engages in various interactions where important structural and dynamic aspects of the environment are perceived. Therefore, it is of major importance for a self-adaptive system to acquire and structure comprehensive knowledge in such a way that it can be effectively and efficiently processed, so such a system becomes aware of itself

---

* This research was supported by the European project IP 257414 (ASCENS).

M. Wirsing et al. (eds.): Collective Autonomic Systems, LNCS 8998, pp. 221–247, 2015.
© Springer International Publishing Switzerland 2015

and its environment. Such a system needs to be developed with initial knowledge and learning capabilities based on knowledge processing and awareness. In this approach, it is very important how the system knowledge is both structured and modeled to provide essence of self-adaptation.

In this chapter, we present an approach to implementing self-adaptation capabilities with KnowLang, a special framework for KR&R. KnowLang provides for a special knowledge context and a special reasoner operating in that context. The approach is formal and demonstrates how knowledge representation and reasoning help to establish the vital connection between knowledge, perception, and actions realizing the self-adaptive behavior. The knowledge is used against the perception of the world to generate appropriate actions in compliance to some goals and beliefs. KnowLang [22,24] is an initiative undertaken by Lero–the Irish Software Engineering Research Center within Lero's mandate in the ASCENS Project [1].

The rest of this chapter is organized as follows. Section 2 introduces the KnowLang formal language as an approach to knowledge representation of self-adaptive systems. The section also presents a proof-of-concept case study. Section 3 presents the KnowLang Reasoner. Section 4 presents a mechanism for awareness in software-intensive systems and how this mechanism is implemented by the KnowLang platform. Section 5 presents related work and finally, Section 6 presents a brief conclusion and future work.

2   KnowLang – Language for Knowledge Representation of Self-adaptive Systems

KnowLang [22,24,23,20,21] is a framework for KR&R that aims at efficient and comprehensive knowledge structuring and awareness based on *logical* and *statistical reasoning*. Knowledge specified with KnowLang takes the form of a Knowledge Base (KB) that outlines a Knowledge Representation (KR) context. A special KnowLang Reasoner operates in this context to allow for knowledge querying and update. In addition, the reasoner can infer special self-adaptive behavior.

2.1   Multi-tier Specification Model

A key feature of KnowLang is a formal language with a multi-tier knowledge specification model allowing for integration of ontologies together with rules and Bayesian networks [13]. The language aims at efficient and comprehensive knowledge structuring and awareness based on logical and statistical reasoning. It helps us tackle [22]: 1) explicit representation of domain concepts and relationships; 2) explicit representation of particular and general factual knowledge, in terms of predicates, names, connectives, quantifiers and identity; and 3) uncertain knowledge in which additive probabilities are used to represent degrees of belief. Other remarkable features are related to knowledge cleaning (allowing for efficient reasoning) [22] and knowledge representation for autonomic behavior [24]. By applying the KnowLang's multi-tier specification model (see

Figure 1) we build a Knowledge Base (KB) structured in three main tiers [22]: 1) *Knowledge Corpuses*; 2) *KB Operators*; and 3) *Inference Primitives.* The tier of Knowledge Corpuses is used to specify KR structures. The tier of KB Operators provide access to Knowledge Corpuses via special classes of *ASK* and *TELL Operators* where ASK Operators are dedicated to knowledge querying and retrieval and TELL Operators allow for knowledge update. When we specify knowledge

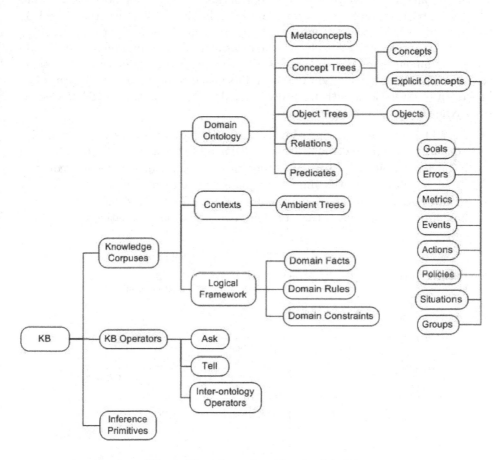

Fig. 1. KnowLang Specification Model

with KnowLang, we build a KB with a variety of knowledge structures such as *ontologies, facts, rules* and *constraints* where we need to specify the ontologies first in order to provide the "vocabulary" for the other knowledge structures. A KnowLang ontology is specified over *concept trees, object trees, relations* and *predicates.* Each concept is specified with special properties and functionality and is hierarchically linked to other concepts through *PARENTS* and *CHILDREN* relationships. For reasoning purposes every concept specified with KnowLang has an intrinsic *STATE* attribute that may be associated with a set of possible *state values* the concept instances may be in. The concept instances are considered as objects and are structured in object trees - a conceptualization of how objects existing in the world of interest are related to each other. The relationships in an object tree are based on the principle that objects have properties, where the value of a property is another object, which in turn also has properties. Moreover, concepts and objects might be connected via *relations*. Relations are binary and may have probability-distribution attribute (e.g., over time, over situations, over concepts' properties, etc.). Probability distribution is provided to support probabilistic reasoning and by specifying relations with probability distributions we actually specify Bayesian networks connecting the concepts and objects of an ontology. Figure 2 shows a KnowLang specification sample demonstrating both the language syntax [17] and its visual counterpart - a concept map based on interrelations with no probability distributions. Modeling knowledge with KnowLang requires a few phases:

– Initial knowledge gathering - involves domain experts to determine the basic notions, relations and functions (operations) of the domain of interest.
– Behavior definition - identifies situations and behavior policies as "control data" helping to identify important self-adaptive scenarios.
– Knowledge structuring - encapsulates domain entities, situations and behavior into KnowLang structures like concepts, objects, relations, facts and rules.

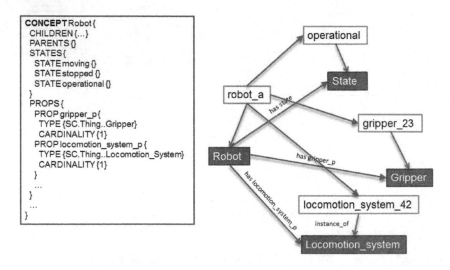

Fig. 2. KnowLang Specification Sample

Note that the full presentation of the KnowLang specification model is beyond the scope of this chapter. For further reading, covering other parts of the specification model, such as *Contexts, Logical Framework, Inter-ontology Operators,* and *Inference Primitives,* the interested reader is advised to refer to [25].

2.2 Knowledge Representation for Self-adaptive Behavior

KnowLang employs special knowledge structures and a reasoning mechanism for modeling autonomic self-adaptive behavior [24]. Such a behavior can be expressed via KnowLang *policies, events, actions, situations* and *relations* between policies and situations (see Definitions 1 through 10). Policies (Π) are at the core of autonomic behavior. A policy π has a *goal* (g), *policy situations* (Si_π), *policy-situation relations* (R_π), and *policy conditions* (N_π) mapped to *policy actions* (A_π) where the evaluation of N_π may eventually (with some degree of probability) imply the evaluation of actions (denoted $N_\pi \xrightarrow{[Z]} A_\pi$) (see Definition 6). A condition is a Boolean expression over an ontology (see Definition 2), e.g., the occurrence of a certain event.

Policy situations Si_π are situations (see Definition 7) that may trigger (or imply) a policy π, in compliance with the policy-situations relations R_π(denoted by $Si_\pi \xrightarrow{[R_\pi]} \pi$), thus implying the evaluation of the policy conditions N_π(denoted by $\pi \to N_\pi$)(see Definition 6). Therefore, the optional policy-situation relations (R_π) justify the relationships between a policy and the associated situations (see Definition 10). Note that in order to allow for self-adaptive behavior, *relations* must be specified to connect policies with situations over an optional probability distribution (Z) where a policy might be related to multiple situations and vice versa. Probability distribution (Z) is provided to support probabilistic reasoning and to help the reasoner to choose the most probable situation-policy "pair". Thus, we may specify a few relations connecting a specific situation to different policies to be undertaken when the system is in that particular situation and the probability distribution over these relations (involving the same situation) should help the reasoner decide which policy to choose (denoted by $si \xrightarrow{[Z]} \pi$ – see Definition 10). Hence, the presence of *probabilistic beliefs* (Z) in both mappings and policy relations justifies the probability of policy execution, which may vary with time.

A goal g is a desirable transition to a state, or from a specific state to another state, (denoted by $s \Rightarrow s'$) (see Definition 5). A state s is a Boolean expression over ontology ($be(O)$)(see Definition 4), e.g., "a specific property of an object must hold a specific value". A situation is expressed with a state (s), a history of actions ($A \overleftarrow{si}$) (actions executed to get to state s), actions A_{si} that can be performed from state s and an optional history of events $E \overleftarrow{si}$ that eventually occurred to get to state s (see Definition 8).

Definition 1. $\Pi := \{\pi_1, \pi_2, ..., \pi_m\}, m \geq 0$ *(policies)*

$\quad A_\pi \subset A, N_\pi \xrightarrow{[Z]} A_\pi$ *(A_π - policy actions; A - the set of all actions)*

$\quad Si_\pi \subset Si, Si_\pi \xrightarrow{[R_\pi]} \pi \to N_\pi$ *(Si_π - policy situations)*

$\quad R_\pi \subset R$ *(R_π-policy-situation relations)*

Definition 2. $n := be(O)$ *(Boolean expression over ontology)*

Definition 3. $N_\pi := \{n_1, n_2, ..., n_k\}, k \geq 0$ *(policy conditions)*

Definition 4. $s := be(O)$ (state)

Definition 5. $g := \langle \Rightarrow s' \rangle | \langle s \Rightarrow s' \rangle$ (goal)

Definition 6. $\pi := < g, Si_\pi, [R_\pi], N_\pi, A_\pi, map(N_\pi, A_\pi, [Z]) >$

Definition 7. $Si := \{si_1, si_2, ..., si_n\}, n \geq 0$ (situations)

Definition 8. $si := < s, A \overset{\leftarrow}{si}, [E \overset{\leftarrow}{si}], A_{si} >$ (situation)
$$A \overset{\leftarrow}{si} \subset A^* \quad (A \overset{\leftarrow}{si} \text{ - executed actions;}$$
$$A^* \text{ - the set of all finite sequences with elements in } A)$$
$$A_{si} \subset A \quad (A_{si} \text{ - possible actions})$$
$$E \overset{\leftarrow}{si} \subset E^* \quad (E \overset{\leftarrow}{si} \text{ - situation events})$$
$$E^* \text{ - the set of all finite sequences with elements in } E)$$

Definition 9. $R := \{r_1, r_2, ..., r_n\}, n \geq 0$ (Relations)

Definition 10. $r := < \pi, [rn], [Z], si >$ (rn - Relation Name)
$$si \in Si, \pi \in \Pi, si \overset{[Z]}{\rightarrow} \pi$$

Ideally, KnowLang policies are specified to handle specific situations, which may trigger the application of policies. A policy exhibits a behavior via actions generated in the environment or in the system itself. Specific conditions determine, which specific actions (among the actions associated with that policy – see Definition 6) shall be executed. These conditions are often generic and may differ from the situations triggering the policy. Thus, the behavior not only depends on the specific situations a policy is specified to handle, but also depends on additional conditions. Such conditions might be organized in a way allowing for synchronization of different situations on the same policy. When a policy is applied, it checks what particular conditions N_π are met and performs the mapped actions A_π ($map(N_\pi, A_\pi, [Z])$ – see Definition 6). An optional probability distribution Z may additionally restrict the action execution. Although specified initially, the probability distribution at both mapping and relation levels is recomputed after the execution of any involved action. The re-computation is based on the consequences of the action execution, which allows for *reinforcement learning*.

2.3   Case Study: Knowledge Representation for Autonomic Clouds

To better understand the concepts behind KnowLang, in this section, we present an example of using the approach to specify a KB for autonomic ensemble described by the ASCENS Science Clouds case study (see Chapter IV.3 [11]).

2.4   Science Clouds

Science Clouds is a cloud computing scientific platform for application execution and data storage Chapter IV.3 [11]. Individual users or universities can join a cloud to provide (and consume of course) resources to the community. A science cloud is a collection of cloud machines - notebooks, desktops, servers, or virtual machines, running the Science Cloud Platform (SCP). Each machine is usually running one instance of the Science Cloud Platform (Science Cloud Platform instance or SCPi). Each SCPi is considered to be a Service Component (SC) in the ASCENS sense. To form a cloud, multiple SCPis communicate over the Internet by using the IP protocol. Within a cloud, a few SCPis might be grouped into a Service Component Ensemble (SCE), also called a Science Cloud Platform ensemble (SCPe). The relationships between the SCPis are dynamic and the formation of a SCPe depends mainly on the properties of the SCPis. The common characteristic of an ensemble is SCPis working together to run one application in a fail-safe manner and under consideration of the Service Level Agreement (SLA) of that application, which may require a certain number of active SCPis, certain latency between the parts, or have restrictions on processing power or memory. The SCP is a *platform as a service* (PaaS), which provides a platform for application execution [15]. Thus, SCP provides an execution environment where special applications might be run by using the SCP's application programming interface (API) and SCP's library [15]. These applications provide a *software as a service* (SaaS) cloud solution to users. The data storage service is provided in the same manner, i.e., via an application.

2.5   Formalizing Science Clouds with KnowLang

Recall that KnowLang is exclusively dedicated to knowledge specification where knowledge is specified as a Knowledge Base (KB) comprising a variety of knowledge structures, e.g., *ontologies*, *facts*, *rules*, and *constraints*. In order to formalize the KB of Science Clouds, the first step is to specify the KB representing the cloud, SCPes, SCPis, applications, etc. To do that, we need to specify ontology structuring the knowledge domains of the cloud. Note that these domains are described via domain-relevant *concepts* and *objects* (concept instances) related through *relations*. To handle explicit concepts like *situations*, *goals*, and *policies*, we grant some of the domain concepts with explicit state expressions.

A big question here is what to specify. The answer can be obtained by performing the initial two phases of the *process of knowledge modeling* with KnowLang, i.e., 1) initial knowledge requirements gathering; and 2) behavior definition (see Section 2.1). By applying the Autonomy Requirements Engineering (ARE) approach to capture the autonomy requirements for Science Clouds, we actually perform these two phases, as described above (see Chapter III.3 [26]).

Science Cloud Ontology. Figure 3, depicts a graphical representation of the *Cloud_Thing* concept tree relating most of the concepts within the Science Cloud Ontology (SCCloud). Most of the concepts presented in Figure 3 were derived from the *Science Clouds Goals Model* built during the autonomy requirements engineering (see Chapter III.3 [26]). Other concepts are considered as "explicit" and were derived from the KnowLang's multi-tier specification model (see Section 2.1).

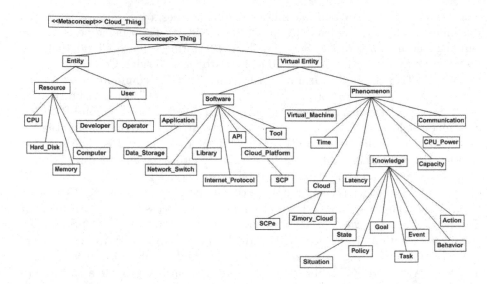

Fig. 3. Science Clouds Ontology: Cloud_Thing Concept Tree

The following is a sample of the KnowLang specification representing two important concepts: the SCP concept and the Application concept (partial specification only). As specified, the concepts in a concept tree might have *properties* of other concepts, *functionalities* (actions associated with that concept), *states* (Boolean expressions validating a specific state), etc.

```
// Science Cloud Platform
CONCEPT SCP {
  CHILDREN {}
  PARENTS { SCCloud.Thing..Cloud_Platform }
  STATES {
    STATE Running { this.PROPS.platform_API. STATES.Running AND this.PROPS.platform_Library.STATES.Running }
    STATE Executing { IS_PERFORMING(this.FUNCS.runApp) }
    STATE Observing { IS_PERFORMING(this.FUNCS.runApp)  AND SCCloud.Thing..Application.PROPS.initiator=this }
    STATE Down { NOT this.STATES.Running }
    STATE Overloaded { this.STATES.OverloadedCPU OR this.STATES.OverloadedStorage OR this.STATES.OverloadedMemory }
    STATE OverloadedCPU { SCCloud.Thing..Metric.CPU_Usage.VALUE > 0.95 }
    STATE OverloadedMemory { SCCloud.Thing..Metric.Memory_Usage.VALUE > 0.95 }
    STATE OverloadedStorage { SCCloud.Thing..Metric.Hard_Disk_Usage.VALUE > 0.95 }
    STATE ApplicationTransferred { LAST_PERFORMED(this, this.FUNCS.transferApp) }
    STATE InCommunication { this.FUNCS.hasActiveCommunication }
    STATE InCommunicationLatency { this.STATES.InCommunication  AND this.FUNCS.getCommunicationLatency >0.5 }
    STATE InLowTrafic { this.FUNCS.getDataTrafic <= 0.5 }
    STATE Started { LAST_PERFORMED(this, this.FUNCS.start) }
    STATE Stopped { LAST_PERFORMED(this, this.FUNCS.stop) }
  }
  PROPS {
    PROP platform_API { TYPE {SCCloud.Thing..API} CARDINALITY {1} }
    PROP platform_Library { TYPE {SCCloud.Thing..Library} CARDINALITY {1} }
    PROP platform_CPU { TYPE {SCCloud.Thing..CPU} CARDINALITY {1} }
    PROP platform_Memory { TYPE {SCCloud.Thing..Memory} CARDINALITY {1} }
    PROP platform_Storage { TYPE {SCCloud.Thing..Data_Storage} CARDINALITY {1} }
    PROP platform_Applications { TYPE {SCCloud.Thing..Application} CARDINALITY {*} }
  }
  FUNCS {
    FUNC run { TYPE { SCCloud.Thing..Action.RunSCP } }
    FUNC down { TYPE { SCCloud.Thing..Action.StopSCP } }
    FUNC runApp { TYPE { SCCloud.Thing..Action.RunApplication } }
    FUNC startApp { TYPE { SCCloud.Thing..Action.StartApplication } }
    FUNC stopApp { TYPE { SCCloud.Thing..Action.StopApplication } }
    FUNC transferApp { TYPE { SCCloud.Thing..Action.TransferApplication } }
    FUNC startNewCommunication { TYPE { SCCloud.Thing..Action.StartCommunication } }
    FUNC stopNewCommunication { TYPE { SCCloud.Thing..Action.StopCommunication } }
```

```
    FUNC hasActiveCommunication { TYPE { SCCloud.Thing..Action.HasActiveCommunication } }
    FUNC getCommunicationLatency { TYPE { SCCloud.Thing..Action.GetCommunicationLatency } }
    FUNC getDataTraffic { TYPE { SCCloud.Thing..Action.GetTraffic } }
  }
  IMPL { SCCloud.SCPImpl }
}

// Science Cloud Application
  CONCEPT Application {
    CHILDREN {}
      PARENTS { SCCloud.Thing..Software }
    STATES {
      STATE Running { PERFORMED(this.FUNCS.Started) AND NOT PERFORMED(this.FUNCS. Stopped) }
      STATE Started { LAST_PERFORMED(this, this.FUNCS.start) }
      STATE Stopped { LAST_PERFORMED(this, this.FUNCS.stop) }
    }
    PROPS {
      PROP needed_CPU_Power { TYPE {SCCloud.Thing..CPU_Power} CARDINALITY {1} }
      PROP needed_Memory { TYPE {SCCloud.Thing..Capacity} CARDINALITY {1} }
      PROP needed_Storage { TYPE {SCCloud.Thing..Storage} CARDINALITY {1} }
      PROP distributiveness { TYPE {Boolean} CARDINALITY {1} }
      PROP requiredSCPis { TYPE {Integer} CARDINALITY {1} }
      PROP requiredLatency { TYPE { SCCloud.Thing..Latency } CARDINALITY {1} }
      PROP initiator { TYPE {SCCloud.Thing..SCP} CARDINALITY {1} }
    }
    FUNCS { .... }
    IMPL { SCCloud.ApplicationImpl }
  }
```

As mentioned, the states are specified as Boolean expressions. For example, the state Executing is true while the SCP is performing the runApp function. The KnowLang operator IS_PERFORMING evaluates actions and returns true if an action is currently performing. Similarly, the operator LAST_PERFORMED evaluates actions and returns true if an action is the last successfully performed action by the concept realization. A concept realization is an object instantiated from that concept, e.g., a SCP instance (SCPi). A complex state might be expressed as a Boolean function of other states. For example, the *Running* state is expressed as a Boolean function of two other states, particularly, states of concept's properties, e.g., the SCP is running if both its API and Library are running:

```
STATE Running { this.PROPS.platform\_API.STATES.Running AND this.PROPS.platform\_Library.STATES.Running }
```

States are extremely important to the specification of goals (objectives), situations, and policies. For example, states help the KnowLang Reasoner determine at runtime whether the system is in a particular situation or a particular goal (objective) has been achieved. Note that to specify some of the SCP states, we used the KnowLang *metric* concept..

```
STATE OverloadedCPU { SCCloud.Thing..Metric.CPU_Usage.VALUE > 0.95 }
```

The *Cloud_Thing* concept tree (see Figure 3) is the main concept tree of the SCCloud Ontology. Due to space limitations, Figure 3 does not show all the concept tree branches. Moreover, some of the concepts in this tree are "roots" of other trees. For example, the *Action* concept, expressing the common concept for all the actions that can be realized by the cloud, is the root of the concept tree shown in Figure 4. As shown, actions are grouped by subsystem (or part) they are associated with. For example, the SCP actions are: *RunSCP*, *StopSCP*, *LeaveSCPe*, and *JoinSCPe*.

Note that in the KnowLang specification models, in addition to concepts we also specify *concept instances*, which are considered as objects and are structured in *object trees*. The latter are a conceptualization of how objects existing in the

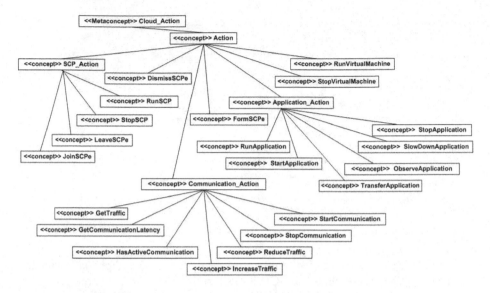

Fig. 4. Science Clouds Ontology: Cloud_Action Concept Tree

world of interest (e.g., Science Clouds) are related to each other. The relationships in an object tree are based on the principle that objects have properties, where the value of a property is another object, which in turn also has properties [25]. Therefore, the object trees are the realization of concepts in the ontology domain (e.g., Science Clouds). To better understand the relationship between concepts and objects, we may think of concepts as similar to the OOP classes and objects as instances of these classes. For example, the SCP concept might be regarded as a class and the SCPis as SCP "instances" of that class. In this exercise, we specified a few exemplary SCPis as object trees, which we do not present here due to space limitations.

Self-adaptive Behavior. To specify self-adaptive behavior, we use goals, policies, and situations (see Section 2.2). These are defined as explicit concepts in KnowLang and for the Cloud Ontology (SCCloud) we specified them under the concepts *Virtual_entity->Phenomenon->Knowledge* (see Figure 3). Figure 5, depicts a concept tree representing the specified Science Clouds goals. Note that most of these goals were derived from the goals model build for Science Clouds by applying the ARE approach (see Chapter III.3 [26]).

KnowLang specifies goals as *functions of states* where any combination of states can be involved. A goal has an *arriving state* (Boolean function of states) and an optional *departing state* (another Boolean function of states) (see Section 2.2). The following code samples present the specification of two simple goals. Note that their arriving and departing states can be either single SCP states or Boolean functions involving more than one state. Note that the states used to specify these goals are specified as part of the *SCP* concept.

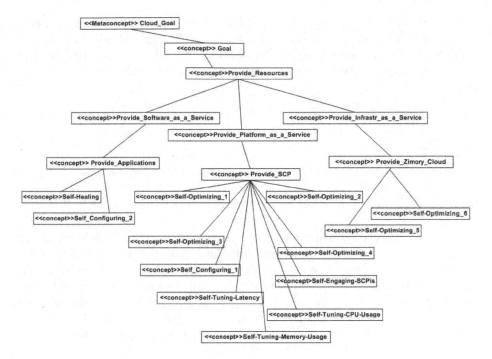

Fig. 5. Science Cloud Ontology: Cloud_Goal Concept Tree

```
//
//==== Cloud Goals ==============================================================
//
CONCEPT_GOAL Self-optimizing_1 {
  SPEC {
    DEPART { SCP.STATES.OverloadedCPU }
    ARRIVE { SCP.STATES.ApplicationTransferred AND NOT SCP.STATES.OverloadedCPU }
  }
}
CONCEPT_GOAL Self-optimizing_3 {
  SPEC {
    DEPART { SCP.STATES.InCommunicationLatency }
    ARRIVE { SCP.STATES.InLowTrafic AND NOT SCP.STATES.InCommunicationLatency }
  }
}
```

According to the KnowLang semantics, in order to achieve specified goals (objectives), we need to specify *policies* triggering *actions* that will eventually change the system states, so the desired ones, required by the goals, will become effective (see Section 2.2). All the policies in KnowLang descend from the explicit *Policy* concept. Recall that the KnowLang policies allow the specification of self-adaptive behavior. As a rule, we need to specify at least one policy per single goal, i.e., a policy that will provide the necessary behavior to achieve that goal. Of course, we may specify multiple policies handling same goal (objective) and let the system decides which policy to apply taking into consideration the current situation and conditions.

The following is a specification sample showing a simple policy called *ReduceCPUOverhead* – as the name says, this policy is intended to reduce the

CPU overhead of a SCPi. As shown, the policy is specified to handle the goal *Self-Opimizing_1* and is triggered by the situation *HighCPUUsage*. Further, the policy triggers conditionally (the *CONDITONS* directive requires that a SCPi is executing an application) the execution of a sequence of actions.

```
CONCEPT_POLICY ReduceCPUOverhead {
  SPEC {
    POLICY_GOAL { SCCloud.Thing..Self-Optimizing_1 }
    POLICY_SITUATIONS { SCCloud.Thing..HighCPUUsage }
    POLICY_RELATIONS { SCCloud.Thing..Policy_Situation_1 }
    POLICY_ACTIONS {SCCloud.Thing..Action.StartCommunication, SCCloud.Thing..Action.TransferApplication,
                    SCCloud.Thing..Action.StopCommunication }
    POLICY_MAPPINGS {
      MAPPING {
        CONDITIONS { SCCloud.Thing..SCP.STATES.Executing }
        DO_ACTIONS { SCCloud.Thing..SCP.Action.StartCommunication, SCCloud.Thing..SCP.Action.TransferApplication,
                     SCCloud.Thing..SCP.Action.StopCommunication }
      }
    }
  }
}
```

Policies are triggered by situations (see Section 2.2). Therefore, while specifying policies, we need to think of important situations that may trigger those policies. A single policy requires to be associated with (related to) at least one situation, but for polices handling self-adaptation we eventually will need more situations. Therefore, a single situation may need more policies, those providing alternative behaviors or execution paths departing from that situation. The following code represents the specification of the *HighCPUUsage* situation, used for the specification of the *ReduceCPUOverhead* policy.

```
//
//==== Cloud Situations ===================================================================
//
CONCEPT_SITUATION HighCPUUsage {
  CHILDREN {}
  PARENTS { SCCloud.Thing..Situation}
  SPEC {
    SITUATION_STATES { SCCloud.Thing..SCP.STATES.OverloadedCPU}
    SITUATION_ACTIONS { SCCloud.Thing..Action.TransferApplication, SCCloud.Thing..Action.SlowDownApplication,
                        SCCloud.Thing..Action. StopApplication }
  }
}
```

As shown, the situation is specified with states and *possible actions*. To consider a situation effective (the system is currently in that situation), its associated states must be respectively effective (evaluated as true). For example, the situation *HighCPUUsage* is effective if the SCP state *OverloadedCPU* is effective. The possible actions define what actions can be undertaken once the system falls in a particular situation. For example, the *HighCPUUsage* situation has three possible actions: *TransferApplication*, *SlowDownApplication*, and *StopApplication*. The following code represents another policy intended to handle the *HighCPUUsage* situation. In this policy, we specified three *MAPPING* sections, which introduce three possible alternative execution paths.

```
CONCEPT_POLICY AIReduceCPUOverhead {
  SPEC {
    POLICY_GOAL { SCCloud.Thing..Self-Optimizing_1 }
    POLICY_SITUATIONS { SCCloud.Thing..HighCPUsage }
    POLICY_RELATIONS { SCCloud.Thing..Policy_Situation_2 }
    POLICY_ACTIONS { SCCloud.Thing..Action.SlowDownApplication, SCCloud.Thing..Action. StopApplication }
    POLICY_MAPPINGS {
      MAPPING {
        CONDITIONS { SCCloud.Thing..SCP.STATES.Executing }
        DO_ACTIONS { SCCloud.Thing..Action. SlowDownApplication }
        PROBABILITY {0.5}
      }
```

```
MAPPING {
    CONDITIONS { SCCloud.Thing..SCP.STATES.Executing }
    DO_ACTIONS { SCCloud.Thing..Action. StopApplication }
    PROBABILITY {0.4}
}
MAPPING {
    CONDITIONS { SCCloud.Thing..SCP.STATES.Executing }
    DO_ACTIONS { GENERATE_NEXT_ACTIONS(SCCloud.Thing..SCP) }
    PROBABILITY {0.1}
    }
  }
 }
}
```

Recall that situations are related to policies via relations (see Section 2.2). The following code demonstrates how we related the *HighCPUUsage* situation to two different policies: *ReduceCPUOverhead* and *AIReduceCPUOverhead*.

```
//
//==== Cloud Relations ===================================================================
//
RELATIONS {
  RELATION Policy_Situation_1 {
    RELATION_PAIR { SCCloud.Thing..HighCPUUsage, SCCloud.Thing..ReduceCPUOverhead } PROBABILITY {0.5}
  }
  RELATION Policy_Situation_2 {
    RELATION_PAIR { SCCloud.Thing..HighCPUUsage, SCCloud.Thing..AIReduceCPUOverhead} PROBABILITY {0.4}
  }
}
```

As specified, the probability distribution gives initial designer's preference about what policy should be applied if the system ends up in the *HighCPUUsage* situation. Note that at runtime, the KnowLang Reasoner maintains a record of all the action executions and re-computes the probability rates every time when a policy has been applied. Thus, although initially the system will apply the *ReduceCPUOverhead* policy (it has the higher probability rate of 0.5), if that policy cannot achieve its goal due to action fails (e.g., the communication link with another SCPi is broken and application transfer is not possible), then the probability distribution will be shifted in favor of the *AIReduceCPUOverhead* policy and the system will try to apply that policy. Note that in this case both policies share the same goal.

Monitoring. In general, a self-adaptive system has sensors that connect it to the world and eventually help it listen to its internal components. These sensors generate raw data that represent the physical characteristics of the world. In our approach, we assume that cloud sensors are controlled by a software driver (e.g., implemented in C++) where appropriate methods are used to control a sensor and read data from it. In KnowLang, by specifying a *Metric concept* we introduce a class of sensors to the KB and by specifying objects, instances of that class, we represent the real sensor. KnowLang allows the specification of four different types of metrics [25]:

- *RESOURCE* - measure resources like capacity;
- *QUALITY* - measure qualities like performance, response time, etc.;
- *ENVIRONMENT* - measure environment qualities and resources;
- *ENSEMBLE* - measure complex qualities and resources where the metric might be a function of multiple metrics both of *RESOURCE* and *QUALITY* type.

The following is a specification of metrics mainly used to assist the specification of states in the specification of the SCP concept (see Section 2.5).

```
//Cloud Metrics
CONCEPT_METRIC CPU_Usage {
  SPEC {    METRIC_TYPE { RESOURCE } METRIC_SOURCE { CPU.Usage }
    DATA { DATA_TYPE { Number } VALUE { 0.00 } }
  } }
CONCEPT_METRIC Memory_Usage {
  SPEC {    METRIC_TYPE { RESOURCE } METRIC_SOURCE { Memory.Usage }
    DATA { DATA_TYPE { Number } VALUE { 0.00 } }
  } }
CONCEPT_METRIC Hard_Disk_Usage {
  SPEC {    METRIC_TYPE { RESOURCE } METRIC_SOURCE { HDD.Usage }
    DATA { DATA_TYPE { Number } VALUE { 0.00 } }
  } }
```

3   KnowLang Reasoner

A very challenging task is the R&D of the inference mechanism providing for *knowledge reasoning and awareness*. In order to support reasoning about self-adaptive behavior and to provide a KR gateway for communication with the KB, we have developed a special KnowLang Reasoner. The reasoner communicates with the system and operates in the KR Context, a context formed by the represented knowledge (see Figure 6).

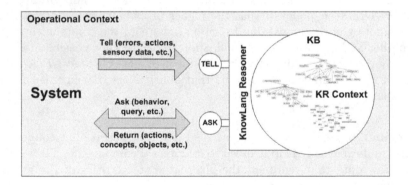

Fig. 6. KnowLang Reasoner

The KnowLang Reasoner should be supplied as a component hosted by the system and thus, it runs in the system's Operational Context as any other system's component. However, it operates in the KR Context and on the KR symbols (represented knowledge). The system talks to the reasoner via special ASK and TELL Operators allowing for knowledge queries and knowledge updates (see Figure 6). Upon demand, the KnowLang Reasoner can also build up and return a self-adaptive behavior model - a chain of actions to be realized in the environment or in the system.

3.1   ASK and TELL Operators

KnowLang provides for a predefined set of *ASK* and *TELL Operators* allowing for communication with the KB. TELL Operators feed the KR Context with important information driven by errors, executed actions, new sensory data, etc., thus helping the KnowLang Reasoner update the KR with recent changes in both the system and execution environment. The system uses ASK Operators to receive recommended behavior where knowledge is used against the perception of the world to generate appropriate actions in compliance to some goals and beliefs. In addition, ASK Operators may provide the system with awareness-based conclusions about the current state of the system or the environment and ideally with behavior models for self-adaptation.

So far, we have developed the operational semantics of the following TELL and ASK Operators [18]:

- *TELL_ERR* - tells about a raised error;
- *TELL_SENSOR* - tells about new data collected by a sensor;
- *TELL_ACTION* - tells about action execution;
- *TELL_ACTION* (behavior) - tells about action execution as part of behavior performance;
- *TELL_OBJ_UPDATE* - tells about a possible object update;
- *TELL_CNCPT_UPDATE* - tells about a possible concept update;
- *ASK_BEHAVIOR* - asks for self-adaptive behavior considering the current situation;
- *ASK_BEHAVIOR(goal)* - asks for self-adaptive behavior to achieve certain goal;
- *ASK_BEHAVIOR(situation, goal)* - asks for self-adaptive behavior to achieve certain goal when departing from a specific situation;
- *ASK_BEHAVIOR(state)* - asks for self-adaptive behavior to go to a certain state;
- *ASK_RULE_BEHAVIOR(conditions)* - asks for rule-based behavior;
- *ASK_CURR_STATE(object)* - asks for the current state of an object;
- *ASK_CURR_STATE* - asks for the current system state;
- *ASK_CURR_SITUATION* - asks for the current situation.

3.2   The ASK_BEHAVIOR Operator

This subsection provides a brief presentation of the *operational semantics* of the *ASK_BEHAVIOR* KB Operator [18]. For more information on the operational semantics of the other KnowLang KB Operators, please consult [18].

ASK_BEHAVIOR Operator is used by the system to ask the KnowLang Reasoner for self-adaptive behavior considering the current situation the system is in. The following rules reveal the operational semantics of the ASK_BEHAVIOR Operator - σ states for Operational Context (OC) and σ' states for Knowledge Representation Context (KRC) (see Figure 6). For clarity reasons, we do not show the change in KRC after updates have been made in that context.

$$(1) \frac{\sigma \xrightarrow{ask\_behavior()} \sigma'}{\langle ASK\_BEHAVIOR, \sigma' \rangle \longrightarrow \langle findCurrentSituation(), \sigma' \rangle}$$

$$(2) \frac{\sigma \xrightarrow{ask\_behavior()} \sigma' \ \langle findCurrentSituation(), \sigma' \rangle \longrightarrow \langle si, \sigma' \rangle}{\langle findSitnPolcyRltns(si), \sigma' \rangle \longrightarrow \langle R_{si}, \sigma' \rangle}$$

$$(3) \frac{\sigma \xrightarrow{ask\_behavior()} \sigma' \ \langle findSitnPolcyRltns(si), \sigma' \rangle \longrightarrow \langle R_{si}, \sigma' \rangle}{\langle max(R_{si}), \sigma' \rangle \longrightarrow \langle \pi_{si}, \sigma' \rangle}$$

$$(4) \ \langle \pi, \sigma' \rangle \longrightarrow \langle applyPolicy(\pi), \sigma' \rangle$$

$$(5) \frac{\langle \pi_{si}, \sigma' \rangle \longrightarrow \langle applyPolicy(\pi_{si}), \sigma' \rangle}{\forall n_\pi \in N_\pi \bullet \langle n_\pi, \sigma' \rangle \longrightarrow \langle TRUE, \sigma' \rangle} \ A'_\pi \subseteq A_\pi$$

$$(6) \frac{\begin{array}{c} \langle \pi_{si}, \sigma' \rangle \longrightarrow \langle applyPolicy(\pi_{si}), \sigma' \rangle \\ \langle map(\pi_{si}, N_\pi, A_\pi, Z), \sigma' \rangle \longrightarrow \langle <A'_\pi, Z'>, \sigma' \rangle \\ \langle max(Z'), \sigma' \rangle \longrightarrow \langle z, \sigma' \rangle \end{array}}{\langle getProbableActions(<A'_\pi, Z'>, z), \sigma' \rangle \longrightarrow \langle <A''_\pi, z>, \sigma' \rangle}$$

$$(7) \frac{\begin{array}{c} \langle \pi_{si}, \sigma' \rangle \longrightarrow \langle applyPolicy(\pi_{si}), \sigma' \rangle \\ \langle map(\pi_{si}, N_\pi, A_\pi, Z), \sigma' \rangle \longrightarrow \langle <A'_\pi, Z'>, \sigma' \rangle \\ \langle getProbableActions(<A'_\pi, Z'>, z), \sigma' \rangle \longrightarrow \langle <A''_\pi, z>, \sigma' \rangle \end{array}}{\langle recordBehavior(\pi_{si}, A''_\pi), \sigma' \rangle \longrightarrow \langle b_{si}^\pi, \sigma' \rangle}$$

$$(8) \frac{\sigma \xrightarrow{ask\_behavior()} \sigma' \ \langle recordBehavior(\pi_{si}, A_\pi), \sigma' \rangle \longrightarrow \langle b_{si}^\pi, \sigma' \rangle}{\sigma' \xrightarrow{return(b_{si}^\pi)} \sigma}$$

As shown in Rule 1, to ask for behavior, the system calls the $ask\_behavior()$ function (a method implementing the system call of the ASK_BEHAVIOR Operator), which triggers a context switching $\sigma \xrightarrow{ask\_behavior()} \sigma'$. This passes the process control to the KnowLang Reasoner operating in the KRC. Further, this context switching initiates an internal for KRC call of the ASK_BEHAVIOR Operator, which starts an internal operation (denoted with the $findCurrentSituation()$ abstract function) to find the situation the system is currently in.

The current situation will be approximately determined based on the *global system state*. Once the current situation is successfully determined (see the second premise in Rule 2), the reasoner needs to find all the policies associated with that situation. Thus, the reasoner looks up all the *situation-policy relations* the current situation participates in (denoted with the $findSitnPolcyRltns(si)$ - see the conclusion in Rule 2). Next, the relation with the *highest probability rate* is selected (recall that KnowLang Relations may be associated with a probability rate - see Definition 10 in Section 2.2), which helps to determine the *most appropriate policy* for that particular situation (see the conclusion in Rule 3). The selected policy is applied (see Rule 4). The evaluation of a policy triggers a *mapping operation* where any *policy condition* that is held (the conditions are Boolean expressions) is mapped to appropriate actions with eventual *probability rate* (see Definition 6 in Section 2.2). This operation selects *pairs "actions subset"-"probability rate"* (see the conclusion in Rule 5). Next, the reasoner selects from these pairs the one with the highest probability rate to extract the *sub-*

set of actions to be executed (see the last premise and conclusion in Rule 6). The extracted subset of possible actions has to be recorded as a *behavior model* (see the conclusion in Rule 7 where this is denoted with the $recordBehavior(\pi_{si}, A''_\pi)$ abstract function). Finally, the KnowLang Reasoner returns the recorded behavior model to the system with a context switching back to OC σ (see Rule 8). Note that the behavior model must comprise only actions allowed to be executed from the actual situation (see Definition 8 in Section 2.2).

4 Awareness in Software-Intensive Systems

In general, any autonomic system engages in interactions where it is not just able to interact with its operational environment, but also to perceive important structural and dynamic aspects of the same [8,19]. To become interaction-aware such a system needs to be aware of its physical environment and whereabouts and its current internal status. This ability is defined as awareness and it helps intelligent computerized systems to sense, draw inferences for their own behavior and react. The notion of awareness should be generally related to perception, recognition, thinking and eventually prediction. Closely related to artificial intelligence, awareness depends on the knowledge we must transfer to a computerized system and make it use that knowledge, so it can exhibit intelligence. However, in addition to computerized knowledge, artificial awareness also requires a means of sensing changes (e.g., event perception and data gathering), so the external and internal worlds can be perceived through their raw events and data. Thus, self-monitoring and monitoring the environment is the key to awareness, i.e., to exhibit awareness, computerized systems must sense and analyze their internal components and the environment where they operate. Such systems should be able to notice a change and understand its implications. Moreover, an aware system should be able to determine normal and abnormal states. See Chapter II.4 [6] for a formal description of awareness based on the GEM model.

4.1 Classes of Awareness

Awareness can be classified into two major classes: self-awareness about the internal world and context awareness about the external world. The autonomic computing research [8] defines these two classes as following:

- *self-awareness* - a system has detailed knowledge about its own entities, current states, capacity and capabilities, physical connections and ownership relations with other (similar) systems in its environment;
- *context-awareness* - a system knows how to sense, negotiate, communicate and interact with environmental systems and how to anticipate environmental system states, situations and changes.

Another intriguing class of awareness could be the so-called *situational awareness*, which is related to situations. Situation awareness considers circumstances particularly relevant to important situations a computerized system can be involved in. Other classes might be more specific and draw our attention to specific problems, e.g., operational conditions and performance (operational awareness), control processes (control awareness), interaction processes (interaction awareness), navigation processes (navigation awareness), etc. Note that although classes of awareness may differ by their subject, basically they all require perception of events and data from the subjective context "within a volume of time and space, the comprehension of their meaning, and the projection of their status in the near future" [2].

To better understand the idea of awareness in computerized systems, we may think of an example with *exploration robots* where we may consider navigation awareness, which requires context-relative plots of position so that the system can infer robot speed and direction. Landmarks should be represented as part of the environment knowledge. Moreover, at the beginning of the navigation process a special "navigation map" can be built on the fly by the navigation awareness mechanism. Then, basically navigation awareness is reading the sensor data from cameras and plotting the position of the robot at the time of observation. Via repeated position plots, the course and land-reference speed of the robot is established.

4.2   Structuring Awareness

To function, the mechanism implementing awareness must be structured taking into consideration possible different stages of an awareness process. The mechanism of awareness might be built over a complex chain of functions pipelining the stages of the awareness process such as: 1) *raw data gathering*; 2) *data passing*; 3) *filtering*; 3) *conversion*; 4) *assessment*; 5) *projection*; and 6) *learning*. As shown in Figure 7, ideally all the *awareness functions* might be structured as a **Pyramid of Awareness** forming the mechanism that converts raw data (facts, measures, raw events, etc.) into conclusions, problem prediction and eventually may trigger learning.

As shown in Figure 7, the different pyramid levels represent awareness functions that can be grouped into four function groups determining specific *awareness tasks*. The first three pyramid levels compose the group of *monitoring tasks*.

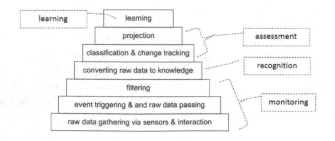

Fig. 7. The Pyramid of Awareness

Further, the fourth level forms the group of *recognition tasks*. The fifth and the sixth levels compose the group of *assessment tasks*, and finally, the last seventh level form the group of *learning tasks*. In addition, *aggregation* can be included as a sub-task at any function level. Note that aggregation is intended to improve the overall awareness performance, e.g., aggregation techniques can be applied to aggregate large amounts of sensory data during the filtering stage, or can be applied by the recognition tasks to improve classification.

Ideally, the four awareness function groups require a comprehensive and well-structured KB representing knowledge in KR Symbols expressing the system itself with its proper internal structures and functionality and the environment. Moreover, the awareness process is not as straightforward as one might think. Instead, it is a cyclic with many iterations over the awareness functions. Thus, by closing the chain of awareness functions we form a special *awareness control loop* [19] where different classes of awareness may emerge (see Figure 8).

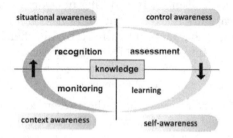

Fig. 8. Awareness Control Loop

An elaborated description of the awareness function groups is the following:

- *monitoring* - collects, aggregates, filters, manages, and reports internal and external details such as metrics and topologies gathered from the system's internal entities and its context;
- *recognition* - uses knowledge structures and data patterns to aggregate and convert raw data into knowledge symbols;
- *assessment* - tracks changes and determines points of interest, generates hypotheses about situations involving these points, and recognizes situational patterns;
- *learning* - generates new situational patterns and maintains a history of property changes.

Its cycling nature is the main reason to regard awareness as complex product with several *levels of exhibition* and eventually *degree of awareness*. The levels of awareness might be related to data readability and reliability, i.e., it could happen to have noisy data that must be cleaned up and eventually interpreted with some degree of probability. Other levels of awareness exhibition might be *early awareness*, which is supposed to be a product of one or two passes of the

Awareness Control Loop and *late awareness*, which should be more mature in terms of conclusions and projections. Similar to humans who may react to their first impression and then the reaction might shift together with a late but better realization of the current situation, an aware computerized system should rely on early awareness to react quickly to situations when fast reaction is needed and on late awareness when more precise thinking is required.

4.3   Implementing Awareness with KnowLang

Ideally, awareness should be a part of the cognitive process where it might support learning. An efficient awareness mechanism should rely on both past experience and new knowledge introduced to the system. Moreover, awareness via learning is the basic mechanism for introducing new facts into the cognitive system - other possible ways are related to interaction with a human operator who may manually introduce new facts into the KB. An efficient awareness mechanism needs to properly integrate the Pyramid of Awareness. The baseline is to provide a means of *monitoring* and *knowledge representation* with proper reasoner supporting the Pyramid of Awareness.

By the time of that chapter writing, the presented awareness mechanism was partially implemented in the KnowLang Reasoner. As shown in Section 3, a KR with KnowLang adds a new context to the program and the KnowLang Reasoner operates in this context taking into account the monitoring activities driven by the system's sensors and reported via TELL Operators to the reasoner (see also Figure 6). The KnowLang Reasoner drives the Awareness Control Loop and delivers awareness results to the system as outputs of the ASK Operators.

In addition to the awareness abilities initiated via ASK and TELL operators, a further implementation of the KnowLang Reasoner envisions an additional awareness capability based on *self-initiation* where the KnowLang Reasoner may initiate actions without being asked for it. In this approach, we consider a behavior model based on the so-called Partially Observable Markov Decision Processes (POMDP) [10]. Note that this model is appropriate when there is uncertainty and lack of information needed to determine the state of the entire system. For example, individuals in complex systems like Science Clouds (see Section 2.4) often might be idle, i.e., not actively participating in the cloud's activities, because they are not certain about the current global state of the cloud. The POMDP model helps individuals reason on the current cloud state (or that of the environment) and eventually self-initiate when an action is needed to be performed. Therefore, according to a POMDP-based model, built for the Science Clouds case study, a SCPi (a service component - SC) takes as input observable situations, involving other SCPis and the environment, and generates as output actions initiating SCPi activity (see Section 2.4). Note that the generated actions affect the global cloud state.

Formally, this model is a tuple $M :=< S, A, T, R, X, O >$ where:

- S is a finite set of system states.
- An initial belief state $s_0 \in S$ is based on $z_0(s_0; s_0 \in S)$, which is a *discrete probability distribution* over the set of system states S, representing for each state a SCPi's belief that it is currently occupying that state.
- A is a finite set of actions that may be undertaken by a SCPi. Note that the system state determines the current situation and thus, the possible set of actions is reduced only to those able to cope with that situation.
- $T : S \times A \longrightarrow Z(S)$ is a state transition function, giving for each system state s and action a, a probability distribution over states. Here, $T(s; a; s')$ computes the probability of ending in state s', given that the start state is s and a SCPi takes action a, $z(s'|s; a)$.
- $O : A \times S \longrightarrow Z(X)$ is the observation function giving for each system state s and action a, a probability distribution over observations X. For example, $O(s'; a; x)$ is the probability of observing x, in state s' after performing action a, $z(x|s'; a)$.
- $R : S \times A \longrightarrow R$ is a reward function, giving the expected immediate reward gained by a SCPi for performing an action a while staying in a state s, e.g., $R(s; a)$. The reward is a scalar value in the range $[0..1]$ determining, which action (among many possible) should be undertaken by a SCPi in compliance with the system goals.

Interpretation. To illustrate this model, let's assume that a cloud is currently occupying the state $s =$ *"there is an SCPi with overloaded both CPU and storage, but no application transfer procedure has been initiated yet and still no SCPi has self-initiated for new application hosting"*. Let's assume there is at least one idle SCPi in the cloud ready to undertake a few actions A, including the action $a =$ *"self-initiation for new application hosting"*. That SCPi performs the following reasoning steps in order to self-initiate for new application hosting:

1. The SCPi computes its current belief state s_0 - the SCPi picks up the state with the highest probability z_0 and eventually $s_0 = s$.
2. The SCPi computes the probability z_1 of the cloud occupying the state s' = *"there is an SCPi with overloaded both CPU and storage and a SCPi has self-initiated for new application hosting"* if the action a is undertaken from state s_0.
3. The SCPi computes the probability $z_2(x|s'; a)$ of observation $x =$ *"there are sufficient CPU and storage resources to host a new application"*.
4. The SCPi computes the reward $r(s_0; a)$ for taking the action a (self-initiation for new application hosting) in state s_0. If no other immediate actions should be undertaken (forced by other cloud goals), the reward r should be the highest possible, which will determine the execution of a.

Probability Computation. The POMDP model for self-initiation requires the computation of a few probability values. Our *model for assessing probability* applicable to the computation of POMDP probability values (probability of the

Table 1. Transition Matrix Z

	s_1	s_2	...	s_i	...	s_n
s_1	z_{11}	z_{12}	...	z_{1j}	...	z_{1n}
s_2	z_{21}	z_{22}	...	z_{2j}	...	z_{2n}
...	...	...	... ...	... ...
s_i	z_{i1}	z_{i2}	...	z_{ij}	...	z_{in}
...	...	...	... ...	... ...
s_n	z_{n1}	z_{n2}	...	z_{nj}	...	z_{nn}

cloud being in a state and probability of observation) is basically based on the probability distributions at the levels of *situation-policy relations* and *policy mappings* connecting conditions to actions (see definitions 10 and 6 in Section 2.2). Therefore, we need to provide the system with initial probability distributions at these levels, which practically is building Bayesian networks in our KR model. In our approach, the *probability assessment* is an indicator of the number of possible execution paths a SCPi may take meaning the amount of certainty (excess entropy) in the cloud's behavior. To assess that behavior prior to the KR, it is important to understand the complex interactions among the SCPis in a cloud. This can be achieved by modeling the behavior of individual reactive SCPis together with the cloud's behavior as *Discrete Time Markov Chains* [3], and assessing the level of probability through calculating the probabilities of the state transitions in the corresponding models. We assume that the SCPi-cloud interaction is a stochastic process where the cloud events are not controlled by the SCPi and thus the probabilities of occurring these events are considered equal. The theoretical foundation for our Probability Assessment Model is the property of Markov chains, which states that, given the current state of the cloud, its future evolution is independent of its history, which is also the main characteristic of a reactive autonomic SCPi. An algebraic representation of a Markov chain is a matrix (called transition matrix) (see Table 1) where the rows and columns correspond to the states, and the entry z_{ij} in the i-th row, j-th column is the transition probability of being in state s_j at the stage following state s_i. The following property holds for the calculated probabilities:

$$\sum_j z_{ij} = 1$$

We contend that probability should be calculated from the steady state of the Markov chain. A *steady state* (or equilibrium state) is one in which the probability of being in a state before and after a transition is the same as time progresses. Here, we define probability for a cloud SCPe (a SCE - Service Component Ensemble) composed of k SCPis as the level of certainty quantified by the source excess entropy, as follows:

$$Z_{SCPe} = \sum_{i=1,k} H_i - H$$
$$H_i = -\sum_j z_{ij} log_2(z_{ij})$$
$$H = -\sum_i v_i \sum_j z_{ij} log_2(z_{ij})$$

Here,

- H is an entropy that quantifies the level of uncertainty in the Markov chain corresponding to a SCPe;
- H_i is a level of uncertainty in the Markov chain corresponding to a SCPi;
- v is a steady state distribution vector for the corresponding Markov chain;
- z_{ij} values are the transition probabilities in the extended state machines that model the behavior of the i-th SCPi.

Note that for a transition matrix Z, the steady state distribution vector v satisfies the property $v * Z = v$, and the sum of its components v_i is equal to 1. The level of uncertainty H is exponentially related to the number of statistically typical paths in the Markov chain. Having an entropy value of 0 means that there is no level of uncertainty in a Markov system for a specific SCPi's behavior. Here, a higher value of a probability measure implies less uncertainty in the model, and thus, a higher level of predictability.

5 Related Work

Developing self-adaptive systems with Knowledge Representation and Reasoning (KR&R) has been an increasingly interesting topic for years. Examples are found in semantic mapping [4], improving planning and control aspects [12], and most notably in human-robotic interaction (HRI) systems [5,9]. Overall, KR&R strives to solve complex problems where the operational environment is non-deterministic and a system needs to reason at runtime to find missing answers. Decision-making is a complex process that is often based on more than logical conclusions. Probability and statistics may provide for the so-called probabilistic and statistical reasoning intended to capture uncertain knowledge in which additive probabilities are used to represent degrees of belief of rational agents in the truth of statements. For example, the purpose of a statistical inference might be to draw conclusions about a population based on data obtained from a sample of that population. Probability theory and Bayes' theorem [14] lay the basis for such reasoning where Bayesian networks [13] are used to represent belief probability distributions, which actually summarize a potentially infinite set of possible circumstances. The key point is that nodes in a Bayesian network have direct influence on other nodes; given values for some nodes, it is possible to infer the probability distribution for values of other nodes. How a node influences another node is defined by the conditional probability for the nodes, usually based on past experience. The experience can be associated with the success of the actions generated in the physical environment by the intelligent system. Maintaining an execution history of the actions shall help that system eventually compute the success probability for those actions. In that way, the system may learn (infer new knowledge) not to execute actions that traditionally have low success rate.

Today, knowledge representation for self-adaptive systems is a wide open research area with only a limited number of approaches yet considered. The work that is most similar in spirit to our own is that on developing cognitive robots relying on the so-called *deliberative controllers*. Architectures for autonomous control in robotic systems require concurrent embedded real-time performance, and are typically too complex to be developed and operated using conventional programming techniques. The core of an autonomous controller is an execution system that executes commands and monitors the environment [7]. Execution systems with deliberative controllers are based on knowledge that contains an explicitly represented symbolic model of the world. Deliberation is the explicit consideration of alternative behaviors (courses of actions).

In [27] an agent programming language called Goal is used to program a cognitive robot control architecture that combines low-level sub-symbolic control with high-level symbolic control. The Goal language helps to realize a cognitive layer where low-level execution control and processing of sensor data are delegated to components in other layers. Similar to KnowLang, Goal supports a goal-oriented behavior and decomposition of complex behavior by means of modules that can focus their attention on relevant sub-goals. However, KnowLang is far more expressive than Goal, especially at the level of modeling self-adaptive behavior, which is not supported by Goal. The integration of situations, goals, policies, and actions with a Bayesian network probability distribution allows for self-adaptation based on both logical and statistical reasoning.

In [16] the high-level language Golog is used for robot programming. Golog supports writing control programs in a high-level logical language, and provides an interpreter that, given a logical axiomatization of a domain, will determine a plan. Similar to KnowLang, Golog also supports actions and situations (actually the language incorporates Situation Calculus), but again, KnowLang is far more expressive with its Ontology-logical framework knowledge structuring. Moreover, Golog does not provide a means for self-adaptive KR, which is provided by KnowLang.

Lately, there have been significant research efforts in the implementation of awareness for computerized systems. For example, commercially-available server monitoring platforms, such as NimSoft's NimBUS and JJ Labs' Watch Tower, offer robust, lightweight sensing and reporting capabilities across large server farms. Note that these solutions are oriented towards massive data collection and performance reporting, and leave much of the final analysis and decision-making to the administrator. In other approaches, awareness is achieved through a model-based detection and response based on offline training and models (e.g., Markov models) constructed to represent different scenarios.

6   Conclusions

This chapter has presented the KnowLang approach to knowledge representation and reasoning for self-adaptive and aware systems. The approach was developed by the ASCENS project and used to build and operate knowledge models for the ASCENS case studies. KnowLang provides a special knowledge context and a special reasoner operating in that context, these helping to establish the vital connection between knowledge, perception, and actions realizing the self-adaptive behavior. The knowledge is used against the perception of the world to generate appropriate actions in compliance to some goals and beliefs.

A proof-of-concept example has been presented where we formalized a knowledge model for the ASCENS Science Clouds case study. With this example, we have demonstrated how KnowLang can be used to handle self-adaptive behavior at the level of knowledge representation.

Further, we have discussed the reasoning capabilities of the KnowLang Reasoner based on special KB Operators implemented by KnowLang. An approach to awareness capabilities of self-adaptive systems has been also discussed in this chapter. Basically, artificial awareness depends on the knowledge we transfer to software-intensive systems so they can use it to exhibit intelligence. In addition to knowledge, artificial awareness also requires a means of sensing changes so that the system can perceive both external and internal worlds through raw events and data. The KnowLang mechanism implementing the awareness capabilities of the knowledge-represented systems is structured in a way taking into consideration different stages and different degrees of awareness, thus helping SCs to self-initiate for performing actions part of self-adaptive behavior.

Future work is mainly concerned with full implementation of the KnowLang Reasoner including the presented POMDP model for self-initiation. Moreover, a further integration of KnowLang in the ARE (Autonomy Requirements Engineering) Framework is envisioned. This includes the development of special ARE Test Bed tool based on the KnowLang Reasoner. With such a test bed, we shall be able to evaluate capabilities that might manifest system awareness about situations and conditions.

References

1. ASCENS: ASCENS - Autonomic Service-Component Ensembles (2012), http://www.ascens-ist.eu/
2. Endsley, M.R.: Toward a theory of situation awareness in dynamic systems. Human Factors 37(1), 32–64 (1995)
3. Ewens, W.J., Grant, G.R.: Stochastic processes (i): poisson processes and Markov chains. In: Statistical methods in Bioinformatics, 2nd edn., Springer, New York (2005)
4. Galindo, C., Fernandez-Madrigal, J., Gonzalez, J., Saffiotti, A.: Robot task planning using semantic maps. Robotics and Autonomous Systems 56(11), 955–966 (2008)
5. Holzapfel, H., Neubig, D., Waibel, A.: A dialogue approach to learning object descriptions and semantic categories. Robotics and Autonomous Systems 56(11), 1004–1013 (2008)
6. Hölzl, M., Gabor, T.: Reasoning and Learning for Awareness and Adaptation. In: Wirsing, M., Hölzl, M., Koch, N., Mayer, P. (eds.) Software Engineering for Collective Autonomic Systems. LNCS, vol. 8998, pp. 247–288. Springer, Heidelberg (2015)
7. J. Ocón et al.: Autonomous controller - survey of the state of the art, ver. 1.3. Tech. Rep. GOAC, GMV-GOAC-TN01, Contract No. 22361/09/NL/RA, Oct. 31, ESTEC (2011)

8. Kephart, J.O., Chess, D.M.: The vision of autonomic computing. IEEE Computer 36(1), 41–50 (2003)
9. Kruijff, G.J.M., Lison, P., Benjamin, T., Jacobsson, H., Hawes, N.: Incremental, multi-level processing for comprehending situated dialogue in human-robot interaction. In: Proceedings of the Symposium on Language and Robots (2007)
10. Littman, M.L.: Algorithms for sequential decision making, phD Thesis, Department of Computer Science, Brown University (1996)
11. Mayer, P., Velasco, J., Klarl, A., Hennicker, R., Puviani, M., Tiezzi, F., Pugliese, R., Keznikl, J., Bureš, T.: The Autonomic Cloud. In: Wirsing, M., Hölzl, M., Koch, N., Mayer, P. (eds.) Software Engineering for Collective Autonomic Systems. LNCS, vol. 8998, pp. 493–510. Springer, Heidelberg (2015)
12. Mozos, O., Jensfelt, P., Zender, H., Kruijff, G.J.M., Burgard, W.: An integrated system for conceptual spatial representations of indoor environments for mobile robots. In: Proceedings of the IROS 2007 Workshop: From Sensors to Human Spatial Concepts (FS2HSC), pp. 25–32 (2007)
13. Neapolitan, R.: Learning Bayesian Networks. Prentice-Hall, Englewood Cliffs (2003)
14. Robinson, P., Bauer, S.: Introduction to Bio-Ontologies. CRC Press, Boca Raton (2011)
15. Serbedzija, N., Reiter, S., Ahrens, M., Velasco, J., Pinciroli, C., Hoch, N., Werther, B.: D7.1: First Report on WP7 Requirement Specification and Scenario Description of the ASCENS Case Studies, ASCENS Deliverable (2011)
16. Soutchanski, M.: High-level robot programming and program execution. In: Proceedings of the ICAPS'03 Workshop on Plan Execution, AAAI Press, Menlo Park (2003)
17. Vassev, E.: KnowLang Grammar in BNF. Tech. Rep. Lero-TR-2012-04, Lero, University of Limerick, Ireland (2012)
18. Vassev, E.: Operational semantics for KnowLang ASK and TELL operators. Tech. Rep. Lero-TR-2012-05, Lero, University of Limerick, Ireland (2012)
19. Vassev, E., Hinchey, M.: The challenge of developing autonomic systems. IEEE Computer 43(12), 93–96 (2010)
20. Vassev, E., Hinchey, M.: Towards a formal language for knowledge representation in autonomic service-component ensembles. In: Proceedings of the 3rd International Conference on Data Mining and Intelligent Information Technology Applications (ICMIA2011). AICIT, IEEE Xplore, pp. 228–235. IEEE Computer Society Press, Los Alamitos (2011)
21. Vassev, E., Hinchey, M.: Awareness in software-intensive systems. IEEE Computer 45(12) (2012)
22. Vassev, E., Hinchey, M.: Knowledge representation for cognitive robotic systems. In: Proceedings of the 15th IEEE International Symposium on Object/Component/Service-oriented Real-time Distributed Computing Workshops (ISCORCW 2012), pp. 156–163. IEEE Computer Society Press, Los Alamitos (2012)
23. Vassev, E., Hinchey, M.: Knowledge representation with KnowLang - the marXbot case study. In: Proceedings of the 11th IEEE International Conference on Cybernetic Intelligent Systems (CIS 2012), IEEE Computer Society Press, Los Alamitos (2012)
24. Vassev, E., Hinchey, M., Gaudin, B.: Knowledge representation for self-adaptive behavior. In: Proceedings of C* Conference on Computer Science & Software Engineering (C3S2E '12), pp. 113–117. ACM Press, New York (2012)

25. Vassev, E., Hinchey, M., Montanari, U., Bicocchi, N., Zambonelli, F., Wirsing, M.:
    D3.2: Second Report on WP3: The KnowLang Framework for Knowledge Modeling
    for SCE Systems, ASCENS Deliverable (2012)
26. Vassev, E., Hinchey, M.: Engineering Requirements for Autonomy Features. In:
    Wirsing, M., Hölzl, M., Koch, N., Mayer, P. (eds.) Software Engineering for Col-
    lective Autonomic Systems. LNCS, vol. 8998, pp. 377–401. Springer, Heidelberg
    (2015)
27. Wei, C., Hindriks, K.V.: An agent-based cognitive robot architecture. In: Program-
    ming Multi-Agent Systems (ProMAS) Workshop Affiliated with AAMAS 2012,
    Valencia, Spain, pp. 55–68 (2012)
28. Wirsing, M., Hölzl, M., Koch, N., Mayer, P. (eds.): Software Engineering for Col-
    lective Autonomic Systems. LNCS, vol. 8998. Springer, Heidelberg (2015)

CHAPTER II.4

Reasoning and Learning for Awareness and Adaptation*

Matthias Hölzl and Thomas Gabor

Ludwig-Maximilians-Universität München, Germany

Abstract. Reasoning and learning for awareness and adaptation are challenging endeavors since cogitation has to be tightly integrated with action execution and reaction to unforeseen contingencies. After discussing the notion of awareness and presenting a classification scheme for awareness mechanisms, we introduce Extended Behavior Trees (XBTs), a novel modeling method for hierarchical, concurrent behaviors that allows the interleaving of reasoning, learning and actions. The semantics of XBTs are defined by a transformation to SCEL so that sophisticated synchronization strategies are straightforward to realize and different kinds of distributed, hierarchical learning and reasoning—from centrally coordinated to fully autonomic—can easily be expressed. We propose novel hierarchical reinforcement learning strategies called Hierarchical (Lenient) Frequency-Adjusted Q-learning, that can be implemented using XBTs. Finally we discuss how XBTs can be used to define a multi-layer approach to learning, called teacher-student learning, that combines centralized and distributed learning in a seamless way.

Keywords: Autonomic Computing, Learning, Reasoning, Planning, Behavioral Adaptation, Self-awareness, Computational Reflection

1 Introduction

An autonomic ensemble performing challenging tasks in an open-ended, dynamic environment cannot rely solely on data and information provided by its developers while it was designed—there are too many contingencies, too many possible alterations of the environment, too many differences between the real environment and its development model for that to be feasible. Instead the ensemble has to have some way to gather data about the environment, account for its previous experience and modify its behavior accordingly. This can take many forms: for example, agents may leave traces in the environment that lead to stigmergic coordination of actions, agents may modify their behavior based on feedback from the environment, or a central controller may evaluate the performance of agents

* This research was supported by the European project IP 257414 (ASCENS).

M. Wirsing et al. (eds.): Collective Autonomic Systems, LNCS 8998, pp. 249–290, 2015.
© Springer International Publishing Switzerland 2015

and modify those that fail to reach certain performance criteria. While the details of these techniques vary considerably, each leads to some form of *learning*, and most of these techniques employ some form of *automated reasoning*. Learning and reasoning are based on the knowledge that a system has about itself and its environment—whether it was pre-specified by its developers or gathered dynamically during execution. We call this knowledge the ensemble's *awareness*; and the capability of an ensemble to choose actions based on its awareness *self-expression*. Since there is a plethora of possible methods for a system to obtain and update data and to process it into information and knowledge, it is not helpful to classify some of them as "aware" and some as "not aware," or even to say that an ensemble is "more aware" than another without further qualification. We will instead identify various dimensions along which the awareness of a system and its capabilities for self-expression can be classified.

Automated reasoning and machine learning are difficult problems when applied to single agents operating in a well-defined, static environment. Extending them to multi-agent settings poses several additional challenges. To mention two examples: (1) The computational complexity—which is already significant in the single-agent case—increases exponentially since joint actions and joint results of many agents have to be taken into account. (2) Evaluating the performance of actions becomes much more difficult, since actions of an agent A now depend not only on a stochastic but stationary environment; instead the results of actions are influenced by the actions of other agents, and these agents also learn new behaviors and may, in competitive scenarios, actively try to undermine the success of A. Therefore, many properties that hold in static, single-agent settings are no longer true in dynamic, multi-agent environments. Empirically, reinforcement-learning algorithms that provably converge to the optimal strategy in the single-agent case often result in non-optimal solutions when naively applied to multi-agent settings in which the expectations underlying the proof of optimality are no longer satisfied. It is therefore necessary to develop improved learning techniques that take into account the effects of other agents and a dynamic environment, and to reduce the computational effort expended for computing solutions, e.g., by reusing learned results in multiple contexts or by exploiting the hierarchical nature inherent in many problems. This is a very active area of research, and no completely satisfactory solution has been found so far. Recently, significant progress has been made in developing theoretical foundations, based on evolutionary game theory, for multi-agent learning, and in adapting reinforcement techniques to cooperative multi-agent scenarios.

Besides algorithmic difficulties, designers of learning and reasoning mechanisms face another problem: the components of the ensemble have to *act*, even if they are resource constrained and have only limited information about the environment. As has been pointed out, e.g., by Ghallab et al. [18], this imposes requirements on the system architecture that are often a poor fit to the assumptions made in the literature. For example, a planner in an adaptive ensemble will not be able to plan the execution of a task and then pass that plan to an executive that performs the completed plan; instead the planning and execution stages have to be interwoven, high-level plans have to take into account uncertainty about the possible actions at lower levels and consider new information as it becomes available. Often, the planner in such a scenario will itself be distributed among agents with only local information about the environment and the overall state of the ensemble. This means that the reasoning system cannot exist as a "black box" that provides complete solutions to the rest of the system; reasoning and learning has to be incremental, integrated with the distributed structure of the ensemble, and tightly interwoven with action execution; often different reasoning and execution mechanisms have to be active simultaneously. This chapter presents several techniques that can be helpful in achieving these goals.

In the next section we review various notions of awareness, self-awareness and self-expression discussed in the literature and present a classification scheme for awareness based on the one initially proposed by Hölzl and Wirsing in [21].

In Sect. 3 we give a short review of behavior trees, a behavioral modeling technique; then we introduce Extended Behavior Trees (XBTs) and give their semantics in SCEL. XBTs are a novel graphical language for modeling hierarchical, concurrent behaviors based on behavior trees; they allow modelers to interleave reasoning, learning and actions in a goal-directed manner, but they can also react flexibly to external events. We also show that XBTs can express hierarchical plans and generalize a variant of total-order HTN-planning.

We introduce (hierarchical) reinforcement learning, the main learning technique used in ASCENS, in Sect. 4. After a short overview of Markov-Decision Processes and the dynamic-programming approach to solving them we review the TD(0) algorithm as an example for flat single-agent reinforcement learning and indicate how function approximation and hierarchical structure can allow reinforcement-based approaches to scale to larger problems. We then give a brief overview of Markov games and evolutionary game theory, the foundations for multi-agent learning, before addressing the topic of multi-agent learning. At the end of the section we propose new reinforcement-learning strategies for hierarchical, cooperative multi-agent learning, Hierarchical (Lenient) Frequency-Adjusted Q-learning.

Sect. 5 shows how ideas from the previous two sections can be combined into teacher-student learning, a multi-layer approach that integrates centralized and decentralized learning and is therefore particularly applicable in the context of the Ensemble-Development Life Cycle (EDLC) proposed by the ASCENS project and presented in Chapter III.1 [20] of this volume. The final sections discuss related work and conclude.

This chapter focuses on learning and reasoning methods and their integration with the mechanisms the system has for achieving awareness and self-expression. Since the chapter covers a broad range of topics the later sections are mostly introductory and point to other publications for in-depth treatments of the topic. Several related aspects are discussed in more detail in other chapters of this book: The awareness of a system depends on its knowledge; KnowLang, a mechanism for representing and updating knowledge is introduced in Ch. II.3 [42].

Awareness, reasoning and learning are not objectives in themselves, rather they are techniques that enable a system to adapt to different environments and to perform well in unforeseen situations. Different conceptions of adaptation are discussed in Ch. II.1 [9].

2   Awareness and Self-expression

A theory of awareness should state what we consider to be part of a system's awareness, and explain how its own notion of awareness relates to the rich published literature on the subject. In this section we propose a simple model that defines behavioral self-expression as well as operational and non-operational notions of "degree of awareness" and that identifies various dimensions of awareness that can usefully be distinguished.

2.1   Classifying Awareness and Self-expression

We will at first focus on a structural, or white-box, definition of awareness; an observational notion can be based on this definition (see p. 257). We therefore assume for the time being that we can conceptually inspect and analyze the internal structure of the ensemble. We use GEM as the formal basis of our definition and therefore describe ensembles by their *state space*. All possible trajectories a system can take through its state space over time form its *trajectory space*. An introduction to the formal model underlying GEM is given in Ch. II.1 [9] of this volume, a more in-depth discussion can be found in [22].

We base our model of awareness on the notion of an *awareness mechanism,* a conceptual set of features for describing awareness. Awareness mechanisms may be compared along different dimensions, each of which represents a particular aspect of the general notion of awareness. A discussion of other approaches to awareness and self-awareness and their relationship to the work presented in this section can be found in [21].

Elements of the Awareness Mechanism. A system that can be called aware should be able to sense or store at least some information about its environment or itself. We call this information the *awareness model M* of system S. The awareness model does not have to be centralized in a single location or node of S; it can be distributed between the nodes of S and even the environment. Therefore, our concept of awareness models also encompasses, e.g., system architectures based on stigmergy, such as a swarm of robots that communicate by placing tokens in their environment.

Since ensembles operate in non-static environments the awareness model will often take into account the dynamics of their environment E (which may include, from the point of view of S, other agents active in E): changes in E should be reflected in the awareness model M and, if S is to make use of its awareness, *vice versa*. Adapting the definition of Smith [38] for procedurally reflective systems to ensembles, we call a subset $N \subseteq M$ and E *causally connected* if changes to

N eventually influence E. In many systems, this influence happens only after a delay, since activities taken by the system need time to affect the the environment. Similarly, we say that $N \subseteq M$ is *inversely (causally) connected* to E if certain changes in E lead to corresponding changes in N. However, the change might only take place after S reaches some state in which it can perceive the changes. We call the parts of S that are responsible for maintaining the inverse connection between E and M the *sensor system* of S. As with the awareness model, the sensor system does not necessarily have to be a single, dedicated component.

Most environments are only partially observable: S cannot directly perceive all relevant information. In this case, S may employ various *reasoning* techniques to obtain the information required for action. We use the term "reasoning" in a very broad sense: in the simplest case it might simply mean querying the data stored in an agent's awareness model. More sophisticated reasoning engines might perform complex computations or inferences, run simulations or develop plans as part of their reasoning process. A system may include several, distributed reasoning engines operating simultaneously.

In the following we identify the results of the reasoning process with their (model-theoretic) interpretation, and we assume that predicates relating to the system's state space are interpreted in the state space itself; see [22] for details. We call the set of all inferences the reasoning engines may draw from the awareness model the *inference closure* of the awareness model. We allow empty inferences, hence the inference closure includes the awareness model. If an inference depends on an inversely connected subset of the awareness model we call the result *transitively connected*. Given our choice of models, the inference closure intersects the state space as long as the awareness model contains any information about the state of the system, and the transitively connected inferences contain the intersection of the state space with the awareness model.

We call the combination of sensor system, awareness model and reasoning engines of a system its *awareness mechanism*. Its components need not be dedicated to the awareness mechanism, they can also be used by other parts of the system.

A White-Box Definition of Awareness. We classify awareness mechanisms along three different axes: *expressivity*, *quality* and *interface* with the rest of the system.

Expressivity. An awareness mechanism will only contain some dimensions of the state space, often with limited precision, and it will only store a limited amount of information about past events. Expressivity measures how much information about the state space an awareness mechanism retains. Basing our notion of awareness on GEM alleviates the problems involved in comparing the expressivity of different languages, since we can regard both the state space and the awareness mechanism as sets. Therefore, scope and depth can be defined as follows:

Scope: The *scope* of an awareness mechanism is the intersection of the awareness mechanism with the phase space of the system, i.e., the subspace of the
trajectory space contained in the awareness-mechanism.

Depth: The *depth* of an awareness mechanism is the transitive closure of its
scope.

Note that scope and depth are defined with relation to the state space; both
"M_1 has larger scope than M_2" and "M_1 is deeper than M_2" mean that M_1
contains more information than M_2, the difference is whether this information
is part of the system's state or whether it is meta-information about the system.
Intuitively, the scope of an awareness model M describes how big the slice of
the world represented by M is and the depth of M describes the richness of the
model's ontology. The transitive connection between depth and scope prevents
information that is completely unrelated to the system's behavior from counting
as deeper awareness.

Quality. Scope measures the part of the phase space that is contained in an
awareness model, depth measures the inferences an awareness mechanism may
draw from this information. However, neither tells us about whether the data
in the awareness model corresponds to the actual situation or whether the inferences drawn by the reasoning engines are correct. Therefore we are not only
interested in the expressivity of awareness mechanisms but also in their *quality*,
which we subdivide into accuracy, predictive power, precision and performance:

Historical accuracy: The *historical accuracy* of an awareness mechanism at a
point of time t is a measure of the distance between the trajectory of the
system stored in the awareness mechanism and the projection of the system's
trajectory in the state space into the awareness mechanism for times $t' \leq t$.

Predictive power: The *predictive power* of an awareness mechanism at a point
of time t is a measure of the distance between the trajectory of the system
predicted by the awareness mechanism and the projection of the system's
trajectory in the state space into the awareness mechanism for times $t' > t$.

Precision: The *precision* of an awareness mechanism is a measure for the variance of the awareness mechanism, i.e., how close the values for identical
states are to each other, independent of their distance to the "real" value.

Performance: We define the performance of an awareness mechanism as the
average time it takes to answer queries of a certain complexity.

Accuracy (as well as predictive power) and precision capture the usual definitions for measurement systems, and correspond to the terms "trueness" and
"precision" as specified by the ISO 5724-1 standard. An awareness mechanism
is accurate if the values stored in the awareness model or inferred by reasoners
are close to the corresponding values in the real world. It is precise if it always
represents the same real world state in the same manner. An awareness mechanism may be precise without being accurate, e.g., a robot that stores its latitude
and longitude as $(0°, 0°)$ irrespectively of its real location is very precise but
wildly inaccurate. For decisions about actions it is often important to predict

future developments; therefore we introduce the notion of predictive power that represents the accuracy of awareness mechanisms for estimating future events.

Interface. Another aspect that distinguishes different awareness mechanisms is the *interface* they expose to the ensemble. The interface can be divided into its *interaction* with the rest of the system, its *accessibility*, its *traceability* and its *configurability*.

Interaction: There are various ways how awareness mechanisms may interact with the rest of the system. Ensembles often consist of components that communicate via well-defined ports and protocols, in contrast to biological systems, e.g., within which responsibilities of and interactions between different parts of the system are often much more complex.

Accessibility: An interface may restrict access to some features of the awareness mechanism. We call the subset of the awareness mechanism's scope that is exposed to the rest of the system its *accessible scope*, and similarly for depth, quality, etc.

Traceability: It is often necessary that users of an awareness mechanism can comprehend or analyze the reasoning that led to certain conclusions. We call this property the *traceability* of the awareness mechanism.

Configurability: Some awareness mechanisms allow users to modify the structure of the awareness model, add or remove sensors from the sensor system, and add, replace or reconfigure reasoners. The extent to which these operations are possible is called the (run-time) *configurability* of the awareness mechanism.

The design of the interfaces of awareness mechanisms plays an important role in awareness engineering [21] since awareness mechanisms generally have to balance many competing demands: extensible awareness mechanisms often require more resources, demand complex interactions from the rest of the system, and often produce results that are difficult to comprehend. Accessible awareness mechanism may enable more features but pose privacy or security problems for the ensemble.

A White-box Definition of Awareness. We call the functionality of a system's awareness mechanism its *(internal) awareness* and the accessible functionality of the awareness mechanism its *(structurally) accessible* or *exposed awareness*. Since this notion is based on the internal workings of the system's awareness mechanism and not on an operational description of its behavior, this is a non-operational (or structural, white-box) definition of awareness.

By defining measures m_d or partial orders $\prec_d$ on the different dimensions of the awareness mechanism discussed in the previous sections, we can classify or compare the *degree of awareness* of different systems with regard to the measure $\prod_d m_d$ or the order $\prod_d \prec_d$. We call the degree of awareness of the awareness mechanism itself the *internal degree of awareness* of the system with regards to $\prod_d m_d$ or $\prod_d \prec_d$ and the degree of awareness of the functionality exposed by the interface of the awareness mechanism's interface the *(structurally) exposed degree of awareness* of a system.

Various (non-operational) notions of self-awareness found in the literature can be expressed using our definition by placing constraints on the expressivity of the awareness mechanism. See [21] for further details.

Self-expression. Given a structural definition of awareness or self-awareness, we know whether a system has enough information about itself, its environment and the behaviors required to achieve certain goals, but unless this information can actually influence the behavior of the system it serves no operational purpose. Therefore we are usually interested in systems whose knowledge representation is causally connected. Recall that a system and its model are causally connected if a change in the model can affect the system's behavior and thereby eventually the environment.

We call a system S *bicausally connected* to E (via its model M) if it is causally and inversely connected to E. The idea behind this notion is that a change in the model that a system has of its environment will have the potential to affect its behavior, and a change in the environment will eventually trigger an update of the system's internal model when the system reaches a state in which it can perceive the change.

Whereas inverse connection is required to maintain high-quality awareness in changing environments, causal connection (and hence bicausal connection) is not a necessary ingredient of awareness. For example, a passive monitoring system might possess a deep, high-quality awareness mechanism for the circumstances in a room, but no effectors to change the room. According to our classification this system would have an inverse connection to the room and a high degree of awareness about its environment, but it would not be causally connected to the room.

We propose to define the level of *self-expression* exhibited by a system in a decision-theoretic way that is similar to the one presented in [26] and weaker than the one by Zambonelli et al. [47]. To this end, we suppose that the desirability of various courses of action can be described by a *value function V*, which may or may not be explicitly known to the system; see Sect. 4.1 of this chapter. Using V we can express goals of the system and preferences over the system's behavior in a unified manner.

Recall that causal connection means that the awareness model influences the behavior of the system, but causal connection does not imply any expectation that these behavioral changes are positively correlated with either goals of the system itself or the externally provided value function. For self-expression we strengthen this notion slightly and demand that a change in the awareness model M of a system that is *self-expressive with respect to V* influences its behavior so that it improves the expected value of V given M. Note that the dependence on M is crucial for this definition; a system with an inaccurate awareness model M may exhibit perfect self expression (because it optimizes the expected value of V based on M) but bad overall performance (because M bears no relationship to the actual environment). Also, the degree of self-expression depends crucially on V; we call a system *self-expressive* if it is self-expressive with regards to its own value function.

Put another way, the degree of self-expression of a system with respect to V can be defined as the degree of rationality that the system's actions exhibit relative to the value function V and its awareness model, i.e., a system expresses itself perfectly, if it uses its awareness mechanism to maximize the expected total value of its actions over its lifetime.

A Black-Box Definition of Awareness. From the definitions of non-operational awareness and self-expression we can recapture a notion of *operational* (or *black-box*) *awareness*. To analyze the awareness of a system S without relying on knowledge about its internal structure, we require a fixed value function V. We can then compare the performance of S, as measured by V for the tasks we are interested in to systems S_i with known awareness mechanisms exhibiting perfect self-expression with respect to V. If S achieves a performance measure that is at least as good as S_i, we define its (operational) awareness to be at least the same as that of S_i.

For example, in certain environments it is not possible for a robot to efficiently navigate to a target location without knowing its own position. If a robot R is consistently able to navigate to a desired target location, we say it is *(operationally) aware* of its location, without knowing anything about its internal structure. If, on the other hand, a robot R' is unable to find the target location, it is not operationally aware of its location. This may mean that the awareness mechanism of R' does not contain the necessary data to make good decisions, or the failure of R' may be due to a lack of self-expression; this distinction cannot be established by the chosen experiment.

Having defined a model of awareness, subsequent sections will introduce learning and reasoning techniques that can be used to increase the expressivity and quality of awareness mechanisms. In the next section we introduce a modeling approach that facilitates the integration of awareness-based decision into the behavior of autonomic components.

3   Extended Behavior Trees

Behavior Trees are a flexible behavioral modeling approach that was developed for the AI-component of computer games and has recently been used in robotics and avionics. In this section we introduce *Extended behavior trees (XBTs)*, an extension of behavior trees that support many kinds of reasoning and learning beyond the reactive planning that behavior trees perform.

3.1   Behavior Trees

As mentioned in the introduction, exploiting the hierarchical nature and inherent structure of many tasks is essential to learning in and reasoning about non-trivial systems. Various formalisms for specifying hierarchical behaviors have been proposed and are being used, the most popular being state machines [13]. State-based models excel at specifying reactive behaviors; they can concisely describe different state configurations of a system, the transitions between configurations, and the behaviors exhibited by each configuration. But it has also been noted, e.g., by Zhang and Hölzl [48], that state machines exhibit significant modularity deficiencies and, e.g., by Millington and Funge [29] that they are poorly suited for expressing goal-based behaviors. Behavior trees are a modeling technique that was initially developed for computer games [23] and has recently gained popularity in other areas, such as robotics [28] and aircraft control [33].[1]

Whereas state machines represent the state of a system and behaviors are triggered by transitions between states, each node in a behavior tree represents a task, i.e., some kind of (instantaneous or ongoing) behavior that the system exhibits. We use the terms *task*, *behavior* and *node* interchangeably. Children of a task represent the subtasks that are executed (either sequentially or concurrently) to perform the parent task.

Since behavior trees have been integrated into various systems, often with pre-existing scheduling and distribution architectures, there is a wide variety of "behavior tree dialects." For example, behavior trees have been implemented with event-based scheduling of behaviors [16], or their semantics has been described in a highly concurrent manner as CSP processes by Colvin and Hayes [11]. In the following we give an overview of a commonly used model for behavior trees; the SCEL-based semantics presented in Figs. 5–9 formalize and extend this informal description.

In the following we assume that each behavior tree is integrated into an event loop that repeatedly triggers execution of the topmost node of the tree; this is called *ticking* the tree. We say a task in the tree is *ticked* if its execution is started. This is an architecture that is frequently used for reactive systems, e.g., in the ARGoS [35] swarm robotics runtime and simulator used for the ASCENS case study described in Chapter IV.2 [34]. Ticks sometimes have an associated integer counter so that nodes can determine whether they are triggered in successive steps. Since we want to integrate behavior trees with reinforcement learning techniques in later sections we assume for concreteness that a behavior tree operates on a Markov Decision Process (MDP, see Sect. 4.1), and that the primitive actions performed by the tasks in the behavior tree trigger transitions in this MDP.

In each iteration of the loop, each ticked node in the behavior tree performs a small amount of computation (potentially ticking one or more of its child nodes or executing actions in the process) and then returns control to its parent. The return value passed to the parent can either be succeeded if the behavior terminated successfully, running if the behavior did not terminate in this tick but can continue to run in future ticks, and failed when the behavior cannot be continued but also did not produce the desired result. The presence of the

---

[1] Note that there is also a graphical requirements modeling language called Behavior Trees; this language is different from the one discussed in this paper.

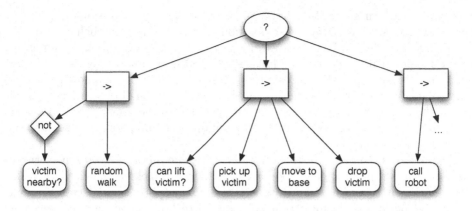

Fig. 1. Behavior tree for simple rescue robot

running return value allows the integration of long-lasting computations into an event-loop based control mechanism if the behavior can be structured in a co-routine like manner.

A behavior can either be *atomic* or *composite*; the simplest atomic behaviors correspond to triggering single actions in the MDP associated to the behavior tree. However, it is not necessary for atomic actions to consist of a single instruction or to be instantaneous. For example, an atomic behavior might perform actions a_1 and a_2 on the MDP and return running; when it is triggered again in the next tick it might perform action a_3 and return succeeded if the associated MDP is in state s_1 and failed otherwise. The important property of atomic behaviors is thus that they are leaves in the behavior trees.

A composite behavior has one or more children in the behavior tree; these children are ordered. The simplest behavior trees provide just two composite actions with multiple children: *sequence* and *choice*. A sequence node executes its children from left to right; when a child returns running the node returns running as well and resumes executions with this child if it is ticked again in the next step. When a child returns failed the sequence node returns failed as well and resumes execution with its leftmost child when it is triggered again. When a child returns succeeded, the sequence node continues with the evaluation of the next child; when the rightmost node returns succeeded the sequence node returns succeeded as well. Choice nodes exhibit the reverse behavior: they evaluate their children until one returns succeeded and then immediately return succeeded; if all children return failed they return failed as well. When we interpret succeeded as **t** and failed as **f**, sequence nodes correspond to an *and* operation and choice nodes to an *or*. With this interpretation a behavior tree can be seen as an *and/or* tree and evaluation of the tree as a non-strict depth-first walk.

A composite node with just a single child is called a *decorator*. The addition of a decorator that "negates" succeeded and failed and an action that does nothing and always return succeeded allows the embedding of propositional logic in a behavior tree, so that *if/then/else* decisions can be modeled by behavior trees.

Many different kinds of decorators have been proposed for behavior trees or implemented in behavior tree libraries [29]. One common usage scenario for decorators is the protection of resources via semaphores: A semaphore decorator tries to acquire a semaphore and executes its child if it can obtain the semaphore. When the child returns a value the decorator releases the semaphore and passes the value to its parent. When it cannot obtain the semaphore, the semaphore decorator fails immediately.

Fig. 1 shows the behavior tree for a simple rescue robot: the robot performs a random walk until it happens upon a victim. If it can pick up the victim it picks it up, moves it to the base and drops the victim off; otherwise it calls another robot and performs a joint rescue mission. Note how certain actions serve as guards: The robot only performs a random walk if there is no victim nearby. If victim nearby? evaluates to succeeded the negation decorator inverts it into failed and the sequence node fails.

One feature that makes behavior trees well-suited to modeling adaptive behaviors is their uniform handling of failures. For physical systems it is, in general, not possible to perform a reliable test whether an action will succeed since there may be failure conditions that cannot be easily tested before trying the action. Therefore a guard can avoid unnecessary execution of operations that are likely to fail, but when a task fails after evaluating a guard that predicted its success, the same fallback behavior is triggered as if the guard had correctly predicted the task's performance. For example, if the can lift victim? guard returns succeeded in Fig. 1, the pick up victim behavior can still fail, e.g., because the victim is heavier than expected. In this case the sequence node will fail and the topmost choice node will continue with the joint rescue behavior.

Behavior trees, as described in this section, provide no way for nodes to communicate data values. In practice this is often too restrictive, therefore behavior trees often provide a knowledge repository (typically called *blackboard*) that can be read and written by tasks, so that communication of values between tasks becomes possible.

3.2   Extended Behavior Trees

While behavior trees are a convenient way to model behavior, in the simple form presented in the previous section they are not sufficient to seamlessly integrate learning and reasoning. *Extended Behavior Trees (XBTs)* are an extension of the behavior-tree language that allows them to represent different hierarchical multi-agent learning and reasoning mechanisms.

To achieve this, XBTs modify the conceptual model of behavior trees in the following way

- During evaluation, a state object is passed from parent nodes to their children. Actions and access to global state are mediated by the state object.
- Each XBT has a name, and it is possible to call other XBTs as subroutines.

- The **succeeded** result returns two values: a performance indicator *quality* taken from an ordered monoid specifies the quality of the evaluated tree, and a Boolean flag *cont?* indicates whether the tree can continue executing to try and improve the result achieved so far.

The actions performed by tasks of a behavior tree are, conceptually, directly executed, i.e., they either modify the state of the associated MDP that represents the world if the behavior tree is used as part of a simulation, or they invoke the actuators of a system that modify the real world. In either case, an action that has been performed by the behavior tree is visible to the rest of the system, even if the subtree containing this action later fails. Since choice nodes can be used to try different behaviors when some behaviors fail, the execution strategy of behavior trees is sometimes called *reactive planning* [29]: While, in contrast to planning techniques, behavior trees exhibit no foresight when selecting their tasks, the reaction to failed tasks closely resembles the manner in which some forward planning algorithms build plans. For example, the widely-used Hierarchical-Task-Network (HTN) planner SHOP2 [6] performs this kind of forward planning. In XBTs, in contrast to traditional behavior trees, all actions and state accesses are performed via a state object, and the state object can be *virtualized*, i.e., a snapshot of the state object can be created so that updates to the virtual state do not influence the original state. This extension allows the straightforward definition of a new type of composite XBT-task that performs HTN-planning: This node first executes its child nodes on a virtualized state and prunes tasks resulting in failure as well as choices that do not achieve the desired goal from (a copy of) its children. The result is a new XBT that contains only those paths that correspond to valid plans; this XBT is executed with the original (non-virtual) state. In contrast to the plans produced by most planners, the resulting XBT still retains the flexibility to try different alternatives should one of the generated plans fail during execution.[2]

To illustrate the use of the additional features of XBTs, Figs. 2–4 show XBTs for the rescue scenario that modularize the structure of the behavior tree shown in Fig. 1 and refine the rescue strategy in various ways. The top-level XBT in Fig. 2 is a sequence of calls to other behavior trees so that the structure of the rescue task becomes more explicit and the behaviors expressed by the subtrees can more easily be reused.

The top-level node in the **locate victim** tree in Fig. 3 is a reinforcement learning node. These nodes are similar to choice nodes, but the order of their child nodes is not fixed, but chosen by a learning system to maximize the performance of the agent. The reinforcement learning techniques used by these nodes are described in Sect. 4; note that the integration of reinforcement learning techniques

---

[2] The input language of SHOP2 can describe more general plans than the XBTs presented in this section since it allows more general constraints between nodes in the task network than XBTs allow between behaviors. The planning problems directly expressible in XBTs correspond to totally-ordered Simple Task Networks (STNs) in the nomenclature of Ghallab et al. [17], but we believe it would be straightforward to extend XBTs to the expressivity of full HTN planning.

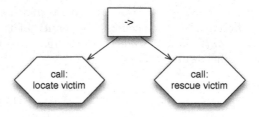

Fig. 2. Top-level XBT

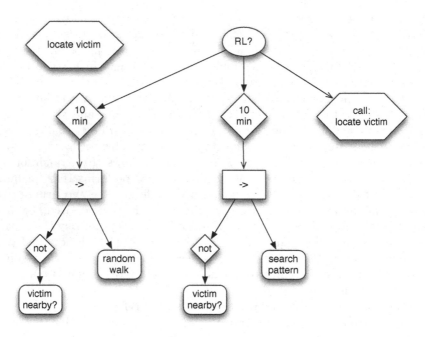

Fig. 3. XBT for locating victims

into XBTs relies on the performance indicator returned by child nodes to their parent. In this example the rescue robot has two strategies to locate victims: it can perform a random walk or it can follow a fixed search pattern. The locate victim XBT tries each strategy for 10 minutes and then switches to the other one if no victim has been found yet. After both strategies have been tried the XBT calls itself recursively to continue the search. Initially the robot performs the random walk before switching to the predefined search pattern. However, if the search pattern results in higher average performance, the reinforcement learning node will swap the order of its child branches and turn to a random walk strategy only when the search pattern fails. As this example shows, XBTs can use recursive function calls to express behavioral strategies of indefinite length.

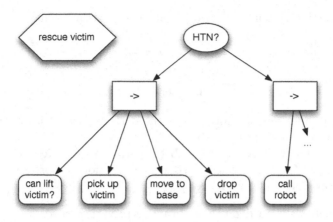

Fig. 4. XBT for rescuing victims

The XBT for rescuing victims is shown in Fig. 4; it mimics the rescue behavior shown in Fig. 1. However, the topmost node in this scenario is a planning node that first executes its subtrees on a virtual state and discards branches of the tree that are not successful. Therefore, while a robot using the original behavior tree always tries to lift the victim and only resorts to a collective rescue operation if this action fails, a robot using the rescue victim XBT will first execute the rescue mission on a virtual state. If the simulation fails to achieve the desired result, the left subtree will be pruned and the robot will start the rescue mission by calling another robot.

3.3 SCEL Semantics

In the following we specify the semantics of XBTs in SCEL.[3] We use a slight syntax extension for SCEL that can be expressed by the following pre-processing rules for:

– placing common follow-up processes outside of brackets of a sum,

$$[a_{1,1}.a_{1,2}.\ldots.a_{1,m_1} + \cdots + a_{n,1}.a_{n,2}.\ldots.a_{n,m_n}].P \rightarrow$$
$$a_{1,1}.a_{1,2}.\ldots.a_{1,m_1}.P + \cdots + a_{n,1}.a_{n,2}.\ldots.a_{n,m_n}.P$$

– combining otherwise identical processes starting with actions with different parameters

$$(\mathbf{qry}(x_1,\ldots,x_{m-1},a \sqcup b,x_{m+1},\ldots,x_n)@t).P \rightarrow$$
$$(\mathbf{qry}(x_1,\ldots,x_{m-1},a,x_{m+1},\ldots,x_n)@t).P$$
$$+ (\mathbf{qry}(x_1,\ldots,x_{m-1},b,x_{m+1},\ldots,x_n)@t).P$$

---

[3] A detailed discussion of SCEL can be found in chapter I.1 [32] of this volume. Note that just like the definition of SCEL, the realization of XBTs in SCEL presented here is parametrized for $\mathcal{K}$ and Π.

– and supporting a short notation for updating existing values.

$$(\textbf{put}(x_1, \ldots, x_{m-1}, !x_m, x_{m+1}, \ldots, x_n)@t).P \rightarrow$$
$$(\textbf{get}(x_1, \ldots, x_{m-1}, ?\_, x_{m+1}, \ldots, x_n)@t).$$
$$(\textbf{put}(x_1, \ldots, x_{m-1}, x_m, x_{m+1}, \ldots, x_n)@t).P$$

To simplify the notation, we don't write the performance indicator and the improvement flag for succeeded results.

We assume that we have an XBT B consisting of N nodes $n_1, \ldots, n_N$ with root n_1. We write T_i for the node type of n_i and also for the corresponding SCEL process; the possible node types are

– *DoNothingNode* for a node that always returns succeeded.
– *CallNode$_F$* for node representing a call to an (externally defined) process that communicates via the knowledge repository at target F. A call node passes the state as argument to the external process, therefore it can be used to invoke other behavior trees.
– *ChoiceNode* for a choice node.
– *SequenceNode* for a sequence node.
– *ExternalChoiceNode$_F$* for a generalized form of choice node where an external function communicating via the knowledge repository at target F can modify the children of the node before it is ticked.
– *VirtualizationNode* for a node that virtualizes the current state.
– *DecoratorNode$_F$* for an (externally defined) decorator node communicating via the knowledge repository at target F.

We translate the structure of the XBT into SCEL components that make the following components' knowledge repositories available:

– A component *children* models the parent-child relationships of the XBT by providing a knowledge repository acting as a tuple space containing the following tuples:
  • For each decorator n_P decorating a tree node n_C, the knowledge repository of *children* contains the tuple $(n_P, \mathsf{only}, n_C)$.
  • For each non-leaf node n_P of the XBT, which has the children $n_{i_1}, \ldots, n_{i_M}$, the knowledge repository of *children* contains the tuples $(n_P, \mathsf{first}, n_{i_1})$, $(n_P, \mathsf{last}, n_{i_M})$ to mark the first and last child, and $(n_P, \mathsf{next}, n_{i_1}, n_{i_2})$, $(n_P, \mathsf{next}, n_{i_2}, n_{i_3})$, $\ldots$, $(n_P, \mathsf{next}, n_{i_{M-1}}, n_{i_M})$ to encode the order of the child nodes.
  • For each node n_i of the XBT, it contains the tuple (n_i, all, c) where c is some vector representation of all child nodes of n_i which is understood by the tuple space of *states*.
– A component *states* providing a tuple space to all other XBT components, which initially contains the tuples $(n_1, \mathsf{inactive}), \ldots, (n_N, \mathsf{inactive})$. Note that *states* is able to recognize and accept parameters of some vector format as a first parameter to **put** and processes each of the vector's elements separately.

$$\begin{aligned}
BehaviorTree \quad &= \mathbf{new}(\mathcal{I}_1, \mathcal{K}, \Pi, T_1(n_1)) \\
&\mid \dots \\
&\mid \mathbf{new}(\mathcal{I}_N, \mathcal{K}, \Pi, T_N(n_N)) \\
&\mid children \\
&\mid states \\
&\mid virtualizer \\
&\mid ticks
\end{aligned}$$

$$\begin{aligned}
DoNothingNode(n_P) = \ &\mathbf{get}(n_P, ?state)@ticks. \\
&\mathbf{put}(n_P, !\mathsf{succeeded})@states. \\
&DoNothingNode(n_P)
\end{aligned}$$

$$\begin{aligned}
CallNode_F(n_P) \quad = \ &\mathbf{get}(n_P, ?state)@ticks. \\
&\mathbf{put}(\mathsf{invoke}, n_P, state)@F. \\
&[\ \mathbf{get}(\mathsf{running})@F.\mathbf{put}(n_P, !\mathsf{running})@states \\
&+ \mathbf{get}(\mathsf{succeeded})@F.\mathbf{put}(n_P, !\mathsf{succeeded})@states \\
&+ \mathbf{get}(\mathsf{failed})@F.\mathbf{put}(n_P, !\mathsf{failed})@states\ ]. \\
&CallNode_F(n_P)
\end{aligned}$$

Fig. 5. SCEL semantics for XBTs (top-level and atomic processes)

- A component *virtualizer*, which returns a virtual world state on request via **get**. This requires a SCEL instantiation that provides reflection over tuple spaces.
- A component containing a tuple space *ticks* and a user-defined process which invokes the execution of B by executing the operation $\mathbf{put}(n_1, state)@ticks$ for world state *state*. This process can then retrieve the status of the execution by **qry**-ing the tuple space of *states* for the root node n_1.

Given these preparations, Figs. 5 – 9 give the process structure of the XBT. We write $T[P_2/P_1]$ for the process definition of T where each occurrence of the syntactic *token* P_1 is replaced by the token P_2 to avoid unnecessary duplication of similar node definitions.

When execution of an XBT B is started, a new SCEL component is instantiated for each node of B; this node initially runs a single process controlling the execution of the node. The structure of the process for the different nodes is similar: Atomic nodes (like the *DoNothingNode* or *CallNode* in Fig. 5) perform a **get** operation with their name as parameter on the *ticks* knowledge repository to block until they are ticked; this **get** also retrieves the current state. They then perform their slice of work and put their current state in the knowledge repository of the *states* component. An atomic node that performs a long-lasting task repeatedly performs this **get** operation followed by a work slice, followed by a **put** on the *states* knowledge repository.

Similarly, compound nodes (cf. Figs. 8 and 9, which use the same program structure) start by waiting for a tick. However, if they have previously reached the end of one execution run (i.e., they have returned succeeded or failed), they

$$
\begin{aligned}
ChoiceNode(n_P) \quad = [\ &\mathbf{qry}(n_P, \mathsf{running} \sqcup \mathsf{inactive})@states \\
+ \ &\mathbf{qry}(n_P, \mathsf{succeeded} \sqcup \mathsf{failed})@states. \\
&\mathbf{qry}(n_P, \mathsf{all}, ?c)@children. \\
&\mathbf{put}(c, !\mathsf{inactive})@states \ ]. \\
&\mathbf{get}(n_P, ?state)@ticks \\
&\mathbf{qry}(n_P, \mathsf{first}, ?n_c)@children. \\
&Choice(n_P, n_C, state) \\
Choice(n_P, n_C, state) = [\ &\mathbf{qry}(n_C, \mathsf{running} \sqcup \mathsf{inactive})@states. \\
&\mathbf{put}(n_C, !\mathsf{inactive})@states. \\
&\mathbf{put}(n_C, state)@ticks \\
+ \ &\mathbf{qry}(n_C, \mathsf{succeeded} \sqcup \mathsf{failed})@states \ ]. \\
(\ &\mathbf{qry}(n_C, \mathsf{running})@states. \\
&\mathbf{put}(n_P, !\mathsf{running})@states. \\
&Choice(n_P) \\
+ \ &\mathbf{qry}(n_C, \mathsf{succeeded})@states. \\
&\mathbf{put}(n_P, !\mathsf{succeeded})@states. \\
&ChoiceNode(n_P) \\
+ \ &\mathbf{qry}(n_C, \mathsf{failed})@states. \\
(\ &\mathbf{qry}(n_P, \mathsf{next}, n_C, ?n_N)@children. \\
&Choice(n_P, n_N, state) \\
+ \ &\mathbf{qry}(n_P, \mathsf{last}, n_C)@children. \\
&\mathbf{put}(n_P, !\mathsf{failed})@states. \\
&ChoiceNode(n_P) \ ) \ )
\end{aligned}
$$

Fig. 6. SCEL semantics for XBTs (choice)

first "clean up" their children by setting their respective states to inactive. Then, they iterate over all children from left to right, transitioning into a new process with the current child as one if its parameters. These sub-processes (like *Choice* or *Sequence*) tick the current child if it was previously running or inactive, i.e., if it has still slices of work to run or it has never been run at all. Then, they wait for the child to enter one of the states {running, succeeded, failed}.[4] In the example of *Choice*, the states running and succeeded are passed on to the parent, since they indicate that the execution of the current slice of work or the whole parent node, respectively, has finished. Previously failed children are skipped over, unless all children have failed, which again indicates that the whole parent node is failed. For *Sequence* nodes, the child states succeeded and failed are treated reversely.

Decorators (cf. Fig. 8) invoke an external process with their only child node as argument and return the same value as the external process. Virtualization

---

[4] For a *ChoiceNode* n_P with children $< n_{i_1}, \ldots, n_{i_M} >$, these children are in the states:

- $<$ failed, $\ldots$, failed, running, inactive, $\ldots$, inactive $>$ if n_P is running,
- $<$ failed, $\ldots$, failed, succeeded, inactive, $\ldots$, inactive $>$ if n_P is succeeded,
- $<$ failed, $\ldots$, failed $>$ if n_P is failed.

For a *SequenceNode*, succeeded and failed are reversed. Note that a succeeded or failed parent resets its children's states to inactive quickly, as previously discussed.

$$SequenceNode(n_P) \quad = ChoiceNode[Sequence/Choice](n_P)$$
$$Sequence(n_P, n_C, state) = Choice[Sequence/Choice, SequenceNode/ChoiceNode,$$
$$\text{succeeded/failed, failed/succeeded}](n_P, n_C, state)$$

Fig. 7. SCEL semantics for XBTs (sequence)

$$DecoratorNode_F(n_P) \quad = \mathbf{get}(n_P, ?state)@ticks.$$
$$\mathbf{qry}(n_P, \text{only}, ?n_C)@children.$$
$$\mathbf{put}(\text{invoke}, n_P, n_C, state)@F.$$
$$[\ \mathbf{get}(\text{running})@F.\mathbf{put}(n_P, \text{!running})@states$$
$$+ \mathbf{get}(\text{succeeded})@F.\mathbf{put}(n_P, \text{!succeeded})@states$$
$$+ \mathbf{get}(\text{failed})@F.\mathbf{put}(n_P, \text{!failed})@states\ ].$$
$$DecoratorNode_F(n_P)$$

$$VirtualizationNode(n_P) = \mathbf{fresh}(F).(\ DecoratorNode_F(n_P)\ |\ Virtualization_F()\ )$$
$$Virtualization_F() \quad\quad = \mathbf{get}(\text{invoke}, ?n_P, ?n_C, ?state)@F.$$
$$\mathbf{get}(state, ?virtualState)@virtualizer.$$
$$\mathbf{put}(n_C, \text{!inactive})@states.$$
$$\mathbf{put}(n_C, virtualState)@ticks.$$
$$[\ \mathbf{qry}(n_C, \text{running})@states.\mathbf{put}(\text{running})@F$$
$$+ \mathbf{qry}(n_C, \text{succeeded})@states.\mathbf{put}(\text{succeeded})@F$$
$$+ \mathbf{qry}(n_C, \text{failed})@states.\mathbf{put}(\text{failed})@F\ ].$$
$$Virtualization_F()$$

Fig. 8. SCEL semantics for XBTs (decorators and virtualization)

nodes have the same structure as decorators, but also create a new process that receives the decorator's child n_C as a message through a fresh shared channel F.[5] It then continues to virtualize the received *state* and tick n_C with the virtualized state, thereby executing the respective subtree of B under n_C using the virtual state. On its own this is not particularly useful, but together with external choice nodes this allows the implementation of different kinds of planning strategies as described at the beginning of this section.

An *ExternalChoiceNode* (cf. Fig. 9) is a choice node that allows another process to transform its children before it behaves as a choice node. Together with virtualization nodes, external choice nodes can be used to integrate planning techniques into XBT evaluation; without virtualization of the state, external choice nodes can be used to perform reinforcement learning by reordering the choices according to their expected value. We will examine this in greater detail in the next section.

---

[5] This message marked by its first component invoke is part of the interface every *DecoratorNode* provides and contains the decorating node n_P and the current *state* as well.

$$\begin{aligned}
ExternalChoiceNode_F(n_P) \quad &= [\ \mathbf{qry}(n_P, \text{running} \sqcup \text{inactive})@states \\
&\quad + \mathbf{qry}(n_P, \text{succeeded} \sqcup \text{failed})@states \\
&\qquad \mathbf{qry}(n_P, \text{all}, ?c)@children. \\
&\qquad \mathbf{put}(c, !\text{inactive})@states \\
&\qquad \mathbf{put}(\text{reorder\_please}, n_P)@F. \\
&\qquad \mathbf{get}(\text{reordering\_complete}, n_P)@F\ ]. \\
&\quad \mathbf{get}(n_P, ?state)@ticks. \\
&\quad \mathbf{qry}(n_P, \text{first}, ?n_C)@children. \\
&\quad ExternalChoice(n_P, n_C, state) \\
ExternalChoice_F(n_P, n_C, state) &= Choice[ExternalChoice_F/Choice, \\
&\qquad ExternalChoiceNode_F/ChoiceNode](n_P, n_C, state)
\end{aligned}$$

Fig. 9. SCEL semantics for XBTs (external choice)

Note that the basic XBT model given in this section can be extended in a multitude of ways. Since the semantics are based on SCEL one obvious extension is the introduction of composite nodes that execute their child nodes concurrently and fail or succeed based on a predicate over the children, e.g., it is straightforward to define a node that runs its children concurrently and succeeds if at least two of its children succeed. Another important addition is the possibility to interrupt a running configuration. Currently, once a path is activated it runs until it either succeeds or fails. Interrupts can be introduced by defining decorators that evaluate the condition that should trigger the interrupt and reset the tree below them to its initial state when the condition becomes true. A similar construction can be used to define state-based behaviors that abort even long-running tasks of the XBT when an external state machine switches into a different state.

4   Reinforcement Learning

Many learning problems for adaptive agents can be expressed as controlling a Markov decision process (MDP, see [39]), and the corresponding problem for ensembles is control of a Markov Game [40]. We briefly introduce these models and solution algorithms based on dynamic programming. Reinforcement learning can then be understood as an approximate version of the dynamic-programming algorithms. Two characteristics of reinforcement learning are problematic for many applications to realistic problems: (1) By expressing the problem as a "flat" MDP, all information about the solution structure of the problem is lost, and no learning from shared sub-problems is possible. (2) For all but the smallest state spaces it is impractical to maintain a table of all state/action or state/value mappings. These problems can be addressed by hierarchical reinforcement learning, which only considers solutions that follow a certain structure, and by state approximation techniques, which approximate the state by a smaller number of parameters. Following the introduction of single-agent reinforcement learning we discuss issues arising in a multi-agent setting and extensions of reinforcement learning for multiple independent agents.

4.1   Single-Agent Learning

Markov Decision Processes. The behavior of an agent and its environment can often be modeled in the following way: At each point in time, agent and environment are in some (combined) state s from a nonempty, finite state set S. Whenever the agent performs an action a from a finite, nonempty set A of actions, the system probabilistically transitions into state s'; we write $P^a_{ss'}$ for the probability of reaching s' after performing action a in state s. Obviously $P^a_{ss'} \in [0,1]$ and

$$\forall s \in S : \forall a \in A : \sum_{s' \in S} P^a_{ss'} - 1$$

Whenever it performs an action, the agent receives reward $R^a_{ss'} \in \mathbb{R}^6$. The distribution of the initial state is $I : S \to [0,1]$; typically this is either a uniform distribution over all states or a deterministic distribution, i.e., a distribution that assigns all weight to a single state s_0. We are interested in the total reward that the agent obtains when it performs a sequence of actions. It is possible to consider finite and infinite sequences of actions; in this chapter we concern ourselves only with infinite action sequences.[7] We write a sequence of transitions, where the agent starts in state s_0, performs action a_0 and transitions to state s_1 with reward r_0, and so on, as

$$s_0, a_0, r_0, s_1, a_1, r_1, s_2, \ldots$$

and call this sequence a trajectory. A finite sequence of the form $s_0, a_0, r_0, \ldots$, s_n, a_n, r_n, s_{n+1} is called a *history*; H is the set of all histories. To ensure that the sum of rewards is finite, we define the *value* V of a sequence of rewards

$$V((r_i)_{i \in \mathbb{N}}) = \sum_{i \in \mathbb{N}} \gamma^i r_i$$

where $\gamma \in [0,1)$ is called a *discount factor*[8]. If each sequence of actions eventually leads to an absorbing state we also allow $\gamma = 1$.

The six-tuple (S, A, P, R, I, γ) is called a *Markov decision process*. A mapping $\pi : H \to A \to [0,1]$ from histories to probability distributions over A is called a *strategy* or *policy*, Π is the set of all policies. If $\pi(h)$ is a deterministic distribution

---

[6] MDPs may be defined in a more general manner: S and A can be infinite, e.g., Borel subsets of Polish spaces, the possible actions may depend on the state, and the reward may be a random variable. This has no significant impact on the following discussion.

[7] A finite sequence of actions can always be extended to an infinite one by adding a transition into an additional (absorbing) state $s^\#$ with $P^a_{s^\# s^\#} = 1$ and $R^a_{s^\# s^\#} = 0$ for every action a.

[8] For infinite state or action spaces we also have to ensure that $(r_i)_{i \in \mathbb{N}}$ is bounded

for every history h we call π *deterministic*, i.e., a deterministic strategy prescribes a single action for every situation the agent may encounter; we then regard it as function $\pi : H \to A$. If π depends only on the last state s_n of each history, i.e., it can be written in the form $\pi : S \to A \to [0, 1]$, it is a *stationary policy*. Deterministic, stationary policies can be regarded as functions $\pi : S \to A$.

Value Functions. Since transitions are probabilistic we cannot determine the exact value an agent will obtain when starting in state s_0 and following a policy π. Instead we define the value of s_0 when following π, written $V^\pi(s_0)$, as the expected value of the discounted rewards obtained when starting from s_0 and following π:

$$V^\pi(s) = \mathbb{E}\Big(\sum_{n=0}^{\infty} \gamma^n r_n \; \Big| \; s_0 = s, \pi\Big) \tag{1}$$

V is called the *state-value* or simply *value function*, or the V-function, for strategy π. Under the assumptions we have made the value of every state is finite, therefore (r_i) is bounded, and V maps each state to a real number, $V : S \to \mathbb{R}$. There is always at least one optimal strategy which is written π^*. It is easy to see that π^* has the value function

$$V^*(s) = V^{\pi^*}(s) = \max_{\pi \in \Pi} V^\pi(s)$$

and that, if several optimal strategies exist, their value functions are identical. Since $V^*(s)$ is independent of the history with which s was reached, we can restrict ourselves to stationary policies in the rest of this section.

When trying to find a good behavior it is often useful to compute the value of a state s if the agent performs action a and *then* follows strategy π. This function is called the *action-value* or *Q-function* for π, $Q^\pi : S \times A \to \mathbb{R}$. As for the state-value function there is always at least one optimal action-value function Q^*, and its value can be computed from the expected reward for the transition on a and the state-value of the successor state:

$$Q^\pi(s, a) = \mathbb{E}\Big(\sum_{n=0}^{\infty} \gamma^n r_n \; \Big| \; s_0 = s, a_0 = a, \pi\Big) \tag{2}$$

$$Q^*(s, a) = \max_{\pi \in \Pi} Q^\pi(s, a) \tag{3}$$

$$= \mathbb{E}\Big(r_0 + \gamma V^*(s_1) \; \Big| \; s_0 = s, a_0 = a\Big) \tag{4}$$

Bellman Equations. By computing the expected values in equations (1) and (2) we easily obtain two recursive equations for V^π and Q^π, the so-called *Bellman* *equations*:

$$V^\pi(s) = \sum_{a \in A} \pi(s, a) \sum_{s' \in S} P_{ss'}^a \left(R_{ss'}^a + \gamma V^\pi(s') \right) \tag{5}$$

$$Q^\pi(s, a) = \sum_{s' \in S} P_{ss'}^a \left(R_{ss'}^a + \gamma \sum_{a' \in A} \pi(s', a') Q^\pi(s', a') \right) \tag{6}$$

The Bellman equation for V^π computes the value for a state s from the values of its successor states. It is easy to see intuitively how this works: When going from s to s' the agent obtains immediate reward $R_{ss'}^a$ and enters a state with value $V^\pi(s')$, however this value has to be discounted with γ since it is obtained one step in the future. The probability of ending up in state s' after having chosen action a in state s is given by $P_{ss'}^a$, therefore the inner sum in Eq. (1) is the expected value of s if the agent chooses action a. The sum of all these values, weighted by the probability of choosing each action a is exactly the expected value of s.

For the optimal state- and action-value functions, the Bellman equations are:

$$V^*(s) = \max_{a \subset A} \sum_{s' \in S} P_{ss'}^a \left(R_{ss'}^a + \gamma V^*(s') \right) \tag{7}$$

$$Q^*(s, a) = \sum_{s' \in S} P_{ss'}^a \left(R_{ss'}^a + \gamma \max_{a' \in A} Q^*(s', a') \right) \tag{8}$$

They are obtained from equations (5) and (6) by maximizing over a or a', i.e., by picking the best possible action, either immediately (in Eq. (7)) or after performing one transition, and then following the optimal strategy.

The Bellman equations provide a way to compute optimal strategies using dynamic programming. We sketch one possible method for achieving this, called *policy iteration* [39] in Fig. 10. The intuition behind this algorithm is that policy evaluation will improve the value function V to match the current policy π, policy improvement will then set π to the greedy policy for V. Since there are only finitely many policies, it is easy to see that this process converges to the optimal policy. The idea of using an existing approximation to generate a better approximation is called *bootstrapping*. See Sutton and Barto [39] for a more detailed discussion of this algorithm. Ch. II.2 [19] in this volume contains other applications of dynamic programming techniques.

Reinforcement Learning. The algorithm presented in the previous section has two serious drawbacks for applications in autonomic systems:

1. Each iteration sweeps the whole state space of the problem and the algorithm computes the whole policy, even for parts of the state space that the system may never reach. An algorithm for online use should focus the evaluation on the parts of the state space that are actually relevant for the agent.

1. Choose V and π arbitrarily
2. Repeat the following algorithm until Δ becomes smaller than a (small) positive number θ:

   $\Delta \leftarrow 0$
   for all $s \in S$ **do**
   $\quad v \leftarrow V(s)$
   $\quad V(s) \leftarrow \sum_{s' \in S} P_{ss'}^{\pi(s)} \left(R_{ss'}^{\pi(s)} + \gamma V(s') \right)$
   $\quad \Delta \leftarrow \max(\Delta, |v - V(s)|)$
   end for

   This step is called *policy evaluation*
3. Run the following algorithm:

   policy-stable $\leftarrow$ **t**
   for all $s \in S$ **do**
   $\quad b \leftarrow \pi(s)$
   $\quad \pi(s) \leftarrow \arg\max_a \sum_{s' \in S} P_{ss'}^a \left(R_{ss'}^a + \gamma V(s') \right)$
   $\quad$ **if** $b \neq \pi(s)$ **then**
   $\quad\quad$ *policy-stable* $\leftarrow$ **f**
   $\quad$ **end if**
   end for

   If *policy-stable* is **t** then V approximates V^*, otherwise continue with the policy evaluation of step 2. Step 3 is called *policy improvement*.

Fig. 10. Policy iteration

2. The algorithm relies on a model of the MDP, i.e., it needs the reward function and the transition probabilities as input. In most scenarios an agent will have no way of obtaining this model; even in cases where generating an exact model would theoretically be feasible, it is often too complicated or expensive to do so.

TD-learning uses the bootstrapping principle presented in the dynamic-programming algorithm. However, the improvement is not based on values computed from a model but on experience gained by either operating in the real environment, or by exploring a simulated environment.

Before describing TD-algorithms in more detail we note that moving from a model that contains the whole dynamics of the MDP to feedback obtained while traversing the environment introduces another issue: If the agent can only update the value of states it is exploring, there is a trade-off between utilizing the knowledge it has already gained and exploring parts of the state space that it has not yet seen. This is known as the exploration/exploitation trade-off: If the agent is too eager to exploit the knowledge it has gained so far it may converge to a sub-optimal solution, either because it has not sampled the best states at all or because the initial samples of the best states were worse than average. If, on the other hand, the agent spends too much time exploring the state space it may not gain enough value from the accumulated knowledge. There are various ways to choose actions that try to achieve a good balance; in the rest of this

Initialize $V(s)$ arbitrarily, s according to I
loop
    $a \leftarrow \varepsilon[\pi(s)]$
    Perform a, obtaining reward r and moving to state s'
    $V(s) \leftarrow V(s) + \alpha\big(r + \gamma V(s') - V(s)\big)$
    $s \leftarrow s'$
end loop

Fig. 11. Tabular TD(0) learning for policy π and constant learning rate α

chapter we assume that the agent uses a simple ϵ-greedy strategy: It will choose the action a proposed by the current policy with probability $1 - \epsilon$, and otherwise choose equiprobably between the other actions. We write this selection as $\varepsilon[a]$.

Another question that has to be addressed when learning from experience is the question of *temporal credit assignment:* If rewards for actions are not received immediately but only after a sequence of actions, how should the reward be distributed among the actions? For example, when winning a game of chess, all the reward is obtained with the final mate, but the actual winning move has likely taken place long before.

TD-Learning. The main idea behind TD-learning is to use Eq. (1) (or, for algorithms improving the action-value function, Eq. (2)) to bootstrap an estimate of the state (or action) value function. The improvement is not based on a value computed from a model, but on values obtained while exploring the environment: if $V(s)$ is an estimate of the value of V^{π} and following π results in reward r and a state s' then $r + \gamma V(s')$ can be used as a better estimate for the value of $V(s)$. This is easy to see for the case of deterministic, episodic environments and a deterministic strategy: If we reach a final state s_f then no more reward will be received, hence the reward r_f of the final transition is the value of the previous state s_p. Every state immediately before s_p therefore has value $r_p + \gamma V(s_p)$. By backward iteration we can find the exact values of all states.

When applying TD-learning the situation is not so simple, since the agent usually has to learn while it is operating, and since the environment is stochastic. Therefore the agent cannot perform a simple backward induction step. Instead it updates its current estimate while it is operating; but it only updates $V(s)$ by a percentage α of the difference between $r + \gamma V(s')$ and $V(s)$. The value of α is called the *learning rate*. Often the learning rate will be reduced with time, so that the algorithm learns rapidly in the beginning and becomes more robust against random fluctuations later. Since $(r + \gamma V(s')) - V(s)$ represents the difference between estimates of the value of s at two different times (after and before performing the transition to s'), the update is according to the *temporal difference*, hence the name TD-learning. It is possible to take longer temporal differences into account, leading to a class of reinforcement learning algorithms called TD(λ).

Initialize $Q(s, a)$ arbitrarily, s according to I
loop
    $a \leftarrow \varepsilon[\pi(s)]$
    Perform a, obtaining reward r and moving to state s'
    $Q(s, a) \leftarrow Q(s, a) + \alpha(r + \gamma \max_{a' \in A} Q(s', a') - Q(s, a))$
    $s \leftarrow s'$
end loop

Fig. 12. One-step Q-learning for policy π and constant learning rate α

In the simplest case, when only the temporal difference between a state and its immediate successor is taken into account we obtain the following equations for the estimates V and Q of the state-value and action-value functions:

$$V(s_n) \leftarrow V(s_n) + \alpha_n(r_s + \gamma V(s_{n+1}) - V(s_n))$$
$$Q(s_n, a_n) \leftarrow Q(s_n, a_n) + \alpha_n(r_s + \gamma Q(s_{n+1}, a_{t+1}) - Q(s_n, a_n))$$

Fig. 11 gives pseudo-code for the TD(0) algorithm. Note that, in contrast to the dynamic programming algorithm, TD(0) updates a single value of V when new information becomes available and does not perform a sweep through the state space. The TD(0) algorithm can be used to perform policy evaluation, either interleaved with policy improvement as shown in Fig. 10, or with π as the greedy policy with respect to V.

It is sometimes advantageous to learn the Q function instead of the V function, and to be able to learn even when not following the policy being learned (off-policy learning). One of the important breakthroughs in reinforcement learning was the discovery of Q-learning by Watkins [43], an off-policy algorithm for learning action-value functions. Q-learning updates an estimate of the Q function according to the temporal difference

$$Q(s, a) \leftarrow Q(s, a) + \alpha(r + \gamma \max_{a' \in A} Q(s', a') - Q(s, a))$$

when action a leads to a transition from s to s'. It can be shown to converge to Q^* independently of the policy being followed.[9]

Fig. 12 contains the complete algorithm.

Function Approximation. The algorithms presented in the previous section represent the value for each state (or state-action pair) exactly. Since they conceptually maintain a table of values for each state they are called *table-based* algorithms. For most application this is neither feasible nor desirable. Obviously, the full state space is typically too large to be represented explicitly, and in continuous state spaces learning becomes impossible since the probability of reaching the same state twice is zero. There is another reason why learning an

---

[9] Convergence is always subject to some constraints, e.g., that the exploration policy samples each state infinitely often.

individual value for every state is counter-productive: this does not allow the system to reuse learned behaviors in similar situations. For example, if a robot has learned how to pick up a red object it should be able to use this knowledge to pick up a blue object as well, since the color of the object does not influence how to grasp it. Therefore, in practice value functions are typically represented using parameterized approximations, e.g., as a linear combinations of a fixed number of basis functions. Updates of the value functions then consist in finding a parameter change that moves the approximation closer to the desired function.

For factored state spaces (i.e., state spaces that are subsets of a Cartesian product space), approximations are often defined in terms of their individual features. Therefore function approximators are sometimes called featurizers. While they are indispensable for practical applications, function approximators generally lead to learning systems that no longer converge to the optimal solution.

4.2 Hierarchical and Multi-agent Learning

Function approximation allows reinforcement learning agents to generalize about states: if two states are approximated in the same way the behavior in both states is identical. Hierarchical structure is another frequently-used abstraction mechanism, and it is not surprising that this kind of decomposition is also useful for learning: If several tasks rely on a common subroutine, this subroutine can often learn much more efficiently if it reuses its knowledge across all tasks. Consider, as an example, a rescue robot that learns the location of a victim, finds a path to get there, picks up the victim and transports it to a rescue zone. Clearly the task of the robot consists of several phases in which different behavior is required, and it has several sub-problems (e.g., navigation) that can be reused across different phases. When representing the problem as a single MDP this "phase structure" is lost and the space of possible solutions becomes intractably large. Furthermore, it is difficult to deal with concurrent, ongoing activities in a pure MDP framework. For example, the robot should look for additional victims as it moves through the environment and, depending on several factors such as the severity of the victim's injuries and the topology of the environment, modify its currently planned actions.

The reinforcement learners described in the previous section and the MDP model on which they are based are not well-suited to express hierarchical and concurrent problems. We will therefore look at two extensions to MDPs and the extended capabilities they allow: Semi-Markov Decision Processes (SMDPs) for hierarchical reinforcement learning and Markov games for multi-agent learning. Due to limited space we only provide short conceptual overviews and refer to the literature for details.

Hierarchical Learning and SMDPs. The main idea behind hierarchical reinforcement learning (HRL) is to group sets of actions together so that the agent can execute them as a single unit. Then reinforcement learning techniques can be applied at different levels of the hierarchy, and results learned at lower levels can be reused whenever the low-level operation is invoked by a higher-level system. For example, if a robot has learned the motor commands for a ninety-degree turn it can simply execute these commands whenever a turn is requested by a higher level. A flat reinforcement learner cannot do this, since the concept of "ninety-degree-turn" does not even exist in the flat MDP.

The distinguishing feature of high-level commands is that they often take variable amounts of time, and that subsequent actions are therefore discounted with variable factors. Therefore, high-level commands are no longer strictly Markovian even though the low-level actions still are. To capture this feature, Semi-Markov Decision Processes (SMDPs) have been introduced by Tanaka and Wakuta [40]. SMDPs extend MDPs by associating a distribution over times to each transition. This extension is sufficient to add hierarchical actions to the MDP framework.

To provide an execution model for hierarchical learners, Andre [5] introduced the notion of reinforcement learning machines (RLMs). A RLM is a model for a computer program that can be composed with a MDP so that the combined system is a SMDP. To this end, RLMs contain different types of states, among them *choice* and *action* states. Choice states represent choices in the execution of the program where the programmer has specified different alternatives; the task of the RLM in choice states is to learn an optimal strategy. Action states are states in which the program triggers actions in the associated MDP and therefore a non-deterministic transition of the MDP. Additionally, RLMs support *subroutines* which are responsible for the hierarchical decomposition of the learning task.

It is not guaranteed that an optimal policy respects the constraints imposed by the hierarchical decomposition of the problem. For example, assume that the high-level task decomposition for a rescue robot is

$$\mathsf{nav(victim)} \to \mathsf{pickup(victim)} \to \mathsf{nav(base)} \to \mathsf{drop(victim)}$$

If this robot has picked up a victim and is navigating back to its base, it will not be able to pick up a second victim, even if it has the means to carry it and that is the optimal solution. Therefore the best strategies we can expect a hierarchic learning algorithm to learn are only optimal among strategies that respect the hierarchical task decomposition, which is called *hierarchically optimal.*

RLMs guarantee a number of interesting properties, in particular that the composition of a RLM $\mathcal{H}$ and an MDP $\mathcal{M}$ results in a joint SMDP $\mathcal{H} \odot \mathcal{M}$, and that optimal solutions for (a minimized version of) $\mathcal{H} \odot \mathcal{M}$ constitute an optimal policy for $\mathcal{M}$ that is consistent with $\mathcal{H}$. This result allows us to use SMDP solution algorithms to solve HRL problems. In particular, reinforcement learning techniques can be modified to work with the joint SMDP without explicitly building $\mathcal{H} \odot \mathcal{M}$. The basic idea thereby is to operate on the product space of the states of $\mathcal{H}$ and $\mathcal{M}$, to collect the rewards and times accumulated by $\mathcal{M}$ for all transitions that do not lead into a choice state of $\mathcal{H}$. Upon reaching a choice state of $\mathcal{H}$, the algorithm updates the Q-function with the collected reward and discounts future rewards with the accumulated time. Fig. 14 shows an example of a hierarchical learning algorithm for a multi-agent setting.

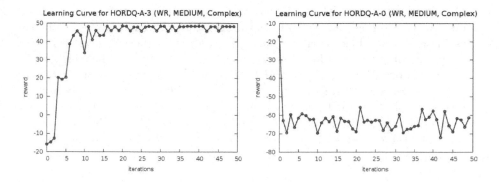

Fig. 13. Learning curves with good and bad choice of features for hierarchy

There exists a class of function approximations for hierarchical reinforcement learners based on RLMs that preserves hierarchical optimality; we call them *admissible*. The existence of admissible featurizers is important, since badly chosen abstractions can lead to very low performance of hierarchical learners. Fig. 13 shows an example of this effect. The plots in this figure show the learning performance of a robot performing a simulation of the rescue task. The x-axis represents the number of rescue missions the robot performed to learn a strategy, the y-axis shows the performance achieved by this strategy (i.e., how quickly the robot could rescue victims). The left learning curve uses an admissible function approximator whereas the right curve shows an experiment where the approximator was deliberately chosen to conflict with the learning hierarchy. The robot using an admissible featurizer starts with the performance of a random walk, since initially the robot has no information about its environment. It then converges quickly towards the optimal strategy and consistently obtains a reward close to the maximum achievable in this environment (approximately 48.5). The other strategy performs even worse than even a random walk, since the featurizer used for this strategy is deliberately designed so that the robot cannot learn to return to the base when it learns a solution that navigates to the victim, and *vice versa* (note the different offsets of the y axis for the graphs). We emphasize that this is an extreme example in which the hierarchy and featurizers have deliberately been designed to show the possible problems; in practice non-admissible featurizers will often lead to a performance that is worse than that obtained by an admissible featurizer but still better than random actions.

The best-known language for hierarchical reinforcement learning is ALisp [5], which allows developers to write programs in which some choices are unspecified, so-called *partial programs*. The ALisp system learns strategies for the choices appearing in a partial program during execution and uses them to guide the execution of the program. The set of all learned strategies is called the *completion* of a partial program and can be shown to converge to the hierarchically optimal solution given admissible featurizers and learning strategies, e.g., a hierarchical version of the Q-learning algorithm from Fig. 12.

The integration of an ALisp-like facility for hierarchical reinforcement learning into XBTs is straightforward: choices in ALisp correspond to external choice nodes in the XBT which learn a Q function and order their child nodes, e.g., ϵ-greedy according to the value of the Q function.[10] As in ALisp the hierarchy is provided by subroutine calls. A *partial XBT* is an XBT in which certain external choice nodes are controlled by a learning process, and the *completion* of a partial XBT consists of all learned strategies. The correctness results for reinforcement learning machines can immediately be applied to partial XBTs: The completion of a partial XBT converges to the hierarchically optimal solution as long as the Q-learning algorithm and the featurizers are admissible.

Multi-agent Learning and Markov Games. The reinforcement-learning techniques we have seen so far can scale to large, complex problems. But they are restricted to scenarios in which there is a single learning agent operating in a mostly static environment. If an environment contains multiple learning agents the problem becomes much more complex, and currently available techniques are much more restricted in their scope of applicability. There are several reasons for this:

— The different agents may cooperate, compete, or mix cooperation and competition. In many scenarios a mix of cooperation and competition happens, even for agents belonging to the same ensemble. For example, different rescue robots may cooperate to rescue victims but compete for space in recharging stations. Utility functions of individual robots therefore have to take into account the utility for the robot itself as well as for the ensemble. This often leads to performance problems for learners, since utility functions that correspond well to the ensemble utility are difficult to learn for individual agents, and *vice versa* [2].
— With several agents operating simultaneously, the state and action spaces both become exponentially larger: One state of the MDP is now the product of the states of *all* agents and the environment. If learning agents in such an environment have to consider the actions of other agents in addition to their own, reasoning about actions has to take place in the cross-product space of actions of all relevant agents. To avoid this state explosion problem each agent in a multi-agent system is often treated as an individual learner and the other agents are aggregated into the environment. However, while this works well for some practical applications, few theoretical considerations for the single-agent case apply, since in this scenario the environment of each agent is neither Markovian nor stationary.
— In addition to the temporal credit assignment problem there also exists a *structural credit assignment problem*: If an agent receives a high or low re-

---

[10] Actually a slight extension of external choice nodes as we have presented them in Sect. 3.2 is required: Whenever a choice is performed the value of the choice has to be recorded in the choice node. It is straightforward, although somewhat tedious, to add this extension to the SCEL model.

ward, how much of this reward should it attribute to its own actions, and
how much should it assign to actions of other agents?
- For hierarchical multi-agent learning there is another, similar complication:
  When performing a high-level action that spawns a series of lower-level actions, the activities of the other agents while the actions are running may
  lead to a large number of possible traces through the SMDP, which makes it
  difficult to identify which action in the hierarchy is ultimately responsible for
  the credit obtained. We call this the *hierarchical credit assignment problem*.
- When different types of agents operate in an environment, they will often
  use different learning algorithms. Thus the analysis of multi-agent scenarios has to encompass *heterogeneous* scenarios, where different learners are
  interacting with each other.

Another contrast to the single-agent case is that the theoretical foundations of
multi-agent learning are much less definite than in the single agent case. The
basic model for most work is that of a Markov game, a generalization of both
repeated games (by introducing states for the individual stages of a game) and
MDPs (by introducing multiple players acting on the environment).

However, whereas in the single-agent case different algorithms can be mean-
ingfully compared by evaluating their performance on example problems, e.g., in
terms of rate of convergence to an optimal solution, this alone is not sufficient
to analyze the multi-agent case: These environments are dynamical systems in
which convergence to a single learned strategy for all agents of a type (i.e., a fixed-
point attractor) is not guaranteed. Instead we should expect agents to converge
towards a mixture of different learned behaviors, or even settle into periodic
or chaotic oscillations between learned behaviors. In the analysis of multi-agent
learning, the dynamics of the learning process therefore plays a much greater
role than in the single-agent case.

Following the work of Boörgers and Sarin [8], evolutionary game theory, and
in particular the notion of replicator dynamics, is becoming a common framework
for understanding the dynamical behavior of multi-agent learning algorithms.
Replicator dynamics describe how the likelihood of players using a certain strategy π_i varies over time, based on the success that π_i has when playing against
the strategies played by other players. If A and B are the payoff matrices of
players x and y, respectively, and if we identify players with the vector of probabilities with which they play each strategy (so that x_i is the probability of player
x playing strategy i), then the change of strategies over time can be described
by the differential equations

$$\dot{x}_i = x_i\big((Ay)_i - x^T Ay\big)$$
$$\dot{y}_i = y_i\big((Bx)_i - y^T Bx\big)$$

(assuming that the players play continuously). $\dot{x}_i$ is the derivative of x_i, i.e., the
rate of change of x over time. (Ay) is the payoff vector for player x given the
distribution of strategies that y plays. $x^T Ay$ is the average payoff that x achieves
against y. If strategy i fares better than average, the replicator dynamics will

cause x to play i more frequently, if i is less successful than average, x will play it less frequently in the future. The replicator equations provide a tool to forecast the steady states of a multi-agent learning system (if they exist) and the trajectory to arrive there.

(Lenient) Frequency Adjusted Q-Learning. As we have discussed previously, there are two major ways in which multi-agent learning can be performed: it is possible to learn in the joint state and action space, so that an optimal policy for all agents performing choices together is learned, or it is possible to learn individual actions for each individual agent operating in the joint state space, without taking the actions of the other agents into account. Concurrent ALisp by Marthi [27] is an example for the first approach; each agent runs a hierarchical learning algorithm in a single thread and waits at choices points for the other agents to perform a shared choice.

While the approach of Concurrent ALisp can be very successful in practice and has nice theoretical properties, the notion of a central planner that computes joint actions is not well suited for ensembles of individual components. Therefore we will focus on the second approach.

The Q-learning algorithm from Fig. 12 can be applied to the multi-agent case by simply treating the actions of other agents as stochastic. Since the environment is no longer Markovian because of the actions of the other agents, no convergence guarantees can be given, and in fact the algorithm typically converges to a sub-optimal solution. The comparison of the learning behavior predicted by the evolutionary model of Q-learning with observed behavior shows significant differences between prediction and observed behavior, with the actual behavior often being less desirable than the predicted behavior. The reason for the difference is that the derivation of the evolutionary behavior supposes that the update frequency is the same for all actions, which does not hold in practice. Kaisers and Tuyls [24] propose a modification of Q-learning which addresses this discrepancy by adjusting the learning rates for different actions according to their probability, so that the frequency difference is eliminated. This variant of Q-learning is called Frequency-Adjusted Q-learning (FAQ-learning).

The approximation of the action-value function Q used by FAQ-learning is thus

$$Q(s,a) \leftarrow Q(s,a) + \min\left(\frac{\beta}{P(\pi(s') = a')}, 1\right) \alpha\left(r + \gamma \max_{a' \in A} Q(s', a') - Q(s,a)\right)$$

where the new factor $\min(\beta/P(\pi(s') = a'), 1)$ is used to simulate the desired synchronous updates of actions, all occurring with equal frequencies, by increasing the update rate of less-frequently used actions.[11] The value of $P(\pi(s') = a')$, the probability that action a' is selected by strategy π is state s', changes according to a replicator dynamics of the form $\dot{P}(\pi(s') = a') = f(s', a')$ where f depends of the reward matrices of the players, see Bloembergen et al. [7] for details.

---

[11] The factor β is not necessary in theory but introduced for pragmatic reasons to adjust the convergence of the algorithm.

Initialize $Q([m, s], a)$ arbitrarily, $[m, s]$ according to I
Initialize $m_0 \leftarrow m$, $s_0 \leftarrow s$, $r_c \leftarrow 0$, $\gamma_c \leftarrow 0$
loop
    $a \leftarrow \varepsilon[\pi(s)]$
    Perform a, obtaining reward r and moving to state $[m', s']$
    if m' is a choice state **then**
        $Q([m_0, s_0], a) \leftarrow Q([m_0, s_0], a) +$
                $\min\left(\frac{\beta}{P(\pi(s')=a')}, 1\right)\alpha\left(r + \gamma V([m', s'], a') - Q([m_0, s_0], a)\right)$
    else
        $r_c \leftarrow r + r_c$, $\gamma_c \leftarrow \gamma\gamma_c$
    end if
    $m \leftarrow m'$, $s \leftarrow s'$
end loop

Fig. 14. One-step HFAQ-learning for policy π and constant learning rate α; as in Q-learning, $V([m', s'], a') = \max_{a' \in A} Q([m', s'], a')$

One important discovery in the area of cooperative multi-agent reinforcement learning is that, particularly in the early stages of the learning process, it is often advantageous for agents to be lenient with respect to actions that result in low rewards, i.e., to not reduce the value estimates for these rewards. Intuitively, this can be explained by the observation that in the early stages of learning no good synchronization strategy has yet been learned by the cooperating players, and therefore they may inadvertently perform joint actions that result in bad outcomes, even though the individual actions might be beneficial. One possible action update rule for lenient learning is that rewards are not updated immediately but only after κ samples for a state action pair have been collected, and the highest of these κ values is then taken as the first reward. When using a lenient update strategy for Q values together with the Q-function for FAQ-learning, we obtain the Lenient Frequency-Adjusted Q-learning (LFAQ) algorithm [7].

LFAQ-learning operates on a flat state space. Since the reasons for hierarchical learning given in Sect. 4.2 apply in the multi-agent case as well, we propose to extend (L)FAQ-learning to the hierarchical case, resulting in the H(L)FAQ-learning update rule. The definition of an HFAQ-learning algorithm with constant learning rate is given in Fig. 14. It can be seen that this algorithm operates on the joint state space of the XBT (or, more generally, RLM) and the MDP. If the values of Q are initialized lazily it is not necessary to store the whole action-value table but only the states that are actually reached. r_C and γ accumulate the reward and discount accrued while executing actions that do not result in a choice state; the update rule adjusts the value of the *previous* choice state according to r_C and γ when the next choice state is reached, i.e., the whole reward and discount factor count towards the value of the choice state from which the current path started.

5   Passing Knowledge to Other Components: Teacher-Student Learning

There are manifold possibilities for an ensemble to engage in learning. While previous studies tend to focus on offline learning, which is as of now yielding "better" results, online learning is much more practical since simulations have consistently proven not to be able to fully mimic the physical world.[12]

In the general case, considering the lifetime of an adaptive ensemble, there will be several learning periods as well as operational periods. In the case of offline learning, the learning and operational periods will be mutually exclusive.[13] Typically, any ensemble utilizing offline learning will also provide dedicated resources capable of and responsible for reasoning and simulation.[14] Offline learning tends to produce more consistent and predictable results but is obviously highly dependent on the quality and efficiency of available simulations. Conversely, in the "clean" approach of online learning, the periods of learning and operation are strictly congruent, i.e. the ensemble is supposed to work its defined purpose from day one and is not simulating nor reviewing scenarios when shut down. This approach removes any dependency on simulation, but tends to require a long operational time in the real world to produce results comparable to offline learning and may thus be rather costly. Since both approaches provide advantages (and come with disadvantages),[15] it only seems reasonable to combine both approaches into one more general framework allowing both "pure" online and offline learning as boundary instances and thus abstracting from the previously described distinction between them.

In order to do so, we introduce the *teacher-student* approach: It does not model learning as occurring at certain time periods only, but as a continuous process, through which information flows into and spreads inside the ensemble. By not limiting learning to certain components or specific time periods, this approach combines online and offline learning into one model. In general though, there will be components more concerned with or able to produce knowledge valuable to the ensemble, which will be called "teachers" for simplicity, while components that tend to play a relative small role in producing new model information will be called "students". Note that this distinction is built upon

---

[12] Considering ASCENS's rescue scenario e.g., complete offline planing is highly unrealistic by the very definition of the scenario, with robots acting in a randomly altered version of the world model available for planning.

[13] By this definition, offline learning includes "review" approaches where learning takes place after an actual run of the scenario and can use results gathered there to improve further planning.

[14] Most scenarios embrace a view where simulation resources are considered external to an ensemble made up of agents which actually interact with the environment and thus directly working towards the goal of the scenario. However, considering the complete life-cycle of an ensemble, it is natural to regard every part involved in computing its observable behavior as a component of the ensemble.

[15] Cf. Watson et al. [44] for further discussion of the (dis-)advantages. Although that article is more focused on evolutionary algorithms, most points apply regardless.

tendency and thus not a strict dichotomy nor fixed in time (i.e., it is reasonable to talk about students becoming teachers and vice versa), but referring to components by the task they excel at seems most practical.[16]

This approach allows us to integrate different models not only statically for a new model description, but also dynamically during run-time. Thus, it also helps formalize and automate the feedback/deployment loop of the Ensemble Development Life Cycle (EDLC) as described in chapter III.1 [20]: The learned behavior that proved to be successful among the agents describes strategies to be considered during the next design cycle while deploying new strategies can be as simple as adjusting the teaching environment, e.g. by favoring said strategies or adding a new teaching component. In practice, our ensembles feature dedicated learning entities, which act as teachers, that try to learn agent behavior through different learning mechanisms (cf. Sect. 4). They can then pass the knowledge they gained on to agents controlling robots e.g., which continue to adapt their behavior to concrete environmental changes. They use online learning through an embodied genetic algorithm[17] to exchange their execution plans between one another. Using a genetic algorithm here is the obvious choice because the agents implicitly form a framework suitable for it: Since students usually are not capable of enhancing their current action plans on their own (because they lack the reasoning resources), they need to exchange plans with other agents to improve on their current fitness. If the agents' environment favors the passage of more fit plans (or parts of plans) over less fit ones, evolution on plans (or plan parts) happens "naturally". That can easily be achieved by granting (more) teaching functionality to agents considered more fit by some means of evaluation.[18] Interestingly, as robotic agents promoted to (possibly part-time) teachers can still interact with the environment and change their location in particular, the teacher-student framework naturally includes the means necessary for the development of local optimization, i.e. group forming or even speciation. This follows Karafotias et al. [25], which suggests using an island model for a self-adaptive embodied evolutionary algorithm.[19]

---

[16] For example, a typical robot swarm scenario may feature dedicated servers running reasoning software acting as teachers while the actual robots are equipped with much less computational power and will be acting as students. It is obvious that basically all online information collecting will be done by the robots which actually act in and observe the environment through their sensors, thus generating a lot of data. However, as long as the bulk of the processing and distributing is not done at the robot side, they still fit the "student" description.

[17] That is a genetic algorithm running on actual agents where gene transfer follows agent interaction in the real world. For more information on so-called *embodied evolution*, cf. Karafotias et al. [25] and Watson et al. [44].

[18] Also note that it may be necessary to include some space constraint on concurrently "active" plans in order to introduce selection pressure. However, this usually coincides with restrictions of the physical world, i.e. computer hardware, anyway.

[19] Island models for evolutionary algorithms model several separate populations (solving the same problem), which evolve independently most of the time, but do exchange individuals on some occasions. Cf. Tomassini [41] for further information.

In other cases, arguably well-working agents and/or suitable reasoning engines are already available, making it only necessary to pass on their abilities to an ensemble of agents. When the knowledge representations of their plans are available in the format expected by the agents, these can just be copied over to the students. However, instead of copying the internal data structure, *teaching* is the wider approach and works across different learning models as well: In the most general case, "teaching" encompasses re-learning a behavior by applying a learning method with the original behavior as a fitness/goal function. Again, in the boundary cases, when the student is able to understand the teacher's knowledge representation anyway, the learning method may be the *id* function. In most cases, however, this method can be used to bridge different models and reasoning approaches if necessary. In another boundary case, it may even allow operationally very distinct components like a human teacher manually assigning grades to agent behavior to be integrated into the ensemble. The inherent loss of precision due to the usually non-exact re-learning process and the model conversion is negligible or even advantageous as the re-learned model are later used as individuals in a the embodied evolutionary algorithm, which is inherently resistant to random distortions and needs mutation to function properly anyways.

Thus, it is easy to include manually adjusted teachers into an ensemble, pushing the evolutionary process into a certain direction deemed fruitful by having said teachers constantly spreading relevant knowledge (without giving in to "peer pressure" even when most students diverge towards other regions of the solution space). Including a fixed set of teachers then gives rise to an implicit, fuzzy version of the utility space as described by Abeywickrama and Zambonelli [1]: The agents' plans are able to diverge into other regions of the solution space, but are quite unlikely to do so due to the constant influence of the teachers.[20] Using the notion of an *adaptation domain* as defined in III.1 [20], this approach can be interpreted as a utility-based system: The system may potentially adapt to very wide range of adaptation requirements, but has a preference attached to each of them.

Ensemble behavior can be learned by teaching a suitable single-agent strategy for the task, which should include solutions to "atomic" problems like navigation e.g., and have the agents use a distributed learning algorithm to adapt it into a viable ensemble strategy.[21]

Obviously, this presupposes a common communication language: Extended behavior trees (XBTs) as described in section 3 provide a powerful yet concise

---

[20] However, for this approach to function it is necessary to include parameters previously fixed by external constraints in the genome to be decided by the evolutionary mechanic, with all the performance overhead that comes with this design. Note that it is in no way prohibited for student agents to use further optimization techniques suited for own capabilities (like greedy search algorithms for example) to alleviate that problem.

[21] This phenomenon is suspected by and discussed by Dinu et al. [12]: Even under widely different circumstances, robotic agents previously trained (even for a different problem) tend to perform distinctively better than randomly initialized ones.

tool for expressing agent programs that is easily visualizable and human-readable as well, which allows for using the same representation in the manual part of the development process. In the end, the goal of this approach is to specify a common framework, which helps using and most of all combining different concrete approaches to machine learning, thus enabling the design of very heterogeneous ensembles that are still able to work together in a reasonable way. In the end, knowledge always dies out without proper means of passing it on.

6 Related Work

The notions of "awareness" and "self-awareness" have been investigated in various disciplines. The arguably most famous experiments about self-awareness arose from research in biology and psychology: They are the "mirror tests" going back to Charles Darwin and performed in a systematic manner by Gallup [15], amongst others. An extensive overview of biologically inspired notions of self awareness is contained in Lewis et al. [26]. The authors of this paper also provide a definition of awareness in terms of two essential and four optional characteristics. Mitchell [30] defines four "principles of self-awareness and control in decentralized systems" based on studies of the human immune system and ant colonies. Anderson and Perlis [4] give convincing arguments for the need to build self-aware systems in order to achieve non-brittle behavior in complex environments. They present active logic and the *metacognitive loop* as components for aware systems.

The notion of *situation awareness* and methods to measure situation awareness have been developed in human factors research starting in the 1980s. A comprehensive treatment is Endsley [14].

Behavior trees are extensively covered in the literature on game programming; Millington and Funge [29] gives a good introduction that also discusses the strengths and weaknesses of the approach. Applications to robotics and avionics are given by Marzinotto et al. [28] and Ögren [33].

Machine learning is a large and diverse research area. Alpaydin [3] and Murphy [31] provide book-length introduction into the subject area. Sutton and Barto [39] is the standard introductory text to reinforcement learning; Busoniu et al. [10] provide more information on techniques for function approximation. Andre [5] comprehensively covers hierarchical reinforcement learning; Marthi [27] extends this work to the concurrent case. Schwartz [36] covers reinforcement learning in the context of multi-agent systems. Wiering and van Otterlo [46] describe the major current developments in reinforcement learning.

Shoham and Leyton-Brown [37] and Weiss [45] provide a broad overview over topics relevant to multi-agent systems and include chapters about reasoning and learning in this context. Ghallab et al. [17] is a comprehensive overvies of single-agent planning techniques. More specialized references have been included in their respective sections of the text.

7   Conclusions and Future Work

Despite (or maybe because of) their reduced expressiveness when compared to other formalisms, behavior trees are gaining popularity as modeling tool for control and artificial intelligence in different areas. There are several reasons for this, among them the simplicity of the basic execution model, the ease with which behavior trees can be visualized, and their straightforward behavior in case of task failure, which is a common occurrence when interacting with an external world.

We have introduced Extended Behavior Trees (XBTs), an extension of behavior trees, as a way to model and implement reasoning and learning mechanisms for adaptive and self-aware agents. While XBTs are more expressive, and hence more complicated, than behavior trees, we hope that the additional capabilities do not significantly diminish the usability of XBTs when compared to behavior trees. The semantics of XBTs are defined in terms of SCEL, therefore many more sophisticated concurrency and control features can be defined. It remains to investigate which ones are the most useful ones to increase the expressive power, and how they impact the cognitive complexity of XBTs.

We have indicated how XBTs can be used to define reasoning and learning mechanisms for single-agent and multi-agent applications and in particular how reinforcement learning techniques can be integrated into XBTs. For the multi-agent case we have proposed H(L)FAQ-learning, which is to our knowledge the first proposal for a hierarchical, cooperative multi-agent reinforcement-learning technique that does not presuppose simultaneous execution of actions. XBTs are also well suited to the requirements of teacher-student learning since they allow agents with very different capabilities to share structurally equivalent programs.

Despite the tremendous progress that has been made in the last decades, the field of machine learning and reasoning for adaptation and awareness is still in its infancy, and its methods are neither as universally applicable nor as robust as would be desirable. Experimental validation of the techniques proposed in this paper is therefore an important area for future work; specific guidelines when individual techniques can usefully be employed and which circumstances are counter-indications would be extraordinarily valuable to practitioners. For this a derivation of the replicator dynamics of H(L)FAQ-Learning would be highly desirable. It would also be interesting to better understand the combination of different techniques, e.g., the interaction between planning and learning used within a single decision mechanism.

The ASCENS project has proposed the Ensemble Development Life Cycle as a guideline for developing robust ensembles. The teacher-student approach to learning is one example how learning techniques might be integrated into this life cycle in such a manner that the feedback inside each development phase, as well as the feedback from run-time to design-time can be exploited to improve the learning behavior over the lifetime of an ensemble. There are many aspects of the EDLC that teacher-student learning in its current form does not take into account, e.g., how knowledge representation or formal verification interact with learning. It would also be beneficial to gain knowledge about the behavioral properties of the evolutionary algorithms implicitly defined by a teacher-student environment. Further progress on both theoretical properties of as well as practical experience with the EDLC and teacher-student learning is required.

References

1. Abeywickrama, D., Zambonelli, F.: Model Checking Goal-oriented Requirements for Self-Adaptive Systems. In: 19th IEEE Conference on the Engineering of Computer-based Systems, Novi Sad, Serbia, April 2012, IEEE CS Press, Los Alamitos (2012),
http://pmi.ascens-ist.eu/text_files/0000/0017/ECBS12.pdf
2. Agogino, A.K., Tumer, K.: Analyzing and visualizing multiagent rewards in dynamic and stochastic domains. Autonomous Agents and Multi-Agent Systems 17(2), 320–338 (2008), doi:10.1007/s10458-008-9046-9
3. Alpaydin, E.: Introduction to Machine Learning, 2nd edn. Adaptive Computation and Machine Learning. MIT Press, Cambridge (2010)
4. Anderson, M.L., Perlis, D.: Logic, self-awareness and self-improvement: the metacognitive loop and the problem of brittleness. J. Log. Comput. 15(1), 21–40 (2005)
5. Andre, D.: Programmable Reinforcement Learning Agents. Ph.D. thesis, University of California at Berkeley (2003)
6. Au, T., Ilghami, O., Kuter, U., Murdock, J.W., Nau, D.S., Wu, D., Yaman, F.: SHOP2: an HTN planning system. CoRR abs/1106.4869 (2011),
http://arxiv.org/abs/1106.4869
7. Bloembergen, D., Kaisers, M., Tuyls, K.: Lenient frequency adjusted Q learning. In: Proc. of 22nd Belgium-Netherlands Conf. on Artificial Intelligence (BNAIC 2010), pp. 19–26 (2010)
8. Börgers, T., Sarin, R.: Learning Through Reinforcement and Replicator Dynamics. Journal of Economic Theory 77, 1–14 (1997)
9. Bruni, R., Corradini, A., Gadducci, F., Hölzl, M., Lafuente, A.L., Vandin, A., Wirsing, M.: Reconciling White-Box and Black-Box Perspectives on Behavioral Self-adaptation. In: Wirsing, M., Hölzl, M., Koch, N., Mayer, P. (eds.) Software Engineering for Collective Autonomic Systems. LNCS, vol. 8998, pp. 163–184. Springer, Heidelberg (2015)
10. Busoniu, L., Babuska, R., Schutter, B.D., Ernst, D.: Reinforcement Learning and Dynamic Programming Using Function Approximators. CRC Press, Boca Raton (2012)
11. Colvin, R.J., Hayes, I.J.: A semantics for Behavior Trees using {CSP} with specification commands. Science of Computer Programming 76(10), 891–914 (2011),
http://www.sciencedirect.com/science/article/pii/S0167642310002066
12. Dinu, C.M., Dimitrov, P., Weel, B., Eiben, A.E.: Self-adapting fitness evaluation times for on-line evolution of simulated robots. In: Proceedings of the 15th Annual Conference on Genetic and Evolutionary Computation. GECCO '13, pp. 191–198. ACM Press, New York (2013), doi:10.1145/2463372.2463405
13. Drusinsky, D.: Modeling and Verification Using UML Statecharts. Elsevier, Amsterdam (2006)
14. Endsley, M.: Design and evaluation for situation awareness enhancement. In: Proceedings of the Human Factors Society 32nd Annual Meeting, pp. 97–101. Human Factors Society (1988)

15. Gallup, G.G.: Self recognition in primates: A comparative approach to the bidirectional properties of consciousness. American Psychologist 32(5), 329–338 (1977)
16. Games, E.: How Unreal Engine 4 Behavior Trees Differ (2014), https://docs.unrealengine.com/latest/INT/Engine/AI/BehaviorTrees/HowUE4Behavior TreesDiffer/index.html, last accessed 2014-11-28
17. Ghallab, M., Nau, D.S., Traverso, P.: Automated planning - theory and practice. Elsevier, Amsterdam (2004)
18. Ghallab, M., Nau, D.S., Traverso, P.: The actor's view of automated planning and acting: A position paper. Artif. Intell. 208, 1–17 (2014), doi:10.1016/j.artint.2013.11.002
19. Hoch, N., Monreale, G.V., Montanari, U., Sammartino, M., Siwe, A.T.: From Local to Global Knowledge and Back. In: Wirsing, M., Hölzl, M., Koch, N., Mayer, P. (eds.) Software Engineering for Collective Autonomic Systems. LNCS, vol. 8998, pp. 185–220. Springer, Heidelberg (2015)
20. Hölzl, M., Koch, N., Puviani, M., Wirsing, M., Zambonelli, F.: The Ensemble Development Life Cycle and Best Practices for Collective Autonomic Systems. In: Wirsing, M., Hölzl, M., Koch, N., Mayer, P. (eds.) Software Engineering for Collective Autonomic Systems. LNCS, vol. 8998, pp. 325–354. Springer, Heidelberg (2015)
21. Hölzl, M., Wirsing, M.: Issues in engineering self-aware and self-expressive ensembles. In: Pitt, J. (ed.) The Computer After Me: Awareness and Self-awareness in Autonomic Systems, October 2014, Imperial College Press (2014)
22. Hölzl, M.M., Wirsing, M.: Towards a system model for ensembles. In: Agha, G., Danvy, O., Meseguer, J. (eds.) Formal Modeling: Actors, Open Systems, Biological Systems. LNCS, vol. 7000, pp. 241–261. Springer, Heidelberg (2011)
23. Isla, D.: Handling complexity in the halo 2 ai. In: Proceedings of the Game Developer's Conference 2005 (GDC2005) (2005), http://www.gamasutra.com/view/feature/130663/gdc_2005_proceeding_handling_.php, last accessed 2014-11-28
24. Kaisers, M., Tuyls, K.: Frequency adjusted multi-agent q-learning. In: van der Hoek, W., Kaminka, G.A., Lespérance, Y., Luck, M., Sen, S. (eds.) 9th International Conference on Autonomous Agents and Multiagent Systems (AAMAS 2010), vol. 1–3, Toronto, Canada, May 10-14, 2010, pp. 309–316. ACM Press, New York (2010), doi:10.1145/1838206.1838250
25. Karafotias, G., Haasdijk, E., Eiben, A.E.: An algorithm for distributed on-line, on-board evolutionary robotics. In: Proceedings of the 13th Annual Conference on Genetic and Evolutionary Computation, pp. 171–178. ACM Press, New York (2011), doi:10.1145/2001576.2001601
26. Lewis, P.R., Chandra, A., Parsons, S., Robinson, E., Glette, K., Bahsoon, R., Torresen, J., Yao, X.: A Survey of Self-Awareness and Its Application in Computing Systems (2011)
27. Marthi, B.: Concurrent hierarchical reinforcement learning. In: Veloso, M.M., Kambhampati, S. (eds.) Proceedings, The Twentieth National Conference on Artificial Intelligence and the Seventeenth Innovative Applications of Artificial Intelligence Conference, Pittsburgh, Pennsylvania, USA, July 9-13, 2005, pp. 1652–1653. AAAI Press / The MIT Press (2005), http://www.aaai.org/Library/AAAI/2005/dc05-009.php
28. Marzinotto, A., Colledanchise, M., Smith, C., Ögren, P.: Towards a unified behavior trees framework for robot control. In: 2014 IEEE International Conference on Robotics and Automation, ICRA 2014, Hong Kong, China, May 31 -

June 7, 2014, pp. 5420–5427. IEEE Computer Society Press, Los Alamitos (2014), doi:10.1109/ICRA.2014.6907656

29. Millington, I., Funge, J.: Artificial Intelligence for Games, 2nd edn. Morgan Kaufmann, San Francisco (2009)

30. Mitchell, M.: Self-awareness and control in decentralized systems. In: Metacognition in Computation, pp. 80–85 (2005)

31. Murphy, K.P.: Machine Learning: A Probabilistic Perspective. Adaptive Computation and Machine Learning. MIT Press, Cambridge (2013)

32. De Nicola, R., Latella, D., Lafuente, A.L., Loreti, M., Margheri, A., Massink, M., Morichetta, A., Pugliese, R., Tiezzi, F., Vandin, A.: The SCEL Language: Design, Implementation, Verification. In: Wirsing, M., Hölzl, M., Koch, N., Mayer, P. (eds.) Software Engineering for Collective Autonomic Systems. LNCS, vol. 8998, pp. 3–71. Springer, Heidelberg (2015)

33. Ogren, P.: Increasing Modularity of UAV Control Systems using Computer Game Behavior Trees. AIAA Guidance, Navigation and Control Conference, Minneapolis, Minnesota, pp. 13–16 (2012)

34. Pinciroli, C., Bonani, M., Mondada, F., Dorigo, M.: Adaptation and Awareness in Robot Ensembles: Scenarios and Algorithms. In: Wirsing, M., Hölzl, M., Koch, N., Mayer, P. (eds.) Software Engineering for Collective Autonomic Systems. LNCS, vol. 8998, pp. 471–494. Springer, Heidelberg (2015)

35. Pinciroli, C., Trianni, V., O'Grady, R., Pini, G., Brutschy, A., Brambilla, M., Mathews, N., Ferrante, E., Caro, G.D., Ducatelle, F., Stirling, T.S., Gutiérrez, Á., Gambardella, L.M., Dorigo, M.: ARGoS: A modular, multi-engine simulator for heterogeneous swarm robotics. In: IROS, pp. 5027–5034. IEEE Computer Society Press, Los Alamitos (2011)

36. Schwartz, H.M.: Multi-Agent Machine Learning: A Reinforcement Approach. Wiley, Chichester (2014)

37. Shoham, Y., Leyton-Brown, K.: Multiagent Systems: Algorithmic, Game-Theoretic, and Logical Foundations. Cambridge University Press, New York (2008)

38. Smith, B.C.: Reflection and semantics in LISP. In: POPL '84: Proceedings of the 11th ACM SIGACT-SIGPLAN symposium on Principles of programming languages, pp. 23–35. ACM Press, New York (1984)

39. Sutton, R.S., Barto, A.G.: Reinforcement Learning. MIT Press, Cambridge (1998)

40. Tanaka, K., Wakuta, K.: On Continuous Time Markov Games With The Expected Average Reward Criterion. Science Reports of Niigata University. Series A, Mathematics 14, 15–24 (1977), http://projecteuclid.org/euclid.nihmj/1273779029

41. Tomassini, M.: Spatially Structured Evolutionary Algorithms: Artificial Evolution in Space and Time. Natural Computing Series. Springer, Heidelberg (2005), http://books.google.de/books?id=z7Hf6bL3x7MC

42. Vassev, E., Hinchey, M.: Knowledge Representation for Adaptive and Self-aware Systems. In: Wirsing, M., Hölzl, M., Koch, N., Mayer, P. (eds.) Software Engineering for Collective Autonomic Systems. LNCS, vol. 8998, pp. 221–247. Springer, Heidelberg (2015)

43. Watkins, C.: Learning from Delayed Rewards. Ph.D. thesis, Cambridge (1989)

44. Watson, R.A., Ficici, S.G., Pollack, J.B.: Embodied evolution: Distributing an evolutionary algorithm in a population of robots. Robotics and Autonomous Systems 39(1), 1–18 (2002), http://dblp.uni-trier.de/db/journals/ras/ras39.html#WatsonFP02

45. Weiss, G. (ed.): Multiagent Systems, 2nd edn. MIT Press, Cambridge (2013)

46. Wiering, M., van Otterlo, M. (eds.): Reinforcement Learning. Adaptation, Learning, and Optimization, vol. 12. Springer, Heidelberg (2012)

47. Zambonelli, F., Bicocchi, N., Cabri, G., Leonardi, L., Puviani, M.: On self-adaptation, self-expression, and self-awareness in autonomic service component ensembles. In: SASO Workshops, pp. 108–113. IEEE Computer Society Press, Los Alamitos (2011)

48. Zhang, G., Hölzl, M.M.: HiLA: High-Level Aspects for UML State Machines. In: Ghosh, S. (ed.) MODELS Workshops 2009. LNCS, vol. 6002, pp. 104–118. Springer, Heidelberg (2010)

CHAPTER II.5

Supporting Performance Awareness
in Autonomous Ensembles*

Lubomír Bulej[1], Tomáš Bureš[1], Ilias Gerostathopoulos[1], Vojtěch Horký[1],
Jaroslav Keznikl[1], Lukáš Marek[1], Max Tschaikowski[2], Mirco Tribastone[2], and
Petr Tůma[1]

[1] Department of Distributed and Dependable Systems, Faculty of Mathematics and
Physics, Charles University, Czech Republic
[2] Electronics and Computer Science, University of Southampton, United Kingdom

Abstract. The ASCENS project works with systems of self-aware, self-adaptive and self-expressive ensembles. Performance awareness represents a concern that cuts across multiple aspects of such systems, from the techniques to acquire performance information by monitoring, to the methods of incorporating such information into the design making and decision making processes. This chapter provides an overview of five project contributions – performance monitoring based on the DiSL instrumentation framework, measurement evaluation using the SPL formalism, performance modeling with fluid semantics, adaptation with DEECo and design with IRM-SA – all in the context of the cloud case study.

Keywords: performance, monitoring, modeling, adaptive systems, autonomic systems

1 Introduction

The ASCENS project deals with adaptive systems formed as ensembles of components that both possess and exchange knowledge. In general, an ensemble achieves awareness by observing the state of its components and the state of its environment, deriving knowledge from thus collected information, and deciding how to act on this knowledge through reasoning.

Each of the individual steps that combine to achieve awareness can be related to performance. Consider the example of an adaptive cloud application, used throughout this chapter and outlined in more detail in Chapter IV.3 [38]. Components of such an application may measure the request arrival rate or the request processing time, aiming to adjust resource pool sizes – such as caches or threads – to match the actual workload. Additionally, the components may also monitor the utilization of the host platform and form ensembles with components of other applications on the same host, reacting to possible overload with

---

* This research was supported by the European project IP 257414 (ASCENS).

M. Wirsing et al. (eds.): Collective Autonomic Systems, LNCS 8998, pp. 291–322, 2015.
© Springer International Publishing Switzerland 2015

coordinated migration. Besides utilizing the measurements directly, the components may also derive useful knowledge by analyzing long term trends or periodic behavior observed in performance, or by comparing observed performance with model based predictions, to support proactive rather than reactive adaptation.

Many research contributions of the ASCENS project deal with awareness in general, rather than focusing on a particular aspect such as location awareness or performance awareness. These include results described in other chapters of this book – such as reasoning and learning in Chapter II.4 [23], SOTA in Chapter II.1 [4], SCEL in Chapter I.1 [41], IRM-SA in Chapter III.4 [12] – whose neutral character makes the project results more broadly applicable. Performance awareness represents a concern that cuts across these results, we therefore focus on contributions that facilitate integration of performance awareness in the broader awareness context.

The integration starts with the need for observing performance – while many tools for performance monitoring exist, the dynamic nature of ensembles requires that we are able to start and stop monitoring performance of any component on demand, with managed overhead. Towards this goal, we work on dynamic instrumentation support in the context of DiSL [37], described in Section 2.

The next requirement of integration concerns the output of monitoring – typically, this output takes the form of a series of measurements listing function durations or event times, complete with noise and outliers due to interfering activities. Such output is difficult to use, we therefore work on a formalism that allows reasoning about performance while abstracting away the technical measurement details. The formalism, SPL [9], is presented in Section 3.

Besides integration in system behavior specification, the SPL formalism can be embedded in system implementation, permitting smooth transition between the specification and the implementation. The SPL formalism also does not require differentiating between measurements of a real system and predictions of a high level model, which allows us to efficiently integrate performance modeling activities. The support for SPL at the implementation level is outlined in Section 4 and available in the form of prototype tools with open source licensing [25].

The performance modeling techniques for ensembles are introduced in Section 5. Ensemble performance modeling is challenging due to a high number of potentially interacting components. Models that track the state of individual components encounter state explosion issues. The ASCENS project investigates fluid modeling techniques that rely on symmetries in the behavior of individual components to keep the model both accurate and tractable.

Finally, Section 6 demonstrates the integration of performance awareness in the DEECo component model, and Section 7 presents the process of designing for performance adaptation with the IRM-SA method.

This is an overview text that connects multiple previously published research results of the ASCENS project. We refer the reader to the original publications as appropriate, especially where the detailed formal proofs and experimental evaluation is concerned. In particular, a broader overview of the ASCENS project can be found in [57], more information about the DiSL instrumentation framework is in [37,35], the SPL formalism description is cited and summarized from [9,25,8], the introduction on performance modeling with fluid semantics is condensed from [54], and various elements of the case study with DEECo and IRM-SA have been published in [7]. Where reasonably possible, we have also refrained from printing code, and instead encourage the reader to access our evolving research prototypes directly on the ASCENS project website.

2 Instrumentation for Performance Monitoring

The ability of ensembles to reason about the performance of the constituent components or the surrounding environment requires support for performance monitoring with particular dynamic properties. To avoid limiting the reasoning process, the ensemble must be able to monitor performance at any location that the reasoning process can consider. At the same time, the ensemble must avoid continuous monitoring of many locations, which would induce high overhead and therefore unduly influence the ensemble behavior.

The combination of the two requirements necessitates performance monitoring with dynamic instrumentation that can be inserted and removed on demand. To execute on a specific platform, such an instrumentation has to solve various issues of highly technical nature. The focus of the ASCENS project with dynamic instrumentation is on Java, a platform used in the autonomic cloud case study and the jRESP and jDEECo frameworks.

At a glance, Java provides several technologies with potential use for performance monitoring, each with a particular set of advantages and limitations. The *JVM Tool Interface* (JVMTI) [43] is a powerful native interface used for monitoring, debugging, profiling and similar application analyses. The *java.lang.instrument* API provides class-loading hooks that allow instrumenting an application using a custom Java agent. In addition, Java also provides a standard interface for delivering performance data to applications, based on *Java Management Extensions* (JMX).

To combine the available Java technologies in a robust instrumentation solution, we participate in the development of DiSL [37], a domain specific language and framework that allows to conveniently monitor an application using instrumentation. Using the aspect oriented programming model, DiSL can insert code fragments into Java applications. We use DiSL to specify and execute the performance monitoring code, whose output events are processed by the custom SPL framework, described in Sections 3 and 4.

Listing 1 illustrates a simple method invocation profiling code written in DiSL. The responsibility of the profiling code is to sample the time before and after a method invocation and print the method duration after the invocation. In real monitoring code, the duration is recorded rather than printed.

The method entry time is sampled in the onMethodEntry method. DiSL is guided by the @Before annotation to insert the entire body of onMethodEntry at

Listing 1. Simple method invocation profiling in DiSL

```
public class SimpleProfiler {

  @SyntheticLocal
  static long entryTime;

  @Before(marker=BodyMarker.class)
  static void onMethodEntry() {
    entryTime = System.nanoTime();
  }

  @After(marker=BodyMarker.class)
  static void onMethodExit(MethodStaticContext msc) {
    long exitTime = System.nanoTime();
    System.out.println(msc.thisMethodFullName()
      + " duration is "
      + (exitTime − entryTime));
  }
}
```

the beginning of each monitored method. Similarly, the method exit time is sampled and the method duration calculated in onMethodExit, which is inserted at the end of each monitored method. The use of DiSL removes the need for manual instrumentation, as well as complex handling of situations such as exceptional method exits.

DiSL provides other features useful for dynamic instrumentation, including the ability to insert monitoring routines at arbitrary code locations. DiSL contains specialized *SyntheticLocal* and *ThreadLocal* variables that allow efficient communication between the monitoring code that handles related events. To access additional event context information, DiSL introduces constructs called *StaticContext* and *DynamicContext*. *StaticContext* exposes information about location like method or class name. *DynamicContext* allows to access dynamic information like field or variable values. In the listed example, MethodStaticContext is used to retrieve a name of the profiled method.

Insertion of monitoring code can be restricted using two mechanisms, *Scopes* and *Guards*. *Scope* is a language construct for defining patterns restricting class and method instrumentation. *Guard* is a standard Java class that allows to evaluate complex instrumentation conditions during weaving. As a vital property from the performance monitoring perspective, DiSL does not insert any instrumentation besides snippets, and therefore does not incur any hidden overhead. The monitoring code is prevented from modifying the control flow of the application and the instrumentation does not violate the virtual machine hotswapping rules. As a result, the monitoring code can be dynamically inserted and removed during application execution. Finally, DiSL has very few limitations on which code can be instrumented, making it possible to monitor any arbitrary location in both the application components and the Java class library.

Related to DiSL are instrumentation frameworks such as AspectJ [33], which offers similar features but less control over the instrumentation process and limited dynamic instrumentation support. Better control over the glue code is offered by Javassisst [15] or ASM [2], however, this requires working at the bytecode level. Higher level tools, such as Perf4J [44], rely on these instrumentation frameworks for inserting probes into code. On the whole system level, generic monitoring tools such as DTrace [13] or SystemTap [49] are also available. For more thorough comparison and information about DiSL, we refer the reader to [37]. The DiSL framework is available for download at [36], the monitoring prototype is available at [48].

3 Expressing Performance Properties

In its raw form, the monitoring output contains records of performance relevant events, such as times when particular requests or responses were observed, or execution durations of particular methods. Further processing of the monitoring output depends on the context. For example, an application that needs to be aware of Service Level Agreement (SLA) violations would count those request processing times that exceed a given threshold, including potential outliers. In contrast, an application that needs to adapt an algorithm for the processor cache layout would look for minimum or median algorithm execution times, removing outliers.

To provide a suitable level of abstraction for processing the monitoring output, we introduce a formalism where the performance measurements are represented as observations of random variables and operators allow comparing measurements in a statistically rigorous manner, depending on the adopted interpretation. The formalism is called Stochastic Performance Logic (SPL) and was originally introduced in [9] in the context of software performance evaluation, with broader applications discussed in [7] and practical experience reported in [25]. See [8] for formal proofs of the SPL properties presented here.

SPL is related to previous research on languages for expressing performance properties. An early example of such a language is PSpec [45], a language for expressing performance assertions in performance tests. Unlike SPL, it requires that the performance expectations are specified against absolute bounds. Performance expectations are associated with behavior specification in PIP [46]. Assertion checking and runtime adaptation are also possible with the PA language [55]. The SPL framework implementation offers features similar to JUnit-Perf [17], an extension of JUnit [50] is for unit testing of performance.

3.1 Stochastic Performance Logic

We illustrate the SPL concepts on an example of two methods whose performance needs to be related to each other – this example finds an application in systems that adapt by choosing the faster of two method implementations or the faster of two execution platforms. We formally define the performance of a method as a random variable representing the time it takes to execute the method with random input parameters drawn from a particular distribution. The nature of the random input is formally represented by *workload class* and *method workload*. The workload is parametrized by *workload parameters*, which capture the dimensions along which the workload can be varied, e.g. array size, matrix sparsity, graph density, etc.

Definition 1. Workload class *is a function* $\mathfrak{L} : P^n \to (\Omega \to I)$, *where for a given* $\mathfrak{L}$, P *is a set of* workload parameter *values*, n *is the number of parameters*, Ω *is a sample space, and* I *is a set of objects (method input arguments) in a chosen programming language.*

Definition 2. Method workload *is a random variable* $L^{p_1,\ldots,p_n}$ *such that*

$$L^{p_1,\ldots,p_n} = \mathfrak{L}(p_1,\ldots,p_n)$$

for a given workload class $\mathfrak{L}$ *and parameters* $p_1,\ldots,p_n$.

Unlike conventional random variables that map observations to a real number, method workload is a random variable that maps observations to object instances, which serve as random input parameters for the measured method. Note that without loss of generality, we assume in the formalization that there is exactly one $\mathfrak{L}_M$ for a particular method M and that M has just one input argument.

Definition 3. *Let* $M(in)$ *be a method in a chosen programming language and* $in \in I$ *its input argument. Then method performance* $P_M : P^n \to (\Omega \to \mathbb{R})$ *is a function that for given workload parameters* $p_1,\ldots,p_n$ *returns a random variable, whose observations correspond to execution duration of method* M *with input parameters obtained from observations of* $L_M^{p_1,\ldots,p_n} = \mathfrak{L}_M(p_1,\ldots,p_n)$, *where* $\mathfrak{L}_M$ *is the workload class for method* M.

To facilitate comparison of method performance, SPL is based on regular arithmetics, in particular on axioms of equality and inequality adapted for the method performance domain.

Definition 4. *SPL is a many-sorted first-order logic defined as follows:*

- *There is a set* $FunPe$ *of function symbols for method performances with arities* $P^n \to (\Omega \to \mathbb{R})$ *for* $n \in \mathbb{N}^+$.
- *There is a set* $FunT$ *of function symbols for performance observation transformation functions with arity* $\mathbb{R} \to \mathbb{R}$.
- *The logic has equality and inequality relations* $=, \leq$ *for arity* $P \times P$.
- *The logic has equality and inequality relations* $\leq_{p(tl,tr)}$, $=_{p(tl,tr)}$ *with arity* $(\Omega \to \mathbb{R}) \times (\Omega \to \mathbb{R})$, *where* $tl, tr \in FunT$.
- *Quantifiers (both universal and existential) are allowed only over finite subsets of* P.

– *For $x, y, z \in P$ and $P_M, P_N \in FunPe$, the logic has the following axioms:*

$$x \leq x \tag{1}$$

$$(x \leq y \wedge y \leq x) \leftrightarrow x = y \tag{2}$$

$$(x \leq y \wedge y \leq z) \rightarrow x \leq z \tag{3}$$

For each pair $tl, tr \in FunT$ such that

$$\forall o \in \mathbb{R} : tl(o) \leq tr(o), \text{there is an axiom} \tag{4}$$
$$P_M(x_1, \ldots, x_m) \leq_{p(tl,tr)} P_M(x_1, \ldots, x_m)$$

$$(P_M(x_1, \ldots, x_m) \leq_{p(tm,tn)} P_N(y_1, \ldots, y_n) \wedge$$
$$P_N(y_1, \ldots, y_n) \leq_{p(tn,tm)} P_M(x_1, \ldots, x_m)) \leftrightarrow \tag{5}$$
$$P_M(x_1, \ldots, x_m) =_{p(tm,tn)} P_N(y_1, \ldots, y_n)$$

Using SPL, we can express assumptions about method performance. The lambda notation [3] with $id = \lambda x.x$ is introduced for brevity:

Example 1. "On arrays of 100, 500, 1000, 5000, and 10000 elements, the sorting algorithm A is at most 5% faster and at most 5% slower than sorting algorithm B."

$$\forall n \in \{100, 500, 1000, 5000, 10000\} :$$
$$P_A(n) \leq_{p(id, \lambda x.1.05x)} P_B(n) \wedge P_B(n) \leq_{p(id, \lambda x.0.95x)} P_A(n)$$

3.2 Logic Interpretations

To ensure correspondence between the SPL formula in Example 1 and its textual description, we need to introduce the appropriate semantic that provides the intended SPL interpretation. In [9], we first introduce an expected-value-based interpretation, where the SPL relations are defined over expected values of the random variables that represent execution duration. This interpretation is useful when the expected values are known, such as when performance is computed using analytical models. When performance is observed through monitoring, an interpretation based on the observed samples is needed.

Simple Sample-Based Interpretation. To formulate the sample-based interpretation from [9], we first fix the set of observations for which the relations will be interpreted. We define an *experiment*, denoted $\mathcal{E}$, as a finite set of observations of method performances under a particular method workload.

Definition 5. *Experiment $\mathcal{E}$ is a collection of $\mathcal{O}_{P_M(p_1, \ldots, p_m)}$, where*

$$\mathcal{O}_{P_M(p_1, \ldots, p_m)} = \{P_M^1(p_1, \ldots, p_m), \ldots, P_M^V(p_1, \ldots, p_m)\}$$

is a set of V observations of method performance P_M subjected to workload $L_M^{p_1, \ldots, p_m}$, and where $P_M^i(p_1, \ldots, p_m)$ denotes i-th observation of performance of method M.

For a particular experiment, we define the sample-based interpretation of SPL.

Definition 6. *Let $tm, tn : \mathbb{R} \to \mathbb{R}$ be performance observation transformation functions, P_M and P_N be method performances, $x_1, \ldots, x_m, y_1, \ldots, y_n$ be workload parameters, and $\alpha \in \langle 0, 0.5 \rangle$ be a fixed significance level.*

For a given experiment $\mathcal{E}$, the relations $\leq_{p(tm,tn)}$ and $=_{p(tm,tn)}$ are interpreted as follows:

- $P_M(x_1, \ldots, x_m) \leq_{p(tm,tn)} P_N(y_1, \ldots, y_n)$ *iff the null hypothesis*

$$H_0 : E(tm(P_M^i(x_1, \ldots, x_m))) \leq E(tn(P_N^j(y_1, \ldots, y_n)))$$

cannot be rejected by one-sided Welch's t-test [56] at significance level α based on the observations gathered in the experiment $\mathcal{E}$;
- $P_M(x_1, \ldots, x_m) =_{p(tm,tn)} P_N(y_1, \ldots, y_n)$ *iff the null hypothesis*

$$H_0 : E(tm(P_M^i(x_1, \ldots, x_m))) = E(tn(P_N^j(y_1, \ldots, y_n)))$$

cannot be rejected by two-sided Welch's t-test at significance level 2α based on the observations gathered in the experiment $\mathcal{E}$;

where $E(tm(P_M^i(\ldots)))$ and $E(tn(P_N^j(\ldots)))$ denote the mean value of performance observations transformed by function tm or tn, respectively.

The sample-based interpretation is reasonable for situations where it is possible to collect a relatively large number of samples to be used for the statistical testing. Experience suggests tens of thousands of samples suffice [25]. When SPL is used to make adaptation decisions at runtime, the number of collected samples might be smaller by several orders of magnitude, and the individual samples might suffer from many kinds of disruptive artefacts.

We discuss two kinds of disruptive artefacts – initial transient conditions and run-to-run fluctuations. We assume that system execution consists of stationary episodes termed *runs*.[3] Within a run, system performance would be considered stable, except for initial transient conditions disrupting the run. From run to run, system performance can exhibit fluctuations that are measurable and statistically significant, but not controllable and not significant from the adaptation perspective [30]. The interpretations in the following sections explicitly handle runs.

3.3 Handling Initial Transient Conditions

On many computing platforms, runs are exposed to mechanisms that may introduce transient execution time changes. Measurements performed under these

---

[3] Practical reasons for the existence of runs are for example rejuvenation episodes with virtual machine restarts.

conditions are typically denoted as warmup measurements, in contrast to steady state measurements.[4]

One well known mechanism that introduces warmup is just-in-time compilation. With just-in-time compilation, the method whose execution time is measured is initially executed by an interpreter or compiled into machine code with selected optimizations based on static information. During execution, the same method may be compiled with different optimizations based on dynamic information and therefore exhibit different execution times. This effect is illustrated on Figure 1.[5]

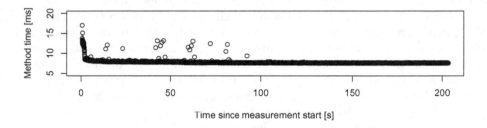

Fig. 1. Example of how just-in-time compilation influences method execution time

The warmup measurements are not necessarily representative of steady state performance and are therefore typically avoided. Sometimes, such measurements can be identified by analyzing the collected observations. Intuitively, long sequences of observations with zero slope (such as those on the right side of Figure 1) likely originate from steady state measurements, in contrast to initial sequences of observations with downward slope (such as those on the left side of Figure 1), which likely come from warmup. This intuition is not always reliable, because the warmup measurements may exhibit very long periods of apparent stability between changes. These would look like steady state measurements when analyzing the collected observations. Furthermore, the mechanisms that introduce warmup may not have reasonable bounds on warmup duration. As one example, just-in-time compilation can be associated with events such as change in branch behavior or change in polymorphic type use, which may occur at any time during measurement.

---

[4] The illustrative measurements in this section were collected on an Intel Xeon E5-2660 machine with 2 sockets, 8 cores per socket, 2 threads per core, running at 2.2 GHz, 32 kB L1, 256 kB L2 and 20 MB L3 caches, 48 GB RAM, running 64 bit Fedora 20 with OpenJDK 1.7.

[5] The method is SAXBuilder::build, used to build a DOM tree from a byte array stream, from the JDOM library [29]. The selection is ad hoc, made to illustrate practical behavior.

Given these obstacles, we believe that warmup should not be handled at the level of logic interpretation. Instead, knowledge of the relevant mechanisms should be used to identify and discard observations collected during warmup.

In addition to the transient initial conditions, the logic interpretation has to cope with run-to-run fluctuations. In contemporary computer systems, the execution conditions include factors that stay relatively stable within each run but differ between runs – for example, a large part of the process memory layout on both virtual and physical address level is determined at the beginning of each run. When these factors cannot be reasonably controlled, as is the case with the memory layout example, each run will execute with possibly different conditions, which can affect the measurements. The memory layout example is one where a significant impact was observed in multiple experiments [30,40]. Therefore, no single run is entirely representative of the observable performance.

A common solution to the problem of changing conditions between runs is collecting observations from multiple runs. In practice, each run takes some time before performing steady state measurements, the number of observations per run will therefore be high but the number of runs will be low. In this situation, the sample variance S^2 (when computed from all the observations together) is not a reliable estimate of the population variance σ^2 and the sample-based logic interpretation becomes more prone to false positives, rejecting performance equality even between measurements that differ only due to changing conditions between runs. The problem can be avoided by introducing a sensitivity limit [25], or by explicitly considering runs in the logic interpretations, done next.

3.4 Parametric Mean Value Interpretation

From the statistical perspective, measurements taken within a run have a conditional distribution depending on a particular run. This is typically exhibited as a common bias shared by all measurements within the particular run [31]. Assuming that each run has the same number of observations, the result statistics collected by a benchmark can be modeled as the sample mean of sample means of observations per run (transformed by tm as necessary):

$$\overline{M} = \frac{1}{ro} \sum_{i=1}^{r} \sum_{j=1}^{o} tm(P_M^{i,j}(x_1, \ldots, x_m))$$

where $P_M^{i,j}(x_1, \ldots, x_m)$ denotes the j-th observation in the i-th run, r denotes the number of runs and o denotes the number of observations in a run.

From the Central Limit Theorem, $\overline{M}$ and the sample means of individual runs $\overline{M}_i = \frac{1}{o}\sum_{j=1}^{o} tm(P_M^{i,j}(x_1, \ldots, x_m))$ are asymptotically normal. In particular, a run mean converges to the distribution $N(\mu_i, \sigma_i^2/n)$. Due to the properties of the normal distribution, the overall sample mean then converges to the distribution

$$\overline{M} \sim N\left(\mu, \frac{\rho^2}{r} + \frac{\overline{\sigma^2}}{ro}\right)$$

where $\overline{\sigma^2}$ denotes the average of run variances and ρ^2 denotes the variance of run means [31].

This can be easily turned into a statistical test of equality of two means, used by the interpretation defined below. Note that since the variances are not known, they have to be approximated by sample variances. That makes the test formula only approximate, though sufficiently precise for large r and o [31].

Definition 7. *Let $tm, tn : \mathbb{R} \to \mathbb{R}$ be performance observation transformation functions, P_M and P_N be method performances collected over r_M, r_N runs, each run having o_M, o_N observations respectively, $x_1, \ldots, x_m, y_1, \ldots, y_n$ be the workload parameters, and $\alpha \in \langle 0, 0.5 \rangle$ be a fixed significance level.*

For a given experiment $\mathcal{E}$, the relations $\leq_{p(tm,tn)}$ and $=_{p(tm,tn)}$ are interpreted as follows:

– $P_M(x_1, \ldots, x_m) \leq_{p(tm,tn)} P_N(y_1, \ldots, y_n)$ *iff*

$$\overline{M} - \overline{N} \leq z_{(1-\alpha)} \sqrt{\frac{o_M R_M^2 + \overline{S_M^2}}{r_M o_M} + \frac{o_N R_N^2 + \overline{S_N^2}}{r_N o_N}}$$

where $z_{(1-\alpha)}$ is the $1 - \alpha$ quantile of the normal distribution,

$$\overline{S_M^2} = \frac{1}{r_M(o_M - 1)} \sum_{i=1}^{r} \sum_{j=1}^{o} \left(tm(P_M^{i,j}(x_1, \ldots, x_m)) - \frac{1}{o} \sum_{k=1}^{o} tm(P_M^{i,k}(x_1, \ldots, x_m)) \right)^2$$

$$R_M^2 = \frac{1}{r_M - 1} \sum_{i=1}^{r} \left[\left(\frac{1}{n} \sum_{j=1}^{o} tm(P_M^{i,j}(x_1, \ldots, x_m)) \right) - \overline{M} \right]^2$$

and similarly for $\overline{S_N^2}$ and R_N^2.
– $P_M(x_1, \ldots, x_m) =_{p(tm,tn)} P_N(y_1, \ldots, y_n)$ *iff*

$$\left| \overline{M} - \overline{N} \right| \leq z_{(1-\alpha)} \sqrt{\frac{o_M R_M^2 + \overline{S_M^2}}{r_M o_M} + \frac{o_N R_N^2 + \overline{S_N^2}}{r_N o_N}}$$

3.5 Non-parametric Mean Value Interpretation

The interpretation given by Definition 7 requires a certain minimal number of runs to work reliably. This is because the distribution of run means $\overline{M}_i = o^{-1} \sum_{j=1}^{o} tm(P_M^{i,j}(x_1, \ldots, x_m))$ is not normal even for relatively large values of o – illustrated on Figure 2.[6] Again, for a small number of runs this typically results in a high number of false positives, we therefore provide an alternative

---

[6] Each run collects $o = 20000$ observations after a warmup of 40000 observations. The method is SAXBuilder::build, used to build a DOM tree from a byte array stream, from the JDOM library [29]. The selection is ad hoc, made to illustrate practical behavior.

interpretation that uses the distribution of $\overline{M}_i$ directly. It works reliably with any number of runs (including only one run), however, the price for this improvement is that the test statistics has to be learned first (e.g. by observing performance across multiple runs of similarly behaving methods).

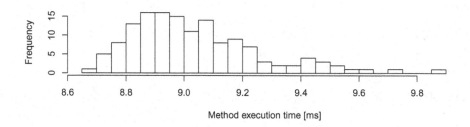

Fig. 2. Example histogram of run means from multiple measurement runs of the same method and workload

We assume that all observations $P_M^{i,j}(x_1, \ldots, x_m)$ in a run i are identically and independently distributed with a conditional distribution depending on a hidden random variable C. We denote this distribution as $B_M^{C=c}$, meaning the distribution of observations in a run conditioned by drawing some particular c from the hidden random variable C.

We further define the distributions of the test statistics as follows:

- $B_{\overline{M}, r_M, o_M}$ is the distribution function of

$$(r_M o_M)^{-1} \sum_{i=1}^{r_M} \sum_{j=1}^{o_M} tm(\dot{P}_M^{i,j}(x_1, \ldots, x_m))$$

where $\dot{P}_M^{i,j}(x_1, \ldots, x_m)$ denotes a random variable with distribution $B_M^{C=c}$ for c drawn randomly once for each i. In other words, $B_{\overline{M}, r_M, o_M}$ denotes a distribution of a mean computed from r_M runs of o_M observations each.

- $B_{\overline{M}, r_M, o_M - \overline{N}, r_M, o_M}$ is the distribution function of the difference $\tilde{M} - \tilde{N}$, where $\tilde{M}$ is a random variable with distribution $B_{\overline{M}, r_M, o_M}$ and $\tilde{N}$ is a random variable with distribution $B_{\overline{N}, r_N, o_N}$.

After adjusting the distributions $B_{\overline{M}, r_M, o_M}$ and $B_{\overline{N}, r_N, o_N}$ by shifting to have an equal mean, the performance comparison can be defined as:

- $P_M(x_1, \ldots, x_m) \leq_{p(tm, tn)} P_N(y_1, \ldots, y_n)$ iff

$$\overline{M} - \overline{N} \leq B_{\overline{M}, r_M, o_M - \overline{N}, r_N, o_N}^{-1} (1 - \alpha)$$

where $\overline{M}$ denotes the sample mean of $tm(P_M(x_1, \ldots, x_m))$, $\overline{N}$ is defined similarly, and $B^{-1}_{\overline{M},r_M,o_M-\overline{N},r_N,o_N}$ denotes the inverse of the distribution function $B_{\overline{M},r_M,o_M-\overline{N},r_N,o_N}$ (i.e. for a given quantile, it returns a value).

- $P_M(x_1, \ldots, x_m) =_{p(tm,tn)} P_N(y_1, \ldots, y_n)$ iff

$$B^{-1}_{\overline{M},r_M,M-\overline{N},r_N,o_N}(\alpha) \leq \overline{M} - \overline{N} \leq B^{-1}_{\overline{M},r_M,o_M,-\overline{N},r_N,o_N}(1-\alpha)$$

An important problem is that the distribution functions $B_{\overline{M},r_M,o_M}$, $B_{\overline{N},r_N,o_N}$, and consequently $B_{\overline{M},r_M,o_M-\overline{N},r_N,o_N}$ are unknown. To get over this problem, we approximate the B-distributions in a non-parametric way by bootstrap and Monte-Carlo simulations [47]. This can be done either by using observations $P_M^{i,j}(x_1, \ldots, x_m)$ directly, or by approximating from observations of other methods whose performance behaves similarly between runs.

Finally, we define a non-parametric interpretation of the logic as follows:

Definition 8. *Let* $tm, tn : \mathbb{R} \to \mathbb{R}$ *be performance observation transformation functions,* P_M *and* P_N *be method performances,* $x_1, \ldots, x_m, y_1, \ldots, y_n$ *be workload parameters,* $\alpha \in \langle 0, 0.5 \rangle$ *be a fixed significance level, and let* X, Y *be methods (including* M *and* N*) whose performance observations are used to approximate the distributions of* P_M *and* P_N*, respectively.*

For a given experiment $\mathcal{E}$*, the relations* $\leq_{p(tm,tn)}$ *and* $=_{p(tm,tn)}$ *are interpreted as follows:*

- $P_M(x_1, \ldots, x_m) \leq_{p(tm,tn)} P_N(y_1, \ldots, y_n)$ *iff*

$$\overline{M} - \overline{N} \leq B^{*-1}_{\overline{X},r_X,o_X-\overline{Y},r_Y,o_Y}(1-\alpha)$$

- $P_M(x_1, \ldots, x_m) =_{p(tm,tn)} P_N(y_1, \ldots, y_n)$ *iff*

$$B^{*-1}_{\overline{X},r_X,o_X-\overline{Y},r_Y,o_Y}(\alpha) \leq \overline{M} - \overline{N} \leq B^{*-1}_{\overline{X},r_X,o_X-\overline{Y},r_Y,o_Y}(1-\alpha)$$

4 Coding for Performance Awareness

The basic role of SPL is to provide a versatile mechanism to express performance properties at various stages of the software development process – the design requirements, the developer assumptions, the test conditions, the health indicators, the adaptation triggers, and so on. Every specialized use of the formalism brings additional considerations, which must be addressed to achieve fitness for purpose. Here, we outline how the formalism is connected to data and code in the implementation environment, additional considerations in the context of adaptive systems are discussed in [10], the context of software documentation is examined in [26], software testing in [25].

4.1   Performance Data Sources

The introduction of SPL in Section 3 formalized performance as the execution time of a particular method under a particular workload, as collected by performance monitoring from Section 2. However, SPL provides considerable freedom as far as the input data is concerned. For example, in the autonomic cloud case study from Chapter IV.3 [38], applications migrate from busy to idle nodes and it is therefore useful to compare the system load metric to identify the busy and idle nodes.

The system load is typically represented as the number of ready threads on the node. If this number is normalized to the number of processors, it can be used as a criterion in a distributed environment for finding the least loaded machine. The formula for deciding whether machine A is less loaded than machine B then remains rather simple, $L_A < L_B$. When comparing the load, we can rely on a trivial SPL interpretation – both L_A and L_B are scalars and plain comparison can therefore be used. If multiple observations of load are available, the comparison can rely on any of the sample-based interpretations. We note that the two cases differ – one is concerned with the current system load, one evaluates the mean system load over a longer time period. There are other practical differences – for example, when a new observation arrives, evaluating the formula with sample-based interpretation is more resource intensive than evaluating with plain comparison. For environments with restricted resources, this can be important.

More systematically, applying SPL to data other than method execution times gives rise to the concept of *data sources*. The performance data is abstracted as a random variable and the data source is responsible for providing information on the random variable that the particular interpretation requires – for example, the expected value for the expected-value-based interpretation, the sample mean $\overline{X}$, sample size V_X and sample variance S_X^2 for the simple sample-based interpretation, and so on. Introducing data sources provides an important level of abstraction in the software development process. In particular, the same SPL formulas can be used in multiple software development phases from modeling to execution – the only difference is what data source is *bound* to the actual random variables in the SPL formula.

We illustrate the concept on an example of an adaptive application. Consider a problem that can be solved using two different algorithms, A and B, with A performing better on larger and B on smaller inputs. The adaptation consists of choosing the better performing algorithm depending on the actual input size. The adaptation is simple when the limit size – size s_{limit} such that A performs better for inputs larger than s_{limit} and B for inputs smaller than s_{limit} – is known, however, s depends on the execution platform and therefore cannot be included in the application design. Instead, an equally simple SPL formula can be used to describe the condition for selecting particular algorithm for given input size s – we use A if $A(s) \leq B(s)$ and B otherwise.

In the early application design phase, modeling might be used to assess the application behavior – and because data on the actual performance would not yet be available, the model would bind $A(s)$ and $B(s)$ to data sources that roughly estimate performance from the algorithm complexity. In the testing phases of the application development process, the same formula would be bound to data sources that measure the performance of the (already implemented) algorithms in a potentially restricted testing environment. The formula would be used as a base indicator that the implementation works as expected. Where needed, artificial data injection (similar to fault injection) through the same data sources could be used to test corner cases. Finally, at runtime, the same formula would be bound to data sources collecting runtime measurements, allowing the application to adapt itself to the actual timing of the particular execution platform.

4.2 Language Integration Support

The outlined uses of SPL require integrating the support for performance monitoring and formula evaluation with data source binding in a particular implementation environment. In the ASCENS project, the choice for the prototype integration environment is Java– it is a well-known multi-platform language that is used in the case studies and in the jRESP and jDEECo frameworks. We note, however, that the choice of Java is without loss of generality – in principle, most methods developed in the ASCENS project are implementation-language-agnostic.

To indicate performance properties (requirements, expectations, conditions) at code level, SPL formulas are attached in the form of annotations to the relevant method, as outlined in the example in Listing 2.

Listing 2. Java annotation expressing performance requirements

```
@SPL(
    methods = "javaSort=java.util.Arrays#sort(long[])",
    generators = "data=SPL:LongUniform('0;1000')",
    formula = "for ( i {100, 1000, 10000} ) SELF[data](i) <=(2, 1) javaSort[data](i)"
)
public void fasterSort(long[] data) {
    // Measured method ...
}
```

The annotation states that *fasterSort* should be at least two times faster than *javaSort*, a library implementation. The generator provides the workload that is being measured, that is, the objects used as arguments when calling the measured methods.

The annotations are suitable for use by external tools that evaluate the performance properties at development time or deployment time – such as with testing, outlined in [25]. It is also possible to include the formula evaluation in the component system runtime, where it can direct mechanisms related to component lifecycle or connector binding, as outlined in [6].

Besides the static language integration based on annotations, we have also designed an API for evaluating SPL formulas directly from application code at runtime. Listing 3 depicts a code fragment that uses the API to check whether a method execution time does not exceed the given threshold – where the example simply prints a warning, an adaptive application would take an action to remedy the problem.

Listing 3. Checking method execution time

```
/*
 * Preparation.
 * The SPL.instrument() creates the data source and also
 * adds the measuring code automatically to the measured
 * method.
 */
SourceData data = SPL.instrument("pkg.MyClass#myMethod");
Formula formula = SPL.createFormula("A < 100");
formula.bind("A", data);

/*
 * Check the formula (once enough samples were collected).
 */
if (formula.evaluate() == Result.FALSE) {
    logger.warn("myMethod is too slow!");
}
```

The *SPL.instrument()* method uses DiSL, outlined in Section 2, to instrument the running Java application with code that measures the method execution time. The instrumentation is also performed on demand, whenever the need to measure a particular method arises – this happens when an annotation uses a formula to refer to the method performance. In addition to plain Java, the prototype implementation includes support for OSGi, where the use of class loaders for component isolation poses additional technical challenges.

4.3   Integrating Predictive Models

A degree of performance awareness can be achieved entirely based on the knowledge of current and past performance. A simple example of this is a server that increases the number of threads in reaction to the observed response time using a simple rule – when the response time grows, more threads are added. The SPL formulas used to express this rule only need to rely on current and past measurements, provided by the appropriate data sources.

In some situations, performance awareness can augment the information about current and past events by using predictive models – following the example, it may be possible to use trend estimation methods to predict a rise in request frequency and adjust the number of service threads accordingly [19]. This option is handled in the support for performance awareness by presenting predictive models as data sources – that way, the same SPL formulas that were used to react to current events can react to predicted behavior.

The integration of predictive models on an application migration example is exemplified Section 6, where the Planner may rely on modeling to pick a suitable deployment alternative. Relying on the modular solution with pluggable data sources simplifies the technical integration of such models in the SPL framework.

5 Modeling Performance

Reasoning about the performance of ensembles introduces a level of difficulty due fact to the system under study comprises of potentially many interacting components. To cope with this inherent complexity, in the ASCENS project we followed an established line of research on finding symmetries at the model level which induce a suitable coarsening of the state space that retains some information about the original one. In this respect, the classical results on bisimilarity allow to relate processes of possibly different state space sizes which are however equivalent with respect to an external observer [39]. Analogous notions have been developed form Markovian process algebra with a discrete-state Markov chain semantics. For instance, the notions of Markovian bisimulation for MTIPP [20] and strong equivalence for PEPA [22] are equivalence relations that give an exactly aggregated Markov chain in terms of the theory of CTMC *lumpability* [5].

A similar line of research in the ASCENS project leads to exact as well as approximate notions of aggregation for Markovian process algebra. Different from the listed literature, we targeted *fluid semantics*. This has recently emerged as an alternative to the classical Markovian semantics, describing the model dynamics in terms of a system of ordinary differential equations (ODEs) [21,34]. These can be interpreted as a deterministic approximation to the expectation of the Markov chain [14,16,18,51]. When the model under consideration consists of many copies of processes in parallel, the ODE system size is independent of the multiplicities of such copies. This is considerably more convenient than the Markovian representation which suffers from the well-known problem of *state explosion*, where the number of states grows exponentially (in the worst case) with the number of concurrent processes in the model.

5.1 Fluid Process Algebra

The motivating observation here is that not all models of ensemble-based systems enjoy a compact ODE description [53]. Indeed, the problem of aggregating large-scale models based on ODEs has attracted the attention of researchers in a variety of other disciplines including control theory [1], theoretical ecology [28], and chemical engineering [42]. Here we consider a *Fluid Process Algebra*, presented in [52] as a fragment of the Markovian process algebra PEPA [22].

Exact Fluid Lumpability. In [52] we define the notion of *exact fluid lumpability* (EFL). It establishes an equivalence relation between processes such that their associated ODE solutions have equal trajectories whenever they are initialized with the same conditions. To be concrete yet informal for the purpose of overviewing our results, let us consider the process

$$\left(P_1[N_1] \parallel_K P_2[N_2] \parallel_K \cdots \parallel_K P_D[N_D]\right) \parallel_L Q[M] \tag{6}$$

where, for all $1 \leq i \leq D$, P_i is some sequential component that is replicated N_i times, and $\parallel_K$ is the parallel operator, parameterised by an action set K, in a CSP-like fashion. EFL may essentially reduce the analysis of such a model by considering the fluid trajectory of a *representative* P_i, which is shown to be equal to that of any other P_j if, for all $1 \leq i, j \leq D$, it holds that $N_i = N_j$ and P_i and P_j are isomorphic. Thus, denoting by $V_S(t)$ the ODE solution related to the sequential component S, EFL would yield $V_{P_i}(t) = V_{P_j}(t)$ for all t. EFL has been exploited in [53] as a building block to automatically simplify models that feature a pattern of *replicated composites* – large ensembles of composite processes which themselves consist of replicated copies of other composites, with an arbitrary level of nesting. However, in general symmetries are required both at the level of the sequential component and at the compositional level, by ensuring that all populations have the same size.

Taking EFL as the starting point of our investigation, it is possible to extend it along two orthogonal directions [54]. In one direction, we define a new notion of lumpability, called *ordinary fluid lumpability* (OFL), which relaxes assumptions on certain symmetries whilst still guaranteeing exactness of the aggregated system. In the other direction, we consider approximate versions of both EFL and OFL which can yield coarser aggregations, at the cost of losing exactness.

Ordinary Fluid Lumpability (OFL). Similarly to EFL, ordinary fluid lumpability considers symmetry through isomorphism at the sequential level; thus, it still requires that P_i and P_j be isomorphic for all i, j. However, it allows *heterogeneity* at the compositional level: in the example above, it may yield an exactly aggregated ODE system even if $N_i \neq N_j$. However, unlike EFL, where all the trajectories of the original ODE system can be obtained from the solution of the aggregate, in OFL the aggregate gives the exact sum of the solutions of its parts, but their individual trajectories cannot be recovered. Thus, for instance, OFL would define an aggregate ODE for some variable $W_P(t)$ and show that $W_P(t) = V_{P_1}(t) + V_{P_2}(t) + \ldots + V_{P_D}(t)$. More precisely, OFL identifies an aggregate ODE system where the solution to each ODE is the linear combination of solutions of ODEs belonging to the original system.

Approximate Aggregations. To relax the requirement on the *exactness* of the aggregation, we study ε-variants of both EFL and OFL as a means of relaxing symmetries at the sequential level. These variants allow non-isomorphic processes to be aggregated if there exists a *perturbation* in the rates that makes them isomorphic. For instance, let us take $P_i \xrightarrow{(\alpha, r)} P_k$ and $P_j \xrightarrow{(\alpha, r+\varepsilon)} P_k$, for some P_k, where the edges give the action/rate pair, specifying a label that identifies the activity and the rate of an exponential distribution determining its duration, with $r > 0$ and $\varepsilon > 0$. Then, these processes cannot be aggregated with either EFL or OFL because $\varepsilon > 0$ does not make them isomorphic. However, there exists a perturbation on the parameters of P_i and P_j that makes them isomorphic. For instance, one can take $P_j \xrightarrow{(\alpha,r)} P_k$ such that ε represents the degree of such perturbation. In fact, there exist infinitely many such perturbations. For instance, it would be possible to consider $P_i \xrightarrow{(\alpha,r+\varepsilon/2)} P_k$ and $P_j \xrightarrow{(\alpha,r+\varepsilon/2)} P_k$. In all these cases, it would hold that the model is ε-ordinarily fluid lumpable for any N_i and N_j. Clearly, the aggregated system will not be in exact correspondence with the original one. However, a theoretical bound shows that the aggregation error depends *linearly* in the intensity of the perturbation $|\varepsilon|$.

Exhibiting such near-symmetries may appear quite limiting for practical applications; however, there are models in the literature that do exhibit this characteristic. This has been recently studied also in [27], where a similar notion of approximate aggregation has been presented.

Characterisation of ODE Aggregations. When the aggregation is induced by a process algebra, it is possible to study the nature of such aggregation in two main ways.

1. The ODE aggregations can be induced by suitable notions of behavioural equivalence, which turn out to be congruences with respect to the parallel operator of Fluid Process Algebra.
2. We consider the nonrestrictive (syntactic) notion of model well-posedness originally defined in [52]. Under this assumption, processes which can be aggregated according to either EFL or OFL are related by *semi-isomorphism*. This is an extension of graph isomorphism to labelled transition systems with transition multi-sets, which does not distinguish between the multiplicity of arcs connecting two nodes whenever the total rate is the same. Furthermore, under well-posedness it holds that ε-EFL and ε-OFL imply the behavioural notion of ε-semi-isomorphism, the natural extension of semi-isomorphism which relates graphs up to changes in the transition rates. At the same time, however, processes that are semi-isomorphic cannot be aggregated according to EFL or OFL in general, essentially because two semi-isomorphic processes may be present in different contexts, which may impact their ODE expressions due to possibly different synchronisations.

5.2   Aggregation Error

To provide some numerical evidence of the aggregation error introduced by ε-EFL and ε-OFL, let us consider the model in (6) where the sequential components are defined, for $1 \leq d \leq D$, as

$$P_d \stackrel{def}{=} (\alpha, r_d).P_d' \qquad P_d' \stackrel{def}{=} (\beta, s).P_d \qquad Q \stackrel{def}{=} (\alpha, r).Q' \qquad Q' \stackrel{def}{=} (\gamma, w).Q \ . \qquad (7)$$

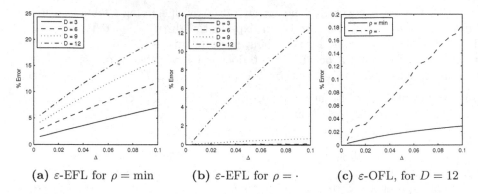

(a) ε-EFL for $\rho = $ min   (b) ε-EFL for $\rho = \cdot$ (c) ε-OFL, for $D = 12$

Fig. 3. Numerical evaluation of ε-lumpability

These model two agents, P_d and Q, which cycle through states P'_d and Q', respectively. With this choice, the model can be interpreted as a high-level description of a *multi-class* service system where one resource, modelled by Q, can be accessed by different classes of clients, P_d, each with its own service demand characterized by r_d. We arbitrarily chose the rates of the independent actions, fixing $s = 0.5$ and $w = 15.0$, while we varied the values of r_d.

Our intent is to approximate ODEs systems where P_i and P_j are aggregated for some $1 \leq i, j \leq D$. Thus, in order to obtain non-isomorphic sequential components, we made r_d dependent on $1 \leq d \leq D$, setting $r_d = 1.0 + (d-1)\Delta$. Here, Δ is a parameter that was varied between 0.0005 and 0.1000 at 0.005 steps in our tests. In this way, it is directly proportional to the intensity of the perturbation. For instance, in a model with $D = 12$ and $\Delta = 0.1000$, we have $r_{10}/r_1 = 2.1$, showing a non-negligible difference between the rate parameters of P_1 and those of P_{10}. In order to enforce asymmetry also in the initial populations, we made the initial populations of P_d components dependent on d. Specifically, we considered initial conditions defined as $V_{P_d}(0) = 200 + (d-1)$, $V_{P'_d}(0) = 0$, $V_Q(0) = 400$, and $V_{Q'}(0) = 0$; thus, the components have initial populations separated by a few percent. For evaluating both ε-EFL and ε-OFL, we considered a perturbed model where r_d in (7) was made independent of d and set equal to the average value in the original model, i.e.,

$$\tilde{r}_d = 1.0 + (\Delta/D) \sum_{d=1}^{D}(d-1).$$

In such a perturbed model, all P_d sequential components are now isomorphic.

Assessment of ε-EFL We considered different values of D to numerically evaluate the impact of different initial conditions on the quality of the aggregation of ε-EFL. Specifically, we set $D = 3, 6, 9, 12$. Let us recall that (6) has $2D + 2$ ODEs. For each value of D and Δ, the model solution was compared against that of the perturbed model with the initial conditions set as follows: $V^{\varepsilon}_{\tilde{P}_d}(0) = $

$200 + (1/D) \sum_{d=1}^{D}(d-1)$, $V_{P_d'}^{\varepsilon}(0) = 0$, $V_Q^{\varepsilon}(0) = 400$, and $V_{Q'}^{\varepsilon}(0) = 0$. In this way, the initial population of P_d sequential components is made independent from d and is set equal to the average initial population across d, similarly to what done for the perturbation on r_d. It follows that, in the perturbed model, $\{\{P_1, \ldots, P_D\}, \{Q\}\}$ is an exactly fluid lumpable partition. Hence, the original model and the perturbed one are related by ε-EFL. Both models were solved over the time interval $[0; 100]$, so as to ensure convergence of the ODE solution to equilibrium for all parameterisations considered. Solutions were registered at 0.2 time steps. The approximation relative error for ε-EFL is as:

$$100 \times \max_{t \in \{0, 0.02, \ldots, 100\}} \max_{S \in \{P_1, \ldots, P_d, Q\}} \frac{|V_S(t) - V_S^{\varepsilon}(t)|}{V_S(0)},$$

where $V_S(t)$ is the solution of the original model and $V_S^{\varepsilon}(t)$ is the corresponding solution in the perturbed one. The absolute difference is normalised with respect to the total population of the component.

The results are presented in Figures 3a and 3b, for two distinct interpretations of the synchronisation operator. The first one defines synchronisation as the minimum of the rates of the synchronising components ($\rho = \min$) while the second one takes the product of their rates ($\rho = \cdot$). In both cases, it is possible to observe a linear growth of the error as a function of the perturbation Δ. For any fixed D, the case $\rho = \cdot$ yields more accurate aggregates than $\rho = \min$, with particularly small errors for $D = 3, 6, 9$. These tests show that even non-negligible perturbations (i.e., up to Δ ca 0.04) can produce acceptable errors (i.e., less than 10%) in practice.

Assessment of ε-OFL Analogous tests were performed for the assessment of ε-OFL, since in the perturbed model $\{\{P_1, \ldots, P_D\}, \{Q\}\}$ is also an ordinarily fluid lumpable partition. We analysed only the case $D = 12$, which yielded the worst accuracy in ε-EFL; the other cases showed the same errors (up to numerical precision of the ODE solver). A different error metric was used, to reflect the fact that OFL involves sums of ODE solutions of the unaggregated model. The approximation relative error is defined as:

$$100 \times \max_{t \in \{0, 0.02, \ldots, 100\}} \max \left\{ \frac{\left| \sum_{d=1}^{D} V_{P_d}(t) - W_P^{\varepsilon}(t) \right|}{\sum_{d=1}^{D} V_{P_d}(0)}, \frac{|V_Q(t) - W_Q^{\varepsilon}(t)|}{V_Q(0)} \right\}.$$

The numerical results are shown in Figure 3c. Overall, both for $\rho = \min$ and $\rho = \cdot$, the ε-OFL appears to be much more robust, with negligible errors across all values of Δ.

6   Performance Aware Ensembles

We present performance aware ensembles in the context of the cloud case study from Chapter IV.3 [38]. We assume a heterogeneous cloud where mobile devices, such as smart phones, can offload computationally intensive applications to the nearby available computational nodes to improve battery lifetime [7]. To elaborate the example, we use the DEECo component model [11], which realizes the concepts of the SCEL formalism for developing adaptive ensembles. As a major feature, the ensembles consist of components that communicate exclusively through shared knowledge – we therefore include performance measurements among the knowledge elements.

6.1   Scenario Description

The scenario elaborated in this section is that of a person travelling in a train or a bus, who wants to do productive work using a tablet computer or review travel plans and accommodation. The tablet notes the presence of a cloud server machine located in the bus itself, and to save battery, it offloads the most computationally intensive tasks to that machine. Later, when the bus approaches its destination, the server notifies the tablet that its service will soon become unavailable and tasks will start moving back to the tablet. When the bus enters the terminal, the tablet will discover another server, provided by the terminal authority, and move some of the tasks to the newly found machine. The challenge is in predicting which deployment scenario will deliver the expected performance – that is, when is it worth migrating parts of the application to a different computer.

For our example, we assume that the application has a frontend component that cannot be migrated (such as the user interface, which obviously has to stay with the user, Af in our example) and a backend component that can be offloaded (typically the computationally intensive tasks, Ab in our example). Figure 4 depicts the adaptation architecture (the used notation is that of component systems, except for interfaces which are based on exchanging knowledge rather than invoking methods, various types of arrows denote various instances of interaction through knowledge described next).

6.2   Adaptation Architecture Components

The adaptation architecture on Figure 4 forms an overlay that reflects the application architecture. Central to the adaptation architecture is the Planner component, responsible for computing the optimum application component deployment. The Planner relies on Monitor components to provide information about application performance – each Monitor is a surrogate of one application component on one machine. The machines are represented by Device components. In more detail:

Planner. Each adaptive application is managed by a Planner component, whose implementation includes the application adaptation preferences. Specifically, given the alternatives for deploying each of the application components, the Planner selects the application deployment that best satisfies the preferences. We assume that the resulting deployment is described by a deployment plan,

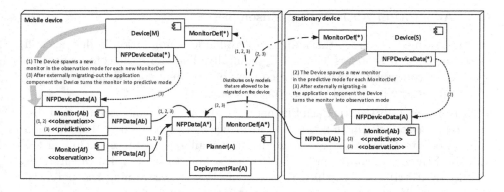

Fig. 4. Adaptation architecture. Numbers denote adaptation phases, 1 for Ab located at M, 2 for S discovered, 3 for Ab migrated to S.

and an external mechanism is responsible for performing the adaptation (for example by migrating components) as directed by the plan. To select among the available alternatives, the Planner is provided with data on non-functional properties (such as estimated frame rate or power consumption) that characterize the performance of the corresponding application component in a particular deployment (NFPData). The Planner also advertises definitions of Monitors for individual application components (MonitorDef).

Monitor. A single Monitor component exists for every application component in every deployment alternative. The Monitor component is responsible for providing NFPData for that particular combination of component and alternative. Depending on the actual deployment of the corresponding application component, the Monitor operates in one of two modes:

- The Monitor is in the *observation mode* if it resides on the same machine as the corresponding application component and therefore can observe the actual component execution. In this mode, NFPData is obtained by performance measurement of the running application component.
- The Monitor is in the *predictive mode* if it resides on a different machine than the one where the application component currently executes, and therefore represents a potential deployment alternative. NFPData is estimated from machine parameters in NFPDeviceData (such as estimating frame rate from the CPU and GPU parameters as a function $CPU \times GPU \rightarrow FPS$). In other words, the Monitor roughly predicts the performance that the application component would exhibit if it were deployed on a particular machine, relying on machine-specific data passed in NFPDeviceData.

Device. Each machine is represented by the Device component, which is responsible for instantiating Monitors advertised by newly discovered Planners and providing NFPDeviceData for Monitors operating in the predictive mode.

6.3   Adaptation Architecture Ensembles

In the assumed scenario, the number of available computation nodes, as well as the number of Monitors, changes dynamically. Therefore, the communication among the components exploits the concept of emergent component ensembles. The architecture involves the following ensembles (Figure 4):

Planner and Device(s). Each Planner is a coordinator of an ensemble that distributes MonitorDefs (including the performance prediction model) of application components to Devices representing currently available machines (including the one the Planner is running on). The Planner is able to limit which MonitorDefs should be distributed to which Devices (effectively constraining the potential migration destinations for a particular application component).

Planner and Monitor(s). Each Planner is a coordinator of an ensemble that aggregates NFPData from all Monitors corresponding to the components of the application managed by the Planner. Thus, this ensemble aggregates all the deployment alternatives for the application.

Device and Monitor(s). Each Device component is a coordinator of an ensemble that distributes NFPDeviceData to the Monitors in the predictive mode residing on the corresponding machines.

6.4   Adaptation Interaction Example

Initially (phase 1, Figure 4), the ensemble distributes the MonitorDefs of both Af and Ab from Planner(A) to the Device(M) component of the mobile device, which subsequently spawns Monitors for both components and sets them to the observation mode. The Monitors start measuring NFPData of the locally executing components, which are eventually aggregated and delivered as knowledge to the Planner. So far, no deployment alternatives are discovered.

After the stationary device is discovered (phase 2, Figure 4), the ensemble propagates MonitorDefs of the components that could be (potentially) migrated (here only Ab) to the Device(S) component, which spawns a new Monitor. Because Ab is deployed on Device(M), this Monitor runs in the predictive mode. The Device(S) component feeds the Monitor with NFPDeviceData and, based on this NFPDeviceData and the performance prediction model of Ab, the Monitor produces NFPData describing the expected performance of Ab on S. Consequently, another ensemble delivers all the currently produced NFPData for Af and Ab to the Planner. The Planner thus eventually discovers that there are two deployment alternatives for Ab (the one currently executing on M and the one modeled on S) and, assuming the adaptation is perceived as beneficial, decides to deploy Ab on the stationary device.

After Ab is migrated to the stationary device (phase 3, Figure 4), the Monitor on S switches to the observation mode. In turn, the Monitor on M is set to the predictive mode and the whole monitoring and planning process repeats.

When further stationary devices are discovered, new Monitors in the predictive mode are spawned, eventually providing new deployment alternatives for consideration by the Planner. Disappearing devices are handled similarly (but the overlay does not tackle state loss).

7 Designing Performance-Based Adaptation

The dynamic membership and communication features of ensembles, the formal methods of expressing and evaluating performance properties, and the availability of dynamic instrumentation at implementation level are all elements that contribute to the support for building adaptive applications. Complementing these elements is a method for designing adaptation strategies – the Invariant Refinement Method for Self-Adaptation (IRM-SA), described in detail in Chapter III.4 [12]. IRM-SA is an extension to IRM [32] and guides the design of an application from high-level strategic goals and (performance) requirements to their realization in terms of system architecture with design choices that correspond to different adaptation alternatives.

Design with IRM-SA captures the high-level system goals and requirements in terms of interaction *invariants*. The invariants describe the desired state of the system-to-be at every time instant, and, in general, are to be maintained by the cooperation of the system elements (actors, components, ensembles). A special type of invariant, called *assumption*, describes a condition that is expected to hold about the environment – an assumption is not intended to be maintained explicitly by the system-to-be. In a sequence of design decisions, the identified top-level invariants are decomposed into combinations of more specific invariants forming a decomposition graph. By this decomposition, we strive to get to the level of abstraction where the (leaf) invariants represent detailed design of the particular system constituents – components, component processes, and ensembles. Two special types of invariants, the *process* and *exchange* invariants, are used to model the component computation (processes) and interaction (ensembles), respectively.

To facilitate design with alternatives, IRM-SA features two decomposition types, *AND-decomposition* and *OR-decomposition*. The AND-decomposition is essentially a refinement in the traditional interpretation, where the composition of the children exhibits all the behavior expected from the parent and (potentially) some more. Formally, the AND-decomposition of a parent invariant I_p into a conjunction of sub-invariants $I_{s1} \dots I_{sn}$ is a refinement if the conjunction of the sub-invariants can guarantee the parent invariant:

1. $I_{s1} \wedge \dots \wedge I_{sn} \Rightarrow I_p$ (entailment)
2. $I_{s1} \wedge \dots \wedge I_{sn} \not\Rightarrow false$ (consistency)

For the OR-decomposition, in the context of adaptation alternatives, we introduce the concept of *situations*. A situation is a state that the system and its environment can reside in. Situations should not be confused with system (operating) modes – whereas the former refer to the perceived environment, which is inherently impossible to control, the later describe different system configurations, whose choice is under the control of the running software.

The OR-decomposition is used for invariants that can be decomposed into two or more sub-invariants, with each sub-invariant corresponding to a different situation. The OR-decomposition of a parent invariant I_p into two or more sub-invariants I_{s1} ... I_{sn} is correct if in any situation (corresponding to some of the invariants I_{s1} ... I_{sn}) there is at least one sub-invariant that refines the parent invariant I_p. It is important to notice that the situations identified and elaborated in an OR-decomposition can potentially overlap. Overlapping of situations can add to the overall robustness of the system, as it essentially means that more than one design solution is applicable to the same situation. Of course, situations can also be nested, following the observation that certain situations arise only in the context of other ones.

Technically, each situation in the IRM-SA graph is associated with one or more assumptions (see Figure 5). These assumptions describe the conditions that are expected to hold under a given situation in a declarative way, and can in fact be understood as evaluation conditions or adaptation triggers for a given situation. The formalism used for describing the assumptions depends on the nature of the assumptions, especially on whether the assumption conditions can be observed and quantified.

7.1   Scenario Description

To illustrate the IRM-SA method, we return to the cloud case study and the computation offloading example. In the case study, multiple heterogeneous network nodes form an open cloud platform that runs user applications, some possibly computationally intensive. When such an application executes on a mobile device, it can take advantage of the nearby cloud nodes by offloading the computationally intensive processing to those nodes. These nodes can even be a part of a traditional cloud infrastructure, leased on demand when there is a need for computational resources. The general assumptions are that (i) the application can be partitioned to run on multiple nodes, and (ii) a mechanism for effectively migrating application components across cloud nodes exists. Given this scenario, the goal of the system-to-be is two-fold: (1) to guarantee an upper limit in the response time observed by the user; (2) to guarantee that the application components are distributed in line with the maximum capacity constraints and load of each node.

Figure 5 shows a possible IRM-SA graph for the above scenario. The design starts with the identified top-level invariant stating that *"Load is balanced while expected QoS is kept"*. The "expected QoS" has been quantified by the SPL formula that specifies an upper bound on the application's response time (500 ms). This invariant can be decomposed into two possible sub-invariants, based on the situation the system resides in and specifically based on whether extra computational power from a cloud data center is needed.

In the first case (left alternative from top) invariant (1) is decomposed into one assumption (2) and two invariants, (3) and (4), following Figure 5. Assumption (2) specifies that *"Mobile nodes have enough capacity to handle application*

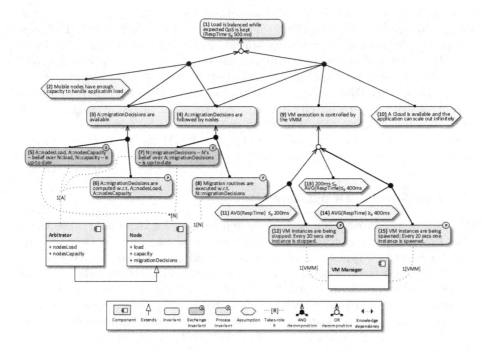

Fig. 5. Cloud case study with situations – IRM-SA graph

load" – it is an example of an assumption specified in an informal way in natural language. Obviously, this kind of assumption cannot be formally specified or checked at execution time, but has to be included for design completeness and consistency. Invariants (3) and (4) are further refined into lower level semantics which specify the architecture of the load balancing mechanism. Specifically, the Arbitrator component (which is a specialization of the Node component, indicating that it contributes both to the invariants it takes a role in and to its parent's invariants, and inherits the knowledge of its parent) implements the load balancing logic by acquiring a view over every node's capacity and load (5), and devising a migration plan (6). In order for the migration plan to be followed, it has to be distributed to all nodes (7) and executed in every node separately (8).

In the second case (right alternative from top) invariant (1) is now decomposed into one assumption (10), and three invariants, (3), (4), and (9). Whereas invariants (3) and (4), which describe the load balancing mechanism, are shared between the two situations, invariant (9) is local to the second situation. In particular, invariant (9) specifies that virtual machine execution is controlled by the VM Manager component (VMM) in a manner described by the sub-invariants (12) and (15).

Here, three situations are distinguished, depending on the response time of the application: Low RespTime, Normal RespTime, and High RespTime, each associated with a different assumption regarding the average response time over some period in time (assumptions (11), (13) and (14) respectively). These assumptions refer to a measurable system attribute and as such can be formally verified and checked at execution time – indeed, all three assumptions are specified as SPL formulas, which can be evaluated at runtime using the SPL engine in conjunction with DiSL, as exemplified in Listing 1. The idea here is to use the concept of situations to specify a simple control logic: if the average response time is less than 200 ms (11), the VMM needs to react by stopping virtual machines (12); if it is more than 400 ms (14), the VMM has to start new virtual machines (15); otherwise (13), do nothing.

7.2   Transforming Design into Code

IRM-SA is tailored towards producing system designs for DEECo [11]. The leaves of the IRM-SA graph can be process invariants, exchange invariants or assumptions. The first two types are mapped to the DEECo concepts of processes and ensembles, respectively. For assumptions, we distinguish between the ones that can be formally specified, observed and verified, and the informal ones, typically specified in natural language. Whereas informal assumptions cannot be checked at runtime (thus we optimistically assume that they hold during system execution), formal assumptions are checked at runtime by mapping them to runtime monitors.

When the formal assumptions concern performance, they can be specified using SPL. This is especially useful when the assumptions concern alternative decompositions that model different adaptation strategies – the performance properties described in SPL can be used to identify what situation the system is currently in, and to react accordingly (e.g. invariants (11), (13) and (14) on Figure 5). SPL can also specify performance invariants that are checked to validate the design (e.g. invariant (1) on Figure 5). Finally, the presence of SPL formulas in the IRM-SA graph gives an early (design time) indication of the need for monitoring, whose potential overhead needs to be balanced against the adaptation capabilities.

8   Summary

Besides dealing with many individual challenges inherent to the construction of collective autonomic systems, the ASCENS project also examines the overall lifecycle of such systems, considering where and how the proposed individual solutions interact and complement each other. Chapter III.1 [24] describes this perspective in general terms, introducing the concept of continuous development lifecycle, where repeated design and runtime activities interact with each other through deployment and feedback to manage system evolution.

In this chapter, we present the support for performance awareness in the same lifecycle context – starting with the runtime cycle, where instrumentation is used to monitor performance relevant system properties (Section 2), which are evaluated (Section 3) by the system implementation (Section 4). Both the design and the runtime cycles may reflect on system performance through modeling (Section 5), the design cycle also provides the concept of dynamic ensembles to structure the implementation (Section 6), which can be architected by gradual refinement from the initial system requirements (Section 7).

References

1. Aoki, M.: Control of large-scale dynamic systems by aggregation. IEEE Trans. Autom. Control 13(3) (1968)
2. ASM (2014), http://asm.ow2.org/
3. Barendregt, H.: The Lambda Calculus: Its Syntax and Semantics. Mathematical Programming Study. North-Holland Publishing Company, Amsterdam (1984)
4. Bruni, R., Corradini, A., Gadducci, F., Hölzl, M., Lafuente, A.L., Vandin, A., Wirsing, M.: Reconciling White-Box and Black-Box Perspectives on Behavioral Self-adaptation. In: Wirsing, M., Hölzl, M., Koch, N., Mayer, P. (eds.) Software Engineering for Collective Autonomic Systems. LNCS, vol. 8998, pp. 163–184. Springer, Heidelberg (2015)
5. Buchholz, P.: Exact and ordinary lumpability in finite Markov chains. Journal of Applied Probability 31(1) (1994)
6. Bulej, L., Bureš, T., Horký, V., Keznikl, J., Tůma, P.: Performance awareness in component systems: Vision paper. In: Proc. COMPSAC 2012 CORCS (2012)
7. Bulej, L., Bureš, T., Horký, V., Keznikl, J.: Adaptive deployment in ad-hoc systems using emergent component ensembles: Vision paper. In: Proceedings of the 4th ACM/SPEC International Conference on Performance Engineering (ICPE '13), ACM Press, New York (2013)
8. Bulej, L., Bureš, T., Horký, V., Kotrč, J., Marek, L., Trojánek, T., Tůma, P.: SPL: Unit testing performance. Tech. Rep. D3S-TR-2014-04, Dep. of Distributed and Dependable Systems, Charles University in Prague (2014)
9. Bulej, L., Bureš, T., Keznikl, J., Koubková, A., Podzimek, A., Tůma, P.: Capturing performance assumptions using stochastic performance logic. In: Proc. ICPE 2012, ACM Press, New York (2012)
10. Bureš, T., Horký, V., Kit, M., Marek, L., Tůma, P.: Towards performance-aware engineering of autonomic component ensembles. In: Margaria, T., Steffen, B. (eds.) ISoLA 2014, Part I. LNCS, vol. 8802, pp. 131–146. Springer, Heidelberg (2014)
11. Bures, T., Gerostathopoulos, I., Hnetynka, P., Keznikl, J., Kit, M., Plasil, F.: DEECo – an ensemble-based component system. In: Proc. of the International ACM SIGSOFT Symposium on Component Based Software Engineering (CBSE '13), Vancouver, Canada, ACM, New York (2013)
12. Bures, T., Gerostathopoulos, I., Hnetynka, P., Keznikl, J., Kit, M., Plasil, F.: The Invariant Refinement Method. In: Wirsing, M., Hölzl, M., Koch, N., Mayer, P. (eds.) Software Engineering for Collective Autonomic Systems. LNCS, vol. 8998, pp. 405–428. Springer, Heidelberg (2015)
13. Cantrill, B.M., Shapiro, M.W., Leventhal, A.H.: Dynamic instrumentation of production systems. In: Proceedings of the USENIX Annual Technical Conference (ATC'04), Berkeley, CA, USA (2004)
14. Cardelli, L.: On process rate semantics. Theor. Comput. Sci. 391 (2008)

15. Chiba, S.: Load-time structural reflection in Java. In: Bertino, E. (ed.) ECOOP 2000. LNCS, vol. 1850, p. 313. Springer, Heidelberg (2000)
16. Ciocchetta, F., Hillston, J.: Bio-PEPA: A framework for the modelling and analysis of biological systems. Theor. Comput. Sci. 410(33–34) (2009)
17. Clark, M.: JUnitPerf (2014), http://www.clarkware.com/software/JUnitPerf
18. Hayden, R.A., Bradley, J.T.: A fluid analysis framework for a Markovian process algebra. Theor. Comput. Sci. 411(22-24) (2010)
19. Herbst, N.R., Huber, N., Kounev, S., Amrehn, E.: Self-adaptive workload classification and forecasting for proactive resource provisioning. In: Proceedings of the 4th ACM/SPEC International Conference on Performance Engineering (ICPE '13), ACM Press, New York (2013)
20. Hermanns, H., Rettelbach, M.: Syntax, semantics, equivalences, and axioms for MTIPP. In: Proceedings of Process Algebra and Probabilistic Methods, Erlangen (1994)
21. Hillston, J.: Fluid flow approximation of PEPA models. In: Proceedings of Quantitative Evaluation of Systems, IEEE Computer Society Press, Los Alamitos (2005)
22. Hillston, J.: A compositional approach to performance modelling. Cambridge University Press, New York (1996)
23. Hölzl, M., Gabor, T.: Reasoning and Learning for Awareness and Adaptation. In: Wirsing, M., Hölzl, M., Koch, N., Mayer, P. (eds.) Software Engineering for Collective Autonomic Systems. LNCS, vol. 8998, pp. 249–290. Springer, Heidelberg (2015)
24. Hölzl, M., Koch, N., Puviani, M., Wirsing, M., Zambonelli, F.: The Ensemble Development Life Cycle and Best Practices for Collective Autonomic Systems. In: Wirsing, M., Hölzl, M., Koch, N., Mayer, P. (eds.) Software Engineering for Collective Autonomic Systems. LNCS, vol. 8998, pp. 325–354. Springer, Heidelberg (2015)
25. Horký, V., Haas, F., Kotrč, J., Lacina, M., Tůma, P.: Performance regression unit testing: a case study. In: Balsamo, M.S., Knottenbelt, W.J., Marin, A. (eds.) EPEW 2013. LNCS, vol. 8168, pp. 149–163. Springer, Heidelberg (2013)
26. Horký, V., Libič, P., Marek, L., Steinhauser, A., Tůma, P.: Utilizing performance unit tests to increase performance awareness. In: Proc. ICPE 2015, ACM Press, New York (2015)
27. Iacobelli, G., Tribastone, M.: Lumpability of fluid models with heterogeneous agent types. In: DSN (2013)
28. Iwase, Y., Levin, S.A., Andreasen, V.: Aggregation in model ecosystems I: perfect aggregation. Ecological Modelling 37 (1987)
29. JDOM Library (2013), http://www.jdom.org
30. Kalibera, T., Bulej, L., Tůma, P.: Benchmark precision and random initial state. In: Proc. SPECTS 2005, pp. 853–862. SCS (2005)
31. Kalibera, T., Bulej, L., Tuma, P.: Automated detection of performance regressions: the Mono experience. In: 13th IEEE International Symposium on Modeling, Analysis, and Simulation of Computer and Telecommunication Systems, Sep. 2005, IEEE Computer Society Press, Los Alamitos (2005)
32. Keznikl, J., Bures, T., Plasil, F., Gerostathopoulos, I., Hnetynka, P., Hoch, N.: Design of ensemble-based component systems by invariant refinement. In: Proc. of the 16th International ACM SIGSOFT Symposium on Component Based Software Engineering (CBSE '13), Vancouver, Canada, ACM, New York (2013)
33. Kiczales, G., Hilsdale, E., Hugunin, J., Kersten, M., Palm, J., Griswold, W.G.: An overview of aspectJ. In: Knudsen, J.L. (ed.) ECOOP 2001. LNCS, vol. 2072, p. 327. Springer, Heidelberg (2001)

34. Kwiatkowski, M., Stark, I.: The continuous π-calculus: A process algebra for bio-chemical modelling. In: Heiner, M., Uhrmacher, A.M. (eds.) CMSB 2008. LNCS (LNBI), vol. 5307, pp. 103–122. Springer, Heidelberg (2008)
35. Marek, L., Zheng, Y., Ansaloni, D., Bulej, L., Sarimbekov, A., Binder, W., Tůma, P.: Introduction to dynamic program analysis with DiSL. Science of Computer Programming (2014)
36. Marek, L., Zhen, Y., Binder, W.: DiSL (2012), http://d3s.mff.cuni.cz/software/disl
37. Marek, L., Zheng, Y., Ansaloni, D., Binder, W., Qi, Z., Tuma, P.: DiSL: An extensible language for efficient and comprehensive dynamic program analysis. In: Proc. 7th Workshop on Domain-Specific Aspect Languages (DSAL '12), ACM Press, New York (2012)
38. Mayer, P., Velasco, J., Klarl, A., Hennicker, R., Puviani, M., Tiezzi, F., Pugliese, R., Keznikl, J., Bureš, T.: The Autonomic Cloud. In: Wirsing, M., Hölzl, M., Koch, N., Mayer, P. (eds.) Software Engineering for Collective Autonomic Systems. LNCS, vol. 8998, pp. 495–512. Springer, Heidelberg (2015)
39. Milner, R.: Communication and Concurrency. Prentice-Hall, Inc., Upper Saddle River (1989)
40. Mytkowicz, T., Diwan, A., Hauswirth, M., Sweeney, P.F.: Producing wrong data without doing anything obviously wrong. In: Proceedings of ASPLOS 2009, ACM Press, New York (2009)
41. De Nicola, R., Latella, D., Lafuente, A.L., Loreti, M., Margheri, A., Massink, M., Morichetta, A., Pugliese, R., Tiezzi, F., Vandin, A.: The SCEL Language: Design, Implementation, Verification. In: Wirsing, M., Hölzl, M., Koch, N., Mayer, P. (eds.) Software Engineering for Collective Autonomic Systems. LNCS, vol. 8998, pp. 3–71. Springer, Heidelberg (2015)
42. Okino, M.S., Mavrovouniotis, M.L.: Simplification of mathematical models of chemical reaction systems. Chemical Reviews 2(98) (1998)
43. Oracle: JVM Tool Interface (2006), http://docs.oracle.com/javase/6/docs/platform/jvmti/jvmti.html
44. Perf4J (2014), http://perf4j.codehaus.org/
45. Perl, S.E., Weihl, W.E.: Performance assertion checking. SIGOPS Oper. Syst. Rev. 27 (1993)
46. Reynolds, P., Killian, C., Wiener, J.L., Mogul, J.C., Shah, M.A., Vahdat, A.: Pip: Detecting the Unexpected in Distributed Systems. In: NSDI'06. USENIX (2006)
47. Sheskin, D.J.: Handbook of Parametric and Nonparametric Statistical Procedures. CRC Press, Boca Raton (2011)
48. SPL Tool (2013), http://d3s.mff.cuni.cz/software/spl
49. SystemTap (2014), http://sourceware.org/systemtap/
50. Tahchiev, P., Leme, F., Massol, V., Gregory, G.: JUnit in Action, 2nd edn. (2010)
51. Tribastone, M., Gilmore, S., Hillston, J.: Scalable differential analysis of process algebra models. IEEE Transactions on Software Engineering 38(1) (2012)
52. Tschaikowski, M., Tribastone, M.: Exact fluid lumpability for Markovian process algebra. In: Koutny, M., Ulidowski, I. (eds.) CONCUR 2012. LNCS, vol. 7454, pp. 380–394. Springer, Heidelberg (2012)
53. Tschaikowski, M., Tribastone, M.: Tackling continuous state-space explosion in a Markovian process algebra. Theoretical Computer Science 517 (2014)
54. Tschaikowski, M., Tribastone, M.: A unified framework for differential aggregations in Markovian process algebra. Journal of Logical and Algebraic Methods in Programming (2014)

55. Vetter, J.S., Worley, P.H.: Asserting Performance Expectations. In: Proc. 2002 ACM/IEEE Conf. on Supercomputing (Supercomputing '02), IEEE Computer Society Press, Los Alamitos (2002)
56. Welch, B.L.: The generalization of student's problem when several different population variances are involved. Biometrika 34(1/2) (1947)
57. Wirsing, M., Hölzl, M.M., Tribastone, M., Zambonelli, F.: ASCENS: Engineering Autonomic Service-Component Ensembles. In: Beckert, B., Damiani, F., de Boer, F.S., Bonsangue, M.M. (eds.) FMCO 2011. LNCS, vol. 7542, pp. 1–24. Springer, Heidelberg (2013)

Part III:
Engineering Techniques for Collective Autonomic Systems

In order to guide developers in the construction and maintenance of ensembles, the ASCENS project provides engineering techniques and tools.

The first chapter describes a cornerstone of the ASCENS approach to developing ensembles: the Ensemble Development Life Cycle (EDLC). It is comprised of two feedback loops for activities that take place during design time and during run time of an ensemble. Since many ensembles are long-running systems that are continuously improved and adapted over the course of their lifetime, a third feedback loop is established by deployment and feedback of runtime data to the design phase. These interlocking cycles serve as a framework for the whole development process. Solutions to more specific development issues arising in the individual activities of the design cycle are provided by a catalog of patterns that capture best practices for designing ensembles.

The second chapter addresses issues that arise from the interaction of many autonomous components in a system: self-organization and emergence. To build reliable ensembles these phenomena have to be engineered such that they support the goals of the system and do not lead to unintended consequences. The chapter shows how a strategy of design that follows the problem organization helps to address the issues presented by self-organization and emergence.

Chapters three and four represent two complementary methods for requirements engineering: the goal-oriented Autonomy Requirements Engineering approach that focuses mainly on high-level aspects of the system and its knowledge requirements, and the Invariant Refinement Method that relies on invariants to model both high-level system goals and low-level software obligations.

The fifth chapter describes tools that were developed as part of the ASCENS project and that support the development process, for example a compiler for the BIP language that allows the execution and verification of BIP models, the jRESP runtime environment for the SCEL language or the FACPL policy IDE and evaluation library.

M. Wirsing et al. (eds.): Collective Autonomic Systems, LNCS 8998, p. 323, 2015.
© Springer International Publishing Switzerland 2015

CHAPTER III.1

The Ensemble Development Life Cycle and Best Practices for Collective Autonomic Systems⋆

Matthias Hölzl[1], Nora Koch[1], Mariachiara Puviani[2], Martin Wirsing[1], and Franco Zambonelli[2]

[1] Ludwig-Maximilians-Universität München, Germany
[2] University of Modena and Reggio Emilia, Italy

Abstract. Collective autonomic systems are adaptive, open-ended, highly parallel, interactive and distributed software systems. Their key features are so-called self-* properties, such as self-awareness, self-adaptation, self-expression, self-healing and self-management. We propose a software development life cycle that helps developers to engineer adaptive behavior and to address the issues posed by the diversity of self-* properties. The life cycle is characterized by three feedback loops, i.e. based on verification at design time, based on monitoring and awareness in the runtime, and the feedback provided by runtime data to the design phases. We illustrate how the life cycle can be instantiated using specific languages, methods and tools developed within the ASCENS project. In addition, a pattern catalog for the development of collective autonomic systems is presented to ease the engineering process.

Keywords: software development life cycle, patterns, ensembles, awareness, adaptation, autonomic systems

1   Introduction

Software is increasingly used to model or control massively distributed and dynamic collective autonomic systems. These systems consist of a set of usually open-ended, highly parallel and interactive components, which operate in highly variable, even unpredictable, environments. Their key features are so-called self-* properties, such as self-awareness, self-adaptation, self-expression, self-healing and self-management.

Self-awareness is concerned with knowledge the system has about the system's behavior and the environment, which may be centrally held or distributed in nature. However, in designing autonomic self-aware systems, it is useful to explicitly and separately consider the process of determining system's actions as a result of this knowledge. This process is called self-adaptation or self-expression.

⋆ This work has been sponsored by the EU project ASCENS IP 257414 (FP7).

M. Wirsing et al. (eds.): Collective Autonomic Systems, LNCS 8998, pp. 325–354, 2015.
© Springer International Publishing Switzerland 2015

In particular, if the autonomic system is recovering from some failure, the term self-healing is used. We distinguish also a self-management property as the ability collective autonomic systems have to manage local and global knowledge in order to be aware of their own state and the state of the environment. The knowledge is used for reasoning, learning and adapting at runtime to the system's and environmental changes.

One of the main challenges for software engineers is then to find reliable methods and tools to build the software that implement those self-* features required by collective autonomic systems. The main aim of the ASCENS project[3] is to tackle these issues using an engineering approach based on service components and ensembles. Ensembles are dynamic groups of components that are formed on demand to fulfill specific goals by taking into account the state of the (changing) environment they are operating in. One distinguishing characteristic of the approach is the use of formal methods to guarantee that the behavior of the software complies to the specifications.

In this chapter we present the Ensemble Development Life Cycle (EDLC) that covers the full design and runtime aspects of collective autonomic systems. It is a conceptual framework that defines a set of phases and their interplay mainly based on feedback loops as shown in Figure 1. The life cycle comprises a "double-wheel" and two "arrows" between the wheels providing three different feedback control loops: *(1)* at design time, *(2)* at runtime and *(3)* between the two of them allowing for the system's evolution. The *design feedback control loop* enables continuous improvement of models and code due to changing requirements and results of verification or validation. The *runtime feedback control loop* implements self-adaptation based on awareness about the system and its environment. Finally, the *evolution feedback control loop* provides the mechanisms to change architectural models and code on the basis of the runtime behavior of the continuous evolving system.

We illustrate the EDLC using methods and tools, mostly developed within the ASCENS project. Examples are SOTA [2] for requirements engineering of awareness and adaptive issues, SCEL ([31], Chapter I.1 [54]) for modeling and programming, SBIP ([9], Chapter I.3 [28]) for verification, SPL ([20], Chapter II.5 [18]) for monitoring, Iliad (Chapter II.4 [42]) as awareness-engine, and JDEECo [22] and JRESP (Chapter I.1 [54]) as runtime frameworks. These methods and tools are specifically designed to capture the self-* features of autonomic systems.

When complex collective autonomic systems are developed, an important aspect of the development process is the reusability of design choices, i.e. the advantage to identify architectural schemes that can be reused at component and ensemble level. We have defined a *pattern catalog* of interrelated patterns –a so-called *pattern language*. Such a pattern language enables developers to choose different design elements making the resulting models, implementation and selected verification techniques more understandable. We illustrate the pat-

---

[3] ASCENS website: http://www.ascens-ist.eu/

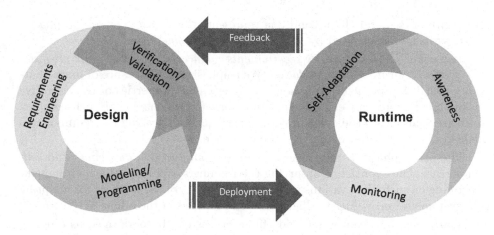

Fig. 1. Ensembles Development Life Cycle (EDLC)

tern catalog with a set of architectural patterns focusing mainly on the feedback control loops they support.

The structure of the chapter is as follows: Section 2 provides an overview of the EDLC. Section 3 focuses on the feedback control loops and their relationship to the phases of the EDLC. Section 4 present a pattern language for ensemble development and a set of pattern examples. Section 5 relates our work to other relevant software engineering approaches, and Section 6 concludes with a summary and future challenges regarding the engineering of collective autonomic systems.

2   Software Development Life Cycle for Ensembles

The development of collective autonomic systems goes beyond addressing the classical phases of the software development life cycle like requirements elicitation, modeling, implementation and deployment. Engineering these complex systems has also to tackle aspects such as self-* properties like self-awareness and self-adaptation. Such properties have to be considered from the beginning of the development process, i.e. during elicitation of the requirements. Therefore, we need to capture how the system should be adapted and how the system or environment should be monitored in order to make adaptation possible.

Models are usually built on top of the elicited requirements, mainly following an iterative process, in which also validation and verification in early phases of the development are highly recommended, in order to mitigate the impact of design errors. A relevant issue is then the use of modeling and implementation techniques for adaptive and awareness features. Our aim is to focus on these distinguishing characteristics of collective autonomic systems along the whole development cycle.

We propose a "double-wheel" life cycle to sketch the main aspects of the engineering process as shown in Figure 1. The "left wheel" represents the *design* or *offline* phases and the second one represents the *runtime* or *online* phases. Both wheels are connected by the transitions *deployment* and *feedback*.

The offline phases comprise *requirements engineering, modeling and programming*, and *verification and validation*. We emphasize the relevance of mathematically founded approaches to validate and verify the properties of the collective autonomic system and enable the prediction of the behavior of such complex software. This closes the cycle providing feedback for checking the requirements identified so far or improving the model or code.

The online phases ("right wheel") comprise *monitoring, awareness* and *self-adaptation*. They consist of observing the running system and the environment, reasoning on such observations and using the results of the analysis for adapting the system and providing feedback that can be used in the offline activities.

Transitions between online and offline phases can be performed as often as needed throughout the system's evolution feedback control loop, i.e. data acquired during monitoring at runtime are fed back to the design cycle to provide information for the system redesign, verification and redeployment.

The process defined by the EDLC can be refined by providing details on the involved stakeholders, the methods and tools they will use in the development as well as the input needed and the output produced in each stage. This will ease the selection of the most appropriate tools for each collective autonomic system to be build. Process modeling languages can be used to specify these details: Either general workflow-oriented modeling languages such as UML activity diagrams[4], and BPMN[5], or a Domain Specific Language (DSL) such as the OMG standard Software and Systems Process Engineering Metamodel (SPEM)[6] and the Multi-View Process Modeling Language (MV-PML) developed by NASA [13].

Figure 2 shows an example of a process model specified in SPEM for the requirements engineering steps of the e-Mobility scenario described in [24]. It illustrates the relationships between stakeholders like the requirements engineer, actions such as the definition of adaptation goals and process inputs like interviews and results such as the SOTA model and the IRM model. Aspects of the runtime phases of the development process of this scenario are shown in Fig. 3 focusing on the monitoring and adaptation activities that use JDEECo components and enables feedback to the phases of the design "wheel".

3   Engineering Feedback Control Loops

Feedback control loops are the heart of any collective autonomic system providing the generic mechanism for adaptation and enabling the creation of flexible runtime solutions by monitoring the subsystem and applying corrections in or-

---

[4] UML website: http://www.uml.org/

[5] BPMN website: http://www.omg.org/spec/BPMN/2.0/

[6] SPEM website: http://www.omg.org/spec/SPEM/2.0/

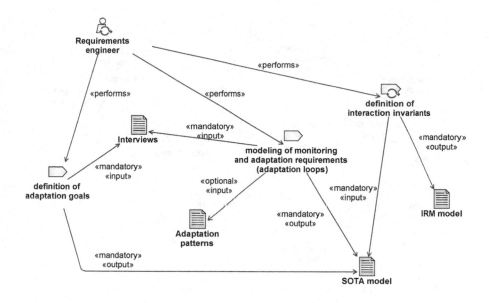

Fig. 2. E-Mobility Scenario Development Process: Requirements Engineering Aspects

der to approach the goals. Moreover they allow a system to become self-aware with respect to the quality of its operations, and self-healing if there are any problems. This is achieved by approaches like MAPE K [30] that collect appropriate runtime data and analyzing it, and by planning and executing adaptation strategies.

Engineering approaches for building collective autonomic systems need to consider feedback control loops from the beginning on and all over the development life cycle. This includes requirements that make such loops necessary, the influence loops have on architecture, deployment aspects to be taken into account, additional features to be supported as monitoring and awareness of the system's and environmental behavior, and implementation of adaptation mechanisms.

These engineering features are considered by the EDLC presented in the previous section, which itself is composed of three feedback loops: at design time, at runtime, and from runtime back to improve the design with the associated redeployment of the evolving software. The development of collective autonomic system offers several engineering challenges that are addressed by the methods, techniques and tools that have been developed in the ASCENS project. The remainder of this section focuses on the feedback loops and provides examples of ASCENS approaches that can be used in the different phases of the development life cycle within each feedback loop.

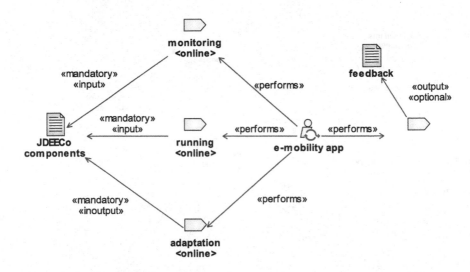

Fig. 3. E-Mobility Scenario Development Process: Runtime Aspects

3.1 Design Cycle

The "design wheel" comprises three phases: *requirements engineering, modeling and programming, and verification and validation.* At first glance it resembles a traditional software development life cycle. However, an autonomic ensemble, has to be aware of other autonomic ensembles and take into account its environment. It has to provide and consume knowledge, manage policies specified in form of goals, rules and/or constraints and infer lower-level actions [46]. These features of collective autonomic systems have to be addressed in the stages prior to *programming*, too, i.e. *requirements engineering* and *modeling*. In particular, goal-oriented approaches are in these stages promising techniques used for requirements elicitation and specification. Particularly challenging are also the *validation and verification* of large-scale autonomic systems as it will be harder to anticipate their environment.

Requirements Engineering. Traditionally, software engineering divides requirements in two categories: functional requirements (what the system should do) and non-functional requirements (how the system stands for achieving its functional requirements in terms of performance, quality of service, etc.). In the area of adaptive systems, and more in general of open-ended systems, both functional and non-functional requirements are better expressed in terms of "goals" [53]. A goal, in most general terms, represents a desirable state of the affairs that a software component or software system, aims to achieve. In fact, a self-adaptive system/component should be engineered not simply to "achieve" a functionality or state of the affairs, but rather to "strive to achieve" such functionality perhaps in several steps, i.e., be able to take self-adaptive decisions and actions so as to preserve its capability of achieving despite contingencies.

Within the ASCENS project a couple of different *goal-oriented* approaches were proposed to elicitate and specify the requirements of collective autonomic systems, i.e. State of the Affairs (SOTA), General Ensemble Model (GEM), Invariant Refinement Method (IRM) and Autonomy Requirements Engineering (ARE) that we briefly sketch below.

The SOTA approach [2] proposes an extension of existing goal-oriented requirements engineering approach that integrates elements of dynamic systems modeling. SOTA models the entities of a self-adaptive system as if they were immersed in n-dimensional space S, each of the n dimensions of such space representing a specific aspect of the current situation of an entity/ensemble and of its operational environment. As the entity executes, its position in S changes either due to its specific actions or because of the dynamics of environment. Thus, we can generally see this evolution of the system as a movement in S. For example, in the ASCENS e-mobility scenario described in [24], the space S includes the spatial dimensions related to the street map, but also dimensions related to the current traffic conditions, the battery conditions, etc. Once the SOTA space is defined, a goal is specified in SOTA; for instance, a goal for a vehicle could imply reaching a position in the SOTA space that, for the dimensions representing the spatial location, trivially represents the final destination and for the dimension representing the battery condition may represent a charging level ensuring safe return.

Along these lines, the activity of requirements engineering for self-adaptive systems in SOTA implies: *(i)* identifying the dimensions of the SOTA space, which means modeling the relevant information that a system/entity has to collect to become aware of its location in such space, a necessary condition to recognize whether it is correctly behaving and adapt its actions whenever necessary; *(ii)* identifying the set of goals for each entity and for the system as a whole, which also implies identifying when specific goals get activated and any possible constraint on the trajectory to be followed while trying to achieve such goals.

The General Ensemble Model (GEM) is a mathematical formalization of the SOTA approach that gives precise semantics to SOTA models and provides ways to specify model properties in various logics [44], such as the higher-order logic of the PVS system [55] or various temporal logics. The precise semantics that GEM provides for SOTA models enables developers to analyze requirements models using mathematical techniques; Chapter II.1 [16] in this volume shows how a SOTA/GEM model may be used to derive an adaptation strategy for a swarm of robots operating in an adversarial environment by applying concepts from (differential and evolutionary) game theory.

The Autonomy Requirements Engineering (ARE) (described in detail in Chapter III.3 [59]) of this volume uses a goal-oriented approach, too, along with a special model for generic autonomy requirements (GAR). ARE starts with the creation of a goals model that represents system objectives and their inter-relationships. In the next phase, the GAR model is used to refine each one of the system goals with elicited environmental constraints to come up with self-* objectives providing autonomy requirements for achieving these goals. The autonomy requirements are derived in the form of goal-supportive and alternative self-* objectives, along with required capabilities and quality characteristics. Finally, these autonomy requirements can be specified with KnowLang, a framework dedicated to knowledge representation for self-adaptive systems.

For the refinement of the high-level strategic goals defined in SOTA to the architecture of the collective autonomic system in terms of low-level components and ensemble, we can use the Invariant Refinement Method (IRM) [47] (see also Chapter III.4 [23]of this volume). The main idea of IRM is to capture the high-level goals and requirements in terms of invariants, which describe the desired state of the system-to-be at every time instant. Invariants are to be maintained by the coordination of the different system components. As a design decision, top-level invariants are iteratively decomposed into more concrete sub-invariants, forming a decomposition graph with traceability of design decisions.

The IRM approach has been used e.g. to model the functional and adaptive requirements of the e-Mobility scenario, capturing the necessity to keep the vehicle's plan updated and to check whether the current plan remains feasible with respect to measured battery level. The identified leaf invariants are easily mappable to component activities, which are further formally specified by (SCEL) [32] or SCPL [21] (see Sec. 3.1).

The requirements engineering approaches SOTA, GEM, ARE and IRM complement each other and are useful to understand and model the functional and adaptation requirements, and to check the correctness of such specifications (as described in [1]). However, when a designer considers the actual design of collective autonomic system, it is necessary to identify which architectural schemes need to be chosen for the individual components and the ensembles. In the next section we give an overview of the taxonomy of architectural patterns we defined [26] for adaptive components and ensemble.

Modeling and Programming. The Service Component Ensemble Language (SCEL) [32,31] (see also Chapter I.1 [54] of this volume) has been designed to deal with adaptation and move toward the actual implementation of the self-* properties identified during the requirements engineering phase, which have been specified e.g. using the IRM approach. It brings together programming abstractions to directly address aggregations (how different components interact to form ensembles and systems), behaviors (how components progress) and knowledge manipulation according to specific policies. SCEL specifications consist of cooperating components which, are equipped with an interface, a knowledge repository, a set of policies, and a process.

The language is equipped with an operational semantics that permits verification of formal properties of systems. Moreover, a SCEL program can rely on separate reasoning components that can be invoked when decisions have to be taken.

To move toward implementation, jRESP[7], a JAVA runtime environment has been developed that provides an API that permits using in JAVA programs the SCEL's linguistic constructs for controlling the computation and interaction of autonomic components, and for defining the architecture of systems and ensembles. Its main objective is to be a faithful implementation of the SCEL programming abstractions, suitable for rapid prototyping and experimentation with the SCEL paradigm. The large use of design patterns greatly simplifies the integration of new features. It is worth noticing that the implementation of jRESP fully relies on the SCEL's formal semantics. This close correspondence enhances confidence in the behavior of the jRESP implementation of SCEL programs, once the latter have been analysed through formal methods made possible by the formal operational semantics. For more details on SCEL and jRESP the reader is referred to Chapter I.1 [54] of this volume.

As a complement to SCEL, within the ASCENS context an approach called Soft Constraint Logic Programming (SCPL) (see Chapter II.2 [39]) has been used and applied to an e-Mobility travel optimization scenario. Besides optimizing trips of single users, so-called local problems, the e-Mobility case study aims to solve global problems involving large ensembles of vehicles. To tackle these a coordination of declarative and procedural knowledge is used and a decomposition of the global problem into local problems, which are solved by SCLP implementations and whose parameters can be iteratively determined by a programmable orchestration.

Complementary approaches to SCEL, like Helena [49] and DEECo, have been developed for the specification of collective autonomic systems as well within the scope of ASCENS. The Helena approach proposes a role-based method for modeling collaborations using a UML-like notation and is founded on a rigorous formal semantics. Helena focuses on the description of the behavior of each role as well as on the behavior on the ensemble level.

DEECo (Dependable Emergent Ensembles of Components) component model [48,22] can be used to provide us with the relevant software engineering abstractions that ease the programmers' tasks. A component in DEECo, features an execution model based on the MAPE-K [30] autonomic loop. In compliance with SCEL, it consists of (i) well-defined knowledge, being a set of knowledge items and (ii) processes that are executed periodically in a soft real-time manner. The component concept is complemented by the first-class ensemble concept. An ensemble stands as the only communication mechanism between DEECo components. It specifies a membership condition, according to which components are evaluated for participation. The evaluation is based on the components' knowledge (their attributes in SCEL). An ensemble also specifies what is to be communicated between the participants, that is, the appropriate knowledge exchange function. Similar to component processes, ensembles are invoked periodically in a soft realtime manner.

In order to bring the above abstractions to practical use we have used jDEECo – our reification of DEECo component model in Java. In jDEECo, components

---

[7] jRESP website: http://code.google.com/p/jresp/

are intuitively represented as annotated Java classes, where component knowledge is mapped to class fields and processes to class methods. Similarly, appropriately annotated classes represent DEECo ensembles. Once the necessary components and ensembles are coded, they are deployed in jDEECo runtime framework, which takes care of process and ensemble scheduling, as well as low-level distributed knowledge manipulation.

Verification and Validation. When dealing with complex collective autonomic systems one needs to face the problem of the development and of the validation of the models used for planning and for execution control. These systems are deployed for increasingly complex tasks; and it becomes more and more important to prove as early as possible in the development life cycle that they are safe, dependable, and correct.

Analysis techniques for collective autonomic systems that capture essential aspects such as adaptive behavior, interactions between the components, and changing environments can only succeed if they exploit as much as possible the specific structure of the considered systems (e.g. large replication of the same component, hierarchical compositions). In ASCENS (see Chapter I.3 [28]) we consider both, *qualitative analyses* targeting boolean properties stating that the system behaves without any flaw, and *quantitative analyses* that evaluate expected performances according to predefined metrics (energy/memory consumption, average/maximum time to accomplish a task, probability to fulfil a goal, etc.). We also address security specific issues such as control policies and information flow.

Our approach for dealing with *qualitative properties* is to use so called formal verification techniques, which provide a mathematical proof, e.g. model-checking and theorem prover. Formal verification is an attractive alternative to traditional methods of testing and simulation that can be used to provide correctness guarantees. Hereby, we mean not just the traditional notion of program verification, where the correctness of code is at question. We more broadly focus on design verification, where an abstract model of a system is checked for desired behavioral properties. Finding a bug in a design is more cost-effective than finding the manifestation of the design flow in the code.

Regarding *quantitative properties* and system performance, the environment in which the system is immersed plays an important role. Therefore the environment behavior has to be modeled as well providing additional information on possible scenarios the system may present. In ASCENS we used stochastic models and frameworks for the evaluation of quantitative properties related to the case studies of the project.

Considering *security aspects*, the focus was on confidentiality issues. We develop a model-driven framework for information flow analysis, named *secBIP* [7], which is suited for checking non-interference, a system property stating that information about higher security levels cannot be inferred from lower security levels. This component-based framework allows for the construction of complex systems by composition of atomic components with communication and coordination operators.

Several tools have been implemented within ASCENS to support these verification and validation methods, some of them as extension of well known existing tools. We mention here the most relevant: D-Finder [10,11], SMC-BIP [6], SBIP [9] and GMC.

The first three are based on BIP, a formal framework for building heterogeneous and complex component-based systems [8]. Notably, thanks to the formal operational semantics of the SCEL language, BIP models can be obtained from static SCEL descriptions (i.e. involving only bounded creation/deletion of components and processes) by exploring a set of transformations rules. D-Finder is a tool used for the compositional verification of safety properties, that is, it aims at producing proofs stating that ensemble of components cannot reach a predefined set of undesirable states. The method developed combines structural analysis for component behaviors with structural analysis of connectors. SMC-BIP is a tool to perform quantitative analysis, using formally-defined models from which it explores the reachable states. Its main characteristic is to provide answers to quantitative questions based on partial state-space coverage. It also evaluates confidence in such results based on stochastic models. SBIP is an extension of BIP that allows stochastic modeling and statistical verification. On one hand, it relies on BIP expressiveness to handle heterogeneous and complex component-based systems. On the other hand it uses statistical model checking techniques to perform quantitative verification targeting non-functional properties. GMC is a model checker that verifies whether properties of service components are satisfied by their implementations in the C or C++ language, i.e. that in any thread interleaving, no deadlock appears and no assertion state in the code is violated. It supports verification of multi-threaded programs.

3.2 Runtime Cycle

The "runtime wheel" comprises the online activities the system performs autonomically: *monitoring, awareness and adaptation*. This cycle is characteristic for the life cycle of collective autonomic systems and a major difference from traditional software which has a much more static runtime behavior.

The runtime collecting of data about the system, its components or its environment is called *monitoring*. Monitoring is an essential feature of adaptive systems. While sometimes systems react directly to the data obtained by the monitor, it is more common for ensembles to pass this data to an *awareness mechanism*, i.e., a subsystem that contains reasoners, planners or learning mechanisms, that allow an autonomic system to come up with responses to the challenges posed by its environment. *Adaptation*, in this context, is then the act of implementing the decisions made by the awareness mechanism, e.g., by performing different actions done before or by reconfiguring the system structure. To manage their collective behavior, self-aware components in an ensemble may need to communicate with each other. Therefore the phases of the runtime cycle are not restricted to actions taken by a single component, they may also involve the joint activities of multiple components. For example, when a robot in a swarm becomes aware of a danger to the swarm it should communicate the presence of the danger to other robots in the swarm.

Monitoring. Monitoring is the first step in the runtime cycle of any adaptive system: without information about the state of the system or environment, any change in behavior can only be a random activity and not a purposeful action of the system. Individual components, subsystems of a collective autonomic system, the whole system or parts of the environment may all be monitored.

In the double-wheel life cycle, monitoring has a dual role. The primary objective is usually to provide information about the current state of the system and its environment to the awareness mechanism, which incorporates this information into the decision making process. A secondary objective is to provide developers feedback about properties of the environment so that they can check whether the behavior of the awareness mechanism is adequate and achieves the desired goals.

One of the technical challenges faced by monitoring systems is *dynamic coverage configuration*: The awareness mechanism may require different information at different points. Monitoring should accommodate these requests for information dynamically, rather than relying only on a statically configured description of what has to be monitored. It is also important to provide *monitoring cost awareness*, to make it possible to reason on the trade off between the cost of monitoring and the awareness benefit provided by the data. Often *high monitoring coverage* is necessary to accommodate the requirements of the awareness mechanism, but sometimes this may lead to monitoring costs that are higher than the benefits gained by the additional situational awareness.

To support easy access to monitoring performance information in ASCENS, we have developed SPL [20], a formalism that makes it possible to express conditions on performance-related observations in a compact manner. To collect the monitoring information from executing components, we use dynamic instrumentation in DiSL [50]. In [19] and the Chapter II.5 [18] of this volume we explain how the two technologies interact in the context of a performance-aware component system.

Awareness. The knowledge a collective autonomic system has on its behavior and environment as well as the reasoning mechanisms that can be employed by the system at runtime comprise its awareness. We divide the notion of awareness along four dimensions: *scope* (which parts of the system and environment are represented by the awareness mechanism), *breadth* (which properties are part of the awareness model), *depth* (which kinds of questions the awareness mechanism can answer) and *quality* (how well the conclusions the ensemble draws correspond to reality). Chapter II.4 [42] contains a more detailed discussion of awareness mechanisms.

To enable problem solving and adaptation in complex domains, *deep awareness mechanisms* may be required. Deep models and reasoners can not only answer questions about the immediately observable state of the system, they also model underlying principles such as causality or physical properties so that they may, e.g., infer consequences of actions or diagnose likely causes of unexpected events.

Designers cannot provide a complete specification of the conditions in which an autonomic system has to operate. To achieve the desired performance and to allow flexible reactions to contingencies not foreseen at design-time, the awareness mechanism may need to learn how to adapt its internal models to the circumstances encountered at runtime.

The POEM language [41] enables developers to specify deep logical and stochastic domain models that describe the expected behavior of the system's environment. System behaviors are specified as *partial programs*, i.e., programs in which certain operations are left as non-deterministic choices for the runtime system. A strategy for resolving non-determinism is called a *completion*. Various techniques can be used to build completions: If precise models of the environment are available for certain situations, completions may be inferred logically or statistically and planning techniques can be used to find a long-term strategy. In cases where models cannot be provided, reinforcement learning techniques can instead be applied, and the ensemble can behave in a more reactive manner.

The Iliad implementation of POEM includes facilities for full first-order inference and special-purpose reasoners for, e.g., temporal and spatial reasoning; their results can be combined with planning methods to compute long-term strategies if enough information about the ensemble's operating conditions is available. In addition, it can compute completions of programs using hierarchical reinforcement-learning techniques. Iliad is fully integrated as knowledge repository and reasoner in jRESP and can therefore be used as awareness engine for SCEL programs.

Self-adaptation. Once the awareness mechanism of a component or ensemble has come to the conclusion that a malfunction, contingency, or simply a performance issue exists, it has to decide how to respond in order to resolve the situation.

In ASCENS we call this response an adaptation action, and we distinguish between two main classes of adaptation actions:

- *Weak-adaptation*, which implies modifying some of the control parameters of a component/ensemble, and possibly adding new functions/behaviors or modifying some of the existing ones.
- *Strong-adaptation*, which implies modifying the very structure of the component or ensemble, and in particular modifying the architecture by which adaptive feedback loops are organized around the component or ensemble.

Weak adaptations are often cheaper and simpler than strong adaptations and still sufficient to respond adequately to changes in its environment: If the path of a rescue robot is blocked it can simply try to take another route to its target; there is no need for the robot to change its configuration to respond to this scenario.

However, for more difficult adaptations, the whole structure of an ensemble may need to be reconfigured: If a swarm of independently operating rescue robots has to move victims that are too heavy for a single robot to carry, several robots may have to form a new sub-ensemble that coordinates their actions using a centralized autonomic manager. The adaptation patterns presented in Sect. 4 support these kinds of strong adaptation.

To the best of our knowledge, ASCENS is the first approach in which both weak and strong forms of self-adaptation are put at work in a unique coherent framework. For white-box and black-box adaptation mechanisms for collective autonomic systems the reader is referred to Chapter II.1 [16] of this volume.

3.3 Evolution Control Loop

The two cycles of EDLC are complemented by transitions from design cycle to runtime cycle and vice versa supporting the long term system's evolution. The collective autonomic system evolution consists in monitoring data at runtime, the fed back to the design cycle to provided basis for system redesign and redeployment. These transitions thus correspond to *deployment* and *feedback* activities.

Deployment. The transition from design to runtime deploys a collective autonomic system preparing it for its execution. This involves installing, configuring and launching the application. The deployment may also involve executable code generation and compilation/linking. In ASCENS, the deployment is addressed by service-component runtime frameworks like JDEECo [22] and JRESP. These frameworks allow for the distributed execution of a service component application and provide their specific means of deployment.

Feedback. The transition from runtime to design provides feedback based on data collected by the monitoring and learning process of the running application. The feedback is used for improving the specification, code or a deeper analysis of the requirements. It connects the online with the offline development process. This connection is made possible by employing design methods that keep the traceability of design decisions to code artefacts and knowledge – e.g. the Invariant Refinement Method (IRM) [47], which has been specifically developed for hierarchical design of a service component application. When used in conjunction with IRM, monitoring *(i)* observes the real functional and non-functional properties of components and situation in components' environment, and *(ii)* provides observed data. At design time these observed data can be compared to assumptions and conclusions captured by IRM; comparison is currently performed manually but we envision automated support. If a contradiction is detected, IRM is used to guide a developer to a component or ensemble which has to be adjusted or extended, e.g. to account for an unexpected situation encountered at runtime. For further details on IRM, see Chapter III.4 [23] of this volume.

4   A Pattern Language for Ensemble Development

In order to design and develop collective autonomic systems, we have defined a catalog of patterns for this kind of systems [56,43]. The importance of the catalog and of patterns in general start from the idea that "software patterns are reusable solutions to recurring design problems and are considered a mainstream of software reuse practice" [52]. So software adaptation can indeed benefit from reuse in a similar way that designing software architectures has benefited from the reuse of software design patterns [37].

Presenting engineering concepts in terms of interrelated patterns enables developers to explore the relationship between different design elements and simplifies an understanding of the trade-offs involved in different modeling, verification and implementation choices. To support the full development life cycle and to be usable for developers who are not already expert in the EDLC and the various technologies developed by ASCENS we have included patterns at different levels of abstraction so that the pattern catalog [40] can also serve as introduction to certain development techniques.

4.1   Pattern Categories

We started identifying adaptation patterns, one of the undoubtedly most important and unique design aspects of ensembles. There are, however, many other parts of the ensemble development process where interrelated design challenges and implementation choices can be clarified and made accessible via a catalog of interrelated patterns, which is often called a pattern language.

Currently our pattern catalog contains patterns in the following areas:

Conceptual Patterns: High-level descriptions of certain techniques or concepts that can serve as introduction to topics with which developers may not be familiar. An example is *Awareness Mechanism* that describes the general concept of those mechanisms to ensure awareness of the system's and environmental behavior.

Architectural Patterns: Patterns that describe the architecture of a system or a component. An example for a pattern in this category is *Distributed Awareness-based Behavior*. These patterns often serve as entry points into the catalog for developers trying to solve an architectural problem.

Adaptation Patterns: Patterns concerned with adaptation and the control-loop structure of ensembles. Examples for patterns in this area are *Reactive Stigmergy Service Components Ensemble Pattern* and *Centralised AM Service Components Ensemble Pattern* described in detail in section 4.3.

Awareness Patterns: Patterns for developing and using awareness mechanisms. An example is *Action-calculus Reasoning*, a pattern that describes the trade-offs in using a logical formalism based on an action calculus for modeling and reasoning about the system's domain.

Coordination Patterns: Patterns that are concerned with coordination aspects of an ensemble. An example for a pattern in this category is *Tuple-space Based Coordination*.

Cooperation Patterns: Patterns that describe mechanisms for cooperation between agents in an ensemble. For example the *Auction* mechanism belongs to this category.

Implementation Patterns: Patterns that are mainly concerned with implementation or low-level design aspects. An example is the *Monkey Patching* (anti)-pattern which deals with a certain method of dynamic code update.

Knowledge Patterns: Patterns that addresses issues arising with the development of knowledge bases and knowledge-based systems. Examples for patterns in this category are *Build Small Ontology* or *Reuse Large Ontology*.

Navigation Patterns: Patterns that address navigation or position keeping in physical space, for example *Build Chain to Target*.

Self-expression Patterns: Patterns that are concerned with self-expression of ensembles, and goal-directed or utility-maximizing behaviors. A simple example is *Decompose Goal into Subgoals*.

These categories are neither exhaustive nor disjoint. Patterns such as *Cooperate to Reach Goal* belong into several categories (cooperation patterns and self-expression patterns), and it is easy to think of patterns which do not fit in any of the categories mentioned above. Therefore, the classification of patterns is done via keywords, which allow m-n relationships between patterns and categories and make it easy to introduce new categories. For each pattern that is concerned with particular phases of the EDLC, these phases are also represented as keywords for the pattern.

As the *Monkey Patching* example shows, the catalog also includes some patterns that describe widely used but potentially dangerous techniques, so-called anti-patterns. We think it is important to also include anti-patterns since there are often good reasons why an anti-pattern has become widely used. In many cases anti-patterns are good solutions for specialized problems which are regularly applied in situations in which they are unnecessary or in which better solutions exist (this is the case for the *Monkey Patching* pattern). Additionally, developers might not even know that a certain practice is considered an anti-pattern, and they might not be aware of superior alternatives, or of ways to mitigate the downside of using the anti-pattern.

When exploring the pattern catalog [40], the first two categories of patterns (conceptual patterns and architectural patterns) serve as good entry points into the pattern system; patterns in these categories provide a coherent overview of a general topic, and the tree of references starting from patterns in these categories transitively spans the whole pattern catalog.

4.2   Pattern Template

In the following paragraphs we describe the template that we use for our pattern language. Since the patterns in our pattern system range from conceptional patterns to implementation patterns, we include a relatively large number of fields, but we allow several of them to be left empty. In the following description, mandatory fields are marked with an asterisk. Except for conceptual patterns, each pattern should either contain a *context* field or the two fields *motivation* and *applicability*, but it should not contain all three.

Name:* A descriptive name for the pattern, e.g., *Algorithmic Planning*.

Specializes: A pattern may inherit properties from another pattern but modify certain fields. In this case the parent pattern is included in the *specializes* field and the differences are described in the respective fields.

Classification:* The set of keywords that describes, e.g., to which phases of the EDLC the pattern applies.

Aliases: Other names by which this pattern is known.

Intent:* The purpose for this pattern, what does the pattern accomplish?

Summary: For patterns which have a very long description, a summary that addresses the most important features may be given in this field.

Context:* The design problem or runtime conditions to which this pattern is applicable. This field is mandatory for adaptation patterns; for other patterns the context is often split into motivation and applicability.

Motivation:* The reasons why this pattern is necessary.

Applicability:* Describes for which systems the pattern is applicable, and which influences might lead to other patterns being preferable.

Diagram/Structure: If applicable a diagram that describes the pattern; e.g., adaptation patterns contain a diagram illustrating the components that are involved in the feedback loops.

Description/Behavior:* A description of the pattern.

Formal Behavior: If applicable a more formal description of the pattern's behavior can be given in this section. For example, all adaptation patterns include a specification using the State-of-the-Affairs (SOTA) [2] notation of their behavior, which comprises the description of the pattern's goals, constraints and utilities.

Consequences: Consequences and trade-offs for using the patterns. If this section is present it often summarizes trade-offs already mentioned in the *description* field.

Implementation: Implementation techniques and practical tips for realizing this pattern. This section also includes references to ASCENS tools that are helpful for implementing the pattern.

Variants: If a pattern has simple variations which are not significant enough to justify their own patterns they are mentioned here.

Related Patterns: Related patterns, e.g., patterns that specialize the current pattern, alternatives for the current pattern or patterns that are useful in the implementation of the current pattern.

Applications: References to applications that apply self-adaptation patterns in different real life scenarios. This is very important because the catalog has to be based on experiences and/or on some solid formal ground, and on a solid organization.

4.3   Pattern Examples

The pattern language described above provides a flexible structure in which many kinds of patterns can be conveniently expressed while still retaining enough commonality to build a coherent system of patterns.

   To give a flavor of the patterns we present an excerpt of five patterns of the ASCENS pattern catalog. Due to space restrictions we omitted the section *applications* for some of the examples. The complete catalog is available on the web [40]. For a detailed description as long as the taxonomy table of the adaptation patterns the reader is referred to [56].

Pattern: *Reactive Stigmergy Service Components Ensemble Pattern.*

- **Name**: Reactive Stigmergy Service Components Ensemble.
- **Classification**: service-components-ensemble, edlc-requirements-engineering
- **Intent**: There are a large amount of components that are not able to directly interact one to each other. The components simply react to the environment and sense the environment changes.
- **Context**: This pattern has to be adopted when:
  - there are a large amount of components acting together;
  - the components need to be simple components, without having a lot of knowledge;
  - the environment is frequently changing;
  - the components are not able to directly communicate one with the other.
- **Structure**: See Figure 4.

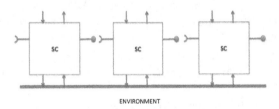

Fig. 4. Reactive Stigmergy Service Components Ensemble

- **Behavior**: This pattern has not a direct feedback loop. Each single component acts like a bio-inspired component (e.g. an ant). To satisfy its simple goal, the Service Component (SC) acts in the environment that senses with its "sensors" and reacts to the changes in it with its "effectors". The different components are not able to communicate one with the other, but are able to propagate information (their actions) in the environment. Than they are able to sense the environment changes (other components reactions) and adapt their behavior due to these changes.

- **SOTA description (Formal Behavior)**:
    - *Goals*: $G_{SC_1}, G_{SC_2}, \ldots, G_{SC_n}$
    - *Utilities*: $U_{SC_1} = U_{SC_2} = \ldots = U_{SC_n}$
    - *Explanation*: In the pattern each Service Component has a separated goal, that is explicit only at the component level.
      Regarding the utilities of the ensemble, they are the same of each SCs that have to be shared by the components.
- **Consequences**: If the component is a proactive one, its behavior is defined inside it with its internal goal. The behavior of the whole system cannot be a priori defined. It emerges from the collective behavior of the ensemble. The components do not require a large amount of knowledge. The reaction of each component is quick and does not need other managers because adaptation is propagated via environment. The interaction model is an entirely indirect one.
- **Related Patterns**: Proactive Service Component.

Pattern: *Centralised AM Service Components Ensemble Pattern.*

- **Name**: Centralised Autonomic Manager (AM) Service Components Ensemble.
- **Classification**: service-components-ensemble, edlc-requirements engineering
- **Intent**: A Service Component necessitates an external feedback loop to adapt. All the components need to share knowledge and the same adaptation logic, so they are managed by the same AM.
- **Context**: This patterns has to be adopted when:
    - the components are simple and an AM is necessary to manage adaptation;
    - a direct communication between components is necessary;
    - a centralised feedback loop is more suitable because a single AM has a global vision on the system;
    - there are few components composing the system.
- **Structure**: See Figure 5.
- **Behavior**: This pattern is designed around an unique feedback loop. All the components are managed by a unique AM that "control" all the components behavior and, sharing knowledge about all the components, is able to propagate adaptation.
- **SOTA description (Formal Behavior)**:
    - *Goals*: $G = G_{SC_1} + G_{SC_2} + \ldots + G_{SC_n} + G_{AM}$
    - *Utilities*: $U = U_{SC_1} + U_{SC_2} + \ldots + U_{SC_n} + U_{AM}$
- **Consequences**: An unique AM is more efficient to manage adaptation over the entire system, but it can became a node of failure.
- **Related Patterns**: Autonomic Service Component.

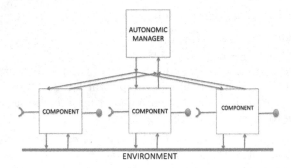

Fig. 5. Centralised AM Service Components Ensemble

Pattern: *P2P AMs Service Components Ensemble Pattern.*

- **Name**: P2P AMs Service Components Ensemble.
- **Classification**: service-components-ensemble, edlc-requirements-engineering
- **Intent**: This pattern is designed around an explicit autonomic feedback loop for each component. The components are able to communicate and coordinate each other through their AMs. Each AM manages adaptation on a single SC.
- **Context**: This pattern has to be adopted when:
    - the components are simple and an external AM is necessary to manage adaptation at the component level;
    - the components need to directly communicate one with the other (throu gh their AMs) to propagate adaptation.
- **Structure**: See Figure 6.

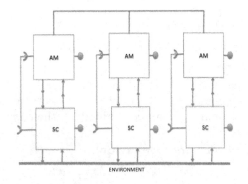

Fig. 6. P2P AMs Service Components Ensemble

- **Behavior**: Each component is managed by an AM and acts as an autonomic component. Than the AMs directly communicate one with the other with a P2P communication protocol. The communication made at the AM's level makes it easier to share not only knowledge about the components, but also the adaptation logic.
- **SOTA description (Formal Behavior)**:
  - *Goals*: $(G_{SC_1}, G_{AM_1}) \bigcup (G_{SC_2}, G_{AM_2}) \bigcup \ldots \bigcup (G_{SC_n}, G_{AM_n})$
  - *Utilities*: $(U_{SC_1}, U_{AM_1}) \bigcup (U_{SC_2}, U_{AM_2}) \bigcup \ldots \bigcup (U_{SC_n}, U_{AM_n})$

  The goal of the ensemble is composed of the goals of every single component. Here a component is composed of a SC and an AM, so its goal is the goal of the SC (if it is a proactive component), along with the goal of the AM.

  At the same way the utilities of the ensemble are composed of the utilities of every single component. In this scenario, it is not necessary that all the components have the same utilities (same for goals), and also some components may have no utilities at all.
- **Consequences**: The use of AMs to communicate between components makes the adaptation management more simple because the components remain simple and the knowledge necessary for adaptation is easily shared between the AMs.
- **Related Patterns**: Autonomic Service Component.
- **Applications**: A lot of case studies about intelligent transportation systems use this pattern. For example a traffic jam monitoring system case study is presented in [4]. The intelligent transportation system consists of a set of intelligent cameras, which are distributed evenly along a highway. Each camera (SC) has a limited viewing range and cameras are placed to get an optimal coverage of the highway. Each camera has a communication unit to interact with other cameras. The goal of the cameras is to detect and monitor traffic jams on the highway in a decentralised way. The data observed by the multiple cameras have to be aggregated, so each camera has an agent that can play different roles in organizations. Agents exploit a distributed middleware, which provides support for dynamic organizations. This middleware acts as an AM; it encapsulates the management of dynamic evolution of organizations offering different roles to agents, based on the current context.

Pattern: *Knowledge-equipped Component.*

- **Name**: *Knowledge-equipped Component*
- **Classification**: architecture, component, edlc-design, edlc-modeling
- **Intent**: Enable an autonomous component to operate in a context-sensitive manner that potentially requires interaction with other components.
- **Motivation**: Various architectures exist that allow components and systems to exhibit these kinds of complex, context-sensitive behaviors and interactions. *Knowledge-equipped Components* are components with individual behaviors and knowledge repositories that can dynamically form aggregations.

These components can often be arranged in a *Flat Architecture* to provide a powerful and flexible, yet simple, architectural choice.

– **Context:** *Knowledge-equipped Components* are well-suited to ensembles in which components need to act autonomously and interact with each other. They can be used in different architectural styles such as *Peer-to-peer* or *Client/Server* systems.

Components need to have at least a modest amount of computational power and local storage; the pattern is not applicable for systems that rely on, e.g., pure stigmergy. Furthermore, if interaction is necessary, components must be equipped with a communication mechanism that enables sender and receiver to establish their identities and sufficient bandwidth must be available.

– **Description:** A knowledge-equipped component, is equipped with *behaviors* and a *knowledge repository.* Behaviors describe the computations each component performs. They are typically modeled as processes executing actions, for example in the style of process calculi or in rewriting logic. In systems using knowledge-equipped components, interaction between components is achieved by allowing components to access the knowledge repositories of other components; access restrictions are mediated by access policies.

Knowledge repositories provide high-level primitives to manage pieces of information coming from different sources. Knowledge is represented through items containing either application data or awareness data. The former are used for determining the progress of component computations, while the latter provide information about the environment in which the components are running (e.g. monitored data from sensors) or about the actual status of an autonomic component (e.g. its current location). This allows components to be both context- and self-aware. The knowledge repository's handling mechanism for knowledge-equipped components has to provide at least operations for adding knowledge, as well as retrieving and withdrawing knowledge from it.

– **Implementation:** SCEL (see Chapter I.1 [54]) defines primitives for modeling and implementing *Knowledge-equipped Components.* An example for the behavior of a component implemented in SCEL is the following monitor for a garbage-collecting robot (which is a simplified version of the controller analyzed in [62]):

$$s \triangleq \mathbf{get}(item)@ctl.p$$

$$p \triangleq \mathbf{get}(items, !x)@master.\mathbf{put}(items, x + 1)@master.c$$

$$c \triangleq \mathbf{get}(arrived)@ctl.\mathbf{put}(dropped)@master.s + \mathbf{get}(done)@ctl$$

This monitor waits until a tuple *item* becomes available in the knowledge repository *ctl*, updates a counter in the knowledge repository *master*, and then waits until either a tuple *arrived* or a tuple *done* is available in *ctl*. In the first case the controller informs the repository *master* that it has *dropped* an item and resumes from the beginning, if instead a tuple *done* is retrieved from *ctl* the monitor stops.

This example also shows how several knowledge-equipped components can interact via a shared knowledge repository *master*. Note that no further synchronization primitives are necessary, even in the case where the *master* repository is shared between different components, since the first component to perform the action **get**(*items*, !*x*)@*master* removes the *items*-tuple from this knowledge repository, and other components will block on their **get**(*items*, !*x*)@*master* operations until the first component has **put** the updated tuple back into *master*.

- **Consequences:** A knowledge-equipped component can exhibit complex behavior that relies on local or shared knowledge. It can adapt its behavior flexibly to knowledge gathered while the ensemble is running. In some cases (e.g., some swarm robotics scenarios with limited sensor input) it may not be possible to extract the required knowledge from the available information. In general knowledge-equipped components have relatively high processing and storage requirements; shared knowledge repositories often require high network bandwidth and low latency.
- **Related Patterns:** The coordination of interactions for knowledge-equipped components is an example of *Tuple-space Based Coordination*; the interaction between components can be performed using *Attribute-based Communication*. If the knowledge of the component is repeatedly or continuously updated to correspond to the environment, the knowledge repository and processes responsible for updating it form an *Awareness Mechanism*. An ensemble containing multiple such components exhibits *Distributed Awareness-based Behavior*.

Pattern: *Statistical Model Checking.*

- **Name:** *Statistical Model Checking*
- **Classification:** ensemble, validation, edlc-verification-and-validation
- **Intent:** Validate quantitative properties of a system at design time.
- **Motivation:** It is desirable to ascertain that a system can perform according to specification as early as possible in the design process, and to validate changes of the system design when requirements or environmental conditions change. Traditional verification and validation techniques are often difficult to scale to the size of ensembles.
- **Context:** *Statistical Model Checking* is applicable in many situations in which quantitative properties of ensembles need to be validated at design time. It is necessary to have (stochastic) models of the system and its environment that match the actual behavior closely enough to ensure meaningful results.

  While it scales well when compared to many other validation techniques, the computational and memory requirements of statistical model checking may be too high for very large systems. Systems that include non-determinism may pose problems for statistical model checkers, although advances in the area of statistical model checking for, e.g., Markov Decision Procedures, have recently been made. Statistical model checking provides only statistical assurances; it can therefore not be applied in situations where a proof of correctness is required. Furthermore, statistical model checking cannot validate properties that can only be established for infinite execution traces. In cases where precise behavioral estimates are required, the effort for statistical model checking may be prohibitive.

- **Description:** In contrast to traditional (numerical) model checking techniques, statistical model checking runs simulations of the system, performs hypothesis testing on these simulations and then uses statistical estimates to determine whether the probability that the system satisfies the given hypotheses is above a certain threshold.

- **Applications:** Several examples for applying the *Statistical Model Checking* pattern to validate properties of ensembles and choose between different implementation strategies are presented in [29].

5   Related Work

In the literature we find several approaches for possible architectures or reference models for adaptive and autonomic systems. A well known approach is the MAPE-K architecture introduced by IBM [30] which comprises a control loop of four phases Monitor, Analyse, Plan, Execute. MAPE-K – in contrast to our approach – focus only on the adaptation process at runtime and does not consider the interplay of design and runtime phases. The second research roadmap for self-adaptive systems [3] also suggests a life cycle based on MAPE-K and proposes the use of a process modeling language to describe the self-adaptation workflow and feedback control loops.

The approach of Inverardi and Mori [45] shows foreseen and unforeseen context changes which are represented following a feature analysis perspective. Their life cycle is also based on MAPE-K, focusing therefore on the runtime aspects. A slightly different life cycle is presented in the work of Brun et al. [15] which explores feedback loops from the control engineering perspective; feedback loops are first-class entities and comprise the activities collect, analyse, decide and act.

Bruni et al. [17] presented a control data based conceptual framework for adaptivity. In contrast to our pragmatic approach supporting the use of methods and tools in the development life cycle, they provide a simple formal model for the framework based on a labelled transition system (LTS). In addition, they provide an analysis of adaptivity in different computational paradigms, such as context-oriented and declarative programming from the control data point of view.

After the original "Gang of Four" book [35] introduced design patterns for object-oriented software development, pattern catalogues in various formats have been proposed for a large and varied number of domains, and covering many areas also addressed in the ASCENS pattern catalogue, e.g., application architecture [34,33], distributed computing [25,58,5], testing [12], resource-constrained devices [36], cooperative interactions [51], or fault-tolerant software [38]. However, many of the specific features of ASCENS and the EDLC, e.g., the use of formal methods or the integration of the design-time and runtime cycle are not addressed in these pattern languages.

In the last years the interest in engineering self-adaptive and autonomic systems is growing, as shown by the number of recent surveys and overviews on the topic [27,57]. However, a comprehensive and rationally-organized analysis of architectural patterns for self-adaptation is still missing.

Salehie and Tahvildari [57] survey and classify the various principles underlying self-adaptation and the means by which adaptation ca be enforced in a system, i.e., the different mechanisms to promote adaptation at the behavioral and structural level. Similarly, Andersson et al. [4] propose a classification of modeling dimensions for self-adaptive systems to provide the engineers with a common set of vocabulary for specifying the self-adaptation properties under consideration and select suitable solutions. However, and although both these works emphasize the importance of feedback loops, nothing is said about the patterns by which such feedback loops can be organized to promote self-adaptation.

Coming to work that have a more direct relation with ours, Brun et al. [14] present a possible classification of self-adaptive systems with the emphasis on the use of feedback loops as first-class entities in control engineering. They unfold the role of feedback loops as a general mechanism for self-adaptation, essential for understanding all types of self-adaptation. Taking inspiration for control engineering, natural systems and software engineering, the authors present some self-adaptive architectures that exhibit feedback loops. They also identify the critical challenges that must be addressed to enable systematic and well-organized engineering of self-adaptive and self-managing software systems. Their analysis of different kinds of feedback loops is very relevant for our work, and in our effort towards a comprehensive and complete taxonomy of patterns for feedback loops we have partially built upon it.

Grounded on earlier works on architectural self-adaptation approaches, the FORMS model [60] (FOrmal Reference Model for Self-adaptation) enables engineers to describe, study and evaluate alternative design choices for self-adaptive systems. FORMS defines a shared vocabulary of adaptive primitives that – while simple and concise – can be used to precisely define arbitrary complex self-adaptive systems, and can support engineers in expressing their design choices, there included those related to the architectural patterns for feedback loops. FORMS does not have the ambition to analyse and classify architectural self-adaptation patterns, and rather has to be considered as a potentially useful complement to our work.

6   Conclusions

In this work we presented a software development life cycle for collective autonomic systems. Its aim is to support developers dealing with self-* properties of ensembles, mainly self-awareness and self-adaptation talking into account environmental situations. A distinguishing feature of the double-wheeled life cycle is the feedback loop from runtime to design (in addition to the feedback loops at design and runtime provided by classical approaches for self-adaptive engineering). It is also important to remark that our life cycle relies on foundational methods used for the verification of the expected behavior; indeed this provides a feedback loop that allows for improvement of an evolving software. We illustrated how the life cycle can be instantiated using a set of languages, methods and tools developed within the ASCENS project.

A first proof of concept of the life cycle was performed for the e-mobility domain [24]. Future plans are the validation of our engineering approach with more challenging scenarios of different application domains. A vision on future engineering approaches should consider to have a look at other disciplines even those that are not so directly related to computer science for ideas and technologies for building collective autonomic systems.

In addition, we have presented a catalog of patterns to provide reusable solutions for the development of collective autonomic systems. We included in the catalog patterns at different levels of abstraction so that the pattern catalog can also serve as introduction to certain development techniques. Therefore, it is useful for developers who are not already experts in the EDLC and the various technologies developed within the scope of the ASCENS project.

References

1. Abeywickrama, D.B., Zambonelli, F.: Model Checking Goal-Oriented Requirements for Self-Adaptive Systems. In: Proceedings of the 19th IEEE International Conference and Workshops on Engineering of Computer-Based Systems, Apr. 2012, pp. 33–42 (2012)
2. Abeywickrama, D., Bicocchi, N., Zambonelli, F.: Sota: Towards a general model for self-adaptive systems. In: IEEE 21st International Workshop on Enabling Technologies: Infrastructure for Collaborative Enterprises (WETICE 2012), June 2012, pp. 48–53 (2012)
3. de Lemos, R.: Engineering for Self-Adaptive Systems: A second Research Roadmap. In: de Lemos, R., Giese, H., Müller, H., Shaw, M. (eds.) Software Engineering for Self-Adaptive Systems. No. 10431 in Dagstuhl Seminar Proceedings, Schloss Dagstuhl - Leibniz-Zentrum fuer Informatik, Germany, Dagstuhl, Germany (2011)
4. Andersson, J., de Lemos, R., Malek, S., Weyns, D.: Modeling dimensions of self-adaptive software systems. In: Cheng, B.H.C., de Lemos, R., Giese, H., Inverardi, P., Magee, J. (eds.) Self-Adaptive Systems. LNCS, vol. 5525, pp. 27–47. Springer, Heidelberg (2009)
5. Babaoglu, O., Canright, G., Deutsch, A., Caro, G.A.D., Ducatelle, F., Gambardella, L.M., Ganguly, N., Jelasity, M., Montemanni, R., Montresor, A., Urnes, T.: Design patterns from biology for distributed computing. ACM Trans. Auton. Adapt. Syst. 1(1), 26–66 (2006)
6. Basu, A., Bensalem, S., Bozga, M., Caillaud, B., Delahaye, B., Legay, A.: Statistical abstraction and model-checking of large heterogeneous systems. In: Hatcliff, J., Zucca, E. (eds.) FORTE 2010 and FMOODS 2010. LNCS, vol. 6117, pp. 32–46. Springer, Heidelberg (2010)
7. Basu, A., Bensalem, S., Bozga, M., Combaz, J., Jaber, M., Nguyen, T.H., Sifakis, J.: Rigorous component-based design using the BIP framework. IEEE Software,

Special Edition – Software Components beyond Programming – from Routines to Services 28(3), 41–48 (2011)

8. Basu, A., Bozga, M., Sifakis, J.: Modeling Heterogeneous Real-time Components in BIP. In: SEFM, pp. 3–12. IEEE Computer Society Press, Los Alamitos (2006)

9. Bensalem, S., Bozga, M., Delahaye, B., Jegourel, C., Legay, A., Nouri, A.: Statistical Model Checking QoS Properties of Systems with SBIP. In: Margaria, T., Steffen, B. (eds.) ISoLA 2012, Part I. LNCS, vol. 7609, pp. 327–341. Springer, Heidelberg (2012)

10. Bensalem, S., Bozga, M., Nguyen, T.H., Sifakis, J.: D-Finder: A Tool for Compositional Deadlock Detection and Verification. In: Bouajjani, A., Maler, O. (eds.) CAV 2009. LNCS, vol. 5643, pp. 614–619. Springer, Heidelberg (2009)

11. Bensalem, S., Griesmayer, A., Legay, A., Nguyen, T.H., Peled, D.: Efficient Deadlock Detection for Concurrent Systems. In: Singh, S., Jobstmann, B., Kishinevsky, M., Brandt, J. (eds.) MEMOCODE, pp. 119–129. IEEE Computer Society Press, Los Alamitos (2011)

12. Binder, R.: Testing Object-Oriented Systems: Models, Patterns and Tools. Addison-Wesley Professional, Reading (2000)

13. Bröckers, A., Lott, C.M., Rombach, H.D., Verlage, M.: MVP-L Language Report Version 2. Tech. Rep. Technical Report Nr. 265/95, University of Kaiserslautern (1995)

14. Brun, Y., Di Marzo Serugendo, G., Gacek, C., Giese, H., Kienle, H.M., Litoiu, M., Müller, H., Pezzè, M., Shaw, M.: Engineering self-adaptive systems through feedback loops. In: Cheng, B.H.C., de Lemos, R., Giese, H., Inverardi, P., Magee, J. (eds.) Self-Adaptive Systems. LNCS, vol. 5525, pp. 48–70. Springer, Heidelberg (2009)

15. Brun, Y., Di Marzo Serugendo, G., Gacek, C., Giese, H., Kienle, H.M., Litoiu, M., Müller, H., Pezzè, M., Shaw, M.: Engineering self-adaptive systems through feedback loops. In: Cheng, B.H.C., de Lemos, R., Giese, H., Inverardi, P., Magee, J. (eds.) Self-Adaptive Systems. LNCS, vol. 5525, pp. 48–70. Springer, Heidelberg (2009)

16. Bruni, R., Corradini, A., Gadducci, F., Hölzl, M., Lafuente, A.L., Vandin, A., Wirsing, M.: Reconciling White-Box and Black-Box Perspectives on Behavioral Self-adaptation. In: Wirsing, M., Hölzl, M., Koch, N., Mayer, P. (eds.) Software Engineering for Collective Autonomic Systems. LNCS, vol. 8998, pp. 163–184. Springer, Heidelberg (2015)

17. Bruni, R., Corradini, A., Gadducci, F., Lluch Lafuente, A., Vandin, A.: A Conceptual Framework for Adaptation. In: de Lara, J., Zisman, A. (eds.) Fundamental Approaches to Software Engineering. LNCS, vol. 7212, pp. 240–254. Springer, Heidelberg (2012)

18. Bulej, L., Bureš, T., Gerostathopoulos, I., Horký, V., Keznikl, J., Marek, L., Tschaikowski, M., Tribastone, M., Tøuma, P.: Supporting Performance Awareness in Autonomous Ensembles. In: Wirsing, M., Hölzl, M., Koch, N., Mayer, P. (eds.) Software Engineering for Collective Autonomic Systems. LNCS, vol. 8998, pp. 291–322. Springer, Heidelberg (2015)

19. Bulej, L., Bures, T., Horky, V., Keznikl, J., Tuma, P.: Performance Awareness in Component Systems: Vision Paper. In: Proceedings of COMPSAC (2012)

20. Bulej, L., Bures, T., Keznikl, J., Koubkova, A., Podzimek, A., Tuma, P.: Capturing Performance Assumptions using Stochastic Performance Logic. In: Proc. 3rd Intl. Conf. on Performance Engineering (ICPE'12), Boston, MA, USA (2012)

21. Bulej, L., Bureš, T., Keznikl, J., Koubková, A., Podzimek, A., Tůma, P.: Capturing performance assumptions using stochastic performance logic. In: Proc. ICPE 2012, pp. 311–322. ACM Press, New York (2012)
22. Bures, T., Gerostathopoulos, I., Hnetynka, P., Keznikl, J., Kit, M., Plasil, F.: DEECO: An Ensemble-Based Component System. In: Proceedings of the 16th International ACM Sigsoft symposium on Component-based software engineering (CBSE '13), pp. 81–90. ACM Press, New York (2013)
23. Bures, T., Gerostathopoulos, I., Hnetynka, P., Keznikl, J., Kit, M., Plasil, F.: The Invariant Refinement Method. In: Wirsing, M., Hölzl, M., Koch, N., Mayer, P. (eds.) Software Engineering for Collective Autonomic Systems. LNCS, vol. 8998, pp. 405–428. Springer, Heidelberg (2015)
24. Bures, T., Nicola, R.D., Gerostathopoulos, I., Hoch, N., Kit, M., Koch, N., Monreale, G.V., Montanari, U., Pugliese, R., Serbedzija, N., Wirsing, M., Zambonelli, F.: A life cycle for the development of autonomic systems: The e-mobility showcase. 2013 IEEE 7th International Conference on Self-Adaptation and Self-Organizing Systems Workshops 0, 71–76 (2013)
25. Buschmann, F., Henney, K., Schmidt, D.C.: A Pattern Language for Distributed Computing. Pattern-Oriented Software Architecture, vol. 4. Wiley, Chichester (2007)
26. Cabri, G., Puviani, M., Zambonelli, F.: Towards a Taxonomy of Adaptive Agent-Based Collaboration Patterns for Autonomic Service Ensembles. In: Proceedings of the 2011 International Conference on Collaboration Technologies and Systems, May 2011, pp. 508–515. IEEE Computer Society Press, Los Alamitos (2011)
27. Cheng, B.H.C., de Lemos, R., Giese, H., Inverardi, P., Magee, J., Andersson, J., Becker, B., Bencomo, N., Brun, Y., Cukic, B., Di Marzo Serugendo, G., Dustdar, S., Finkelstein, A., Gacek, C., Geihs, K., Grassi, V., Karsai, G., Kienle, H.M., Kramer, J., Litoiu, M., Malek, S., Mirandola, R., Müller, H.A., Park, S., Shaw, M., Tichy, M., Tivoli, M., Weyns, D., Whittle, J.: Software engineering for self-adaptive systems: A research roadmap. In: Cheng, B.H.C., de Lemos, R., Giese, H., Inverardi, P., Magee, J. (eds.) Self-Adaptive Systems. LNCS, vol. 5525, pp. 1–26. Springer, Heidelberg (2009)
28. Combaz, J., Bensalem, S., Tiezzi, F., Margheri, A., Pugliese, R., Kofron, J.: Correctness of Service Components and Service Component Ensembles. In: Wirsing, M., Hölzl, M., Koch, N., Mayer, P. (eds.) Software Engineering for Collective Autonomic Systems. LNCS, vol. 8998, pp. 107–159. Springer, Heidelberg (2015)
29. Combaz, J., Lafuente, A.L., Montanari, U., Pugliese, R., Sammartino, M., Tiezzi, F., Vandin, A., von Essen, C.: Verification Results Applied to the Case Studies - ASCENS Joint Deliverable JD3.1 (2013),
http://www.ascens-ist.eu/deliverables/JD31.pdf
30. IBM Corporation: An Architectural Blueprint for Autonomic Computing. Tech. rep., IBM (2005),
http://researchr.org/publication/autonomic-architecture-2005
31. De Nicola, R., Ferrari, G.-L., Loreti, M., Pugliese, R.: A Language-Based Approach to Autonomic Computing. In: Beckert, B., Damiani, F., de Boer, F.S., Bonsangue, M.M. (eds.) FMCO 2011. LNCS, vol. 7542, pp. 25–48. Springer, Heidelberg (2013)
32. De Nicola, R., Loreti, M., Pugliese, R., Tiezzi, F.: SCEL: A Language for Autonomic Computing. Tech. rep., IMT Lucca (January 2013)
33. Erl, T.: SOA Design Patterns, 1st edn. Prentice-Hall, Upper Saddle River (2009)
34. Fowler, M.: Patterns of Enterprise Application Architecture. Addison-Wesley Longman, Amsterdam (2002)

35. Gamma, E., Helm, R., Johnson, R., Vlissides, J.: Design Patterns: Elements of Reusable Object-Oriented Software. Addison-Wesley Longman, Amsterdam (1995)
36. Gay, D., Levis, P., Culler, D.: Software design patterns for TinyOS. Trans. on Embedded Computing Sys. 6(4), 22 (2007)
37. Gomaa, H., Hashimoto, K.: Dynamic self-adaptation for distributed service-oriented transactions. In: International Workshop on Software Engineering for Adaptive and Self-Managing Systems, Zurich, Switzerland, pp. 11–20. IEEE, Los Alamitos (2012)
38. Hanmer, R.: Patterns for Fault Tolerant Software. John Wiley & Sons, Chichester (2007)
39. Hoch, N., Monreale, G.V., Montanari, U., Sammartino, M., Siwe, A.T.: From Local to Global Knowledge and Back. In: Wirsing, M., Hölzl, M., Koch, N., Mayer, P. (eds.) Software Engineering for Collective Autonomic Systems. LNCS, vol. 8998, pp. 185–220. Springer, Heidelberg (2015)
40. Hölzl, M.: APEX: The ASCENS Pattern Explorer. web site, http://www.ascens-ist.eu/pattern
41. Hölzl, M.: The Poem Language (Version 2). Tech. Rep. 7, ASCENS (July 2013), http://www.poem-lang.de/documentation/TR7.pdf
42. Hölzl, M., Gabor, T.: Reasoning and Learning for Awareness and Adaptation. In: Wirsing, M., Hölzl, M., Koch, N., Mayer, P. (eds.) Software Engineering for Collective Autonomic Systems. LNCS, vol. 8998, pp. 249–290. Springer, Heidelberg (2015)
43. Hölzl, M., Koch, N.: D8.3: Third Report on WP8—Best Practices for SDEs (first version) (November 2013)
44. Hölzl, M.M., Wirsing, M.: Towards a system model for ensembles. In: Agha, G., Danvy, O., Meseguer, J. (eds.) Formal Modeling: Actors, Open Systems, Biological Systems. LNCS, vol. 7000, pp. 241–261. Springer, Heidelberg (2011)
45. Inverardi, P., Mori, M.: A Software Lifecycle Process to Support Consistent Evolutions. In: de Lemos, R., Giese, H., Müller, H.A., Shaw, M. (eds.) Software Engineering for Self-Adaptive Systems II. LNCS, vol. 7475, pp. 239–264. Springer, Heidelberg (2013)
46. Kephart, J.O., Chess, D.M.: The vision of autonomic computing. Computer 36(1), 41–50 (2003), doi:10.1109/MC.2003.1160055
47. Keznikl, J., Bures, T., Plasil, F., Gerostathopoulos, I., Hnetynka, P., Hoch, N.: Design of Ensemble-Based Component Systems by Invariant Refinement. In: Proceedings of the 16th International ACM Sigsoft symposium on Component-based software engineering (CBSE '13), pp. 91–100. ACM Press, New York (2013)
48. Keznikl, J., Bures, T., Plasil, F., Kit, M.: Towards Dependable Emergent Ensembles of Components: The DEECo Component Model. In: WICSA/ECSA, pp. 249–252. IEEE Computer Society Press, Los Alamitos (2012)
49. Klarl, A., Hennicker, R.: Design and Implementation of Dynamically Evolving Ensembles with the HELENA Framework. In: Proceedings of the 23rd Australasian Software Engineering Conference, pp. 15–24. IEEE Computer Society Press, Los Alamitos (2014)
50. Marek, L., Villazón, A., Zheng, Y., Ansaloni, D., Binder, W., Qi, Z.: DiSL: a domain-specific language for bytecode instrumentation. In: Proceedings of the 11th annual international conference on Aspect-oriented Software Development (AOSD '12), pp. 239–250. ACM Press, New York (2012)

51. Martin, D., Sommerville, I.: Patterns of Cooperative Interaction: Linking Ethnomethodology and Design. ACM Trans. Comput.-Hum. Interact. 11(1), 59–89 (2004)

52. Morandini, M.: the use of the goal-oriented paradigm for system design and law compliance reasoning. In: iStar 2010–4 th International i* Workshop, Hammamet, Tunisia, p. 71 (2010)

53. Mylopoulos, J., Chung, L., Yu, E.S.K.: From Object-Oriented to Goal-Oriented Requirements Analysis. Communications of the ACM 42(1), 31–37 (1999)

54. De Nicola, R., Latella, D., Lafuente, A.L., Loreti, M., Margheri, A., Massink, M., Morichetta, A., Pugliese, R., Tiezzi, F., Vandin, A.: The SCEL Language: Design, Implementation, Verification. In: Wirsing, M., Hölzl, M., Koch, N., Mayer, P. (eds.) Software Engineering for Collective Autonomic Systems. LNCS, vol. 8998, pp. 3–71. Springer, Heidelberg (2015)

55. Owre, S., Rushby, J.M., Shankar, N.: PVS: A prototype verification system. In: Kapur, D. (ed.) CADE 1992. LNCS, vol. 607, pp. 748–752. Springer, Heidelberg (1992), doi:10.1007/3-540-55602-8_217

56. Puviani, M.: Catalogue of architectural adaptation patterns (2012), http://mars.ing.unimo.it/wiki/papers/TR42.pdf

57. Salehie, M., Tahvildari, L.: Self-adaptive software: Landscape and research challenges. ACM Transactions on Autonomous and Adaptive Systems 4(2), 1–42 (2009)

58. Schmidt, D.C., Stal, M., Rohnert, H., Buschmann, F.: Patterns for Concurrent and Networked Objects. Pattern-Oriented Software Architecture, vol. 2. Wiley, Chichester (2000)

59. Vassev, E., Hinchey, M.: Engineering Requirements for Autonomy Features. In: Wirsing, M., Hölzl, M., Koch, N., Mayer, P. (eds.) Software Engineering for Collective Autonomic Systems. LNCS, vol. 8998, pp. 379–403. Springer, Heidelberg (2015)

60. Weyns, D., Malek, S., Andersson, J.: Forms: Unifying reference model for formal specification of distributed self-adaptive systems. ACM Transactions on Autonomous and Adaptive Systems 7(1), 8 (2012)

61. Wirsing, M., Hölzl, M., Koch, N., Mayer, P. (eds.): Software Engineering for Collective Autonomic Systems. LNCS, vol. 8998. Springer, Heidelberg (2015)

62. Wirsing, M., Hölzl, M.M., Tribastone, M., Zambonelli, F.: ASCENS: Engineering Autonomic Service-Component Ensembles. In: Beckert, B., Damiani, F., de Boer, F.S., Bonsangue, M.M. (eds.) FMCO 2011. LNCS, vol. 7542, pp. 1–24. Springer, Heidelberg (2013)

Methodological Guidelines for Engineering Self-organization and Emergence*

Victor Noël and Franco Zambonelli

University of Modena and Reggio Emilia, Italy

Abstract. The ASCENS project deals with the design and development of complex self-adaptive systems, where self-organization is one of the possible means by which to achieve self-adaptation. However, to support the development of self-organising systems, one has to extensively re-situate their engineering from a software architectures and requirements point of view. In particular, in this chapter, we highlight the importance of the decomposition in components to go from the problem to the engineered solution. This leads us to explain and rationalise the following architectural strategy: designing by following the problem organisation. We discuss architectural advantages for development and documentation, and its coherence with existing methodological approaches to self-organisation, and we illustrate the approach with an example on the area of swarm robotics.

Keywords: Self-organization, software architecture, problem decomposition, swarm robotics

1 Introduction

Engineering complex software intensive systems made up of large ensembles of components, and make them autonomic, requires a number of innovative models and tools. As it has been deeply investigated in the context of the ASCENS project, and is extensively reported in this book, these may include: new approaches to requirements engineering (as discussed in [1]), new programming languages (see Chapter I.1 [39]), and new methodological guidelines (see Chapter III.1 [31]).

In this chapter, we focus on a specific – yet very critical – methodological problem related to the engineering of complex autonomic service ensembles. Although the inherent goal of any software engineering approach is that to achieve – by design – a specific predictable behavior of the system, the complexity of large scale ensembles can sometimes undermine the possibility to fully achieve such goal. Indeed, as the scale of a system grows, the presence of non-linear interactions between its components and the lack of central control can make the appearance of emergent behaviours at the system level [38].

---

* This work has been sponsored by the EU project ASCENS IP 257414 (FP7).

M. Wirsing et al. (eds.): Collective Autonomic Systems, LNCS 8998, pp. 355–378, 2015.
© Springer International Publishing Switzerland 2015

In particular, those systems showing "organised complexity" are of interest: their emergent behaviour can't simply be understood using statistical tools and it is the organisation of the elements that matters [46]. An important mechanism governing complex systems is self-organisation: the autonomous change of the elements organisation without external control [15]. With self-organisation and emergence, complex systems are known for self-adaptivity: they adapt their functioning as a response to internal and environmental changes [29].

Johnson [33] noted that the apparent paradox between emergence and engineering stems from the confusion between emergence approached in a predictive way (i.e., being equated to surprising and often undesirable behaviours of the system) and emergence approached as a construct [27] (i.e., being equated to the appearance of high-level behaviours resulting from low-level simpler rules). Here, embracing the second vision, we assume (without arguing for the correctness of this choice) that self-organisation is the principle followed to design the low-level rules that lead to emergence.

Multi-Agent Systems (MAS) is one field where self-organisation and emergence are studied and applied to engineer self-adaptive systems [16,42]. In such systems, the various agents organise themselves in an autonomous and decentralised way to change how the functionality of the system is realised or even to change the functionality itself. Some aspects of the global behaviour are not explicitly pre-designed but emerge at runtime through this self-organising process in an endogenous and bottom-up way: the agents are unaware of the organisation as a whole [42].

Precisely, the general challenge tackled here is engineering self-adaptive self-organising complex systems that exist in and modify a complex context while meeting complex needs, in the continuation of [12] and [1]. Towards that goal, we propose to look at practical methodological guidelines to accompany their design. In the following, we use the term "Self-Organising MAS" (SOMAS) to denote such engineered system.

The paper presents two strongly interrelated contributions. First, it proposes a clear understanding, using a software architecture and requirements vocabulary, of what it means to engineer a SOMAS. From that, it highlights and explains the role that the decomposition design activity plays for such systems: it acts as a design bridge between the problem and the emergent behaviour. Second, it explains and rationalises an architectural design strategy stating that when designing a SOMAS, the problem organisation can be exploited for decomposition: it is an enabler for emergent behaviours reached through self-organisation to be adequate with respect to the problem. We also discuss implications for the development and documentation of SOMAS in general.

This strategy is not a method by itself but a complement to existing approaches and methods: one of our objectives is to defend these contributions so that they influence existing and future methodological approaches to self-organisation and emergence as well as applications.

They are illustrated with an example taken from swam robotics IV.2 [43]: bots exploring and securing victims in an unknown environment. This example was used to elicit and try-out the contributions but is not the focus of this paper. Nevertheless, it is fully implemented and we propose a short comparison with two other distributed algorithms to show the validity of applying the strategy and illustrate the differences it implies.

In Section 2, we review self-organisation and emergence from a software architecture and requirements points of view, and underline the importance of the role played by decomposition in the design of SOMAS. In Section 3, we present rationalise and discuss the defended strategy. In Section 4, we discuss in more details the example from swarm robotics. In Section 5, we relate the contributions with existing works that can be used to engineer emergence. We conclude in Section 6.

2   Emergence, Engineering and Decomposition

In this section, by interpreting the concepts of self-organisation and emergence from an engineering, i.e., architectures and requirements, point of view, we underline two important things: first, these approaches answer requirements but also impose design constraints, and second, some requirements are answered by the human designer while others are emergently answered at runtime. These facts are of course not novel by themselves but are usually not explained with an architecture and requirements vocabulary. This leads us to conclude on the importance of the role that the decomposition plays in the design of SOMAS.

2.1   Self-organisation and Emergence

Emergence is considered present in a system if from two different point of view on the system (hence it is an observer-relative property), the behaviour exhibited by the first one — called high-level or macro-level — is determined (formally "supervenes on" [36]) by the second one — called low-level or micro-level —, and if the first one is easier to understand than the second one [13]. In other words, we say that a macro-level behaviour emerges from the micro-level interactions, that this macro-level behaviour is not contained in some elements of the micro-level and that the macro-level behaviours we consider are those that are of interest to the engineer of the system.

Even though this definition of emergence does not include self-organisation, emergence most usually appears in self-organising systems. The main important specificities of these systems are that they change their organisation (and thus their behaviour) without external control [15]. Together, self-organisation and emergence imply a decentralisation of control inside the system [29]: without it, there can't be emergence as the elements of the micro-level behaviour would contain the macro-level behaviour.

Here, emergence is about the state of the system at a given moment while self-organisation is about the dynamics that enable to reach this state. There exist other understandings of these concepts (cf. [13, 15, 16, 33, 42]) but they all describe the same reality: the global behaviour is found at runtime and not

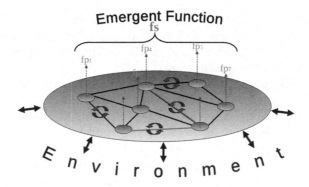

Fig. 1. Components and connectors view about the emergence of the global function from local functions through self-organisation [22]

predefined in the elements or in the way they are composed. Figure 1 illustrates well this principle: the emergent function results from the composition of the local functions of the elements and can be changed by the latter by modifying their function or their relations.

2.2 Software Architecture, Problems and Requirements

In terms of software architecture, and in line with the general component-based approach of ASCENS (see Chapter I.2 [11]) the design activity of SOMAS focuses on producing components and connectors (C&C) views [5, 14] (i.e., the description of the runtime elements, their behaviours and their relations) of the solution to answer the requirements and the constraints of the problem tackled. The components are the agents, their environment connects them together and the relations between agents and with the environment are often dynamically changing at runtime [3]. Figure 1 is thus a SOMAS C&C view. Another important aspect of software architectures concerns modules views (i.e., the description of units of implementation and their relations): while the design of SOMAS does not usually directly cover them [3], as we will see in Section 3.6 the choices made during their engineering still impact them.

Problems of Interest. What we call a problem to answer here is made of a context and requirements [28]: engineering is about finding the software solution, here the SOMAS, satisfying the requirements in that context.

As an example, in a robotics scenario (illustrated in Figure 2), we look at the search and secure problem: bots must explore an unknown environment to look for victims and then secure them (supposedly to rescue them, but this is not covered in our example). The context is composed of the bots (controlled by the software to build) with limited communication capabilities, the environment that have walls, the victims that must each be secured by several bots. The requirements are to

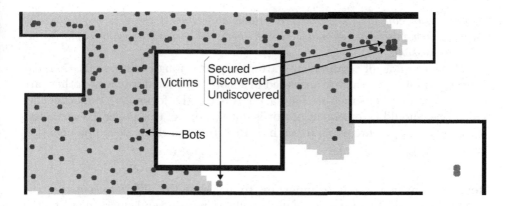

Fig. 2. Robotic scenario with bots, victims and environment to explore

search and secure victims, to secure them all, as fast as possible, to explore the accessible space fairly, to completely explore the space in a non-random way, etc.

Some aspects of the problem won't change in any of its instances (e.g., bots capabilities), while some will be different (e.g., walls and victims positions, bots communication distance) and may even change at runtime (e.g., failure of bots). The type of SOMAS we want to be able to engineer must work in any situation that conforms to such a class of problems.

Requirements and Underspecification. Requirements are usually meant to be explicitly identified, quantified, etc, in order to derive from them precise implementable specifications of the solution to be built. But with the type of problems that interest us, it is often the case that requirements cannot be practically and completely specified at a global level because of the complexity of the system and of its context, or because there is no implementable efficient centralised solution. In other words, these problems can suffer from underspecification.

In the robotic example, it is not clear how to specify from the point of view of each bots the global objective of efficiently exploring and securing all victims as the bots cannot communicate across the whole environment, which they don't even know in advance.

From a software architecture point of view, it is known that using (SO)MAS is an architectural response to a certain problems with requirements such as complexity, distribution, dynamicity, scalability, or adaptation [3, 15, 47, 48]. These are other ways of saying that the actual specification of what the system should do changes at runtime and can't be predefined. One way to tackle such underspecification is the use of self-organisation as a way to make the actual solution to the problem be found at runtime through emergence.

In the robotic example, depending on the state of the environment, the victim found and other contextual facts, the bots collective has to devise at runtime the best exploration and securing strategies to follow. If victims are evenly dis-

tributed, bots can disperse to secure them all, while if there is big groups of victims, then more bots should dispatch themselves to them, while exploring as much as possible.

Of course, not all requirements are answered through self-organisation and emergence: some of them are answered in a more traditional way while others are answered through emergence. The latter is really the focus here, but choosing which ones should be emergent or not is out of scope of this paper. Nevertheless in the following, we are going to see how to distinguish them when documenting the built system.

Design Constraints. It is important to underline the difference between the problem answered by the choice of using self-organisation and emergence, and the constraints this choice implies: most of the works characterising self-organisation and emergence tend to not make this distinction explicit [9, 15, 16, 42].

Indeed, the following can be part of the problem: to have self-adaptation, a distributed deployment context, large-scale system, non-existence of an efficient centralised solution or impossibility of expressing the global behaviour of the system.

Inversely, as said in Section 2.1, the following are mandatory design constraints when embracing self-organisation: the decision must be distributed and decentralised, the global macro-level behaviour and organisation can't be predefined or self-organisation must be a bottom-up process initiated locally by the elements of the system.

Of course, some of these imposed constraints can also be part of the requirements (e.g., distribution of control), but even if they are not (e.g., the system runs on only one computer), they must still be followed when designing a SOMAS.

2.3   Role of the C&C Decomposition Design Activity

In terms of C&C views, designing a SOMAS focuses on two main activities: decomposing in runtime components (the agents) and giving them a self-organising behaviour. For the engineer, these are the two main difficulties to overcome. Often experience and intuition are useful tools to design software systems, but it is accepted that there exist architectural design strategies that can be followed to build good software [4]. Depending on the problem, various strategies are available, and when a strategy is chosen, then it becomes a design constraint for the engineer. We focus on the decomposition activity now.

Following a traditional reductionist approach to software design means to define a global functionality answering the problem requirements, and then, a decomposition in runtime components and their functionalities are chosen *a priori* through a top-down refinement of this predefined functionality. The control is embedded in the way these sub-functionalities are composed: through structural composition (e.g., dataflow components) or by being orchestrated by a central element (e.g., service workflow).

Because of the design constraints highlighted in Section 2.2, such an approach cannot thus be followed if one wants to have adaptation through emergence: the macro-level behaviour is self-designed by a bottom-up autonomous process, and not by following a top-down human-driven process. This shifts of focus from a traditional design choice as an answer to some requirements to a design choice at the local level of elements to have them find the organisation (i.e., the runtime composition) answering the requirements, is where the paradigm change implied by self-organisation and emergence happens. And this is also where the real difficulty rests: how one can engineer such a micro-level behaviour without thinking about the macro-level behaviour? How to answer the requirements by not directly answering them in our design?

We argue here that the decomposition plays the role of a design bridge between the problem and the emergent behaviour. Indeed, the decomposition in agents implies to choose the local function they play in the system (as it was depicted in the Figure 1): it is the runtime composition of such local functions that makes up the global function, and it is the self-organising behaviour of the agents that leads the system in the adequate composition of the local functions for answering the requirements. Thus, the chosen decomposition constrains the possible macro-level behaviours that can be found at runtime through the self-organising process, and choosing the correct decomposition will determine the success of the engineering of a SOMAS.

2.4   How Should the SOMAS Be Decomposed?

Figure 3 summarises all the relations between the concepts discussed in this section.

It shows the different aspects of the problem answered at design time and runtime by the engineered SOMAS. It shows the two main design activities of decomposition and giving a self-organising behaviour to the agents of the SOMAS. It underlines that the engineer does not tackle at design the requirements emergently answered, but that some constraints have to be followed by the design nevertheless. It also shows that the decomposition and local functions of the agents constrain the possible macro-level behaviours that can emerge at runtime. As the focus of the engineering of SOMAS is on the emergent solution of the problem, we call the local function of the agents their "pre-solved" behaviour because they are solved directly in the humanly designed agent and not emerging at runtime as the Figure shows (a similar differentiation of behaviours is present in the AMAS approach [23] which calls them nominal and cooperative behaviours: the difference is mainly on the adopted problem-oriented point of view).

Finally it highlights the questions that this section raises: how should this decomposition be done? What is a good or a bad decomposition? We give our answer in the next section.

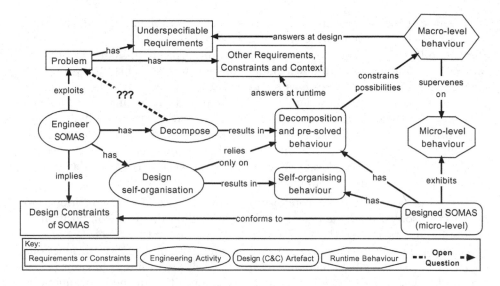

Fig. 3. Relations between Problem, Design Activities and SOMAS

3   Following the Problem Organisation

From our experience in the design of SOMAS and the points discussed in the previous section, we concluded that a strategy to follow when designing SOMAS is to base the software solution on the problem organisation. While we defended previously that decomposition is a design bridge between the problem and the emergent macro-level behaviour, here we explain that following the problem organisation during the decomposition activity is what can make the emergent macro-level behaviour as adapted to the problem as it can be. In the following, we first explain the strategy and present a rational for it. Then we situate it with respect to existing methodological approaches to self-organisation, we underline some open questions, draw lessons for documentation and show architectural advantages for the development.

3.1   The Strategy

It is usual in software engineering to first model the problem space before entering the solution space. However, here we advocate for directly mapping the problem organisation to the solution decomposition, and for only relying on the problem abstractions to design the agents behaviour.

From the Problem Organisation... By problem organisation, we mean the identification of the various elements participating in it and of the role they play with respect to the requirements.

In the robotic example, the elements participating in the problem are the bots, but also the victims and the environment. Furthermore, in relation with the

requirements, the elements play the following role in the problem: bots choose a direction to go to, bots communicate with other bots, bots perceive victim, bots perceive the walls, victims are situated, victims need a specific number of bots to be secured, etc.

The Figure 4a shows such a decomposition of the problem in elements. We call it the "organisation" to avoid confusion with the meaning usually associated to a decomposition of the problem in sub-problems as shown in the Figure 4b. The problem organisation can be imposed by the context (that the engineer can't control or modify, as in the robotic example) or must be chosen by the engineer when building the system.

. . . to the Solution Decomposition. Based on this modelling of the problem, we then advocate for a direct mapping between elements of the solution (software agents) and the elements of the problem, and for giving them the same capabilities (the local function) as in the problem domain and not more. Their behaviour should be designed locally with respect to the relations elements have in the problem. The decisions (including those of the self-organising behaviour) they take should only rely on the problem domain abstractions and no higher-level global abstractions should be introduced.

In the robotic example, bots must choose where is the best direction to go at every given moment. For that, they can use what they directly see (victims and explorable areas), and when they don't know what to choose, they should rely on information shared by other bots about the state of the world with respect to the problem: where they are needed for victims or exploration. Hence, bots that see victims or explorable areas advertise about it. This information can be propagated by the bots and they can use it to decide where to go next.

Of course the complexity of the context and of the requirements (e.g., high number of bots, unknown scattering of the victims or limited perception means) are likely to make all these choices difficult. Correctly choosing the best action to take is thus an important questions: we don't pretend to answer it in this paper, but, as said before, we argue that such decisions must rely on the problem domain abstractions. Still, we comment on this question when relating the defended strategy with existing approaches to self-organisation, which propose such guidelines, in the next section.

3.2   Relation to the Design of Self-organisation

The strategy presented in the previous section can thus be used to design a SOMAS, but, as we highlighted it, is not enough by itself. In particular, a very important point is the problem of taking the correct local decision for the agents.

Some approaches to self-organisation propose guidelines to design the micro-level behaviour of the agents of the system. They propose local criteria to be followed by the agents in order to drive the self-organisation. For example, the work of Gershenson [25] and the AMAS theory [22, 23] are such approaches. In the AMAS approach, the main strategy is that agents must have a cooperative

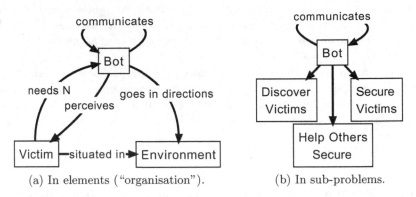

(a) In elements ("organisation").   (b) In sub-problems.

Fig. 4. Different decompositions for the robotic problem example

social attitude: the whole approach rests on the theory that if the agents of a system are cooperative with the system environment as well as internally, then the system will behave adequately with respect to the objectives of the agents and of their environment. In the work of Gershenson, the main strategy proposed is to reduce frictions and increase synergy between the agents of the system. In both, most of the actual engineering is about finding which local information to share in order for the agents to act as cooperatively or synergistically as possible. We detail the AMAS approach in the rest of this section (but the same conclusions can be applied to the work of Gershenson) and discuss the coherence of the defended strategy with it.

In the AMAS approach, by identifying local non-cooperative situations agents can face, the engineer designs the agents so that they prevent or correct such situations in order to put the system in a state as cooperative as possible. Usually, a measure called criticality that is shared amongst agents is used to reflect the importance of some state of the problem and to give an agent a way to decide between several choices.

In the robotic example, a bot often has the choice between several directions and do not see any victims. In order to take the most cooperative decision, he needs some information about the state of the system: bots can advertise for example about the direction they chose to go to and some measure (the criticality) of how much more bots are needed in this direction. When a bot propagates this information (because he chose the direction), it will update this criticality in order to reflect his and others participations in the self-organisation process: its choice means that this direction is a bit less critical now. Because bots assume they are all cooperative, they know that a direction chosen by another bot is presently the most important one to go to: choosing the most critical direction amongst all the neighbouring advertisements is enough for a bot to decide where to go next. Every decision taken will then influence how the bot computes this criticality, and inversely.

The way the self-organising process can be designed with this approach heavily relies on the fact that the agents does not contain any pre-defined behaviour in relation to the expected global behaviour, but only concepts manipulated in the definition of the problem itself, which serves to base the local decision on. For example, the criticality measure used in the AMAS approach reflects some aspect of the problem state in a comparable form: no extra high-level characterisation of what is or not a good global solution is used.

3.3   Rationale

The rationale behind the defended strategy, namely to follow the problem organisation when designing a SOMAS, derives from the points highlighted in Section 2: the global behaviour must emerge, exploiting self-organisation imposes some design constraints and decomposition plays an important role in what can emerge. We discuss here two cases: why the solution shouldn't be based on a decomposition of the problem in sub-problems, and why the solution shouldn't be based on abstractions foreign from the problem organisation. As we are going to see, we do not conclude that these ways of doing are wrong *per se*, but that they have important implications that are usually overlooked.

Sub-problems. A problem decomposition in sub-problems calls for solving each sub-problem separately (if it is not the case, then the decomposition in sub-problems is useless for the design and this is out of the scope of the discussion here). This means that the sub-solutions must then be integrated together, and such integration is embedding the complexity of the problem.

In the robotic example, if the bots have a behaviour to explore and discover victims, and another to go help other bots secure their discovered victims (as in the Figure 4b), it becomes very difficult to handle at the agent level the choice between going in a direction or not: it could be needed to secure a victim, but there may be already other bots going there, so it must gather information about that, and then it could not be needed because other bots are going, but then maybe there is more to explore behind the victim, so it should go anyway, except in the case where there is still enough bots going there for the same reason as it is, and so on. . .

This puts back the complexity of solving the problem at the agent level instead of making it the result of the collective behaviour: this is the very reason why the paradigm shift proposed by self-organisation and emergence engineering was proposed in the first place. This matter has been discussed many times in the literature (the "complexity bottleneck" [30]) and we don't pretend to bring new arguments for it.

Foreign Abstractions. Even if the problem organisation is used to design the SOMAS, the engineer can decide to introduce extra concepts that are foreign to the problem organisation. This means that when facing local decisions, the agents must translate their interpretation of the current state of the problem to the extra abstractions. Going far from the problem implies that we pre-set how situations are interpreted by the agents: it prevents them from interpreting correctly unforeseen situations because the concepts they manipulate can't capture them. In other words, the farther the design is from the problem, the lesser adaptive the system will be, and the lesser adequate behaviours can emerge.

In the robotic example, if the bots are designed so that to explore, they move in the direction of a repulsion vector from other bots (this is a typical algorithm for dispersing bots in an unknown environment), then part of the problem solved is not about exploring while securing anymore, it is about dispersing bots in an environment: for example in a hallway, a stopped bot securing a victim will prevent other bots to go behind him. Inversely, if bots behave as we explained before, when facing a situation where the collective would profit from dispersing, then bots will disperse as a result of going in directions advertised by others where the less bots are going and when facing a situation where there is only one direction to go (e.g., a hallway), bots jut go there because it is the only advertised direction.

3.4   Open Questions

We now look at open questions but don't answer them.

In the light of the discussion, how to make a good modelling of a problem becomes an important question. The strategy and its rationale highlight the impacts of such a decision, but there is many other things to say about it that need more research.

Then, the relation between requirements answered at runtime and the agent's behaviour is not so clear: it seems that it pertains more to strategies for designing the self-organising behaviour than the decomposition and the pre-solved behaviour.

Next, it is obvious that some of the elements identified in the problem can't always be mapped to agents. That means that the other agents are responsible of interpreting the state of such elements and can be many to do so: they must most certainly thus use a common interpretation mechanism (either part of the self-organising or of the pre-solved behaviour) and there may be ways to correctly choose it.

In the robotic example, theoretically, an agent modelling a victim should be responsible of advertising needs for more bots to secure him, but because victims can't be mapped to agents, this responsibility is distributed amongst the bots that locally decide by themselves if they are needed next to a victim as part of their pre-solved behaviour.

Another point is the practical application of the strategy during the design: how much the choices made for the self-organising behaviour impacts the pre-solved behaviour? Does it involve modifying the modelled problem organisation?

3.5   Lessons for Documenting SOMAS

This design strategy and its rationale highlight several points pertaining to documentation and understanding of SOMAS. These "lessons" are useful in our opinion not only when using the proposed strategy but more generally when documenting SOMAS.

First, not following the problem domain and still using self-organisation means that the problem solved is another problem derived from the original. Second, whichever concept emanating from the problem organisation (including the pre-solved behaviour) and used to design the self-organising behaviour has to be considered as being foreseeable in the problem to solve. Taking these two points into account, during the design and the documentation, is useful to better understand what is actually emergently solved in a SOMAS, and what can be adequately used to build SOMAS (including deciding what should be pre-solved or not).

It is particularly relevant to document the relations between the behaviours and the problem. Some parts of the problem are not solved through self-organisation but directly by the human engineer: they are sub-problems whose solution is implemented by the pre-solved behaviour. The rest of the problem is not directly solved at design, but at runtime by the self-organising behaviour that exploits the state of the problem as well as the pre-solved behaviour capabilities to do so.

In the robotic example, bots move in desired directions while avoiding walls, interpret the needs of the victims they can see, exchange and interpret messages, etc. All of this is pre-solved by the human designer either because there is no need for emergence (for requirements) or because it is imposed as part of the problem (constraints and context).

3.6   Architectural Advantages for Development

The defended strategy promotes some interesting advantages in terms of non-functional requirements. Requirements pertaining to the software itself are well studied in the literature, as seen in Section 2.2, but requirements related to the organisation of the development are not so much. This can be explained by the fact that the existing methodological guidelines in the literature do not directly promote such advantages, while the strategy presented here does. Some of these architectural advantages of the strategy were already identified in the context of MAS [3]: here we improve their rationalisations by linking them to the proposed strategy.

Separation of Concerns. First, a design based on the problem tightly reflects the existence of different types of developers of a SOMAS: the developers taking care of the pre-solved behaviour are often expert of the problem domain while those taking care of the self-organising behaviour are often researchers expert in self-organisation. This results in a separation in different implementation modules and thus ease the organisation of the development work.

In the robotic example, roboticians can focus on matters such as vision interpretation, obstacle avoidances, while a self-organisation researcher can exploit these high-level but problem-oriented abstractions.

Furthermore, this is very helpful to well distinguish what are the parts of the behaviour that lead to emergence (the self-organisation behaviour and the aspect of the model it can change) and those that pertain to traditional engineering. The documentation is thus facilitated. Also it is much more difficult to confuse these two aspects: this avoids making mistakes such as changing the problem to be solved while trying to change the self-organising behaviour.

Maintenance and Incremental Design. The way the system is decomposed in various agents that reflects the problem organisation and do not contain sub-solutions to the problem eases the answering of new requirements, either because of a planned incremental design, or unexpected emergent behaviours. Such way of developing is very common from our experience, often because engineering emergence is a bit of an experimental science due to the complexity of the way the system work, and iteration must be done before the system is even in a basic working state.

Handling a new requirement is changing the behaviour of every agents in the same way and not redefining the decomposition in sub-functionality and thus changing the whole architecture. The fact that the system follows directly the problem organisation allows to closely follow the evolutions of the latter: the effort for evolving the software is proportional to the quantity of changes in the problem because of their closeness of structures.

Deployment. It is almost obvious that the correspondence between agents and their deployment environment will be very close as the elements are modelled on the problem, which includes the deployment context when there is one.

Rationalisation. Rationalising the choices taken during the design is very important when following a proper software architecture approach to development [14]: it is an important enabler for the longevity of a software system in an industrial context for example.

As we presently rationalised the strategy of following the problem for designing the system, this strategy can be used safely when rationalisation is needed, on top of the fact that the advantages presented in this section and in Section 3.5 are useful for explaining and thus rationalising the design choices.

4   Engineering a Swarm of Bots

We now discuss the example with bots exploring and securing victims, which originates from the ASCENS[1] project (see Chapter IV.2 [43]). The proposed

---

[1] Autonomic Service Component Ensembles: http://www.ascens-ist.eu/.

SOMAS enables bots to choose where to go and to distribute this decision by exchanging relevant information.

It was fully implemented using the MASON simulator [37] and MAY[2], a tool for supporting the development of MAS using a component-based approach [40]. The sources as well as an executable version are available at the following url: `http://www.irit.fr/~Victor.Noel/unimore-ascens-saso-2015/`.

The objective of this section is to illustrate the contributions and not to present the best solution to this problem, but we still show a simple comparison with two known algorithm in order to discuss the validity of the produced design.

4.1   Problem

Bots are situated in a 2D space where they can move in all direction at limited speed. They can identify and localise other bots in their line of sight up to 20m around 360° using a range-and-bearing (R&B) device. They localise victims in their line of sight up to 6m around 360°. They estimate the distance to walls up to 6m in 36 directions with proximity sensors. Finally, the R&B device can advertise data (without size limit): this allows to share information in a local way. All the numbers can be modulated for the sake of experimentation.

The requirements and context are described in Section 2.2. In terms of requirements answered through emergence, while "exploring" isn't something that will emerge, as it is clear that even one bot is acting to explicitly explore, on the other hand it is the collective way to share such exploration that is difficult to achieve and for which no centralised solution exists. The same applies with victims securing: when a bot sees a victim, securing it is not a problem, but what is difficult to achieve is an efficient dispersion of the bots while securing victims quickly as soon as they are found.

4.2   Proposed Design

The swarm exploration example is particularly interesting because, in our opinion, it is not totally straightforward to see how the strategy can be applied: even though it is easy to see that each bot is an agent, the choice of their self-organising behaviour and the type of information it manipulates can lead to very different solutions as highlighted in Section 3.3. It can thus profit from being rationalised, with respect to the arguments given in this paper, and documented as with a proper software architecture approach to development.

Decomposition and Pre-solved Behaviour. This phase is done following the strategy proposed in Section 3.1: see Figure 4a for a simple model of the problem organisation.

The first design choice is about the pre-solved behaviour. Since the problem is about exploring and securing, and since the bot can perceive directions where

---

[2] Make Agents Yourself: `http://www.irit.fr/MAY-en`.

he can go or not, this behaviour is about choosing a direction to go to, but also about avoiding walls or evaluating state of victims (number of bots needed to secure them). When a victim is seen, the bot will secure it if the number of bots already on it is not enough for the victim's need. When no victim is saw, without any self-organising behaviour, that means choosing randomly one of the available directions.

As we can notice, no prejudgement is done about how the problem (in terms of requirements answered through emergence) is solved yet. Starting from that, we now construct the self-organising behaviour that enables to tune this local pre-solved behaviour.

Self-organising Behaviour. This phase is done following the AMAS approach while respecting the defended strategy as presented in Section 3.2. Incrementally, we add more and more cooperative behaviour to the agents so that they avoid or correct what is called non-cooperative situations: local situation which are uncooperative with respect to the goal of the agent (i.e., explore and secure). For that they can base their decision on exchanged information, on locally observable information and also on their knowledge of the fact that other bots are cooperative. We simplified the behaviour description to ease the understanding.

Selecting Directions to Consider Bots see walls and free directions around them: since they have some information from bots in that direction, they do not consider by themselves the directions where there is another bot but the advertised direction instead (after translating and estimating the direction for their point of view). Bots see victims, and must advertise about them, but if every bot that sees a victim advertise about it, many bots will propagate duplicate and incorrect information: thus, a bot only advertise about victims without a bot closer to them than it.

Sharing Information Since bots do not see far, they advertise their next movement (a direction) using the R&B device: implicitly, because the bot will act cooperatively, it means that this direction is the best place to go from his point of view. To this direction they associate a measure of criticality as explained in Section 3.2. To a direction with victims is associated a criticality proportional to the number of bots needed in that direction. To an empty area is associated a criticality of one. Hence, in a given instance of the problem, the criticality is upper bounded by the number of bots needed by victims that can be seen in a direction. Then criticality is decreased before being used and propagated in order to take into account the fact that the bot and other bots are now going into the chosen direction. This is not the best in terms of cooperation, but it is enough to illustrate this paper.

Choosing between Directions As said before, they prefer going toward a visible victim than a direction they see or shared by others. The rest of the time, they always choose the most critical direction he knows about, but if there is a tie, they choose the closest to their previous move.

4.3 Observed Global Behaviour

A swarm of bots with these behaviours explores the environment and secure victims. Their behaviour is such that only bots on the borders of the swarm actually consider new directions to explore, while those inside the swarm propagate this information. They start as one set and any explorable direction attracts a set of bots which separate when facing multiple directions. A victim attracts a small number of bots which stay around it, without attracting too many bots nor preventing them to continue exploration.

4.4 Discussion on the Strategy

In the example, once the problem is known, we kept all reasoning, decision and exchanged information close to the concepts of "choosing a direction" and perceived information to make that decision. We didn't use other abstractions to simplify the reasoning by making it less close to the problem.

The main illustration of that is the criticality that is driving the self-organisation of the system. Thanks to its dynamics, loops in the path of the information exchanged are avoided as fresher information will always takes precedence. Furthermore bots do not "pre-solve" the global problem for the others: the receiver chooses what to do with all the information it receives, and not the sender. Thus, the criticality as it is instantiated in this example is a constantly updated local representation of the most critical aspects of the problem: it does not make any assumption about what is a global solution to the problem and it enables a runtime exploration of the problem space while solving it at the same time.

4.5 Evaluation: Brief Analysis

In order to show that the produced design is good enough to be seriously considered, we compared its performance with two other algorithms. All algorithms (including ours) relies on the same mechanisms for what does not concern self-organisation: wall avoidance, victim's state interpretation and actual securing. We can notice that this corresponds to the pre-solved behaviour of our solution.

Simple Disperse Behaviour. Bots consider other visible bots and compute a repulsion vector from them.They do not consider other bots on a victim (the only advertised information) to compute the repulsion vector: it is needed so that stopped bots do not prevent other bots to explore behind them or help them secure victims. They then choose the direction closest to this repulsion vector amongst the directions they can go to. In case of a tie, the closest direction to its previous move is chosen.

Levy Walks. As described in [7], bots randomly choose a direction, go in that direction for a random amount of time and when the time is up or they hit a wall or another bot (except if it is to secure a victim), they choose another direction.

Comparisons. The performance we compare is time to secure victims (the more secured, the more the algorithm is considered efficient). We ran the algorithms by modulating various settings: communication range, number of bots, topology of the map. We discuss just some interesting cases.

First, the Levy walks algorithm is bad everywhere (at least with the parameters we used). Then generally, our behaviour is equivalent to the dispersion one when there is a lot of bots (aroung 200) or when the communication range is very low (approx 3 meters). Securing after discovery happens faster with our algorithm (as it is handled by the self-organising process). When the communication range increases too much, the disperse behaviour is less efficient (mainly because bots are too much spaced out and can't see victims in between) while inversely, our behaviour's efficiency increases with the communication range (as they have better information but explore in the same way). When the number of bots decreases, the disperse behaviour efficiency decreases (mainly because they can't cover enough space while staying in contact and thus miss some part of the map) while our behaviour efficiency is more or less unchanged.

What is also interesting is that the design resulting from applying the strategy is completely rationalised and form a coherent whole. With the dispersion algorithm, we had to add some special cases to manage the fact that the repulsion vector was not adequate in some situations, such as when a bot was stopped on a victim in a hallway: this would prevent other bots to go behind the stopped one or helping to secure the victim it is on. Even with these special cases, there is many situations where the disperse behaviour still gives strange results: solving the complexity of the problem has to be done inside the bots behaviours and is not the result of composing self-organising simple bots as with out behaviour. The same comments apply to the Levy walks. Furthermore, the latter was very hard to use because of the parameters that must be tuned by hand for each instance of the problem: we simply didn't succeed doing that, which may explain its bad results.

5   Related Works and Discussion

There exists many research work that can be used to support the engineering of SOMAS, we present and discuss them following various axis.

Applications. Some works apply self-organisation to specific problem in order to build SOMAS: many of them can be for example found in the SASO (Self-Adaptive and Self-Organizing systems) community[3]

They don't provide methodological guidelines to help the design of SOMAS, but recurrent practices or self-organising mechanisms can be extracted from them [45]. Nevertheless, it is sometimes implicit in these works that the problem organisation (as we understand it) plays an important role in their functioning: it has even been highlighted in some [34].

---

[3] See the SASO Conferences at http://www.saso-conferences.org.

Reuse and Generic Mechanisms. Some works propose self-organising mechanisms that were reused or developed specifically for a problem. Even if it is not always explicitly said in all works on the matter, the idea is that such mechanisms are generic and reusable: they enable to engineer emergence in different contexts than those where the mechanisms were first applied. Many works take inspiration from nature [18] to use well-studied self-organisation mechanisms (famous examples to solve optimisation problem are ant colony optimisation [19], or particle swarm optimisation [35]). Also, some works propose generic (hence reusable) frameworks handling and constraining the self-organising aspects of the system [44], or generic external mechanism to adapt the functioning of the agents at runtime [32].

All these works rely on approaches or mechanisms dependent on a certain class of problems: they have the advantage to be easier to apply and to be reused when possible, but in exchange it is needed to translate the concepts manipulated in the problem to the abstractions of the solution reused. As highlighted in Section 3.5, this means that part of the original problem is lost during that translation: depending on the problem, this can be acceptable or not.

Methods and Modelling Approaches. Even though there exist many development methods in the (SO)MAS field [8], very few tackle methodological aspects of engineering emergence itself but focus on other questions not of interest here. We still highlight a type of works that can be mistakenly considered as similar to what is discussed in this paper: ways and models to decompose the problem or the solution. For example, some methods approaches the design with a focus on requirements engineering using goal-oriented notations: an example is the Tropos method [26]. These approaches decompose the problem requirements in goals and sub-goals before attributing them to agents. For example the decomposition shown in Figure 4b is typical in goal-oriented approaches. They do not impose any decomposition in agents, or if they do, it is with a strategy opposite to the one defended here that maps the sub-goals to agents. Another example is role-based decomposition of MAS, used by many methods (the typical example is AgentUML [6]): roles enable to describe a SOMAS and explain its functioning, but the contributions of these works are not about guidelines on what is a good decomposition, which is the main subject of this very paper.

The Ensemble Development Life Cycle proposed within the ASCENS project (see Chapter III.1 [31]), apparently shares a similar endeavour to the above described methodological aspects. However, it has also been explicitly conceived so as to make it possible to easily accommodated problem decomposition approach as the one we have proposed in this chapter.

Design Strategies. As discussed in Section 3.2, there exists methodological guidelines, or design strategies, to accompany the design of the self-organising behaviour leading to the emergence of desired properties. For example we cited the work of Gershenson [25] and the AMAS theory [23]. We also redirect the reader to [17] that presents other such strategies. These works help to build the self-organisation mechanisms themselves as opposite to reuse them (but may of course profit of reuse at other levels of the development), in exchange of a better correspondence between the problem tackled and the built solution. As discussed in Section3.5, this is what can make an emergent behaviour more adapted to a problem.

While this type of works cover well the question of giving a self-organising behaviour to the agents of a SOMAS, very few, if none, works propose clear and rationalised strategies for tackling the decomposition. Nevertheless, the importance of the problem for the decomposition as been sometimes highlighted in these works and as been noted as an important architectural feature of MAS [3]. In the work of Gershenson, an interesting clue is given when self-organisation is defined: it says that "the elements need to divide, but also to integrate, the problem". Similarly, the ADELFE method [10], which supports the applying of the AMAS approach, suggests that the problem domain should help the decomposition in agents. But for all these works, no explanation nor rationalisation are given to support these recommendations.

Experimental Engineering and Simulation. As highlighted in Section 3.6, engineering SOMAS is very similar to an experimental science. Some works note that the interleaving of design and simulation can be used to accompany the engineering of emergence in order to iteratively adapt the design with respect to the observed results: they call it "co-development" [2], "using the experimental method" [20] or "disciplined exploration" [41]. Some goes farther with "living design" [24]: designing while the system is running. The discourse of this paper is well coherent with all these approaches, even though they sometimes adopt a predictive understanding of emergence [33]. Nevertheless, our contributions are of a different nature and show that it is possible to exploit the problem organisation to reduce the development effort of SOMAS.

Problem-Orientation. In traditional software engineering, exploiting the problem domain is not a novel strategy to approach the development, in particular in the Problem-Oriented Software Engineering (POSE) [28] and the Domain-Driven Design (DDD) [21] fields. DDD is particularly successful in a large scale business context: the focus on problem domain helps to better organise the development and influences the implementation of the system. But complex functionalities are separated from the elements modelling the problem and are often as input on how to model the problem domain, while we advocate for the opposite (when the objective is engineering emergence of course). POSE follows a more academic and formal approach with the objective of helping the human designer to explore the problem space, which is well separated from the solution space.

Thus, an important feature promoted by these works is to exploit the problem space and to decompose it in sub-problems to then better explore the solution space. As we have seen in Section 2, in SOMAS, this same problem space is partially explored by the built system and the roles that the decomposition plays influences the design in different ways. We can also note that some of the architectural advantages of the strategy presented in Section 3.6 were already identified in these works on problem-orientation, but here we discussed their specificities in the context of self-organisation and emergence. These approaches are thus compatible with the discourse of this paper and a better characterisation of the links with self-organisation would be beneficial to engineers of SOMAS.

6 Conclusion

By revisiting the concepts of self-organisation, emergence and engineering through the lenses of the software architecture and requirements field, we highlighted that the design activity of decomposition in runtime elements plays the role of a design bridge between the problem to solve and the emergent behaviour of the engineered system. We defended the idea that it rationalises the strategy of designing the system by following what we call the problem organisation, and that it is an enabler for the emergent behaviour to be adapted to the requirements. Using the defended strategy gives much advantages, and not only for the system itself but also for the organisation of the project, on top of being fitted for the design constraints imposed by self-organisation and existing approaches.

Self-organisation and emergence are taking more and more important place in today's engineering of software system. The need for clearer and rationalised strategies and methodological guidelines to approach the engineering of emergence is in our opinion an important challenge. There exist many other issues to explore on this subject, such as better way of documenting and distinguishing between requirements answered by emergence from the others, ways to well model the problem tackled with self-organisation or define more precisely how the problem impacts the decentralised decision making.

References

1. Abeywickrama, D.B., Bicocchi, N., Zambonelli, F.: SOTA: Towards a general model for self-adaptive systems. In: WETICE Conference, pp. 48–53. IEEE Computer Society Press, Los Alamitos (2012)
2. Andrews, P., Stepney, S., Winfield, A.: Simulation as an experimental design process for emergent systems. In: EmergeNET4 Workshop: Engineering Emergence (2010)
3. Arcangeli, J.P., Noël, V., Migeon, F.: Software Architectures and Multiagent Systems. In: Oussalah, M. (ed.) Software Architectures, vol. 2, pp. 171–208. Wiley, Chichester (2014)
4. Bass, L., Clements, P., Kazman, R.: Software Architecture in Practice, 2nd edn. Addison-Wesley, Reading (2003)
5. Basu, A., Bensalem, S., Bozga, M., Combaz, J., Jaber, M., Nguyen, T., Sifakis, J.: Rigorous component-based system design using the BIP framework. IEEE Software 28(3), 41–48 (2011)
6. Bauer, B., Müller, J.P., Odell, J.: Agent uml: A formalism for specifying multiagent software systems. International Journal of Software Engineering and Knowledge Engineering 11(3), 207–230 (2001)

7. Beal, J.: Superdiffusive dispersion and mixing of swarms with reactive levy walks. In: International Conference on Self-Adaptive and Self-Organizing Systems, pp. 141–148. IEEE Computer Society Press, Los Alamitos (2013)

8. Bernon, C., Cossentino, M., Pavón, J.: An Overview of Current Trends in European AOSE Research. Informatica 29, 379–390 (2005)

9. Berns, A., Ghosh, S.: Dissecting Self-* Properties. In: International Conference on Self-Adaptive and Self-Organizing Systems, pp. 10–19. IEEE Computer Society Press, Los Alamitos (2009)

10. Bonjean, N., Mefteh Mejri, W., Gleizes, M.P., Maurel, C., Migeon, F.: ADELFE 2.0. In: Cossentino, M., Hilaire, V., Molesini, A., Seidita, V. (eds.) Handbook on Agent-Oriented Design Processes, pp. 19–64. Springer, Heidelberg (2013)

11. Bruni, R., Montanari, U., Sammartino, M.: Reconfigurable and Software-Defined Networks of Connectors and Components. In: Wirsing, M., Hölzl, M., Koch, N., Mayer, P. (eds.) Software Engineering for Collective Autonomic Systems. LNCS, vol. 8998, pp. 73–106. Springer, Heidelberg (2015)

12. Cabri, G., Puviani, M., Zambonelli, F.: Towards a taxonomy of adaptive agent-based collaboration patterns for autonomic service ensembles. In: International Conference on Collaboration Technologies and Systems, pp. 508–515. IEEE Computer Society Press, Los Alamitos (2011)

13. Chalmers, D.: Strong and weak emergence. In: Clayton, P., Davies, P. (eds.) The Re-Emergence of Emergence, Oxford University Press, Oxford (2006)

14. Clements, P., Bachmann, F., Bass, L., Garlan, D., Ivers, J., Little, R., Nord, R., Stafford, J.: Documenting Software Architectures: Views and Beyond, 2nd edn. Addison-Wesley, Reading (2003)

15. De Wolf, T., Holvoet, T.: Emergence versus self-organisation: different concepts but promising when combined. In: Brueckner, S.A., Di Marzo Serugendo, G., Karageorgos, A., Nagpal, R. (eds.) Engineering Self-Organising Systems. LNCS (LNAI), vol. 3464, pp. 1–15. Springer, Heidelberg (2005)

16. Di Marzo Serugendo, G., Gleizes, M.P., Karageorgos, A.: Self-organisation and emergence in mas: An overview. Informatica 30, 45–54 (2006)

17. Di Marzo Serugendo, G., Gleizes, M.P., Karageorgos, A. (eds.): Self-Organising Software. Natural Computing. Springer, Heidelberg (2011)

18. Di Marzo Serugendo, G., Karageorgos, A., Rana, O.F., Zambonelli, F. (eds.): Engineering Self-Organising Systems. LNCS (LNAI), vol. 2977. Springer, Heidelberg (2004)

19. Dorigo, M., Stützle, T.: Ant Colony Optimization. MIT Press, Cambridge (2004)

20. Edmonds, B.: Using the experimental method to produce reliable self-organised systems. In: Brueckner, S.A., Di Marzo Serugendo, G., Karageorgos, A., Nagpal, R. (eds.) Engineering Self-Organising Systems. LNCS (LNAI), vol. 3464, pp. 84–99. Springer, Heidelberg (2005)

21. Evans, E.: Domain-driven design: tackling complexity in the heart of software. Addison-Wesley, Reading (2004)

22. Georgé, J.P., Edmonds, B., Glize, P.: Making Self-Organising Adaptive Multiagent Systems Work. In: Bergenti, F., Gleizes, M.P., Zombonelli, F. (eds.) Methodologies and Software Engineering for Agent Systems, pp. 319–338. Kluwer Academic Publishers, Dordrecht (2004)

23. Georgé, J.P., Gleizes, M.P., Camps, V.: Cooperation. In: Di Marzo Serugendo, G., Karageorgos, A., Rana, O.F., Zambonelli, F. (eds.) Engineering Self-Organising Systems. LNCS (LNAI), vol. 2977, pp. 193–226. Springer, Heidelberg (2004)

24. Georgé, J.P., Picard, G., Gleizes, M.P., Glize, P.: Living Design for Open Computational Systems. In: International Workshop on Theory And Practice of Open Computational Systems at WETICE, pp. 389–394. IEEE Computer Society Press, Los Alamitos (2003)
25. Gershenson, C.: Towards a general methodology for designing self-organizing systems. In: Bogg, J., Geyer, R. (eds.) Complexity, Science and Society, Radcliffe Publishing (2007)
26. Giorgini, P., Kolp, M., Mylopoulos, J., Castro, J.: Tropos: A requirements-driven methodology for agent-oriented software. In: Henderson-Sellers, B., Giorgini, P. (eds.) Agent-Oriented Methodologies, pp. 20–45. IGI Global (2005)
27. Goldstein, J.: Emergence as a construct: History and issues. Emergence 1(1), 49–72 (1999)
28. Hall, J., Rapanotti, L., Jackson, M.: Problem-oriented software engineering: Solving the package router control problem. Transactions on Software Engineering 34(2), 226–241 (2008)
29. Heylighen, F.: The science of self-organization and adaptivity. The Encyclopedia of Life Support Systems 5(3), 253–280 (2001)
30. Heylighen, F., Gershenson, C.: The meaning of self-organization in computing. IEEE Intelligent Systems, Section Trends & Controversies 18(4), 72–75 (2003)
31. Hölzl, M., Koch, N., Puviani, M., Wirsing, M., Zambonelli, F.: The Ensemble Development Life Cycle and Best Practices for Collective Autonomic Systems. In: Wirsing, M., Hölzl, M., Koch, N., Mayer, P. (eds.) Software Engineering for Collective Autonomic Systems. LNCS, vol. 8998, pp. 325–354. Springer, Heidelberg (2015)
32. Hudson, J., Denzinger, J., Kasinger, H., Bauer, B.: Dependable risk-aware efficiency improvement for self-organizing emergent systems. In: International Conference on Self-Adaptive and Self-Organizing Systems, pp. 11–20. IEEE Computer Society Press, Los Alamitos (2011)
33. Johnson, C.: What are Emergent Properties and How do They Affect the Engineering of Complex Systems? Reliability Engineering and System Safety 91(12), 1475–1481 (2006)
34. Jorquera, T., Georgé, J.P., Gleizes, M.P., Couellan, N., Noë, V., Régis, C.: A Natural Formalism and a Multi-Agent Algorithm for Integrative Multidisciplinary Design Optimization. In: International Workshop on Optimisation in Multi-Agent Systems at AAMAS (2013)
35. Kennedy, J., Eberhart, R.: Particle Swarm Optimization. In: International Conference on Neural Networks, pp. 1942–1948. IEEE Computer Society Press, Los Alamitos (1995)
36. Kim, J.: Making sense of emergence. Philosophical studies 95(1), 3–36 (1999)
37. Luke, S., Cioffi-Revilla, C., Panait, L., Sullivan, K., Balan, G.: Mason: A multi-agent simulation environment. Simulation: Transactions of the society for Modeling and Simulation International (2005)
38. Mitchell, M.: Complexity: A guided tour. Oxford University Press, Oxford (2009)
39. De Nicola, R., Latella, D., Lafuente, A.L., Loreti, M., Margheri, A., Massink, M., Morichetta, A., Pugliese, R., Tiezzi, F., Vandin, A.: The SCEL Language: Design, Implementation, Verification. In: Wirsing, M., Hölzl, M., Koch, N., Mayer, P. (eds.) Software Engineering for Collective Autonomic Systems. LNCS, vol. 8998, pp. 3–71. Springer, Heidelberg (2015)
40. Noël, V.: Component-based Software Architectures and Multi-Agent Systems: Mutual and Complementary Contributions for Supporting Software Development. Ph.D. thesis, Paul Sabatier University (2012)

41. Paunovski, O., Eleftherakis, G., Cowling, T.: Disciplined exploration of emergence using multi-agent simulation framework. Computing and Informatics 28(3), 369–391 (2009)
42. Picard, G., Hübner, J.F., Boissier, O., Gleizes, M.P.: Reorganisation and Self-organisation in Multi-Agent Systems. In: International Workshop on Organizational Modeling, pp. 66–80 (2009)
43. Pinciroli, C., Bonani, M., Mondada, F., Dorigo, M.: Adaptation and Awareness in Robot Ensembles: Scenarios and Algorithms. In: Wirsing, M., Hölzl, M., Koch, N., Mayer, P. (eds.) Software Engineering for Collective Autonomic Systems. LNCS, vol. 8998, pp. 471–494. Springer, Heidelberg (2015)
44. Pitt, J., Schaumeier, J., Artikis, A.: Axiomatization of socio-economic principles for self-organizing institutions: Concepts, experiments and challenges. Transactions on Autonomous and Adaptive Systems 7(4), 1–39 (2012)
45. Snyder, P., Valetto, G., Fernandez-Marquez, J., Di Marzo Serugendo, G.: Augmenting the repertoire of design patterns for self-organized software by reverse engineering a bio-inspired p2p system. In: International Conference on Self-Adaptive and Self-Organizing Systems, pp. 199–204. IEEE Computer Society Press, Los Alamitos (2012)
46. Weaver, W.: Science and complexity. American scientist 36(4), 536–544 (1948)
47. Weyns, D.: Architecture-Based Design of Multi-Agent Systems. Springer, Heidelberg (2010)
48. Weyns, D., Helleboogh, A., Steegmans, E., De Wolf, T., Mertens, K., Boucké, N., Holvoet, T.: Agents are not part of the problem, agents can solve the problem. In: International Workshop on Agent-Oriented Methodologies at OOPSLA, pp. 101–102 (2004)

CHAPTER III.3

Engineering Requirements for Autonomy Features*

Emil Vassev and Mike Hinchey

Lero–the Irish Software Engineering Research Center, University of Limerick,
Limerick, Ireland

Abstract. This chapter outlines an approach to Autonomy Requirements Engineering (ARE). ARE targets the integration and promotion
of autonomy in software-intensive systems by providing a mechanism and
methodology for elicitation and expression of autonomy requirements.
ARE relies on *goal-oriented requirements engineering* to elicit and define system goals, and uses the *generic autonomy requirements* model to
derive and define assistive and, eventually, alternative objectives. The
system may pursue these *"self-* objectives"* in the presence of factors
threatening the achievement of the initial system goals. Once identified,
the autonomy requirements are specified with the KnowLang language.
To demonstrate the ARE's ability to handle autonomy requirements for
autonomic ensembles, the ARE's application to the ASCENS Science
Clouds case study is presented and discussed in detail.

Keywords: autonomic computing, autonomy requirements, requirements engineering, self-adaptive behavior

1 Introduction

Nowadays, requirements engineering for autonomous systems appears to be a
wide open research area with no definitive solution yet. The problem is that
the integration and promotion of autonomy in software-intensive systems is an
extremely challenging task. Among the many challenges engineers must overcome are those related to elicitation and expression of autonomy requirements.
This chapter draws upon our experience with the Autonomy Requirements Engineering (ARE) [31,23] approach to present its ability to handle autonomy requirements for self-adaptive systems such as ASCENS ensembles [2,33]. The
ARE approach has been developed by Lero, the Irish Software Engineering Research Center, within the mandate of a joint project with ESA, the European
Space Agency. The approach is intended to help engineers tackle the integration and promotion of autonomy in software-intensive systems. ARE combines

* This research was supported by the European project IP 257414 (ASCENS).

M. Wirsing et al. (eds.): Collective Autonomic Systems, LNCS 8998, pp. 379–403, 2015.
© Springer International Publishing Switzerland 2015

generic autonomy requirements (GAR) with goal-oriented requirements engineering (GORE). Using this approach, software engineers can determine what autonomic features to develop for a particular system as well as what artifacts that process might generate (e.g., goals models, requirements specification, etc.). For the ASCENS Project [2] in particular, ARE has helped us capture the autonomy requirements for the ASCENS case studies, but also helped us derive efficient and relevant knowledge models for these case studies.

The rest of this chapter is organized as follows. Section 2 introduces in detail the ARE approach. Section 3 presents a proof-of-concept case study where ARE is used to capture autonomy requirements for an autonomic cloud platform. Section 4 presents related work and finally, Section 5 presents a brief conclusion and future work.

2   ARE – Autonomy Requirements Engineering

2.1   Understanding ARE

The first step in developing any new software-intensive system is to determine the system's functional and non-functional requirements. The former requirements define what the system will actually do, while the latter requirements refer to its qualities, such as performance, along with any constraints under which the system must operate. Despite differences in application domain and functionality, all autonomous systems extend upstream the regular software-intensive systems with special *self-managing objectives* (self-* objectives). Basically, the self-* objectives provide the system's ability to automatically discover, diagnose, and cope with various problems. This ability depends on the system's degree of *autonomicity, quality and quantity of knowledge, awareness and monitoring capabilities*, and quality characteristics such as *adaptability, dynamicity, robustness, resilience*, and *mobility*. Basically, this is the basis of the ARE approach [31,23,26,25,24]: autonomy requirements are detected as self-objectives backed up by different capabilities and quality characteristics outlined by the GAR model.

The ARE approach starts with the creation of a *goals model* that represents system objectives and their interrelationships. For this, we use GORE where ARE goals are generally modeled with intrinsic features such as *type, actor*, and *target*, with links to other goals and constraints in the requirements model. Goals models might be organized in different ways copying with the system specifics and engineers' understanding about the system goals. Thus we may have 1) hierarchical structures where goals reside different level of granularity; 2) concurrent structures where goals are considered as concurrent; etc. At this stage, the goals models are not formal and we use natural language along with UML-like diagrams to record them.

The next step in the ARE approach is to work on each one of the system goals along with the elicited environmental constraints to come up with the self-* objectives providing the autonomy requirements for this particular system's behavior. In this phase, we apply our GAR model to a system goal to derive autonomy requirements in the form of goal's supportive and alternative self-* objectives along with the necessary capabilities and quality characteristics. In the first part of this phase, we record the GAR model in natural language. In the second part though, we use a formal notation to express this model in a more precise way. Note that, this model carries more details about the autonomy requirements, and can be further used for different analysis activities, including requirements validation and verification.

2.2   System Goals and Goals Models

Goals have long been recognized to be essential components involved in the requirements engineering (RE) process [18]. To elicit system goals, typically, the system under consideration is analyzed in its organizational, operational and technical settings. Problems are pointed out and opportunities are identified. High-level goals are then identified and refined to address such problems and meet the opportunities. Requirements are then elaborated to meet those goals.

Goal identification is not necessarily an easy task [12,8,17]. Sometimes goals can be explicitly stated by stakeholders or in preliminary material available to requirements engineers. Often though, they are implicit so that goal elicitation has to be undertaken. The preliminary analysis of the current system along with the operational environment is an important source for goal identification. Such analysis usually results in a list of problems and deficiencies that can be formulated precisely. Negating those formulations yields a first list of goals to be achieved by the system-to-be. In our experience, goals can also be identified systematically by searching for intentional keywords in the preliminary documents provided, e.g., ASCENS case study description. Once a preliminary set of goals and goal-related constraints is obtained and validated with stakeholders, many other goals can be identified by *refinement* and by *abstraction*, just by asking HOW and WHY questions about the goals/constraints already available [10]. Other goals are identified by resolving conflicts among goals or obstacles to goal achievement. Further, such goals might be eventually defined as self-* objectives.

Goals are generally modeled by *intrinsic features* such as their type and attributes, and by their links to other goals and to other elements of a requirements model. Goals can be hierarchically organized and prioritized where high-level goals (e.g., main system objectives) might comprise related, low-level, sub-goals that can be organized to provide different alternatives of achieving the high-level goals. In ARE, goals are registered in plain text with characteristics like *actors*, *targets* and *rationale*. Moreover, inter-goal relationships are captured by *goals models* putting together all goals along with associated constraints. ARE's goals models are presented in UML-like diagrams. Goals models can assist us in capturing autonomy requirements in several ways [26,25,24,23]:

1. An ARE goals model might provide the starting point for capturing autonomy requirements by analyzing the environment for the system-to-be and by identifying the problems that exist in this environment as well as the needs that the system under development has to address to accomplish its goals.

2. ARE goals models might be used to provide a means to represent *alternative ways* where the objectives of the system can be met and analyze and rank these alternatives with respect to *quality concerns* and other constraints, e.g., environmental constraints:

   (a) This allows for *exploration and analysis of alternative system behaviors at design time.*

   (b) If the alternatives that are initially delivered with the system perform well, there is no need for complex interactions on autonomy behavior among autonomy components.

   (c) Not all the alternatives can be identified at design time. In an open and dynamic environment, new and better alternatives may present themselves and some of the identified and implemented alternatives may become impractical.

   (d) In certain situations, new alternatives will have to be discovered and implemented by the system at runtime. However, the process of discovery, analysis, and implementation of new alternatives at runtime is complex and error-prone. By exploring the space of alternatives at design time, we are minimizing the need for that difficult task.

3. ARE goals models might provide the traceability mechanism from design to requirements. When a change in requirements is detected at runtime, *goal models can be used to re-evaluate the system behavior alternatives with respect to the new requirements and to determine if system reconfiguration is needed*:

   (a) If a change in requirements affects a particular goal in the model, it is possible to see how this goal is decomposed and which parts of the system implementing the functionality needed to achieve that goal are in turn affected.

   (b) By analyzing a goals model, it is possible to identify how a failure to achieve some particular goal affects the overall objective of the system.

   (c) Highly variable goals models can be used to visualize the currently selected system configuration along with its alternatives and to communicate suggested configuration changes to users in high-level terms.

4. ARE goals models provide a unifying intentional view of the system by relating goals assigned to individual parts of the system (usually expressed as actors and targets of a goal) to high-level system objectives and quality concerns:

   (a) High-level objectives or quality concerns serve as the *common knowledge* shared among the autonomous system's parts (or components) to achieve the global system optimization. In this way, the system can avoid the pitfalls of missing the globally optimal configuration due to only relying on local optimizations.

   (b) Goals models might be used to identify part of the knowledge requirements, e.g., actors or targets.

Moreover, goals models might be used to manage conflicts among multiple goals including self-* objectives. Note that by resolving conflicts among goals or obstacles to goal achievement, new goals (or self-* objectives) may emerge.

2.3 Self-* Objectives and Autonomy-Assistive Requirements

Basically, the GAR (generic autonomy requirements) model follows the principle that despite their differences in terms of application domain and functionality, all autonomous systems are capable of autonomous behavior driven by one or more *self-management objectives* [23] that drive the development process of such systems. ARE uses goals models as a basis helping to derive self-* objectives per a system goal by applying a model for *generic autonomy requirements* to any system goal [25,23]. The self-* objectives represent assistive and eventually *alternative goals* (or objectives) the system may pursue in the presence of factors threatening the achievement of the initial system goals. The diagram presented in Figure 1 depicts the process of deriving the self-* objectives from a goals model of the system to be. Basically, a context-specific GAR model provides some initial self-* objectives, which should be further analyzed and refined in the context of the specific system goal to see their applicability. As shown in Figure 1, in ad-

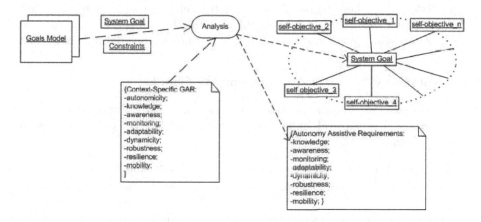

Fig. 1. The ARE Process of Deriving Self-* Objectives per System Goal

dition to the derived self-* objectives, the ARE process also produces *autonomy assistive requirements*. These requirements (also defined as adaptation-assistive attributes) are initially defined by the GAR model [31,26,23] and are intended to support the achievements of the self-* objectives. The autonomy assistive requirements outlined by GAR might be defined as following:

- *Knowledge* - basically data requirements that need to be structured to allow efficient reasoning.
- *Awareness* - a sort of functional requirements where knowledge is used as an input along with events and/or sensor signals to derive particular system states.
- *Resilience* and *robustness* - a sort of soft-goals. For example, such requirements can be defined as *"robustness: system is robust to communication*

latency" and "resilience: system is resilient to hardware failures, node disappearances, or appearances". These requirements can be specified as soft goals leading the system towards *"reducing and copying with communication latency"* and *"keeping system's performance optimal"*. A soft goal is satisfied rather than achieved. Note that specifying soft goals is not an easy task. The problem is that there is no clear-cut satisfaction condition for a soft goal. Soft goals are related to the notion of satisfaction. Unlike regular goals, soft goals can seldom be accomplished or satisfied. For soft goals, eventually, we need to find solutions that are "good enough" where soft goals are satisfied to a sufficient degree. Thus, when specifying robustness and resilience autonomy requirements we need to set the desired degree of satisfaction, e.g., by using probabilities.

– *Monitoring, mobility, dynamicity* and *adaptability* - might also be defined as soft-goals, but with *relatively high degree of satisfaction*. These three types of autonomy requirements represent important *quality requirements* that the system in question needs to meet to provide conditions making autonomicity possible. Thus, their degree of satisfaction should be relatively high. Eventually, adaptability requirements might be treated as hard goals because they determine what parts of the system in question can be adapted (not how).

2.4   Autonomy Needs and Requirements Chunks

To record autonomy requirements, ARE relies on both natural language and formal notation. A natural language description of a self-* objective has the following format [25]:

– **Name of Self-* Objective**: *Rationale of this self-* objective.*
   • **Assisting system goals**: *List of system goals assisted by this self-* objective.*
   • **Actors**: *Actors participating in the realization of this self-* objective.*
   • **Targets**: *Targets of this self-* objective.*

Note that this description is abstract and does not say how the self-* objective is going to be achieved. Basically, as recorded the self-* objectives define the *"autonomy needs"* of the system. How these needs are going to be met is provided by more detailed description of the self-* objectives recorded as ARE Requirements Chunks and/or specified formally.

In general, a more detailed description in a natural language may precede the formal specification of the elicited autonomy requirements. Such description might be written as a scenario describing both the conditions and sequence of actions needed to be performed in order to achieve the self-* objective in question. Note that a self-objective could be associated with multiple scenarios. The combination of a self-* objective and a scenario forms an *ARE Requirements Chunk* (see Figure 2). A requirements chunk can be recorded in a natural language as following:

ARE Requirements Chunk

- **Name of Self-* Objective**: *Rationale of this self-* objective.*
  - **Assisting system goals**: *List of system goals assisted by this self-* objective.*
  - **Actors**: *Actors participating in the realization of this self-* objective.*
  - **Targets**: *Targets of this self-* objective.*
- **Scenario**: *Description of a scenario how this self-* objective can be met by performing the system's functionality.*

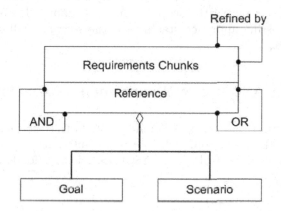

Fig. 2. Requirements Chunk - Goal & Scenario

Requirements chunks associate each goal with scenarios where the *goal-scenario pairs* can be assembled together through *composition, alternative* and *refinement relationships* (see Figure 2). The first two lead to AND and OR structures of requirements chunks, whereas the last leads to the organization of the collection of requirements chunks as a hierarchy of chunks of different granularity. *AND relationships* among requirements chunks link complementary chunks in the sense that everyone requires others to define a completely functioning scenario covering a main goal. Requirements chunks linked through *OR relationships* represent alternative ways of fulfilling the same goal. Requirements chunks linked through a *refinement relationship* are at different levels of abstraction. Internally, the scenarios might introduce additional variability via *conditional requirements* derived from the GAR's requirements such as *monitoring, adaptability, dynamicity, resilience,* and *robustness.*

2.5   Formal Specification

ARE relies on KnowLang for the formal specification of the elicited autonomy requirements. Therefore, we use KnowLang to record these requirements as knowledge representation in a Knowledge Base (KB) comprising a variety of knowledge structures, e.g., *ontologies*, *facts*, *rules*, and *constraints*. The self-* objectives are specified with special *policies* associated with *goals*, special *situations*, *actions* (eventually identified as system capabilities), *metrics*, etc. Thus, the self-* objectives are represented as policies describing at an abstract level what the system will do when particular situations arise. The situations are meant to represent the conditions needed to be met in order for the system to switch to a self-* objective while pursuing a system goal. Note that the policies rely on actions that are a priori-defined as functions of the system. In case, such functions have not been defined yet, the needed functions should be considered as *autonomous functions* and their implementation will be justified by the ARE's selected self-* objectives. ARE does not state neither specify how the system will perform these actions. This is out of the scope of the ARE approach. Basically, any requirements engineering approach states what the software will do not how the software will do it.

3   Capturing Autonomy Requirements for Science Clouds

To better understand the concepts behind ARE, in this section, we present an example of using the ARE approach to capture autonomy requirements for an autonomic ensemble described as the ASCENS Science Clouds case study (see Chapter IV.3 [15]).

3.1   Science Clouds

Science Clouds is a cloud computing scientific platform for application execution and data storage [14]. Individual users or universities can join a cloud to provide (and consume of course) resources to the community. A science cloud is a collection of cloud machines - notebooks, desktops, servers, or virtual machines, running the Science Cloud Platform (SCP). Each machine is usually running one instance of the Science Cloud Platform (Science Cloud Platform instance or SCPi). Each SCPi is considered to be a Service Component (SC) in the ASCENS sense. To form a cloud, multiple SCPis communicate over the Internet by using the IP protocol. Within a cloud, a few SCPis might be grouped into a Service Component Ensemble (SCE), also called a Science Cloud Platform ensemble (SCPe). The relationships between the SCPis are dynamic and the formation of a SCPe depends mainly on the properties of the SCPis. The common characteristic of an ensemble is SCPis working together to run one application in a fail-safe manner and under consideration of the Service Level Agreement (SLA) of that application, which may require a certain number of active SCPis, certain latency between the parts, or have restrictions on processing power or memory. The SCP is a *platform as a service* (PaaS), which provides a platform for application execution [20]. Thus, SCP provides an execution environment where special applications might be run by using the SCP's application programming interface (API) and SCP's library [20]. These applications provide a *software as a service* (SaaS) cloud solution to users. The data storage service is provided in the same manner, i.e., via an application.

Based on the rationale above, we may conclude that the Science Clouds' main objective is to *provide a scientific platform for application execution and data storage* [14]. Being a cloud computing approach, the Science Clouds approach extends the original cloud computing goal to *provide services* (or resources) to the community of users. Note that cloud computing targets three main types of service (or resource):

1. Infrastructure as a Service (IaaS): a solution providing resources such as virtual machines, network switches and data storage along with tools and APIs for management (e.g., starting VMs).
2. Platform as a Service (PaaS): a solution providing development and execution platforms for cloud applications.
3. Software as a Service (SaaS): a solution providing software applications as a resource.

3.2   GORE for Science Clouds

The three different services provided by Science Clouds (see Section 3.1) can be defined as three main goals of cloud computing, and their realization by Science Clouds will define the main Science Clouds goals. Figure 3 depicts the ARE goals model for Science Clouds where goals are organized hierarchically at four different levels. In addition, from the rationale above we may conclude that an underlying system goal is to optimize application execution by minimizing resource usage along with providing a fail-safe execution environment.

As shown in Figure 3, the goals from the first three levels are main system goals captured at different levels of abstraction. The 3rd level is resided by goals directly associated with Science Clouds and providing a concrete realization of the cloud computing goals outlined at the first two levels. Finally, the goals from the 4th level are supporting and preliminary goals that need to be achieved before proceeding with the goals from the 3rd level. Figure 3 puts together all the system goals by relating them via particular relationships such as inheritance and dependency. Goals are depicted as boxes listing both goal actors and targets (note that targets might be considered as a distinct class of actors). The ARE Goals Model for Science Clouds provides the traceability mechanism for autonomy requirements. When a change in requirements is detected at runtime, the goals model can be used to re-evaluate the system behavior with respect to the new requirements and to determine if system reconfiguration is needed. Moreover, the presented goals model provides a unifying intentional view of the system by relating goals assigned to actors and involving targets. Some of the actors can be eventually identified as the autonomy components providing a self-adaptive behavior when necessary to keep up with the high-level system objectives (the goals residing Level 3).

The following elements describe the system goals by goal levels as shown in Figure 3:

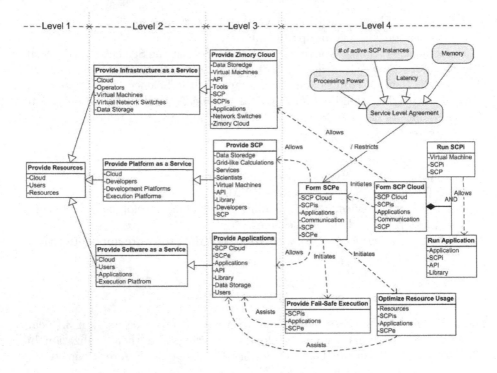

Fig. 3. Science Clouds Goals Model

Level 1 Goals:

- **Provide Resources**: *A cloud computing system (cloud) shall provide computational resources to the community of users.*
  - **Actors**: *cloud (the cloud computing system), users*
  - **Targets**: *resources*

Level 2 Goals:

- **Provide Infrastructure as a Service**: The cloud shall provide resources such as virtual machines, virtual network switches, and data storage. To manage this infrastructure, the cloud provides tools and APIs for management, e.g., starting and stopping VMs or creating new virtual networks.
  - **Actors**: cloud, operators
  - **Targets**: virtual machines, network switches, data storage
- **Provide Platform as a Service**: The cloud shall provide development and execution platforms for cloud applications, e.g., it may provide a framework for writing applications (by developers), which can either be supplied with adequate resources and distributed automatically, or request additional resources.
  - **Actors**: cloud, developers
  - **Targets**: development platforms, execution platforms

- **Software as a Service**: The cloud shall provide software applications that can be run by users within the cloud. Some examples of such applications could be e-mail service, word processor, etc. A good real-life example is Google Apps.
  - **Actors**: cloud, execution platform, users
  - **Targets**: applications platforms

Level 3 Goals:

- **Provide Zimory Cloud**: This goal is to realize the Provide Infrastructure as a Service cloud computing goal by running the Zimory Cloud. The Zimory Cloud shall provide cloud infrastructure based on SCP by running SCPis on virtual machines, as described by the rationale above. In addition, the goal requires that the Zimoty Cloud provide both API and tools needed for infrastructure management.
  - **Actors**: Zimory Cloud, API, tools, SCP, SCPis, operators
  - **Targets**: virtual machines, network switches, data storage, applications
- **Provide SCP**: This goal is to realize the Provide Platform as a Service cloud computing goal by providing the Zimory Cloud's SCP. The SCP must ensure both development and execution platforms where cloud applications can be developed and executed. Therefore, the platform must provide both API and libraries used by developers.
  - **Actors**: SCP, developers, scientists
  - **Targets**: API, library, virtual machines, services, grid-like calculations, data storage
- **Provide Applications**: This goal is to realize the Provide Software as a Service cloud computing goal by providing applications running in the SCP Cloud (or Zimory Cloud). The software applications can be run within a SCPe by users using the SCP's application programming interface (API) and SCP's library. Data storage services might be provided via applications as well.
  - **Actors**: SCP Cloud, SCPe, API, library, users
  - **Targets**: applications, data storage

Level 4 Goals:

- **Form SCPe**: This goal is to form a dynamic SCPe that shall provide the needed computational resources for the realization of either the Provide SCP goal or Provide Applications goal, or both. The Form SCPe goal is supportive to these two goals (see the *allows* relationship in Figure 3). Moreover, the achievement of this goal may initiate two more assistive goals: Provide Fail-safe Execution and Optimize Resource Usage, which assist the Provide Applications goal (see Figure 3). Note that this goal shall take into consideration the Service Level Agreement constraint, which may impose restrictions (or requirements) on the processing power, number of SCPis running within the ensemble, communication latency, memory usage, etc.

- **Actors**: SCP Cloud, SCPis, application, communication, Service Level Agreement
- **Targets**: SCPe

- **Form SCP Cloud**: This goal is to form the SCP Cloud (Zymory Cloud) from the running SCPis joining their resources within that cloud. Note that the cloud allows the individual SCPis voluntarily join in or opt out. In addition, any application that runs on a cloud's SCPi is also added to the cloud as a resource. Thus, the SCP Cloud is formed by both running SCPis and applications (see Figure 3).
  - **Actors**: SCP, SCPis, application, communication
  - **Targets**: SCP Cloud

- **Run SCPi**: This goal is to run a SCPi as an instance of SCP hosted by a virtual machine. Basically, this goal along with the Run Application goal (both connected via AND relationship) might be considered as a sub-goal of the Form SCP Cloud goal.
  - **Actors**: SCP, virtual machine
  - **Targets**: SCPi

- **Run Application**: This goal is to run an application on a SCPi using SCP's API and library. This goal must be achieved as part of the Form SCP Cloud goal, i.e., it might be considered as a sub-goal of this goal.
  - **Actors**: SCPi, API, library
  - **Targets**: application

- **Provide Fail-safe Execution**: This goal is to ensure that running applications will continue working if a hosting SCPi fails. This policy must be provided by a SCPe, eventually formed to provide a fail-safe execution environment. The Provide Fail-safe Execution goal is assistive to the Run Application goal and it may be considered as a self-* objective providing fault tolerance.
  - **Actors**: applications, SCPis, SCPe
  - **Targets**: fail-safe execution of applications

- **Optimize Resource Usage**: This goal is to ensure that running applications will use the cloud resources in the most optimal way. This policy must be provided by a SCPe, eventually formed to provide an optimal use of particular cloud resources, e.g., memory, disk space, etc. The Optimize Resource Usage goal is assistive to the Run Application goal and it may be considered as a self-* objective providing self-optimization.
  - **Actors**: applications, SCPis, SCPe, cloud resources
  - **Targets**: optimized resource usage

3.3   GAR for Science Clouds

After completing the goals model for Science Clouds, the next step of the ARE approach is to put the GAR model in the context of cloud computing to derive a domain-specific GAR that can be applied to the goals captured by the goals model for Science Clouds. To derive the domain-specific GAR we elaborated on the Science Clouds features, issues and goals to come up with self-* objectives and the consecutive autonomy-assistive requirements. For example, some remarkable issues that eventually can turn to autonomy features are [14]:

- *fail-safe operation*: An application should be available even its host SCPi fails (see Provide Fail-safe Execution goal in Section 3.2).
- *load balancing / throughput*: Parallel execution of same applications to distribute the computational/resource overhead (load) when it is high, but not before that.
- *energy conservation*: Shutting down virtual machines or de-configuring virtual networks if not required (this feature requires IaaS support).
- *SCPi fails, disappears, or appears*: A failing SCPi attempts to notify other SCPis, which need to take over responsibilities. If a new SCPi appears, it should engage with applications execution.
- *SCPi (or link) with high load, or idle*: Move applications to another SCPi, receive applications from another SCPi, or run a new SCPi on a virtual machine. If a SCPi is idle, then engage with applications running already on another SCPi, or simply shut down it.

To address these issues, SCPis must be monitored (including self-monitored) along with the cloud environment to detect high computational loads (due to applications), high communication latency, high memory usage, other SCPis that join in or opt out, etc. Basically, monitoring shall go on three levels:

- *network level*: The SCPis forming a SCPe need to know each other and be able to route between themselves.
- *application level*: The SCPis forming a SCPe need to know what applications run on which SCPis.
- *data level*: When an application is deployed, the SCPis that can eventually run that application need to have the application executable (immutable data). Moreover, the SCPis running that application need to monitor the application data (mutable data) and eventually store it through check points, so the application can be resumed in case of a SCPi failure or the failure of the application itself.

Addressing these issues in the context of the system goals (see Section 3.2) will result into self-adaptive behavior realized by self-* objectives. These self-* objectives along with the autonomy-assistive requirements form our domain-specific GAR model for Science Clouds as following:

- *self-* objectives (autonomicity)*:
  - *self-healing*: If a SCPi fails or is shut down, the applications executing on it must be made available on another SCPi in the SCPe hosting those SCPis.
  - *self-configuring_1*: Each SCPi is aware about changes in its hosting SCPe - new SCPis can be added to the hosting SCPe or other can voluntarily leave of shut down. A SCPi should adapt itself to take into consideration both the newly available resources and recently disappeared resources provided by other SCPis.
  - *self-configuring_2*: A SCPi is aware about the performance of the hosted applications. If an application is slowing down due to a lack of resources, this application can be distributed among different SCPis (run/resumed in parallel) if the application itself supports distributed execution.

- *self-optimizing_1*: If a SCPi reaches its capacity (e.g., consistent high CPU load or swapping due to high memory usage), it may transfer some of the computational load to another SCPi from the same SCPe.
- *self-optimizing_2*: If the communication latency within a SCPe is relatively high, due to overloaded links in the network, the SCPe may engage new SCPis to reduce the communication traffic.
- *self-optimizing_3*: If the communication latency within a SCPe is relatively high, due to overloaded links in the network, the SCPe may reduce the load transfer within the SCPe itself.
- *self-optimizing_4*: If SCPis are no longer required, the hosting SCPe may reconfigure to engage the idle SCPis in computational processes.
- *self-optimizing_5*: If certain SCPis are no longer required, they may shut down along with their hosting virtual machines to save energy.
- *self-optimizing_6*: If the computational load in certain SCPes is relatively high, due to overloaded application executions, the SCPe may start new SCPis along with the hosting virtual machines (if necessary) to reduce the computational overload.

- *knowledge*: cloud objectives; SCPes (engaged SCPis, ensemble's applications, ensemble's virtual machines, service level agreement, states), SCPis (applications, CPU, memory, storage capacity, states); applications (needed resources, distributiveness, states); communication links;
- *awareness*: application awareness (resource consumption, execution stage, load distribution, data-transfer); SCPi self-awareness (applications, resources, hosting virtual machine, user); SCPe awareness (participating SCPis, communication links, distributed applications, service level agreement); cloud awareness (SCPes, SCPis); communication awareness (communicating SCPis, data-transfer);
- *monitoring*: SCPi self-monitoring (running applications, CPU load, memory usage, storage capacity); SCPe monitoring (ensemble's SCPis, communication latency between SCPis, data transfer within SCPe);
- *adaptability*: adaptable load balancing; adaptable communication;
- *dynamicity*: dynamic communication links; dynamic SCPe formation;
- *robustness*: robust to SCPi failures; robust to data-transfer failures; robust to application execution failures;
- *resilience*: resilient communication links (communication losses must be repairable); network resilience (the routing needs to work in a dynamic environment where SCPis voluntarily join in and opt out of SCPes); application resilience; data resilience;
- *mobility*: data distribution; application distribution; SCPi mobility (SCPis may run on different virtual machines);

3.4   ARE Requirements Chunks for Science Clouds

The next step is to *merge* the GORE model for Science Clouds with the GAR model for science clouds, by applying the GAR model to the system goals captured in the first phase of the ARE process. Considering the fact that the Level 3 goals (see Figure 3 and Section 3.2) present the main system goals, we applied the GAR model to these goals to derive self-adaptive behavior supporting the common Science Clouds behavior realized by the goals *Provide Zimory Cloud*, *Provide SCP*, and *Provide Applications*. Note that not all the self-* objectives derived by the GAR model in Section 3.3 are relevant to every one of these three goals. In this section, we present the self-* objectives derived for these three goals. The self-* objectives are presented as autonomy requirements chunks (see Section 3.5).

For the *Provide Zimory Cloud* goal we derived the following self-* objectives:

- **Self-optimizing_5**: If certain SCPis are no longer required, they may shut down along with their hosting virtual machines to save energy.
  - **Assisting system goals**: Provide Zimory Cloud
  - **Actors**: SCPis, virtual machines
  - **Targets**: SCPis shut down
  - **Scenario**: If a SCPi is in idle mode during a certain interval of time, then it can autonomously shut down. If a hosting virtual machine detects that it is not running any SCPis for a certain period of time, it can autonomously shut down.
- **Self-optimizing_6**: If the computational load in a SCPe is relatively high, due to overloaded application executions, the SCPe may start new SCPis along with the hosting virtual machines (if necessary) to reduce the computational overload.
  - **Assisting system goals**: Provide Zimory Cloud
  - **Actors**: SCPe, SCPis, virtual machines, applications
  - **Targets**: SCPis started,
  - **Scenario**: If a SCPe detects a high computational load in the entire ensemble of SCPis, i.e., all the engaged SCPis run heavy application executions, then it may start new SCPis. If there is a lack of virtual machines that can host SCPis, then such machines can be started as well.

For the *Provide SCP* goal we derived the following self-* objectives:

- **Self-configuring_1**: Each SCPi is aware about changes in its hosting SCPe - new SCPis can be added to the hosting SCPe or other can voluntarily leave of shut down. A SCPi should adapt itself to take into consideration both the newly available resources and recently disappeared resources provided by other SCPis.
  - **Assisting system goals**: Provide SCP
  - **Actors**: SCPe, SCPis, applications
  - **Targets**: SCPis updated on changes in resource availability
  - **Scenario**: If a SCPi detects absence of a previously active SCPi it stops collaborating with that SCPi, i.e., it stops all the joint operations on applications execution and data transferring. Moreover, the active SCPi may need to reconsider the resource availability and eventually reschedule the controllable application executions to cope with the new situation. If a SCPi detects presence of a new SCPi that recently joined the SCPe, it shall reconsider the resource availability and eventually it may ask this new SCPi share part of the computational workload.

- **Self-optimizing_1**: If a SCPi reaches its capacity (e.g., consistent high CPU load or swapping due to high memory usage), it may transfer some of the computational load to another SCPi from the same SCPe.
  - **Assisting system goals**: Provide SCP
  - **Actors**: SCPe, SCPis, resources, applications
  - **Targets**: application executions shared among SCPis
  - **Scenario**: If a SCPi detects high resource usage (consistent high CPU load or high swapping) it may ask another SCPi to take over some of the application executions.
- **Self-optimizing_2**: If the communication latency within a SCPe is relatively high, due to overloaded links in the network, the SCPe may engage new SCPis to reduce the communication traffic.
  - **Assisting system goals**: Provide SCP
  - **Actors**: SCPe, SCPis, communication
  - **Targets**: low communication latency
  - **Scenario**: If a SCPi detects high communication latency while communicating with another SCPi, it may start collaborating with other SCPis to reduce the data transfer with the initial SCPi and consecutively, reduce the communication latency.
- **Self-optimizing_3**: If the communication latency within a SCPe is relatively high, due to overloaded links in the network, the SCPe may reduce the load transfer within the SCPe itself.
  - **Assisting system goals**: Provide SCP
  - **Actors**: SCPe, SCPis, communication, transferred data
  - **Targets**: low communication latency
  - **Scenario**: If a SCPi detects high communication latency while communicating with another SCPi, it may reduce the amount of transferred data.
- **Self-optimizing_4**: If SCPis are no longer required, the hosting SCPe may reconfigure to engage the idle SCPis in computational processes.
  - **Assisting system goals**: Provide SCP
  - **Actors**: SCPe, SCPis, applications
  - **Targets**: SCPis involved in application executions
  - **Scenario**: If a SCPi stays in idle mode for a specific period of time, it may request from other SCPis to take over some of the ongoing application executions.

For the *Provide Application* goal we derived the following self-* objectives:

- **Self-healing**: If a SCPi fails or is shut down, the applications executing on it must be made available on another SCPi in the SCPe hosting those SCPis.
  - **Assisting system goals**: Provide Application
  - **Actors**: SCPe, SCPis, applications
  - **Targets**: applications transferred for execution to other SCPis
  - **Scenario**: If a SCPi fails or is shut down while performing application executions, other SCPis shall detect the SCPi failure and shall take over the application executions carried by the failed SCPi.

- **Self-configuring_2**: A SCPi is aware about the performance of the hosted applications. If an application is slowing down due to a lack of resources, this application can be distributed among different SCPis (run/resumed in parallel) if the application itself supports distributed execution.
  - **Assisting system goals**: Provide Application
  - **Actors**: SCPe, SCPis, application, resources
  - **Targets**: application distributed for execution to other SCPis
  - **Scenario**: If a SCPi detects low performance in application executions due to a lack of resources, the SCPi may request other SCPis to take over some of the hosted application executions, which will eventually release resources in the initial SCPi and improve the performance of its still hosted applications.

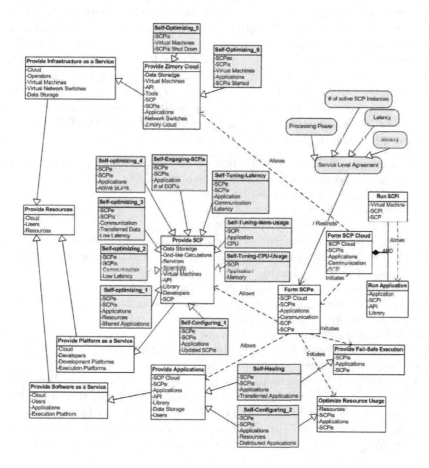

Fig. 4. Science Clouds Goals Model with Self-* Objectives Assisting System Goals from Level 3

In addition to the self-* objectives derived from the context-specific GAR model, more self-* objectives might be derived from the constraints associated with the targeted system goal. Note that the analysis step in Figure 1 (see Section 2.3) uses the context-specific GAR model and elaborates on both system goal and constraints associated with that goal. Often environmental constraints introduce factors that may violate the system goals and self-* objectives will be required to overcome those constraints. Actually, such constraints might represent obstacles to the achievement of a goal. Constructing self-* objectives from goal constraints can be regarded as a form of *constraint programming*, in which a very abstract logic sentence describing a goal with its actors and targets (it may be written in a natural language as well) is extended to include concepts from *constraint satisfaction* and *system capabilities* that enable the achievement of the goal. In ARE, the capabilities are actually abstractions of system operations that need to be performed to maintain the goal fulfillment along with constraint satisfaction. In this approach, we need to query the provability of the targeted goal, which contains constraints, and then if the system goal cannot be fulfilled due to constraint satisfaction, a self-* objective is derived as an assistive system goal preserving both the original system's goal targets and constraint satisfaction.

An example demonstrating this process can be deriving self-* objectives from the Service Level Agreement (SLA) constraints (see Section 3.2). SLA may impose constraints on application execution, e.g., certain number of active SCPis, certain latency between the communicating SCPis, or restrictions on processing power or on memory [20]. In this exercise, we derived the following self-* objectives copying with the SLA constraints:

- **Self-engaging-SCPis**: A SCPe formed for the execution of a certain application may need a certain number of involved SCPis.
  - **Assisting system goals**: Provide SCP
  - **Actors**: SCPe, SCPis, application
  - **Targets**: exact number of SCPis
  - **Scenario**: If an application requires an exact number of SCPis to run, then SCPe shall engage the exact number of SCPis needed for the execution of that application.
- **Self-tuning-Latency**: A SCPe formed for the execution of a certain application may need a certain latency between the communicating SCPis needed for the execution of that application.
  - **Assisting system goals**: Provide SCP
  - **Actors**: SCPe, SCPis, application, communication
  - **Targets**: latency
  - **Scenario**: If an application requires a certain communication latency between the SCPis engaged to run that application, then each one of these SCPis shall maintain its communication latency by either speed up the communication (by applying the self-* objective Self-optimizing-3) or slow it down (by introducing certain delay before sending the data packages).
- **Self-tuning-CPU-Usage**: A SCPi executing a certain application might be restricted by maximum CPU power allowed to this application.

- **Assisting system goals**: Provide SCP
- **Actors**: SCPi, application
- **Targets**: CPU power
- **Scenario**: If an application is consuming more CPU power than the maximum allowed, then the hosting SCPi should slow down the application execution to minimize the CPU usage.

- **Self-tuning-Memory-Usage**: A SCPi executing a certain application might be restricted by maximum memory allowed to this application.
  - **Assisting system goals**: Provide SCP
  - **Actors**: SCPi, application
  - **Targets**: memory
  - **Scenario**: If an application is consuming more memory than the maximum allowed, then the hosting SCPi should enforce lower memory use by this application.

Figure 4 depicts the Science Clouds Goals Model (shown in Figure 3), but enriched with the self-* objectives described above. As shown, these self-* objectives (depicted in gray color) inherit the system goals they assist by providing behavior alternatives with respect to these system goals. Note that, due to the "inheritance" relationship, the targets of the assisted system goals are kept in all of those self-* objectives. Note that the Science Clouds system switches to one of the assisting self-* objectives when alternative autonomous behavior is required (e.g., an SCPi fails to perform).

3.5   Formalizing Science Clouds with KnowLang

The next step after deriving the autonomy requirements per system goal is their specification with KnowLang. Note that the autonomy requirements carry all the necessary information that needs to be represented as knowledge for Science Clouds. Therefore, by specifying the captured self-* objectives we build the necessary knowledge model for Science Clouds, which is the ultimate goal of this exercise. Specifying with KnowLang goes over a few phases:

1. Initial knowledge requirements gathering - involves domain experts to determine the basic notions, relations and functions (operations) of the domain of interest.
2. Behavior definition - identifies situations and behavior policies as "control data" helping to identify important self-adaptive scenarios.
3. Knowledge structuring - encapsulates domain entities, situations and behavior policies into KnowLang structures like concepts, properties, functionalities, objects, relations, facts and rules.

By applying the ARE approach to capture the autonomy requirements for Science Clouds, we actually perform the first two phases, as described above. KnowLang [28] is exclusively dedicated to knowledge specification where knowledge is specified as a Knowledge Base (KB) comprising a variety of knowledge structures, e.g., *ontologies*, *facts*, *rules*, and *constraints*. Here, in order to specify the *autonomy requirements for Science Clouds*, the first step is to specify the KB representing the cloud, SCPes, SCPis, applications, etc. To do that, we need to specify ontology structuring the knowledge domains of the cloud. Note that these domains are described via domain-relevant *concepts* and *objects* (concept instances) related through *relations*. To handle explicit concepts like *situations*, *goals*, and *policies*, we grant some of the domain concepts with explicit state expressions (a state expression is a Boolean expression over ontology) [28]. Note that being part of the autonomy requirements, knowledge plays a very important role in the expression of all the autonomy requirements: *autonomicity, knowledge, awareness, monitoring, adaptability, dynamicity, robustness, resilience,* and *mobility* outlined by GAR (see Section 2.3).

Note that a full presentation of the specified with KnowLang KB for Science Clouds is beyond the scope of this chapter. For more information on the specified KB, the interested reader is advised to consult Chapter II.3 [32].

4   Related Work

An autonomous system is able to monitor its behavior and eventually modify the same according to changes in the operational environment, thus being considered as self-adaptation. As such, autonomous systems must continuously monitor changes in its context and react accordingly. But what aspects of the environment should such a system monitor? Clearly, the system cannot monitor everything. And exactly what should the system do if it detects less than optimal conditions in the environment? Presumably, the system still needs to maintain a set of *high-level goals* that should be satisfied regardless of the environmental conditions, e.g., mission goals of unmanned spacecraft used for space exploration. But non-critical goals could be not that strict [27], thus allowing the system a degree of flexibility during operation. These questions (and others) form the core considerations for building autonomous systems.

Traditionally, requirements engineering is concerned with what a system should do and within which constraints it must do it. Requirements engineering for autonomous systems and self-adaptive systems, therefore, must address what adaptations are possible and under what constrains, and how those adaptations are realized. In particular, questions to be addressed include: 1) *"What aspects of the environment are relevant for adaptation?"*; and 2) *"Which requirements are allowed to vary or evolve at runtime, and which must always be maintained?"*. Requirements engineering for autonomous systems must deal with uncertainty, because the execution environment often is dynamic and the information about future execution environments is incomplete, and therefore the requirements for the behavior of the system may need to change (at runtime) in response to the changing environment.

Requirements engineering for autonomous systems appears to be a wide open research area with only a limited number of approaches yet considered. The ASCENS Project approaches the requirements problem from a few angles. In addition to ARE, ASCENS also considers a design method called Invariant Refinement Method (IRM) (see Chapter III.4 [3]) and a generic approach called SOTA (States Of The Affairs) [1] (see Chapter III.1 [9]). IRM relies on goal-based requirements and refines system goals down to the responsibilities of individual components, component processes, and ensembles. IRM captures goals and requirements as invariants that describe desired system states over time. The SOTA approach proposes an extension of existing goal-oriented requirements engineering approaches that integrates elements of dynamic systems modeling. SOTA models the entities of a self-adaptive system as if they were immersed in multi-dimensional space where each of the dimensions represents a specific aspect of a particular situation involving the system and/or the environment. While ARE provides a complete approach for capturing autonomy requirements, both IRM and SOTA are rather complimentary to ARE approaches, which do not provide mechanisms for determining the autonomy requirements, but rather extend the options for handling some of the autonomy requirements, once these have been identified.

The Autonomic System Specification Language (ASSL) [30,29,22] is a framework providing for a formal approach to specifying and modeling autonomous (autonomic) systems by emphasizing the self-* requirements. Cheng and Atlee [4] report on work on specifying and verifying adaptive software. In [6,19], research on runtime monitoring of requirements conformance is described. In [21], Sutcliffe, S. Fickas and M. Sohlberg demonstrate a method (called PC-RE) for personal and context requirements engineering that can be applied to autonomous systems. In addition, some research approaches have successfully used goal models as a foundation for specifying the autonomic behaviour [13] and requirements of adaptive systems [7].

A major breakthrough of the past decade in Software Requirements Engineering is the *goal-oriented approach* to capturing and analyzing stakeholder intentions to derive functional and non-functional (hereafter quality) requirements [5,16]. In essence, this approach has extended upstream the software development process by adding a new phase (*early requirements analysis*) that is also supported by engineering concepts, tools and techniques.

The fundamental concepts used to drive the goal-oriented form of analysis are those of *goal* and *actor*. To fulfill a stakeholder goal, the Goal-Oriented Requirements Engineering (GORE) [11] approach provides for analyzing the *space of alternatives*, which makes the process of generating functional and non-functional (quality) requirements more systematic in the sense that the designer is exploring an explicitly represented space of alternatives. It also makes it more rational in that the designer can point to an explicit evaluation of these alternatives in terms of stakeholder criteria to justify her choice.

ARE uses GORE as the first phase of the Autonomy Requirements Engineering process. ARE uses GORE to build goal models that can help us derive autonomy requirements in several ways:

1. Goal models can be used to capture and refine requirements for autonomic systems. A goal model provides the starting point for the development of such a system by analyzing the environment for the system-to-be and by

identifying the problems that exist in this environment as well as the needs that the system under development has to address. Thus, requirements goal models can be used as a baseline for validating software systems.

2. Goal models provide a means to represent alternative ways in which the objectives of the system can be met and analyze and rank these alternatives with respect to stakeholder quality concerns and other constraints. This allows for exploration and analysis of alternative system behaviors at design time, which leads to more predictable and trusted autonomic systems. It also means that if the alternatives that are initially delivered with the system perform well, there is no need for complex social interactions among autonomic elements. Of course, not all alternatives can be identified at design time. In an open and dynamic environment, new and better alternatives may present themselves and some of the identified and implemented alternatives may become impractical. Thus, in certain situations, new alternatives will have to be discovered and implemented by the system at runtime. However, the process of discovery, analysis, and implementation of new alternatives at runtime is complex and error-prone. By exploring the space of alternative process specifications at design time, we are minimizing the need for that difficult task.

3. Goal models provide the traceability mechanism from AC system designs to stakeholder requirements. When a change in stakeholder requirements is detected at runtime (e.g., a major change in the global mission goal), goal models can be used to re-evaluate the system behavior alternatives with respect to the new requirements and to determine if system reconfiguration is needed. For instance, if a change in stakeholder requirements affected a particular goal in the model, it is possible to see how this goal is decomposed and which components/autonomic elements implementing the goal are in turn affected. By analyzing the goal model, it is also easy to identify how a failure to achieve some particular goal affects the overall objective of the system. At the same time, highly variable goal models can be used to visualize the currently selected system configuration along with its alternatives and to communicate suggested configuration changes to users in high-level terms.

4. Goal models provide a unifying intentional view of the system by relating goals assigned to individual autonomic elements to high-level system objectives and quality concerns. These high-level objectives or quality concerns serve as the common knowledge shared among the autonomic computing elements to achieve the global system optimization. This way, the system can avoid the pitfalls of missing the globally optimal configuration due to only relying on local optimizations.

5   Conclusions

This chapter has presented an Autonomy Requirements Engineering approach, used by the ASCENS project to capture the autonomy requirements for the ASCENS case studies. A proof-of-concept example has been presented where we have applied the proposed ARE model to the ASCENS Science Clouds case study. With this example, we have demonstrated how ARE can be used to both elicit and express autonomy requirements for software-intensive, yet self-adaptive, systems. Note that ARE relies on Goal-Oriented Requirements Engineering (GORE) to elicit and define the system goals, and uses a Generic Autonomy Requirements (GAR) model to derive and define *assistive* and eventually *alternative goals* (or objectives) of the system. The system may pursue these *"self-* objectives"* in the presence of factors threatening the achievement of the initial system goals. Once identified, the autonomy requirements including the self-* objectives have been further specified with KnowLang.

Future work is mainly concerned with development of tools for our ARE model. An efficient ARE Tool Suite incorporating an *autonomy requirements validation* approach is the next logical step needed to complete the ARE Framework. Moreover, an efficient ARE Framework shall adopt KnowLang as a formal notation and provide tools for specification and validation of autonomy requirements. Runtime knowledge representation and reasoning shall be provided along with monitoring mechanisms to support the autonomy behavior of a system at runtime. We need to build an ARE Test Bed tool that will integrate the KnowLang Reasoner and will allow for validation of self-* objectives based on simulation and testing. This will help engineers validate self-* objectives by evaluating the system's ability to perceive the internal and external environment and react to changes. Therefore, with the ARE Test Bed tool, we shall be able to evaluate capabilities that might manifest system awareness about situations and conditions. Ideally, both the autonomy requirements model specified in the form of knowledge representation and the reasoner, can be further implemented in autonomous systems as an engine responsible for the adaptive behavior. Eventually, a code generator shall be able to generate stubs supporting the operations of the KnowLang Reasoner. These stubs can be further used as a basis for the real implementation of the mechanism controlling the autonomic behavior of the system.

References

1. Abeywickrama, D., Bicocchi, N., Zambonelli, F.: SOTA: Towards a general model for self-adaptive systems. In: The IEEE 21st International Workshop on Enabling Technologies: Infrastructure for Collaborative Enterprises (WETICE), June 2012, pp. 48–53 (2012)
2. A.S.C.E.N.S.: ASCENS - Autonomic Service-Component Ensembles (2012), http://www.ascens-ist.eu/
3. Bures, T., Gerostathopoulos, I., Hnetynka, P., Keznikl, J., Kit, M., Plasil, F.: The Invariant Refinement Method. In: Wirsing, M., Hölzl, M., Koch, N., Mayer, P. (eds.) Software Engineering for Collective Autonomic Systems. LNCS, vol. 8998, pp. 405–428. Springer, Heidelberg (2015)
4. Cheng, B., Atlee, J.: Research directions in requirements engineering. In: Proceedings of the 2007 Conference on Future of Software Engineering (FOSE 2007), pp. 285–303. IEEE Computer Society Press, Los Alamitos (2007)

5. Dardenne, A., van Lamsweerde, A., Fickas, S.: Goal-directed requirements acquisitions. Science of Computer Programming 20, 3–50 (1993)

6. Fickas, S., Feather, M.: Requirements monitoring in dynamic environments. In: Proceedings of the IEEE International Symposium on Requirements Engineering (RE 1995), pp. 140–147. IEEE Computer Society Press, Los Alamitos (1995)

7. Goldsby, H., Sawyer, P., Bencomo, N., Hughes, D., Cheng, B.: Goal-based modeling of dynamically adaptive system requirements. In: Proceedings of the 15th Annual IEEE International Conference on the Engineering of Computer Based Systems (ECBS), IEEE Computer Society Press, Los Alamitos (2008)

8. Haumer, P., Pohl, K., Weidenhaupt, K.: Requirements elicitation and validation with real world scenes. IEEE Transactions on Software Engineering – Special Issue on Scenario Management, 1036–1054 (1998)

9. Hölzl, M., Koch, N., Puviani, M., Wirsing, M., Zambonelli, F.: The Ensemble Development Life Cycle and Best Practices for Collective Autonomic Systems. In: Wirsing, M., Hölzl, M., Koch, N., Mayer, P. (eds.) Software Engineering for Collective Autonomic Systems. LNCS, vol. 8998, pp. 325–354. Springer, Heidelberg (2015)

10. van Lamsweerde, A.: Requirements engineering in the year 00: A research perspective. In: Proceedings of the 22nd International Conference on Software Engineering (ICSE'2000), pp. 5–19. ACM Press, New York (2000)

11. van Lamsweerde, A.: Requirements engineering in the Year 00: A research perspective. In: Proceedings of the 22nd IEEE International Conference on Software Engineering (ICSE-2000), pp. 5–19. ACM Press, New York (2000)

12. van Lamsweerde, A., Darimont, R., Massonet, P.: Goal-directed elaboration of requirements for a meeting scheduler: Problems and lessons learnt. In: Proceedings of the 2nd International IEEE Symposium on Requirements Engineering, pp. 194–203. IEEE Computer Society Press, Los Alamitos (1995)

13. Lapouchnian, A., Yu, Y., Liaskos, S., Mylopoulos, J.: Requirements-driven design of autonomic application software. In: Proceedings of the 2006 Conference of the Center for Advanced Studies on Collaborative Research (CASCON 2006), p. 7. ACM Press, New York (2006)

14. Mayer, P., Klarl, A., Hennicker, R., Puviani, M., Tiezzi, F., Pugliese, R., Keznikl, J., Bures, T.: The autonomic cloud: A vision of voluntary, peer-2-peer cloud computing. In: Proceedings of the 3rd Workshop on Challenges for achieving Self-Awareness in Autonomic Systems, Philadelphia, USA, September 2013, pp. 1–6 (2013)

15. Mayer, P., Velasco, J., Klarl, A., Hennicker, R., Puviani, M., Tiezzi, F., Pugliese, R., Keznikl, J., Bureš, T.: The Autonomic Cloud. In: Wirsing, M., Hölzl, M., Koch, N., Mayer, P. (eds.) Software Engineering for Collective Autonomic Systems. LNCS, vol. 8998, pp. 495–512. Springer, Heidelberg (2015)

16. Mylopoulos, J., Chung, L., Nixon, B.: Representing and using non-functional requirements: a process-oriented approach. IEEE Transactions on Software Engineering 18(6), 483–497 (1992)

17. Rolland, C., Souveyet, C., Achour, C.: Guiding goal-modeling using scenarios. IEEE Transactions on Software Engineering – Special Issue on Scenario Management, 1055–1071 (1998)

18. Ross, D., Schoman, K.: Structured analysis for requirements definition. IEEE Transactions on Software Engineering 3(1), 6–15 (1977)

19. Savor, T., Seviora, R.: An approach to automatic detection of software failures in real-time systems. In: Proceedings of the IEEE Real-Time Technology and Applications Symposium, pp. 136–147. IEEE Computer Society Press, Los Alamitos (1997)

20. Serbedzija, N., Reiter, S., Ahrens, M., Velasco, J., Pinciroli, C., Hoch, N., Werther, B.: D7.1: First Report on WP7 Requirement Specification and Scenario Description of the ASCENS Case Studies, aSCENS Deliverable (2011)

21. Sutcliffe, A., Fickas, S., Sohlberg, M.: PC-RE a method for personal and context requirements engineering with some experience. Requirements Engineering Journal 11, 1–17 (2006)

22. Vassev, E., Hinchey, M.: ASSL: A software engineering approach to autonomic computing. IEEE Computer 42(6), 106–109 (2009)

23. Vassev, E., Hinchey, M.: Autonomy requirements engineering. IEEE Computer 46(8), 82–84 (2013)

24. Vassev, E., Hinchey, M.: Autonomy requirements engineering. In: Proceedings of the 14th IEEE International Conference on Information Reuse and Integration (IRI'13), pp. 175–184. IEEE Computer Society Press, Los Alamitos (2013)

25. Vassev, E., Hinchey, M.: Autonomy requirements engineering: A case study on the BepiColombo Mission. In: Proceedings of the C* Conference on Computer Science & Software Engineering (C3S2E'13), pp. 31–41. ACM Press, New York (2013)

26. Vassev, E., Hinchey, M.: On the autonomy requirements for space missions. In: Proceedings of the 16th IEEE International Symposium on Object/Component/Service-oriented Real-time Distributed Computing Workshops (ISCORCW 2013), IEEE Computer Society Press, Los Alamitos (2013)

27. Vassev, E., Hinchey, M., Balasubramaniam, D., Dobson, S.: An ASSL approach to handling uncertainty in self-adaptive systems. In: Proceedings of the 34th annual IEEE Software Engineering Workshop (SEW 34), pp. 11–18. IEEE Computer Society Press, Los Alamitos (2011)

28. Vassev, E., Hinchey, M., Montanari, U., Bicocchi, N., Zambonelli, F., Wirsing, M.: D3.2: Second Report on WP3: The KnowLang Framework for Knowledge Modeling for SCE Systems, aSCENS Deliverable (2012)

29. Vassev, E.: Towards a Framework for Specification and Code Generation of Autonomic Systems. Ph.D. thesis, Computer Science and Software Engineering Department, Concordia University, Quebec, Canada (2008)

30. Vassev, E.: ASSL: Autonomic System Specification Language - A Framework for Specification and Code Generation of Autonomic Systems. LAP Lambert Academic Publishing, Germany (2009)

31. Vassev, E., Hinchey, M.: Autonomy Requirements Engineering for Space Missions. NASA Monographs in Systems and Software Engineering. Springer, Heidelberg (2014), doi:10.1007/978-3-319-09816-6

32. Vassev, E., Hinchey, M.: Knowledge Representation for Adaptive and Self-aware Systems. In: Wirsing, M., Hölzl, M., Koch, N., Mayer, P. (eds.) Software Engineering for Collective Autonomic Systems. LNCS, vol. 8998, pp. 221–247. Springer, Heidelberg (2015)

33. Wirsing, M., Hölzl, M., Tribastone, M., Zambonelli, F.: ASCENS: Engineering Autonomic Service-Component Ensembles. In: Beckert, B., Damiani, F., de Boer, F.S., Bonsangue, M.M. (eds.) FMCO 2011. LNCS, vol. 7542, pp. 1–24. Springer, Heidelberg (2013), http://www.pst.ifi.lmu.de/~hoelzl/fmco-2011.pdf

CHAPTER III.4

The Invariant Refinement Method*

Tomáš Bureš, Ilias Gerostathopoulos, Petr Hnetynka, Jaroslav Keznikl, Michal Kit, and Frantisek Plasil

Charles University in Prague,
Faculty of Mathematics and Physics,
Department of Distributed and Dependable Systems,
Prague, Czech republic

Abstract. The chapter describes IRM, a method that guides the design of smart-cyber physical systems that are built according to the autonomic service-component paradigm. IRM is a requirements-oriented design method that focuses on distributed collaboration. It relies on the invariant concept to model both high-level system goals and low-level software obligations. In IRM, high-level invariants are iteratively decomposed into more specific sub-invariants up to the level that they can be operationalized by autonomous components and component collaborations (ensembles). We present the main concepts behind the method, as well the main decomposition patterns that back up the design process, and illustrate them in the ASCENS e-mobility case study.

Keywords: system design, dependability, self-adaptivity

1 Introduction

Business needs and technological breakthroughs have been recently pushing towards the cost-effective and manageable development of increasingly complex, software-intensive systems that feature close connection to the physical world – so-called smart *cyber-physical systems* (CPS). Examples of such systems are numerous: smart electric grids, emergency coordination systems, autonomous robots, fleets of cooperating vehicles, smart spaces, to name just a few.

Within the ASCENS project, we have created a comprehensive software engineering solution for the development of smart CPS. The solution takes the form of a framework consisting of:

(i) a specialized software component model, based on the paradigm of *autonomic component ensembles* (ACEs), with clear execution and interaction semantics;

(ii) an execution environment that allows for distributed and decentralized operation of systems composed of the specialized software components;

---

* This research was supported by the European project IP 257414 (ASCENS).

M. Wirsing et al. (eds.): Collective Autonomic Systems, LNCS 8998, pp. 405–428, 2015.
© Springer International Publishing Switzerland 2015

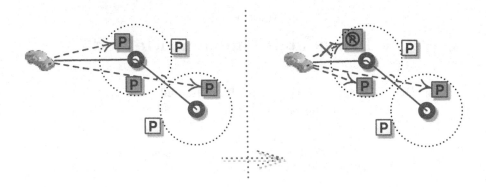

Fig. 1. E-mobility case study: electric cars need to proactively re-plan according to the availability of parking stations.

(iii) design-time and runtime analysis (e.g., timing analysis) based on a well-defined computational model; and

(iv) a specialized requirements-oriented design method that focuses on distributed collaboration and complements (i).

In this chapter, we focus on the last element of our framework and present the design method and associated model – the *Invariant Refinement Method* (IRM). IRM features contractual design based on the iterative refinement of system-level requirements, and provides both *dependability* in form of traceability of software artifacts to system-level goals, and *adaptability*, as it captures the design alternatives pertaining to different operational contexts/situations and translates them into different system and component modes. From the overall perspective of the Ensemble Development Life Cycle (see Chapter III.1 [13]), IRM thus serves as a method to guide the transition from early high-level requirements (featured by SOTA/GEM and ARE, see Chapters III.2 [20] and III.3 [23]) to software architecture of autonomic components and ensembles.

The chapter is based on the authors' papers [7,10,15] and technical reports [6] and is structured as follows. Section 2 presents our running example and illustrates the basic principles behind our ACEs-based component model. Section 3 details on the limitations of traditional software engineering methods when designing CPS via ACEs. Section 4 presents the basics of IRM, while Sections 5 details on the specific refinement patterns that can be employed in the IRM-based design. Finally, Section 6 concludes the chapter and discusses the yet-to-be-addressed challenges.

2   Running Example

To illustrate the IRM approach, we use a scenario taken from the ASCENS e-mobility case study (Chapter IV.4 [12]). In this case study, a fleet of *electric vehicles* (e-vehicles) is used to distribute people to their *places of interest* (POIs) in a city. Due to their limited autonomy compared to conventional vehicles, e-vehicles need to regularly stop at parking lots with energy charging capabilities located in designated parking stations in the city. After recharging, e-vehicles become again fully operational and join the rest of the fleet.

Careful planning is needed in order to avoid traffic bottlenecks and high recharging times. The problem in such planning is threefold:

(i) The whole system is very dynamic, as vehicles change their routes according to the passengers calendars (which can also change at runtime), streets/parking stations can be temporarily closed, and the load of parking stations is typically hard to predict as it changes according to the incoming parking requests from the vehicles (which change as vehicles re-plan).

(ii) No central communication and coordination point is assumed. This results into having an inherently scalable system which is harder to control, as each vehicle plans its own route according to its partial view of the rest of the system and independently of the rest of the vehicles.

(iii) Each element of the system may be in different modes (e.g., "low battery" vs. "fully operational" for the e-vehicles) which prescribes also different local actions to be taken. In combination with the fully decentralized operation, local decision making based on partial views of the whole system can introduce inconsistencies and oscillations.

As a running example, we use a simplified scenario from the above mentioned case study. It is based on the following assumptions:

(i) drivers are bound to their vehicles, i.e., there is no car sharing or car pooling possibility;

(ii) vehicles do not send parking requests to parking stations, but just use the parking stations' availability information in order to plan their trip (and re-plan if needed);

(iii) when planning, vehicles consider parking at parking stations that are within a fixed distance to the POIs in the driver's calendar.

The last point is illustrated in Fig. 1, where a vehicle follows a route that leads to two available parking stations close to its POIs (left hand-side); when one of them becomes unavailable, the vehicle has to head to the next available parking station within the radius of its first POI (right hand-side).

2.1   DEECo Model of the Running Example

The above scenario has been implemented in the DEECo component model [5]. DEECo is a component model developed within ASCENS, that targets the development and deployment of CPS following the paradigm of ACEs.

In DEECo, each component is an independent unit of development and deployment. Examples of two DEECo components in the DEECo domain specific language (DSL) are depicted in Listing 1. It consists of *knowledge*, i.e., component's data (e.g., lines 9-10 and 19), and one or more *processes* (e.g., lines 11-14

```
1  role AvailabilityConsumer:
2      calendar, availabilityList
3
4  role AvailabilityProvider:
5      position, availability
6
7  component Vehicle42 features AvailabilityConsumer:
8      knowledge:
9          calendar = {(WORK,09:00,(50.846232,49.469774)),...}, availabilityList = {(23,8),... },
10         plan = {(20m,LEFT),...}, planFeasibility = TRUE, ...
11     process computePlanWhenFarFromPOI(in calendar, in availabilityList, in planFeasibility, out plan):
12         plan ← JourneyPlanner.computePlan(calendar,availabilityList, planFeasibility)
13         scheduling: periodic( 6000ms ) and triggered(changed(planFeasibility) ∨ changed(availabilityList))
14         mode: farFromPOI
15     ...
16
17 component ParkingStation23 features AvailabilityProvider:
18     knowledge:
19         position = {50.846296, 49.461009}, availability = 8, ...
20     process monitorAvailability(out availability):
21         availability ← Sensors.getCurrentAvailability()
22         scheduling: periodic( 3000ms )
23         mode: closeToPOI, farFromPOI
24     ...
25 ...
26 // updates Vehicles' belief over the availability of relevant Parking Stations
27 ensemble UpdateAvailabilityWhenFarFromPOI:
28     coordinator: AvailabilityConsumer
29     member: AvailabilityProvider
30     membership:
31         ∃ poi ∈ coordinator.calendar: distance(member.position, poi.position) ≤ THRESHOLD
32     knowledge exchange:
33         coordinator.availabilityList ← {m.availability | m ∈ members}
34     scheduling: periodic( 6000ms )
35     mode: farFromPOI
36 ...
```

Listing 1. Example of a DEECo component and ensemble definition in DSL

and 20-23). Each process is essentially a thread that operates upon the knowledge by reading the input knowledge, executing the process body and writing the output knowledge. Process execution can be periodic (e.g., line 22), event-based (where an event is a change in the knowledge of the component), or both (e.g., line 13). Each process is bound to one (e.g., line 14) or more (e.g., line 23) *modes* and gets executed only if the containing component is in one of the process's modes. Finally, each component features one or more *roles* (e.g., line 7 and 17). A role is a collection of knowledge fields (e.g., lines 1-2 and 4-5).

In our running example, the two components depicted at the instance level in Listing 1 are `Vehicle` and `ParkingStation`. The former features the role of aggregating the parking availability information, which the later should provide. Among others, `Vehicle` comprises a process responsible for the computing the `Vehicle`'s plan, while `ParkingStation` comprises a process responsible for sensing the current availability (equivalently occupancy) of the station.

DEECo components do not have explicit bindings to each other and are not allowed to communicate directly. Instead, communication in DEECo is implicit and takes the form of *knowledge exchange* within emerging groups called *ensembles*. Forming of ensembles is one of the tasks of the DEECo runtime framework.

An ensemble in DEECo DSL is an interaction template (e.g., Listing 1, lines 27-35) that consists of the specification of the roles of the interacting parts, termed *coordinator* (line 28) and *member* (line 29), the specification of the condition of interaction, termed *membership* (lines 30-31), and the specification of the actual *knowledge exchange* function (lines 32-33). Similar to DEECo processes, knowledge exchange within an ensemble is triggered in a periodic (e.g., line 34) or event-triggered fashion, and is bound to the mode of the evaluating component (line 35).

In the running example, the `UpdateAvailabilityWhenFarFromPOI` ensemble specifies that whenever two component that feature the roles of `Availability-Consumer` and `AvailabilityProvider` and satisfy the condition of the latter being close to one of the POI of the former (according to their knowledge valuations), then the `availability` knowledge of the provider has to be copied to the consumer side. This models the scenario of a car that communicates with a parking station in order to obtain the station's availability and plan accordingly.

In the rest of the chapter, we will focus on the problem of *how to come up with a specification of a DEECo-based system* (such as the one depicted in Listing 1) based on the initial requirements and domain assumptions. Throughout the rest of the text, we illustrate the approach on the running example.

3   The Need for a Tailored Design Method for ACEs

Although DEECo provides a set of concepts (autonomous components, periodic processes, ensembles) that effectively deal with the dynamicity and distribution at a middleware level, the systematic design of CPS based on ACEs remains a significant challenge. Contemporary design methods for complex systems typically consist of the phases of (i) eliciting and analyzing the goals of the system-to-be, i.e., what is to be achieved and why, (ii) translating them into requirements specifications of the the system-to-be, and (iii) deriving the architecture of the system-to-be by mapping each requirement to one or more runtime entities (usually referred to as components). KAOS [18,19] and Tropos [3,11] are two prominent goal-oriented requirements engineering methodologies that are primarily concerned with the first two design phases. SOTA [1] and ARE [22] are two requirements modeling approaches developed within ASCENS and tailored to the domain of autonomous and self-adaptive systems that also focus exclusively on the first two design phases.

The underlying idea of KAOS is to use goals to capture the intent (the "why") behind the functionality of the system-to-be. Goals in KAOS are iteratively decomposed into sub-goals until they reach the level where they can be mapped to requirements or assumptions of the system-to-be. The process then continues with assigning each requirement to an individual system agent. Goals in KAOS can be formalized in real-time linear temporal logic (LTL) [2] and used to check a requirements specification for consistency, completeness and pertinence. Although KAOS is a well-established methodology in requirements engineering with strong focus on formal specification and reasoning, its application in the design of ACEs is not straightforward. The main issue is that, although there have been preliminary efforts towards this [17], KAOS does not provide a smooth alignment between requirements with architecture (third design phase mentioned in the previous paragraph). For instance, if a goal in our running example is to "maintain the availability of the parking stations up-to-date", the way to reflect this goal in system architecture is open to interpretation and heavily depends on the underlying component model used for development and deployment.

Tropos is an agent-oriented methodology where goals, soft-goals, tasks and dependencies are analyzed from the perspective of the individual agents in the system-to-be. Tropos uses the i* notation [24] for producing goal and actor models, which are later mapped to agent architectures that follow the Belief-Desire-Intention (BDI) reference model [21]. In this respect, it is more effective than KAOS in aligning system requirements with system architecture and implementation. When applied to the design of ACEs, the main shortcoming of Tropos is that it fails to address the special concerns of the ACEs domain, i.e., that of distributed dynamic feedback loop-based systems. In such systems, it is important to capture the relation of the system with the environment at every time instant, as opposed to focus on future states (the case of goals in Tropos).

SOTA [1] is a requirements modeling approach for the domain of ACEs and autonomic systems in general. The key idea of SOTA is to abstract the behavior of a system with a single trajectory through a state space, which represents the set of all possible states of the system at a single point of time. The requirements of a system in SOTA are captured in terms of goals. A goal is an area of the SOTA space that a system should eventually reach, and it can be characterized by its pre-condition, post-condition, and utilities. Thus SOTA provides the means to capture the early requirements of different component cooperation schemes, but not to guide the requirements-driven design of ACEs. A mathematical formalization of SOTA is provided by the *General Ensemble Model* (GEM) [14] The GEM semantics of SOTA is based on timed streams of domain states which closely corresponds to the higher-order predicate semantics of IRM (cf. Section 5). Chapter II.1 [4] in this volume discusses GEM in more detail.

Autonomy Requirements Engineering (ARE) (see Chapter III.3 [23] and [22]) is a methodology for elicitation and expression of autonomy requirements developed within ASCENS. ARE relies on goal-oriented requirements engineering approaches (such as KAOS and Tropos) to elicit and define the system goals, and uses a Generic Autonomy Requirements (GAR) model to derive and define *assistive* and eventually alternative goals (or objectives) of the system. However, similar to classical goal oriented approaches, ARE focuses on the requirements phase and not on the mapping between requirements and architecture.

A key challenge in the design of ACEs is to provide a concept that, contrary to the system goal, captures the *operational normalcy* at every time instant, i.e., the property of being within certain limits that define the range of normal operation of the system. The next challenge is to use this concept in order to

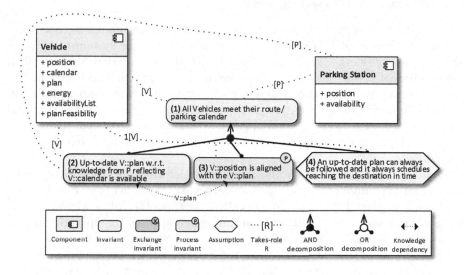

Fig. 2. Top-level design of the case study

systematically map situation-specific high-level goals to low-level artifacts of system architecture (e.g., component processes, ensemble specifications, component modes) so that the compliance of design decisions with the overall system goals and requirements is explicitly captured and (if possible) formally verified.

4 Invariant Refinement Method

We have addressed the above challenge by introducing a novel design method called IRM (Invariant Refinement Method), which specifically focuses on ACEs. IRM builds on goal-based requirements elaboration as pioneered by [16]. Similar to [16], IRM focuses on the system-to-be from a global perspective and reasons about the goals and requirements of the system as whole. By gradual refinement it allows refining these goals down to the responsibilities of individual components, component processes, and ensembles.

IRM captures goals and requirements of the systems as *invariants* that describe the desired state of the system-to-be at every time instant. This corresponds to the operational normalcy of the system-to-be and thus it aligns well with the need of continuous operation of ACEs.

Fig. 2 illustrates an IRM refinement tree reflecting the running example. Each rounded rectangle represents system's requirements represented by an invariant – e.g., the top-level invariant (1): "All Vehicles meet their route/parking calendar".

4.1   Invariants and Assumptions

The IRM tree employs first class entities – *invariants, assumptions,* and *components.* A component is a primary functional entity of the system-to-be (e.g., Vehicle and Parking Station in Fig. 2). At the abstraction level of IRM, each component comprises specific knowledge, i.e., its domain-specific data. The valuation of components' knowledge evolves over time as the result of their autonomous behavior (i.e., execution of the associated component processes) and knowledge exchange. Also, a component may take up a particular role (i.e., a responsibility) in the system-to-be. This is a consequence of being referred to by an invariant.

Technically, an invariant establishes a condition over the knowledge valuation of a set of components. An invariant references components by role names – e.g., in the invariant (1) the component Vehicle takes the *role* V while Parking Station takes the role P. This way, an invariant captures the operational normalcy of the system-to-be or its logical parts (i.e., groups of components).

Invariants need not only describe the responsibilities of components, but they may also express *assumptions* about the environment. An *assumption* is thus a condition that is expected to hold during knowledge evolution and is not intended to be maintained explicitly by the system-to-be (in figures depicted as yellow hexagon; e.g., (4) in Fig. 2).

4.2   Invariants vs. Computation Activities

The core idea of IRM is that each invariant which is not an assumption is associated with a *computation activity* – an abstract computation that produces *output knowledge* given a particular *input knowledge* such that the invariant (over the input and output knowledge) is satisfied. This way, the computation activity provides a dual view on the invariant – while the invariant reflects the operational normalcy, the computation activity represents means for maintaining it.

For instance, Fig. 3 provides the dual view of computation activities reflecting the invariants in Fig. 2.

The duality of the invariants and computation activities gives a convenient option of refer to invariants for the purpose of logic-based reasoning and refer to computation activities when low-level implementation aspects are of concern.

An abstract computation activity can be related to an invariant at any level in the IRM tree. The computation activity however gets a special significance for the leaves of the IRM tree, where it corresponds to a component process or a knowledge exchange. Thus, following the dual perspective, the goal of IRM is to refine high-level invariants (i.e., the abstract activities) to the very concrete invariants which via their computation activities lead to the design of component processes and knowledge exchange.

Note that the activities associated with high-level system goals are abstract, representing the whole system implementation. At this level of abstraction, not all input knowledge can be precisely identified, this is exemplified in Fig. 3, where

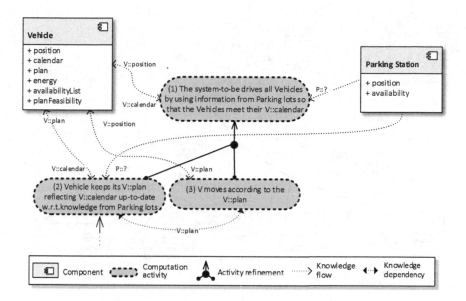

Fig. 3. Dual, activity-based view on the top-level design of the case study from Fig. 2

the input knowledge of the activity associated with (1) comprises V::calendar and potentially some knowledge of parking lots, which is not yet clear, thus denoted by P::?. The output knowledge comprises V::position, which is the knowledge the evolution of which the system can effectively control by the activity.

The relations between component knowledge and input/output knowledge of activities are captured as *knowledge flows* on the IRM diagram. For example, Fig. 3 shows the knowledge flow between the Vehicle and the activity associated with (3) (with V::plan, resp., V::position as its input, resp., output knowledge).

4.3 Invariant Refinement

The basic process in IRM is a systematic, gradual refinement of a higher-level invariant by means of its decomposition (i.e., structural elaboration) into a conjunction or disjunction of lower-level sub-invariants, i.e., $I_p \rightsquigarrow I_{s1} \wedge \ldots \wedge I_{sn}$ and $I_p \rightsquigarrow I_{s1} \vee \ldots \vee I_{sn}$.

Formally, decomposition of a parent invariant I_p into a conjunction of sub-invariants $I_{s1},\ldots,I_{sn}$ is a refinement if the conjunction of the sub-invariants entails the parent invariant, i.e., if it holds that:

$$I_{s1} \wedge \ldots \wedge I_{sn} \Rightarrow I_p \quad (entailment)$$
$$I_{s1} \wedge \ldots \wedge I_{sn} \not\Rightarrow false \quad (consistency)$$

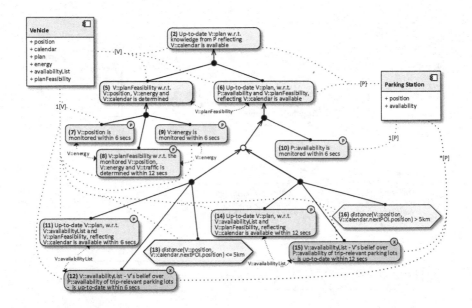

Fig. 4. Invariant refinement of "Up-to-date V::plan w.r.t. knowledge from P reflecting V::calendar is available"

This definition follows the classical interpretation of refinement, where the composition of the children exhibits all the behaviors expected from the parent and (potentially) some more.

Similarly, the OR-decomposition of a parent invariant I_p into the sub-invariants $I_{s1},...,I_{sn}$ is a refinement if it holds that:

$$I_{s1} \vee \ldots \vee I_{sn} \Rightarrow I_p \quad \text{(alternative entailment)}$$
$$I_{s1} \vee \ldots \vee I_{sn} \nRightarrow false \quad \text{(alternative consistency)}$$

The refinement via AND- and OR-branching is applied recursively. This starts with high-level invariants that reflect the overall system goals and involve a number of components and ends with low-level invariants that involve a single component or an ensemble of components.

To keep the semantics of the refinement, only the components that take a role in the parent invariant may also take a role in the sub-invariants. However, as the refinement also leads to concretization of the problem and its solutions, new knowledge can be added to the components that take a role in the sub-invariants (e.g., V::planFeasibility in Fig. 4).

The process of refinement is demonstrated in Fig. 2. As a design decision the invariant (1) is refined into a conjunction of three sub-invariants: (2) having an up-to-date plan, (3) keeping the vehicle's position in alignment with the plan, and (4) an assumption that an up-to-date plan can always be followed by the vehicle (i.e., the environment dynamics – traffic, parking availability, etc. – will never prevent the car from following an up-to-date plan) and that it always schedules reaching the destination in time. The refinement further continues in Fig. 4, where the invariant (2) is further refined, up to the leaves.

Note the OR-decomposition below the invariant (6). Formally, the IRM refinement allows only AND-refinement or OR-refinement, but not a combination of both. If a combination is necessary, it has to be formally modeled by introduction of synthetic invariants following the abstract-syntax tree of the desired formula. As these synthetic invariants do not provide any additional knowledge, the graphical notation used in the figure omits them and permits direct connection of refinement symbols.

Seeing the refinement from the dual perspective of computation activities, the computation activity of a parent is formed by parallel execution of its sub-activities. In case of AND-refinement, this involves all sub-activities. In case of OR-refinement, this involves executing exactly one sub-activity. To help determine which sub-activity of an OR-refinement to execute, the design practice is to equip each OR-branch with an assumption which acts as a guard to the branch (see assumptions (13) and (16) in Fig. 4).

4.4   Leaves of Refinement

As the rule of thumb the refinement is finished when each leaf invariant of the refinement tree is either an assumption or is a computation activity corresponding to a *process* or *knowledge exchange* (see Section 2.1). In particular, the invariant corresponds to a process if it captures the operational normalcy of a single component (technically it means that it refers only to knowledge of a single component). Such an invariant is called a *process invariant* (in diagrams marked by P, e.g., (3) in Fig. 2).

Similarly, an invariant corresponds to knowledge exchange (called *exchange invariant*) if it captures the fact that the knowledge of one component is in certain relationship (typically in "identity" relationship) to knowledge of another component. Invariant (12) in Fig. 4 is an example of an exchange invariant. Exchange invariants are marked by X.

Generally, it is possible to refine invariants where several components take a role (e.g., (5)) to process and exchange invariants which are eventually associated with "real" computation activities. This typically involves a number of refinement steps in which (a) the invariants are gradually split by roles and (b) exchange invariants are introduced that collect needed knowledge.

Specifically, to refine an invariant I_p, referencing the components $C_1,...,C_m$ into sub-invariants $I_{s1},...,I_{sn}$ we introduce the *belief of C_1 over the knowledge of $C_2,...,C_m$*. In this context, the belief $B_{C_1}^{C_2,...,C_m}(K)$ is knowledge of C_1 that represents C_1's snapshot of a part K of the knowledge of $C_2,...,C_m$. For instance, in Fig. 4, the belief V::availabilityList of Vehicle over the knowledge P::availability of Parking Stations is an example of such a knowledge snapshot (denoted as V::availabilityList=$B_{Vehicle}^{ParkingStation}$(P::availability)).

Thus, I_{s1} formulates the normalcy properties of $B_{C_1}^{C_2,...,C_m}$, whereas $I_{s2},...,I_{sn}$ refine I_p while substituting the references to the knowledge of $C_2,...,C_m$ by references to $B_{C_1}^{C_2,...,C_m}$. Note that $B_{C_1}^{C_2,...,C_m}$ is a new knowledge introduced into C_1. For example, (15) formulates the condition on creating the belief `V::availabilityList`$=B_{Vehicle}^{ParkingStation}$(`P::availability`), whereas (14) refines (6) while substituting the references to `P::availability` by references to `V::availability-List`.

Furthermore, $I_{s2},...,I_{sn}$ are potentially process/exchange invariants, since, in general, the number of components taking a role in $I_{s2},...,I_{sn}$ is, compared to I_p, decreased at least by one due to references to the belief $B_{C_1}^{C_2,...,C_m}$ (such as when comparing (6) and (14)).

4.5 From Invariants to Final Architecture

Once the refinement reaches the level of process and exchange invariants, the design continues to the implementation level by refining each process invariant into a component process and each exchange invariant into an ensemble. For example, in Listing 1 `Vehicle` is reified by `Vehicle42`, while (14) is refined into the `Vehicle42`'s `computePlanWhenFarFromPOI` process, and (15) is refined into the `UpdateAvailabilityWhenFarFromPOI` ensemble. Thus, determined by the invariant refinement, this step yields the final architecture of the system. The details are beyond the scope of this text; we refer the interested reader to [8].

5 IRM Abstraction Levels and Invariant Patterns

There is a significant abstraction gap between the high-level and low-level invariants. The former ones capture general operational normalcy while the latter ones reflect architectural elements and thus capture the ACEs-specific aspects. In this section we provide a detailed description of bridging the gap during the invariant refinement, i.e., during generation of low-level invariants from high-level ones. We have identified five patterns of invariants that reflect the way operational normalcy is captured at four adjacent abstraction levels that are covering the abstraction gap. With these patterns we can precisely set out the rules and guidelines for refinement of the invariants on the same/adjacent abstraction levels. The rules/guidelines allow for iterative refinement to continuously lower the level of abstraction until the architectural elements level is reached.

In particular, the patterns are as follows (from the most abstract to the least abstract):

1. *general invariants,*
2. *present-past invariants,*
3. *activity invariants,*
4. *process invariants,* and
5. *exchange invariants* (patterns 4. and 5. are at the same level of abstraction).

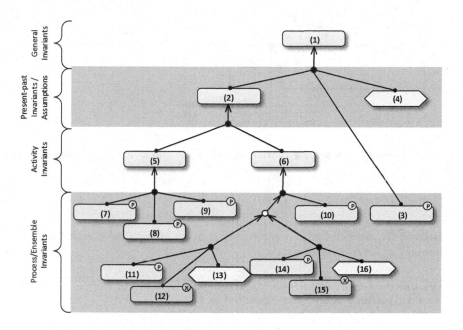

Fig. 5. Patterns of invariants in the case study

The patterns of invariants in the case study are illustrated in Fig. 5.

In the rest of the section we use a predicate formalization of the invariants in order to allow their precise definition and, in particular, to highlight the differences between the patterns. In principle, an invariant expresses the operational normalcy in terms of a condition to be maintained during knowledge evolution in time. Using this formalization, it is possible to refer to timed sequences of the knowledge values, and thus it allows for viewing the complete knowledge value evolution in time. An important aspect of ACEs-based systems is that they are inherently asynchronous. Thus, the formalization has to capture the evolution in terms of asynchrony and delays. As an example, the knowledge evolution shown in Fig. 6 can be assumed. In it, we are interested in a formalization of the form "*The value of V::pAvailable always equals the value of P::available that is not older than the period*" rather than in "*V::pAvailable equals P::available*" (which does not always hold).

5.1 Formalization

We formalize the invariants as follows.

Definition 1. *Time is represented by a non-negative real number, i.e.,* $\mathbb{T} \stackrel{def}{=} \mathbb{R}_0^+$.

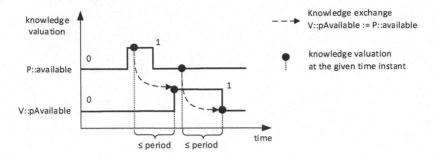

Fig. 6. Example of knowledge evolution in time when employing (periodic) knowledge exchange

Definition 2. *Knowledge is a set $K = k_1, ..., k_n$ of knowledge elements, where the domain of k_i is denoted as V_i.*

Definition 3. *Knowledge valuation of element k_i is a function $T \rightarrow V_i$ which for a time t yields a value of k_i (denoted as $k_i[t]$).*

Definition 4. *Invariant is a predicate (in a higher-order predicate logic with arithmetic) over knowledge valuations and time.*

Of course, the invariant definition above is not the only possible one. For example, real-time LTL [2] can be used too. Nevertheless, we use the proposed formalization as our primary goal is not model checking but rather a description of invariant refinement. For it, we believe the formalization is more suitable and allows for straightforward formulating and proving relevant theorems.

In the rest of this section, we detail the identified invariant patterns and provide formal definitions as well as macros to ease their usage.

5.2   General Invariants

General invariants are defined at the top-level of abstraction and they capture the operational normalcy by relating the past and current knowledge valuations to a future knowledge valuation.

An example of this pattern is the invariant (1): *"All Vehicles meet their route/parking calendar"*, which can be formalized as follows (for the sake of brevity, it assumes only the calendar with a single POI not changing in time):

$$\exists t \in \mathbb{T}, t \leq DEADLINE : v.pos[t] = DEST$$

Importantly, the invariant does not refer to current time; instead, it refers to a particular time instant in the future.

5.3   Present-Past Invariants

On the lower level of abstraction, there are *present-past* invariants that capture the operational normalcy employing the current and/or past knowledge valuations. This corresponds with the fact that software systems can work with current and/or past data and cannot depend on future data. This fact has been abstracted away at the level of general invariants. To limit the amount of needed past data, the *lag* of a present-past invariant is defined as the maximal distance in the past that is needed to formulate the operational normalcy of the invariant. As in real-time software control systems, it is assumed that the smaller the lag, the bigger precision and robustness and vice-versa. An idealized and unreachable case is the zero lag, which would mean that the beliefs of all components are always up-to-date and their actions are instant.

Importantly, when a general invariant is refined into present-past invariants (or more precisely into a conjunction of them), assumptions have to be added that guarantee that maintaining the operational normalcy based on the current/past knowledge valuation will eventually result in reaching the operational normalcy based on a future knowledge valuation. An example of such an assumption is the assumption (4) in Fig. 2.

Definition 5. *(Present-past invariants) For a predicate P capturing the relation between valuation of knowledge elements $I_1, \ldots, I_n$ and $O_1, \ldots, O_m$, and the lag L, the expression $P_{p-p}^L[I_1, \ldots, I_n][O_1, \ldots, O_m]$ denotes the following present-past invariant:*

$$\forall t \in \mathbb{T}, \exists t_1, \ldots, t_n : 0 \leq t - t_i \leq L, i \in 1..n :$$
$$P(I_1[t_1], \ldots, I_n[t_n], O_1[t], \ldots, O_m[t])$$

In this context, we call $I_1, \ldots, I_n$ "input" variables and $O_1, \ldots, O_m$ "output" variables of the invariant so as to denote the correspondence of these variables to the inputs/outputs of the computation that is responsible for maintaining the invariant.

Invariant (2): "*Up-to-date V::plan, w.r.t. knowledge from P, reflecting V::calendar is available*" is an example of a present-past invariant. For parking lots $P_1..P_n$ and lag L it can be formalized as follows:

"*At any time, for the current valuation of `V::plan` there is a valuation of knowledge of P_1, ..., P_n and `V::calendar` not older than the lag L such that they together meet the condition expressed by the `UpToDatePlan` predicate.*"
    In the predicate logic, it can be captured as follows:

$$\forall t_{cur} \in \mathbb{T}, \exists t_1, ..., t_n, t_{cal} \in \mathbb{T}, 0 \leq t_{cur} - t_i \leq L, i \in 1..n, cal :$$
$$UpToDatePlan(P_1[t_1], ..., P_n[t_n], V::calendar[t_{cal}], V::plan[t])$$

In this predicate, if the lag L greater than zero, it means that the `V::plan` is outdated regarding the current knowledge of the parking lots (the greater $L \Rightarrow$ more outdated parking-lot knowledge valuation). The zero lag would mean the plan is up-to-date at any moment.

Using the shortcut introduced in Definition 5, we can rewrite the expression as:

$$UpToDatePlan^L_{p-p}[P_1, ..., P_n, V::calendar][V::plan]$$

Such an shortcut can be also used during invariant refinement for introducing new present-past invariants. It would serve as a "macro" that transforms a time-oblivious predicate (e.g., `UpToDatePlan`) into a formalized present-past invariant of the above-described structure.

5.4   Activity Invariants

Frequently, properties of a (soft) real-time activity have to be assumed. A commonly used property is then that each output knowledge valuation is based on the same or newer input knowledge valuation than the previous one. Fig. 7 illustrates this.

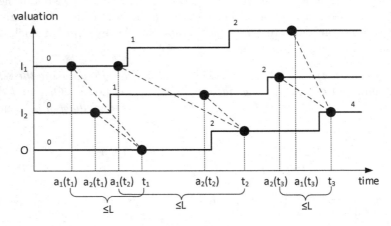

Fig. 7. Illustration of a valid knowledge valuation with respect to an activity where the output O represents the sum of inputs I_1 and I_2, while meeting lag L.

An *activity invariant* expresses the fact that the output knowledge valuation changes only as a result of performing the activity. Moreover, the activity never exceeds the corresponding time limit (the lag). More rigorously, at any time the output knowledge valuation corresponds to the outcome of the activity applied on input knowledge valuation not older than the lag. Plus, each output is based on the same or newer inputs than the previous output.

Definition 6. *(Activity invariant) For a predicate P reflecting the post-condition of an activity with inputs $I_1, \ldots, I_n$ and outputs $O_1, \ldots, O_m$, and for lag L, the expression $P^L_{act}[I_1, \ldots, I_n][O_1, \ldots, O_m]$ denotes the following activity invariant:*

$$\exists a_1, \ldots, a_n : \mathbb{T} \to \mathbb{T}, \forall t \in \mathbb{T}, 0 \leq t - a_i(t) \leq L, a_i \text{ non-decreasing}, i \in 1..n :$$
$$P(I_1[a_1(t)], \ldots, I_n[a_n(t)], O_1[t], \ldots, O_m[t])$$

where the non-decreasing function a_i gives for each time t the corresponding time t' such that the valuation of I_i at t' was "used to compute" the valuation of $O_1, \ldots, O_m$ at t, as shown in Fig. 7.

Invariant (6) can serve as an example of the activity invariant: *"Up-to-date V::plan, w.r.t. P::availability and V::planFeasibility, reflecting V::calendar is available"*. For parking lots $P_1..P_n$ and lag L it can be formalized as follows:

"There is an execution of the planning activity maintaining the condition UpToDatePlan *such that at any time the valuation of* V::plan *corresponds to the outcome of the activity applied on the valuation of the input knowledge* P::availability, V::planFeasibility, *and* V::calendar *not older than lag L. Moreover, each valuation of* V::plan *is based on newer valuation of the input knowledge than the previous one."*

Using the predicate logic, it can be expressed as follows:

$$\exists a_1, ..., a_n, a_{pF}, a_{cal} : \mathbb{T} \to \mathbb{T},$$
$$0 < x - a_i(x) \leq L, \forall i \in \{1..n, pF, cal\},$$
$$a_i(x) \leq a_i(y), \forall x, y : x \leq y, \forall i \in \{1..n, pF, cal\},$$

$$UpToDatePlan \begin{pmatrix} P_1{::}availability[a_n(t)], \\ \vdots \\ P_n{::}availability[a_n(t)], \\ V{::}planFeasibility[u_{pF}(t)], \\ V{::}calendar[a_{cal}(t)], \\ V{::}plan[t] \end{pmatrix}$$

The aspect that V::plan may change only as the result of an execution of a planning activity is captured by the usage of the non-decreasing function $a_i : \mathbb{T} \to \mathbb{T}$ rather than a particular $t_i \in \mathbb{T}$. The a_i function also captures the read consistency.

Similarly as in the previous invariant, the lag greater than zero means that the outdated valuation of P::availability and V::planFeasibility is considered. The zero lag reflects the case where the valuation of V::plan is at each time instant up-to-date with respect to the current valuation of P::availability of the parking lots and V::planFeasibility of the vehicle (i.e., the activity computes infinitely fast and infinitely often).

Using the shortcut introduced in Definition 6, we can write the formalization of invariant (6) as:

$$UpToDatePlan^L_{act} \begin{bmatrix} P_1{::}availability[a_n(t)], \\ \vdots \\ P_n{::}availability[a_n(t)], \\ V{::}planFeasibility[a_{pF}(t)], \\ V{::}calendar[a_{cal}(t)], \\ V{::}plan[t] \end{bmatrix} \begin{bmatrix} V{::}plan \end{bmatrix}$$

5.5   Process Invariants

Process invariants are in the leaves of invariant decomposition, i.e., at the lowest level of abstraction. Such an invariant captures a periodic real-time component process. Into it, an activity invariant capturing local computation (while assuming read consistency) is refined.

Contrary to the activity invariants, the process invariant adds a constraint that the activity is executed exactly once in every *period*. Therefore, the period can be seen as a refinement of the activity lag and the output knowledge evaluation is determined by the release time (time at which a task becomes ready for execution) and finish time in each period [9].

Specifically, such an invariant captures that if the current time is before the finish time of the process in the current period, then the outputs are the same as in the previous period (i.e., they correspond to the inputs used in the previous period). Otherwise, the outputs correspond to the inputs at the release time of the process in this period.

Definition 7. *(Process invariant) For a predicate P reflecting the post-condition of a periodic real-time process with inputs* $I_1, \ldots, I_n$, *outputs* $O_1, \ldots, O_m$, *and period L, the expression* $P^L_{proc}[I_1, \ldots, I_n][O_1, \ldots, O_m]$ *denotes the following process invariant:*

$$\forall x \in \mathbb{N}, \exists R, F : \mathbb{N} \to \mathbb{T} : E(x-1) \leq R(x) < F(x) < E(x),$$
$$\forall p \in \mathbb{N}, \forall t \in \langle E(p-1), E(p)\rangle :$$
$$t < F(p) \Rightarrow P(I_1[R(p-1)], \ldots, I_n[R(p-1)], O_1[t], \ldots, O_m[t])$$
$$t \geq F(p) \Rightarrow P(I_1[R(p)], \ldots, I_n[R(p)], O_1[t], \ldots, O_m[t])$$

where $E : \mathbb{N}_0 \to \mathbb{T}$ *and* $E(n) = n \cdot L$, *i.e., the end of the n-th period.* $R(n)$ *and* $F(n)$ *denote the release and finish time of the real-time process in the n-th period.*

In contrast to the activity invariant, there is the same R for every input I. It reflects the fact that at the release time, all the inputs are read by the process atomically.

The invariant (11) can be taken as an example of the process invariant: "*Up-to-date V::plan, w.r.t. V::availabilityList and V::planFeasibility, reflecting V::calendar is available*". For period L, it can be formalized as follows:

"*If the current time is before the finish time of the process in the current period, then the V::plan valuation is the same as in the previous period; i.e., it corresponds to the outcome of the process w.r.t. the inputs V::availabilityList, V::planFeasibility, and V::calendar at the release time of the process in the previous period. Otherwise, V::plan corresponds to the outcome of the process w.r.t. the inputs at the release time in this period.*"

In the predicate logic, it can be captured as follows:

$$\forall x \in \mathbb{N}, \exists R, F : \mathbb{N} \to \mathbb{T}, E(x-1) \le R(x) < F(x) < E(x),$$
$$\forall p \in \mathbb{N}, \forall t \in \langle E(p-1), E(p) \rangle :$$

$$t < F(p) \Rightarrow UpToDatePlan \begin{pmatrix} V::availabilityList[R(p-1)], \\ V::planFeasibility[R(p-1)], \\ V::calendar[R(p-1)], \\ V::plan[t] \end{pmatrix}$$

$$t \ge F(p) \Rightarrow UpToDatePlan \begin{pmatrix} V::availabilityList[R(p)], \\ V::planFeasibility[R(p)], \\ V::calendar[R(p)], \\ V::plan[t] \end{pmatrix}$$

where $E : \mathbb{N}_0 \to \mathbb{T}$ and $E(n) = n \cdot L$, i.e., the end of the n-th period. $R(n)$ and $F(n)$ denote the release and finish time of the real-time process in the n-th period, as per Definition 7.

In the process invariant case, the zero L means that the `V::plan` is at each time instant infinitely close to the up-to-date plan with respect to the current `V::availability`, `V::planFeasibility`, and `V::calendar` of the vehicle.

With the help of the shortcut from Definition 7, the formalization of (11) can be shortened as:

$$UpToDatePlan_{proc}^{L} \begin{bmatrix} V::availabilityList, \\ V::planFeasibility, \\ V::calendar \end{bmatrix} \begin{bmatrix} V::plan \end{bmatrix}$$

5.6 Exchange Invariants

The activity invariants that capture the establishment of a belief (that can be addressed by ensemble knowledge exchange) while assuming distributed read consistency, are refined into *exchange invariants*, which capture periodic knowledge exchange of an ensemble.

In contrast to process invariants, the input values in exchange invariants can be obtained at different times (but the times still have to belong to the same period), as the input values are potentially distributed. Additionally, knowledge propagation delays are also considered. These delays can arise for example from delays in network communication.

In summary, the exchange invariants depict a composite activity composed of knowledge transfer and periodic evaluation of the knowledge exchange and membership condition.

Importantly, each component processes the incoming knowledge exchange by itself. The required input knowledge is sent asynchronously by other components. If the knowledge transfer time is larger than the knowledge exchange period, the composite activities may partially overlap.

Definition 8. *(Exchange invariant) Let P be a predicate reflecting the post-condition of a periodic knowledge exchange with inputs $I_1, \ldots, I_n$, outputs $O_1, \ldots,$*

O_m, and period L. Provided that it takes at most T for the knowledge to become available at the component executing the knowledge exchange, the expression $P_{exc}^{L,T}[I_1, \ldots, I_n][O_1, \ldots, O_m]$ denotes the following exchange invariant:

$$\exists a_1, \ldots, a_n : \mathbb{T} \to \mathbb{T}, \forall t \in \mathbb{T}, 0 \le t - a_i(t) \le T, a_i \text{ non-decreasing}, i \in 1..n :$$
$$\exists R, F : \mathbb{N} \to \mathbb{T} : E(x-1) \le R(x) < F(x) < E(x) \; \forall x \in \mathbb{N},$$
$$\forall p \in \mathbb{N}, \forall t \in \langle E(p-1), E(p) \rangle :$$
$$t < F(p) \Rightarrow P(I_1[a_1(R(p-1))], \ldots, I_n[a_n(R(p-1))], O_1[t], \ldots, O_m[t])$$
$$t \ge F(p) \Rightarrow P(I_1[a_1(R(p))], \ldots, I_n[a_n(R(p))], O_1[t], \ldots, O_m[t])$$

where $E : \mathbb{N}_0 \to \mathbb{T}$ and $E(n) = n \cdot L$, i.e., the end of the n-th period. $R(n)$ and $F(n)$ denote the release and finish time of the real-time knowledge exchange in the n-th period. Finally, a_i gives for each time t the corresponding time t' such that the valuation of I_i that was available to the component executing the knowledge exchange at t was sent to the component at t'.

For every input I_i, the a_i can be a different value as the component executing the knowledge exchange can receive the inputs at different times. On the other hand, the knowledge exchange is assumed to be unidirectional. It means that that the exchange is written into the knowledge of a single component only, and therefore these writes can be atomic. Thus, for every output O_i there is the same t.

The invariant (12) of the running example can taken as a representative of the exchange invariant: "V::availabilityList – V's belief over P::availability of trip-relevant parking lots – is up-to-date". For parking lots $P_1..P_n$, period L, and upper bound for knowledge transfer T it can be formalized as follows:

"If the current time is before the finish time of the knowledge exchange for V in the current period, then the V::availabilityList valuation is the same as in the previous period. Otherwise, V::availabilityList equals the set of P::availability for all relevant P_i as available at V at the release time in this period. It takes at most T for the knowledge of P_i to become available at V. Further always the newest knowledge of P_i is taken into account."

The predicate logic can capture it as follows:

$$\exists a_1, ..., a_n : \mathbb{T} \to \mathbb{T}, 0 < x - a_i(x) \le T, \forall i \in \{1..n\},$$
$$\exists R, F : \mathbb{N} \to \mathbb{T}, E(x-1) \le R(x) < F(x) < E(x),$$
$$\forall p \in \mathbb{N}, \forall t \in \langle E(p-1), E(p) \rangle :$$

$$t < F_V(p) \Rightarrow EqualsRelevant \begin{pmatrix} P_1::availability[a_1(R(p-1))], \\ \vdots \\ P_n::availability[a_n(R(p-1))], \\ V::availabilityList[t] \end{pmatrix}$$

$$t \ge F_V(p) \Rightarrow EqualsRelevant \begin{pmatrix} P_1::availability[a_1(R(p))], \\ \vdots \\ P_n::availability[a_n(R(p))], \\ V::availabilityList[t] \end{pmatrix}$$

In this case, zero L means that, at each time instant, the `V::availability-List` is infinitely close to the set of the current `P::availability` of all the relevant parking lots.

With the help of the shortcut from Definition 8, the invariant (12) can be formalized as:

$$
EqualsRelevant_{exc}^{L,T}
\begin{bmatrix}
P_1::availability, \\
\vdots \\
P_n::availability,
\end{bmatrix}
\begin{bmatrix}
V::availabilityList
\end{bmatrix}
$$

5.7   Refinement Between Invariant Patterns

With the invariant patterns described, we can now introduce the guidelines for decomposition at the corresponding levels of abstraction. The goal of these guidelines is to guarantee the refinement between invariants following the patterns. The guidelines are presented here informally only; the formal definitions and proofs are in [7].

General → *Present-past*. As already mentioned in section 5.3, when a general invariant is refined into (a conjunction of) present-past invariants, assumption invariants have to be introduced (e.g., invariant (4) in Fig. 2). From the formal point of view, this refinement is the most demanding one as it is necessary to proof each case separately.

Present-past → *Present-past*. When a single present-past invariant is refined into a conjunction of other present-past invariants, the combined lag of the sub-invariants is not greater that the parent's lag. The combination is figured out by the knowledge dependencies among the sub-invariants. (By knowledge dependency, we mean here a situation, when an invariant uses knowledge produced by the activity associated with another invariant.)

Present-past → *Activity*. It holds that the activity invariant pattern is a strict refinement of the present-past invariant pattern; i.e., $P_{act}^{L}[I][O] \Rightarrow P_{p-p}^{L}[I][O]$ for each P, I, and O.

Activity → *Activity*. As in the case of present-past → present-past invariant refinement, an activity invariant can also refined into a conjunction of other activity invariants. For our predicate formalization, it is possible to determine this form of refinement solely based on the time-oblivious skeletons of the invariants and the structure of the decomposition (i.e., without interpreting the full invariants via a theorem prover).

Activity → *Process*. It holds that the process invariant pattern is a refinement of the activity invariant pattern with lag equal twice the period of the process invariant pattern; i.e., $P_{proc}^{L}[I][O] \Rightarrow P_{act}^{2L}[I][O]$ for each P, I, and O. This complies with the well-known fact in the area of real-time scheduling: in order to achieve a particular end-to-end response time with a real-time periodic process with relative deadline equal to period, the period needs to be at most half of the response time [9].

Activity → *Exchange*. Similarly, it holds that the exchange invariant pattern is a refinement of the activity invariant pattern with lag equal twice the period of the exchange invariant pattern plus the time for distributed transfer of the knowledge; i.e., $P_{exc}^{L,T}[I][O] \Rightarrow P_{act}^{2L+T}[I][O]$ for each P, I, and O.

Impact of IRM Design on the Case Study. By identifying invariants in the case study, classifying them into the available invariant patterns (Sections 5.2-5.6), and subsequently refining them using the above guidelines, we systematically constructed the IRM tree of the case study. This can be used in turn to derive the DEECo specification of the case study (Listing 1 in Section 2.1).

6   Conclusions

In this chapter, we have presented IRM – a requirements elicitation and architectural design method that guides the design of ACEs. With respect to the Ensemble Development Life Cycle (cf. Chapter III.1 [13]), IRM lies in the transition between the Requirements Engineering and the Modeling Phase of the design wheel. IRM takes similar approach as found in goal-oriented requirements engineering, but specifically focuses on "maintain" goals, as these are critical for continuously running systems that constantly interact and control their environment (such as cyber-physical systems).

The core idea of IRM is to describe the variability of a system by AND and OR invariant decompositions that capture the required functionality of the system under different runtime situations. IRM establishes systematic refinement between high-level requirements and low-level architectural concepts, i.e., components, component processes, and knowledge exchange functions as defined in the DEECo component model. This directly allows deriving an architecture of ACEs and brings about strong traceability.

References

1. Abeywickrama, D.B., Bicocchi, N., Zambonelli, F.: SOTA: Towards a General Model for Self-Adaptive Systems. In: Proc. of WETICE '12, pp. 48–53. IEEE Computer Society Press, Los Alamitos (2012)
2. Bauer, A., Leucker, M., Schallhart, C.: Monitoring of Real-Time Properties. In: Arun-Kumar, S., Garg, N. (eds.) FSTTCS 2006. LNCS, vol. 4337, pp. 260–272. Springer, Heidelberg (2006)
3. Bresciani, P., Perini, A., Giorgini, P., Giunchiglia, F., Mylopoulos, J.: Tropos: An Agent-Oriented Software Development Methodology. Autonomous Agents and Multi-Agent Systems 8(3), 203–236 (2004)

4. Bruni, R., Corradini, A., Gadducci, F., Hölzl, M., Lafuente, A.L., Vandin, A., Wirsing, M.: Reconciling White-Box and Black-Box Perspectives on Behavioral Self-adaptation. In: Wirsing, M., Hölzl, M., Koch, N., Mayer, P. (eds.) Software Engineering for Collective Autonomic Systems. LNCS, vol. 8998, pp. 163–184. Springer, Heidelberg (2015)

5. Bures, T., Gerostathopoulos, I., Hnetynka, P., Keznikl, J., Kit, M., Plasil, F.: DEECo – an Ensemble-Based Component System. In: Proc. of CBSE'13, pp. 81–90. ACM Press, New York (2013)

6. Bures, T., Gerostathopoulos, I., Hnetynka, P., Keznikl, J., Kit, M., Plasil, F., Plouzeau, N.: Adaptation in Cyber-Physical Systems: from System Goals to Architecture Configurations. Tech. rep., D3S-TR-2014-01, Dep. of Distributed and Dependable Systems, Charles University in Prague (Jan 2014), http://d3s.mff.cuni.cz/publications/download/D3S-TR-2014-01.pdf

7. Bures, T., Gerostathopoulos, I., Keznikl, J., Plasil, F., Tuma, P.: Formalization of Invariant Patterns for the Invariant Refinement Method. To appear in Springer LNCS volume dedicated to Wirsing-Festschrift (2015), preliminary version available at http://d3s.mff.cuni.cz/publications/download/D3S-TR-2013-04.pdf

8. Bures, T., Gerostathopoulos, I., Horky, V., Keznikl, J., Kofron, J., Loreti, M., Plasil, F.: Language Extensions for Implementation-Level Conformance Checking, ASCENS deliverable 1.5 (Nov. 2012), http://www.ascens-ist.eu/deliverables

9. Buttazo, G., Lipari, G., Abeni, L., Caccamo, M.: Soft Real-Time Systems: Predictability vs Efficiency. In: Computer Science, Springer, Heidelberg (2005)

10. Gerostathopoulos, I., Bures, T., Hnetynka, P.: Position Paper: Towards a Requirements Driven Design of Ensemble-Based Component Systems. In: Proc. of HotTopiCS workshop at ICPE '13, pp. 79–86. ACM Press, New York (2013)

11. Giorgini, P., Kolp, M., Mylopoulos, J., Pistore, M.: The Tropos Methodology: An Overview. In: Methodologies and Software Engineering for Agent Systems, pp. 89–106. Kluwer Academic Publishers, Dordrecht (2004)

12. Hoch, N., Bensler, H.-P., Abeywickrama, D., Bures, T., Montanari, U.: The E-mobility Case Study. In: Wirsing, M., Hölzl, M., Koch, N., Mayer, P. (eds.) Software Engineering for Collective Autonomic Systems. LNCS, vol. 8998, pp. 513–533. Springer, Heidelberg (2015)

13. Hölzl, M., Koch, N., Puviani, M., Wirsing, M., Zambonelli, F.: The Ensemble Development Life Cycle and Best Practices for Collective Autonomic Systems. In: Wirsing, M., Hölzl, M., Koch, N., Mayer, P. (eds.) Software Engineering for Collective Autonomic Systems. LNCS, vol. 8998, pp. 325–354. Springer, Heidelberg (2015)

14. Hölzl, M.M., Wirsing, M.: Towards a System Model for Ensembles. In: Agha, G., Danvy, O., Meseguer, J. (eds.) Formal Modeling: Actors, Open Systems, Biological Systems. LNCS, vol. 7000, pp. 241–261. Springer, Heidelberg (2011)

15. Keznikl, J., Bures, T., Plasil, F., Gerostathopoulos, I., Hnetynka, P., Hoch, N.: Design of Ensemble-Based Component Systems by Invariant Refinement. In: Proc. of CBSE '13, pp. 91–100. ACM Press, New York (2013)

16. Lamsweerde, A.V.: Goal-Oriented Requirements Engineering: A Guided Tour. In: Proc. of RE'01, pp. 249–262. IEEE Computer Society Press, Los Alamitos (2001)

17. van Lamsweerde, A.: From System Goals to Software Architecture. In: Bernardo, M., Inverardi, P. (eds.) SFM 2003. LNCS, vol. 2804, pp. 25–43. Springer, Heidelberg (2003)

18. Lamsweerde, A.V.: Requirements Engineering: From Craft to Discipline. In: Proc. of SIGSOFT '08/FSE-16, pp. 238–249. ACM Press, New York (2008)

19. Lamsweerde, A.V.: Requirements Engineering: From System Goals to UML Models to Software Specifications. John Wiley and Sons, Chichester (2009)
20. Noël, V., Zambonelli, F.: Methodological Guidelines for Engineering Self-organization and Emergence. In: Wirsing, M., Hölzl, M., Koch, N., Mayer, P. (eds.) Software Engineering for Collective Autonomic Systems. LNCS, vol. 8998, pp. 355–378. Springer, Heidelberg (2015)
21. Rao, A., Georgeff, M.P.: BDI Agents: From Theory to Practice. In: Proc. of ICMAS '95, pp. 312–319 (1995)
22. Vassev, E., Hinchey, M.: Autonomy Requirements Engineering. IEEE Computer 46(8), 82–84 (2013)
23. Vassev, E., Hinchey, M.: Engineering Requirements for Autonomy Features. In: Wirsing, M., Hölzl, M., Koch, N., Mayer, P. (eds.) Software Engineering for Collective Autonomic Systems. LNCS, vol. 8998, pp. 379–403. Springer, Heidelberg (2015)
24. Yu, E.: Towards Modelling and Reasoning Support for Early-Phase Requirements Engineering, pp. 226–235. IEEE Computer Society Press, Los Alamitos (1997)

CHAPTER III.5

Tools for Ensemble Design and Runtime*

Dhaminda B. Abeywickrama[2,6], Jacques Combaz[10], Vojtěch Horký[1],
Jaroslav Keznikl[1], Jan Kofroň[1], Alberto Lluch Lafuente[3], Michele Loreti[5],
Andrea Margheri[5], Philip Mayer[4], Valentina Monreale[7], Ugo Montanari[7],
Carlo Pinciroli[8], Petr Tůma[1], Andrea Vandin[3], and Emil Vassev[9]

[1] MFF, Charles University, Czech Republic
[2] FOKUS, Fraunhofer-Gesellschaft, Germany
[3] SySMA, Institute for Advanced Studies Lucca, Italy
[4] PST, Ludwig-Maximilians-Universität München, Germany
[5] CMG, Università di Firenze, Italy
[6] APCG, Università di Modena e Reggio Emilia, Italy
[7] DI, Università di Pisa, Italy
[8] IRIDIA, Université Libre de Bruxelles, Belgium
[9] LERO, University of Limerick, Ireland
[10] DCS, VERIMAG Laboratory, France

Abstract. The ASCENS project deals with designing systems as ensembles of adaptive components. Among the outputs of the ASCENS project are multiple tools that address particular issues in designing the ensembles, ranging from support for early stage formal modeling to runtime environment for executing and monitoring ensemble implementations. The goal of this chapter is to provide a compact description of the individual tools, which is supplemented by additional downloadable material on the project website.

Keywords: tools, software development, adaptive systems, autonomic systems

1 Introduction

The ASCENS project tackles the challenge of building systems that are open ended, highly parallel and massively distributed. Towards that goal, the ASCENS project considers designing systems as ensembles of adaptive components. Properly designed, such ensembles should operate reliably and predictably in open and changing environments. Among the outputs of the ASCENS project are multiple tools that address particular issues in designing the ensembles.

The ASCENS tool landscape reflects the ASCENS approach to the software development lifecycle, illustrated on Figure 1 and described in detail in Chapter III.1 [30].

* This research was supported by the European project IP 257414 (ASCENS).

M. Wirsing et al. (eds.): Collective Autonomic Systems, LNCS 8998, pp. 429–448, 2015.
© Springer International Publishing Switzerland 2015

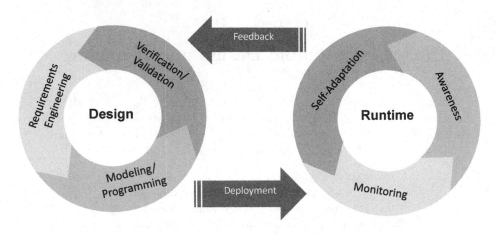

Fig. 1. ASCENS Ensemble Software Development Life Cycle

On the design cycle side, ASCENS provides several early stage formal modeling tools – the jSAM stochastic model checker (Section 2.1) for the modeling approaches that rely on process algebras and the Maude Daemon Wrapper (Section 2.2) for the modeling approaches that rely on rewriting logic – three tools that rely on Maude, MAIA (Section 2.5), MESSI (Section 2.3) and MISSCEL (Section 2.4), have also been developed. The SimSOTA tool (Section 2.6) can evaluate the behavior of complex feedback driven adaptation mechanisms using simulation. The FACPL framework (Section 2.7) can be used to capture policies that regulate interaction and adaptation of SCEL components. The KnowLang Toolset (Section 2.8) serves to describe knowledge models which are then compiled into a binary knowledge base, to be used for subsequent knowledge reasoning tasks.

Tools for transition from modeling to programming include the BIP compiler (Section 2.9) for the approaches that rely on correctness by construction, and two frameworks that reify the formal modeling concepts for manual implementation, namely jRESP (Section 3.2) and jDEECo (Section 3.3).

Because the manual implementation approaches do not guarantee preserving the correspondence between the model and the code, we also examine methods and tools to verify whether code complies to models. For C code, we have developed the GMC model checker (Section 2.10), for Java code, we have integrated the JPF model checker in jDEECo (Section 3.3).

On the runtime cycle side, our tool support focuses on simulation and monitoring. Our simulation environment for the robotic swarms is ARGoS (Section 3.1), a simulation environment that provides built in observation and introspection capabilities. For the cloud case study, we have similarly developed the Science Cloud Platform (Section 3.5). Two generic runtime environments for ensemble prototypes are jRESP (Section 3.2) and jDEECo (Section 3.3).

Visualisation support for ensemble structure and component state is provided by AVis (Section 3.4). Additional ensemble introspection capabilities rely on the

DiSL instrumentation framework [35], which has enough flexibility to observe most Java applications. On top of DiSL, the SPL evaluation tool (Section 3.6) is used to reason about performance.

The next sections contain a brief description of each of the tools, arranged in two large groups following the ASCENS development lifecycle. In Section 2, we place tools that deal mostly with the design cycle side, such as the modeling activities. Section 3 contains tools that provide runtime frameworks for executing either ensembles or simulations. Of necessity, the classification categories are not entirely distinct – some tools would fall into both groups. Such tools are listed only once, but the tool description reflects the complete purpose of the tool.

For access to the tools, the reader is encouraged to consult the ASCENS project website at http://www.ascens-ist.eu. For most tools, links to sources, installation and documentation is provided (depending on licensing).

2   Design Cycle Tools

The design phase of the ASCENS development lifecycle focuses on requirements engineering, modeling and programming, and verification and validation. The prototype tools developed for the design phase focus on connection to the mathematical foundations of the proposed approaches from Chapters I.1 [41], I.2 [14] and I.3 [20], together with knowledge representation as described in Chapter II.3 [53].

2.1   jSAM: Java Stochastic Model-Checker

jSAM is an Eclipse plugin integrating a set of tools for stochastic analysis of concurrent and distributed systems specified using process algebras. More specifically, jSAM provides tools that can be used for interactively executing specifications and for simulating their stochastic behaviors. Moreover, jSAM integrates a statistical model-checking algorithm [17,26,47] that permits verifying if a given system satisfies a CSL-like [7,8] formula.

jSAM does not rely on a single specification language, but provides a set of basic classes that can be extended in order to integrate any process algebra. One of the process algebras that are currently integrated in jSAM is StoKlaim [22]. This is the stochastic extension of Klaim, an experimental language aimed at modeling and programming mobile code applications. Properties of StoKlaim systems can be specified by means of the mobile stochastic logic MoSL [23]. This is a stochastic logic inspired by CSL that, together with qualitative properties, permits specifying time-bounded probabilistic reachability properties, such as the likelihood to reach a goal state within t time units while visiting only legal states is at least p. MoSL is also equipped with operators that permit describing properties resulting from resource production and consumption. In particular, state properties incorporate features for resource management and context verification. Context verification allows the verification of assumptions on resources

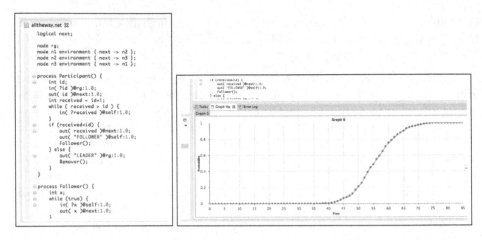

Fig. 2. A jSAM specification (left) and the result of model-checking (right)

and processes in a system at the logical level, i.e. without having to change the model to investigate the effect of each assumption on the system behavior.

As its input, jSAM accepts a text file containing a system specification. For instance, Figure 2 (left) contains a portion of a StoKlaim system. The results of stochastic analyses (both simulation and model-checking) are plotted in graphs, see Figure 2 (right).

On-The-Fly Model Checking. Model checking approaches can be divided into two broad categories: global approaches that determine the set of all states in a model $\mathcal{M}$ that satisfy a temporal logic formula Φ, and local approaches in which, given a state s in $\mathcal{M}$, the procedure determines whether s satisfies Φ. When s is a term of a process language, the model-checking procedure can be executed on-the-fly, driven by the syntactical structure of s. For certain classes of systems, e.g. those composed of many parallel components, the local approach is preferable because, depending on the specific property, it may be sufficient to generate and inspect only a relatively small part of the state space. In [34] an efficient, on-the-fly, PCTL model checking procedure that is parametric with respect to the semantic interpretation of the language has been proposed. The proposed model checking algorithm has been integrated in jSAM together with a module for supporting specification and analysis of systems via the PRISM language.

FlyFast Model Checker. Typical self-organising collective systems consist of a large number of interacting objects that coordinate their activities in a decentralised and often implicit way. Design of such systems is challenging and requires suitable, scalable analysis tools to check properties of proposed system designs before they are put into operation. The exploitation of mean field approximation in model-checking techniques seems a promising approach to overcome scalability issues raised by the size of such collective systems. In [32,33] we have presented a scalable, on-the-fly model-checking procedure to verify bounded PCTL properties of selected individuals in the context of very large systems of independent interacting objects. The proposed procedure combines on-the-fly model checking techniques with deterministic mean-field approximation in discrete time. A prototype implementation of the model-checker, named FlyFast, has been integrated into jSAM and used to verify properties of a selection of simple and more elaborate case studies.

SCEL Development. To support design, analysis and deployment of autonomous and adaptive systems developed in SCEL, jSAM integrates a plug-in that enables the use of selected formal tools by relying on the jRESP simulation environment. The plug-in takes a SCEL specification as input and automatically generates the Java classes used to simulate and execute the considered system.

2.2   Maude Daemon Wrapper

Maude [19] is a high-performance reflective language and system supporting both equational and rewriting logic specification and programming for a wide range of applications. It is a flexible and general framework for giving executable semantics to a wide range of languages and models of concurrency, and has been also used to develop several tools comprising theorem provers and model checkers. Maude is used within the ASCENS project as a convenient formalism for modeling and analysis of self-adaptive systems, as outlined for example in [10,13,9]. Maude can be used to prototype semantic models and then either execute or check them. Maude can also be used as a semantic framework for SCEL dialects, for instance to develop interpreters or analysis tools for SCEL specifications. Maude can also be used to model the case studies. Sections 2.3 and 2.4 present two tools that pursue these research lines.

The Maude Daemon Wrapper is a plugin integrating the Maude framework in the SDE environment. Our tool is a minimal wrapper for the Maude Daemon plugin, an existing Eclipse plugin which embeds the Maude framework into the Eclipse environment by encapsulating a Maude process into a set of Java classes. The Maude Daemon plugin provides an API to use and control a Maude process from a Java program, allowing to programmatically configure the Maude process, to execute it, send commands to it, and get the results from it.

2.3   MESSI: Maude Ensemble Strategies Simulator and Inquirer

Maude has been used to model and analyze self-assembly robotic strategies proposed by IRIDIA [42], outlined in [12,10,13,11]. The resulting implementation is a framework named MESSI (Maude Ensemble Strategy Simulator and Inquirer) [10,13,39] that helps model, debug and analyze scenarios where s-bots self-assemble to solve tasks (e.g. crossing holes or hills). Debugging is done via animated simulations, while analysis can be done by exploiting the Maude toolset, and in particular the distributed statistical analyzer and statistical model checker PVeStA [5,51], or via recently proposed MultiVeStA [50], which extends PVeStA.

The inputs of MESSI are the initial configuration and the self-assembly strategy, provided as Maude modules. The former provides information about the environment (an arena), specifying the presence of obstacles and targets (e.g. particular sources of light), and about the numbers and positions of the robots. The latter specifies the behaviour of the robots in the form of a finite state machine, which will be independently executed by each robot. Figures 3 and 4 provide a pictorial view of the two inputs. Figure 3 depicts an initial configuration with 9 robots distributed in an arena. The robots have to reach the target (the orange circle) situated behind a hole too large to be crossed by any single robot. Figure 4 depicts the *basic self-assembly response strategy* (BSRS) proposed in [42]. The strategy specifies the possible states (each circle is a bird-eye view of a robot) of the robots (i.e. the different mode of operation that the robots have) and the status of the robots LED signals (used to communicate with other robots) in each state. The transitions among the states provide the conditions that trigger a change of state of a robot, i.e., an adaptation.

MESSI provides a library of predefined basic behaviours (e.g. *move towards light*, or *search a given color emission and grab its source*), thus a self-assembly strategy is specified by just providing the list of states, the correspondence between the states and the basic behaviours, the status of the LED signals in each state, and a conditional rewrite rule for each transition of the finite state machine, with the condition as the label of the transition.

Given an initial configuration and a self-assembly strategy, MESSI allows to generate probabilistic simulations. As discussed, such simulations can be used to debug the strategy, or to measure its performance via statistical quantitative analysis.

2.4   MISSCEL: A Maude Interpreter and Simulator for SCEL

The SCEL language comes with solid semantics foundations laying the basis for formal reasoning. MISSCEL is a rewriting-logic-based implementation of the SCEL operational semantics. MISSCEL is written in Maude, which allows to

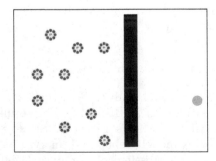

Fig. 3. A pictorial representation of an initial configuration for MESSI

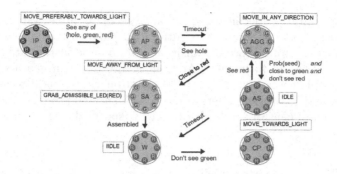

Fig. 4. A pictorial representation of a self-assembly strategy for MESSI

execute rewrite theories – what we obtain is an executable operational semantics for SCEL, that is, an interpreter. Given a SCEL specification, thanks to
MISSCEL it is possible to use the rich Maude toolset [19] to perform (i) automatic state-space generation, (ii) qualitative analysis via Maude invariant and
LTL model checkers, (iii) debugging via probabilistic simulations and animations generation, (iv) statistical quantitative analysis via the recently proposed
MultiVeStA [50] statistical analyser that extends PVeStA [5,51].

With MISSCEL, SCEL specifications can be intertwined with raw Maude
code, exploiting its great expressiveness. This allows to obtain cleaner specifications in which SCEL is used to model behaviours, aggregations, and knowledge
manipulation, leaving scenario-specific details like environment sensing abstractions or robot movements to Maude.

Among the features of MISSCEL, the state space of a SCEL specification can
be generated by exploiting the Maude *search* command (these can also be just
the states satisfying boolean conditions definable as Maude operations on SCEL
configurations). After the generation of the state space, it is possible to obtain
the path that generated one of the returned states, or the whole search graph
(similar to a labelled transition system). Moreover, it is possible to model-check
SCEL specifications, resorting to the LTL model checker. Finally, by resorting
to a set of schedulers that we defined to transform the non-determinism of SCEL
in probabilistic choices, it is possible to generate probabilistic simulations of a
SCEL specification. We have also defined an exporter from SCEL configurations
to DOT terms [6], using which we can obtain images from SCEL configurations
and animate the simulations.

2.5   MAIA

Inspired by white-box approaches to adaptation [12], the ASCENS project has
presented a model of adaptable transition systems [11], based on earlier foundational models of component based systems [4,3]. The key feature of adaptable
transition systems are control propositions, a subset of the atomic propositions
labelling the states of our transition systems, imposing a clear separation between ordinary, functional behaviours and adaptive ones. Control propositions

can be exploited in the specification and analysis of adaptive systems, focusing on various notions like adaptability, control loops, and control synthesis.

The cited model of adaptive transition systems was instantiated on Interface Automata (IA) [4,3], yielding Adaptable Interface Automata (AIA) [11]. MAIA is an implementation of AIA in Maude that can be used to specify and draw an AIA and to perform operations on AIA such as product, composition, decomposition and control synthesis (an AIA is specified as a Maude term).

2.6   SimSOTA

The SimSOTA tool supports modeling, simulating and validating of self-adaptive systems with multiple interacting feedback loops [1,2]. The tool adopts the model-driven development process to model and simulate complex self-adaptive architectural patterns, and to automate the generation of Java implementation code for the patterns. Our work integrates both decentralized and centralized feedback loop techniques to exploit their benefits.

The SimSOTA tool provides a set of pattern templates for the key SOTA patterns, depicted on Figure 5. This facilitates general-purpose and application-independent instantiation of models for complex systems based on feedback loops. The SimSOTA tool applies model transformations to automate the application of UML architectural design patterns and generate infrastructure code for the patterns in Java. The generated Java files of the SOTA patterns can be further adjusted by the engineer to derive a complete implementation for the patterns. To assist this process, we provide a set of context-independent Java templates, which can be instantiated to a particular domain.

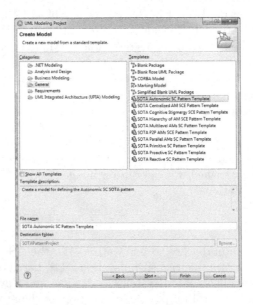

Fig. 5. SOTA pattern templates available to facilitate modeling

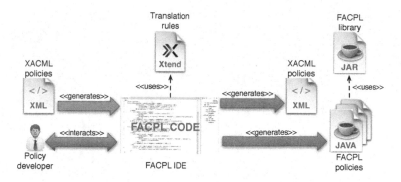

Fig. 6. FACPL Toolchain

2.7 FACPL: Policy IDE and Evaluation Library

FACPL [37] is a policy language for writing policies and requests. It has a mathematically defined semantics and can be used to regulate interaction and adaptation of SCEL components. FACPL provides user-friendly, uniform, and comprehensive linguistic abstractions for policing various aspects of system behaviour, as e.g. access control, resource usage, and adaptation. The result of a request evaluation is an authorisation decision (e.g. permit or deny), which may also include some obligations, i.e. additional actions to be executed for enforcing the decision.

The development and the enforcement of FACPL policies is supported by an Integrated Development Environment (IDE), in the form of an Eclipse plugin, and a Java implementation library. Figure 6 shows the toolchain supporting the use of the language. The policy designer can use the IDE for writing the desired policies in FACPL syntax, by taking advantage of the supporting features provided, e.g. code completion and syntax checks. Then, the tool automatically produces a set of Java classes implementing the FACPL code by using the specification classes defined in the FACPL library. The library, according to the rules defining the language semantics, implements the request evaluation process, given as input a set of Java-translated policies and the request to evaluate.

The policy and request specification is made through a graphical interface, shown on Figure 7. Alternatively, FACPL code can be also automatically created starting from policies and requests written in XACML. The IDE can also generate XML code compliant with the XACML 3.0 syntax corresponding to a given FACPL code.

2.8 KnowLang Toolset

The KnowLang Toolset is a comprehensive environment that delivers tools for creating and reasoning with the KnowLang notation – a suite of editors, parsers, compilers and checkers. The KnowLang knowledge representation (KR) can be written using either text editing tools or visual modeling tools, and then checked for syntactic integrity and model consistency.

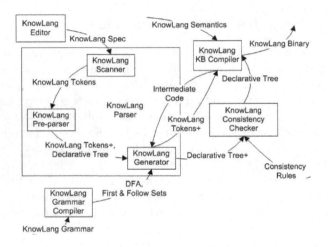

Fig. 7. FACPL Eclipse IDE

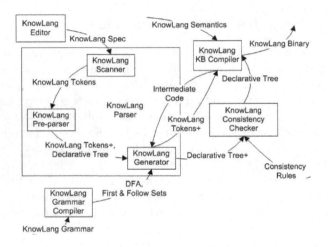

Fig. 8. KnowLang Specification Processor

The KnowLang Toolset organizes its tools in five distinct components (or modules), outlined in Figure 8. These are the KnowLang Editor (which combines both the Text Editor and the Visual Editor), the Grammar Compiler, the KnowLang Parser, the Consistency Checker and the Knowledge Base (KB) Compiler. These components are linked together to form a special *Know Lang Specification Processor* that checks and compiles the KR models specified in KnowLang into a KnowLang Binary. As the output of the KnowLang Toolset, the KnowLang Binary is a compiled form of the specified KB which the KnowLang Reasoner (a distinct KnowLang component to be integrated within the system that uses KR) operates upon.

Figure 8 presents an abstract view where the KnowLang Toolset operation is broken down into the *data source group* (KnowLang Editor + KnowLang Grammar Compiler), which prepares the input data (grammar and specification), the *analysis group* (KnowLang Parser + Consistency Checker), which performs the lexical analysis, syntax analysis and semantic analysis, and the *synthesis group* (KnowLang KB Compiler), which is responsible for generating output.

2.9 BIP Compiler

The BIP (behaviour, interaction, priority) component framework supports the construction of composite, hierarchically structured components from atomic components characterised by their behaviour and interfaces. It lets developers compose components by layered application of interactions and priorities. Architecture is a first-class concept in BIP, with well-defined semantics that system designers can analyse and transform.

BIP is model-based, describing an entire system with a single semantic model. This maintains the overall coherency of the design flow by guaranteeing that a description at step $n+1$ meets the essential properties of a description at step n. BIP is component-based, providing a family of operators for building composite components from simpler components. This overcomes the poor expressiveness of theoretical frameworks based on a single operator, such as the product of automata or a function call. BIP provides correctness by construction, avoiding monolithic a posteriori verification as much as possible.

The BIP framework is supported by a toolchain including model-to-model transformations and code generators, outlined on Figure 9. The BIP compiler is organized in Java packages in a modular way, allowing a dynamic invocation of model-to-model transformers and backends.

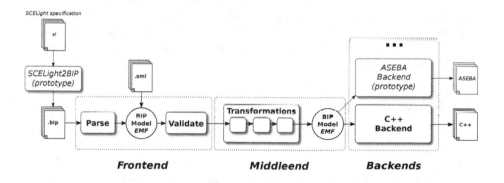

Fig. 9. The BIP Compiler tool-chain

2.10 Gimple Model Checker

Gimple Model Checker (GMC) is an explicit-state code model checker for C and C++ programs, useful especially for revealing errors that manifest themselves in rare thread interleavings that are hard to find via testing. In ASCENS, GMC can check certain ensemble related properties, such as particular sequences of accesses to the ensemble knowledge (using custom assertion statements).

On the technical side, GMC detects low-level programming errors such as invalid memory usage (buffer overflows, memory leaks, use-after-free defects, uninitialized memory reads), null-pointer dereferences, and assertion violations. GMC understands not only the pthread library [46], but also offers means to add support for other thread libraries based on the same principles.

Similar to other explicit model checkers, GMC requires that the actions (steps) of the verified program are revertible. When this is not the case (for example when accessing hardware or external services), the user can provide models that describe how a given action modifies the program state and how to revert the action. GMC already contains models for the basic functions from the standard C library.

The input of GMC is the source code of a complete program. The source code is processed via an extended GCC compiler [25], which dumps a GIMPLE file – the intermediate representation of the program used in GCC. The serialized GIMPLE representation is passed to the model checker, which interprets it and exhaustively searches for errors. If an error is found, GMC dumps a brief error description and an error trace which leads to the error.

3   Runtime Cycle Tools

The runtime phase of the ASCENS development lifecycle focuses on monitoring, awareness and adaptation. The prototype tools developed for the runtime phase focus on providing ensemble implementation environments whose features closely correspond to the theoretical ensemble abstractions. In particular, the tools are used to execute or simulate case studies from Chapters IV.1 [52], IV.2 [44], IV.3 [38] and IV.4 [28].

3.1   ARGoS

ARGoS [45] is a physics-based multi-robot simulator. ARGoS aims to simulate complex experiments involving large swarms of robots of different types in the shortest time possible. It is designed around two main requirements: efficiency, to achieve high perfomance with large swarms, and flexibility, to allow the user to customize the simulator for specific experiments.

To marry efficiency and flexibility, ARGoS is based on a number of novel design choices. First, in ARGoS, it is possible to partition the simulated space into multiple sub-spaces, managed by different physics engines running in parallel. Second, ARGoS architecture is multi-threaded, thus designed to optimize the usage of modern multi-core CPUs. Finally, the architecture of ARGoS is highly modular. Based on advanced concepts from C++ templates, it allows users to extend any aspect of ARGoS without touching the core, add custom features (enhancing flexibility) and allocate computational resources where needed (thus decreasing run-time and enhancing efficiency).

To use ARGoS, the user provides an XML configuration file and user code compiled into a library. The XML configuration file contains complete information required to set up the simulation arena, the individual robots, the physics engines, the controllers, and so on. The user code includes the robot controllers and, optionally, hook functions to be executed in various parts of ARGoS to interact with the running experiment. ARGoS can also interface with external controllers written in the Lua scripting language, experimental extensions include integration with the MultiVeStA distributed statistical analyzer [50].

Screenshots, as well as an example of use are reported in Chapter IV.2 [44]. ARGoS is open-source software released under the MIT license. It can be downloaded at http://iridia.ulb.ac.be/argos.

3.2 jRESP: Runtime Environment for SCEL Programs

jRESP is a runtime environment that provides Java programmers with a framework for developing autonomic and adaptive systems based on the SCEL concepts. SCEL [21,40] identifies the linguistic constructs for modelling the control of computation, the interaction among possibly heterogeneous components, and the architecture of systems and ensembles. jRESP provides an API that permits using the SCEL paradigm in Java programs.

In SCEL, some specification aspects, such as the knowledge representation, are not fixed but can be customized depending on the application domain or the taste of the language user. Other mechanisms, for instance the underlying communication infrastructure, are not considered at all and remain abstracted in the operational semantics. For this reason, the entire jRESP framework is parametrised with respect to specific implementations of these particular features. To simplify the integration of new features, recurrent patterns are largely used in jRESP.

The jRESP communication infrastructure has been designed to avoid any centralised control. A SCEL program typically consists of a set of (possibly heterogeneous) components, equipped with a knowledge repository. The components execute and cooperate in a highly dynamic environment, where the underlying communication infrastructure is not fixed, but can change dynamically during the computation. To simplify the integration with other tools and frameworks, jRESP communication infrastructure relies on open data interchange technologies, including JSON. These technologies simplify interactions between heterogeneous network components and provide the basis on which different runtimes for SCEL programs can cooperate.

Policies can be used in jRESP to authorise local actions and to regulate the interactions among components. Policies can authorise or prevent the execution of an action, and possibly adapt the agent behaviour by returning additional actions to be executed. jRESP can integrate different policy types, including stateful policies based on policy automata and FACPL.

To support analysis of adaptive systems specified in SCEL, jRESP also provides a set of classes that permit simulating jRESP programs. These classes allow the execution of virtual components over a simulation environment that is able to control component interactions and to collect relevant simulation data.

Based on the simulation environment, jRESP also supports statistical model-checking. Following this approach, a randomized algorithm is used to verify whether the implementation of a system satisfies a specific property with a certain degree of confidence. The statistical model-checker is parameterized with respect to a given tolerance ε and error probability p. The used algorithm guarantees that the difference between the value computed by the algorithm and the exact one is greater than ε with a probability that is less than p. The model-checker included in jRESP can be used to verify reachability properties. These permit evaluating the probability of reaching, within a given deadline, a configuration where a given predicate on collected data is satisfied.

To simplify the development process and to simplify the use of formal tools, jRESP extends the concepts provided in SCEL by more conventional programming constructs (e.g. control flow constructs, such as while or if-then-else, or structured data types). The constructs are supported by a high-level extension of SCEL, the jRESP code is generated automatically by an XText transformation.

3.3   jDEECo: Java Runtime Environment for DEECo Applications

jDEECo is a Java-based implementation of the DEECo component model [16] runtime framework. It allows for convenient management and execution of jDEECo components and ensemble knowledge exchange.

The main tasks of the jDEECo runtime framework are providing access to the knowledge repository, storing the knowledge of all the running components, scheduling execution of component processes (either periodically or when a triggering condition is met), and evaluating membership of the running ensembles and, in the positive case, carrying out the associated knowledge exchange (also either periodically or when triggered). The jDEECo runtime framework allows both local and distributed execution (currently, the distribution is achieved on the level of knowledge repository). The local version of jDEECo also supports verification of application properties using Java PathFinder.

The jDEECo runtime framework can be initialized and executed either manually, via its Java API, or inside the OSGi infrastructure [27]. In the latter case, the modules of the jDEECo runtime framework are managed as regular OSGi services (building upon the OSGi Declarative Services).

The input of the jDEECo runtime framework is a set of definitions of the components and ensembles to be executed. In general, such definitions are represented as specifically annotated Java classes [16]. Thus, technically, the input of the jDEECo runtime framework is either a set of Java class files, a JAR file containing the class files, or a set of class objects (in case the jDEECo runtime is accessed directly via its Java API). Thanks to the OSGi integration, component and ensemble definitions may be also packaged into OSGi bundles, each containing any number of the definitions. This way, component and ensemble data can be automatically loaded whenever the bundle is deployed in an OSGi context.

For realistic simulation of ensemble communication, jDEECo can be connected with the OMNeT++ network simulation framework and the MATSim transport simulator.

3.4 AVis

Awareness Visualizer (AVis) is an Eclipse plugin for tracing the awareness and adaptation capabilities of an application executing in the jRESP runtime environment. The AVis plugin has been developed as a rich client application with Graphical Editing Framework (GEF) capabilities. Figure 10 shows how the AVis plugin connects to the jRESP runtime to facilitate monitoring and visualization of changes to the awareness data of an autonomic system at runtime.

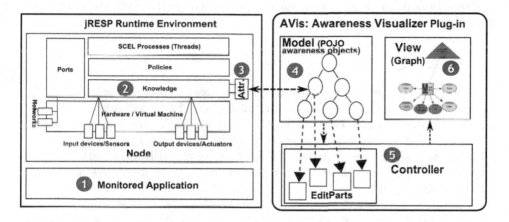

Fig. 10. AVis plug-in system architecture and jRESP

The monitored awareness attributes are extracted at runtime from the knowledge information encapsulated in jRESP nodes. The visualization relies on a standard visual graph representation and can highlight features such as node types or adaptation states, which help investigate the ensemble adaptation behavior.

3.5 Science Cloud Platform

The Science Cloud Platform (SCP) is the software system developed as part of the autonomic cloud case study of ASCENS, described in Chapter IV.3 [38]. SCP is a PaaS cloud computing infrastructure prototype which enables users to run applications when node participation is voluntary, data is stored redundantly, and applications are moved according to current load and availability of node resources. When available, SCP can also take advantage of an IaaS platform such as the Zimory Cloud [54]. In this case, new virtual machines running the SCP can be started on demand, and shut down to conserve energy when no longer needed.

The role of SCP is to serve as the main technical demonstrator for the cloud case study of ASCENS, integrating many of the newly researched methods and techniques into one software system. Outside the project, SCP can act as a prototype platform for experiments.

The network layer of SCP is based on the Pastry peer-to-peer substrate [48], and the accompanying data exchange protocols, specifically the PAST hash-table [49] and the Scribe publish/subscribe middleware [18]. On top of these layers, a variant of the ContractNET [24] protocol is used for application failover. An alternative implementation for communication on the application level integrates a gossip (endemic) strategy, which uses dedicated roles at each node as specified in the Helena approach [31]. This solution increases scalability, because it does not depend on global broadcasts, and serves to structure the implementation along role-based lines.

3.6   SPL

SPL is a Java framework for implementing application adaptation based on observed or predicted application performance [15]. The framework relies on the Stochastic Performance Logic, a many-sorted first-order logic with inequality relations among performance observations. The logic allows to express assumptions about program performance ; the purpose of the SPL framework is to give software developers an elegant way to use the logic to express rules controlling program adaptation.

Internally, the SPL framework consists of three parts that work together, but each can be (partially) used independently. The first part is a Java agent that instruments the application at runtime and collects performance data. The agent uses the Java instrumentation API [43], the byte code transformation is done using DiSL [36]. The second part of the framework offers an API to access the collected data and evaluate SPL formulas. The third part of the framework implements the interface between the application and the SPL framework – this API is used for the actual adaptation.

The purpose of the SPL framework is to support the adaptation of an application, however, the adaptation itself happens through means provided by the application. The framework itself does not add the actual ability to adapt, instead it focuses on providing performance monitoring and evaluation features.

4   Summary

The ASCENS tools provide a collection of features that cover multiple phases of the software development lifecycle from Chapter III.1 [30]. The tools also reflect the explorative character of the ASCENS project – as the mathematical foundations of ensembles developed, so did the tools change. Thus, the tools should not be viewed as definite products, but as research prototypes that encourage further experiments.

This chapter focuses on those tools that have reached a reasonable maturity level. The reader is invited to visit the ASCENS project website, which contains not only the tools described in this chapter, but also links to additional software such as the framework for adaptation through reasoning that was outlined in Chapter II.4 [29], or the role based adaptation framework from Chapter IV.3 [38].

References

1. Abeywickrama, D.B., Hoch, N., Zambonelli, F.: SimSOTA: Engineering and simulating feedback loops for self-adaptive systems. In: Proceedings of the 6th International C* Conference on Computer Science & Software Engineering (C3S2E'13) (In Press), ACM Press, New York (2013)
2. Abeywickrama, D.B., Zambonelli, F., Hoch, N.: Towards simulating architectural patterns for self-aware and self-adaptive systems. In: Proceedings of the 2nd Awareness Workshop co-located with the SASO'12 Conference, IEEE Computer Society Press, Los Alamitos (2012)
3. de Alfaro, L.: Game models for open systems. In: Dershowitz, N. (ed.) Verification: Theory and Practice. LNCS, vol. 2772, pp. 269–289. Springer, Heidelberg (2004)
4. de Alfaro, L., Henzinger, T.A.: Interface automata. In: ESEC/SIGSOFT FSE 2001. ACM SIGSOFT Software Engineering Notes 26(5). ACM (2001)
5. AlTurki, M., Meseguer, J.: PVeStA: A parallel statistical model checking and quantitative analysis tool. In: Corradini, A., Klin, B., Cîrstea, C. (eds.) CALCO 2011. LNCS, vol. 6859, pp. 386–392. Springer, Heidelberg (2011)
6. AT&T Labs, Inc.: Graphviz: Graph visualization software, http://graphviz.org
7. Aziz, A., Sanwal, K., Singhal, V., Brayton, R.: Model checking continuous time Markov chains. Transations on Computational Logic 1(1) (2000)
8. Baier, C., Katoen, J.P., Hermanns, H.: Approximate symbolic model checking of continuous-time Markov chains.
9. Belzner, L., De Nicola, R., Vandin, A., Wirsing, M.: Reasoning (on) service component ensembles in rewriting logic. In: Iida, S., Meseguer, J., Ogata, K. (eds.) Specification, Algebra, and Software. LNCS, vol. 8373, pp. 188–211. Springer, Heidelberg (2014)
10. Bruni, R., Corradini, A., Gadducci, F., Lluch Lafuente, A., Vandin, A.: Modelling and analyzing adaptive self-assembly strategies with Maude. In: Durán, F. (ed.) WRLA 2012. LNCS, vol. 7571, pp. 118–138. Springer, Heidelberg (2012)
11. Bruni, R., Corradini, A., Gadducci, F., Lluch Lafuente, A., Vandin, A.: Adaptable transition systems. In: Martí-Oliet, N., Palomino, M. (eds.) WADT 2012. LNCS, vol. 7841, pp. 95–110. Springer, Heidelberg (2013)
12. Bruni, R., Corradini, A., Gadducci, F., Lluch Lafuente, A., Vandin, A.: A conceptual framework for adaptation. In: de Lara, J., Zisman, A. (eds.) Fundamental Approaches to Software Engineering. LNCS, vol. 7212, pp. 240–254. Springer, Heidelberg (2012)
13. Bruni, R., Corradini, A., Gadducci, F., Lluch Lafuente, A., Vandin, A.: Modelling and analyzing adaptive self-assembly strategies with Maude. Science of Computer Programming (2013)

14. Bruni, R., Montanari, U., Sammartino, M.: Reconfigurable and Software-Defined Networks of Connectors and Components. In: Wirsing, M., Hölzl, M., Koch, N., Mayer, P. (eds.) Software Engineering for Collective Autonomic Systems. LNCS, vol. 8998, pp. 73–106. Springer, Heidelberg (2015)

15. Bulej, L., Bures, T., Horky, V., Keznikl, J., Tuma, P.: Performance awareness in component systems: Vision paper. COMPSAC '12 (2012)

16. Bures, T., Gerostathopoulos, I., Horky, V., Keznikl, J., Kofron, J., Loreti, M., Plasil, F.: Language extensions for implementation-level conformance checking. ASCENS Deliverable D1.5 (2012)

17. Calzolai, F., Loreti, M.: Simulation and analysis of distributed systems in KLAIM. In: Clarke, D., Agha, G. (eds.) COORDINATION 2010. LNCS, vol. 6116, pp. 122–136. Springer, Heidelberg (2010)

18. Castro, M., Druschel, P., Kermarrec, A.M., Rowstron, A.I.: SCRIBE: A large-scale and decentralized application-level multicast infrastructure. IEEE Journal on Selected Areas in Communications 20(8) (2002)

19. Clavel, M., Durán, F., Eker, S., Lincoln, P., Martí-Oliet, N., Meseguer, J., Talcott, C.: All About Maude - A High-Performance Logical Framework. LNCS, vol. 4350. Springer, Heidelberg (2007)

20. Combaz, J., Bensalem, S., Tiezzi, F., Margheri, A., Pugliese, R., Kofron, J.: Correctness of Service Components and Service Component Ensembles. In: Wirsing, M., Hölzl, M., Koch, N., Mayer, P. (eds.) Software Engineering for Collective Autonomic Systems. LNCS, vol. 8998, pp. 107–159. Springer, Heidelberg (2015)

21. De Nicola, R., Ferrari, G., Loreti, M., Pugliese, R.: Languages primitives for coordination, resource negotiation, and task description. ASCENS Deliverable D1.1 (September 2011), http://rap.dsi.unifi.it/scel/

22. De Nicola, R., Katoen, J.P., Latella, D., Loreti, M., Massink, M.: Klaim and its stochastic semantics. Tech. rep., Dipartimento di Sistemi e Informatica, Università di Firenze (2006), http://rap.dsi.unifi.it/~loreti/papers/TR062006.pdf

23. De Nicola, R., Katoen, J.P., Latella, D., Loreti, M., Massink, M.: Model checking mobile stochastic logic. Theoretical Computer Science 382(1) (2007)

24. Foundation for Intelligent Physical Agents: FIPA contract net interaction protocol specification (March 2013),
http://www.fipa.org/specs/fipa00029/SC00029H.html

25. GNU compiler collection, http://gcc.gnu.org/

26. Younes, H., Kwiatkowska, M., Norman, G., Parker, D.: Numerical vs. statistical probabilistic model checking. International Journal on Software Tools for Technology Transfer 8(3) (June 2006)

27. Hall, R., Pauls, K., McCulloch, S., Savage, D.: Osgi in Action: Creating Modular Applications in Java. Manning Pubs Co Series. Manning Publications (2011)

28. Hoch, N., Bensler, H.-P., Abeywickrama, D., Bures, T., Montanari, U.: The E-mobility Case Study. In: Wirsing, M., Hölzl, M., Koch, N., Mayer, P. (eds.) Software Engineering for Collective Autonomic Systems. LNCS, vol. 8998, pp. 513–533. Springer, Heidelberg (2015)

29. Hölzl, M., Gabor, T.: Reasoning and Learning for Awareness and Adaptation. In: Wirsing, M., Hölzl, M., Koch, N., Mayer, P. (eds.) Software Engineering for Collective Autonomic Systems. LNCS, vol. 8998, pp. 249–290. Springer, Heidelberg (2015)

30. Hölzl, M., Koch, N., Puviani, M., Wirsing, M., Zambonelli, F.: The Ensemble Development Life Cycle and Best Practices for Collective Autonomic Systems. In: Wirsing, M., Hölzl, M., Koch, N., Mayer, P. (eds.) Software Engineering for Collective Autonomic Systems. LNCS, vol. 8998, pp. 325–354. Springer, Heidelberg (2015)
31. Klarl, A., Mayer, P., Hennicker, R.: Helena@work: Modeling the science cloud platform. In: Margaria, T., Steffen, B. (eds.) ISoLA 2014, Part I. LNCS, vol. 8802, Springer, Heidelberg (2014)
32. Latella, D., Loreti, M., Massink, M.: On-the-fly fast mean-field model-checking. In: Abadi, M., Lluch Lafuente, A. (eds.) TGC 2013. LNCS, vol. 8358, Springer, Heidelberg (2014)
33. Latella, D., Loreti, M., Massink, M.: On-the-fly fast mean-field model-checking: Extended version. CoRR abs/1312.3416 (2013)
34. Latella, D., Loreti, M., Massink, M.: On-the-fly probabilistic model checking. In: Lanese, I., Lluch-Lafuente, A., Sokolova, A., Vieira, H.T. (eds.) Proceedings 7th Interaction and Concurrency Experience, ICE 2014, Berlin, Germany, 6th June 2014. EPTCS, vol. 166 (2014)
35. Marek, L., Villazón, A., Zheng, Y., Ansaloni, D., Binder, W., Qi, Z.: DiSL: a domain-specific language for bytecode instrumentation. In: AOSD '12: Proceedings of the 11th International Conference on Aspect-Oriented Software Development (2012)
36. Marek, L., Zheng, Y., Ansaloni, D., Binder, W., Qi, Z., Tuma, P.: DiSL: An extensible language for efficient and comprehensive dynamic program analysis. In: Proc. 7th Workshop on Domain-Specific Aspect Languages (DSAL '12), ACM Press, New York (2012)
37. Margheri, A., Masi, M., Pugliese, R., Tiezzi, F.: A formal software engineering approach to policy-based access control. Tech. rep., DiSIA, Univ. Firenze (2013), http://rap.dsi.unifi.it/facpl/research/Facpl-TR.pdf
38. Mayer, P., Velasco, J., Klarl, A., Hennicker, R., Puviani, M., Tiezzi, F., Pugliese, R., Keznikl, J., Bureš, T.: The Autonomic Cloud. In: Wirsing, M., Hölzl, M., Koch, N., Mayer, P. (eds.) Software Engineering for Collective Autonomic Systems. LNCS, vol. 8998, pp. 495–512. Springer, Heidelberg (2015)
39. Modelling, M.S., Lucca, A.I.: Maude ensemble strategies simulator and inquirer, http://sysma.lab.imtlucca.it/tools/ensembles/
40. De Nicola, R., Ferrari, G.-L., Loreti, M., Pugliese, R.: A language-based approach to autonomic computing. In: Beckert, B., Damiani, F., de Boer, F.S., Bonsangue, M.M. (eds.) FMCO 2011. LNCS, vol. 7542, pp. 25–48. Springer, Heidelberg (2013)
41. De Nicola, R., Latella, D., Lafuente, A.L., Loreti, M., Margheri, A., Massink, M., Morichetta, A., Pugliese, R., Tiezzi, F., Vandin, A.: The SCEL Language: Design, Implementation, Verification. In: Wirsing, M., Hölzl, M., Koch, N., Mayer, P. (eds.) Software Engineering for Collective Autonomic Systems. LNCS, vol. 8998, pp. 3–71. Springer, Heidelberg (2015)
42. O'Grady, R., Groß, R., Christensen, A.L., Dorigo, M.: Self-assembly strategies in a group of autonomous mobile robots. Autonomous Robots 28(4) (2010)
43. Oracle: java.lang.instrument (Java platform, standard edition 6, API specification) (2012), http://docs.oracle.com/javase/6/docs/api/java/lang/instrument/package-summary.html
44. Pinciroli, C., Bonani, M., Mondada, F., Dorigo, M.: Adaptation and Awareness in Robot Ensembles: Scenarios and Algorithms. In: Wirsing, M., Hölzl, M., Koch, N., Mayer, P. (eds.) Software Engineering for Collective Autonomic Systems. LNCS, vol. 8998, pp. 471–494. Springer, Heidelberg (2015)

45. Pinciroli, C., Trianni, V., O'Grady, R., Pini, G., Brutschy, A., Brambilla, M., Mathews, N., Ferrante, E., Di Caro, G., Ducatelle, F., Birattari, M., Gambardella, L.M., Dorigo, M.: ARGoS: a modular, parallel, multi-engine simulator for multi-robot systems. Swarm Intelligence 6(4), 271–295 (2012)

46. Information technology - portable operating system interface (POSIX). ISO/IEC/IEEE 9945 (First edition 2009-09-15) (2009)

47. Quaglia, P., Schivo, S.: Approximate model checking of stochastic COWS. In: Wirsing, M., Hofmann, M., Rauschmayer, A. (eds.) TGC 2010. LNCS, vol. 6084, pp. 335–347. Springer, Heidelberg (2010)

48. Rowstron, A., Druschel, P.: Pastry: Scalable, decentralized object location, and routing for large-scale peer-to-peer systems. In: Guerraoui, R. (ed.) Middleware 2001. LNCS, vol. 2218, p. 329. Springer, Heidelberg (2001)

49. Rowstron, A., Druschel, P.: Storage management and caching in PAST, a large-scale, persistent peer-to-peer storage utility. In: ACM SIGOPS Operating Systems Review, vol. 35, ACM Press, New York (2001)

50. Sebastio, S., Vandin, A.: MultiVeStA: Statistical model checking for discrete event simulators, submitted., http://eprints.imtlucca.it/1798

51. Sen, K., Viswanathan, M., Agha, G.A.: VESTA: A statistical model-checker and analyzer for probabilistic systems. In: Baier, C., Chiola, G., Smirni, E. (eds.) QEST 2005, IEEE Computer Society Press, Los Alamitos (2005)

52. Šerbedžija, N.: The ASCENS Case Studies: Results and Common Aspects. In: Wirsing, M., Hölzl, M., Koch, N., Mayer, P. (eds.) Software Engineering for Collective Autonomic Systems. LNCS, vol. 8998, pp. 451–469. Springer, Heidelberg (2015)

53. Vassev, E., Hinchey, M.: Knowledge Representation for Adaptive and Self-aware Systems. In: Wirsing, M., Hölzl, M., Koch, N., Mayer, P. (eds.) Software Engineering for Collective Autonomic Systems. LNCS, vol. 8998, pp. 221–247. Springer, Heidelberg (2015)

54. Zimory Software: Zimory cloud suite. (August 2014), http://www.zimory.com/

Part IV:
Case Studies: Challenges and Feedback

Any method, technique, or tool proposed for the development of software systems needs to be evaluated in the context of realistic case studies, which in turn also feed and challenge the research process according to the expectation of the concrete application domain. Thus, this last part of the book discusses three case studies which cover a large spectrum of autonomous systems: swarm robotics, autonomic cloud computing, and electrically-powered vehicle ensembles.

The first chapter introduces the three ASCENS case studies and describes the role they played in the project. While it is easy to see the differences, the case studies also contain many similarities and common abstract characteristics in the domain of knowledge-based, self-aware and adaptive behaviors, which are highlighted in this chapter.

Adaptation and awareness in robot ensembles are described in the second chapter. This domain is studied using a disaster recovery scenario in which a search-and-rescue operation must be performed by robots in a hazardous environment. The scenario has been used throughout ASCENS as a reference to coordinate the study of distributed algorithms for robot ensembles, and has led to the demonstration of awareness on the ensemble level without requiring awareness on the level of individual robots.

The third chapter discusses the autonomic cloud, which is a cloud providing a platform-as-a-service computing infrastructure formed by a loose collection of voluntarily provided heterogeneous nodes. The individual nodes communicate in a peer-to-peer manner and need to work together in the presence of problems such as failing or disappearing nodes to keep applications running. This requires a certain degree of self-awareness, monitoring, and self-adaptation, which is achieved by the ASCENS ideas and methods.

Finally, the last chapter of this part and the book discusses electro-mobility (e-mobility), one of the promising technologies for replacing combustion engines as a means of propulsions for automobiles. In particular, this case study deals with characteristics and challenges that arise when people travel with privately owned electric vehicles in a resource-constrained road environment. Predictive environment information such as traffic information and car park availability is used to make travel decisions which affect the environment and, in turn, future predictions. As in the other cases, the challenges are addressed by a combination of ASCENS approaches.

M. Wirsing et al. (eds.): Collective Autonomic Systems, LNCS 8998, p. 449, 2015.
© Springer International Publishing Switzerland 2015

CHAPTER IV.1

The ASCENS Case Studies: Results and Common Aspects*

Nikola Šerbedžija

Fraunhofer FOKUS, Berlin, Germany

Abstract. This chapter focuses on pragmatic aspects of the ASCENS project illustrating the role and significance of the three major application domains (swarm robotics, cloud computing and e-mobility) that motivate and pragmatically justify the approach to construct autonomous systems. A special insight is given into similarities and differences of the ASCENS case studies and their common abstract characteristics that led to a general-purpose methodology for expressing, evaluating and deploying knowledge-based, self-aware and adaptive behaviors. From this perspective selected ASCENS tools and methods to support the system development lifecycle are further discussed and illustrated on concrete examples. Finally future plans are given pointing out to the use and further evolvement of the ASCENS technology.

Keywords: application of collective adaptive systems, service component ensembles, software development life cycle, real-life systems

1 Introduction

The application domain, represented by three major case studies, namely swarm robotics, science cloud and e-mobility, played a central role in the ASCENS project[1]. They provide a source of motivation for the ASCENS technology and a treasury of trial examples upon which ASCENS solutions could be tested in practice. Case studies also served as a gravity for joint work among different partners and work packages as the whole spectrum of results had to be put together and applied on the case studies scenarios. This constant interaction between theory and practice made the ASCENS highly theoretical approach unified, pragmatic and well suited for a range of application domains, far beyond the specific areas of the ASCENS case studies.

The ASCENS project deals with the development and deployment of autonomous systems with special attention paid to technical awareness and adaptive behavior of the underlying systems on one side and to rigorous and formal reasoning about the correct system functioning on the other. In the early project

---

* This work has been sponsored by the EU project ASCENS IP 257414 (FP7).
[1] ASCENS website: http://www.ascens-ist.eu/

M. Wirsing et al. (eds.): Collective Autonomic Systems, LNCS 8998, pp. 451–469, 2015.
© Springer International Publishing Switzerland 2015

phase the development lifecycle for autonomous systems has been proposed (see Chapter III.1 [16] of this book) tracing the methodology and the roadmap for system design and development. A number of distinct phases of the development process have been identified and many tools have been developed to support the modeling and development in each of the lifecycle stages. Due to a highly non-deterministic character of the autonomous systems, whose behavior is dynamic and sensitive to unpredicted situation, system validation and verification plays an important role in the project.

Contrary to the majority of computing systems now in use, autonomous systems' behavior is highly dynamic and reactive to unexpected situation. This makes the system verification process extremely difficult as the system alters its behavior at run-time replying to changes of the state of the environment and to new knowledge acquired about its own state. Those circumstances cannot be predicted in advance and a system cannot be fully tested and debugged before it is used. Furthermore, when an autonomous system is deployed, its variable behavior is a run-time response to a live situation and it is hard to distinguish correct behavior from malfunctioning. The ASCENS response to such difficulties is to verify and validate the system in all of its development and deployment phases applying rigorous methodologies and formal methods, from requirement analyses and modeling up to the run-time monitoring.

Having all these challenges in mind, ASCENS strategy was to demonstrate its methodology throughout the development process with the concrete and non-trivial applications. That makes the role of ASCENS case studies manifold:

- Inspirational
- Experimental
- Verifiable
- Pragmatic

From the very beginning of the project, initial concepts for requirement specification, awareness, adaptation and overall system modeling have been taken from the problem-rich application domains of swarm robotics, cloud computing and e-mobility. Both typical examples from the application domain and concrete trial scenarios were thoroughly studied. Inspired and motivated by a wide problem space of ASCENS case studies, a number of new methods have been developed, almost from scratch, and a number of existing methods were modified to reply to these challenges. Out of thorough problem specification, a structured knowledge representation in form of KnowLang [31] approach has been designed allowing for a sound (self-) awareness definition based on knowledge. Further system modeling could use this knowledge to exercise awareness rich behavior, making a system aware of its functional and non-functional requirements. It furthermore led to development of a unique adaptation model called SOTA [1] that defines adaptation as a system journey in a multidimensional space where the coordinates are awareness aspects of the system. By deploying SOTA on case studies a general-purpose catalog of adaptation patterns have been defined that help designer express and exercise with adaptive behavior.

The SCEL language [10] (see also Chapter I.1 [25]) is another ASCENS pillar that allows for system modeling and reasoning on their behavior. It offers means for defining a system as a set of service components extended with local knowledge to express awareness and adaptive policies for predicate-based bindings to express autonomous behavior. The *Helena* approach [21] has been further developed for modeling collaborations using a UML-like notation focusing on the description of the behavior at individual and collective (ensemble) level. Further design steps from high-level strategic goals (requirements, adaptation patterns) to their low-level system architecture realization (components and ensembles) are supported by the Invariant Refinement Method (IRM) (see chapter III.4 [7] and [19]).

Experimental significance of the case studies could be seen through numerous pragmatic examples which were used to model and verify corresponding system behavior. Each concrete problem from the case studies domain has been modeled, and analyzed by the corresponding ASCENS tool, testing simultaneously the analytical power of the tool itself and the pragmatic significance of the solution. Throughout the project this interaction between theory and practice contributed to achieve (1) sound and usable methodology and (2) useful pragmatic results for the application domain and industrial partners. The ASCENS work has been characterized by this interaction and mutual influence that enrich both the theory and the practice. Two major software tools developed from the scratch and for the specific needs of the project were used to deploy and test ASCENS case studies in practice. The two tools are JRESP [18] and JDEECO [20] and are both based on SCEL's linguistic abstractions and integrate also other softwares developed within the ASCENS project.

Verifiable significance of the case studies is present in all the development phases. The case studies offered realistic, pragmatic and complex examples of use, making the highly theoretical validation/verification means both sound and pragmatic. Each concept developed within ASCENS has been first validated in its generic form and then applied on a concrete example from the application domain for further evaluation. For example, SOTA adaptation patterns allow for high-level reasoning and proofs for adaptive behavior and appropriate selection of the adaptation patterns for each of pragmatic problem. High level modeling led to further reasoning on important system properties like safety (e.g. proving that e-vehicles will never deadlock while using common resources e.g. parking lots or charging station) and liveness (e.g. proving that the system will really find the optimal route for a vehicle respecting major constraints e.g. battery level, timing etc.). D-Finder [4] tool has been used for the compositional verification. Further examples of validating coordination and collaboration algorithms and local vs. global goal optimization are taken from a rich problem space of swarm robotics, cloud computing and e-mobility (e.g. guaranteeing that each e-vehicle obtains a parking place nearby its target destination, taking into account that the garage needs to satisfy the needs of hundreds of other e-vehicles. The ASCENS approach also integrates existing BIP (Behavior, Interaction, Priority [3]) framework and its analysis tools with ASCENS novel tools to perform quantitative/qualitative verification (see chapter I.3 [9]).

The rest of the chapter further elaborates on a mutual influence between theory and practice by detailing the application challenges (section 2) that are used to motivate and develop a common approach (section 3) to model, develop and deploy autonomous systems. The set of ASCENS generic tools (section 4) re-visits a wide spectrum of developed means to support the use of ASCENS approach in solving concrete pragmatic problems illustrating ASCENS results and solutions in real application deployments (section 5). Finally, the conclusion (section 6) summarizes the results and discusses a wider pragmatic significance and influence that the ASCENS project has in the domain of adaptive and autonomous systems.

2   Application Challenges

A thorough analysis of the application problem space is crucial, both for successful application design and development and for assessing the impact of the ASCENS methods. This dual role of the case studies has been especially important at the beginning of the project, when the ASCENS approach was defined and developed. The approach has been to decompose the application fields to low-level details, provide partial solutions and to compose those solutions into harmonized methodology that defines complete development lifecycle for autonomous systems.

2.1   Application Overview

To explore the system requirements for autonomous systems, three complex application domains have been closely examined: swarm robotics, cloud computing and e-mobility. The overall strategy has been to analyze separate application domains, find out the characteristics that make these system knowledge aware and autonomous, and finally to generalize these characteristics into a possibly common set of joint features that could be modeled according to a general methodology.

Swarm robotics application domain deals with creation of multi-robot systems that through interaction and coordination among participating simple robots and their environment can accomplish a common goal, which would be impossible to achieve by a single robot. The basic idea behind the application scenario is to organize and control a rescue operation in an emergency situation. Figure 1 illustrates a multi-robot system containing two types of robots with circles showing possible different grouping (ensemble building) among different or similar robot type.

Cloud computing is an approach that exploits Internet to make computing resources available to users in a service-oriented way. By sharing computing resources among many users, significant throughput can be achieved leading to energy and costs savings. This approach to providing computing resources calls

Fig. 1. Swarm robotics

for novel techniques that guarantee the offer of highly dynamic and secure virtual resources that would maintain throughput and efficiency high, wile reducing the number of used resources. Fulfillment of these requirements ensure enormous reduction in energy consumption and computing costs, making powerful computing resources available to everyone. Figure 2 illustrates a collection of computing resources brought together to form a cloud that further offer its services to the users.

E-mobility is a vision of future transportation by means of a network of electric vehicles allowing people to fulfill their individual mobility needs in an environmental friendly manner (decreasing pollution, saving energy, sharing vehicles, etc). Due to limited battery capacity, e-vehicles cannot cover long distances, as it is the case with traditional vehicles (and re-filling energy lasts much longer). The ultimate goal of e-mobility is to overcome that problem by offering a range of supporting activities that would allow energy-aware passengers to master distances in required time. Figure 3 illustrates a fleet of e-vehicles with indicated parking lots and charging stations.

2.2   Common Characteristics

A closer examination the three application areas reveals that, although very different in nature, they share a number of characteristics.

Fig. 2. Cloud Computing

Unique simple entities with clearly identified individual goals. In swarm robotics, those are elementary robots with their simple functionality and single role (e.g. a foraging robot moves and explores the area until it finds the target or come too far away from other robots – then it stops). In cloud computing, elements are specific computing resources with their characteristics (e.g. a CPU with its energy consumption, execution speed, throughput etc.). In e-mobility, elements are e-vehicles, parking and/or charging stations and traffic conditions (e.g. a parking lot has its location, price and availability/occupation schedule). Obviously, all three applications can be described by a huge number of (1) single entities with (2) unique individual goals.

Distribution and grouping around global goal. In swarm robotics, simple elements are grouped into multi-robot system in order to perform the function that individual robots cannot do alone. In cloud computing, more CPUs could be grouped together to offer more computational power. In e-mobility, multiple resources like charging station and parking lots can be combined to provide better overall service. Further characteristics are existence of (3) global goals, (4) grouping principles to express these global goals and (5) massive interaction that exploits these principles of sharing and collectiveness in order to (6) coordinate and harmonize local and global goals.

Awareness and knowledge are characteristics which are pre-conditions for autonomous behavior. Maintaining the knowledge of their own functional and operational capabilities make both single units and their collections self-aware and capable of runtime dynamic responsiveness. Multi-robot system is aware of location and functionality of neighboring robots so that groups of robots can

Fig. 3. E-mobility

coordinate along the common interest. Cloud computing deals with dynamic (re-)scheduling of available (not fully used) computing resources. Maximal utilization can only be achieved if the cloud is aware of the users' processing needs and the on-going states of the deployed cloud resources. Only with such knowledge, a cloud can make a good utilization of computers while serving at best individual users' needs. E-mobility can support coordination only if e-vehicles know their own restrictions (battery state), destinations of users, re-charging possibilities, parking availabilities, the state of other e-vehicles nearby. With such knowledge collective behavior may take place, respecting individual goals, energy consumption and environmental requirements. Consequently, (7) self-awareness allows for knowledge-rich (8) adaptation and (9) optimization within the three case studies.

Robustness and continuous operation are crucial features of real-life systems, where an application needs to run non-interrupted, despite possible malfunctioning. A multi-robot system does not stop when one robot is down. The cloud computing is, by definition, a set of boundless resources that can overcome the failure of a single component. E-mobility aims at operating non-stop while overcoming the restrictions imposed by battery life-time making (10) the robustness a major aim of the overall concept.

When taking into account all the above mentioned common characteristics, it can be seen that all together they contribute to make a target system behave (11) autonomously, which is the ultimate goal of the ASCENS approach. All the mentioned generic common features (with their interpretations within all three case studies) are summarized in the table 1.

Table 1. Common features of the ASCENS case studies

Common feature	Swarm Robots	Cloud computing	E-Mobility
Single entities	Different types of robots	Computing resources	E-vehicles , parking lot, charging station, infrastructure
Individual goals	Find the victim, carry the obejct, ...	compute, store, ...	reach the destination, charge the battery, ...
Global goals	Build the wall, ...	increase throughput, ...	allocate all parking lots, ...
Grouping principles	"All foraging robots close to the target", ...	"Connect idle processors", ...	All available parking lots in radius of 500m of the meeting place, ...
Massive interaction	Among robots, ...	Among computing resources, ...	Among vehicles, parking lots, charging stations, ...
Coordination	Coordinate search algorithm, ...	Coordinate free resources, ...	Coordinate park lot allocation, ...
Self-awareness	"About battery state", ...	"About its usage", ...	"About own location", ...
Optimization	Time, energy, performance, ...	Availability, computational task execution, ...	Arriving in time, vehicle/infrastructure usage, ...
Adaptation	To changing plans, single robot malfunction, ...	To resource failure, ...	To traffic situation, battery shortage ...
Robustness	Sensory noise, limited sensory range and battery life, ...	Failing resources, sudden intense computing requirements, ...	Range limitation, battery shortage, infrastructure problems,...
Autonomous behavior	Run-time plan change,	Decentralised decision making, global optimization, ...	Changing the route, re-allocate parking lot, ...

3   Common Approach

This spectrum of common features serves as a basis for modeling of massively distributed behaviors leading to a generic framework for developing and deploying complex autonomic systems [17]. To behave autonomously, a control system needs to maintain knowledge about itself (specific objectives, capabilities, execution state and restrictions) and about its environment. Such knowledge yields awareness of a specific component about its functionality and about the effects it has on the environment which enable adaptive behavior. Being capable of operating according to the principles of knowledge, awareness, adaptation, a system can re-configure, re-tune and act appropriately and thus to behave autonomously.

The ASCENS approach breaks up a complex control problem into its basic constituents. It deals with complications at a bottom level, solving issues at a lower scale and then harmonizing these solutions at a more global level. Localization and de-centralization is the fourth major principle of the approach. Service components with clearly defined elementary objectives are basic system elements. They gather in larger symbiosis called ensembles in order to fulfill collective goals. As the controlled situation changes, e.g. goals are (partially) fulfilled, re-grouping takes place and the symbiosis re-structures. The criteria to construct an ensemble of service-components is the result of joint interests which can be expressed as a logical sentence, e.g. "connect all robots that can carry up to 4kg and are in the radius of 100m with the aim to cooperatively transport 25kg heavy object" or "select all free parking lots in the radius of 300m that have a charging plug". That makes the very useful resorting to communication mechanisms that select partners implicitly by resorting to predicates. Connections are established at run-time, and depend on the live situation at particular instant. These logical rules for highly dynamic grouping are further used for formal reasoning on optimization and coordination among distributed elements.

The overall system development life cycle consists of the following phases: rigorous design (requirement specification, modeling and validation/verification), deployment (programming) and run-time monitoring (live examination of awareness, adaptation and autonomous behavior). A number of tools have been devised that support the development process at each step, thus guiding and facilitating the whole development process. Requirement specification is a phase where the dissection of the problem to be solved takes place (requirement engineering is described in the Chapter III.1 [16] of this book). Each system element is separately defined both functionally (what to do) and non-functionally (how to do) yielding a set of goals that embrace the terms of functioning and description of environment. The knowledge required for system awareness and adaptation is used as a major attribute repository for system construction (formal approach to knowledge awareness and adaptation is described in the Chapters II.1 [6], II.2 [13], II.3 [32] and II.4 [15] of this book). The SCEL (service-component ensembles language) [10] has been developed for high-level system modeling with service components and their ensembles. Both service-components and ensembles have local knowledge used to express their goals. SCEL is parametric with respect to the way of representing knowledge. In its simple instance the knowledge repositories of SCEL components are nothing more than multi set of tuples that can be read, added or withdrawn. The final aim is representing components' knowledge as ontologies that contain hierarchical and meaningful description of system properties and system goals. The goals are described as rules i.e. logical expressions with system properties. A simple version of the SCEL language, its design, implementation and verification is described in the Chapter I.1 [25] of this book.

The adaptation phenomenon is formally modeled as a progress in a multidimensional space where each axis represents one orthogonal aspect of system awareness (facts about its own functional, operational, or any other necessities defined within requirement specification phase). Adaptation actually happens when the system state moves from one position to another within a predefined space according to the pre and post- conditions on each of its awareness- dimensions. Adaptation is a continuous process where a system acts appropriately, i.e., in harmony with components capabilities and the observed environment. The SOTA adaptation model is used to extract major application requirements and offer appropriate adaptation patterns that effectively control system dynamics with numerous feedback-loops. In order to guarantee correct and timely behavior in such demanding and highly dynamic circumstances this approach relies on formal methods. The major safety and liveness properties are formally proved using SCEL (e.g. prove that two e-vehicles will never block each other while competing for a free charging station, or prove that the foraging algorithm of a robot converges in a given time). Further validation and verification of specific optimization algorithms are performed in order to guarantee correct system behavior in early design phase (e.g. prove that the optimization method will deliver the most energy-efficient route for a given multi-routing problem). Once the system is rigorously modeled and validated, the actual deployment may take place sewing together the different components. The jRESP and jDEECo deployment tools offer direct Java programming support for the SCEL and SOTA models. Other modeling tools, such as the POEM language [14], are used to specify deep logical and stochastic functioning that describe the system behavior.

Due to a seamless functioning of autonomous systems, where system changes are means for appropriate behavior, possible malfunctions are difficult to discover. Therefore, a number of tools have been developed for run-time monitoring where internal system knowledge and topology (ensemble construction) as well as awareness and adaptive characteristics are observed. For example, the monitoring tools can visualize how the robots, close to the target and with enough battery-charge, are grouped into ensemble to perform joint transport of a heavy object. Once the task is performed, the ensembles are dismantled freeing robots for another assignment. Monitoring inspects and displays major system principles: knowledge, awareness and adaptation, offering a visualization of dynamic ensemble building criteria, thus directly observing autonomous behavior. If some malfunctioning is discovered at run-time, a system modification is considered by going back to modeling and design system development phases. Monitoring is performed by means of the following tools: ARGoS [27], AVis Plug-in[2] and POEM for swarm robotics; the Zimory cloud platform [35] and SCP for science cloud; and jDEECo and IRM for e-mobility.

The detailed description of ensemble development life cycle and ASCENS best practice for collective adaptive system is given in the Chapter I.1 [25] of this book.

---

[2] see the ASCENS User Guide

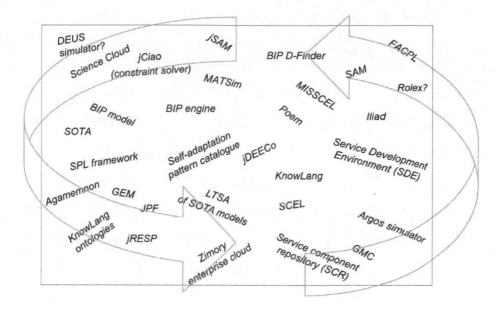

Fig. 4. ASCENS development and deployment tools

4 Generic Set of Common Tools

The set of common features, as described in the previous section, served as a basis for further work and experimenting in each of the case studies. At the same time it led to a generic set of common tools that could be used and tested within scenarios from the case studies domains. Figure 4 shows some of the generic tools which are available in the rich ASCENS tool repository. Most of them are newly developed or adjusted to the ASCENS purposes. The cyclic arrows indicates a multi-level feedback loop - present in all development phases, as described in the ASCENS development life cycle. On one side, the project has given rise to a comprehensive set of generic tools that could be used in any deployment scenario (fully independent from the ASCENS application domain), on the other side, these tools were tested and fine-tuned using complex practical problems with real data.

The tool integration has been allocated to a separate work package whose aim has been to generate a standard integrated development environment where the modeling and editing tools are placed together with profilers and debuggers, making it possible to practically follow the whole development life cycle as described in the previous chapter of this book. All of the tools previously described are stored in a common repository making it a common place to apply ASCENS technology and follow ASCENS development life cycle.

All mentioned tools were separately tested in a theoretical context, or using single problems from the case studies domains. Once fully tested, the tools were applied on a large scale practical scenarios from the ASCENS case studies.

Table 2. ASCENS tools used for the case studies development

EDLC Phase	Swarm Robots	Cloud computing	E-Mobility
Requirements Engineering	SOTA, Gem, POEM	Knowlang, IRM	simSOTA, IRM
Modeling/ Programming	SCEL, jRESP, Poem	SOTA, SCEL, KnowLang	SCEL, SCLP
Verification/ Validation	BIP, jRESP	jRESP	jDEECO
Deployment	ARGoS	SCP SPL, Java, Zimory	jDEECo. Java, MatSim
Monitoring	ARGoS, AVI Plug-In Tool	Zimory, SCP	jDEECO/DiSL/SPL MatSim
Awareness	POEM, ARGoS, AVI	SCP	jDEECo
Self-adaptation	ARGoS, AVI, POEM	Zimory, SCP	jDEECo, IRM
Feedback	POEM	SPL	MatSim

Table 2 describes which ones of the the main ASCENS tools have been used within each of the case study according to the EDLC (Ensemble Development Life Cycle).

The ASCENS tool repository with numerous deployment examples has played an important and dual role: (1) tools were tested in a real and large scale application domain - proving a wide applicability and a strong practical orientation of the ASCENS approach, (2) the end users and corresponding industrial parties could see the benefits (and challenges) of a fully scientific approach to construct and deploy large practical systems, insuring their reliable and correct functioning.

5   Application Deployments

From the very beginning, the project theoretical development has been interleaved with practical exercising, taking various examples from the main ASCENS application areas. Most of these practical results were reported in the theoretical project deliverables. Nevertheless, three major applications served as a pragmatic guideline during the project and they were specified, modeled and developed step-wise during the project (in a separate work package). The task structure of the case study work package is similar to the ASCENS development life cycle and had a following major subtasks:

- Requirements analysis and specification
- Model synthesis
- Integration and simulation
- Implementation and evaluation/validation

In the first project year a thorough requirement analyses took place, first in an informal way and then using a rich set of ASCENS tools for knowledge expression, self-awareness and adaptive behavior. In the second project stage, major system modeling took place synthesizing most of the modeling techniques developed within project. The third stage has been characterized by numerous integration effort, interfacing different tools and languages as well as undertaking numerous simulations in order to pre-check the system behavior before doing final implementations. In the last project stage, the three ASCENS case studies were deployed, tested, monitored and evaluated.

This sections only gives a short reference to the case studies developments, as each of the case study is fully described in the following chapters (IV.2 [26], IV.3 [23] and IV.4 [12]) of this book. However, one further special example is described here: a robot race exhibition, presented at the ICT conference in Vilnius in November 2013. The significance of the exhibition was not only to demonstrate pragmatic ASCENS technology by having real robots performing in real-life settings. It also justified the ASCENS complete ensemble development life cycle as numerous concrete theoretical tools were demonstrated on a concrete example.

5.1 ASCENS Case Studies

The ASCENS project took three major application domain as a major pragmatical inspiration domain: swarm robotics, cloud computing and e-mobility. Each of the area is complex per se, up to date and a subject of many other contemporary research and developments.

Swarm Robotics. The swarm robotics case study deals with a disaster recovery scenario. Numerous separate problems from the scenario were separately specified, modeled and verified during the project work. A special attention has been paid to local vs. global behaviors [34] and distributed algorithms which represent typical class of problems within swarm robotics theory. An engineering approach to apply EDLC in designing a multi-robot system is described in [29] and a separate chapter (Chapter IV.2 [26]) of this book has been fully dedicated to the swarm robotics case study.

Science Cloud. The science cloud case study deals with a vision of an autonomic cloud, providing a platform-as-a-service computing infrastructure, which is created and maintained by a free collection of ad hoc connected heterogeneous voluntary computers forming a peer-to-peer network. The science cloud has been developed from scratch fully deploying ASCENS ensemble development lifecycle [22,28]. A special focus in science cloud case study is on self* features, making the cloud fully aware of its functional and operational state, thus autonomously providing resilience, data redundancy, and failover mechanisms. A separate chapter (Chapter IV.3 [23]) of this book has been fully dedicated to science cloud.

E-mobility. The e-mobility case study deals with a vision of a future transportation that will include more and more e-vehicles as means of transportation, posing a whole range of problems that need to be solved in order to ensure the transition and better acceptance of the new generation of e-vehicles. The e-mobility case study was engineered by strictly applying ASCENS methodology [30,8]. A special attention in the case study has been paid to finding optimal energy routes [11], and overcoming the local vs. global goal optimization, using constraint logic programming techniques [24]. A separate chapter (Chapter IV.4 [12]) of this book has been fully dedicated to e-mobility.

Fig. 5. Robot race

5.2   Robot Race

The challenges of controlling the robot behavior in performing certain task can be better understood if seen from the robot perspective. The complexity does not primarily come from the task itself, but rather from the interaction that goes on between the robot sensory system, environment and self-directed robot performance. To illustrate that, an exhibition has been organized at the well attended ICT conference (Vilnius, November 2013) where ASCENS autonomous robot competed with a human-controlled robot[3]. The task given to the robots was to find building blocks in a closed area, grab them (one by one), and carry them to the place where a wall should be constructed. The competition arena[4].

---

[3] See the ASCENS blog "Beauty is in the eye of the beholder" at: http://blog. ascens-ist.eu/2013/11/beauty-is-in-the-eye-of-the-beholder/.

[4] A video clip of the exhibition is available at: http://www.aware-project.eu/2013/ ascens-ict-2013/ from ICT Conference is illustrated in Figure 5.

The ASCENS robot was fully autonomous and a "competitor robot" was operated by a joystick which could move the robot left/right; forward/backwards and instruct it to grab/release the building blocks (the competitor robot had no knowledge on how to find, grab and carry objects and relied completely on the human operator). Both robots belong to the marXbot robot generation [5], a modular and easily re-configurable robots equipped with numerous devices that allow for sensing and acting in the deployed environment. The tasks allocated to the robots seemed trivial to the audience, so that most of the competitors believed that ASCENS autonomous robot does not stand a chance, against the robot controlled by a human. That proved to be wrong. Most people lost; only a couple of young, joystick-virtuous, competitors won.

But for those who could outperform the ASCENS autonomous robot, a "fair-play" rule has been introduced: since the robots sensory system is less sophisticated than ours, the vision of the human competitor has been reduced to the visual system of the robot (a competitor was not supposed to look to the competing arena with own eyes, but rather to the screen which mirror "what robot sees" (in the left-upper corner of the Figure 5 a screen shot of the robot vision is illustrated). That gave the competitors equal chances. When both competitors have exactly the same information about environment, ASCENS robot performed much better. That shows how seemingly simple assignment (from human point of view) is actually complex for a fully autonomous robot. Taking into account relatively primitive robot sensory system, the robot performance has been quite good and reliable.

Showing ASCENS results at well attended congress with several thousand visitors provided a great audience for the ASCENS demo which attracted more than a hundred competitors (people who really competed with the ASCENS robot). The significance of the demonstration at the Vilnius exhibition has been multifold:

1. ASCENS pragmatic approach has been demonstrated in a vivid and successful error free settings. It has been one of most attended stall at the

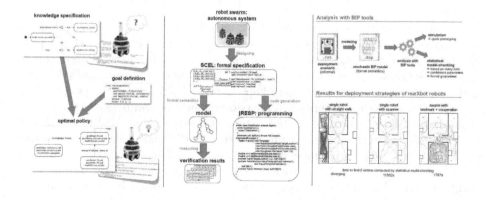

Fig. 6. Elements of the ASCENS EDLC

congress and the ASCENS robots has been running 3 days non-stop from early morning to late evening

2. ASCENS theoretical work has also been demonstrated through several model descriptions, simulation and verification tools. Figure 6 contains three posters from the conference illustrating the specification, modeling and verification phase of the "robot race" demo. It has been a unique situation to discuss the high-level tools in front of the running example, who used those tools.

3. ASCENS evaluation and monitoring approach has been illustrated by the design architecture of the monitoring tool, as shown on Figure 7. The AVI monitoring can show the internal awareness structures of the running example, monitoring and analyzing properties used for ensemble creation.

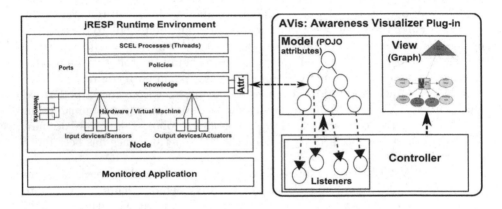

Fig. 7. Monitoring tool

6   Conclusion

This chapter has presented the ASCENS achievements as a continuous balancing between theory and practice. At one side, a number of scientists put their efforts together to make abstract and generic high-level methods and tools to model, analyze, validate and develop autonomous systems. At another side, pragmatic and business driven partners kept the ASCENS achievements applicable and down to deployment terrain. This constant interaction between theory and practice have been beneficial for both sides: theoreticians got real problems and numerous practical data descriptions that they traditionally do not have, so that their work has been confronted with real world problems. Industrial partners, at another side, were in the position to directly influence the theoretical work and tailor its solution towards pragmatic goals, which could be used to improve products and achieve results which could not be achievable without such collaboration.

A wider significance and influence of the ASCENS outcomes is expected also in other application domains. Namely, the ASCENS generic results are applicable in any area where autonomic control is needed. Further exploitation activities like planned summer school and publication of project results on scientific journals and conferences should re-enforce already well known ASCENS methodology. Pragmatic exploitation of ASCENS results is guaranteed by the project industrial partners. Moreover, for encouraging a wider use, a tool repository (see the Chapter III.5 [2] of this book) and an ASCENS user's manual have been made available on-line to any interested party. A close collaboration with other EU projects, especially within collective adaptive initiative opens further perspectives of continuing the development and deployment of the work done in the ASCENS project.

Acknowledgements. All the achievements described here are the results of the common work of the whole ASCENS project team. A special thanks go to the reviewers, Saddek Bensalem and Rocco De Nicola for numerous constructive criticism and text improvement suggestions.

References

1. Abeywickrama, D., Bicocchi, N., Zambonelli, F.: Sota: Towards a general model for self-adaptive systems. In: IEEE 21st International Workshop on Enabling Technologies: Infrastructure for Collaborative Enterprises (WETICE 2012), June 2012, pp. 48–53 (2012)
2. Abeywickrama, D.B., Combaz, J., Horký, V., Keznikl, J., Kofroň, J., Lafuente, A.L., Loreti, M., Margheri, A., Mayer, P., Monreale, V., Montanari, U., Pinciroli, C., Tůma, P., Vandin, A., Vassev, E.: Tools for Ensemble Design and Runtime. In: Wirsing, M., Hölzl, M., Koch, N., Mayer, P. (eds.) Software Engineering for Collective Autonomic Systems. LNCS, vol. 8998, pp. 429–448. Springer, Heidelberg (2015)
3. Basu, A., Bozga, M., Sifakis, J.: Modeling Heterogeneous Real-time Components in BIP. In: SEFM, pp. 3–12. IEEE Computer Society Press, Los Alamitos (2006)
4. Bensalem, S., Bozga, M., Sifakis, J., Nguyen, T.-H.: Compositional verification for component-based systems and application. In: Cha, S(S.), Choi, J.-Y., Kim, M., Lee, I., Viswanathan, M. (eds.) ATVA 2008. LNCS, vol. 5311, pp. 64–79. Springer, Heidelberg (2008)
5. Bonani, M., Longchamp, V., Magnenat, S., Rétornaz, P., Burnier, D., Roulet, G., Vaussard, F., Bleuler, H., Mondada, F.: The marXbot, a miniature mobile robot opening new perspectives for the collective-robotic research. In: Proceedings of the IEEE/RSJ International Conference on Intelligent Robots and Systems (IROS), pp. 4187–4193. IEEE Press, Piscataway, NJ (2010)
6. Bruni, R., Corradini, A., Gadducci, F., Hölzl, M., Lafuente, A.L., Vandin, A., Wirsing, M.: Reconciling White-Box and Black-Box Perspectives on Behavioral Self-adaptation. In: Wirsing, M., Hölzl, M., Koch, N., Mayer, P. (eds.) Software Engineering for Collective Autonomic Systems. LNCS, vol. 8998, pp. 163–184. Springer, Heidelberg (2015)

7. Bures, T., Gerostathopoulos, I., Hnetynka, P., Keznikl, J., Kit, M., Plasil, F.: The Invariant Refinement Method. In: Wirsing, M., Hölzl, M., Koch, N., Mayer, P. (eds.) Software Engineering for Collective Autonomic Systems. LNCS, vol. 8998, pp. 405–428. Springer, Heidelberg (2015)

8. Bures, T., Nicola, R.D., Gerostathopoulos, I., Hoch, N., Kit, M., Koch, N., Monreale, G.V., Montanari, U., Pugliese, R., Serbedzija, N., Wirsing, M., Zambonelli, F.: A life cycle for the development of autonomic systems: The e-mobility showcase. In: 2013 IEEE 7th International Conference on Self-Adaptation and Self-Organizing Systems Workshops, pp. 71–76 (2013)

9. Combaz, J., Bensalem, S., Tiezzi, F., Margheri, A., Pugliese, R., Kofron, J.: Correctness of Service Components and Service Component Ensembles. In: Wirsing, M., Hölzl, M., Koch, N., Mayer, P. (eds.) Software Engineering for Collective Autonomic Systems. LNCS, vol. 8998, pp. 107–159. Springer, Heidelberg (2015)

10. De Nicola, R., Loreti, M., Pugliese, R., Tiezzi, F.: A Formal Approach to Autonomic Systems Programming: The SCEL Language. TAAS 9(2), 7 (2014)

11. Hoch, N., Zemmer, K., Werther, B., Siegwarty, R.Y.: Electric Vehicle Travel Optimization - Customer Satisfaction Despite Resource Constraints. In: Proc. of IEEE IVS, IEEE Computer Society Press, Los Alamitos (2012)

12. Hoch, N., Bensler, H.-P., Abeywickrama, D., Bures, T., Montanari, U.: The E-mobility Case Study. In: Wirsing, M., Hölzl, M., Koch, N., Mayer, P. (eds.) Software Engineering for Collective Autonomic Systems. LNCS, vol. 8998, pp. 513–533. Springer, Heidelberg (2015)

13. Hoch, N., Monreale, G.V., Montanari, U., Sammartino, M., Siwe, A.T.: From Local to Global Knowledge and Back. In: Wirsing, M., Hölzl, M., Koch, N., Mayer, P. (eds.) Software Engineering for Collective Autonomic Systems. LNCS, vol. 8998, pp. 185–220. Springer, Heidelberg (2015)

14. Hölzl, M.: The Poem Language (Version 2). Tech. Rep. 7, ASCENS (July 2013), http://www.poem-lang.de/documentation/TR7.pdf

15. Hölzl, M., Gabor, T.: Reasoning and Learning for Awareness and Adaptation. In: Wirsing, M., Hölzl, M., Koch, N., Mayer, P. (eds.) Software Engineering for Collective Autonomic Systems. LNCS, vol. 8998, pp. 249–290. Springer, Heidelberg (2015)

16. Hölzl, M., Koch, N., Puviani, M., Wirsing, M., Zambonelli, F.: The Ensemble Development Life Cycle and Best Practices for Collective Autonomic Systems. In: Wirsing, M., Hölzl, M., Koch, N., Mayer, P. (eds.) Software Engineering for Collective Autonomic Systems. LNCS, vol. 8998, pp. 325–354. Springer, Heidelberg (2015)

17. Hölzl, M.M., Wirsing, M.: Towards a system model for ensembles. In: Agha, G., Danvy, O., Meseguer, J. (eds.) Formal Modeling: Actors, Open Systems, Biological Systems. LNCS, vol. 7000, pp. 241–261. Springer, Heidelberg (2011)

18. jRESP Java Run-time Environment for SCEL Programs (2012)

19. Keznikl, J., Bures, T., Plasil, F., Gerostathopoulos, I., Hnetynka, P., Hoch, N.: Design of Ensemble-Based Component Systems by Invariant Refinement. In: Proceedings of the 16th International ACM Sigsoft symposium on Component-based software engineering (CBSE '13), pp. 91–100. ACM Press, New York (2013)

20. Keznikl, J., Bures, T., Plasil, F., Kit, M.: Towards Dependable Emergent Ensembles of Components: The DEECo Component Model. In: WICSA/ECSA, pp. 249–252. IEEE Computer Society Press, Los Alamitos (2012)

21. Klarl, A., Hennicker, R.: Design and Implementation of Dynamically Evolving Ensembles with the HELENA Framework. In: Proceedings of the 23rd Australasian Software Engineering Conference, pp. 15–24. IEEE Computer Society Press, Los Alamitos (2014)

22. Mayer, P., Klarl, A., Hennicker, R., Puviani, M., Tiezzi, F., Pugliese, R., Keznikl, J., Bures, T.: The autonomic cloud: A vision of voluntary, peer-2-peer cloud computing. In: 2013 IEEE 7th International Conference on Self-Adaptation and Self-Organizing Systems Workshops (SASOW), Sep. 2013, pp. 89–94 (2013)

23. Mayer, P., Velasco, J., Klarl, A., Hennicker, R., Puviani, M., Tiezzi, F., Pugliese, R., Keznikl, J., Bureš, T.: The Autonomic Cloud. In: Wirsing, M., Hölzl, M., Koch, N., Mayer, P. (eds.) Software Engineering for Collective Autonomic Systems. LNCS, vol. 8998, pp. 495–512. Springer, Heidelberg (2015)

24. Monreale, G.V., Montanari, U., Hoch, N.: Soft Constraint Logic Programming for Electric Vehicle Travel Optimization. CoRR abs/1212.2056 (2012)

25. De Nicola, R., Latella, D., Lafuente, A.L., Loreti, M., Margheri, A., Massink, M., Morichetta, A., Pugliese, R., Tiezzi, F., Vandin, A.: The SCEL Language: Design, Implementation, Verification. In: Wirsing, M., Hölzl, M., Koch, N., Mayer, P. (eds.) Software Engineering for Collective Autonomic Systems. LNCS, vol. 8998, pp. 3–71. Springer, Heidelberg (2015)

26. Pinciroli, C., Bonani, M., Mondada, F., Dorigo, M.: Adaptation and Awareness in Robot Ensembles: Scenarios and Algorithms. In: Wirsing, M., Hölzl, M., Koch, N., Mayer, P. (eds.) Software Engineering for Collective Autonomic Systems. LNCS, vol. 8998, pp. 471–494. Springer, Heidelberg (2015)

27. Pinciroli, C., Trianni, V., O'Grady, R., Pini, G., Brutschy, A., Brambilla, M., Mathews, N., Ferrante, E., Caro, G.D., Ducatelle, F., Stirling, T.S., Gutiérrez, Á., Gambardella, L.M., Dorigo, M.: ARGoS: A modular, multi-engine simulator for heterogeneous swarm robotics. In: IROS, pp. 5027–5034. IEEE Computer Society Press, Los Alamitos (2011)

28. Serbedzija, N., Mayer, P., Klarl, A.: Constructing Autonomous Systems: Major Development Phases. International Journal on Advances in Intelligent Systems 6(4) (December 2013)

29. Serbedzija, N.: Constructing Autonomous Multi-Robot System. In: The Third International Conference on Intelligent Systems and Applications, Sevilla, Spain (June 2013)

30. Serbedzija, N., Bures, T., Keznikl, J.: Engineering Autonomous Systems. In: PCI'13 Proceedings of the 17th Panhellenic Conference on Informatics, Thessaloniki, Greece, September 2013, pp. 128–135 (2013)

31. Vassev, E., Hinchey, M.: Autonomy Requirements Engineering. IEEE Computer 46(8), 82–84 (2013)

32. Vassev, E., Hinchey, M.: Knowledge Representation for Adaptive and Self-aware Systems. In: Wirsing, M., Hölzl, M., Koch, N., Mayer, P. (eds.) Software Engineering for Collective Autonomic Systems. LNCS, vol. 8998, pp. 221–247. Springer, Heidelberg (2015)

33. Wirsing, M., Hölzl, M., Koch, N., Mayer, P. (eds.): Software Engineering for Collective Autonomic Systems. LNCS, vol. 8998. Springer, Heidelberg (2015)

34. Yamins, D.: Towards a theory of local to global in distributed multi-agent systems (i). In: Kudenko, D., Kazakov, D., Alonso, E. (eds.) AAMAS 2004, pp. 183–190. ACM Press, New York (2005)

35. Zimory Software: Zimory Cloud Suite (August 2014), http://www.zimory.com/

CHAPTER IV.2

Adaptation and Awareness in Robot Ensembles: Scenarios and Algorithms[*]

Carlo Pinciroli[1], Michael Bonani[2], Francesco Mondada[3], and Marco Dorigo[1]

[1] Université Libre de Bruxelles, Belgium
[2] Association Mobsya, Switzerland
[3] École Polytechnique Fédérale de Lausanne, Switzerland

Abstract. This chapter presents a disaster recovery scenario that has been used throughout the ASCENS project as a reference to coordinate the study of distributed algorithms for robot ensembles. We first introduce the main traits and open problems in the design of behaviors for robot ensembles. We then present the scenario, highlighting its generality as a framework to compare algorithms and methodologies for distributed robotics. Subsequently, we summarize the main results of the research conducted in ASCENS that used the scenario. Finally, we describe an example algorithm that solves a selected problem in the scenario. The algorithm demonstrates how awareness at the ensemble level can be obtained without requiring awareness at the individual level.

Keywords: swarm robotics, mobile robotics, autonomous robotics

1 Introduction

Large multi-robot systems (*robot swarms*) [2] have the potential to display desirable properties, such as robustness to individual failures through redundancy, and enhanced performance through parallelism and cooperation [11,20]. Realizing such potential is challenging because of the lack of sound design methodologies [5].

In the literature, coordination among multiple robots has been achieved in several ways. Existing approaches span from complete centralization to complete decentralization, with hybrid centralized-decentralized systems in between. With complete centralization, a master system must collect the data from the robots, analyze it and send the actions to perform to each robot. In many applications, the advantages of this approach do not counterbalance its drawbacks. Although centralized control is usually simpler to design and can result in a globally optimized behavior, it suffers from poor robustness (the master system is a single point of failure) and poor scalability (the master system's CPU and network connectivity are shared resources), and it requires global sensing and communication (which is not always available).

[*] This research was supported by the European project IP 257414 (ASCENS).

M. Wirsing et al. (eds.): Collective Autonomic Systems, LNCS 8998, pp. 471–494, 2015.
© Springer International Publishing Switzerland 2015

In contrast, completely distributed coordination algorithms do not exploit any kind of master system, global knowledge, or planning. Instead, coordination is the result of the parallel pairwise interactions of the system's components. Completely distributed coordination algorithms achieve scalability through local sensing and communication, and achieve robustness and high performance by leveraging the natural parallelism and redundancy of the system. However, it is very hard to design effective coordination algorithms of this kind [10].

To date, the design of swarm robotics systems follows two general types of approaches: behavior-based and automatic methods. Behavior-based methods [1] are typically bottom-up design methods whereby the designer gradually refines the individual robot behaviors until the desired global (i.e., ensemble-level) behavior is achieved. The results obtained with behavior-based methods strongly depend on the experience and ingenuity of the designer. The lack of methodologies above mentioned is partially circumvented by taking inspiration from models of biological systems that display some form of *swarm intelligence* [3,13], such as colonies of ants, bees and termites. However, the complexity currently achieved by these methods is limited, and very far from that of the natural models which inspire the design.

In automatic methods, such as reinforcement learning [36] evolutionary robotics [28], and optimization-based approaches [15], the individual robot behavior is regulated by a set of parameters that are set by a suitable algorithm. These methods allow the designer to focus efforts more on the task to solve, rather than on the individual robot behavior. However, the performance of these methods is known to scale poorly with the complexity of the task to solve and of the robot interactions.

A promising approach to the design of swarm robotics systems is a combination of behavior-based (compositional, pattern-based) aspects and automatic procedures (not restricted to optimization methods). The work in the ASCENS project followed the line of research that leads to the definition of such a combined approach.

In this chapter, we describe the research activities we conducted to apply the ASCENS concepts to state-of-the-art problems in swarm robotics. These activities involved two primary tasks:

1. The definition of a class of application scenarios that provides sufficient complexity to motivate the ASCENS research;
2. The development of algorithms that solve selected problems in the application scenario, in order to nurture and showcase ASCENS techniques and tools.

This chapter is structured as follows. In Section 2, we discuss the mapping of the concept of service component ensemble to robot swarms, introduce the robotic platform employed for experimentation, and present the scenario and its variants. In Section 3, we discuss awareness and adaptation in robot swarms, illustrating the work we made throughout the project. In Section 4 we present two algorithms that demonstrate some of the concepts studied in ASCENS. We conclude the paper in Section 5, summarizing our work and proposing ideas for future investigation.

2   Scenario: Disaster Recovery

In this section, we present the application scenario on which we based the robotics case study. In Section 2.1 we discuss the mapping between the concepts of *service component ensemble* and *robot swarms*. In Section 2.2 we present the robotic platform we employed for the work in this case study. In Section 2.3 we provide a general description of the scenario. In Section 2.4 we illustrate the possible variants of the robotics scenario.

2.1   Robot Swarms as Service Component Ensembles

Robots swarms can be cast as *service component ensembles* in several ways, depending on the focus of the designer.

A first approach is to consider a single robot as a service component and robot swarms as service component ensembles. In this case, the design neglects the internals of the robot, which becomes a black box that exposes a set of functionalities. The focus of the design is set on the coordination of the robot swarm as a whole and on the correctness of the individual actions with respect to a common goal.

Alternatively, one might represent a single robot as a distributed system composed of a collection of microprocessors. Each microprocessor is responsible for the control of a subset of the available devices. To achieve coordination, the microprocessors communicate. Under this light, in ASCENS parlance each microprocessor is a service component, and a robot is a service component ensemble. Robot swarms, in turn, become *ensembles of service component ensembles*. Thus, the focus of the design spans two layers: at the lower layer, the design must ensure that each robot device behaves correctly; at the higher layer, the common goal of the swarm must be achieved.

The choice between these two approaches is ultimately dictated by the requirements of the algorithm under development. Considering individual robots as SCEs does not fit the scope of the ASCENS project, in that SC do not join or leave the system dynamically. Moreover, this approach increases considerably the complexity of system design and analysis. Thus, for the purposes of the ASCENS project, we chose to limit our scope to the first approach—considering single robots as service components. In this way, we could target the most interesting aspects of ensemble coordination directly.

A particularly important aspect for ASCENS is the fact that robot swarms possess a dual nature. Being physical objects acting in an environment, robots can be modeled through classical mechanics as bodies interacting through forces (e.g. motion, collisions, assembly, transport). At the same time, a robot swarm can be seen as a classical communication network, in which robots exchange messages to achieve coordination.

This dual nature of robot swarms affects every phase of the ensemble development life cycle. Requirement specification, for instance, might include statements regarding the correctness of the swarm state throughout an experiment. Such statement might include spatial aspects, such as moving while maintaining a cohesive formation (also known as *flocking* [30]), as well as network aspects, such as achieving consensus on the direction to follow. By the same token, modeling might need to consider the position of each robot at any time during an experiment (space), as well as the opinion of each robot on the direction to follow (network) [32].

The duality of robot swarms is apparent also in the so-called *global-to-local* problem [39,40]. The goals of a swarm, as well as its properties, are typically expressed and analyzed at the global (i.e., swarm) level. However, the actions that realize the dynamics of a swarm are executed at the local level (i.e., by each robot individually). A principled methodology to map local actions to global properties is currently an open problem, for which research is ongoing [10,16,34,19].

The design of the robotics scenario for ASCENS follows these considerations. The primary aim of the scenario was to expose the ASCENS researchers to complex, real-world problems for which partial or no solutions exist today.

2.2   The marXbot Robot

The marXbot [4] is a mobile robot developed during the Swarmanoid project [12] and the ASCENS project.[4] The marXbot is equipped with several devices that allow it to sense and act in the environment. The marXbot's modular architecture renders it easy to add new devices and configure the robot to suit the needs of particular experiments.

Lower Module. The marXbot is a non-holonomic, differential-drive robot equipped with a combination of wheels and tracks named *treels*. The treels allow the marXbot to move on mildly rough terrain while maintaining good stability. A ring of 24 equally-spaced infrared sensors placed around the lower module of the robot body double as *proximity sensors* and *light sensors*. Through these sensors, the marXbot can be programmed to avoid close obstacles and to detect the direction to a light source. The lower module also offers two sets of *ground sensors*. The first set is composed of 4 sensors located close to the treel motors, which allow the marXbot to detect 255 levels of gray on the ground. The second set, composed of 8 sensors intertwined with the infrared sensors, provides the robot with binary information to detect the presence or absence of holes on the ground.

LED-Gripper Module. Above the lower module, the marXbot houses a multipurpose module. It is designed to allow two marXbots to dock into each other

---

[4] The robot is also called *foot-bot* to highlight its capabilities with respect to the other Swarmanoid robots, the *hand-bot* and the *eye-bot*.

Fig. 1. The marXbot robot is a modular robot that can be configured to suit the needs of the experimenter. License: Creative Commons 3.0.

to form complex multi-robot assemblies. To this aim, the module is composed of a gripper designed to lock inside the same module of a kin robot. The gripper can be rotated freely around the yaw axis of the robot, making it possible for complex assemblies to move while connected. Another important feature of this module is the presence of 8 RGB LED embedded in the module frame. The color of each LED can be set independently and is detectable through the cameras. With these LEDs, a robot can convey its state or encode directional information for other robots.

Range-and-Bearing Module. The *range-and bearing communication system* [33] is located above the LED-gripper module. This device allows two marXbots to exchange 12 bytes of data every 100 ms. The particularity of this device is that each robot, upon receipt of a message, also detects the location (distance and angle) of the message sender with respect to its own reference frame. This device realizes the notion of *situated communication*, an important communication modality to achieve coordination in swarm systems [35].

Distance Scanner Module. The marXbot also offers a *long-range rotating distance scanner*, which can be used to map the surroundings and to localize the robot in a static environment [25].

Top Module. The top module equips the marXbot with two cameras: *(i)* an *omni-directional camera*, whose images are analyzed to detect colored blobs around the robot; and *(ii)* a *perspective camera*, that can be oriented frontally or towards the ceiling to detect objects. The top module also offers a *beacon*, a high-power RGB LED that can be used in combination with the cameras to highlight the position of a robot and convey its state through specific colors. Finally, the top module is also home to the Linux board of the robot, equipped with a 512 MHz ARM7 processor and 256 Mb of RAM.

2.3   General Scenario Description

The application scenario can be summarized as *disaster recovery*. We imagine that a disaster happened, such as the catastrophic failure of a nuclear plant, or a major fire in a large building. We also imagine that an activity of search-and-rescue must be performed. For instance, people may be trapped inside the building and they must be found and brought to safety. Given the high danger of operating in such environment, it is realistic to think that an ensemble of robots could be used to perform the most dangerous activities. Among these activities, two are the focus of our attention: exploring the environment and finding targets to rescue.

The screenshot in Figure 2 depicts an instantiation of the essential elements of the scenario. The environment is a large rectangular area structured by several walls. The victims to find are scattered throughout the environment. For the purposes of the ASCENS project, there was no real need to design a specific object to be retrieved. Thus, we used a marXbot that we suppose unable to move. This choice enabled us to test variants of the scenario in which the object is able to signal its location to nearby robots, and variants in which the object is completely passive. The robots are initially deployed in the *deployment area* marked in gray in Figure 2.

An important constraint is the fact that robots possess limited battery lifetime. The exhaustion of battery power is as critical an hazard as exposure to radiations. In fact, in low battery power conditions, various sensors tend to provide noisy or wrong readings, which in turn affect a robot's performance. The complete exhaustion of battery power is equivalent to the loss of a robot.

2.4   Parameters

The scenario can be formalized in a matrix of parametric activities with "tunable" complexity as illustrated in Table 1. Within ASCENS, the aim of such complexity matrix was not to enumerate the entire set of possibilities we intended to tackle—such set is too wide and general to be studied realistically. Rather, complexity tuning enabled us to isolate the relevant aspects of a certain problem, and develop new algorithms in a manageable, step-by-step process whereby further complexity was introduced gradually. In the following, we present the main features of the complexity matrix.

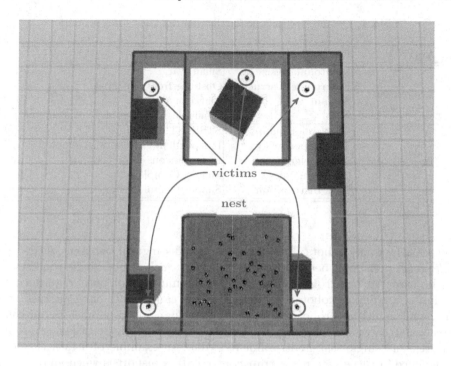

Fig. 2. The environment in which we studied collective exploration. Screenshot taken with the ARGoS robot simulator.

Exploration. To rescue the victims, the robots must first find them. Exploration serves this purpose. Exploration complexity depends on a number of factors related to the environment. Depending on the number of robots, a small environment is easier to navigate than a large one. Navigation is also easier in an obstacle-free environment than in a cluttered one. Typically, in a small, obstacle-free environment the best exploration strategy is diffusion through random walk. In a large, maze-like environment, more complex strategies are necessary. Analogously, navigation is simpler on a flat terrain than on a rough one. Another important aspect is whether the robots can exploit a map of the environment or not. The easiest situation is when a map is available beforehand. In this case, the robots can use this information to locate themselves and the interesting points in the environment, making navigation easier. Alternatively, a map could be constructed during the experiment through SLAM (simultaneous localization and mapping) techniques. The third and most challenging option is that the robots do not possess nor construct a map, but navigate in a cooperative way. An algorithm demonstrating the latter option is presented in Section 4.

Task Allocation. Task allocation is the activity of assigning robots to specific tasks [17]. In this scenario, tasks can be manifold. For instance, some robots could be explorers, other transporters. Transport, in turn, could require co-

Table 1. Complexity matrix for the robotics case study scenario

Activity	Parameter	Alternatives
Exploration	Environment size	Small/Large
	Environment structure	Obstacle-free/Cluttered
	Terrain	Flat/Rough
	Map	Available/Computable/Not available
Task allocation	Task-robot mapping	STSR/STMR
	Task dependency	Independent/Sequential/Complex
	Task assignment	Instantaneous/Time-extended
	Task dynamics	Simple/Complex
	Task distribution	Simple/Complex

operation by many robots. In general, we can distinguish between *single-* and *multi-robot tasks*, and between *single-* and *multi-task robots*. Single-robot tasks can be executed by a robot individually, while multi-robot tasks require cooperation of a group of robots. Single-task robots can execute only one task at a time, while multi-task robots execute more than one in parallel. In our complexity matrix, we consider only the following two cases: single-task-single-robot (STSR), and single-task-multi-robot (STMR). An example of a task that can be declined in these variants is transport. STSR transport is when an object is light enough for a robot to move it. If the object requires many robots to move it, transport is STMR. Furthermore, in a realistic scenario, tasks may possess activation dynamics, i.e., each task must be executed in certain time periods [8]. We can model this by defining a function $T_i(t)$ such that its value over time t is 1 when task $i \in [1, K]$ is active, and 0 otherwise. In general, $T_i(t)$ takes the form of a square wave function, i.e., a task undergoes periods of activation and periods of de-activation. Task activation periods can be correlated to each other, for instance when some tasks are dependent on other tasks (e.g., task i must be executed before task j). Furthermore, assignment of tasks to robots can be *time-extended* or *instantaneous*. In time-extended assignment, $T_i(t)$ (or an approximation of it) is assumed known and tasks are assigned to robots according to a pre-calculated schedule. Instantaneous assignment refers to methods in which $T_i(t)$ is not known. Another important aspect in task allocation is the distribution of tasks in the environment. Task distribution has consequences on the efficiency of task discovery and execution by the robots. Task distribution is linked to the organization of the environment, i.e., how cluttered or structured the environment is. When dealing with robot swarms, in general a task must be executed by a certain number of robots, called *quota*. In practical problems, quotas are rarely precise. For example, moving a heavy object requires a minimum number of robots to compensate for the object weight. Employing more robots usually results in better performance (i.e., the object is transported faster or with less effort by the robots' motors). However, above a certain number of robots, coordination becomes an issue that negatively impacts performance. Therefore, typically quotas can be expressed as ranges [min,max].

3   The Robotics Scenario and the EDLC

The Ensemble Development Life Cycle (EDCL) introduced in Chapter III.1 [22] is composed of several phases. In this section, we report on the main findings regarding each phase. A case study relating several phases can be found in [38].

3.1   Requirement Engineering

Property-Driven Design. As explained in Section 2.1, the dynamics of a robot ensemble comprises two levels—the ensemble level and the individual level. The requirements are typically expressed at the ensemble level, but the mechanisms that realize the wanted behavior are executed at the individual level. A natural approach to reconcile the two levels is to work in step-by-step fashion, gradually refining the ensemble requirements by expressing them in more detailed forms that, eventually, lead to a practical implementation. This idea is the core of the work of Brambilla *et al.* [6], who demonstrated their approach on typical swarm behaviors such as aggregation and foraging.

Engineering Self-organization and Emergence. In Chapter III.2 [27], Noël and Zambonelli illustrate a number of methodological guidelines to engineer the basic self-organization mechanisms that lead to coordinated ensemble behaviors. The author demonstrate their approach through a variant of the scenario in which the robots must spread in an unknown environment and find victims.

3.2   Modeling/Programming and Verificaton/Validation

SCEL Modelling. In Chapter I.1 [26], De Nicola *et al.* present a complete SCEL model of a scenario variant in which robots must find and rescue victims. The robots can take the role of *explorers* or *rescuers*. Explorers search for victims; when a robot detects a victim, it becomes a rescuer. A rescuer, beside assisting a victim, informs other robots of the victim's position, thus attracting more rescuers. The SCEL model considers also the possibility that the battery charge reaches a low level, in which case the robots pause their activity and turn to the battery charging state. The authors describe two models: one based on PSCEL (a SCEL variant which includes *policies*), and one based on StocS (a stochastic extension of the SCEL semantics).

jRESP Implementation. In Chapter I.1 [26], De Nicola *et al.* also describe an implementation of the SCEL model in the jRESP framework, a Java run-time environment that realizes the SCEL paradigm. The remarkable aspect of this exercise is that the primitive concepts of jRESP closely resemble those of SCEL. Thus, through jRESP, an abstract model of a distributed algorithm for robotics can find a direct, practical implementation whose performance can be studied and characterized. In fact, jRESP programs can be simulated and analyzed through a statistical model checker. De Nicola *et al.* report the results of such an analysis on the robotics scenario, studying the probability that a victim is rescued within a given time using different numbers of robots.

Maude Implementation. Another contribution of Chapter I.1 [26] is an analysis of a specific aspect of the scenario modeled in SCEL through a tool called MISSCEL (Maude Interpreter and Simulator for SCEL). MISSCEL is an implementation of SCEL in the Maude framework, a software for model checking. De Nicola *et al.* focus on collision avoidance, a basic behavior the robots perform while exploring the environment. In particular, they analyze the efficiency of collision avoidance when the robots are informed (i.e., can use the proximity sensors) and uninformed (i.e., they choose their direction at random).

Physics-Based Modeling and Implementation. A common technique to study behaviors in robotics is employing physics-based simulation. The advantage of this kind of simulation is the close resemblance of the simulated system dynamics with respect to its real counterpart. Physics-based simulation typically include every relevant aspect that affects the behavior of the robot ensemble—body collisions, network communication errors, etc. For the work in ASCENS, we employed the ARGoS multi-robot simulator [31], a state-of-the-art software capable of accurately simulating experiments involving thousands of robots in a fraction of real time. An example experiment developed with ARGoS is presented in Section 4.

SMC-BIP Verification. In Chapter I.3 [9], Combaz *et al.* present an approach to the verification of distributed robot behaviors based on the BIP statistical model checker. The main advantage of BIP over other modeling techniques is that BIP models can be transformed into executable programs *automatically*, making it possible to link modeling and implementation seamlessly. The authors model the scenario variant described in detail in Section 4, analyzing the effects of several alternatives for each robot behavior on the overall system performance.

3.3   Awareness and Adaptation

The notion of *awareness* and *adaptation* in robot swarms can manifest themselves at the individual level and at the ensemble level. For the purposes of ASCENS, our primary focus is modeling and achieving ensemble-level awareness and adaptation. However, the two levels are deeply intertwined—a study of ensemble awareness/adaptation cannot neglect the individual level. *Individual* awareness and adaptation can be defined as the ability of the robot to estimate its own state, as well as a relevant portion of the ensemble state, and react effectively to state changes. By *relevant portion*, here we mean that the robot must be capable of retrieving enough information about the ensemble state to make decisions leading to correct ensemble behaviors. *Ensemble* awareness and adaptation refer to the capability of the ensemble to behave as a coherent unit, by distributing information correctly and acting in a coordinated fashion.

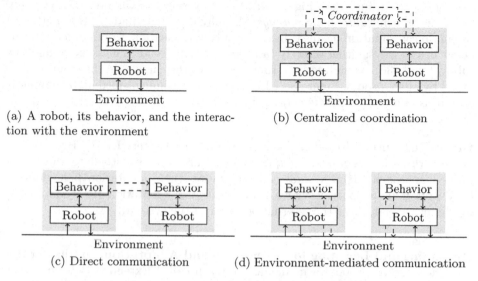

(a) A robot, its behavior, and the interaction with the environment

(b) Centralized coordination

(c) Direct communication

(d) Environment-mediated communication

Fig. 3. Coordination patterns for groups of robots. The solid lines indicate generic interactions among entities. The dashed lines indicate coordination-aimed interactions among entities.

The relationship between the individual and the ensemble levels is complex For instance, a high degree of individual awareness is not required to produce complex ensemble behaviors which display high degrees of awareness [24]. Research on social insects show that individuals following simple rules based on short-range information about the environment are capable of highly complex and efficient behaviors such as nest construction and food foraging. The algorithm described in Section 4 is an example of an individual behavior based on short-range information and little individual awareness that result in a complex ensemble behavior.

Adaptation Patterns. In the robotics case study, each individual robot is considered as a Service Component (SC). Each SC is associated to a program that controls its actions, here referred to as *behavior* (see Figure 3a). Groups of connected robots (physically or networked) form Service Component Ensembles. To achieve adaptation in robot ensembles, we identify four general patterns. These adaptation patterns can be expressed following the approach described in Chapter III.1 [22] for the mapping between SCs and autonomic managers. In this context, the robots are *proactive service components*, and the concept of robot behavior coincides with that of *internal autonomic manager*. The adaptation patterns can be classified into two general categories: *(i)* patterns that include an element of centralization, and *(ii)* fully distributed patterns. In patterns that include an element of centralization, such element is typically meant as dedicated SCs that collect information from the robot SCE, make decisions, and instruct the robots accordingly (see Figure 3b). In the approach of Chapter III.1 [22] this SC is an *external autonomic manager*. In fully distributed adaptation patterns, the main coordination means is inter-robot communication. Communication can occur in two ways: either directly (a robot explicitly sends a message to another robot, Figure 3c), or indirectly (a robot reacts to the changes in the environment made by other robots, Figure 3d). Indirect, or environment-mediated communication, is also known as *stigmergy* [18].

Black-Box and White-Box Adaptation. In Chapter II.1 [7], Bruni *et al.* employ the robotics scenario depicted in Figure 2 as a testbed to validate a unified approach to both *black-box* adaptation (i.e., adaptation behaviors as they appear to an outside viewer) and *white-box* adaptation (i.e., adaptation mechanisms that affect the internal behavior of the system).

Reasoning and Learning for Awareness and Adaptation. In Chapter II.4 [21], Hölzl *et al.* propose a modeling approach called Extended Behavior Trees (XBTs). This approach targets hierarchical, concurrent behaviors that interleave reasoning, learning, and actions. XBTs can be translated into SCEL, thus integrating the EDLC and enriching its scope. The approach is validated on a variant of the proposed scenario.

4   Implementation and Demonstration

In this section, we present a fully distributed algorithm for collective exploration. The algorithm works under the assumption that the robots are initially unaware of the whereabouts of the victims and of the structure of the environment. The concepts of awareness and adaptation play a fundamental role in this application.

In terms of awareness, as discussed in Section 3.3, the most important requirement is that the ensemble *as a whole* is capable of representing the current knowledge regarding the structure of the environment. The ultimate purpose of exploration is to allow a second set of robots, the *rescuers*, to reach the victims that need assistance.

To achieve this result, one could endow each robot with an algorithm for simultaneous localization and mapping (SLAM) [37] and let the robots integrate each others' maps through communication. With this approach, the representation of the whole environment is a composition of the individual representations of each robot. While this approach is effective, it requires adequate sensing and computation capabilities on the robots, which are mostly lacking on the marXbot. Moreover, this approach does not target the intrinsically *distributed* nature of the systems we studied throughout the project—in principle, a robot could solve the exploration task alone, given sufficient time and resources.

In this section we focus on an alternative solution, in which the robots construct a coherent collective representation of the environment without requiring

(a) An explorer robot   (b) Victims are simulated with robots

Fig. 4. The robots involved in the exploration scenario. Screenshot taken with the ARGoS robot simulator.

SLAM capabilities. In terms of awareness, this algorithm demonstrates how little (or even zero) individual awareness can result in effective and coherent ensemble awareness.

4.1 Scenario Instantiation

The scenario consists of a structured environment of width W and depth D, initially unknown to the robots. As reported in Figure 2, the structure of the environment mimics that of a building floor. A team of R robots called *explorers* (Figure 4a) is deployed in a special area called the *nest* within the environment. The size of the nest is always assumed sufficient to house the entire explorer ensemble.

We imagine that a number V of victims (Fig. 4b) are scattered throughout the environment and must be found by the robots. The robots construct a representation of the environment such that a second robot ensemble, the *rescuers*, can promptly reach the victims.

4.2 Algorithm Structure

The core idea behind the algorithm is to employ the robots as *landmarks*. A landmark robot occupies a specific location of the environment and maintains communication with a number of immediate neighboring landmarks. Upon receipt of a request for direction to a specific victim by a wandering robot, two situations can occur:

1. The landmark can see the victim directly: in this case, the landmark sends the direction to the victim;
2. The landmark cannot see the victim: in this case, the landmark propagates the request to its neighbors, and then picks the shortest suggested path.

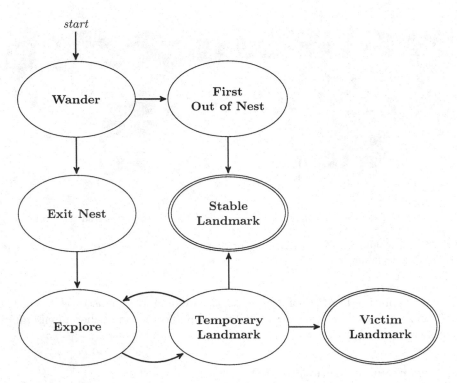

Fig. 5. A finite state machine representation of the exploration algorithm. Double-bordered nodes represent final behaviors, i.e., behaviors after which no further transition is possible.

The algorithm presented here concentrates on the creation of the network of landmarks and is inspired to the approach of Nouyan *et al.* [29]. For an algorithm that uses the landmark network to guide robots to their destination, see Ducatelle *et al.* [14].

A diagrammatic representation of the algorithm is reported in Fig. 5, while the main phases of a typical execution of this behavior are illustrated in Figure 6. In the rest of this section, we will present the main behaviors along with a snippet of their implementation in the Lua language.

Wander. The robots are initially deployed in the nest. Their first task is to find the exit of this area, which leads to the environment to explore. This first behavior makes the robot navigate randomly following an adapted version of the diffusion algorithm of Howard *et al.* [23]. To facilitate the detection of the nest exit, we color-coded the ground. The nest ground is gray, while the rest of the environment is white. Through its ground sensors, a marXbot can monitor the floor color, thus detecting when it exits the nest.

```
function rescuer:wander()
  -- State transition logic
  if rescuer:should_exit() then
    -- The robot should exit the nest because there is
    -- a landmark nearby, or because other robots are
    -- already exiting
    rescuer:switch_to_exiting()
    return
  end
  -- If we get here, the robot is out of the nest, nobody
  -- else is exiting, and no landmark is nearby
  if rescuer:is_out_of_nest() then
    -- The robot just exited the nest
    -- It's the first, so become a landmark
    rescuer:set_state(RESCUER_STATE__FIRST_LANDMARK,
                 rescuer.first_landmark)
    return
  end
  -- State logic
  -- Get vector to escape from obstacles
  local repulsion = rescuer:repulsion_vector()
  if(repulsion.x * repulsion.x +
     repulsion.y*repulsion.y > 0.001) then
    rescuer:vector_to_wheel_velocity_noscale(repulsion)
  else
    robot.wheels.set_velocity(5,5)
  end
end
```

First Out of Nest. A robot switches to this behavior when its ground sensors detect white and no robot in range is in this behavior nor in any landmark-related behaviors. When a robot is in this behavior, it keeps moving for a few seconds to free space in front of the nest exit. Subsequently, the robot switches to **Stable Landmark**. It is not strictly necessary to ensure that a single robot is the 'first out of nest'. The probability that more than one robot follow this behavior is related to the ease with which a robot can find the exit of the nest (e.g., the width of the exit, the initial position and the sensor range of the robot).

```
function rescuer:first_landmark()
  -- State transition logic
  rescuer.counter = rescuer.counter + 1
  -- If 15 seconds have expired, become landmark
  if rescuer.counter > 150 then
    -- Become a stable landmark
    rescuer:set_state(RESCUER_STATE__STABLE_LANDMARK,
                      rescuer.stable_landmark)
    rescuer.landmark_data.mark = 1
    -- Stop the robot
    robot.wheels.set_velocity(0,0)
```

```
    -- Change LED color to green, for visual confirmation
    robot.leds.set_all_colors("green")
    -- Set the mark for the current landmark
    robot.range_and_bearing.
      set_data(3, rescuer.landmark_data.mark)
    robot.debug.message = robot.debug.message .. "(1)"
    return
  end
  -- State logic
  -- Just keep going straight
  robot.wheels.set_velocity(5,5)
end
```

Stable Landmark. A stable landmark is a robot that occupies a specific location of the environment and acts as a node in the communication network. A stable landmark receives requests for direction, propagates them to neighbors, and returns an answer to the robot which issued the request. For the purposes of this algorithm, once a robot has become a stable landmark, it simply acts as a beacon signalling its own position.

Exit Nest. The robots that are following the **Wandering** behavior close to the nest exit detect when the first stable landmark appears. Upon detecting this event, a robot switches to the **Exit Nest** behavior. In this behavior, the robot propagates the information about the direction to the exit throughout its neighbors. In this way, the robots that cannot detect the first landmark directly are informed of its presence and switch to this behavior as well. To exit the nest, a robot follows the direction to the landmark, if directly visible, or to the closest robot that is aware of such direction. When a robot exits the nest, it switches to the **Explore** behavior.

```
function rescuer:exit_nest()
  -- Buffer for the averaged sum of contributions of exiting
  -- robots nearby
  local exiting = { count = 0, accum = {x = 0, y = 0} }
  -- Buffer for the direction to the closest landmark
  local landmark = {
    direct = false,
    dist = INF_DISTANCE,
    angle = 0 }
  -- The current RAB message being processed
  local msg
  -- Go through RAB messages
  for i=1,#robot.range_and_bearing do
    msg = robot.range_and_bearing[i]
    if (msg.data[2] >= RESCUER_STATE__TEMPORARY_LANDMARK) and
      (msg.range < landmark.dist) then
      -- Landmark detected, and it's the closest so far
```

```
      landmark.dist = msg.range
      landmark.angle = msg.horizontal_bearing
      landmark.direct = true
  elseif msg.data[2] == RESCUER_STATE__EXIT_NEST then
    -- Exiting robot detected
    exiting.count = exiting.count + 1
    -- Calculate distance to landmark of this robot
    local land_dist =
      msg.data[4] + msg.data[3] * 256 + msg.range
    if land_dist < landmark.dist then
      -- Found the robot who knows the closest way to a
      -- landmark
      landmark.dist = land_dist
      landmark.angle = msg.horizontal_bearing
      landmark.direct = false
    end
    -- Calculate the contribution of this robot
    local lj = rescuer:lennard_jones(
      msg.range,
      RESCUER_EXITING_DISTANCE,
      RESCUER_EXITING_GAIN)
    local contr = {
      x = lj * math.cos(msg.horizontal_bearing),
      y = lj * math.sin(msg.horizontal_bearing)
    }
    exiting.accum.x = exiting.accum.x + contr.x
    exiting.accum.y = exiting.accum.y + contr.y
  end
end
-- State transition logic
-- If you can see the landmark directly and you're out
-- of the nest, explore
if landmark.direct and rescuer:is_out_of_nest() then
  rescuer:switch_to_explore()
  return
end
-- State logic
-- Postprocess the data collected
-- Take the average of the exiting robot interaction
if (exiting.count > 1) then
  exiting.accum.x = exiting.accum.x / exiting.count
  exiting.accum.y = exiting.accum.y / exiting.count
end
-- Calculate the LJ interaction to the landmark
local landmark_contr = { x = 0, y = 0 }
if landmark.dist < INF_DISTANCE then
  magnitude = 2
  if landmark.dist < 1.5 * RAB_RANGE then
    magnitude = rescuer:lennard_jones(
      landmark.dist,
```

```
          RESCUER_LANDMARK_DISTANCE ,
          RESCUER_LANDMARK_GAIN )
  end
  landmark_contr.x = magnitude * math.cos(landmark.angle)
  landmark_contr.y = magnitude * math.sin(landmark.angle)
  -- Send around the closest direction to landmark known
  robot.range_and_bearing.set_data(3, landmark.dist / 256)
  robot.range_and_bearing.set_data(4, landmark.dist % 256)
else
  robot.range_and_bearing.set_data(3, 256)
  robot.range_and_bearing.set_data(4, 256)
end
-- Calculate the direction
local direction = {
  x = exiting.accum.x + landmark_contr.x,
  y = exiting.accum.y + landmark_contr.y
}
-- Actuate wheels
rescuer:vector_to_wheel_velocity_scale(direction)
end
```

Explore. A robot in this behavior performs random walk in the environment. While wandering, the robot keeps track of the closest landmark detected. If the distance to this landmark becomes too high (i.e., more than 80% of the maximum range of the range-and-bearing system), the exploring robot stops and becomes a **Temporary Landmark**.

```
function rescuer:explore()
  -- State transition logic
  if rescuer:is_out_of_nest() then
    -- Get the landmarks around
    local landmarks = rescuer:landmarks_in_range()
    if landmarks then
      -- Get the data of the closest landmark
      local dist = RAB_RANGE
      local marker
      local is_victim_landmark = false
      for i = 1, #landmarks do
        if landmarks[i].range < dist then
          dist = landmarks[i].range
          marker = landmarks[i].data[3]
          is_victim_landmark =
            (landmarks[i].data[2] ==
             RESCUER_STATE__VICTIM_LANDMARK)
        end
      end
      -- Are we getting too far from the closest?
      if (not is_victim_landmark) and
        (dist > 0.8 * RAB_RANGE) then
```

```
        -- The closest landmark is getting too far
        -- Become a landmark!
        rescuer:become_landmark(marker)
        return
      end
    end
  else
    -- Explorer got back to the nest
    -- Switch back to exiting state
    rescuer:switch_to_exiting()
    return
  end
  -- State logic
  -- Wander in the environment
  local repulsion = rescuer:repulsion_vector()
  if(repulsion.x * repulsion.x +
     repulsion.y * repulsion.y > 0.001) then
    rescuer:vector_to_wheel_velocity_noscale(repulsion)
  else
    robot.wheels.set_velocity(5,5)
  end
end
```

Temporary Landmark. When a robot switches to this behavior, it stops its motion and waits for a few seconds while monitoring the environment for other nearby landmarks. If a nearby landmark is located and is too close, the robot switches back **Explore**. Otherwise, at the end of the monitoring period, the robot switches to **Stable Landmark** or **Victim Landmark**, depending on whether a victim is visible or not. The rationale for this behavior is to optimize the diffusion of landmarks across the environment. The motion of explorers around a temporary landmark might hide (for a short period) the presence of other stable landmarks; the monitoring period is designed to allow the robot to collect information and discover nearby landmarks despite the motion of the explorers.

```
function rescuer:temporary_landmark()
  -- Increase counter
  rescuer.counter = rescuer.counter + 1
  -- Switch green LEDs depending on how far we are from
  -- making a decision
  if (rescuer.counter %
      RESCUER_TEMPORARY_PROGRESS_PERIOD) == 0 then
    robot.leds.set_single_color(
      rescuer.counter / RESCUER_TEMPORARY_PROGRESS_PERIOD ,
      "green")
  end
  -- Collect data
  -- Go through the messages
  if #robot.range_and_bearing > 0 then
```

```
  -- local msg
  for i = 1, #robot.range_and_bearing do
    local msg = robot.range_and_bearing[i]
    if msg.data[1] == ROLE__VICTIM then
      -- Detected a victim in range
      rescuer.landmark_data.victim_nearby = true
    elseif msg.data[2] >=
             RESCUER_STATE__TEMPORARY_LANDMARK then
      -- Detected a landmark in range
      if rescuer.landmark_data.dist_to_closest_landmark >
           msg.range then
        rescuer.landmark_data.
          dist_to_closest_landmark = msg.range
      end
      if msg.data[2] == RESCUER_STATE__VICTIM_LANDMARK then
        rescuer.landmark_data.victim_landmark_nearby = true
      end
    end
  end
end
-- If 10 seconds have expired, make a decision
if rescuer.counter > RESCUER_TEMPORARY_PERIOD then
  if rescuer.landmark_data.victim_nearby and
     (not rescuer.landmark_data.victim_landmark_nearby) then
    -- There's a victim and no victim landmark
    -- Become victim landmark
    rescuer:set_state(RESCUER_STATE__VICTIM_LANDMARK,
                      rescuer.victim_landmark)
    robot.debug.message =
      robot.debug.message .. "(" ..
      rescuer.landmark_data.mark .. ")"
    -- Set the mark for the current landmark
    robot.range_and_bearing.
      set_data(3, rescuer.landmark_data.mark)
  elseif (not rescuer.landmark_data.victim_nearby) and
         (rescuer.landmark_data.dist_to_closest_landmark >
           0.3 * RAB_RANGE) then
    -- No victim around and no landmark is too close
    -- Become a stable landmark
    rescuer:set_state(RESCUER_STATE__STABLE_LANDMARK,
                      rescuer.stable_landmark)
    robot.debug.message =
      robot.debug.message .. "(" ..
      rescuer.landmark_data.mark .. ")"
    -- Set the mark for the current landmark
    robot.range_and_bearing.
      set_data(3, rescuer.landmark_data.mark)
  else
    -- Either there's both a victim nearby and a victim
    -- landmark, or there's no victim but a landmark is too
    -- close. Either case, go back exploring
```

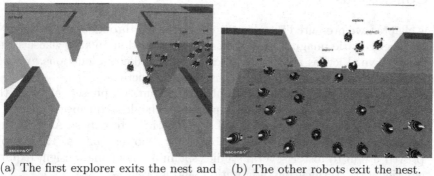

(a) The first explorer exits the nest and (b) The other robots exit the nest.
becomes a stable landmark.

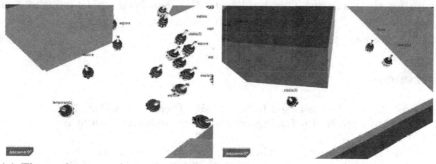

(c) The explorers navigate the environ-(d) Explorers that are close to a victim
ment, occasionally becoming stable land-become victim landmarks.
marks.

Fig. 6. The essential phases of the exploration behavior. Screenshots taken with the ARGoS robot simulator

```
      rescuer:switch_to_explore()
    end
  end
end
```

Victim Landmark. When a robot is eligible to become a stable landmark, it checks for the presence of nearby victims. If at least a victim is detected, the robot becomes a victim landmark. This behavior is similar to a stable landmark in that a robot becomes part of the communication network, receiving and replying requests from the rescuers. However, the role of a victim landmark is to act as the leaf node of the network when the direction to a victim in range is requested. For the purposes of this algorithm, once a robot has become a victim landmark, it simply acts as a beacon signalling its own position.

5   Conclusions

In this chapter, we presented the robotics scenario used throughout the ASCENS project. The scenario imagines that a disaster happened in an area whose structure is unknown. Victims are assumed scattered at unknown locations. A robot ensemble is deployed to the area and must save the victims.

We decoupled the scenario in a number of parametric phases, allowing the ASCENS researchers to "tune" the complexity of the desired aspects at will.

The choice of this scenario stemmed from the need to expose ASCENS researchers to real-world coordination problems for robot ensembles. These problems proved useful to foster several studies spanning modeling, design, requirement specification, verification, adaptation, and awareness.

We presented an implementation that demonstrates a possible, albeit simple, solution for the scenario. This implementation has been used throughout the project as a reference, allowing researchers to analyze its properties and improve on its limitations.

References

1. Arkin, R.C.: Behavior-Based Robotics. MIT Press, Cambridge (1998)
2. Beni, G.: From Swarm Intelligence to Swarm Robotics. Swarm Robotics 3342, 1–9 (2005)
3. Bonabeau, E., Dorigo, M., Theraulaz, G.: Swarm Intelligence: From Natural to Artificial Systems. Santa Fe Institute Studies in the Sciences of Complexity. Oxford University Press, New York (1999)
4. Bonani, M., Longchamp, V., Magnenat, S., Rétornaz, P., Burnier, D., Roulet, G., Vaussard, F., Bleuler, H., Mondada, F.: The marXbot, a miniature mobile robot opening new perspectives for the collective-robotic research. In: Proceedings of the IEEE/RSJ International Conference on Intelligent Robots and Systems (IROS), pp. 4187–4193. IEEE Press, Piscataway (2010)
5. Brambilla, M., Ferrante, E., Birattari, M., Dorigo, M.: Swarm robotics: a review from the swarm engineering perspective. Swarm Intelligence 7(1), 1–41 (2013)
6. Brambilla, M., Pinciroli, C., Birattari, M., Dorigo, M.: Property-driven design for swarm robotics. In: Proceedings of the 11th International Conference on Autonomous Agents and Multiagent Systems, pp. 139–146. International Foundation for Autonomous Agents and Multiagent Systems (2012)
7. Bruni, R., Corradini, A., Gadducci, F., Hölzl, M., Lafuente, A.L., Vandin, A., Wirsing, M.: Reconciling White-Box and Black-Box Perspectives on Behavioral Self-adaptation. In: Wirsing, M., Hölzl, M., Koch, N., Mayer, P. (eds.) Software Engineering for Collective Autonomic Systems. LNCS, vol. 8998, pp. 163–184. Springer, Heidelberg (2015)
8. Brutschy, A., Pini, G., Pinciroli, C., Birattari, M., Dorigo, M.: Self-organized task allocation to sequentially interdependent tasks in swarm robotics. Autonomous Agents and Multi-Agent Systems 28(1), 101–125 (2014)
9. Combaz, J., Bensalem, S., Tiezzi, F., Margheri, A., Pugliese, R., Kofron, J.: Correctness of Service Components and Service Component Ensembles. In: Wirsing, M., Hölzl, M., Koch, N., Mayer, P. (eds.) Software Engineering for Collective Autonomic Systems. LNCS, vol. 8998, pp. 107–159. Springer, Heidelberg (2015)

10. Crespi, V., Galstyan, A., Lerman, K.: Top-down vs bottom-up methodologies in multi-agent system design. Autonomous Robots 24(3), 303–313 (2008)
11. Dorigo, M., Birattari, M., Brambilla, M.: Swarm robotics. Scholarpedia 9(1), 1463 (2014)
12. Dorigo, M., Floreano, D., Gambardella, L., Mondada, F., Nolfi, S., Baaboura, T., Birattari, M., Bonani, M., Brambilla, M., Brutschy, A., Burnier, D., Campo, A., Christensen, A., Decugnière, A., Di Caro, G., Ducatelle, F., Ferrante, E., Förster, A., Guzzi, J., Longchamp, V., Magnenat, S., Martinez Gonzales, J., Mathews, N., Montes de Oca, M., O'Grady, R., Pinciroli, C., Pini, G., Rétornaz, P., Roberts, J., Sperati, V., Stirling, T., Stranieri, A., Stützle, T., Trianni, V., Tuci, E., Turgut, A., Vaussard, F.: Swarmanoid: a novel concept for the study of heterogeneous robotic swarms. IEEE Robotics & Automation Magazine 20(4), 60–71 (2013)
13. Dorigo, M., Birattari, M.: Swarm intelligence. Scholarpedia 2(9), 1462 (2007)
14. Ducatelle, F., Di Caro, G., Förster, A., Bonani, M., Dorigo, M., Magnenat, S., Mondada, F., O'Grady, R., Pinciroli, C., Rétornaz, P., Trianni, V., Gambardella, L.M.: Cooperative navigation in robotic swarms. Swarm Intelligence 8(1), 1–33 (2014)
15. Francesca, G., Brambilla, M., Brutschy, A., Trianni, V., Birattari, M.: AutoMoDe: A novel approach to the automatic design of control software for robot swarms. Swarm Intelligence, 1–24 (2014)
16. Gazi, V., Fidan, B.: Coordination and control of multi-agent dynamic systems: Models and approaches. In: Şahin, E., Spears, W.M., Winfield, A.F.T. (eds.) SAB 2006. LNCS, vol. 4433, pp. 71–102. Springer, Heidelberg (2007)
17. Gerkey, B.P., Matarić, M.J.: A formal analysis and taxonomy of task allocation in multi-robot systems. The International Journal of Robotics Research 23(9), 939–954 (2004)
18. Grassé, P.: La reconstruction du nid et les coordinations inter-individuelles chez bellicositermes natalensis et cubitermes sp. la théorie de la stigmergie: Essai d'interprétation des termites constructeurs. Insects Sociaux 6, 41–83 (1959)
19. Hamann, H.: Towards swarm calculus: Urn models of collective decisions and universal properties of swarm performance. Swarm Intelligence 7(2-3), 145–172 (2013)
20. Hinchey, M.G., Sterritt, R., Rouff, C.: Swarms and swarm intelligence. Computer 40(4), 111–113 (2007)
21. Hölzl, M., Gabor, T.: Reasoning and Learning for Awareness and Adaptation. In: Wirsing, M., Hölzl, M., Koch, N., Mayer, P. (eds.) Software Engineering for Collective Autonomic Systems. LNCS, vol. 8998, pp. 249–290. Springer, Heidelberg (2015)
22. Hölzl, M., Koch, N., Puviani, M., Wirsing, M., Zambonelli, F.: The Ensemble Development Life Cycle and Best Practices for Collective Autonomic Systems. In: Wirsing, M., Hölzl, M., Koch, N., Mayer, P. (eds.) Software Engineering for Collective Autonomic Systems. LNCS, vol. 8998, pp. 325–354. Springer, Heidelberg (2015)
23. Howard, A., Matarić, M., Sukhatme, G.: Mobile sensor network deployment using potential fields: A distributed, scalable solution to the area coverage problem. In: Proceedings of the International Symposium on Distributed Autonomous Robotic Systems (DARS), pp. 299–308. Springer, New York (2002)
24. Self-organized, M.G.J.C.W.L.T.J.D.R.G.: aggregation without computation. International Journal of Robotics Research 33(8), 1145–1161 (2014)

25. Magnenat, S., Longchamp, V., Bonani, M., Rétornaz, P., Germano, P., Bleuler, H., Mondada, F.: Affordable slam through the co-design of hardware and methodology. In: 2010 IEEE International Conference on Robotics and Automation (ICRA 2010), pp. 5395–5401. IEEE Press, Piscataway (2010)

26. De Nicola, R., Latella, D., Lafuente, A.L., Loreti, M., Margheri, A., Massink, M., Morichetta, A., Pugliese, R., Tiezzi, F., Vandin, A.: The SCEL Language: Design, Implementation, Verification. In: Wirsing, M., Hölzl, M., Koch, N., Mayer, P. (eds.) Software Engineering for Collective Autonomic Systems. LNCS, vol. 8998, pp. 3–71. Springer, Heidelberg (2015)

27. Noël, V., Zambonelli, F.: Methodological Guidelines for Engineering Self-organization and Emergence. In: Wirsing, M., Hölzl, M., Koch, N., Mayer, P. (eds.) Software Engineering for Collective Autonomic Systems. LNCS, vol. 8998, pp. 355–378. Springer, Heidelberg (2015)

28. Nolfi, S., Floreano, D.: Evolutionary robotics. MIT Press, Cambridge (2000)

29. Nouyan, S., Campo, A., Dorigo, M.: Path formation in a robot swarm. Swarm Intelligence 2(1), 1–23 (2008)

30. Olfati-Saber, R.: Flocking for multi-agent dynamic systems: Algorithms and theory. IEEE Transactions on Automatic Control 51(3), 401–420 (2006)

31. Pinciroli, C., Trianni, V., O'Grady, R., Pini, G., Brutschy, A., Brambilla, M., Mathews, N., Ferrante, E., Di Caro, G., Ducatelle, F., Birattari, M., Gambardella, L.M., Dorigo, M.: ARGoS: a modular, parallel, multi-engine simulator for multi-robot systems. Swarm Intelligence 6(4), 271–295 (2012)

32. Ren, W., Beard, R.: Distributed consensus in multi-vehicle cooperative control: theory and applications. Springer, Berlin (2007)

33. Roberts, J., Stirling, T., Zufferey, J.C., Floreano, D.: 2.5d infrared range and bearing system for collective robotics. In: IEEE/RSJ International Conference on Intelligent Robots and Systems (IROS 2009), IEEE Press, Piscataway (2009)

34. Schmickl, T.: How to engineer robotic organisms and swarms? In: Bio-Inspired Self-Organizing Robotic Systems, pp. 25–52. Springer, Berlin (2011)

35. Støy, K.: Using situated communication in distributed autonomous mobile robots. In: Proceedings of the 7th Scandinavian Conference on Artificial Intelligence, pp. 44–52. IOS Press, Amsterdam (2001)

36. Sutton, R.S., Barto, A.G.: Introduction to reinforcement learning. MIT Press, Cambridge (1998)

37. Thrun, S., Leonard, J.J.: Simultaneous localization and mapping. In: Springer handbook of robotics, pp. 871–889. Springer, Heidelberg (2008)

38. Wirsing, M., Hölzl, M., Tribastone, M., Zambonelli, F.: ASCENS: Engineering Autonomic Service-Component Ensembles. In: Beckert, B., Damiani, F., de Boer, F.S., Bonsangue, M.M. (eds.) FMCO 2011. LNCS, vol. 7542, pp. 1–24. Springer, Heidelberg (2013), http://www.pst.ifi.lmu.de/~hoelzl/fmco-2011.pdf

39. Yamins, D.: Towards a theory of local to global in distributed multi-agent systems (i). In: Proceedings of the fourth international joint conference on autonomous agents and multiagent systems (AAMAS'04), pp. 183–190. ACM Press, New York (2005)

40. Yamins, D.: Towards a theory of local to global in distributed multi-agent systems (ii). In: Proceedings of the fourth international joint conference on autonomous agents and multiagent systems (AAMAS'04), pp. 191–198. ACM Press, New York (2005)

The Autonomic Cloud*

Philip Mayer[1], José Velasco[2], Annabelle Klarl[1], Rolf Hennicker[1],
Mariachiara Puviani[3], Francesco Tiezzi[4], Rosario Pugliese[5], Jaroslav Keznikl[6], and
Tomáš Bureš[6]

[1] Ludwig-Maximilians-Universität München, Germany
[2] Zimory Software, Berlin, Germany
[3] Università di Modena e Reggio Emilia, Italy
[4] IMT Institute for Advanced Studies Lucca, Italy
[5] Università degli Studi di Firenze, Italy
[6] Charles University in Prague, Faculty of Mathematics and Physics, Czech Republic

Abstract. The cloud case study within ASCENS explores the vision of an *autonomic cloud*, which is a cloud providing a platform-as-a-service computing infrastructure which, contrary to the usual practice, does not consist of a well-maintained set of reliable high-performance computers, but instead is formed by a loose collection of voluntarily provided heterogeneous nodes which are connected in a peer-to-peer manner. Such an infrastructure must deal with network resilience, data redundancy, and failover mechanisms for executing applications. As such, the autonomic cloud thus requires a certain degree of self-awareness, monitoring, and self-adaptation to reach its goals, which has been achieved with the integration of ASCENS methods and techniques.

Keywords: case study, cloud computing, voluntary computing, peer-to-peer computing, awareness, monitoring, adaptation

1   Introduction

Cloud computing is a recent trend in large scale computing that involves the provisioning of IT resources in a dynamic and on-demand fashion. It supports both conventional scenarios such as scaleout, in which companies opt to extend locally available, internal resources with additional external capacities from a cloud temporarily or for a longer period of time, and new cloud-specific usage scenarios like purely cloud-based applications that may be offered in a cost-efficient, demand-driven way.

Cloud computing services are usually classified into three layered solutions, which are Infrastructure-as-a-Service (IaaS), Platform-as-a-Service (PaaS), and Software-as-a-Service (SaaS). The first is the lowest level and refers to the provisioning of virtual machines; the second is one step higher and provides a development and execution

---

* This research was supported by the European project IP 257414 (ASCENS).

M. Wirsing et al. (eds.): Collective Autonomic Systems, LNCS 8998, pp. 495–512, 2015.
© Springer International Publishing Switzerland 2015

platform regardless of the actual machine, and the last involves the provisioning of complete applications on an on-demand basis.

The goal of the *Autonomic Cloud* case study of ASCENS — also called the *Science Cloud* case study due to its envisioned use within the scientific community — is building a cloud system whose components are self-aware, self-monitoring, and able to self-adapt in the face of problems. As such, this cloud is built following the concepts of a Platform-as-a-Service, that is, it provides a development and runtime platform for applications. However, the scenario where this cloud will be deployed and the parts it consists of are very different from that of a classical cloud implementation. In particular, the nodes forming this cloud will not be well-maintained and secured servers. Instead, the cloud relies on *autonomic nodes* — machines and software which will be provided on a case-by-case basis, mostly voluntarily, and can be withdrawn or change in load at any time.

This environment necessitates a different way of organizing application execution, resilience, data storage, and communication — the autonomic cloud computing platform must be able to *execute applications* in the presence of difficulties such as leaving and joining nodes, fluctuating load, and hard- and software requirements of applications which some of the nodes may not be able to fulfill. This vision has been achieved with the integration of key ASCENS concepts and methods in the implementation of this case study, where the basic nodes of the cloud are realized using *service components* (also called SCPi, for Science Cloud Platform instance). Those components which work together to execute an application dynamically form a *service component ensemble* (called an SCPe, or Science Cloud Platform ensemble).

Although the cloud relies on voluntarily provided nodes, participation of centrally-controlled entities such as IaaS providers is by no means prevented. In fact, parts of the autonomic cloud may run on IaaS solutions which enables it to spawn new virtual machines or shut them down again. This additional functionality is used to balance load or to conserve energy, and has been integrated into the commercial cloud infrastructure of the ASCENS partner Zimory [28].

This chapter describes the autonomic cloud case study, its origins, use of ASCENS methods, implementation, and evaluation. The next section will discuss influencing areas of computing for the case study (Section 2). In Section 3, we will discuss handling awareness and adaptation in the cloud by means of the ASCENS methods. The implementation of the cloud is discussed in Section 4, followed by an evaluation in Section 5. We conclude in Section 6.

This chapter presents an extended version of the publication "The Autonomic Cloud: A Vision of Voluntary, Peer-2-Peer Cloud Computing", previously published at the 2013 AWARENESS workshop [18].

2   Influencing Areas of Computing

Before delving into the deeper details of the cloud, we discuss the three major computing areas which have been influential for realizing the autonomic cloud vision, which are cloud computing, voluntary computing, and peer-to-peer computing.

2.1   Cloud Computing

Firstly and obviously, we deal with *cloud computing* [20]. Cloud computing refers to provisioning resources such as virtual machines, storage space, processing power, or applications to consumers "on the net": Consumers can use these resources without having to install hardware or software themselves and can dynamically add and remove resources.

There are three commonly accepted levels of provisioning in cloud computing, which are infrastructure, platform, and software. In the first, low-level resources such as virtual machines are offered. In the second, a platform for executing custom client software is provided. On the third level, complete applications (such as an office suite) are provided, mostly directly to end users. In any case, clouds are usually offered from one or more centrally managed locations; the servers providing the infrastructure run in a well-maintained data center and are under the control of a single entity.

In the ASCENS cloud computing case study, we will be concerned with a Platform-as-a-Service (PaaS) solution. The goal of the case study is providing a software system (called the Science Cloud Platform, SCP) which will, installed on multiple virtual or non-virtual machines, form a cloud providing a platform for application execution (these applications in turn providing SaaS solutions). The applications running on top of the platform are assumed to have requirements similar to Service Level Agreements (SLAs), which includes where they can and want to be run (regarding CPU speed, available memory, or even closeness in network terms such as latency to other applications or nodes).

2.2   Voluntary Computing

The second area is *voluntary computing*. This term usually refers to solutions in which individuals (consumers) offer part of their computing power to take part in a larger computing effort. The classic examples are the *@home* programs, of which SETI@Home [15] where personal computers are used in the search for extra-terrestrial intelligence is probably the most famous. Usually, voluntary computing is focused on computation; it depends on an agency which provides a centralized infrastructure into which people may plug-in, get their data from, perform calculations, and report back.

In the ASCENS cloud computing case study, we adopt the voluntary computing approach insofar as we imagine individual entities (which includes natural persons, but universities as well) to voluntarily provide computing power in the form of cloud nodes which they can add or remove at any time as they see fit; i.e. nodes can come and go without warning, and their load may change outside of cloud concerns. They may include vastly different hardware, which includes CPU speed, available memory, and also specialized hardware as, for example, graphics processing chips.

2.3   Peer-to-Peer Computing

Finally, the last area is *peer-to-peer computing* [2]. First popularized in the infamous area of file sharing, the basic idea of peer-to-peer computing is the lack of a centralized structure. There is no single node in the network on which the functionality of the overall system depends; rather, a decentralized communication approach is used which ideally is stable through the process of nodes coming and going, and offers no single point of failure, or single point of attack.

The ASCENS cloud computing case study is based on this idea; i.e. there is no centralized component in this cloud and nodes have to use some protocol to agree, in a decentralized manner, on where and what to execute. As already discussed above in the voluntary computing part, nodes may thus come and go without having to inform a central entity.

2.4 Bringing It All Together

Thus, all in all, we have a voluntary, peer-to-peer based platform-as-a-service solution. Such an infrastructure requires autonomic nodes which are (self-)aware of changes in load (either from cloud applications or from applications external to the cloud) and of the network structure (i.e. nodes coming and going) which requires self-healing properties (network resilience). Another issue is data redundancy in case nodes drop out of the system, which requires preparatory actions. Finally, executing applications in such an environment requires a fail-over solution, i.e. self-adaptation of the cloud to provide what we may call application execution resilience.

To sum up in one sentence, the goal of the SCP is *to deploy and run user-defined applications on the p2p-connected web of voluntarily provided machines which form the cloud.*

3 Handling Awareness and Adaptation

The ASCENS project has contributed many techniques and methods to the area of self-aware and self-adapting systems. In this section, we will focus on four important areas which have been influential for the design of the Adaptive Cloud, and in turn have been validated on the Science Cloud Platform implementation.

The first of these are *adaptation patterns* which serve as a way of structuring the cloud on an architectural level (section 3.1). Following this, we discuss modeling of ensemble behavior in a rigorous way by using the *Helena approach* (section 3.2). System specification is best executed using specifically developed language primitives, namely from the *SCEL language* (section 3.3). The nodes in the autonomic cloud may be personal computers and as such may be mobile. Issues relating to this fact have been investigated in the *DEECo approach* (section 3.4).

Other ASCENS methods have been used on the cloud case study as well, which are not described in detail here due to space limitations. We discuss an overview of these, including the lifecycle which ASCENS defines for the development of autonomous systems, in section 3.5.

3.1 Adaptation Patterns

A common approach to understanding, categorizing, and designing IT systems is the use of patterns, i.e. descriptions of characteristics which have proven to be beneficial for the implementation of a system. Within ASCENS, a catalog of architectural design patterns has been developed [7] which are intended to be used to build adaptive components and systems. The design patterns have been studied with regard to the cloud case study. In this section, we will discuss two patterns which have been used in the cloud.

Firstly, we need to discuss individual cloud nodes (which we call SCPis, for Science Cloud Platform instances). In this regard, the *proactive service component pattern* [21] best captures the behavior of such a node. This pattern enables the SCPi, which is a *Service Component* (SC) in the terms of ASCENS and the adaptation pattern itself, to have an internal feedback loop, or, in other words, implicitly contain an *Autonomic Manager* (AM) which is responsible for driving the adaptation through this feedback loop. These kinds of components are used because nodes in the cloud are goal-oriented in nature and actively try to adapt their behavior, even without an external call (e.g. for saving energy). A visualization of such a component is shown in Fig. 1.

In the cloud, one such node uses its sensor to read environmental values such as CPU speed, current load, etc.; effectors may be used to configure an IaaS solution. Inputs and outputs refer to a user interacting with deployed applications. The control and emitter ports are used for ensemble adaptation (see below).

By using the proactive service component pattern, individual SCP nodes are self-aware and able to self-adapt, each following the goal of achieving best performance for deployed apps while saving energy. The internal feedback loop created through the AM part of the node is used for checking these conditions and adapting properly.

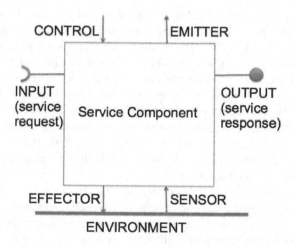

Fig. 1. Proactive Service Component

Furthermore, multiple nodes work together to execute applications. On this level, the *p2p negotiation service components ensemble pattern* [21] is a fitting description of this behavior, since each node (potentially) communicates with every other node for adaptation, there is no central coordinator, and each node follows a goal (which in this case is the same for each node, though with different data depending on deployed apps). The use of this pattern is also possible because the components that form the ensemble are proactive and need to communicate with others to propagate adaptation. This is done, as indicated above, through the control and emitter interfaces of the service component.

Using this pattern, multiple SCP nodes work together: For each application, one ensemble consisting of a subset of the overall cloud nodes is formed which is then responsible for executing the application (which includes deployment, finding an executor, executing, and monitoring). We call such an ensemble an SCPe (Science Cloud Platform ensemble).

Obviously, there are also other ways in which a cloud can be organized. In [21], the applicability of the *centralized AM service components ensemble pattern* was discussed as well. This pattern proposes a completely different setup which does not use a peer-to-peer ogranization but instead uses a centralized autonomic manager. Dynamically adapting the cloud to such a structure might be advisable in the case of a partial blackout of the cloud, that is, a large percentage of the cloud goes down. If only a few nodes remain, switching to a centralized mode in which one AM coordinates many individual nodes (which give up their own adaptivity mechanisms for the time being) might prove to be more effective. Nevertheless, this pattern can only be applied as long as its context of applicability is the same as in the observed case. When the context changes again, the pattern has to be changed as well.

3.2   Modeling Ensemble Behavior

Modeling the behavior of the individual components and the ensembles which implement the cloud functionality is challenging due to the complexity and dynamics of the participating ensembles. In ASCENS, existing techniques such as component-based software engineering ([25,22]) have thus been augmented with features that focus on the particular characteristics of ensembles. Among these is the fact that ensembles are dynamically formed on demand, realizing collective, goal-oriented behavior through communication between the individual participants; furthermore, multiple ensembles may run concurrently using the same basic resources, but dealing with different tasks on a higher level. To be able to model these issues on a first-class basis, the *Helena* approach [12] has been developed, which uses a UML-like notation for collaborations founded on a rigorous formal semantics.

A particular property of ensembles is the fact that although the platform on which ensembles run may itself be plain component-based, each component can take part in different ensembles and in the course of doing so take up different, ensemble-specific *roles*. A service component may play different roles at the same time, both in one ensemble and in different, concurrently running ensembles; it may also dynamically change its role(s) in order to adapt to new situations.

The Helena approach is centered on this notion of roles and the collaboration of roles in ensembles for pursuing the ensemble goal. In the present case study, there may be multiple such ensembles; one for each of the applications which are executed within the cloud. Each ensemble has the goal of deploying the application, finding an execution target node, executing, and finally monitoring the application execution. This is illustrated in Fig. 2.

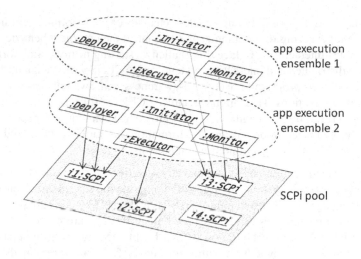

Fig. 2. Ensembles in the *Helena* approach

The first or basic level (on the bottom of the figure) shows the pool of all SCPi nodes which are, in principle, able to provide resources to the cloud. In the figure, these are the four nodes labeled i1 to i4, which may be physical or virtual machines on which instances of the science cloud platform (SCPis) are running. Each of these may participate in ensembles for executing an application.

As indicated in the figure, executing an application requires different responsibilities taken up by different roles in the ensemble; in total, there are six roles of which four are shown in this overview figure. These are the *deployer* (node from which the application originates), the initiator (leading the search for an execution node), the actual *executor*, and a *stopper* which deals with application shutdown. As an example, the figure shows two different ensembles, each executing one application, where nodes concurrently play different roles or do not participate at all.

Helena allows the fine-grained specification of the role interactions as well as the description of the behavior of each role (for details, see [14]). These descriptions are given a rigorous formal foundation, which can then be exploited for ensuring that the ensemble behavior actually reaches the desired goal. We believe that the analysis of ensembles of collaborating roles is beneficial to developers due to the reduction of the complexity of the models, since the combination of all roles within one service component must only be integrated into a component-based architecture in the following implementation phase.

This phase is discussed in the next section, where a language is presented to which a systematic transition from Helena is currently being investigated.

3.3   System Specification in SCEL

The challenge for language designers posed by autonomic systems is to devise appropriate abstractions and linguistic primitives to deal with the large dimension of systems, to guarantee adaptation to (possibly unpredicted) changes of the working environment, to take into account evolving requirements, and to control the emergent behaviors resulting from complex interactions. To face this challenge, starting from existing formalisms for specifying distributed and interacting systems, in ASCENS a new language has been designed that supports programming context-awareness, self-awareness, adaptation and ensemble-wide interactions. This language, called SCEL (Software Component Ensemble Language) [10], provides a complete set of linguistic abstractions for specifying the behavior of autonomic components and the formation of their ensembles, and for controlling the interaction among autonomic components.

SCEL is, somehow, minimal; its syntax fully specifies only a small set of constructs for specifying autonomic systems naturally, avoiding the intricacies due to encoding in lower level languages. SCEL can be thought of as a "kernel" language based on which different full-blown languages can be designed. In particular, here we consider PSCEL (see Chapter I.1 [19]), the instantiation of SCEL obtained by using tuple spaces for managing components' knowledge and the language FACPL for expressing the policies regulating components' behaviour.

In the rest of this section, we consider the PSCEL specification of a scenario in the cloud where an SCPi is overloaded, i.e. the CPU load exceeds a certain threshold, and an application needs to be moved to a different node. This scenario requires the use of an IaaS solution, as it demands the ability to dynamically spawn a new virtual machine and move the application there (indeed, it also prescribes that the application is a *singleton*). The full specification of the scenario can be found in [17]. Here we only outline the general idea.

The SCPi where the application is initially running is a PSCEL component of the form $\mathcal{I}[\mathcal{K}, \Pi, P]$. The interface $\mathcal{I}$ makes available information about the component itself in terms of *attributes*. $\mathcal{K}$ is the knowledge of the SCPi. Π is the policy regulating the component behaviour. P is the set of concurrent processes running in the component.

SCPis follow the proactive service component pattern (described in Section 3.1). Thus, the application logic, implemented as part of process P, uses a group-oriented action to retrieve an application from a member of the SCPe within a given geographical area. This ensemble is dynamically determined when the action is executed and consists of all components that expose in their interface the *location* attribute with the given value (indeed, the notion of ensemble in SCEL matches the notion of SCPe, as both are based on components' attributes). Then, the process sends the retrieved application for execution.

The adaptation logic (i.e., when to adapt) is implemented by the policy Π. Indeed, the component's interface $\mathcal{I}$ exposes the attribute *CPULoad*, whose value (i.e., a percentage of load) is a context information sensed by the component from the underlying infrastructure. The policy Π then detects when the attribute value is over a given threshold (e.g., 90%) and, in that case, triggers a self-adaptive behaviour. More specifically, the policy states that a new application can be retrieved as long as *CPULoad* is less than the threshold. If the process running in the component attempts to retrieve a new application and the threshold is exceeded, then the policy evaluation returns an *obligation* action for spawning a new SCPi.

An interesting aspect in this context is that in a dynamically created SCPi $\mathcal{K}$, Π and P are the same as those of the creating SCPi. However, the application logic, which is part of P, may only be executed on one SCPi at a time (because, due to the scenario requirements, no two instances of the application can run simultaneously). To ensure such behavior, the component relies on a policy automaton, whose states are policies and transitions represent adaptation events. In this way, the policy in force at the component can be dynamically switched according to adaptation events. In our example, the policy automaton ensures that whenever a new component has been created and the application is moved there, if the run-time value of the attribute *CPULoad* of the 'old' component decreases and becomes less than 90%, the application instance running there cannot resume its execution.

3.4 Supporting Mobile Nodes with jDEECo

An interesting aspect of the case study is the fact that the individual nodes can be personal computers. As such, the concept also includes mobile nodes: laptops, tablets, or even smartphones. Mobile devices have some noteworthy properties in addition to standard nodes. They are devices (a) whose neighbors – in the sense of network proximity – may change, (b) whose battery capacity is limited, and (c) whose computing capacity may be (severely) limited as well.

Applications running on top of the autonomic cloud may want to take those properties into consideration. In fact, we can imagine that applications intended to run on mobile devices be effectively split into two components, or smaller applications, communicating with one another. In one scenario, they may both run on one SCPi — if the node is powerful enough and access to power is not an issue; in another, they may be split between two SCPis, one on a mobile node (which handles UI) and another on a stationary node (which handles the computationally extensive background work). In order to keep the user interface responsive, the network latency between the two nodes may not exceed a certain threshold, which becomes problematic in the presence of (physical) node mobility.

This scenario has been investigated as described in [5] and is further detailed in Chapter II.5 [4]. It uses the jDEECo framework of ASCENS, which is described in Chapter III.4 [6]. The envisioned solution for this case uses a specialized adaptation architecture which, through two components, takes care of the planning and monitoring involved.

The first component involved is the *monitor*, which works within an application and can operate in one of two modes:

Observation mode. In observation mode, the monitor executes as part of a running application, i.e. it reflects the actual deployment. The monitor gathers data about the current node, which includes the performance and battery life. This non-functional properties data (*NFPData*) is used by the planner (see below) to decide on adaptation.

Predictive Mode. A monitor may also be detached from its application and spawned on a different node where it runs in predictive mode, testing the performance of the node with the performance model of the application (*MonitorDef*) in mind, but without actually moving the whole application. Again, NFPData is generated which can be used by the planner.

The second component is the *planner*. The planner provides the SCPi with Moni-torDefs for the monitors involved, which the SCPi can distribute to interesting nodes for gathering NFPData. Based on information about the application, which is included in a deployment plan, the planner is able to restrict which nodes are interesting; for example, this may include nodes which are a limit of two hops away. Based on the information in the NFPData from affected nodes, the planner instructs the underlying SCPi(s) to deploy the applications appropriately given the data.

A particular advantage of the monitor approach with predictive modes is the avail-ability of real data: The monitor deployed on remote nodes is able to report, based on its MonitorDef, precisely those measurements which are relevant for the application. As usual, the nodes which may take part in the execution of an application form an ensem-ble with the specific task to figure out the best configuration for all entities involved.

Fig. 3 shows a simplified definition of such an ensemble.

```
1  ensemble PlannerToDevice:
2     coordinator: Planner
3     member: Device
4     membership: HopDistance(Planner.device, Device) ≤ 2
5     knowledge exchange:
6        Device.monitorDef[Planner.app] := Planner.monitorDef
7     scheduling: periodic( 15s )
```

Fig. 3. Ensemble Definition

All in all, the adaptation architecture based on planners and (mock) monitors allows for a very flexible awareness of the network environment. While this approach is useful for all kinds of nodes the SCP may run on, it is particularly helpful in the presence of mobile nodes.

3.5   The EDLC and Other ASCENS Methods

The ASCENS project defines a lifecycle for the development of ensembles, which is called the EDLC (see Chapter III.1 [13]). This lifecycle, which consists of eight phases, describes how to use the various methods defined in ASCENS in the design of a system such as the autonomic cloud. The EDLC consists of two cycles; the first (the *design* cy-cle) includes the activities *requirements engineering*, *modeling/programming*, and *veri-fication/validation*; the second (the *runtime* cycle) consists of the activities *monitoring*, *awareness*, an *self-adaptation*.

The two cycles are connected by the *deployment* activity (from design to runtime) and the *feedback* activity (from runtime to design); in the cloud, both are handled by the Science Cloud Platform (SCP) implementation.

Each method of ASCENS is associated with a different activity in the EDLC. In the following, we discuss methods of ASCENS which have been applied to the case study, and their place in the EDLC. We first discuss the design time cycle.

Requirements Analysis with ARE The first phase in the Ensemble Development Life Cycle (EDLC), which is about *requirements engineering*, is supported by ARE (Autonomy Requirements Engineering). The ARE method has been used to provide detailed requirements for the autonomous cloud and is described in Chapter III.3 [27].

Adaptation Patterns in the Cloud Following requirements engineering, the architecture of the system can be designed in the *modeling* phase of the EDLC by choosing the correct adaptation patterns for the cloud implementation. This technique has been shown in section 3.1.

Modeling with Helena An important aspect of service components and ensembles is the fact that components may play different roles in different ensembles, which has been shown in section 3.2 and is used in the *modeling* activity in the EDLC.

System Specification in SCEL One level down, we can specify the system in terms of the processes which service components run, and the attribute-based dynamic identification of ensembles as discussed in section 3.3; this activity is part of the *programming* activity in the EDLC.

Analysis of Denial-Of-Service Attacks In the *verification* step of the EDLC, we have investigated the problem of distributed Denial-of-Service (dDoS) attacks which are relevant for all connected systems. Two formal patterns have been identified which can serve as defenses against such attacks (this method is described in [9]).

Verification of Routing Procedures in Pastry The network layer of the science cloud implementation, Pastry, has been modeled in κNCPi. The specific emphasis here has been put on formalizing the conditions for ensuring that messages reach their target within Pastry; again, this technique is part of the *verification* phase in the EDLC. It is described in chapter I.2 [3].

Secondly, we discuss the runtime cycle.

Performance Monitoring and Prediction with SPL On the runtime side of the EDLC, the interactions of running ensembles and service components come into play; a key requirement is *monitoring* which is the first activity in the runtime cycle. Monitoring and prediction regarding performance are described in Chapter II.5 [4].

Supporting Mobile Nodes with jDEECo An interesting aspect of the autonomic cloud is that the nodes may not be servers stored in a data center, but personal machines which may include mobile nodes. This brings into play the dimension of spatial location, which is considered by the jDEECo monitoring approach as discussed in section 3.4. In the EDLC, this affects again the *monitoring* phase.

Cooperative Distributed Task Execution A cooperative approach to task execution by distributed nodes in a cloud has has been investigated in a simulation approach, test-driving the *awareness* and *self-adaptation* activities. This method is described in [8].

4   Implementation

As identified in the previous sections, the cloud system is implemented in a peer-to-peer manner with a heavy focus on being aware of changes in the available nodes and the load of each node.

On a technical level, our implementation is based on the existing peer-to-peer substrate Pastry [24] and accompanying protocols, and uses a gossip-style protocol for communication on the application level. This is discussed in section 4.1. The SCP also uses the Zimory IaaS cloud platform to start and stop virtual machines on demand as required for ensuring application uptime as well as energy conservation (see section 4.2).

4.1   Implementing an Autonomic Cloud

The implementation is split into three layers: a network layer, which implements routing and message passing along with network self-healing properties; a data layer which handles data storage, including redundancy, and an application layer, which handles execution and fail-over of applications. The layer-based organization is shown in Figure 4.

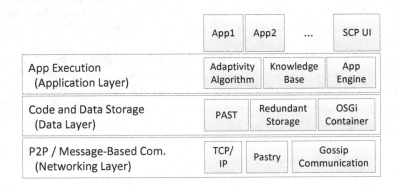

Fig. 4. Science Cloud Platform Implementation

On the *network level*, the nodes which form the science cloud need to know about one another and be able to pass messages, either to single nodes (unicast), a group of nodes (multi- or anycast), or all nodes (broadcast). Given that the network can potentially become large, it is advisable that not all nodes need to know all other nodes. Furthermore, routing needs to be stable under adverse conditions (i.e. nodes that are part of the autonomic cloud leave, or new nodes are added).

We use the existing protocol Pastry [24] in the form of the FreePastry implementation [11] as the basis of this layer, which is in turn based on standard networking protocols (i.e. TCP/IP). The inner workings of Pastry are similar to that of classic Distributed Hash Tables (DHTs), that is, each node is assigned a unique hash and nodes are basically organized in a ring structure, with appropriate shortcuts for faster routing. The protocol has built-in network resilience (self-healing). These properties have been formally analyzed in [16]. The SCP uses a gossip-style protocol for passing on information about individual nodes, which works along the usual epidemic paths.

The second layer handles *data*. When an application is deployed, the code needs to be available to all nodes which can possibly execute it; furthermore, application data needs to be stored in such a way that resuming an application, after a node which ran it failed, is possible. We thus need data storage with data redundancy, not only of immutable data (application code) but also of mutable data (application data). Data is handled on top of Pastry using gcPAST, which is an implementation of the PAST protocol [23] with support for mutable data. PAST basically implements a DHT and includes a data redundancy mechanism which works by keeping k copies of a data package in the nodes surrounding the primary storage node (which is the one the data package hash is closest to). Application code is stored as Java byte code, and the OSGi container is used to inject this code at runtime into the Java virtual machine.

The final layer, and the one implementing the actual platform-as-a-service idea, is the *application layer*. This layer first of all implements a *Knowledge Base* in the KnowLang [26] style which keeps track of the knowledge about its own and all other nodes. An App(lication) Engine, again based on OSGi, is responsible for starting and stopping applications in the form of OSGi *bundles*. Finally, adaptivity is implemented by different roles (such as initiator or executor), based on the Helena principles outlined above. Since applications can only run on some machines (based on requirements), these must first be found in the network. Every user of the cloud runs (at least) one instance of an SCPi and uses this instance both for deploying and using applications.

Deploying an application first means simply storing the executable code (as an OSGi bundle), which is based on the primary storage node idea introduced above. The primary storage node assumes an initiator role which is responsible for finding an executor based on the requirements of the application and, once an executor is found, for monitoring its continued existence. If the executor fails, another will take its place, preserving data of the application through redundant storage. Likewise, if the initiator fails, another node (which is closest to the hash of the application) will take over.

4.2 Integrating Zimory IaaS

The company Zimory, an ASCENS partner, provides the Zimory Cloud Suite [28], a full Infrastructure-as-a-Service (IaaS) solution which facilitates end-to end management of the Virtual Machine (VM) lifecycle: VMs can be created, started, killed, backed-up and destroyed via the Zimory Manage component. Having such management of the VM lifecycle provides two main advantages: instantiation of SCPs through the use of VMs and starting and stopping of VMs as needed (supporting the "joining at will" principle in the Autonomic Cloud).

The Zimory platform provides the ability to store blueprints for VMs which are called *appliances*. An appliance is a preconfigured virtual machine which can be *deployed* to the cloud in order to start it; likewise, it can be undeployed. For the autonomic cloud, one such appliance was created which includes the Science Cloud Platform installation which is triggered to automatically launch when the VM is started.

The process of starting a new virtual machine and stopping those no longer needed for energy conservation is integrated into the core SCP logic. A fallback mechanism is triggered if none of the available non-virtual SCPs is able to execute an application — whether due to lack of nodes which can handle the application requirements or because the load of existing nodes is too high. In this case, the initiator contacts the Zimory platform and creates a new deployment from the preconfigured appliance discussed above. As soon as the appliance is started, the SCP running on it will register with the autonomic cloud and take over execution of the application. Likewise, integration of a virtual machine shutdown is achieved by monitoring apps running on virtualized machines and checking for possible non-virtualized executors, which are chosen over virtualized ones when available. Again, idle virtualized nodes are instructed to shut down via the API.

Both processes are integrated into the role-based mechanism of starting and stopping apps with two new roles (*DeploymentCreator* and *DeploymentStopper*) [1].

5   Evaluation and Demonstrator

As shown in the previous sections, many ideas of the ASCENS project have been integrated into the working implementation of the Science Cloud Platform, and vice versa. A full prototype implementation has been created which makes use of the Zimory IaaS and can be instrumented for test-driving and investigating the supported functionality.

For allowing researchers as well as students to interact with the software, a monitoring server has been created which visualizes the network structure, which, being based on peer-to-peer principles, can not otherwise be observed in a centralized manner. The monitoring server includes options for instrumenting the network to produce particular results, for example, forcing the creation of a new virtual machine.

As an example, we show how the start of a virtual machine is triggered in a network and then used for executing an application. The first step is shown in Figure 5, which shows a Pastry ring of eight nodes, each running one instance of the Science Cloud platform. The caption on the left shows the meaning of the colors and shapes; in particular, there is no virtualized node at the moment and all of the nodes are overloaded (CPU over 80% load, as shown by the red background in the CPU line). Furthermore, the lower left shows a variety of buttons with which to instrument the platform.

The node 2D5EC1 in the lower center has the Initiator role for the application *Exchange* (a collaboration platform), as well as the Main Storage role. The node has futhermore already determined that no node in the network is able to execute this application and thus has instantiated an instance of the Deployment Creator role which instructs the underlying Zimory platform to start a new node.

A short time later, a new node is up and running and has been selected to run the application, as is shown in Figure 6. As can be seen, the new virtualized node 96A591 is executing the application. The figure also shows that the CPU load on node AEF29E has fallen below 80%, which the initiator is bound to notice in a short while.

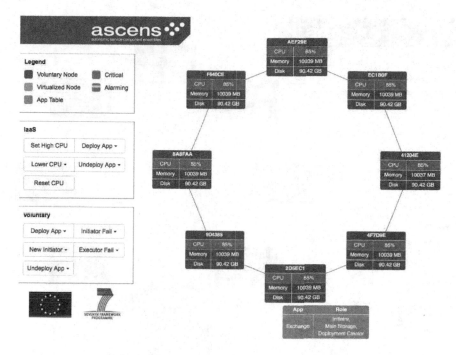

Fig. 5. Science Cloud Platform Demo — Step 1

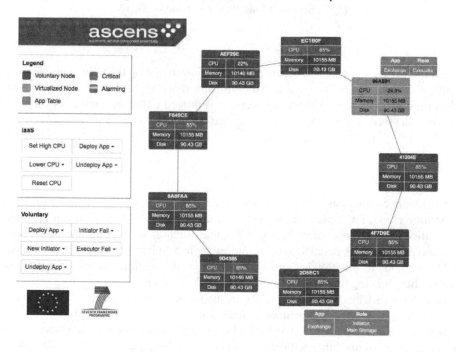

Fig. 6. Science Cloud Platform Demo — Step 2

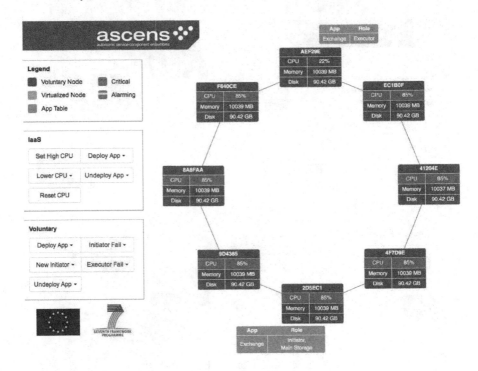

Fig. 7. Science Cloud Platform Demo — Step 3

Since AEF29E is able to execute the application (based on the application requirements, and since it is not overloaded) the virtualized node is no longer required. Thus, it is shut down and the application execution is moved to the new node, as shown in Figure 7. In this example, the initiator node has stayed the same.

6   Summary

The autonomic cloud case study has been used within ASCENS as a test case for an autonomic cloud, i.e. a platform-as-a-service infrastructure intended to run customer applications in the presence of certain difficulties such as voluntarily provided nodes. In this report, we have detailed several interesting hand-picked results of applying AS-CENS methods to the cloud. Our implementation of an autonomic cloud uses these results, thus showing their applicability in a working system.

The Science Cloud Platform (SCP), including the monitor server, is available on the ASCENS web site for download[7]. Since some of the demonstration functionality requires the Zimory platform, we have also created videos showing the starting and stopping of virtual machines within the visualization; these are available online as well.

---

[7] http://www.ascens-ist.eu/cloud/

Acknowledgements. The authors would like to thank all ASCENS members who contributed to the autonomic cloud case study. Furthermore, thanks go out to Alexander Dittrich, Ansgar Zeblin, and Elias Englmeier who contributed to the implementation of the SCP.

References

1. Dittrich, A.: Integration einer Virtualisierungslösung in Peer-to-Peer Cloud Computing, Bachelor Thesis, Ludwig-Maximilians-Universität München (2014)
2. Androutsellis-Theotokis, S., Spinellis, D.: A survey of peer-to-peer content distribution technologies. ACM Comput. Surv. 36(4), 335–371 (2004)
3. Bruni, R., Montanari, U., Sammartino, M.: Reconfigurable and Software-Defined Networks of Connectors and Components. In: Wirsing, M., Hölzl, M., Koch, N., Mayer, P. (eds.) Software Engineering for Collective Autonomic Systems. LNCS, vol. 8998, pp. 73–106. Springer, Heidelberg (2015)
4. Bulej, L., Bureš, T., Gerostathopoulos, I., Horký, V., Keznikl, J., Marek, L., Tschaikowski, M., Tribastone, M., Tůma, P.: Supporting Performance Awareness in Autonomous Ensembles. In: Wirsing, M., Hölzl, M., Koch, N., Mayer, P. (eds.) Software Engineering for Collective Autonomic Systems. LNCS, vol. 8998, pp. 291–322. Springer, Heidelberg (2015)
5. Bulej, L., Bures, T., Horký, V., Keznikl, J.: Adaptive deployment in ad-hoc systems using emergent component ensembles: vision paper. In: Proceedings of the 4th ACM/SPEC International Conference on Performance Engineering (ICPE '13), pp. 343–346. ACM Press, New York (2013)
6. Bures, T., Gerostathopoulos, I., Hnetynka, P., Keznikl, J., Kit, M., Plasil, F.: The Invariant Refinement Method. In: Wirsing, M., Hölzl, M., Koch, N., Mayer, P. (eds.) Software Engineering for Collective Autonomic Systems. LNCS, vol. 8998, pp. 405–428. Springer, Heidelberg (2015)
7. Cabri, G., Puviani, M., Zambonelli, F.: Towards a Taxonomy of Adaptive Agent-based Collaboration Patterns for Autonomic Service Ensembles. In: Proc. of CTS, May 2011, pp. 508–515. IEEE Computer Society Press, Los Alamitos (2011)
8. Celestini, A., Lluch Lafuente, A., Mayer, P., Sebastio, S., Tiezzi, F.: Reputation-based cooperation in the clouds. In: Zhou, J., Gal-Oz, N., Zhang, J., Gudes, E. (eds.) Trust Management VIII. IFIP Advances in Information and Communication Technology, vol. 430, pp. 213–220. Springer, Heidelberg (2014), doi:10.1007/978-3-662-43813-8_15
9. Combaz, J., Lluch Lafuente, A., Montanari, U., Pugliese, R., Sammartino, M., Tiezzi, F., Vandin, A., von Essen, C.: Software engineering for self-aware sces. Tech. rep., ASCENS Project, deliverable JD3.1 (2013)
10. De Nicola, R., Loreti, M., Pugliese, R., Tiezzi, F.: A Formal Approach to Autonomic Systems Programming: The SCEL Language. TAAS 9(2), 7 (2014)
11. Druschel, P., Haeberlen, A., Hoye, J., Iyer, S., Mislove, A., Nandi, A., Post, A., Singh, A., Castro, M., Costa, M., Kermarrec, A.M., Rowstron, A., Iyer, S., Wallach, D., Hu, Y.C., Jones, M., Theimer, M., Wolman, A., Mahajan, R.: FreePastry. (March 2013), http://www.freepastry.org/
12. Hennicker, R., Klarl, A.: Foundations for Ensemble Modeling – The HELENA Approach. In: Iida, S., Meseguer, J., Ogata, K. (eds.) Specification, Algebra, and Software. LNCS, vol. 8373, pp. 359–381. Springer, Heidelberg (2014)
13. Hölzl, M., Koch, N., Puviani, M., Wirsing, M., Zambonelli, F.: The Ensemble Development Life Cycle and Best Practices for Collective Autonomic Systems. In: Wirsing, M., Hölzl, M., Koch, N., Mayer, P. (eds.) Software Engineering for Collective Autonomic Systems. LNCS, vol. 8998, pp. 325–354. Springer, Heidelberg (2015)

14. Klarl, A., Mayer, P., Hennicker, R.: Helena@work: Modeling the science cloud platform. In: Margaria, T., Steffen, B. (eds.) ISoLA 2014, Part I. LNCS, vol. 8802, pp. 99–116. Springer, Heidelberg (2014)

15. Korpela, E., Werthimer, D., Anderson, D., Cobb, J., Lebofsky, M.: Seti@home-massively distributed computing for seti. Computing in Science and Engineering 3(1), 78–83 (2001)

16. Lu, T., Merz, S., Weidenbach, C.: Towards verification of the pastry protocol using TLA+. In: Bruni, R., Dingel, J. (eds.) FORTE 2011 and FMOODS 2011. LNCS, vol. 6722, pp. 244–258. Springer, Heidelberg (2011)

17. Margheri, A., Pugliese, R., Tiezzi, F.: Linguistic Abstractions for Programming and Policing Autonomic Computing Systems. In: 10th International Conference on Autonomic and Trusted Computing, UIC/ATC, pp. 404–409. IEEE Computer Society Press, Los Alamitos (2013)

18. Mayer, P., Klarl, A., Hennicker, R., Puviani, M., Tiezzi, F., Pugliese, R., Keznikl, J., Bures, T.: The autonomic cloud: A vision of voluntary, peer-2-peer cloud computing. In: 2013 IEEE 7th International Conference on Self-Adaptation and Self-Organizing Systems Workshops (SASOW), Sep. 2013, pp. 89–94 (2013)

19. De Nicola, R., Latella, D., Lafuente, A.L., Loreti, M., Margheri, A., Massink, M., Morichetta, A., Pugliese, R., Tiezzi, F., Vandin, A.: The SCEL Language: Design, Implementation, Verification. In: Wirsing, M., Hölzl, M., Koch, N., Mayer, P. (eds.) Software Engineering for Collective Autonomic Systems. LNCS, vol. 8998, pp. 3–71. Springer, Heidelberg (2015)

20. Mell, P., Grance, T.: The NIST Definition of Cloud Computing, Special Publication 800-145, NIST - National Institute of Standards and Technology (2011)

21. Puviani, M., Frei, R.: Self-management for cloud computing. In: SAI Conference, London, UK (2013)

22. Rausch, A., Reussner, R., Mirandola, R., Plášil, F. (eds.): The Common Component Modeling Example. LNCS, vol. 5153. Springer, Heidelberg (2008)

23. Rowstron, A., Druschel, P.: Storage management and caching in past, a large-scale, persistent peer-to-peer storage utility. In: ACM SIGOPS Operating Systems Review, vol. 35, pp. 188–201. ACM Press, New York (2001)

24. Rowstron, A.I.T., Druschel, P.: Pastry: Scalable, decentralized object location, and routing for large-scale peer-to-peer systems. In: Guerraoui, R. (ed.) Middleware 2001. LNCS, vol. 2218, pp. 329–350. Springer, Heidelberg (2001)

25. Szyperski, C.: Component Software: Beyond Object-Oriented Programming, 2nd edn. Addison-Wesley, Boston (2002)

26. Vassev, E., Hinchey, M.: Implementing artificial awareness with knowlang. In: 2013 IEEE International Systems Conference (SysCon), April 2013, pp. 580–586 (2013)

27. Vassev, E., Hinchey, M.: Engineering Requirements for Autonomy Features. In: Wirsing, M., Hölzl, M., Koch, N., Mayer, P. (eds.) Software Engineering for Collective Autonomic Systems. LNCS, vol. 8998, pp. 379–403. Springer, Heidelberg (2015)

28. Zimory Software: Zimory Cloud Suite. (August 2014), http://www.zimory.com/

CHAPTER IV.1

The E-mobility Case Study*

Nicklas Hoch[1], Henry-Paul Bensler[1], Dhaminda Abeywickrama[2], Tomáš Bureš[3], and Ugo Montanari[4]

[1] Volkswagen AG,
Corporate Research Group, Wolfsburg, Germany,
[2] Fraunhofer FOKUS,
Berlin, Germany
[3] Charles University Prague,
Faculty of Mathematics and Physics,
Department of Distributed and Dependable Systems,
Prague, Czech Republic
[4] Università di Pisa,
Dipartimento di Informatica, Pisa, Italy

Abstract. Electro-mobility (e-mobility) is one of the promising technologies being considered by automotive OEMs as an alternative to internal combustion engines as a means of propulsion. The e-mobility case study provides a novel example of a relevant industry application within the ASCENS framework. An overview of the system design is given which describes how e-mobility is conceptualized and then transformed using the ensemble development life cycle (EDLC) approach into a distributed autonomic (i.e self-aware, self-adaptive) component-based software system. The system requirements engineering is based on the state-of-the-affairs (SOTA) approach and the invariant refinement method (IRM) which are both revisited and applied. Regarding the implementation and deployment of the system, a dependable emergent ensembles of components (DEECo) approach is utilized. The DEECo components and ensembles are coded and deployed using the Java-based jDEECo runtime environment. The runtime environment integrates the multi-agent transport simulation tool (MATSim), which is used to predict the effects of the physical interactions of users, vehicles and infrastructure resources. jDEECo handles multiple MATSim instances to allow for different belief states between components and ensembles.

Keywords: software engineering methodologies, requirements analysis, autonomic systems, self-organization, ensemble-oriented systems, scheduling

---

* This research was supported by the European project IP 257414 (ASCENS).

M. Wirsing et al. (eds.): Collective Autonomic Systems, LNCS 8998, pp. 513–533, 2015.
© Springer International Publishing Switzerland 2015

1   Introduction

This chapter describes the characteristics and challenges arising when people travel with privately owned electric vehicles (EVs) in a resource constraint road environment. In particular, it addresses the dual problem of decision making in transportation systems, where drivers use predictive environment information (PEI), such as traffic information and car park availability, to make travel decisions (e.g. route choice, parking choice), and in return, these decisions influence the PEI on which the drivers base their decisions. The challenges give rise to the various ASCENS approaches, which collectively enable an efficient coordination of travelers and resources. The scenario is referred to as electric vehicle travel problem (EVTP).

The transportation system involves a large number of nodes and complex interactions between them. It is open-ended, not allowing for a precise definition of the number of vehicles entering and exiting a reference area. Most importantly, the system involves highly dynamic decision making and information distribution, with the additional challenge that decisions and information are mutually dependent (dual problem). All of these characteristics give rise to important software design challenges, which include the question of knowledge distribution, the efficient handling of timeliness of information and the management of different belief states of the entities of the system.

The software design challenges can be addressed in different ways, comprising (1) a centralized approach, where a single coordinator controls the system behavior of all nodes, and (2) a decentralized agent-based approach, where reasoning capabilities are distributed across software agents and where system states are emerging from the interaction of the agents.

In a first step, a centralized system was implemented; although the approach was well-suited for simulation purposes, it was not real-world applicable, which was due to its scaling characteristics over the large number of nodes in the real-world traffic environment. In a second step, an agent-based system was developed which is described in [12]. This approach produced very promising results, but showed that agent-based systems require ensemble engineering approaches, where components with congruent goals group in ensembles in order to coordinate knowledge exchange on a group-level. The ASCENS approach is the third step, which addresses the shortcomings of the aforementioned centralized and decentralized approaches.

The application of the general ASCENS theory to EVTP real-world challenges is shown in this chapter. A conceptualization of the EVTP is presented in Section 2.1. The ASCENS life cycle for the development of autonomic systems is shown in Section 2.2. The design loop of the ASCENS life cycle comprises the design of distributed system architecture and the design of distributed reasoning. The design of distributed reasoning for EVTP is discussed in greater detail in Chapter II.2 [11]. The design of the distributed architecture is discussed in Section 3, where a discussion of functional and non-functional system requirements is given. Architecture design involves the state-of-the-affairs (SOTA) approach and the invariant refinement method (IRM). As to the runtime loop of the AS-

CENS life cycle, the distributed emergent ensembles of components (DEECo) approach is described in Section 4, giving rise to the jDEECo runtime environment, as described in Section 5. The runtime environment interfaces with a MATSim traffic simulator, which models the real-world physical interactions of vehicles, users and road network resources.

2   System Design

The goals of this section are to provide a conceptualization of the real-world problem being considered and to discuss how this is transformed into a distributed, autonomous software system.

A conceptualization of a real-world problem can be understood as an abstract ontology, describing stakeholders and their relations within the given system boundaries. It is the highest abstraction level and is not yet confined to a specific software engineering approach. Section 2.1 presents a conceptualizing of the real-world electric vehicle travel problem (EVTP). The characteristics of the software system are determined during system design, which involves requirements specification, modeling, validation and verification approaches. Section 2.2 describes the ASCENS specific design approach and how it is used to transform the EVTP concept to a distributed, autonomous software system.

2.1   Conceptualizing E-mobility

A transportation system can be understood as a market where infrastructure resources reflect the supply side and people that take advantage of the infrastructure resources represent the demand side. In general, transportation systems allow for modal shifts. This study considers the case of individual motorized travel; more specifically, it assumes that people exclusively travel with privately owned electric vehicles.

These electric vehicles are competing for infrastructure resources of the transportation system. Infrastructure resources such as parking lots, roads and charging stations are constrained thereby imposing restrictions on travel demand. The cost for a vehicle to use infrastructure resources is variable. It may change with scale, time and location or dynamically depend on the market situation. Situations exist in which demand exceeds resource availability, at least locally. The ASCENS approach addresses these situations both from a driver and operator perspective.

Departing from the local perspective of the driver, each driver has a set of appointments $A = \{A_1, \ldots, A_n\}$, where each appointment is defined by a location L_i, a starting time $_i t_S^A$ and a duration $_i d^A$. A route alternative from appointment A_i to appointment A_{i+1} is denoted as iR^D. It connects the departure location L_i and the destination location L_{i+1} and is defined in terms of time and energy consumption. The departure time is denoted as $_i t_S^D$ and the arrival time as $_i t_E^D$. The electric vehicle (EV) battery level at departure is denoted as $_i e_S^D$, while $_i e_E^D$ defines the battery energy level at the time of arrival. The user must arrive in time at the appointment location, so it is required that $_it_E^D \leq {}_it_S^A$. The vehicle should never run out of energy, so that it is required that $_ie_E^D > 0$. A charging event may be scheduled during appointment duration. It is assumed that a set of charging stations exists, where each one is defined by a name $CSname$. The number of available charging spots at a location L is defined as $SpotsNum$. Given this notation, the local travel problem is presented in [17,13] and is described in greater detail in Chapter II.2 [11].

Continuing now from the local perspective of an infrastructure operator, each operator has individual interests such as achieving a specific capacity usage or profit margin. Private operators of parking lots (resp. car parks) and charging stations generally aim at maximum capacity usage. In order to achieve their objective, they provide incentives such as specific price scales. In contrast, public road operators want to avoid traffic congestion and therefore avoid limit capacity usage. Their objective is a road capacity usage around the free flow limit.

From a group-level perspective, individually optimal solutions of the drivers and infrastructure operators may conflict, giving rise to a local-global optimization of the transportation system. As human behavior is not entirely deterministic, it cannot be expected that a transportation system is fully controllable, giving rise to contingency situations. State-of-the art approaches which handle local-global optimization and contingency situations have major drawbacks. First off on a functional level, they do not provide adequate adaptation mechanisms to ensure goal satisfaction in contingency situations; secondly, they do not effectively compromise the local traveler and global resource perspective; and thirdly, they do not allow for different belief states amongst travelers or groups of travelers. On a non-functional level, up-to-date approaches are not real-time capable and do not provide the means to adequately cope with the failure of individual nodes. The ASCENS approach addresses the aforementioned shortcomings of state-of-the art approaches through adequate architecture and logic design, which is discussed in greater detail in the subsequent sections.

The key challenge of an ASCENS conceptualization is the identification of stakeholder goals, their awareness and their adaptation capabilities. The main stakeholders of the system are drivers, vehicles, and operators, encompassing both public road operators and private parking (resp. charging station) operators.

Drivers are assumed to travel with private vehicles only. A driver and a vehicle are therefore treated as a single stakeholder, denoted in the following as a vehicle. A vehicle is aware of its current position, battery energy level, current traffic information, route alternatives, points-of-interest (e.g. parking lots, charging stations) and the traveler's sequence of appointments $A = \{A_1, \ldots, A_n\}$ and the adherence thereof. Adaptation actions of the vehicle comprise a departure time change, route change and a change of parking lot and charging strategy.

A road operator manages a predefined reference area. Given the reference area, the operator is aware of the current traffic level, the projected travel demand, the vehicles entering and leaving the boundaries of the reference area and their alternative travel options. Adaptation actions of the road operator comprise of road pricing and requesting vehicles to change plans which implies choosing a different route out of the vehicle's set of route alternatives.

A parking operator (resp. charging station operator) manages a predefined set of entities. Given the predefined set, the operator is aware of its capacity, the current capacity usage, future requests, the vehicles entering and leaving the car parks (resp. charging stations) and their alternative parking (resp. charging) options. Adaptation actions of the parking operator (resp. charging station operator) comprise of pricing changes and requesting vehicles to change plans; this implies choosing a different parking lot (resp. charging station) out of the vehicle's set of alternatives.

2.2 Software Development Life Cycle

The design of distributed, autonomous software systems is cross-inspired from multiple disciplines, comprising of agent-based systems (e.g. [21], [22]), control engineering (e.g. [9]), artificial intelligence (e.g. [20]) and operations research. In the view of these existing approaches, this section presents a conceptual discussion of the design stage of a distributed, autonomous software system, explaining both EVTP and ASCENS specific concepts and highlighting the links between them.

ASCENS provides a general framework for the structured design and development of autonomous, distributed systems, in particular their self-awareness and self-adaptation properties. The framework is denoted as *ensemble development life cycle* (EDLC) and is discussed in [4] and revisited in Chapter III.1 [14]. The EDLC comprises of two loops: a design loop which describes the offline engineering tasks, and a runtime loop which defines the online engineering tasks. The design loop is an iterative process, departing from requirements engineering, going on to modeling and programming and arriving at verification and validation. The design loop results in system deployment, giving rise to the runtime loop. The runtime loop includes the activities corresponding to runtime monitoring, awareness and self adaptation. The engineering activities in the design loop and the runtime loop are distinguished from traditional approaches in that they focus on the aspects of self-awareness and self-adaptation.

Self-awareness and self-adaptation enable the system to continuously infer decisions that guarantee goal adherence. In tangible terms, self-awareness describes the capability to interpret information with respect to a given goal and self-adaptation describes the capability to manipulate knowledge or execute real-world actions in order to achieve the goal. Self-awareness and self-adaptation define knowledge processes, namely, perception, communication and reasoning processes. Knowledge processes occur at two levels: the intra-component and the inter-component level. The intra-component level defines processes within the component. The inter-component level defines processes between the components. An ASCENS ensemble can technically be understood as an inter-component process which controls the knowledge exchange between its members; it thereby manipulates the belief states and decisions of its members.

Given this context, the objective of the design stage is two-fold: (1) design an architecture of components and ensembles that allows for efficient knowledge distribution, and (2) design reasoning that allows the knowledge processes to efficiently manipulate the environment in order to reach the system goals.

As is depicted in Figure 1, the design objective is solved in two loops: the loop of architecture design and the loop of reasoning design. The loop of architecture design evolves from the EDLC requirements engineering stage, while the loop of reasoning design is part of the EDLC modeling stage, with the EDLC being discussed in chapter III.1 [14]. Architecture design departs from a conceptual-

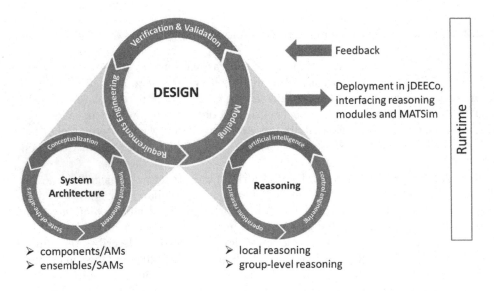

Fig. 1. Designing knowledge architecture and knowledge processes for electric vehicle travel planning

ization of the EVTP. It then uses the state-of-the-affairs (SOTA) approach, as discussed in Chapter III.1 [14], and the invariant refinement method (IRM), as discussed in Chapter III.4 [6], to infer both functional and non-functional system requirements. Components and ensembles are derived and a set of feedback loops connecting them. Feedback loops are described in terms of autonomic managers (AMs) and super autonomic managers (SAMs).

IRM and SOTA are partly converse approaches. While SOTA takes a dynamic systems engineering perspective, IRM is a top-down approach with a goal-refinement perspective. Yet, both SOTA and IRM infer a system architecture of the system-to-be, departing from the same conceptualization and arriving at the level of components, ensembles and AMs/SAMs. The analogy of the two partly converse approaches allows for an iterative improvement of the system specification, by using one approach to correct the other.

While architecture design requires an understanding of the flow of control data at the input/output level, it does not require an understanding of the inner control logic. Control logic is designed by the reasoning loop. Multiple levels of control logic are distinguished, namely, control logic within-subsystems of a component ($level_1$), control logic between-subsystems of a component ($level_2$) and control logic between-components, respectively within-ensembles ($level_3$). $Level_1$ mostly employs conventional control engineering approaches, where the control path is described by a set of differential equations as a closed-form expression. $Level_1$ logic is developed for EVTP entities, yet, the discussion is beyond the scope of this chapter. $Level_2$ logic can be understood as local component reasoning, which is embedded in the knowledge processes of a component and is architecturally represented by AMs. $Level_3$ logic can be understood as group-level reasoning, which is embedded in the ensemble processes and is architecturally represented by SAMs. Both $level_2$ and $level_3$ logic use approaches from operations research and artificial intelligence, such as the dynamic programming strategy in Chapter II.2 [11].

As described in [4], the EDLC design loop defines a programming stage. Here the programming step is implicit in the sense that IRM by definition results in a DEECo specification (a component-based reification of SCEL concepts – see Chapter I.1 [18]), which can be directly mapped to a jDEECo program. The jDEECo program inherits the architecture defined in the architecture loop, and inherits the reasoning processes defined in the reasoning loop. While some reasoning processes are directly coded in jDEECo, others are called externally such as the EV planning modules and the MATSim traffic simulator.

3   Goal-Oriented Requirements Engineering for Self-adaptive Autonomic Systems

With reference to the previous discussion, SOTA is an approach, which is inspired from dynamic systems modeling. IRM is a top-down approach, which is inspired from goal-refinement. This section demonstrates how the combination of the two approaches improves the specification of the system-to-be.

Section 3 is organized in the following manner. Section 3.1 discusses requirements engineering using SOTA. Section 3.2 revises requirements engineering using IRM. Section 3.3 explains how an iterative requirements engineering process involving SOTA and IRM improves system design.

3.1   High-Level Requirements Engineering with SOTA

SOTA is designed for goal-oriented requirements engineering of self-adaptive systems. It adapts a dynamical systems modeling approach to model feedback loops, which are used to control service component (SC) goal achievement in autonomic distributed systems [4]. Conventional approaches to model and control systems use closed-form models, which comprise of a set of differential equations that are solved at every time step in order to minimize the error between the actual behavior and the intended behavior of a system. If a closed-form model does not exist, as is the case for complex agent-based systems, conventional approaches do not hold.

In SOTA a state space S is defined by the state variables of the SCs and the operational environment. Given the state space representation, a SC goal is described by a point in the state space, whereby a SC evolution is described as a vector in the state space. The evolution of SCs has to satisfy constraints, which are denoted by utilities. The optimal SC evolution over time satisfying all utilities is defined by the goal trajectory U. A SC is activated to strive for a goal, respectively follow U, once a precondition is met, which is defined as a region in S. Self-adaptation actions are initiated once the deviation of a SC trajectory from the optimal goal trajectory U exceeds a critical threshold, respectively satisfies an adaptation condition.

Self-adaptation is defined by the feedback control loops, which define a set of actions that allow a component to reach its goal. A complex system inherits multiple interacting control loops. They support adaptation mechanisms either on an intra-loop level or an inter-loop level. Intra-loops are encapsulated within a component. Inter-loops coordinate adaptation across components, whereby three mechanisms of inter-loop coordination are distinguished, namely, hierarchy, stigmergy and direct interaction. Feedback control loops can be classified by structural properties and assigned to categories, denoted by patterns, giving rise to a taxonomy of hierarchical patterns as presented in [7].

Requirements engineering with SOTA involves two major tasks: first, the identification of the dimensions of the SOTA state space, and second, the design of feedback control loops by the help of the mentioned patterns. The key adaptation patterns are conceptually described in [19]. For selected patterns, Abeywickrama et al. [1] presented both platform-independent UML template models and platform-independent Java template models. In particular, the authors describe two SC related patterns, namely the *autonomic SC pattern* and the *parallel AMs SC pattern*, and one ensemble related pattern, namely the *centralized service component ensemble (SCE) pattern*. The *autonomic SC pattern* inherits one autonomic manager (AM) that implements one local feedback loop, thereby controlling a single adaptation aspect of the SC. The *parallel AMs SC pattern* comprises multiple autonomic managers, each controlling a local adaptation aspect of the SC. As an example, Figure 2 shows the UML pattern template model of the *parallel AMs SC pattern* and Figure 3 presents the respective Java pattern template model. For a detailed description of the remaining template models, the reader may refer to [1]. As previously mentioned, the interaction of the feedback loops is coordinated with inter-loop mechanisms either through hierarchy, stigmergy or direct interaction. The *centralized SCE pattern* uses a hierarchical control structure to coordinate the interaction of multiple supervised SCs. It employs a single super autonomic manager (SAM), implementing a single global feedback loop.

For the purpose of engineering and simulating feedback loops for self-adaptive systems, SimSOTA was developed. It is an Eclipse plug-in providing tool sup-

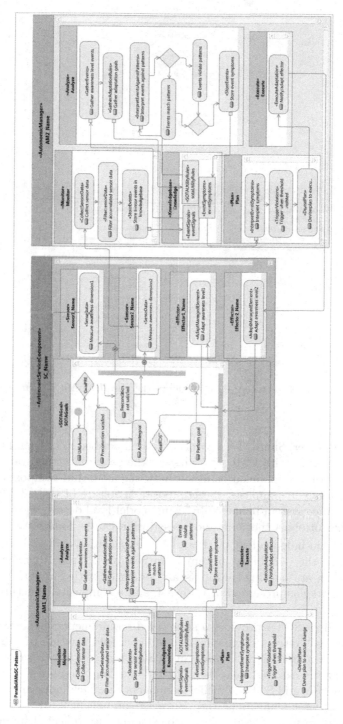

Fig. 2. UML pattern template model of the *parallel AMs SC pattern* [1]

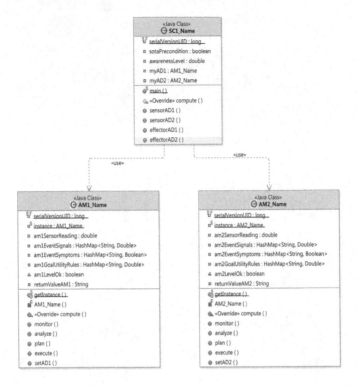

Fig. 3. Java pattern template model of the *parallel AMs SC pattern* [1]

port to the designer. SimSOTA is conceptually described in [2,3] and models the adaptation patterns with UML 2.2, whereby the pattern's structural and behavioral information are modeled using activity, sequence and composite structure diagrams. SimSOTA animates the composite structure of the adaptation patterns and verifies system behavior by using model-level debugging with detailed control of execution. A more detailed description can be found in [2].

The platform-independent UML and Java descriptions of the design patterns are applied to the e-mobility system from Section 2. From this the platform-specific models are obtained. Models are animated with SimSOTA producing an activity model as presented in Figure 4, and a composite structure model as shown in Figure 5.

Summarizing, SOTA provides a structured requirements engineering process for self-adaptive systems. Departing from a conceptualization of the system of interest, SOTA infers SC/SCE goals and a SOTA state space description. SOTA employs a pattern catalog, comprising of feedback loop templates, to assign feedback loops to SCs and SCEs. Within-component feedback loops are expressed in terms of autonomic mangers (AMs). Between-component feedback loops, which are equivalent to within-ensemble feedback-loops, are reflected by super autonomic managers (SAMs). The behavior of the system is modeled and checked

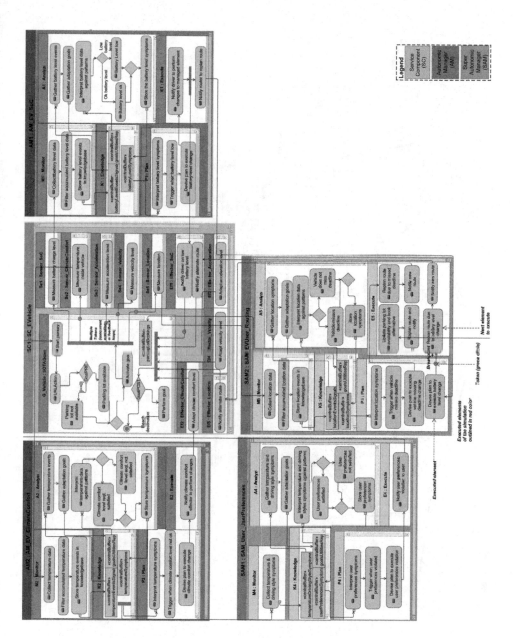

Fig. 4. Patterns simulated as a domain-specific activity model [1]

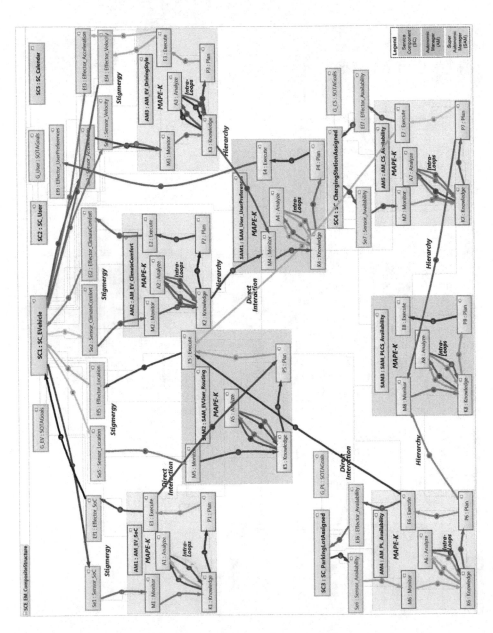

Fig. 5. Patterns simulated as a domain-specific composite structure model [2]

with the eclipse-plugin SimSOTA. Given the final system model, pattern templates are used to derive a UML representation of the system, which is mapped to Java templates with the help of model transformations[5]. SOTA is useful not only to define functional properties from goals but also non-functional properties via utilities.

3.2 Low-Level Requirements Engineering with the Invariant Refinement Method

The invariant refinement method (IRM), which is presented in [15], transforms high level system goals into low-level concepts of system architecture, namely components, component processes and ensembles of the system. IRM builds a hierarchy of invariants through gradual refinement, whereby invariants describe the desired state of the system-to-be as a function of time [15,4]. SOTA and IRM are partially redundant and partially complementary. This fact can be exploited during requirements engineering, as will be discussed later in Section 3.3.

The IRM approach defines an invariant as a condition on the knowledge valuation of a set of components that captures the operational normalcy to be maintained by the system-to-be [15]. In dynamical systems engineering, an invariant represents a control objective. In terms of system conceptualization, it reflects a goal. IRM departs from the most general system goal, as defined by the conceptualization. The decomposition process subdivides parent invariants into mutually exclusive and commonly exhaustive child invariants. The invariants belong to either one of three categories: (1) process invariants which describe within-component processes, (2) exchange invariants which describe between-component processes, respectively ensemble processes, and (3) high-level invariants (e.g. general invariants, present-past invariants) which do not yet define a low-level process. A process invariant can be understood as an intra-component feedback loop that manipulates the component's knowledge. An exchange invariant can be understood as an inter-component feedback loop, which controls the adaptation mechanisms across multiple components. The decomposition process terminates once all high-level invariants are represented by either process invariants or exchange invariants. As a side effect of the decomposition process, assumptions are defined. An assumption describes an environment condition that is to be guaranteed but is not explicitly controlled by the processes. The resulting IRM decomposition graph of the e-mobility scenario is shown in Figure 6. Adherence to child invariants guarantees adherence to parent invariants. In the limit, adherence to leaf invariants guarantees all high-level system goals to be fulfilled.

3.3 Iterative Requirements Engineering with SOTA and IRM

Finally, the question remains to be answered how the combination of the two approaches, namely the requirements engineering with SOTA and the top-down re-

---

[5] The *Fork/Join framework of Java SE7* is employed to represent adaptation patterns in Java.

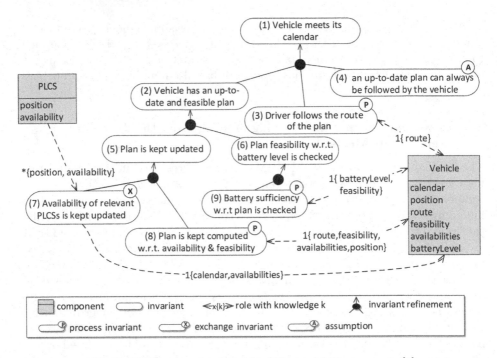

Fig. 6. IRM system level graph of the e-mobility scenario [4]

quirements engineering with IRM, improves the design of autonomic distributed systems.

Recall that in accordance with a dynamical systems engineering perspective, SOTA uses a state space representation of the system to model both within-component and between-component feedback loops. Within-component feedback loops are represented by AMs and between-component feedback loops are represented by SAMs. The design of the feedback loops is supported by a patterns catalog of adaptation templates. The resulting hierarchy of feedback loops describes the complex interplay of adaptation actions in the system. In terms of IRM, AMs represent functional within-component processes, while SAMs represent functional between-component (resp. ensemble) processes. The modeled processes can be most easily compared at the Java/jDEECo level. Discrepancies in the processes, modeled by IRM and SOTA, point at potential modeling errors.

4   Implementation and Deployment

The result of the iterative requirements engineering loop which involves SOTA and IRM (see Section 3), is a low-level specification of the system-to-be. The low-level description of the system architecture is formulated in terms of the DEECo [5] component model which comprises of (1) DEECo components and (2) DEECo

```
1    component Vehicle features AvailabilityAggregator:
2        knowledge:
3            batteryLevel = 90%,
4            position = GPS(...),
5            calendar = [ POI(WORKPLACE, 9AM−1PM), POI(MALL, 2PM−3PM), ... ],
6            availabilities = [ ],
7            plan = { route = ROUTE(...), isFeasible = TRUE }
8        process computePlan:
9            in plan.isFeasible, in availabilities, in calendar, inout plan.route
10           function:
11               if (!plan.isFeasible) plan.route ← planner(calendar, availabilities)
12           scheduling: periodic( 5000ms )
13           ...
14   ensemble UpdateAvailabilityInformation:
15       coordinator: AvailabilityAggregator
16       member: AvailabilityAwareParkingLot
17       membership:
18           ∃ poi ∈ coordinator.calendar:
19   '         distance(member.position, poi.position) ≤ THRESHOLD &&
20               isAvailable(poi, member.availability)
21       knowledge exchange:
22           coordinator.availabilities ← { (m.id, m.availability) | m ∈ members }
23       scheduling: periodic( 2500ms )
```

Fig. 7. Example of DEECo SCs and SCEs in e-mobility modeling [4]

ensembles. As to (1), a DEECo component is defined by three elements: first, local component knowledge, second, knowledge processes that operate on the local component knowledge, and third, interfaces which define the subsets of the local component knowledge that are exposed once the component becomes part of an ensemble. A DEECo knowledge process implements an IRM process invariant. As to (2), a DEECo ensemble is defined as a process that encapsulates the communication between the components of an ensemble. A DEECo ensemble implements the IRM exchange invariant. The assignment of components to an ensemble is controlled via a membership condition. While the knowledge processes of a component control local component knowledge, an ensemble controls the group-level knowledge exchange between its members and its coordinator. An example of DEECo components and DEECo ensembles is shown in Figure 7.

As described in [4], the reification of the DEECo component model in Java is called jDEECo. Components are intuitively represented as annotated Java classes. Component knowledge is mapped to class fields. Component processes are mapped to class methods. Appropriately annotated classes represent DEECo ensembles. Once the necessary components and ensembles are coded, they are deployed using the jDEECo runtime framework, which takes care of process and ensemble scheduling, as well as low-level distributed knowledge manipulation. Figure 8 shows a simplified description of the jDEECo class fields (component knowledge) and class methods (component processes) of the e-mobility scenario. Figure 9 illustrates a jDEECo ensemble.

```
1  @Component
2  public class PLCS {
3      public LatLon location;
4      public Map<String, ReservationRequest> reservationRequests;
5      public Map<String, ReservationResponse> reservationResponses;
6      public Map<Long, Integer> occupancy;
7      public Integer maxCapacity;
8      public String id;
9      ...
10     /**
11      * Processes reservation requests and produce appropriate reservation
12      * responses. As all the vehicles follow the optimal assignment of the
13      * PLCSSAM it is not possible to overbook the PLCS. Nevertheless the check
14      * is performed and the appropriate response is generated.
15      *
16      * In the "occupancy" knowledge we store the map that translates the hourly
17      * intervals into the space occupancy. If the request cannot be satisfied
18      * (i.e. the maximum capacity has been reached for the requested time) the
19      * negative response is created.
20      */
21     @Process
22     @PeriodicScheduling(period = DEFAULT_PERIOD)
23     public static void processReservations(
24             @In("id") String id,
25             @In("reservationRequests") Map<String, ReservationRequest> reservationRequests,
26             @InOut("reservationResponses") ParamHolder<Map<String, ReservationResponse>>
27                     reservationResponses,
28             @InOut("occupancy") ParamHolder<Map<Long, Integer>> occupancy,
29             @In("maxCapacity") Integer maxCapacity) {
30         ReservationResponse response;
31         for (ReservationRequest rr : reservationRequests.values())
32             if (!reservationResponses.value.containsKey(rr.id)) {
33                 //Generate response
34                 response = new ReservationResponse(rr.id, book(rr.fromHour,
35                         rr.toHour, occupancy.value, maxCapacity), rr.vehicleId, id);
36                 reservationResponses.value.put(rr.id, response);
37                 System.out.println(id + " reservation response : " + response);
38             }
39     }
40     ...
41 }
```

Fig. 8. Description of a ParkingLotChargingStation (PLCS) component in jDEECo, where component knowledge is represented by class fields and component processes are represented by class methods

5   Runtime Simulation

The e-mobility case study employs the jDEECo runtime environment to handle monitoring, awareness and self-adaptation during runtime. The e-mobility specific implementation of the jDEECo components (e.g. PLCS component) and the jDEECo ensembles (e.g. vehicle-PLCS SAM) is shown in Section 4.

jDEECo embeds a Multi-Agent Transport Simulation (MATSim) which is an execution environment implementing the physical interaction of drivers, vehicles and infrastructure resources. MATSim implements general concepts of transportation modeling, which is briefly discussed in Section 5.1. The coupling of jDEECo and MATSim is presented in Section 5.2.

```
1  @Ensemble
2  @PeriodicScheduling(period = 1000)
3  public class VehiclePLCS {
4
5      @Membership
6      public static boolean membership(
7              @In("coord.reservationRequest") ReservationRequest reservationRequest
8              @In("member.id") String plcsId) {
9          if (reservationRequest == null || reservationRequest.plcsId == null) return false;
10         return reservationRequest.plcsId.equals(plcsId);
11     }
12
13     @KnowledgeExchange
14     public static void exchange(
15             @In("coord.id") String vehicleId,
16             @In("coord.reservationRequest") ReservationRequest reservationRequest
17             @InOut("coord.reservationResponse") ParamHolder<ReservationResponse>
18                     reservationResponse
19             @In("member.reservationResponses") Map<String, ReservationResponse>
20                     plcsReservationResponses,
21             @InOut("member.reservationRequests") ParamHolder<Map<String, ReservationRequest>>
22                     plcsReservationRequests) {
23         plcsReservationRequests.value.put(vehicleId, reservationRequest);
24         reservationResponse.value = plcsReservationResponses.get(reservationRequest.id);
25     }
26 }
```

Fig. 9. Description of a jDEECo ensemble, exchanging data between a vehicle and a PLCS. The vehicle transfers the reservation request to PLCS's knowledge. The PLCS transfers the request response to the vehicle's knowledge.

5.1 MATSim Transportation Modeling

MATSim is a microscopic traffic simulator. It is used to simulate individual travel patterns and predict aggregate travel demand. It is based on the underlying theory of transportation science which is discussed in [8] and [10]. MATSim specific publications can be found in [16].

MATSim simulates physical interactions of drivers, vehicles and infrastructure resources. In MATSim, a driver is represented as a software agent, which inherits travel preferences and a daily activity chain. A driver agent schedules and executes a day plan, which is defined as a sequence of travel stages (e.g. walking stage, driving stage) that connect the daily activity chain. Driver decisions represent the demand side of transportation, while infrastructure resources reflect the supply side.

Driver decisions produce a demand for infrastructure resources (e.g. road, parking space, charging station). The ratio of supply and demand influences the cost of resource usage (e.g. traffic induced travel time, parking cost), and hence, assigns a utility to driver decisions. Drivers generally aim to find the set of decisions that maximize utility.

MATSim addresses the dual problem of decision making, where drivers use information about the transportation network (e.g. traffic information, parking fee) to make travel decisions (e.g. route choice, parking choice), and in return, these decisions influence the state of the transportation network. MATSim em-

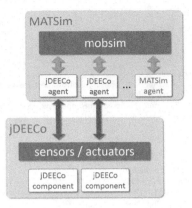

Fig. 10. Coupling of jDEECo and MATSim

ploys an optimization loop to solve the dual problem of transportation. In a first step, agents execute day plans. This produces a travel demand, which for a given supply, determines the cost of resource usage. In a second step, a scoring module computes the generalized cost of the set of travel decisions. In a third step, agents modify travel decisions in order to minimize the generalized cost of travel (resp. maximize the utility). The set of actions of an agent comprises of (i) shifting departure time, (ii) changing travel mode and (iii) changing route. Step 1-3 are iteratively executed until an equilibrium is reached. The loop of optimization is executed in every simulation step.

The e-mobility case study requires several extensions to MATSim. First, mode choice is confined to electric vehicle travel. Second, the optimization loop additionally respects parking choice and charging station choice. Third, vehicles consume energy and they are range restricted, which introduces a need to monitor and manage vehicle energy budgets.

5.2 Integration of jDEECo and MATSim

The jDEECo runtime framework integrates MATSim in order to simulate the states of the traffic environment (e.g. road traffic, parking space availability) and monitor the states of the components, in particular, the state of the vehicle component (e.g. battery capacity, location). MATSim information can be grouped into two categories: (1) current information $x_s(t_0)$, capturing the state of the traffic system at the current time slice t_0, and (2) predictive information $x_s(t_1)$, describing the state of the traffic system at any consecutive time slice t_i, with $i > 0$ and $i \in \mathbf{N}$.

In case of the (1) current information, jDEECo connects all components to an instance of MATSim (see Figure 10). Internally, each jDEECo component is reflected in MATSim by a dedicated instance of MATSim's mobility agent (denoted as "jDEECo agent" in the figure).

As for (2) predictive information, the prediction can be understood as a function $f(x_s(t_0), t_i, A)$, which maps the current state of the traffic system $x_s(t_0)$ to a future state t_i, given a set of actions A, thereby describing the effects of current actions. The particular ASCENS characteristics allow for different perceptions of the same current information $x_s(t_0)$, reflecting a different belief of the current system state. The particular ASCENS characteristics also allow for different future beliefs $x_s(t_1)$, given the same current belief. Consider an example, where a first component uses a prediction logic defined by $f_1(x_s(t_0), t_i, A)$, which differs from the prediction logic $f_2(x_s(t_0), t_i, A)$ of a second component, thereby predicting a different effect from the same set of actions. In order to account for component specific belief states, each jDEECo component contains a separate instance of the MatSim simulation.

In concluding, MATSim is used to predict the effects of the physical interactions of users, vehicles and infrastructure resources. jDEECo assigns MATSim instances to jDEECo components and handles these instances in a way that allows for different belief states between components and potentially synchronized belief states within ensembles.

6   Summary

The e-mobility case study in ASCENS provided a novel example of a relevant industry application. A conceptualization of the e-mobility case study was shown and was used as a basis for the application of the EDLC approach for distributed autonomic software systems. Concerning the requirements engineering phase of the EDLC, the case study utilized the IRM and SOTA approach. Considering the implementation and deployment of the system, DEECo was used for modeling purposes, while jDEECo was used as the runtime environment. The system simulation was performed by using the runtime environment integrated with the MATSim traffic simulator. The combined approach of this study provided a novel method for the simulation of physical interactions between users, e-vehicles and infrastructure resources in a decentralized ensemble-based manner.

References

1. Abeywickrama, D.B., Hoch, N., Zambonelli, F.: Engineering and implementing software architectural patterns based on feedback loops. International Journal for Parallel and Distributed Computing, Special Issue on Enabling Technologies for Collaboration to appear, 19 (2015)
2. Abeywickrama, D.B., Hoch, N., Zambonelli, F.: Simsota: engineering and simulating feedback loops for self-adaptive systems. In: International C* Conference on Computer Science & Software Engineering (C3S2E13), Porto, Portugal, July 10 - 12 (2013)
3. Abeywickrama, D.B., Zambonelli, F., Hoch, N.: Towards simulating architectural patterns for self-aware and self-adaptive systems. In: Sixth IEEE International Conference on Self-Adaptive and Self-Organizing Systems Workshops, SASOW, Lyon, France, September 10-14 (2012)

4. Bures, T., De Nicola, R., Gerostathopoulos, I., Hoch, N., Kit, M., Koch, N., Monreale, G.V., Montanari, U.: Pugliese, Rosario Serbedzija, N.B., Wirsing, M., Zambonelli, F.: A life cycle for the development of autonomic systems: The e-mobility showcase. In: 7th IEEE International Conference on Self-Adaptation and Self-Organizing Systems Workshops (SASOW), Philadelphia, PA, USA, September 9-13 (2013)

5. Bures, T., Gerostathopoulos, I., Hnetynka, P., Keznikl, J., Kit, M., Plasil, F.: Deeco: An ensemble-based component system. In: Proceedings of the 16th International ACM Sigsoft Symposium on Component-based Software Engineering (CBSE '13), pp. 81–90. ACM Press, New York (2013)

6. Bures, T., Gerostathopoulos, I., Hnetynka, P., Keznikl, J., Kit, M., Plasil, F.: The Invariant Refinement Method. In: Wirsing, M., Hölzl, M., Koch, N., Mayer, P. (eds.) Software Engineering for Collective Autonomic Systems. LNCS, vol. 8998, pp. 405–428. Springer, Heidelberg (2015)

7. Cabri, G., Puviani, M., Zambonelli, F.: Towards a taxonomy of adaptive agent-based collaboration patterns for autonomic service ensembles. In: 2011 International Conference on Collaboration Technologies and Systems (CTS), May 2011, pp. 508–515 (2011)

8. Cascetta, E.: Transportation Systems Analysis - Models and Applications, 2nd edn. Springer, Heidelberg (2009)

9. Geering, H.P.: Regelungstechnik. Springer, Heidelberg (2004)

10. Hall, R.W.: Handbook of Transportation Science, 2nd edn. International Series in Operations Research & Management Science, vol. 56. Springer, Heidelberg (2003)

11. Hoch, N., Monreale, G.V., Montanari, U., Sammartino, M., Siwe, A.T.: From Local to Global Knowledge and Back. In: Wirsing, M., Hölzl, M., Koch, N., Mayer, P. (eds.) Software Engineering for Collective Autonomic Systems. LNCS, vol. 8998, pp. 185–220. Springer, Heidelberg (2015)

12. Hoch, N., Werther, B., Bensler, H.P., Masuch, N., Luetzenberger, M., Hessler, A., Albayrak, S., Siegwart, R.Y.: A user-centric approach for efficient daily mobility planning in e-vehicle infrastructure networks. In: Meyer, G., Valldorf, J. (eds.) Advanced Microsystems for Automotive Applications 2011. VDI-Buch, pp. 185–198. Springer, Heidelberg (2011)

13. Hoch, N., Zemmer, K., Werther, B., Siegwart, R.Y.: Electric vehicle travel optimization-customer satisfaction despite resource constraints. In: 2012 IEEE Intelligent Vehicles Symposium IV, Alcal de Henares, Madrid, Spain, June 3-7 (2012)

14. Hölzl, M., Koch, N., Puviani, M., Wirsing, M., Zambonelli, F.: The Ensemble Development Life Cycle and Best Practices for Collective Autonomic Systems. In: Wirsing, M., Hölzl, M., Koch, N., Mayer, P. (eds.) Software Engineering for Collective Autonomic Systems. LNCS, vol. 8998, pp. 325–354. Springer, Heidelberg (2015)

15. Keznikl, J., Bures, T., Plasil, F., Gerostathopoulos, I., Hnetynka, P., Hoch, N.: Design of ensemble-based component systems by invariant refinement. In: Proc. of the 16th International ACM SIGSOFT Symposium on Component Based Software Engineering (CBSE '13), ACM, Vancouver, Canada (2013)

16. MATSim: Multi-Agent Transport Simulation (MATSim) (August 2014), http://www.matsim.org/

17. Monreale, G.V., Montanari, U., Hoch, N.: Soft constraint logic programming for electric vehicle travel optimization. CoRR abs/1212.2056, 17 (2012)

18. De Nicola, R., Latella, D., Lafuente, A.L., Loreti, M., Margheri, A., Massink, M., Morichetta, A., Pugliese, R., Tiezzi, F., Vandin, A.: The SCEL Language: Design,

Implementation, Verification. In: Wirsing, M., Hölzl, M., Koch, N., Mayer, P. (eds.) Software Engineering for Collective Autonomic Systems. LNCS, vol. 8998, pp. 3–71. Springer, Heidelberg (2015)

19. Puviani, M., Cabri, G., Zambonelli, F.: A taxonomy of architectural patterns for self-adaptive systems. In: Proceedings of the International C* Conference on Computer Science and Software Engineering (C3S2E '13), pp. 77–85. ACM Press, New York (2013)

20. Russell, S., Norvig, P.: Artificial Intelligence - a modern approach, 2nd edn. Prentice-Hall, Englewood Cliffs (2002)

21. Wooldridge, M.: An Introduction to MultiAgent Systems, 2nd edn. Wiley, Chichester (2009)

22. Wooldridge, M., Jennings, N.R.: Intelligent agents: Theory and practice. Knowledge Engineering Review 10(2), 115–152 (1995)

Author Index